Edward Lear in Corsica

Uniform with this volume

EDWARD LEAR IN SOUTHERN ITALY

EDWARD LEAR IN GREECE

EDWARD LEAR IN CORSICA

The Journal of a
Landscape Painter

WILLIAM KIMBER
46 WILTON PLACE, LONDON, S.W.1

First published in this edition in 1966 by
WILLIAM KIMBER & CO. LIMITED
46 Wilton Place, London, S.W.1

© William Kimber & Co. Limited 1966

MADE AND PRINTED IN GREAT BRITAIN BY
W. & J. MACKAY & CO LTD, CHATHAM, KENT

To

FRANKLIN LUSHINGTON, Esq.,

of the Inner Temple,

formerly Member of the Supreme Council of Justice,

in the Ionian Islands,

and still earlier the Companion of my Travels in Greece,

These Illustrated Journals in Corsica are Inscribed,

By his Affectionate Friend,

EDWARD LEAR

London, 1869

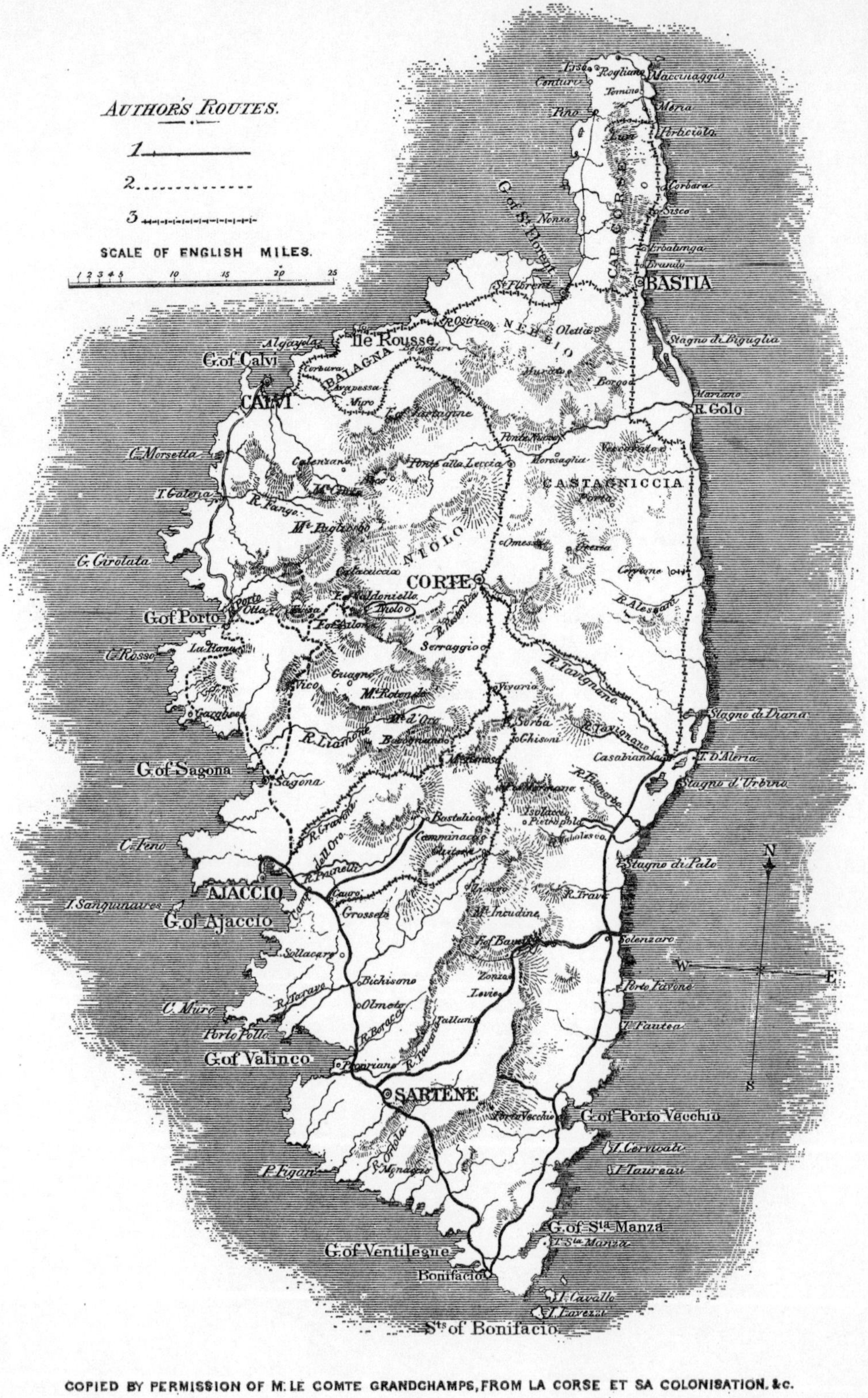
AUTHOR'S ROUTES.
1.
2.
3.
SCALE OF ENGLISH MILES.
1 2 3 4 5 10 15 20 25
Rogliano
Macinaggio
Centuri
Pino
Luri
Nonza
Corbara
Sisco
G. of St Florent
CAP CORSE
BASTIA
St Florent
Oletta
NEBBIO
Stagno di Biguglia
Ile Rousse
Algajola
G. of Calvi
BALAGNA
CALVI
Muro
Murato
Borgo
Mariano
R. Golo
C. Morsetta
Calenzana
Ponte alla Leccia
Morosaglia
CASTAGNICCIA
T. Galeria
R. Fango
Mt. Paglia Orba
NIOLO
G. Girolata
CORTE
G. of Porto
C. Rosso
Serraggio
R. Alesani
R. Tavignano
Vico
Guagno
Mt. Rotondo
Stagno di Diana
R. Liamone
Bocognano
Ghisoni
Casabianda
T. d'Aleria
G. of Sagona
Sagona
Stagno d'Urbino
Bastelica
C. Feno
Stagno di Palo
AJACCIO
I. Sanguinaires
G. of Ajaccio
Grosseto
Mt. Incudine
Solenzara
Sollacaro
Bichisano
Olmeto
C. Muro
Zonza
Levie
Tallano
Porto Favone
Porto Pollo
G. of Valinco
Propriano
SARTENE
G. of Porto Vecchio
Porto Vecchio
I. Cervicali
P. Figari
G. of Sta Manza
G. of Ventilegne
Bonifacio
I. Cavallo
I. Lavezzi
Sts of Bonifacio
N
S
E
W

COPIED BY PERMISSION OF M. LE COMTE GRANDCHAMPS, FROM LA CORSE ET SA COLONISATION, &c.

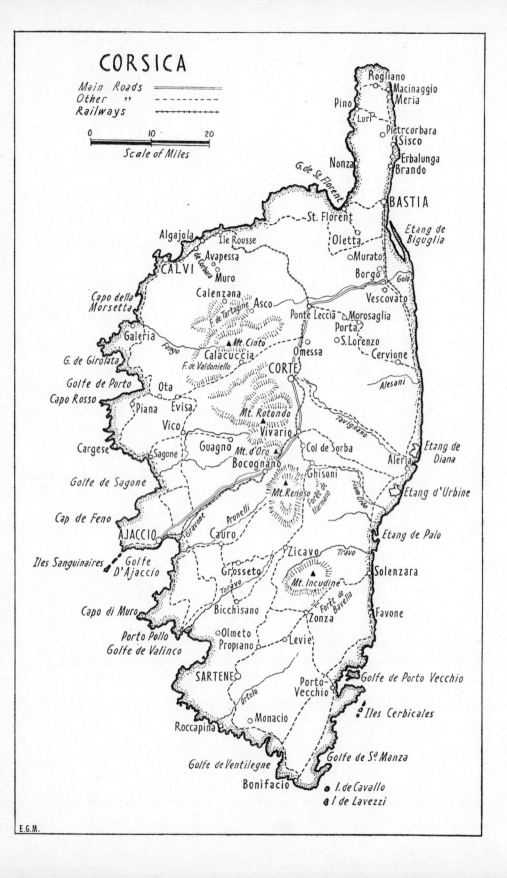

CORSICA

Main Roads ─────
Other " ─ ─ ─
Railways ─┼─┼─┼─

0   10   20
Scale of Miles

Rogliano
Macinaggio
Meria
Pino
Luri
Pietrcorbara
Sisco
Nonza
Erbalunga
Brando
G. de St. Florent
BASTIA
St. Florent
Oletta
Etang de Biguglia
Algajola
Ile Rousse
Murato
de Lonbra
Avapessa
Borgo
CALVI
Muro
Vescovato
Golo
Capo della Morsetta
Calenzana
Asco
F. de Tartagine
Ponte Leccia
Morosaglia
Galeria
Fango
Mt. Cinto
Porta
S. Lorenzo
Cervione
G. de Girolata
Calacuccia
F. de Valdoniello
Omessa
CORTE
Golfe de Porto
Ota
Alesani
Capo Rosso
Piana
Evisa
Mt. Rotondo
Vico
Tavignano
Vivario
Cargese
Guagno
Mt. d'Oro
Col de Sorba
Aleria
Etang de Diana
Sagone
Bocognano
Ghisoni
Golfe de Sagone
Mt. Renoso
Forêt de Marmano
Fium Orbo
Etang d'Urbine
Cap de Feno
Prunelli
Gravone
Cauro
Etang de Palo
AJACCIO
Zicavo
Travo
Iles Sanguinaires
Golfe D'Ajaccio
Grosseto
Mt. Incudine
Solenzara
Toravo
Capo di Muro
Bicchisano
Forêt de Bavella
Favone
Zonza
Porto Pollo
Olmeto
Propiano
Levie
Golfe de Valinco
Golfe de Porto Vecchio
SARTENE
Porto Vecchio
Ortolo
Iles Cerbicales
Monacio
Roccapina
Golfe de Sa Manza
Golfe de Ventilegne
Bonifacio
I. de Cavallo
I. de Lavezzi

E.G.M.

Contents

List of Illustrations

Publishers' Note

Edward Lear in Corsica was first published in 1870 with the title *Journal of a Landscape Painter in Corsica*, though the journey it records was made two years earlier in 1868. The delay was caused by Lear's attempts to find a publisher willing to reproduce his illustrations by colour lithography; in the end he gave up, and the book was published with a series of engravings from Lear's own woodcuts printed in black and white. It is the third volume in the series of the 'Journals of a Landscape Painter'— the earlier two covered Lear's travels in Greece and Southern Italy. (Lear himself in referring to three earlier books was including his *Illustrated Excursions in Italy* published in 1846, but this is not strictly part of the 'Journals of a Landscape Painter' series.)

The Corsican Journal was set in a larger format—the text is also longer—than the earlier volumes, with a page $10\frac{1}{4}$ inches deep by 7 inches wide. In this edition the more conventional size of the earlier volumes has been adopted and twenty of the original plates have been reproduced by lithography, with the introduction of two extra colours, based on the earlier Greek volume. They have not been reduced in size. It is clear from Lear's own letters that he wished to have colour and would himself have undertaken the necessary work; he considered that the uncoloured engravings lacked vitality.

The text itself is reprinted in full, with Lear's own footnotes. The original edition included, as footnotes and in a section called 'Additional Notes', long extracts from standard works on Corsica, and the majority of these have been omitted, though a number of the more interesting 'additional notes' have been retained at the end of the book; a long footnote on King Theodore has also been transferred to this section.

Lear's original map has been reproduced on page 6, with a modern map facing it, showing the more normal spellings.

Preface

In the years 1846, 1849, and 1852, I published illustrated journals of tours in Central and Southern Italy, and in Albania, three books which met with a successful reception from the public, and were very kindly noticed by the Press.

The present volume consists of journals written with the same intent and plan as those which preceded them. They describe, nearly word for word as they were written, my impressions of the nature of the landscape in those portions of Corsica through which I travelled. It is possible that the literary part of this book may not prove of equal interest with that of the publications above named; not, indeed, from any want of merit in the subject, but because I have now no longer the help of friends who then kindly assisted me by their criticisms, especially the late Robert A. Hornby, Esq., and Richard Ford, Esq. But the aim of all these journals should be looked on as the same, simply to be aids to the knowledge of scenery which I have visited and delineated.

I passed last winter at Cannes, intending to return early in the spring to Palestine, for the purpose of completing drawings and journals for a work already partly advanced; but circumstances having prevented me from carrying out this plan, I decided on going to Corsica, rather perhaps on account of its being a place near at hand and easily reached, than from any distinct impression as to the nature of the country, or from any particular interest in its history, inhabitants, or scenery. It is true that the Corsican mountains are sometimes visible from Cannes at sunrise, and latterly I had read M. Prosper Merimée's beautiful little tale of *Colomba*, the scene of which lies in Corsica; but I confess to having been chiefly led to think of going there by that necessity which the wandering painter —whose life's occupation is travelling for pictorial or topographical purposes—is sure to find continually arising, that of seeing some new place, and of adding fresh ideas of landscape to both mind and portfolio—

> For all experience is an arch, wherethrough
> Gleams the untravell'd world, whose margin fades,
> For ever and for ever when I move.

13

It was growing late in the spring when I had decided on going to Corsica, and time did not allow of my procuring books (though plenty have been written on the subject) or maps. Valery's *Voyages en Corse*, published so long back as 1837, was the only guide I could obtain; nor did I happen to fall in with anyone who knew the Corsica of 1868. M. Prosper Merimée's visit to the island had occurred many years back (though he most kindly procured me letters of introduction which proved of great value). One friend wrote that though there were roads, there were no carriages; another that a yacht was the only means of seeing a place, the interior of which was intolerable for want of accommodation. My ignorance was *not* bliss, and I would have got knowledge if I could; but as there was no remedy, and as I intended to pass some eight or ten weeks there, I prepared to go to Corsica as I should have done to any other land of unknown attributes, where I might find the necessity of roughing it daily or nightly, or the contrary; it cannot, I thought, be worse than travelling in Albania or Crete, long journeys through both of which countries I have survived.

A few words on the arrangements preliminary to such travelling may be allowed. Some there are who declaim against carrying much luggage, and who reduce their share of it to a minimum. From these I differ, having far more often suffered from having too little *roba* than too much. Clothing for travelling comfortably in hot or cold climates, such as must be experienced in the plains and mountains of an island so varied in formation as Corsica, and for different phases of social life during an extended tour; great amount of drawing material, folios, paper, etc.; an india-rubber bath; above all, a small folding camp or tent bed, of good use in many a long journey in Albania, Syria, etc., and in which I am sure of sleep anywhere; these, mostly contained in a brace of strong saddle-bags, form a goodly assortment of luggage, and eventually I found it to be not one iota too much.

Then, as to travelling alone, the prospect of which is dreadful to some, I almost always do so by preference, because I cannot otherwise devote every moment to my work, or so arrange plans as to ensure their success. Sometimes, indeed, I have made exceptions to this rule, yet only in cases where my fellow travellers were not only as eager draughtsmen as myself, and where I, being their senior, as well as instructor in sketching, could define and follow all my own plans exactly and without

14

hindrance. Strictly speaking, however, it is long since I made any tours really alone, as various sharp illnesses have taught me the great inconvenience of doing so; and I have frequently been thankful for the care of a good servant who has travelled with me for many years. George Kokali (Giorgio), a Suliot, speaking several languages, sober, honest, and active, saves me all trouble and gives none; now carrying a weight of cloaks and folios and 'daily bread' for a twenty-mile walk or more, anon keeping off dogs and bystanders when I am drawing, or cooking and acting as house-servant when stationary; a man of few words and constant work.

Those who go to Corsica hoping to study antiquities will be disappointed; for the manifold charms of classical countries are wanting there; the long lines of Grecian plains, so crowded with spots full of historic and poetic memories, vast and beautiful remains such as those of Sicily, Syria, or Egypt, do not exist in it; neither will he find the more modern beauties of architecture, the varied forms of tower or castle, mosque, cathedral, or monastery, with which Albania or Italy abound. On the other hand, the ever-varying beauties of light and shade in mountain and valley, the contrast of snowy heights and dark forests, the thick covering of herb and flower, shrub and tree, from the cyclamen and cystus to the ilex, oak, beech, and pine, these are always around him, and he will find that every part of Corisca is full of scenes stamped with original beauty and uncommon interest. Equally will the tourist through the Corsica of our days fail in finding anything of romance there, except in the traditions of the past. If it were, in travelling through Calabria twenty years since, a disappointment to find no pointed hats, and no brigand costume, how much more so is it to find that Corsica, once the very fountain-head of romance, no longer possesses any, that you may walk from Capo Corso to the Straits of Bonifacio in the undisturbed monotony of security, and that all gloomy atmosphere of risk and danger has for years past been dispersed by the broad daylight of French administration and civilisation? With old customs and costumes, mystery and murder have alike disappeared from the Corsica of 1868.

A slight sketch of Corsican history, together with some information concerning its geography, its inhabitants, etc., matters which to many readers will prove of interest, but which it was not easy to incorporate with the *Journal*, will be found separately annexed; and copious details are added in the shape of notes extracted from books I have read since my return from the island,[1] from which may be gathered impressions of the improved state of Corsica now, contrasted with that it was in at the time of the visits of earlier authors.

A certain monotony of narrative must needs be the result of monotony of travel; and the recital of a tour made in a carriage, cannot, I imagine, be made very attractive, if the writer simply records his own impressions. Many of the illustrations, however, were made in short pedestrian excursions, particularly in the forests, at some distance from the high road.

One drawback to my visit, but one I could not avoid, was its shortness: far too little time was devoted to delineating so large a space of country.

To these remarks I will add that, in spite of the want of classical interest throughout Corsica, the memory of my visit to it becomes fresher and more interesting as time goes on; nor do I despair of returning to it, to see some portions of the island I much regret not having visited—Niolo, the Casinca, the Coscione, Rostino, and the coast from Calvi to Porto. Of the Corsicans, too, I would gladly add a word as to their general courtesy and good breeding, and their hospitable welcome in places where no inns exist; and, among other pleasant recollections, this should not pass unnoticed, namely, that there are no beggars in Corsica, a fact contrasting agreeably with the persecutions met with in some other countries.

[1] These quotations from other works have not been reproduced in full in this edition, but some of the more interesting have been retained in the Additional Notes at the end of this book.

Journal of
a Landscape Painter in Corsica

CHAPTER I

APRIL 8, 1868

IT seems a pity to leave Cannes just as the most pleasant and beautiful season is beginning; but if a sketching tour is to be made in Corsica, this is the right and perhaps the only time to choose, at least if all parts of the island are to be visited; earlier, the snow would have made the higher districts unavailable to the landscape painter; later, the heat would prevent work being easy or possible. So I close my rooms in M. Guichard's house, and say good-bye for the present to the cheerful town and its quiet bay, with the beautiful Esterelles on the horizon.

Off by rail to Nice, whence every week a steamer starts for Corsica, going alternately to Ajaccio on the west coast, and to Bastia on the east. This week Ajaccio is the point, and the *Insulaire* is to leave the port at 8 P.M., a roomy and well-appointed steamboat, fares thirty-one and twenty-one francs for first- and second-class places. I go from the pier at seven, and on reaching the boat meet with a pleasant surprise in finding my friend J.A.S., with Mrs. J.S.[1] and the little Janet already on board.

Meanwhile clouds cover the sky—so bright and clear all day—the wind rises before we are fairly off at eight-thirty, and instead of the smooth sea, full moon-light, and other delicacies of a night voyage fondly hoped for, the most ugly forebodings are heard concerning a rough passage, whereby the landscape painter, always a miserable sailor, begins to repent of his decision to draw all Corsica, and, were it possible, would fain return to land. But it is too late; and the only

---

[1] John Addington Symonds and his wife: 'a more charming and good fellow I never met, besides so full of knowledge and learning'—Edward Lear wrote. *The Owl and the Pussy-Cat* was written for their daughter Janet.

alternative is to cultivate sulkiness and retreat instantly to bed; the cabin will be at least a tolerably quiet one, for of passengers there are but few. Neither on deck is any living being left but two fat and perpetually backwards-and-forward trotting poodles.

April 9

The night voyage, though far from pleasant, has not been as bad as might have been anticipated. He is fortunate, who, after ten hours of sea passage, can reckon up no worse memories than those of a passive condition of suffering—of that dislocation of mind and body, or inability to think straightforward, so to speak, when the outer man is twisted, and rolled, and jerked, and the movements of thought seem more or less to correspond with those of the body. Wearily go by

The slow sad hours that bring us all things ill

and vain is the effort to enliven them as every fresh lurch of the vessel tangles practical or pictorial suggestions with untimely scraps of poetry, indistinct regrets and predictions, couplets for a new *Book of Nonsense* and all kinds of inconsequent imbecilities—after this sort—

Would it not have been better to have remained at Cannes, where I had not yet visited Theoule, the Saut de Loup, and other places?

Had I not said, scores of times, such and such a voyage was the last I would make?

Tomorrow, when 'morn broadens on the borders of the dark', shall I see Corsica's 'snowy mountain tops fringing the (Eastern) sky'?

Did the sentinels of lordly Volaterra see, as Lord Macaulay says they did, 'Sardinia's snowy mountain-tops', and not rather these same Corsican tops, 'fringing the southern sky'?

Did they see any tops at all, or if any, which tops?

Will the daybreak ever happen?

Will two o'clock ever arrive?

Will the two poodles above stairs ever cease to run about the deck?

Is it not disagreeable to look forward to two or three months of travelling quite alone?

Would it not be delightful to travel, as J.A.S. is about to do, in company with a wife and child?

Does it not, as years advance, become clearer that it is very odious to be alone?

Have not many very distinguished persons, Œnone among others, arrived at this conclusion?

Did she not say, with evident displeasure—

> And from that time to this I am alone,
> And I shall be alone until I die?—

Will those poodles ever cease from trotting up and down the deck?

Is it not unpleasant, at fifty-six years of age, to feel that it is increasingly probable that a man can never hope to be otherwise than alone, never, no, never more?

Did not Edgar Poe's raven distinctly say 'Nevermore'?

Will those poodles be quiet? 'Quoth the raven, nevermore.'

Will there be anything worth seeing in Corsica?

Is there any romance left in that island? Is there any sublimity or beauty in its scenery?

Have I taken too much baggage?

Have I not rather taken too little?

Am I not an idiot for coming at all?—

Thus, and in such a groove, did the machinery of thought go on, gradually refusing to move otherwise than by jerky spasms, after the fashion of mechanical Ollendorff exercises, or verb-catechisms of familiar phrases—

Are there not Banditti?

Had there not been Vendetta?

Were there not Corsican brothers?

Should I not carry clothes for all sorts of weather?

Must *thou* not have taken a dress coat?

Had *he* not many letters of introduction?

Might *we* not have taken extra pairs of spectacles?

Could *you* not have provided numerous walking boots?

Should *they* not have forgotten boxes of quinine pills?

Shall *we* possess flea-powder?

Could *you* not procure copper money?

19

May *they* not find cream cheeses?

Should there not be innumerable moufflons?

Ought not the cabin lamps and glasses to cease jingling?

Might not those poodles stop worrying?—

thus and thus, till by reason of long hours of monotonous rolling and shaking, a sort of comatose insensibility, miscalled sleep, takes the place of all thought, and so the night passes.

At sunrise there are fine effects of light and cloud; but, alas for my first impression of that grand chain of Corsican Alps about which I have heard so much, and which were to have been seen so long before reaching the island! Nothing is visible at present beyond the leaden, unlovely waves, except a low line of dark grey-green coast, and above this there are glimpses from time to time between thick folds of cloud, disclosing for a moment mysterious phantom heights of far snow and rock, or here and there some vast crag dimly seen and less remote, imparting a sensation of being near a land of lofty mountains, but none of any distinctness or continuity of outline.

As the steamer approaches the island, cape after cape is passed, and on one a village is seen, which the pilot tells me is Carghese, the Greek settlement, of which I had heard from M. Prosper Merimée. The coast is deeply indented in bays and gulfs, and so far as cloud allows of seeing inland, seems remarkable for its greenness.

About ten we arrive at the pointed rocky islets called Les Iles Sanguinaires, and passing between them and the Punto della Parata, enter the Gulf of Ajaccio. The islands, on one of which there is a lighthouse, are picturesque; but the weather has now become cold and windy, and the gulf, presumed by the enthusiastic to be ever lake-like and placid, is anything but calm or beautiful; on the contrary, its aspect is gloomy, and its inquietude disgusting. Thick clouds hide all the hills and this beginning of Corsican travel is certainly far from propitious.

We proceed along the north side of the gulf, and pretty near the shore. Close at the water's edge is a line of buildings, some so small as to be not unlike bathing machines; others resembling tiny dwellings, or rather those little places of worship, Ebenezers or Houses of Sion, observable in many English villages; but these are neither. They are tombs, small chapels, or sepulchral monuments, forming the Campo Santo, or cemetery of Ajaccio, but the pilot tells me that it is a more general usage in Corsica for the inhabitants to bury their relatives either on their own family property or in some conspicuous spot near their dwellings, thus never removing far from the living the memories of those who were with them in life.

Presently we near the head of the gulf, where Ajaccio stands out gloomy and grey on a point of land that forms an inner and an outer harbour. The city does not appear promising in a picturesque point of view, though on this boisterously windy morning, when all is sombre and sunless, and when the surrounding scenery is blotted and half hidden by clouds, it is premature to judge; finer weather may change my opinion.

Before eleven we are anchored not far from the city; boats come off to take the passengers, and I fancy that every one of these leave the *Insulaire* with pleasant recollections of its clean and good arrangements, and its careful and attentive captain and pilot; possibly, too, of the pair of funny little poodles continually trotting about its deck.

On a nearer approach Ajaccio does not seem to me to present any special beauty or interest; no charm either of colour or architecture in public or other buildings salutes the eye of the painter. There are lines of respectable-looking, lofty, and bulky houses—they may be likened to great warehouses, or even to highly magnified dominoes—with regular rows of windows singularly wanting in embellishment and variety; but there is no wealth of tall campanile or graceful spire, no endless arches or perforations or indescribable unevennesses, no balconies, no galleries, as in most parts of Italy, in the dull lines of buildings here; no fragmentary hangings, no stripes, no prismatic gatherings of inconceivable objects, far less any gorgeous hues, as in Eastern worlds. Perhaps the place I thought of at first as being likest to Ajaccio was Rapallo, on the Riviera di Levante, a town, if I remember rightly, one of the least gay or ornamented on that beautiful coast.

Still more striking is the absence of colour, and of any peculiarity of costumes in the dress of both sexes. Almost all are in black, or very dark brown, and to a new-comer who has travelled in the East and South everything has a dull and commonplace, not to say a mournful, air. The boatmen who convey me, my man, and luggage, to the shore, are quiet and solemn; and, on reaching the landing-place—ah, viva! once more the solid ground!—the sober propriety of demeanour in the groups standing round is remarkable; the clamour and liveliness of an Italian port, the wildness and splendour of an Eastern quay are alike wanting; the countenances of both men and women are grave, and the former have an inactive and lazy manner; so that, whether or not I am prejudiced by the damp and overcast gloom of the day, my first impressions of the Gulf of Ajaccio and of the capital of Corsica are not of a lively character. Among the notes I have had forwarded to me by the last post from friends in England who knew of my coming to this island, are some written by a naturalist, who mentions, among other creatures peculiar to Corsica, the *Helix tristis*; and, in my present mood, I feel that the melancholy snail was right when he chose a sympathetic dwelling.

No trouble whatever is given at the Custom House; the officials are civil and obliging. I walk on up a broad street, leading to an open place square—where, or near which, I am told, the best hotels are to be found—in search of a lodging; to the right a street stretches along the quay, to the left appears to stand the more populous part of the city. On the way I pass a large fountain, with lions; how gloomily dressed are the women filling their water-jars! but they carry them gracefully, and are well made—their features regular, and rather of a Greek type, except that the nose is longer. At the top of the street (the Rue Napoléon) is the Place du Diamant (the large open space above alluded to), three-sided; the fourth, open to the sea, containing the equestrian statue of Napoleon and those of his four brothers. And now, for the weather shows signs of clearing, the opposite or southern side of the gulf is for the first time visible. Out of this Grande Place du Diamant the Cours Napoléon opens. In it are barracks, the Préfecture, the theatre, the post, etc., and the Hotel de l'Europe; and at one of its corners stands the Hotel de France, to which I go, but only to find that it contains no vacant rooms. My next trial was at the Hotel de Londres, which stands in a small street at the north-west corner of the Place du Diamant, and is by no means so well situated as the last I had entered. Each of these inns occupies a single flat in a large square building. Here, although the entrance and staircase are very objectionable, being extremely dirty, and encumbered by small children who cling parasitically to the steps and balustrades, and though it is at once evident that the arrangements of the floor used as the hotel leave much to be desired, I find one very clean room looking to the front for myself, and one on the

other side of the establishment for my servant. These are the only two
unlet; my own is far too near the kitchen to be agreeable—abundant
noises, odours, and flies may be expected—yet, for one may go farther
and fare worse, I order my luggage to be brought upstairs and settle
myself for a sojourn of some days, the more readily that my first impressions of the owners of the inn are prepossessing. Valery's volume is
the only book I have with me as a guide to Corsica, and from that I
gather that Ajaccio will be my best point as head-quarters while I remain
in the island.

1 P.M.—My host, M. Ottavi, has produced an excellent breakfast—
fresh whitings, omelette, the famous broccio or cream cheese of Corsica,
etc.; and it must be allowed that the assiduity of the landlord and his
wife go far to atone for the shortcomings of their *salles à manger*—as
various many-tabled roomlets or boxes are with dignity named. Other
apartments there are, and of a larger size, but these are used by officers
of the garrison, and other regular pensioners of the restaurant.[1] Since
breakfast, I have been out to the Préfecture; but M. Géry, the Préfet, to
whom M. Merimée has kindly procured me two introductory letters, is
in France; so I leave these at the office of the Secretary-General, M.
Galloni. The Préfecture, which stands back from the Cours Napoléon, in
a garden, is the handsomest public building I have seen in Ajaccio. The
backs of the houses here have many picturesque accompaniments denied
to their bald staring fronts; from my window in the hotel, as I look at
the back or north side of the houses fronting the sea on the Place du
Diamant, there are clusters of wooden balconies, little flights of glittering
pigeons, and pigeon-houses to suit, mysterious zigzag lines of jars up
and down the walls, unaccountably linked together like the joints of
some mighty serpent, and various other small incidents of interest. On
the whole, however, I feel happy that there is little or nothing for me
to do in the way of street-scenery drawing at Ajaccio.

---

[1] It may be stated here that I had no reason to repent my decision, and that I
cannot speak in too high terms of the Hotel de Londres, or of its proprietors, M.
and Mdme Ottavi. Their constant attention to the wants of their inmates as far as
the limited nature of their hotel allowed, the extreme cleanliness of their rooms,
the good qualities of their cookery, their reasonable charges, and their untiring
civility and cheeriness, it is a pleasure to remember. Nor should the first-rate
coffee of Madame be forgotten (the Ottavi had long kept an hotel at Algiers), nor
the industry and good humour of Boniface, the waiter.

The day becomes finer; crossing the spacious place by the equestrian statue of the first Emperor Napoleon, I go down to the sea by a broad carriage road which, at its outset, is sheltered by a pleasant avenue of plane trees, and afterwards leads on to the Capella de'Greci, and to the public cemetery which I had remarked in steaming up the gulf. I wander on—as is my way in coming to new places—in order that by seeing a little on all sides, the best sites for making characteristic drawings may be ascertained; along this shore there are many beautiful bits, but chiefly about the small mortuary chapels, where cypress trees and various shrubs flourish, and in the frequent combination of granite rocks with the sea and opposite gulf shore. Very few people seem about, though the city is so close by; the cut of the peasant women's dress is much like that of the Ionians, the skirt full, with many small plaits or folds, the bodice and short jacket close-fitting—a graceful costume, but in nearly all cases of a dark hue, brown or purple, more usually black. The elder women—many of whose faces recall the portraits of Madame Mère—mostly wear a black handkerchief tied closely over the head; but the younger, who are not so frequently pretty as they are particularly graceful, wear two handkerchiefs, the one tied round the forehead and fastened behind the head (and of this kerchief only a portion of the front is seen), the other over the top of the head, fastened below the chin and falling on the back of the neck in a point like the head-dress represented in old Italian pictures. As for the men, they have a look as of porters or tradesmen out of work, carrying their hands in their pockets with what seems an idle and disconsolate air, and are in no wise picturesque or remarkable.

Leaving the shore drive—for there is a broad and good road all along the sea-side for some miles—I ascend by a short cut to the Cours Grandval, a noble promenade leading from the Place du Diamant, opposite to the Rue Napoléon, of which, in fact, it may be called a continuation, since from its termination you may see the harbour and the quay at the other extremity, to the hills which shelter Ajaccio on its west side. This Cours Grandval is really fine; a wide carriage road with a footpath on each side, and in its position, high above the sea, most beautiful; and now that the clouds are lifting, disclosing a vast semicircle of lofty mountains at the head of the gulf, besides a prolonged line of lower heights on its southern side, I begin to foresee that my opinions concerning Corsican scenery have yet to be formed—all the more that as I walk on I find a magnificent luxuriance of vegetation filling up, not only every portion of the gardens and of parts of the un-cultivated space on each side of the Cours Grandval, but of the hills beyond, where a profusion of olive growth waves low down, and a rich carpeting of underwood or shrubbery clothes their sides higher up. Close to this beautiful but apparently little-frequented promenade, stand the four houses lately built, known as *Les Cottages* (and calling at one of these, Dr. Ribton's, I learn that my friends the J.S.s are at the Hotel de l'Europe). Nearly opposite these four dwellings stands the fine house of M. Conti, Receveur-Général; and beyond them a large convent school seems at present nearly the only other building on the Cours Grandval, except a solitary house at its termination, where, so to speak, the city ends and the country begins.

Going down again to the shore, I wander on to the Capella de' Greci. Now that the features of this gulf scenery are beginning to be dis-cernible, though even yet the summits of all the higher mountains are cloud-covered, a grand and lofty serenity seems its character. Some-how, a kind of lonely sadness forms part of the landscape, and it is diffi-cult to realise the fact that one is in the near neighbourhood of a city. The vegetation is surprisingly beautiful and vigorous, especially that of the cactus, broom, cistus, myrtle, asphodel, and lentisk; the almond tree in full flower, and the fig tree in leaf, showing how much warmer is the climate here than at Cannes or Nice, where as yet not a leaf of these trees is out.

But—I speculate professionally—what can I make of Ajaccio itself as a drawing? What though some of the very best views of the city are to be found along this walk by the shore and towards the end of the Cours Grandval, how are its blocks of houses seven stories high, square as warehouses, white evenly spotted with black, to be wrought into material for the picturesque? Possibly, at sunrise, when the light will be behind the buildings and all their poverty of good detail hidden, its general form may then be utilised as a single dark mass.

Returning to the town and through the Place du Diamant, I walk along the Cours Napoléon, which runs eastward and at right-angles to the Cours Grandval and the Rue Napoléon; from it, numerous narrow lanes descend to the inner or east harbour, and to the Rue Fesch. But although perhaps there is more appearance of life in this broad street than in any other part of the city, I find little to admire in its uniform lines of tall houses, and am not sorry to come to the end of it, opposite what needs must be, when the mountains are unveiled—for all are now once more invisible—very grand views of the gulf-head and the surrounding shores.

But how rural—now that I have explored most parts of Ajaccio—does this city seem! How little activity and movement in its streets! How abounding with children and how destitute of men! How scantily furnished is the sea with craft! How lazy seem a great portion of its inhabitants! The brisk little French soldiers alone redeem the dullness of the town scenes, their bright red trousers almost the only gleam of colour in a world of black and brown; their lively walk and discourse nearly the only signs of gaiety. City, quotha! might it not, O sympathetic *Helix tristis*, rather be called a village?

Although my friends were out when I called at the Hotel de l'Europe, the landlady begged me to see all the rooms in her inn, consisting, like the other hotels here, of one large flat containing various apartments. The situation of the Hotel de l'Europe certainly has advantages which the de Londres cannot boast of; but for all that, I do not regret having selected to live in the latter.

At six-thirty, having prowled and wandered till too tired to search any longer for the picturesque, I return to Ottavi's, to rest, write, and think what can be extracted from Ajaccio as food for pencil and paint. The Gulf mountain lines seem unmanageable from their great length, and difficult to represent except by portions; but perhaps a clear sky may show things differently tomorrow: '*Bakalum*—we shall see', as the Turk says; and being here for a purpose, all that is possible in topographic illustration must be tried.

By the crowding of officers and others here, and by the narrowness of the allotted space, I am reminded of the inn at Cattaro in Dalmatia, and of its multitudinous frequenters and noises. The cook here, however, is a loftier artist than he at the foot of the Montenegrin mountain; so the discomfort has its compensations. After the dry air of Cannes and Nice, how warm and damp does this feel!

APRIL 10

5 A.M.—It is blowing a hurricane, and pouring with rain. A pleasant beginning for study in Corsica, O painter!

But at seven the rain ceases, and gleams of sunshine gladden the gulf. I walk out, up to the end of the Boulevard or Cours Grandval, to make if possible a commencement of work, but find the wind far too high for any drawing. The solitary house, the last on the left hand on the road, now uninhabited, belonged, they tell me, to Cardinal Fesch, and here at one period the Buonaparte family resided during summer, the great detached group of granite rocks a little farther on, known now by the name of 'Napoleon's Grotto', being, I suppose, at that time within the bounds of the garden. At present these form, one may say, the terminus of the Cours Grandval, and are very picturesque, their grey sides shaded by light olive trees, and surrounded by a wild growth of cactus and all sorts of verdure. At this hour the grotto, and all the neighbourhood of the old Buonaparte house, are gay with French soldiery, and resounding with bugles and drums, this being the practising ground for those art students.

From all about this spot are seen some of the best views of Ajaccio, and of the central chain of mountains, for the ground rises from the city to the end of the Cours Grandval, and commands most extensive prospects eastward; the city, wholly in shadow, looks its best in early morning, as I guessed it would. Beyond the grotto, winding gravel paths lead downward to a most charming little dell; you descend through a wilderness of heath, cistus, broom, and asphodel, till you come to gardens of fig and olive, when, passing one or two tiny cottages, you find yourself on the farther side of the little valley, whence other pleasant paths cross and border the hill-sides down to the Campo Santo on the sea-shore carriage road. Everywhere throughout these rambles there is a sensation of freedom—rarely do you see a creature—nothing interrupts the quiet. A flock of sheep and a shepherd are the only living things I have seen since I left the Cours Grandval; the sheep are the first I have met with in Corsica, diminutive little beasts, all jetty black; black too, is the dress of their guardian.

On by the sea to the Campo Santo; the tombs which had appeared like dwellings from the steamer are very numerous and of every kind, from the large plain or ornamented chapel to the simple headstone or cross. Generally they exhibit good taste, often standing in a small detached garden, walled or railed round, and planted with shrubs and flowers. Many of these plots of ground are evidently kept with care. Beyond them a large space is marked out for a public cemetery, the practice of separate sepulchres in the vicinity of cities being, I am told, now prohibited, or about to be so in a short time. Passing these homes of the dead, the road runs on towards the Iles Sanguinaires, here in full view, but wind and cloud forbid all drawing today, so, giving up further exploring, I return; only two or three peasants in rude carts, and some half a score on foot, all dressed in triste black, passing me on my way back to the city, so quiet and little frequented are these environs of Ajaccio.

At the Hotel de l'Europe I find my friends the J.S.s preparing to migrate today to Dr. Ribton's. The longer I stay in Ajaccio the more I am surprised at the crowds of children, not so much in its streets as in the passages and doorways and on the stairs of the houses. These they lay claim to as their own particular property, and seem to think it odd if you ask them to allow you to pass; nevertheless, it should be added that these little urchins are invariably civil and good-humoured. Another surprise to me is that everybody talks an Italian which is quite easy to understand, especially by one used to the dialects of southern Italy—a facility of communication I was not prepared for, as I had heard the Corsican dialect described as a mere jargon, whereas it is not at all so.

11 A.M.—To breakfast in one of the small *salle à manger* boxes. M. Ottavi is Corse, but has passed most of his life in Algiers; Madame is of Strasbourg, but a Pole in origin: both spare no pains to please, and are profuse of good food and wine—the latter a strong red sort, and not unlike a Burgundy in flavour. An elderly Corsican breakfasts in the same *salle*, who asks what part of the island I intend to see; having, as yet, no fixed plan, I mention the Greek colony of Carghese as one of the places I had some idea of visiting first. 'But,' says my acquaintance, 'you would find that place *triste*!' (To myself I added, *Helix tristis!* If the capital is *triste*, why not the remote villages?) One of the Carghese Greeks, it seems, has married this gentleman's daughter, and he obligingly offers me an introduction to him. 'You will, however,' he adds, 'find no

28

costumes in the present day at Carghese; the people there, who originally came from Maina, in the Morea, have for a long time past intermarried with Corsicans, and, although among themselves they keep up their own language, they can hardly, except in that one particular, be any longer called Greek.'

This is disappointing intelligence; for I have been looking forward to brilliant Greek costumes as a set-off to the paucity of colour here. I decline the friendly offer of this gentleman—a M. Martinenghi—to inscribe my name in the *cercle*, or club; for, should the weather become clear, there will be little enough time for drawing before June, none at all extra for 'dawdling' or 'society'—terms at certain times nearly equivalent.[1]

Noon.—The air is as damp and chill as it used to be at Mountain Civitella di Subiaco after a two days' rain; but I would it were as certain as it was wont to be there, that weeks of clear sunshine would follow this soft weather—there, where rain was so regularly succeeded by a bursting forth of light over that wild space of landscape from Olevano to Segni, one of the most beautiful scenes I have ever known. How would it be to pass whole months here, as of old one did in those Italian hills? Would isolation and undisturbed study atone now, as then, for the want of society and much else? Meanwhile, I write out all M. Prosper Merimée's and Mr. Hawker's notes for use, till, the rain holding up, I try to see the Secretary-General, but he is *indisposto*, and in bed. So I come back and give myself up to the fixed conviction that this is truly the land of the *Helix tristis*, the melancholy snail.

Later, a most violent wind blows; yet who can stay for ever indoors? So I set out eastward, to explore some new ground, with G., cloaks, and a folio, in case there should be an opportunity of pencilling anything beyond the blackness of attire of men, women, and children, and the multitudinous congregating of the latter at doors and on stairs. All about the eastern or inner harbour many interesting drawings might be made, weather permitting; but the boats partake of the unpicturesqueness of all things artificial in Corsica. Oh, for a few of the beautiful

[1] I have been sorry since my return from Corsica, that my short stay there did not admit of seeing more of Corsican society; what little I had the advantage of knowing was pleasant, hearty, and full of intelligence and good taste; and by the warm welcome I received at the only two gentlemen's houses where I stayed, I am convinced that the old hospitable virtues of the island are unaltered.—E.L.

rainbow-tinted boats of Malta or Gozo! But here, like the goats and the sheep, and the dress of the human beings, the boats, too, are all black! (Mems., zoological and others:—Observe 1st Goat tied to tail of a horse; goat greatly disquieted by being obliged to gallop. 2ndly. Swallows in small parties, flitting about, battling with the fierce wind, or sitting puffily-ruffled upon the telegraph wires, saying, 'We have come to Corsica too soon.' 3rdly. Many of the peasant women hereabouts wear low-crowned straw hats, like those in use at Antibes, but not so flat.)

High up, on one of the many hills—for the Gulf of Ajaccio is entirely backed by heights—is a lofty monument, and a wayside man informs one that it is the tomb of Count Andrea Pozzo di Borgo,[1] who was a native of Alata, a village adjoining. Turning off from the main or Bastia road, one less wide leads to the left, and I follow it, as somewhat more sheltered; it goes, they tell me, to two large convict establishments or *penitenciers*, called Castelluccio, and beyond that to Milelli, another old Buonaparte country house; also to the chapel and rocks of St. Antoine, and to one or two more distant villages. And if there is no possibility of work, owing to the wind, at least this walk is interesting, as showing much beautiful landscape all around—in depths of olive-grown valleys, in cultivation near at hand, and in glimpses of the eastern mountains, where, amid gloomy cloud, many grand and transient effects gleam out. The peasants, or, possibly gentry (for all who pass me are dressed alike), are mostly riding the wiry little ponies for which the island is noted. Some of these persons wear hood-cloaks, like those used in Crete; but generally they wear black cloth caps, black beards, and black velveteen dresses. Far down in the leafy valleys, and high up on the hill-sides, everywhere peer forth from the olive or ilex groves solitary tombs, many of them domed, and very much like Mohammedan welys; others are quaint little temple-like structures, or plain chapels. But it becomes too tiresome to fight on against this furious wind, so by 5 P.M. I am again back at the city, and sit a while with the S.s—all three of us indulging

[1] Charles-André, Comte de Pozzo di Borgo, 1764 to 1842. Born at Alata in Corsica; secretary of Paoli, and a personal enemy of Napoleon. Deputy to the Assemblée Legislative, he voted with Paoli to hand over the island to the English in 1793, was forced to flee to England, and went to Russia in 1805. He continued to do everything in his power to harm the Bonaparte family and Napoleon throughout his life.

in disrespectful remarks on the climate of Ajaccio in April 1868, and half wishing we had never visited the native land of *Helix tristis*.

Last of all I went to the Piazza Létitia, one side of which is formed by what was the family dwelling of the Buonapartes when Napoleon I was born, in 1769. But this, the very greatest lion of Ajaccio, it is too late to see this evening; yet one cannot contemplate even the outside of the house without feelings of singular interest. Nor, till now, did I know that the family occupied a palazzo of such size and of so much appearance of well-to-do condition.

April 11

5 A.M.—All is cloud and mist, and small seems the chance as yet of settled fine weather, though rain has fallen all night. But it clears later, as it did yesterday, and allows me a couple of hours for drawing at the end of the Cours Grandval, and at the Grotto of Napoleon, where the lichen-grown granite boulders are a picture, and the growth of vegetation on all sides charming. My work, however, is cut short by a sharp storm of hail, and for nearly ten minutes a fall of sleety snow makes the grotto a welcome refuge. (As usual, they tell me 'such weather in April was never before known in Ajaccio!' but was not the same said to me, April 12, 1864, concerning the weather in Crete?)

At nine, to the Prefecture, where I find M. Galloni d'Istria, the Secretary-General. This gentleman, whose time during the absence of M. le Préfet is so fully occupied that I hardly expected him to be able to devote much attention to the casual bearer of introductory letters, receives me with the greatest friendliness; and the interest he takes in my desire to see Corsica thoroughly, and to portray its scenery, is very encouraging; for the advice of one so intimately acquainted with every part of the island is invaluable. He suggests I should go to Sartène, Bonifacio, and Porto Vecchio (whence I may visit the forests of Spedale named to me by M. Merimée), then cross the mountains from Solenzaro, and return again to Sartène by the pass and forest of Bavella. By this route, he tells me, I shall traverse some of the finest inland Corsican scenery, as well as visit the most interesting towns in the southern part of the island, and that the whole of the tour can be made in a carriage, provided it be a light one; for the broad Route Impériale, or diligence road, does not cross the mountains at Bavella; the last part of the journey, moreover, is not so certain to be effected if any heavy fall of snow should occur in the high forest passes. Nor did the active help of M. Galloni d'Istria cease here. He gave me a first-rate map of the island, and promises letters of introduction to persons residing in the places through which I must go while making the first tour he has thus indicated, and on my return to Ajaccio, he will provide letters to all other parts of the island I may wish to visit. It does not always happen that an artist's topographical tour should be so completely entered into and so warmly assisted by an official personage; and I leave M. Galloni d'Istria, feeling not only much obliged to himself, but also to M. Prosper Merimée for having so kindly procured letters for me to M. le Préfet.

Returning to the hotel, after a visit to the J.S.s, the next step is to decide finally in what mode of travelling I can best manage to make characteristic drawings of so large an island as Corsica during the short time at my disposal. Four plans present themselves, and it becomes urgent that I should fix on one of these, and carry it into execution.

First—To go to the principal towns by diligence—certainly a cheaper plan than any other. But as these public vehicles go by night as well as by day, the object of my visit—to study scenery—would be but half gained, nor, indeed, so much as half, for a diligence could not be stopped for the sake of drawing a landscape, though never so beautiful; and many disadvantages, to wit, jolting, crowding, and dirt, would assuredly more or less interfere with work after some twenty-four hours' journey. Moreover, from Porto Vecchio or Solenzaro no diligence roads cross the island, and once arrived at the first-named of those places, further progress would be stopped, as there are no vehicles for hire at all on the east side of the island, excepting at Bastia. Plan No. 1 is therefore abandoned.

Secondly—To hire horses and ride; doubtless, great freedom of action is ensured by such an arrangement. Yet against it there are numerous personal objections not to be overruled. So exit plan No. 2.

Thirdly—Luggage might be sent on by Diligence, and I might walk, my servant carrying folios and food for the day, a plan I have constantly worked out in Greece, Italy, Crete, etc. But in Corsica this system could

AJACCIO

SCENERY NEAR SARTENE

hardly be effected, for, from what I can learn, the towns are sometimes farther apart than even the longest day's walk could manage, and with no halting-place between them; very often too much time would thus be wasted in such a plan, because great portions of the island would probably not present any interest for the pencil. To go on foot through some of the forest scenery may be necessary; but a quicker process for seeing and drawing the greater part of Corsica in ten weeks must be adopted.

Fourthly—There remains this plan, on which, after looking at the matter in all its bearings, I finally decide—namely, to hire a two-horse carriage for the whole time of my stay, paying for it so much daily, and using it for long or for short journeys, either as there may be much or little to draw, or according to the distance of halting-places. In this way I should be free to make drawings in the neighbourhood of the principal towns, or to make excursions from them to various points; and if any scene on the high road could not easily be returned to, owing to too great distance, I might halt my vehicle while I worked, or perhaps oftener send it on and walk; on the other hand, I could drive as quickly as possible through districts in which there is little of the picturesque. This plan of travelling, though apparently the most expensive, will economise time, and in the end, I believe, will prove the cheapest; for my object in coming to Corsica being that of carrying away the greatest possible number of records of its scenery, the saving some outlay will not compensate for a meagre portfolio, and I might ultimately discover the least costly process to be also the least satisfactory. In support of which hypothesis a fable taught me long years ago by one dead and gone recurs to my memory.

Once upon a time three poor students, all very near-sighted, and each possessing a single pair of horn-rimmed spectacles, set out to walk to a remote university, for the purpose of competing for a professorship.

On the way, while sleeping by the road-side, a thief stole their three pairs of horn-rimmed spectacles.

Waking, their distress was great: they stumbled, they fell, they lost their way; and night was at hand, when they met a pedlar.

'Have you any spectacles?' said the three miserable students.

'Yes,' said the pedlar, 'exactly three pairs; but they are set in gold, and with magnificent workmanship; in fact, they were made for the king, and they cost so much——'

'Such a sum,' said the students, 'is absurd; it is nearly as much as we possess.'

'I cannot,' the pedlar replied, 'take less; but here is an ivory-handled frying-pan which I can let you have for a trifling sum, and I strongly recommend you to buy it, because it is such an astonishing bargain, and you may never again chance to meet with a similarly joyful opportunity.'

Said the eldest of the three students, 'I will grope my way on as I can. It is ridiculous to buy a pair of this man's spectacles at such a price.'

'And I,' said the second, 'am determined to purchase the ivory-handled frying-pan; it costs little, and will be very useful, and I may never again have such an extraordinary bargain.'

But the youngest of the three, undisturbed by the laughter of the two others, bought the gold-rimmed sumptuous spectacles, and was soon out of sight.

Thereon, No. 1 set off slowly, but, falling into a ditch by reason of his blindness, broke his leg, and was carried back, by a charitable passer-by in a cart, to his native town.

No. 2 wandered on, but lost his way inextricably, and, after much suffering, was obliged to sell his ivory-handled frying-pan at a great loss, to enable him to return home.

No. 3 reached the University, gained the prize, and was made Professor of Grumphiology, with a house and fixed salary, and lived happily ever after.

Moral—to pay much for what is most useful is wiser than to pay little for what is not so.

Two other matters have to be settled before starting 'to see all Corsica'. First, the direction in which to travel, and the time at which to undertake certain tours; and, secondly, the division of baggage, with regard to daily and nightly comfort. The first question has been already partly settled by M. Galloni d'Istria's advice, for it is doubtless best to commence with the southern coasts of the island, as in all probability the heat will be soonest felt there; and thence, if possible, to see all that is necessary of the eastern plains, as, at the end of May, they begin to be malarious and unwholesome, that is, for a working painter; since it is one thing to travel rapidly through feverish air, and quite another to sit drawing in it for several hours, or to halt in it when heated, etc. Tours to the higher forests, and the centre of the island, may be postponed till all risk of snow and rain are passed.

Next as to baggage. Not knowing in the least what sort of accommodation is to be met with, I shall carry a good supply. Dividing my *roba*, and leaving part of it with my host, M. Ottavi, I shall take lots of drawing material, and clothing for hot and cold weather, besides my small folding bed; so that, with my servant's help, I may at least be as comfortable as in Albanian khans, Cretan cottages, or Syrian sheds. For it is certain that at fifty-six roughing it is not so easy as at thirty or forty, and if good rest at night is not to be procured, the journey may as well be given up, for there would be an end of work. Last of all, a fitting carriage and driver are to be found, and price, etc., agreed on.

Here is a visit from M. Martinenghi; he kindly offers to show me some pictures in his possession, some by Salvator Rosa, etc., and appears confounded at the little enthusiasm I express on the subject, and at my declining the proposal. In this hotel there resides an English lady —a Miss C.[1]—who has not only been here for some months, but has visited many parts of the island; and before I set off I shall venture on a visit to her, to get some hints about my journey.

Noon.—What is going to happen? A remarkable clattering noise fills the air. I look out of window, and behold a torrent of children—a hundred, at least—all carrying bits of wood, which they knock, and bump, and rattle against all the railings, doorsteps, and walls, as their procession passes on. Now, in most southern places where Christians are desirous of celebrating Easter by triumphant noises, pistols and crackers are fired off at the proper time; every one who has been in Rome at that season is aware of the uproar made on the Saturday preceding Easter Day; and in the Maltese villages, at Alexandria, and other eastern cities, the hullabaloo is fearful. But here, in Corsica, no firearms of any sort are at present allowed to be in the hands of the people,

---

[1] Miss Campbell: she belonged, Angus Davidson writes in *Edward Lear*, 'to that class of slightly eccentric middle-aged Englishwomen of independent means of which a representative is to be found in all the obscurer Mediterranean ports—descendants, however inglorious, of the illustrious tradition of Lady Hester Stanhope'. Lear himself described her as 'a vast and manlike maiden, who roars and raves about Corsica'.

and so the popular piety finds vent in this singular outburst of rattling pieces of wood, which, I am told, has a dim reference to Judas Iscariot, the thumps on the rails and stones being typical of what the faithful consider that person's bones, were he living, should receive.

At 1 P.M. I go out to the broad Cours Grandval, and pass most of the afternoon in making drawings near the Grotto of Napoleon. For the day is now finer, the clouds higher, and the mountains at intervals nearly clear. The view over Ajaccio from this point is indeed fine; the noble range of snowy heights beyond the head of the gulf rise magnificently above the city, and the ugliness of its detail is lost in the midst of so large and glorious a picture, of which it forms so small a part. The colour of this landscape, too, is very beautiful; the deep-green clustering foliage in the middle distance, and the grey olives, the purple nearer the hills, and the dazzling white snow-line more remote, the calm blue of the sea (today really lake-like), and the exquisite variety of vegetation in the foreground, combine to make one of the most delightful of scenes— one, however, by no means easy to convey a just idea of on paper.

I feel that I am beginning to be fascinated by Corsica, and to discover that it is far fuller of landscape beauty than I had thought; those long vistas of valley and mountain must needs contain stores of interest and novelty, and far away the high silver Alp-like points speak of grand and majestic scenery, well worth an effort to visit, all of which has been hidden until now by the thick cloud-covering of the distant hills.

At five-thirty, after a peep at the J.S.s in their new dwelling at Dr. Ribton's, in one of the four cottage villas, I went up the hill on the north side of the town, immediately above the Hotel de Londres; there are very charming walks among olive trees here, as well as on an open kind of common, where cactus growth and granite boulders form a thousand ready-made foregrounds. This is one of the most striking views I have yet seen in the neighbourhood of Ajaccio; far below lies spread out the whole city and the broad gulf, across which you look to the high range of hills stretching out to Capo Moro, while to the east the gorge of Bocognano and the lofty snow-topped walls which shut in the valley of Bastelica rise in great splendour and beauty. The line of the hill cape opposite is, however, one only to be managed in a picture with delicacy, by breaking it with cloud shadows, for its uniform length is wanting in variety of outline. Pitifully barren of interest is the city as to architecture. In what place along the two Riviere, or the Gulf of Spezzia—or, indeed, in what part of Italian coast scenery in general—should one not feel a desire to sketch some arch, some campanile, or even the whole town or village? Here, on the contrary, you seek to avoid drawing a space literally filled by great warehouselike buildings, unrelieved in the slightest way except by parallel lines of windows. This, and the gloomy darkness of the dress of both sexes, are certainly drawbacks to Ajaccio in a picturesque sense.

At dinner, M. Ottavi tells me that from fifteen to twenty-five francs daily may be asked for a two-horse carriage. But he is to inquire further.

APRIL 12

6 A.M.—At the end of the Cours Grandval. The morning is lovely, and there is a delicious fresh and light mountain-air sort of feeling in the atmosphere. The distant heights are absolutely clear, a wall of opal, and today, for the first time, I see this remarkable view in perfection. No amount of building, even should this part of Corsica become eventually as villa-covered as Mentone or Cannes, Torquay or Norwood, can ever affect the character of this exquisite prospect, which depends on elements far above all risk of change; on the wide extent of its horizon and on the great majesty of the two dark ranges of hills opposite, connected by a line of heights still loftier, conveying a forcible impression of the solemn inner-mountain life of the island; on the broad and generally placid gulf; on the long and marked form of the hills to the south side of it; and on the wide expanse of water towards the western sea. All these cannot alter. The olive-grown slopes, the almond groves, the gardens, and the breadth of shrubby wilderness and high cactus may disappear, but the general aspect of the distance cannot change. Why, I ask myself, do people compare this Gulf to the Bay of Naples? To me it seems that no two places more dissimilar can exist.

Scarcely anyone comes to this part of the neighbourhood of Ajaccio; a few boys and girls are seen searching for wild asparagus, and one or two individuals with surprising chimney-pot hats taking a morning walk. So till nine I draw quietly, and, after a talk with the J.S.s, return to the town and get letters from the post. If I wanted any confirmation of my resolve not to go about the island in diligences, I could have none better than an examination of the vehicles which start at 11 A.M. for Sartène and Bonifacio, for Vico, and for Bastia via Corte. To be shut up in one of these might be endured if duty or necessity so ordered; but on no other consideration whatever.

On coming back to the hotel the plague of little boys bursts forth again in a new phase. It pleases some twenty to have instituted a blockade inside the street door of the house, and the fun is to hold it closed against the battering and hammering of some twenty outside, wholly irrespective of the interests of the frequenters of the establishment; and this lasts till the outer party conquer and the door is beaten in, when the calamity ceases, and a passage upstairs becomes possible. At no time does the impression of multitudinous little-boyhood leave me in Ajaccio; no sooner am I upstairs than I happen to look beyond the houses of the Place du Diamant towards two high and slanting walls following the direction of the steep hill-side hard by. Now, in any other place where I ever was, such walls would be infested by cats, or pigeons, or swallows; but here I count twenty-eight little boys, all crawling up the wall-tops after the fashion of lizards, and sliding down again—which pastime goes on all day long.

M. Galloni d'Istria pays me a visit, and obligingly goes over the ground I am about to visit on the Government map with me. He quite concurs with me as to the advantage of a carriage tour, and recommends me to stay first at Sartène, one of the four Sous-préfectures of the island, and where, by means of letters he will supply me with, I can learn more definitely from M. le Sous-Inspecteur of Forests, what may be the condition of the high passes as to snow in the neighbourhood of the Forest of Bavella, through which I am to return to Ajaccio. He recommends me to visit the plains on the east side as early as I can, on account of their great unhealthiness late in the season, and to leave the high forests on the west and in the centre of the island till the snow is melted and the chestnut woods out in leaf. I decide, therefore, to start on the 14th or 15th, if, meantime, I can find a carriage to suit me.

2 P.M.—To the Necropolis on the sea-shore road. Many of these tomb-temples are very pleasing in form, and the view from the last of them looking back to the gulf-head and mountains is striking. They

38

stand all along the shore, at the foot of the hills which form the northern side of the gulf, ending in Punto Parata, separated by the carriage road from the granite rocks that stretch out into the sea, a sad but picturesque landscape, and one somewhat recalling the Via Appia or other sepulchre-bordered roads.

Beyond the Campo Santo all along the road-side the growth of myrtle, lentisk, cactus, and asphodel, is luxuriant beyond description; and the Iles Sanguinaires form numberless combinations with such foregrounds. Masses of pale granite, covered in part with cystus, are at the outer edge of the road, and run out into the gulf in spurs, white foam breaking over them and catching the sunlight, while the pointed islets on the horizon gleam darkly purple against the deepening sky tints.

Returning, there are more persons walking, as it is a fête day, than I have yet seen in the neighbourhood of Ajaccio. The head-dress of the women, so graceful and becoming, is generally, among those not in mourning, of buff or purple, with a broad white border. The short Greek spencer and fluted dress is most frequently worn, though there are a few of more modern or fashionable cut. I observe hardly any girls whom one might call beautiful, but nearly all have a very pleasing expression and a look of intelligence. Among the gloomily dressed men, a group of French soldiers here and there in red and blue form a pictorial relief.

In the town the small-boy plague has gone into another form today, besides the passage-swarming and door-blocking. Crowds of urchins have taken to rushing to and fro with small barrows with shrilly shrieking wheels; each barrow contains three small Corsicans, and is pushed and pulled by twice as many more.

After dinner I visit Miss C., whose acquaintance indeed is well worth cultivating. Her interest in Corsica and all it contains is extreme. The collection of plants and natural history she has made in the island, and her drawings of the numerous fish found here, must have fully occupied her leisure through the winter; she has already accomplished some long mountain excursions, and really knows the island well. A person uniting great activity of mind, physical energy, good judgement and taste, as this lady appears to do, and bent on introducing Corsica to the English south-seeking public, may really become instrumental in bringing about great changes in Ajaccio.

39

APRIL 13

5 A.M.—Off once more to the cactus and asphodel lands beyond the Cours Grandval, to finish or proceed with drawings; mountains perfectly clear—gorgeous purple, silver, and blue. I doubt if any double range can be finer, what though the refinement of Greek outline and the contrast of plains be wanting. If the city were tolerably supplied with picturesque architecture, few finer subjects for a painting could be found, so good is the middle distance of trees, so rich and varied the foreground vegetation. I work, too, this morning at another drawing nearer the city, and quite on the shore; in the first hours of morning this view is very imposing, the vulgar detail of the houses being hidden in shade, and the high snow mountains appearing to rise directly above them.

M. Galloni has not yet sent the promised budget of letters; neither have I found a carriage; so it seems clear that a start tomorrow cannot be accomplished. The landlord here asks me if he shall give me a letter of introduction to some *banditti*, a few of whom are still known to live in the Macchie, or woods of the interior. 'They are rich,' says M. Ottavi, '*ils ne manquent rien*—they have plenty of sheep and do nobody any harm.' But Madame O., on the contrary, says, '*Ah, je vous prie donc, ne vous en allez pas, ils vous abimeront!*—do not go, I implore you, they will destroy you!' At breakfast-time my host and hostess generally supply one of the *broches*, or *broccie*, a sort of cheese or preparation of milk, for which Corsica is famous; it is made of sheep's milk, and is precisely the same as the *ricotta* of Italy. Generally, it is eaten with sugar. With fresh fish, *broccie*, and the good ordinary red wine for daily fare, might not a painter do well to come here—air and landscape being such as they are? Already I begin to feel infected by Corsica-mania, the more that the quiet of the country adjoining this city reminds me of Olevano and Civitella and other mountain places where I studied painting in early days. Assuredly Ajaccio is a place where activity and bustle are little known; very seldom you see a carriage in its streets, barring those of the postal service; and even carts are rare objects.

By and by comes the man who is to let me the carriage and two horses. We agree on the price, fifteen francs a day—this is to include all expenses of driver and horses, and I am to pay neither more nor less, whether I remain stationary or use the trap daily. Tomorrow I am to make a trial excursion.

It is discovered that my man Giorgio (of whom, in some twelve or thirteen years' service, there exists no tradition of his having been known to forget anything), has left my flask on board the steamer, so we must take to gourds, which, indeed, are the popular and appropriate media for carrying fluid in Corsica. Almost every peasant carries one, slung to his shoulder by a string; those in common use are generally of large size, but there are others smaller, very pretty and delicate, and these, when polished and finished with silver stoppers and chains, are really elegant.

2 P.M.—What is there to do? There is Napoleon's house to be seen; or rather that in which he was born. So, not being in an industrious mood (and, indeed, the cloudiness of the day prevents colouring out of doors, as I had intended), I go to the Place Létitia, a small square, of which, as I before mentioned, the Casa Buonaparte forms almost the whole of one side. Although I confess to having gone to this sight with a kind of routine or duty feeling, the visit gave me very great pleasure. The house—there is now an inscription above the door recording that Napoleon I was born there, with the date of his birth—is much more roomy and pleasantly habitable than its exterior would lead one to expect, and it is easy to see that it was one of a superior class in Ajaccio a century back. Nearly all the furniture passed into the possession of the Ramolini (Madame Letitia's family), who inherited the property; but there are still in the apartments mirrors, old framework of chairs (like the walls, they appear to have been formerly covered with red or gilt tapestry), marble chimney-pieces, and large fireplaces, one or two highly ornamented chests, an ancient spinet-piano, the sedan-chair of Madame, her bedstead, and a few portraits; all beside, as far as I saw, is bare unfurnished wall, and much of what I have named has been collected by the present Emperor of the French from various places. The long gallery, the terrace and courtyard at the back of the house, the dining-room, every part of the building has its interest of association, and by walking through the apartments one is carried back to the days when the most wonderful man of modern times lived in it as a boy. To me, who years ago was in the habit of frequently visiting one branch of

the Buonaparte family, the place is doubly interesting; and when I
remember the group of the late Prince Canino's numerous children, of
whom in those days I saw so much, I seem to be more able to realise the
circle of the first Napoleon's mother and her little ones. The elderly
person who showed me the house had lived in the service of Princess
Caroline Buonaparte-Murat, Queen of Naples, and was interested at
hearing me speak of the houses at Musignano and l'Arricia, where I was
wont to be so kindly received in former days. No Buonaparte now
resides at Ajaccio, except the Princess Mariana, wife of Prince Louis
Lucien, a younger brother of Charles Lucien, late Prince of Canino.
There is plenty of food for reflection in a visit to the Casa Buonaparte
in Ajaccio.

3 P.M.—I wander through this town, so like a village in its outskirts,
and sit on a wall to write journal notes and cast up accounts. There is a
statue of General Abbatucci close by, with posts, chain-connected, at a
little distance all round it. I count fifty-three children swinging on these
chains, and rather more swarming up some carts not far off. Certainly,
the multitude of children is a striking feature of Ajaccio street scenery,
and M. Ottavi tells me that numbers of the male population emigrate
to the Continent for a part of the year, so that the apparent comparative
fewness of grown-up men or youths may be thus accounted for. After
walking a mile or two I turned back when near the Palazzo Bacciocchi,
a handsome building which stands in gardens towards the head of the
gulf, and thence, repassing the town, regained my favourite spot at the
end of the Cours Grandval. Here, in spite of the cold and chilly afternoon, I find Mrs. J.S. making a good view of the scene, for she hath an
able hand and eye; but I, too idle to recommence work, employ myself
in constructing an artificial and beautiful foreground of cactus leaves and
asphodel stalks stuck endways into a tall pyramid of stones for that lady
to copy, who, far from applauding, not only censures my performance
as absolutely deficient in natural grace, but absolutely declines to make
a faithful portrait of it in her sketch.

Back to the hotel, after sitting some time with J.A.S., and here I
find that M. Galloni d'Istria has very kindly sent me the promised
budget of introductory letters for Olmeto, Sartène, Bonifacio, and
Porto Vecchio. All today, after the first hour or two of early sunshine,
has been gloomy and cloudy. *Helix tristis* prevails.

CHAPTER II

APRIL 14

STILL thick cloud, not a mountain-top visible: Corsican topography thriveth not. Nevertheless, at seven I go out to the cactus land and granite rocks, for one can make foreground studies; but no, it begins to rain, and I have to return. Is there, as I said this time four years ago in Crete, no settled weather here in April? So I sit down to write letters, especially one to M. Galloni d'Istria, thanking him for his assistance.

Miss C. went yesterday to Bastelica, but as yet those high regions are too heavily laden with snow; so that she came back instead of staying there. This lady is very obliging in answering my innumerable questions about numerous places in Corsica.

At nine, when it rains less, I call at Dr. Ribton's to see the J.S.s. You enter their *salle à manger* straight from the road, a system which—all the world being seated at breakfast—is destructive to the peace of the delicate-minded intruder.

Says a Frenchman to me, and truly—speaking of the slow-walking people in the Piazza here—'*ils se promènent, ces Corses, comme des estropiés, ou commes des limaçons*—these Corsicans walk like cripples or snails'—*Helix tristis* to wit. And, certainly, on a wet day it would be hard to find so dull a place as Ajaccio. Suli, in Albania, is gay by comparison, Wadi Halfa, in Nubia, bustling; for those are places of by-gone times, whereas we are here in a 'city'.

An inevitable necessary, money, is next to be obtained through a letter of credit to M. Conti, Receveur-Général; and after that comes a visit to Miss C., who prophesies that I shall repent employing the people of whom I have hired the carriage. Meanwhile the carriage in question comes; it seems a comfortable and strong trap, and I do not think fifteen francs a day will be dear if the driver and horses are good; of the latter G. remarks, '$εἶναι ὡσὰν ποντικὸι$—they are like rats'—and small they certainly are.

2 P.M.—After hard rain all the morning it is now moderately fine,

43

so I set off to try the vehicle, the driver of which I own has a face—if there be any truth in physiognomy—not at all indicative of good character. The trap does not go badly—which, as it may be one's daily home for a couple of months, it is pleasant to know—and the two poor little horses shuffle along quickly enough. We take the road to Castellucio, the upper Penitencier, or convict establishment, but turn off at the lower building, whence a bridle road goes on to St. Antonio, a place Miss C. recommends me to visit as one of the most picturesque hereabouts. All around the Penitencier convicts are working, and fast changing these bare or *maquis*-covered hills into vineyards.

Leaving the carriage here, I follow a winding track, which, leading to the rocks of St. Antonio, very soon leaves all traces of habitation and humanity, and might be exceedingly remote from cities instead of close to a capital. The walk along the hills is delightful, and the *maquis* of which I have heard and read so much, full of charm—orchids, cyclamen, lavender, myrtle, cystus, absolutely a garden of shrubs and flowers. As the path approaches the mountain which stands immediately above the chapel of St. Antonio, the views of this 'wild waste place' become wondrously grand. Such granite crags and boulders I think I have only seen at Philæ and in the peninsula of Sinai; and from the little platform, whence the whole mountain-side is visible, with the western sea beyond, the strangely desolate prospect is greatly impressive. The chapel, a small and ancient building, can only be portrayed together with the rocks from one or two positions; but the cliff or mountain is in itself a world of study, an endless storehouse of chasms, boulders, and peaks. Many new and great ideas of landscape may be gained by the painter who visits St. Antonio.

Returning to the trap, I drive to the town, and, at G.'s request, go to the fish-market, which is really well worth a visit, for the strange beauty of colour and the novelty of form of the fish there. Then a little more study at the 'grotto gardens' and a visit to J.A.S. wind up the day.

At one or two tomorrow I hope to start on my way to the south of the island, sleeping the first night at Cauro.

April 15

5 A.M.—Heavy rain has fallen all night, and there is much more snow on the mountains, a sign probably of settled fine weather. For a short time I drew at the 'grotto gardens', from which beautiful spot the landscape never tires; this morning the mountains are of the very darkest purple, and the freshness of the flowers and foliage after rain delicious. The drums and bugles of the soldiery make an odd accompaniment to scenery so tranquil and poetical. At Dr. R.'s, where I call to say good-bye to the J.S.s, I find S. far from well, and leave them uneasily with a feeling that his inability to travel may detain them here longer than they anticipate.

Arrangements for the afternoon's start, bill settling, etc., occupy me till noon, and then follows a visit with Miss C. (with whom the *Helix tristis* has nothing in common, for she is always merry and active) to the Hotel de France, where the F.W. family are staying; thence, with two more ladies, we adjourn to the house of the Princess Louis Lucien, or, as she is more generally called, the Princess Mariana Buonaparte. This lady, who has still the remains of great beauty, has much charm of manner, and is much liked by those who know her. Her rooms, pleasant in situation, were full of interesting portraits of the Buonaparte family. Her pleasure in speaking of Musignano, where she found I had formerly been used to study, was very evident, and my offer to send her a small view of the house was received with delight.

Our party then go to the Préfecture, where Miss C. wants to show us some young moufflons or *muffoli*; there are two of them, lambs or kids, call them as you will, well-made, active little creatures, shy and wild, notwithstanding their early captivity. The moufflon, an animal partaking of the goat nature and of that of the sheep, inhabits only the highest and most savage districts of Corsica, and comes down to lower levels only when compelled to do so by winter's heavy snows.

It was two-thirty before the trap came to the hotel, and careful packing commenced; one of my saddle-bags (or *bisacchi*) and the portable bed are stowed behind, well secured against rain by two wild boar skins; inside the carriage, my servant's package and my leather hand-bag for small objects (Valery's volume, my only guide, included) leave

45

good room for self, besides a large folio in the old Coliseum—a case or sack so called by my servant from its extreme antiquity and venerable look, used for holding drawing materials or food in many expeditions— and G. on the outside seat with the coachman, whose appearance is objectionable, and whose name is Peter, complete the arrangement. The kindly Miss C. has sent me a flask in place of the one lost, and calls from the window, cheerfully, 'You should have taken my man Jean! all your luggage will fall off! your horses will tumble! everything will go wrong!' *Absit omen!* and finally we start at three-thirty.

The way is along the Cours Napoléon, and out of the city towards the head of the gulf, leaving on the left the roads to Castelluccio, Alata, and Bastia, and passing the Villa Bacciocchi and its gardens, with some scattered villas and mulberry plantations—all these environs of Ajaccio are considered unhealthy in summer-time, on account of the marshy ground at the end of the gulf, parent of malaria fever. From this side of Ajaccio the view of the city is rather wanting in interest, though with a composition of boats it might be made more worthy; perhaps from near the Lazzaretto, or Fort d'Aspretto it is best. The blackness of the crows on the shore, and that of the dress of the peasantry, alike wanting in liveliness, are the foreground accompaniments. Leaving the coast the road passes along the Campo di Loro (or dell' Oro), a flat plain with here and there those wide spreading marshes, so unfriendly to the health of the city. The rivers Gravona and Prunelli, which flow from the high mountains of Renoso and dell' Oro, by the valleys of Bocognano and Bastelica to the sea, are crossed by long bridges. In winter-time, when the snow lies on the heights at the head of these valleys, many beautiful pictures might be made here among the broad green meadows; just now, heavy storm clouds obscure the distance; flocks of blackest sheep and a world of glittering silver-blossomed asphodels are the chief objects noteworthy. From the River Prunelli, where the road turns inland, and begins to rise, the scenery becomes more rugged and severe, reminding me of that of the valley of the Kalamà in Albania, hemmed in by hills of no great height, above which are glimpses of far purple and snow.

At five the ascent becomes steeper and winding, and I avoid the high road to walk by short cuts, pleasant paths by heath-like slopes above a stream, beside which groups of large and as yet leafless chestnut trees are scattered. Every turn of the way up the hill shows changes of lovely green scenery, dells of crowded ilex, and a bosky richness of foliage, with now and then knots of tall trees on slanting turf, such as Stohard might have painted; and then, looking back, the whole Gulf of Ajaccio is spread out to the western sun, and the capital of the island, the rocky hill of St. Antonio, and the long lines of the hills on the northern side of the gulf, fill up the picture.

Higher up still, the view into the valley of the Prunelli becomes most grand, and from a point in the road near some wayside houses (they call the place Barraconi), the mountains shutting in the valley are particularly imposing, and I am sorry to that it is too late (6 P.M.) to do more than jot down a memorandum of the exquisite effect of sunset which just now makes this scene so fine. As the sun goes down, the high snowy summit of Mont Renoso seems on fire, seen through a rose-coloured veil of mist above the nearer dark purple mountain; below this, in deepest shadow, are great masses of rock, and at their foot lies the rich hollow valley and village of Suarella—a scene which I trust to return to.

6.30 P.M.—The village of Cauro is reached slowly, and by a stiff last pull, just as the sunset hues of gold and crimson—bright as those blazing dying-day glories on the Nile—have turned to lilac and cold grey. The chief part of the village and its church stands back above the high road on the right (you may see it glittering against the hills-side as you stand at the grotto of Napoleon at Ajaccio, or at the end of the Cours Grand-val), that with which I have to do is a row of mean-looking houses by the wayside on the left, and I am curious to know what sort of accommodation Corsican mountain travel will really exhibit. Two of the dwellings are lodging-houses, or, as they are called in this island, hotels, a term applied here to the least pretentious of inns, such as we might call pot-houses in an English village, and of these two the first applied to is full, and cannot take me in. Nor does there seem much better fortune at the second hotel, at the door of which two very civil landladies inform me, with many regrets, that their three rooms are taken up by a party of officials on a tour of inspection of boundaries, and that they have but their own apartment left, which they will give up. This, as a beginning, of Corsican journeys, is not encouraging; but there is no help for it, for it is too late to go on or to go back; and, besides, having undertaken to see all Corsica, the matter must be gone through as it best may. So the

47

roba is brought up to the third floor by a rickety ladder-stair, and in a little while my man sets up my bed, to the extreme amazement of the two hostesses, and makes things tolerably comfortable in one corner, while a mattress in the farther one is to do for himself. The hostesses, with all the family, are to sleep in the kitchen, and Peter, the coachman, inside the trap.

Meanwhile, Mdme Angela Paoloni, the chief landlady, brings notice that M. the Inspector, and the other officials, are about to sit down to supper, and she intimates plainly that unless I and my servant do so, too, no other opportunity may present itself; so that the occasion is seized without delay. Miss C. has already told me that there would rarely be a chance of master and man eating separately, and that in her journeys she and her maid had always been co-partners at meals.

In a small but clean-looking front room there was a large round table, which everyone sat down to. The quality of the food served was quite unexpected in so rough-looking a roadside hostelry; there was a tolerably good soup, and after it the inevitable boiled beef and pickles, then a stew, a timballo, roast lamb and salad, and a superb broccio. Capital wine, and plenty of it, was supplied.

Hardly had I sat down to supper than I found I had committed an error, into which a little previous thought might have prevented my falling; yet, with the very best intentions, a man may sometimes 'rush in where angels fear to tread'. One of the party spoke French with a Parisian accent, the others were Corsicans. '*Vous êtes donc Français, Monsieur?*' said I; a remark which directly produced a sudden chill and pause, and after that came this reply—'*Monsieur, nous sommes tous Français.*' I had yet to learn that the words 'French' and 'Corsican' are not used by the discreet in this island; you should indicate the first by 'Continental', and the second by 'Insulaire' or *du pays*. It is as well, indeed, to recollect that there are old men still living who can remember the hopes of Corsican independence even up to the end of the last century, and, consequently, all allusions by a stranger to differences of race are as well avoided, now that both people are under one government.

The fact, too, that I spoke Italian with greater facility than French evidently puzzled my supper companions, and when I asked questions about the country, there was a kind of occult distrust observable;

SARTENE

PORT OF BONIFACIO

travellers in Corsica—in out-of-the-way places at least—are rare; might I not be a revolutionary agent? I asked about the wines made in the island, but when ill luck urged me to speak about Sardinian produce, dumbness or short replies ensued, and at once I found that Sardinia was a tabooed subject. The better I spoke Italian and the more I hesitated in French, the less respectable I became, and since at the commencement of travelling in a new country one has all to ask and learn, my numerous inquiries were received and answered with caution, and my evil genius having suddenly prompted me to ask something about the Straits of Bonifacio, there was again a full stop, and a sensation as if all Caprera-cum-Garibaldi were about to burst into the room.

After this I confined myself strictly to observations on the nature of the supper and upon the climate of Ajaccio, and as the conversation afterwards was chiefly on local or municipal topics, I was glad to get away to rest for an early start tomorrow.

Earnestly entreating my servant to snore as little as possible (he can hardly occasion more disturbance than F.L.,[1] and I used to suffer in Greek khans from old Andrea), I congratulate myself on my forethought in bringing my little military bed, and think that if Corsican travel brings no greater hardship than this of its first day, it may be very bearable.

April 16

Mdme Angela Paoloni, of the 'Hotel' or 'Café Restaurant du Cours', at Cauro, did not certainly overcharge for her supper and lodging, and for coffee this morning—to wit, three francs per head. A desire to oblige, and a homely sort of friendly manner, are also what I have to note down respecting this the first Corsican country inn I have come to.

By 6 A.M. Peter and the trap are ready, but as the road is an ascent as far as the Col San Giorgio, eight kilomètres onward, and, as the morning is lovely, I set off walking, after having searched in vain for some spot whence I could make a characteristic drawing of Cauro; moreover, the landscape looking westward from above the village, though very beautiful, is of such magnitude and so full of detail as to be

[1] Franklin Lushington.

quite out of the pale of an hour or two's sketching. When the day is but just commenced, and the amount of what may be available for work is as yet unknown, it is not prudent to sit down to make a drawing, the time given to which may be proved later in the day to have been ill bestowed, in comparison with what should have been given to scenes which the painter is then reluctantly compelled to pass by in haste.

All the way up to the Col San Giorgio (the road throughout is broad and good, and the ascent not very steep) a succession of beautiful mountain scenery delights the eye; and from a spot whence the majestic Monte d'Oro forms the principal point above all the surrounding heights, it is impossible not to pause to get a drawing. Yet the fine distance hardly attracts the attention more than the near at hand details of the excessively rich foliage which is the characteristic clothing of all the hills. This *maquis*, or robe of green, covering every part of the landscape except the farthest snowy heights, is beyond description lovely, composed as it is of myrtle, heath, arbutus, broom, lentisk, and other shrubs, while, wherever there is any open space, innumerable crimson cyclamen flowers dot the ground, and the picturesque but less beautiful hellebore flourishes abundantly. Here groups of ilex or chestnut rise above the folds of exquisite verdure; there, but rarely, you pass a plot of cultivation, or a vineyard, in which stands one of those branch-woven towers supported on four poles, and not unlike a Punch and Judy box, called Torri di Baroncello, such as one used to see in days of Calabrian sojourn. The freshness of the morning mountain air adds to the pleasure of this walk, and as it increases higher up, this compensates for the gradually barer scenery of the col, just below the summit of which, marked by a single roadside house, is a plentiful fountain of excellent water.

From the Col San Giorgio the road now turns eastward to descend into the great valley through which the River Taravo flows from the Col di Verde, joined on its way by streams from Zicavo, Sta. Maria, etc., into the Gulf of Valinco. The wide hollow, or basin, presents quite a new prospect full of variety and beauty; on the farther side of it you see the village of Bicchisano, and above that, the road will pass the highest hills that bound the valley, and again dip down to the sea at Propriano, between Olmeto and Sartène.

Meanwhile, the descent to the next village, Grosseto, where Peter the coachman says we must make a midday halt, and whence the road instead of following up the valley towards the mountains runs directly across it, continually increases in beauty; the wild outspread of mountain form beyond, the profuse luxuriance of foliage, the refreshing greenness on all sides are really enchanting; a continual succession of park scenes, groups of large chestnuts and venerable ilex trees, great shadowy snow-topped pine-grown heights far away, or huge granite masses close to the road, giving a constant interest to the scenery. Often I could have liked to make a drawing, but thought it better not to delay at present, for the day's journey may be a long one, and the landscape is of a character to require sustained and attentive work. A landscape painter might well pass months in this valley of foliage, villages, mountain, and river.

9 A.M.—Grosseto is reached, and Peter not a little surprises me by saying it is quite necessary to remain the night there, declaring that the village of Bicchisano is twenty-two kilometres, or some fourteen miles, farther on, but on inquiry I find the distance to be but fourteen kilometres, and that if I prefer doing so I may easily, when the horses have well rested, say by eleven o'clock, get on to Olmeto before evening.

Grosseto is a village of scattered houses, and of the most quiet and rural appearance. Among five or six of its dwellings grouped together is one, neatly white, with Hotel des Amis inscribed on it, to which we have driven; a little beyond the inn, and standing alone, is the church, sheltered by fine ilex trees, and a picture in itself (the ilex grows to an extreme size hereabouts), behind it are more evergreen groves and pastures, and the road which leads by Santa Maria Zicché to Zicavo.

Some time must pass before breakfast, which G. has ordered, can be ready, and I would gladly employ the time in sketching; but, as is usual when an artist is obliged to stop anywhere for some such commonplace cause as horse-baiting, eating, or sleeping, the spot to which destiny nails him happens to be the least picturesque in the neighbourhood, and on the present occasion, without going back some distance, it is not easy to hit upon a subject for drawing, unless one made an elaborate study of an evergreen oak. The whole of this beautiful valley seems full of 'silent woody places', but all the scenery is of a grave, or as some would say a Poussinesque character, for the sombre foliaged cork and ilex give ever a sad and dark tone to landscape, and a hasty sketch can convey but little idea of its character.

51

The village church is the only subject I can commence on, but, perversely enough, this can be done as I wish but from one single spot, to wit, in the road; so I send for a chair and draw in public. But there is no fear of being disturbed; a few men, all grave-looking, and dressed in shabby black and brown, stand round, but are quite well behaved, and do not interrupt me, while groups of children look on silently at a greater distance. These Corsicans all appear to me intelligent; I cannot recall having as yet seen a dull or stupid countenance in man, woman, or child; nor is the intelligent expression one of sharp cunning, but rather of thought and good sense, always, however, with a shade of gravity—very little gaiety have I yet seen in Corsica. During this morning's progress I do not think I saw more than eight or ten peasants, and of those, three were close to a mill hard by this village, yet this is the high road to the south of the island, and the diligence stops to bait at the Hotel des Amis daily.

At nine-thirty I go into the little wayside inn, and through a dirty entrance and by a bad wooden staircase arrive at a middle room, which seems that used by the family, and on each side of this are very clean and tidy little chambers, vastly better than the outside of the house would lead one to expect. In one of these, where prints of the Emperor and Empress, and of some of the acts of Napoleon I, adorn the walls, and in every part of which there are evident marks of attention to neatness and cleanliness, a small table is covered with a clean cloth, and breakfast is soon brought. The hostess, a homely but pleasant-mannered widow, with two rather nice-looking daughters, and a son who acts as waiter, apologise in few words for having little variety of eatables. Travellers, they say, come very unexpectedly, and for long intervals not at all; so that, excepting at the times of arrival of the diligences, they seldom have food in the house beyond such as they now set on the table, namely, eggs and salame (or ham sausage), a plate of good trout, and an indifferent steak, but, above all, a famous broccio, for which, on G. asking if they had any, they had dispatched a messenger half an hour ago to some sheepfolds nearer the hills. Assuredly, after much that one has heard of wild and savage Corsica, the interior accommodation of this little inn surprises me, and the particular civility and desire to please, unaccompanied by any servility, are as satisfactory as the Widow Lionardi's charges, three and a half francs for breakfast for me and my servant, a good bottle of wine, besides coffee, for myself being included in the sum.

11 A.M.—Off again, the road following the course of a clear stream, which makes its way to the Taravo, at times by the edge of steep banks and precipices, which I prefer coasting on foot, because there are no parapets, and Peter the coachman drives 'whiles' more crookedly than is agreeable. The weather just now is delightful, and it is no small pleasure to walk below the beautiful shady trees—groups of immense aged evergreen oaks—through this charming valley, where the first cuckoo of the year is heard, and all along which the scenery, of a grave hue, reminds me frequently of that in 'Epirus' valleys', although both this and that has each its own particular characteristic—Corsica, the broad carriage road which I see ahead for miles; Greece or Albania, pastoral incident and the brightness of gay costume. Now the stream becomes more picturesque, dashing and foaming over granite boulders, like the Tavy or the Lyd; farther on it runs through a deep hollow filled with trees—and such trees! And then it falls into the Taravo, the main river of this fine valley, over which a bridge carries the high road. Hence the landscape generally is less like southern scenery than Welsh or Scotch, though now and then a bit of Greece seems before me, where, as here, the evergreen oak is so characteristic a tree. One or two of these spots completely recall the wood scenes of Eriligova, in Thrace. Would that here there were the village girls of those parts, with their gold and coin chains, their red caps, and their festoon'd flower head-dresses! Meanwhile it is much to sit below huge brown-armed trees, full foliaged, shading a green slope of freshest turf and fern, less green, indeed, than coloured with cranesbill, cyclamen, and forget-me-not; my man the while gathering huge bunches of watercresses from the streams about, aidful of supper supply at the next halt. Where that halt will be does not seem certain, for the sky is becoming cloudy and threatening, and Bicchisano, still far up on the opposite hill, seems to have no especial attraction, though doubtless in fine weather the views from its high position and those of the snow-powdered rocks close above it, would be worth a stay to study.

In winding up the ascent above the Taravo Peter seems less and less to control his horses, which are apt to make for the side of the road with an abruptness that would be alarming were there such precipices as those nearer Grosseto; but Peter, whom I suspect to have been frequently more or less asleep, apostrophises them with a lively fervour—'What, then, did you think that wall a house and stable? Do you want water, and run to that rock to find a fountain?'

At twelve-thirty Bicchisano, the mountain village extolled by some as a good summer residence, is reached; it appears to be a collection of hamlets, and there is said to be one of the best little inns here on the road between Ajaccio and Bonifacio, but the day has now become cold and windy, and as there would not be a chance of exploring the upper valley of the Taravo, I resolve to drive on to Olmeto, a decision clinched by a sharp storm of sleet and rain, which adds to my desire to exchange this high and shivering situation for a warm one, which Olmeto is considered to be.

A long ascent leads from Bicchisano[1] to another village, Casalabriva, passing obliquely up the south side of the valley of the Taravo, commanding a constantly widening view towards Capo di Porto Pollo, on the Gulf of Valinco, in front, and looking back to the high central range near Mont Renoso, now of a dark smalt-blue under the shadow of heavy clouds, with here and there strips of fierce light on the snow. The promontories or spurs which, descending from the mid-island heights form the walls of these deep and long valleys, are evidently constant characteristics of Corsican scenery on its west side. Throughout this ascent the road winds in and out along the mountain-side, now carried round deep recesses or gorges full of enormous ilex, anon passing great masses of granite, shaded by great trees growing from their crevices; at several points clear fountains gush out by the wayside, but neither habitation nor human being was visible for the two hours employed in this part of the journey.

The top or col of this long climb is reached at 2.40 P.M., and turning abruptly round the hill, the long lines of the green valley of Taravo disappear, and Peter halts at Casalabriva, a more compact village than Grosseto or Bicchisano, but, with the exception of some rocks and evergreen oaks at its entrace, not promising in appearance. Nor, even were the weather fine, should I care to draw the place, the houses of which

---

[1] At Bicchisano, a town of 800 inhabitants, there is a charming view from its new chapel and promenade. The prospect extends over a vast cultivated valley, with a glimpse of the sea and the Gulf of Taravo.

have no pretensions to the picturesque, though there are some peculiarities in their structure which speak volumes as to their discomfort and uncleanliness.

From this height[1] the road descends very rapidly into the next valley which adjoins that of the Boracci, a stream flowing into the Gulf of Valinco —and for a while hereabouts I fancy that I see the hills of Sardinia 'fringing the southern sky', but am not sure whether the vision be land or cloud—and sending on Peter and the trap to whatever hotel there may be at Olmeto, I walk down the steep zigzags leading to that little town, which stands perhaps half-way down between the col and the shore. Thick wood, mostly evergreen, is the characteristic of this valley, which, unlike that of the Taravo, is narrow and closely shut in by heights, the tops of which are bare; and their sides are covered with dense *maquis*, as well as groves of ilex and wild olive, and these, as the nook in which Olmeto is built expands lower down into the broad vale of the Boracci, are exchanged for rich plantations of cultivated olive, fruit trees, and corn.

3.30 P.M.—Olmeto, which from this approach you do not see till you are close upon it, is wholly unlike those villages of Corsica I have hitherto seen, and resembles many a hill town in Italy; compact, and very picturesque, its houses looking towards the south and east, and hanging as it were in a steep hollow of hill which entirely shelters it from the west wind; it is gifted with galleries and inequalities, and varieties of light, and shade, and colour, delightful to the painter's eye. The entrance is gloomy and dirty; a narrow street runs through the village from end to end, and it is thronged with people, all in dark dresses, and all sitting or standing idle.

Nearly at the end of the street is Peter with the trap, at the door of the hotel—a most forlorn-looking structure, entered by a flight of steps, eminently suggestive of possible bone fractures, being composed of very high and slippery stones without any parapet; and at the top of this is a small antechamber of equally forbidding appearance, leading to a sitting-room similarly unprepossessing. Half one end of this is occupied by a large open fireplace, with chimney-corners, where a wood-fire is blazing, a not unnecessary set-off against the cold and damp of the day, and

[1] It is called the Col Celaccia separating the valley of the Taravo from that of the Boracci, and is 576 metres in height.

in which a little boy who perpetually coughs is crouched on a small stool. A very tiny bedroom, far cleaner than the appearance of other parts of the house would warrant one to expect, just allows of my camp-bed being set up in it, and my servant can be put up on a sofa in the *salle à manger*; so, as dinner is promised by the landlady at sunset, I consider myself settled at Olmeto for the present. The hostess indeed, Mdme Paolantonuccio, seems to be well satisfied with her hotel, and she tells me two gentlemen have been living for more than a month in it.

Meanwhile I go out in search of a point to make a drawing of Olmeto, which is in truth a beautiful place, and for general position, details, and surrounding scenery, as picturesque in every sense as any Italian town I ever saw. When you have passed out of the west end of the single street—there is a very large fountain here, as at the other extremity of the town—you perceive high above you, among the great towering rocks, one of those solitary sepulchre-chapels so remarkable in this island; and beyond it, a cross on a slight elevation above the high road, at once marks the precise spot from which a view of Olmeto must be made. Thither I went, and laboured at a large drawing, until showers of rain stopped my work.

No more beautiful site than that of Olmeto can be pictured. Immediately below the town the ground dips steeply down, covered with corn or turf, or in terraces of vineyard, varied with large groups of fine olive trees, resembling those thick clustering masses below Delphi in North Greece; and these stretch away to gardens and other olive grounds down to the shore. Above the village a vast growth of vegetation climbs the heights, and besides huge rounded boulders of granite and dark bosky shades of olive and ilex, there are tangles of every shrub the island produces, the wild olive or oleaster being one of the most elegant. Across the valley all the lofty hills seem one solid mass of *maquis*, vivid green where lit by gleams of sunlight, or streaked with dark purple and grey as clouds rest on the upper heights or flit across the sky. And in the midst of this setting of every shade of green the little town of Olmeto stands out full of picturesque accidents of form and light and shade, its lower houses growing as it were out of granite crags, and surrounded by fruit trees. Nor does there lack foreground to this picture in the shape of rocky masses, creeper and lichen grown, and imbedded in foliage of innumerable kinds. Certainly, if Corsica turns out thus increasingly beautiful from day to day, I shall have more than enough to do; but may weather be more propitious!

Every part of the heights close to the town abounds with little picture-subjects—here a chapel, there a tomb exactly like Absalom's Pillar in the Valley of Jehoshaphat; the dress of the peasantry alone is uninteresting in all this catalogue of picturesqueness.

Before sunset, however, I am glad to leave it all, as damp and chill increases, and to come to the hotel, where, having ejected four cats, a dog, and the coughing boy, the rest of the evening is passed. The fare, as usual in these untoward-looking hostelries, is far better than could be expected, though woe to the traveller who cannot eat omelettes! Mdme Paolantonuccio, however, piques herself on abstruse and scientific cookery—eggs dressed with tomatoes, and other surprises, besides boiled and roast lamb, and the unfailing and excellent broccio, and wine of capital quality, the neighbourhood of Sartène producing some of the best in Corsica.

A young man brings in the dinner, the hostess being employed in serving the two English gentlemen, who, it seems, are still in the village, though at another house. One of these two he describes as hopelessly ill, and I think I had better send or call tomorrow to know if any help can be given to a countryman in so out of the way a place.

APRIL 17

5.30 A.M.—This inn, wretched enough as to its exterior and its entrance, is, after all, not intolerable, and again I note in the people of the house the obliging manner which thus far into Corsica I have invariably met with. The view from Olmeto is one marked by extremely delicate beauty. The olives on the slopes below the town more than ever remind me of those at Delphi at this hour, when the landscape is in deep shadow—for, alas! clouds are rapidly rising on all sides, and I fear rain. Most observable is the thickness and redundance of the vegetation here, the mingling of grey granite and green *maquis*. But what could make M. Valery write that Olmeto, a village clustered among rock and woods half-way up a mountain, reminded him of Nice, a place of boulevards and promenades at the edge of the sea?

The weather holds up sufficiently to allow of my working a good bit on the detail of the drawing I commenced yesterday, but cloud and gloom increase every minute. While thus occupied, a good many of the men of Olmeto, going out toward their vineyards, pass where I sit, and some few stand still to see me draw. All are civil; very dusky-looking and slow, clad in the universal black or dark brown, and blackly bearded. But, on the whole, the people here appear a rougher set than those I have seen, and some of the children shout out, '*O Anglais!*' As yet, however, since I landed in Corsica, I have not met with a single beggar.

At seven-thirty there is but just time to return to the hotel before a violent down-pouring commences, and they say it will probably not cease all day. A conviction of dampness impresses me at this place; and today, as well as yesterday, I observe very many people coughing. Fires, they tell me, are generally in use, and I cannot help thinking that the high hill which quite screens the town from the west, depriving it of afternoon sun, must be prejudicial to dwellers in Olmeto, though, on the other hand, it saves them from the mistral.

After breakfast there is nothing better to do than to draw portions of the town out of a side window, and I send a card to the sick English-man to learn if he would like to see me, in case I can in any way help him. To this a messenger brings word that he will gladly do so at noon, on which I am taken to a small house not far off, and by a very dirty staircase reach a floor, where in a room, far more comfortable within than its exterior predicted, was the sick man, whom, to my extreme surprise, I found to be Mr. B., the eldest son of Lord E.B. Already in ill health, he had come to this island in search of a warm winter climate; but by a fall from his horse had received a serious internal injury from which it is next to impossible that he can recover. Though suffering greatly at times, it did not appear to me that he was in want of anything, and he had with him one who seems an attentive and good domestic or companion. When I left him I promised to return and dine with him at seven, if the weather did not hold up, which, they say, it is not likely to do, though I am not without hopes of it. Meanwhile I come back to the hotel and find sleep the best occupation.

At two G. wakes me, saying 'ἰατρεύει ὁ καιρός—the weather is curing itself'—and certainly the rain has not only ceased, but the clouds are breaking, and a decision must be come to at once, since three or three-thirty is the very latest at which I may start from here in time to get to Sartène, my next halt. I write, therefore, to Mr. B., stating that I am going to leave Olmeto, and then ordering Peter to get the trap ready, leave him and G. to follow, and set off on foot. Mdme Paolantonuccio recommends me to go at Sartène to the Hotel d'Italie, where her son is cook.

All the way down to the sea-level the road from Olmeto zigzags and curves through beautiful scenery, of similar character as to luxuriant foliage with that higher up, but opening out more and more to broad green slopes and cornfields dotted with olives, and spreading into wide distances of Claude Lorraine landscape, either looking west or towards the hills at Fozzano,[1] in the valley of the Boracci. At every step there are studies for pictures, if only in the hedges, which are in some places literally blue with a beautiful climbing vetch.

The bridge over the Boracci, which runs into the sea here through some low marshy ground, green and pleasant to see, but exceedingly unwholesome as to air, is passed at 4 P.M. At the head of the Gulf of Valinco, which, spite of the bright sun now once more shining, has a sad and deserted look, the road follows the shore, and soon reaches Propriano, which stands on the sea, and appeared to me a dull and uninteresting place, containing some very tall and particularly ugly houses; once a week the steamer which goes from Ajaccio to Bonifacio touches here, but it seems a place of small traffic.

Striking inland, the road, after an uninteresting ascent, soon dips into the valley of the Tavaria, and here all at once the scenery becomes most beautiful in character, but unlike that I have passed through hitherto. Some of the scenes on the broad part of the river, which runs below exquisitely wooded hills, might be in Scotland or in Wales, and there are masses of granite and tufts of foliage perfect as foreground studies. One of the hills to the right of the valley, with craggy outline and hanging woods, forms infinite fine pictures, and I have seen nothing in Corsica hitherto so classic and poetical. Beyond these succeed levels

[1] Fozzano is said to be the scene of M. Merimée's beautiful romance of 'Colomba'. —E.L.

of cystus and asphodel, and then, after passing the opening of the valley of Tallano, the River Tavaria, which flows down it, is left, and the road begins the long ascent to Sartène, which stands at a great height, and has been visible since I came over the hill close to Propriano.

Sartène, one of the four Sous-préfectures of Corsica, and a large, important place, is truly grand as approached from this side, though its architecture seems of questionable picturesqueness; nevertheless, as a whole, it has an imposing look, and resembles Bova, in South Calabria, more than any place I can compare it to, though wanting in the castle-like groups of buildings which so adorn that Italian town. At Sartène, the massive square houses are more detached; and in that respect it has a certain look of Arghyró-Kastro, in Albania. As the road winds up the very long ascent to the town, the views of the great valley below, so varied with graceful lines and undulations of cultivated ground, and so rich in wood, and of the splendid snowy heights of the long range of mountains opposite, terminating in the lofty regions of the great Monte Incudine, are exceedingly noble, and perhaps give me greater pleasure than all I have hitherto seen of the landscape in this island. The town is approached by a fine bridge over a torrent, and from this point the whole valley, down to the Gulf of Valinco, is seen—one of the wildest and loveliest of prospects, and such as I had not at all anticipated to find in Corsica.

Sartène seems to be a populous place, with many large houses; but it was past sunset when I reached it, and I went at once to the Hotel d'Italie. For the Ajaccio diligence, which leaves Sartène at 6.30 P.M., had come thundering down the hill an hour before we arrived at the top of it, and, I suppose, to avoid any possibility of my being smuggled into any opposition locanda, the son of Mdme Paolantonuccio had come down to meet me, and ensured my going to the right place by piloting me there himself. (Did I not, when I met that public conveyance, feel glad that I had not chosen to travel in it, knowing that the whole of the beautiful scenery from here to Grosseto would have been passed in the dark, seeing that the diligence only arrives at Cauro tomorrow morning at 7 A.M.!)

At the hotel—as usual, occupying only one floor of a house, in this instance a good-sized one—I found several decent apartments untenanted, and was accompanied to the one I chose for myself by the landlady, a person of most astonishing fatness; her face was nice and pleasant, but in figure she was like nothing so much as Falstaff disguised as the 'Fat Woman of Brentford'. This bulky hostess looked on me with great favour, on finding that I was well acquainted with her native place, Como, and went into raptures when I talked about Varese and other Lombard localities. Nevertheless, at one moment I thought our acquaintance was to be of no long duration; for, having discovered me in the act of putting up my camp-bed—which at first, I believe, she thought was a photographic machine, or something connected with art —she suddenly became aware of its nature, and, calling Giovanni and others of her household, shouted out, '*Ecco un signore chi sdegna i letti di Corsica!*—here is one who despises the Corsican beds!'—and I did not know what might have followed this discovery, till my servant assured her that this was my constant habit, and by no means referred to her particular hotel, by which announcement the amiable Fatima allowed herself to be pacified.

Later, the supper she provided was excellent, and she could not be satisfied without bringing far more dishes than were required, with fruits and smaller delicacies, such as olives, pickles, butter, etc., and the best of Tallano wine.

April 18

Coffee was very obligingly got ready some time before sunrise, and the early part of the morning went in making a drawing below the town, some short way down the hill (from a spot whence a wonderfully fine picture might be made), until the sun, shining above the houses, prevented further work. These views of Sartène are most majestic and poetical; and, moreover, while the buildings of the town are in shadow, the commonplace nature of their details is hidden. The great isolated blocks of granite which seem thrown about on all sides on purpose to serve as foreground, the excess of wild vegetation, the silence of the deep valley or plain, and the clear lines of snow crowning all, combine to make a thousand bewitching subjects.

After seven or eight, a walk on the other side of the city, and a long scramble among thick woods, where the ground is literally red with cyclamen, show me more of the Sartène scenery; from the eastern side of the town you look into the quietest of profound valleys, above which the lofty line of what I suppose to be the Incudine mountain range shines crystal clear and bright against a cloudless sky. I shall certainly remain here tomorrow, at least, and try to get as many records as I can of the landscape, which is of a class rarely met with in such perfection, so fertile and so varied, so full of giant rocks, of abundant foliage, and sublime mountain forms.

But it is necessary to give M. Galloni d'Istria's letters to the Sous-préfet and to M. Vico, Sous-Inspecteur of Forests, from whom I am to gain information about the woods of Bavella, which are to be visited from the east side of the island; so I return to the town. The streets of Sartène are not gifted with any charm of liveliness; the lofty square houses are built of blocks of rough granite, dark grey in colour, and many of them are so massive as to look more like prisons than private dwellings.

Signor Vico, a most obliging person, gives me every information about the roads. From Solenzaro, he says, my light carriage can cross the heights of Bavella, at which place I am to have an introduction to the government agent, who resides in the forest, and thence I may re-turn by Zonza, Levie, and Tallano, to Sartène. The whole distance across the mountains he represents as about seventy or seventy-five kilo-metres—forty-five miles, more or less—and provided no new fall of snow occurs, I shall find no difficulty in crossing. He confirms M. Galloni's opinion, that the Bavella forest scenery is among the finest in the island.

At ten I am back at Fatima's hotel for breakfast. That person evi-dently has regrets for her native land, and my acquaintance with the towns and villages of her early days continues to give me great interest in her eyes. She is most profuse of good things; her wine of the best quality; her table cleanly and carefully set out; and her attentions un-failing. But she laments the little traffic of Sartène, and says, what must be true enough, that many articles of perishable nature cannot be kept, because so few passengers come to eat them. Her principal custom seems derived from *pensionati*, civilians, government officials, etc. (the officers of the garrison—for Sartène has a small garrison—go to the opposition hotel), and she makes such efforts to please all that she assuredly merits success.

At eleven I start down the hill for a walk of nine kilometres (about six miles) to get recollections of the river scenery of the Tavaria, and of the great granite boulder foregrounds. The cuckoo sings cheerily, and the cystus flowers scent the air. Up to the seventh kilometre there is comparatively little to interest; but thenceforward, when you have passed a wayside fountain where aged and broken ilex trees and a carpet of fern make a picture, all is charming. Little, however, can be represented of this extremely beautiful scenery by the pencil alone; the colouring of the river and that of the densely foliaged cork and ilex groves, and of the granite fragment-strewn hills—which have a sort of velvety and speckled texture or quality—are characteristics only to be given by hard study with the brush.

Returning, drew some of the great rock foregrounds. How difficult it is to give ever so slight an impression, on a small scale, of objects as full of detail as of grandeur—of those huge wrinkled Philæ-like masses of granite; of that mingling of tall evergreen oak and rock; that smooth bright green turf, dotted with flocks of black sheep! Worked till I was weary, and yet again, upon a view of Sartène, on my way up. The specky greyness of the hill on which the town stands is strongly contrasted with those parts that are covered with green-brown *maquis*.

The long ascent to Sartène—I cannot call it tedious, so varied is the scenery, so delightful at this hour the song of innumerable blackbirds, so opportune the many little rock fountains for refreshment—was accomplished by 7.15 P.M. The last look before you turn towards the street leading into the town it is difficult to cut short—to pass the bridge, without lingering to gaze down the long, long valley westward to the sea.

All through the day I have observed the civility of the passers-by, mostly bearded men in black or brown, with brown cloth caps, riding on spirited little horses, the few women with them always riding astride, and always dressed in black; not a vestige of costume exists. Every one saluted me as I sat drawing. One called out, 'We are glad you are making our Corsica known by drawing it!' Another said, 'Perhaps when you foreigners know us better, you will cease to think us such savages as we are said to be!'

Fatima's reception and supper were as cheery and good as heretofore. Tomorrow I shall devote the whole day to the Tavaria scenery, and all things are to be in order to start at sunrise if possible.

63

APRIL 19

At 5.30 A.M. I walk down the hill, and drawing more or less by the way, gradually reach my farthest point, the bridge over the Tavaria, a distance of some eleven kilometres, or seven miles. Such a walk here, at early morning, is unboundedly full of pleasant items; the whistle and warble of countless blackbirds, and the frequent cuckoo's note; flowers everywhere, especially the red cyclamen, blue vetch, yellow broom, tall white heath, pink cranesbill, and tiny blue veronica; the great rocks—at this hour in deep shadow—overgrown with ivy, moss, and a beautiful red lichen; the slopes of fern and cystus; all these are on each side, and below there is ever the grand valley scene. I must linger yet another day at Sartène; indeed, a week would be a short stay in these parts for an artist who really wished to study this fine order of Coriscan landscape.

About the seventh kilometre the road is lively by groups of peasants going up to the town on the fête day—lively, that is by movement, not by colour, for all are gloomily black, caps, beards, and dresses—trotting on little ponies, many of which carry two riders. While I sit drawing above the Tavaria bridge, a shepherd leaves his large flock of black sheep and stands by me. At length he says, 'Why are you drawing our mountains?' '*Per fantasia e piacere,*' I reply, 'for fun, and because it gives me pleasure to draw such beautiful places.' '*Puole,*' quoth he, '*ma cosa siggriffica?*'—That may be, but what is the meaning of it?—*da qualche parte d'Italia venite certo*—You come, it is plain, from some part of Italy; do you go about mapping all our country?—*facendo tutta la Corsica nostra dentr' una carta geografica?*' But I, who cannot work and talk at the same time, tell him so, on which he says, with an air of wisdom, '*Si capisce*—I understand'—and goes away apparently in the belief that I am constructing a political survey of the island.

At eleven it is time for breakfast, which G. has set, with cloaks and a folio for chair and table, below a large olive tree some way off the road; and Fatima the plentiful has outdone herself by a selection of good things, cold lamb, eggs, tunny, and Sta. Lucia di Tallano wine. I have seen few spots more full of poetical beauty than this, which, though close to the high road, would be completely a solitude but for hosts of birds, of which the woods are full, especially blackbirds, titmice, and

64

BONIFACIO

FOREST OF MARMANO

bee-eaters, with many jays and ravens, whose home is in the crags high up on Monte Lungo. But after midday, all these woodland and mountain dwellers cease to sing or cry, and the bright dead silence of southern noon succeeds to the lively freshness of morning. Once only a living stream of some eighty jet black goats suddenly passes along the green sward by the little brook, sneezing and snuffling after their fashion, and disappearing behind the great crags of granite, leaving silence as they had found it; little greenish lizards playing about the flat stones being now the only sign of life all around—

> For now the noonday quiet holds the hill;
> The lizard, with his shadow on the stone,
> Rests like a shadow.

The whole scene recalls to me many a morning in Greece, and repeats the 'days that are no more' as I had not supposed they could be brought back.

Let a landscape painter, having set out from Sartène, turn off the high road to his left, where, a little beyond the ninth kilometre from the town, he comes upon some fine detached rocks, forming a screen to an opening that leads to a vista of thick wood and noble mountain, and let him follow the winding goat tracks to the foot of the hill; there he will find on every side hundreds of foreground studies of incalculable value. The granite fragments are usually of a pale dove or slate colour, mottled with thousands of vegetable tints, green, white, yellow, orange, and black lichen, tufts of a red kind of stonecrop, moss, and ivy; and of such masses of rock with a portion of the background to make a picture, he will find enough work for months of artist-life.

One more pause before setting out townward, to draw by the river where the wood overhangs the cliffs and masses of granite, and where the clear water reflects the delicate hues of the pallid hill above it. Then as the sun sinks lower (for it is 4.30 P.M.), while the light and shadow on the rocks in the valley and on the exquisite mountain is constantly changing, and silvering the high crags and gilding the tufted trees, I go reluctantly. Since I made drawings at Mount Athos, in 1856, I have seen no heights so poetically wild, so good in form, and so covered with thick wood; and, altogether, as a wild mountain scene this has few rivals. A shepherd tells me they call the chief hill here Monte Lungo.

The ancient Coliseum sack is packed, and I set off on my return. Here, at the seventh kilometre, are twenty Corsicans on just ten horses, no more—a by no means ordinary spectacle—riding back from Sartène.

On the way up the long ascent I am met by the landlord of the Hotel de l'Univers at Sartène; he says he had heard that my worship was coming, by a message from the Secretary-general, and 'had not the son of that woman at Olmeto been so cunning as to seize your honour first, by artfully coming down the hill, you would have come to my hotel, which is wholly the best at Sartène, and most fit for you to have gone to'; to which I can only reply by regrets, and by assuring my host of the Universe that Fatima's inn is as comfortable as need be.

Many a spot on the way up to the town has a charm at this hour which it does not possess earlier in the day, for now the sun has set, the contrast of the almost black ilex against the pallor of the fading blue mountains is lovely and wondrous; so, by reason of lingering to make notes and memoranda, I do not reach Sartène till seven forty-five.

APRIL 20

5.30 A.M.—The first part of the day is passed in completing drawings of the town and valley already commenced, and in making other small sketches characteristic of a place I may perhaps never revisit, at least with leisure for drawing. One or two of these sketches are of the mortuary chapels or sepulchral monuments, which are very numerous and conspicuous about the neighbourhood of Sartène, and are often exceedingly picturesque, some high up peeping from thick woods of wild olive and cork, others in positions close to the road.

Then I pay a visit to M. Peretti, one of the Sous-préfets of the department, who was away when I came here first, a very agreeable and kindly person. To his inquiries as to what I thought of and how I liked Corsica I made a reply which savoured certainly more of the artist than the politician, namely, that I regretted extremely to find no Corsican costume in the island. '*Vous voulez donc, Monsieur, recommencer avec la nationalité Corse?*—Do you wish to re-establish Corsican nationality?' he asked, laughing. Of the present condition of the island he speaks as

having absolutely no afinity with that in existence at the commencement of this century, or rather up to the year 1852, when the general
disarmament of the population took place—'robbery, banditism, vendetta, all beyond that period belongs to the past, and are exchanged in
the present day for security and tranquillity'.

After visit to M. Vico, it becomes requisite to practise letter-writing
and resignation indoors, for, cloudy all the morning, it now rains in
torrents; the weather, however, has been very propitious for drawing
in Sartène, and even this downfall may presage a clear day for tomorrow.

4.30 P.M.—The mists roll up from the higher mountains, and disclosing bright paths of coming sunset, enable me to go out once more
to make some last sketches. All about the Cappuccini—a small convent
just outside the town—there are beautiful bits of landscape; but they
are not easily attainable, because there is an inconvenient custom here
of building up high stone walls, enclosing nothing at all; probably they
mark divisions of property; at the same time they interfere much with
the researches of painters not gifted with kid-like activity. Nevertheless
there is hardly a path round Sartène that does not lead to some surpassingly fine bit of landscape, and excepting Civitella and Olevano, I
have known no such place for study combining so many features of
grandeur and beauty. Perhaps in the finest parts of Calabria there is more
analogy to the class of scenery here, but in that part of Italy there is a
greater amount of culture and less variety of unbroken wildness. As the
sun goes down, a band of golden light beams along the Gulf of Valinco,
and a last shower breaks over the misty grey olive woods and the huge
lichen-grown rocks; so at six-thirty I return to the Hotel d'Italie.

I ask my hostess about the mourning which everyone seems to wear
here. She says, for a parent or a child you mourn for life, as also for
brothers, sisters, husbands, and wives, unless you marry (or remarry)
after their death, on which event you cease to mourn, and a new life is
supposed to commence. '*Allora, il matrimonio taglia il duol*—then
marriage cuts the grief.' For an uncle or aunt you mourn ten years,
and for a cousin seven, so that it is not wonderful that the world is so
mournful as to dress in these parts. On the hostess asking my opinion
on various matters regarding Corsican inns, and on my gently suggesting
that somewhat more cleanliness and attention in the matter of floors,
stairs, etc. (for, indeed, the state of these contrasts strangely with that

67

of the very clean linen, table service, etc.), would be very likely to have beneficial effect on the recommendation of English visitors, Fatima says excitedly: '*Come posso far tutto?*—How can I do all things? In Corsica there are no servants; they consider service a dishonour, and will starve sooner than work.' Yet she promises to do something for the unwashed floors. 'Can I,' she says, 'prevent those who come to my hotel, and through whom chiefly I am able to keep it up, from bringing their dogs, and throwing all the bones and broken fragments of meat on the ground for them? *Cosa volete che faccio?*' Finally she hits on an ingenious compromise: '*So béne che vi dev' essere la pulizia, ma qui in Sarténé non é possibile*—I know well that it is proper that things should be clean, but here cleanliness is impossible—*Dunque, voglio colorire con color' oscuro tutt' il fondo delle camere; cosi appunto non si scoprirà le sporcheri!*—Therefore I will colour with a dark tint the floors of all the rooms, and so nobody will be able to see the dirt!'

Peter the coachman, who has already asked for two supplies of money, comes for more, and it begins to be suspected that the horses do not altogether benefit by this so much as they should in the shape of *orzo* or barley.

CHAPTER III

April 21

6 A.M.—After drawing an outline of the mountains, I am picked up by Peter, G., and the trap. After three days' stay (and I would willingly remain here for as many weeks; for what have I seen of the upper valley or the opposite hills?) I leave Sartène, and can bear witness to the good fare, moderate charges, and constant wish to oblige of Fatima, padrona of the Hotel d'Italie. Poor Fatima, rumour says, is forsaken by her husband, and 'dwells alone upon the hill of storms', as in the literal sense of the expression Sartène must certainly be, for it is exposed to all the winds of heaven, and from its great elevation must needs be bitterly cold in winter.

Just above the town, where the high road to Bonifacio passes the Capuchin convent, there is the finest view of Sartène and the mountains; the whole town stands out in a grand mass from the valley and heights, and there is something rough and feudal in its dark houses that places its architecture far above that of Ajaccio in a picturesque sense. But to halt for drawing now is not to be thought of, inasmuch as this day's journey to Bonifacio is not only a long one, but because in the whole distance (some fifty-three kilometres, or thirty-two miles) there is only a single wayside house, where the horses are to bait, yet where humanity, expecting food, would be severely disappointed. Hearing which, the Suliot has taken care to pack the old Coliseum sack with food for the day.

How grand at this hour is the broad light and shade of these mountains and valleys! (Notwithstanding that such as leave their houses at 10 or 11 A.M. complain of 'want of chiaroscuro in the south'.) How curious are the chapel-tombs, so oddly and picturesquely placed, and frequently so tasteful in design, gleaming among the rocks and hanging woods! At first, after leaving Sartène, the road passes through splendid woods of clustering ilex, and then begins to descend by opener country, shallower green vales and scattered granite tors or boulders, here and

69

there passing plots of cultivation, and ever farther away from the high central mountains of the island. Now the distance sweeps down to lower hills, all clothed in deep green *maquis*, and at every curve of the road are endless pictures of grey granite rocks and wild olive.

While I am thinking how pleasant it would be to get studies of this very peculiar scenery, by living at Sartène, and walking seven or eight miles daily, Peter suddenly halts below the village of Giunchetto, which stands high above the road. 'What is the matter?' says G.; but Peter only points to the village and crosses himself, and looks round at me. 'What has happened?' I repeat. Peter whispers, 'In that village a priest has lately died, and without confessing himself.' In the midst of visions of landscape—'What—' as Charles XII said to his secretary—'What has this bomb to do with what I am dictating?'

Farther on, near the eleventh kilometre, are some enormous granite blocks, with two or three stone huts by the road-side, and then follows a steep descent to the valley of the Ortola; looking back, you see a world of mist-folded mountains in the north-east, while ahead are *maquis*, and cystus carpets, sown with myriads of star-twinkling white flowers, broom, and purple lavender. The descent to the Ortola valley abounds with beauty, and by its verdure reminds me of more than one Yorkshire dale—here, instead of the oak or ash, depths of aged evergreen oak and grey-branched cork-trees, shading pastures and fern.

At eight, the river, a shallow stream, is crossed by a three-arched bridge; and here, near a solitary stone hut, are a few cattle and some peculiarly hideous pigs—the only living things seen since I left Sartène. Then, at the eighteenth kilometre, an ascent on the south side of the valley brings me in sight of the long point and tower of Cape Roccaspina and of the broad sea, above which I halt at 9 A.M., for the great Lion of Roccaspina may not be passed without getting a sketch of it. And, truly, it is a remarkable object—an immense mass of granite perfectly resembling a crowned lion, placed on a lofty ledge of the promontory, and surrounded by bare and rugged rocks.

The road now becomes a regular cornice coast-way, alternately descending and rising, always broad and good, and well protected by parapets; long spurs of rock jut out into the sea beyond odorous slopes of myrtle and cystus, while in some parts enormous blocks and walls of granite form the left side of the picture. Presently the road diverges more inland, and is carried through wild and lonely tracts of *maquis*, varied by patches of corn at intervals, and recalling the valleys of Philistia when you begin to ascend towards the Judæan hills from the plains near Eleutheropolis. Two flocks of goats—of course, black—and a few black sheep and pigs, who emulate the appearance of wild boars, with one man and one boy, are the living objects which a distant hamlet (I think Monaccia) contributes to the life of the scene. Occasionally glimpses of the distant sea occur; but, as far as eye can reach, the wild green unbroken *maquis* spreads away on every side.

At ten-thirty 'half our mournful task is done', and the midday halt at a house (one of some six or seven by the wayside) is reached. The appearance of these dwellings is very poor and wretched; and a gendarme informs me that from the end of May till November they are all deserted, so unwholesome is the air of this district; and that the few peasants at present here go up at that season to the villages of Piannattoli or Caldarello—small clusters of houses higher up on the hill-side. How little cheerful the aspect of this part of the island must be then, one may imagine from what it is even in its inhabited condition.

On a rising ground close by are some of those vast isolated rocks which characterise this southern coast of Corsica—a good spot whereat to halt for Fatima's breakfast. Looking southward, green lines of campagna stretch out into what is the first semblance of a plain that I have seen in this island, and which is exceedingly like portions of Syrian landscape. It was worth while to get a drawing of this, and I would willingly have stayed longer, but at 1 P.M. it is time to start again.

The road continues across comparatively low ground by undulating inequalities, through wide *maquis*-dotted tracts, where here and there the tall giant-hemlock is a new feature in the more moist parts of the ground. Twice we descend to the sea at inlets or small creeks—Figari and Ventilegne—in each case passing the stream which they receive by a bridge, and at these points marshes and 'still salt pools' show the malarious nature of the district. Nor does the landscape painter fail to rejoice that he has chosen this method of 'seeing all Corsica', and that he is able to drive rapidly over this part of it, where there is no need of halt for drawing, for the higher mountains are far away from the south of the island, and the hills nearer the coast stretch seaward with a persistent and impracticable length of line not to be reduced to agreeable

71

pictorial proportion. Once only, at 3 P.M., about seven kilometres from Bonifacio, I stop to draw, more to obtain a record of the topographic character of the south-west coast than for the sake of any beauty of scenery, of which the long spiky promontories hereabouts possess but little, although there is a certain grace in some of those slender points running far out into the blue water, and, though far inland, you may at times catch a glimpse of some heights of varied form; yet, be your drawing never so long or narrow, the length of the whole scene is with difficulty to be compressed within its limits.

At three-thirty I send on Peter and the trap to Bonifacio, and walk, for so many hours of sitting still in a carriage cramps limbs and head. As the hills, from the ascent to which I had made my last drawing, are left behind, Bonifacio, the Pisan or Genoese city, becomes visible; extreme whiteness, cliffs as chalky as those of Dover, and a sort of Maltese look of fortified lines are the apparent characters at this distance of a city so full of interest and history. Opposite, towards the south, a thick haze continues to hide the coast of Sardinia, and this has been no light drawback to the day's journey, since the sight of remote mountains and the blue straits would have gone far to relieve the *maquis* monotony, driving through which has occupied so much of the time passed between Sartène and Bonifacio.

Meanwhile a space of three or four miles has to be done on foot, shut out from all distant view, as well as very uninteresting in its chalky white dryness of road, about which the only features are walls, with olives all bent to the north-east, and eloquently speaking of the force of the south-west wind along this coast. But at 4.30 P.M. fields of tall corn and long-armed olives replace this ugliness, and the road descends to a deep winding gorge or valley, closely sheltered and full of luxuriant vegetation, olive, almond, and fig. After the boulders and crags of granite, which up to this time have been the foregrounds in my Corsican journey, a new world seems to be entered on coming to this deep hollow (where a stream apparently should run, but does not), for its sides are high cliffs of cretaceous formation, pale, crenellated, and with cavernous ledges, and loaded with vegetation.

At 5 P.M. the road abruptly reaches the remarkable port of Bonifacio, which forms one of the most delightful and striking pictures possible. Terminating a winding and narrow arm of the sea, or channel, the nearer part of which you see between overhanging cliffs of the strangest form, it is completely shut in on all sides, that opposite the road by which alone you can reach it being formed by the great rock on which the old fortress and city are built, and which to the south is a sheer precipice to the sea, or rather (even in some parts of it visible from the harbour) actually projecting above it. At the foot of this fort-rock lies a semi-circle of suburban buildings at the water's edge, with a church, and a broad flight of shallow steps leading up to the top of this curious peninsular stronghold; all these combine in a most perfect little scene, now lit up by the rays of the afternoon sun, and which I lose no time in drawing.

A broad and good carriage road leads up to the city, huge grim walls enclose it, and before you enter them you become aware how narrow is the little isthmus that joins the rock-site of Bonifacio to the mainland; from a small level space close below the fort you see the opposite coast of Sardinia, and you look down perpendicularly into the blue straits which divide the two islands. Very narrow streets conduct from the fortifications to the inner town; the houses are lofty and crowded, and Bonifacio evidently possesses the full share of inconveniences natural to garrison towns of limited extent, with somewhat of the neglected and unprepossessing look of many southern streets and habitations. There was no difficulty in finding the Widow Carreghi's hotel, but its exterior and entrance were, it must be owned, not a little dismal, and the stair-case, steep, narrow, wooden, dark, dirty, and difficult, leading to the inn rooms on the third floor, was such as a climbing South American monkey might have rejoiced in. Nevertheless, once safe at the top of this ladder-like climb there are several little and very tolerably habitable rooms; and, as seems to be invariably the rule as to Corsican hostesses, the two here are very obliging and anxious to please.

There was yet time to walk through the town, which I was surprised to find so extensive and populous. Some of the churches are ancient, and near the end of the rock (though the lateness of the hour, together with a powder magazine and obstructive sentry, prevented my getting quite to its extremity) a considerable plateau with barracks and other public buildings exists, and I can well imagine some days might be spent with great interest in this ancient place. As it was, I could but make a slight drawing from the edge of the precipice looking up to the harbour or sea-inlet, but from such examination it was evident that the most characteristic view of this singular and picturesque place must be made from the opposite side of the narrow channel, though it does not appear how, except by boat, such a point can be reached. Bonifacio is doubtless a most striking place and full of subjects for painting; the bright chalky white of the rocks on which it stands, the deep green vegetation, and the dark gulf below it, add surprising contrasts of colour to the general effect of its remarkable position and outline.

Returning to the Widow Carreghi's hotel, confusion prevailed throughout that establishment, owing to its being crowded at this hour by, not only the officers of the garrison, who take their food there, but an additional host of official civilians, gendarmerie, etc., tomorrow being a day of great excitement, on account of the conscription taking place, in consequence of which event the Sous-préfet is here from Sartène, with numerous other dignitaries. It was not wonderful that the two obliging women, who seemed joint hostesses, were somewhat dazed by the unbounded noise in the small and overfull rooms; nevertheless, they got a very good supper for me and my man, only apologising continually that '*le circonstanze*' of the full house, and of the late hour at which I had arrived, prevented their offering more food and in greater comfort and quiet. Everybody seemed to be aware that I was a travelling painter, and all proffered to show me this or that; the Sous-préfet, they said, had gone out to meet me, and the Mayor, for whom I have left a card and a letter from M. Galloni d'Istria (he lives in the Carreghi house), would come and see me tomorrow. Another of the persons at the table gave me his address at Casabianda, and begged that, if I should come there, he might show me the ruins of Aleria. The whole party, Continentals and Insulaires, were full of civility.

All night long there was singing and great noise in the streets, so that in spite of my camp-bed very little sleep was attainable.

April 22

How to obtain the best illustrations of Bonifacio? and in a single day?— that is to say, all that can be got upon dry land; for though I am aware that the grottoes here are considered as some of the finest known, I have resolved not to go into any of them, for they are all situated outside the channel, in the cliffs on the open sea, and I mentally decide to relinquish whatever of seeing Corsica depends on entering a boat.

The attentive Carreghi hostesses bring me coffee at five, in a tumbler, which, it seems, is the mode in South Corsican households, and they give as a reason for doing so, that the coffee keeps hotter in glass than earthernware, which I do not deny; though at this early hour the un-expected feeling suggested by this practice—to wit, of your being about to drink a glass of porter—is objectionable. It is not possible to praise this hotel for its cleanliness, and yet it does not seem fair to judge Corsican inns, as some do, as if they were in Lombardy or Tuscany, constantly frequented by strangers. Take any part of Italy or France, away from the routine line of travellers, and you will find the inns hardly as good as those here.

6 A.M.—The first work of today is to complete the drawings begun yesterday at the head of the port—rather a long task, as much accurate detail is necessary. It is not easy to realise that the sea is on the farther side of the fortress as well as on this. The harbour is really beautiful at this hour, when everything is reflected in the water, and the Genoese tower, which commands a view far up the channel, stands picturesquely in the foreground.

While I work there comes down the hill a large party of what G. calls μεγάλοι ἄνθρωποι—great people—to wit, M. le Sous-préfet, Dr. Montepagano the Maire, with others of the local notables and clergy, and on their arrival at where I sit, introductions, with much lifting of hats, ensue. The mayor seems a particularly agreeable man, and the whole party give an impression of being well-bred and pleasant, nor did they long interrupt my labours; every one offered to show me some portion of the city, or aid me in some way, but from the limited time at my disposal, I could only venture to name the convent of Sta. Trinità as a place I should like to visit, on account of its commanding a distant view of Bonifacio, and it was agreed that Dr. Montepagano should take me there at 2 P.M.

The next thing was to procure a view from the side of the channel opposite the city, and to this end I began, with G., an examination of paths and valleys in that direction, though the heat, and the contrast of the glaringly white soil with the dark vegetation, made the search as uncomfortable as at first it was profitless; for, pursuing a line parallel to the inlet, we diverged at times towards the water, but as often got entangled among vineyards and walls; till growing weary with climbing steep paths that led me no nearer to the point desired, and half blinded with the dazzling and hot white pathways, I was giving up the task. The Suliot, however, persevered, saying, 'ἐντροπὴ εἶναι νὰ πᾶμ' ὀπίσω'— It is a shame to go back', and left me to return in half an hour, having discovered a dell leading down to the water, where a ledge at the end of the rocks seemed to command a view of the other side of the channel. And so it turned out to be, though the path along the cliff edge was so narrow and precipitous, and so giddily overhanging the water, that even with assistance I could hardly manage to arrive at the required height.

From this point there is a perfect view of this curious and interesting old Corsican city, and I know of no scene of the kind more strikingly beautiful. The exceedingly deep colour of the quiet narrow channel contrasts wondrously with the pale hues of the rocks and buildings, and the strange lonely character of the fort, and of the projecting cliffs rising perpendicularly from the water's edge, and striped with long ledges of singular form, is most impressive. A solitary cormorant flitting by is the only sign of life, and a complete silence adds to the charm of this wild spot, so full of memories of the sufferings of the Bonifacio people. I would gladly linger some days to explore more fully the position of this historic medieval city, so unique in appearance and site. When the wind lashes this inland channel, how grandly the foaming waves must beat against the sides and hollows of these cliffs, wrinkled and worn by long buffeting!

While I am drawing, the stillness is broken by two boats, which, from the distant harbour come down the channel, those who are in them singing 'O pescator dell' onde;' at first the sound is feeble, but gradually swells into a loud chorus over the calm water and among the great caverns of the echoing cliffs. The boats steer for the cove near which I am sitting, and twenty individuals land on a ledge of rock just below me, where they place a barrel of wine and provisions, and prepare to pass the day. These are conscripts, chosen as soldiers only yesterday, and this their farewell fête before leaving their native Bonifacio, a place so peculiar in itself, and so remote from the outer world, that the attachment its inhabitants are said to bear towards it is easily understood.

Leaving the cormorant perch or ledge, where I have made my drawing, I return to the town, and after a hot climb, first through the dells near the channel, choked with foliage, airless and stifling, and then by the blinding white stair-paths, reach Mdme Carreghi's hotel before noon.

Fresh red mullet, lobster (or rather crawfish), good fowl, and other dishes more numerous than necessary, were ample proof that the good people of the house were in earnest last night when they promised better fare; and now that the rooms are less noisy and crowded, I look upon the inn as a very tolerable place of sojourn. The Widow Carreghi, like Fatima of Sartène, is also anxious to improve her house, though with very decidedly conservative opinions as to some of its shortcomings, for, to her inquiry, '*Come credete che posso far meglio nostra povera casa?*—What do you think can be done to improve our poor house?' I suggest a cleaning of the remarkably dirty entrance and stairs by way of a commencement. But to this Widow Carreghi gives a flat negative in the most positive manner, '*Signore, qui non e mai uso di polir le scale; le scale non si pulisce mai!*—Here, sir, it is never the custom to clean stairs; stairs are never cleaned, never!' So I was silent.

At two comes Dr. Montepagano, and walks with me through a part of the town, showing me several points of interest, such as the house where the Emperor Charles V lived in 1510, a small abode, and very unimperial in appearance, and that in which Buonaparte resided in 1793. The worthy doctor had insisted, much against my will, that we should use the carriage of one of his friends, but when we arrived at the port, where the vehicle in question awaited us, it was found to carry only one besides the driver, whereon I had to send G. up to the town for Peter and my own trap; and, until its arrival, the doctor and myself sat by a fountain close to the harbour, which is celebrated for the excellence of its water, discoursing on some peculiarities in the ornithology of the district.

Then we drive up by the white cliffs and green hollow, down which I came yesterday on entering the town, and along the bald road, where stand the scanty wind-bent olives, till we come to the foot of the hills of La Trinità. A footpath leads to the great granite rocks, in a nook among which a small Franciscan monastery has now succeeded to the hermitage mentioned by Valery in 1835. The view from the convent garden is very remarkable, and as the day is clear, the north coast of Sardinia is perfectly seen in all its length and detail, in which there is much beauty, though, in some respects, it is rather disappointing, the height of the mountains beyond the straits being inconsiderable compared with those of Corsica, and the long line of hills seem wanting in grandeur. Now that I am acquainted with the position of Bonifacio, I perceive that from here its peculiar character cannot in the least be indicated, as the narrow arm or inlet of the sea is completely hidden by the higher ground on this side of it; consequently, the city seems to stand on a part of the broad level on its western side, instead of rising, as it really does, from a rock platform, almost entirely surrounded by water. Nevertheless, this Santa Trinità view—the monastery itself has nothing picturesque to recommend it—is one very curious and impressive. You feel, as it were, at the end of the world, as you look at the far white fortress through the stems of the large olives growing among great boulders in the convent garden; beyond it is nothing but the wide sea, and the low line of Sardinia on the horizon. At six we drove back to the town.

Dr. Montepagano, the Maire, says that two years ago there were two Englishmen here, one of them Mr. C., the name of the other he cannot remember, but will show me his photograph tomorrow. The Maire's acquaintance has been well worth making; he is a most friendly and well-informed gentleman.

April 23

At 6 A.M. an early visit from M. Trani, to whom I had brought an introductory letter from M. Merimée, but who was absent from the city yesterday. The Corsicans seem most anxious to show every attention to strangers, and I regretted that I could not see more of this gentleman, who was very agreeable, and who evidently entertained a warm recollection of my introducer. Dr. Montepagano also called and brought the promised photograph. Behold, it was of my friend J.B.H.! I was not aware he had ever visited this island.

At seven I left Bonifacio and its kindly inhabitants, with more regret than is usually felt after so short a stay in any place. It is full of an indefinable romance and interest not shared by either Ajaccio or Sartène; a kind of wild and solemn classic grandeur prevails about its lofty fortress walls and in the views from them, either towards the screens of steep rock rising from the deep and narrow channel, or seaward to the strange pale cliffs and the long line of Sardinian hills. The port scene is a little gem, and I feel sure that there are many more beauties in the narrow valley running eastward among the hills, and from the coast towards the lighthouse.

The peasantry about Bonifacio seem of a small stature, and not as well looking as those in other parts of Corsica; among the women I did not see even one tolerably pretty face. All dress in dark brown. As a set-off, the people of Bonifacio are said to be, as their character has been always represented, quiet and well conducted; nor was the savage Vendetta ever know in the territory, which was, indeed, separated from all the rest of Corsica, not more by its isolated position than by the habits and circumstances of its inhabitants. The race of donkeys, of which there seem to be many used, are the smallest I have seen in the island.

The road to my next halting-place, Porto Vecchio, to which I set out at 7 A.M., is for a short way, the same as that by which alone Bonifacio can be entered; but it soon strikes off to the east, and, after passing through beautiful sheltered groves of rich olives, the white chalky soil is quitted, and once more the familiar granite rocks appear, interspersed with slopes of turf, cultivated undulations, and spaces gay with flowers—may or blackthorn in full bloom, and a wilderness of vegetation. The road does not run near the sea—once or twice only are there glimpses of it between heights clothed with high and dense *maquis* —but mostly along a rather flat vale or small plain, half covered with underwood and cork trees, and lying between low granite hills on the left, and a similar but lower ridge on the right. And such is the route for nearly three hours, when, after a dip down to a small bay (the Gulf of Sta. Giulia), and a pull up on the opposite side, the valley of the Stabiaccia, the stream flowing into the Gulf of Porto Vecchio is reached. Hereabouts is the only bad bit of road encountered since leaving Ajaccio—a causeway in process of being raised across some marshy ground, and not as yet complete.

A good way ahead, the town of Porto Vecchio appears on a hill above the Gulf, in the midst of what is characteristic of all the surrounding country, excessively abundant vegetation; in parts a regular jungle, with unhealthy-looking marshes and pieces of water at intervals, in the neighbourhood of which small midges and loud frogs proclaim, even at this early season of the year, a dangerous atmosphere. But apart from its unhealthiness, the wildness of the scenery has a great charm, the more that towards the west, finely formed hills stand forth with a stern beauty, so that I could not resist sending on Peter and the trap, and stopping to draw till 11 A.M. Every shrub and thicket seems alive with the invisible nightingale, whose song

> Fills the soul
> Of that waste place with joy.

Porto Vecchio, about which I make an exploring ramble before entering it, is a place of forlorn appearance, with no little picturesqueness in its old grey walls and towers, but joined to a general look of decay, more agreeable to a painter's eye than indicative of the inhabitants' prosperity. Nor did the interior offer any greater signs of vitality —unfinished houses, heaps of stones, shattery wooden outer stairs and galleries, with much dirt and a large supply of idle loiterers. On one side of a small piazza is a row of somewhat better buildings, among which the 'hotel'—kept by the widow Gianelli, an old woman like one of Michelangelo's Fates—resembles some others I have seen in its very bad and dirty stair entrance, but also in its tolerably decent little apartments; a small public *salle à manger* (the diligence from Bonifacio to Bastia stops here for refreshment), with sofas that do duty for beds, two small bedrooms, by good luck unoccupied, and a sort of kitchen used by the family, complete the hotel arrangements; but no part of it is as tidy or well furnished as the inns of Grosseto or Sartène.

While Mdme Gianelli produces breakfast, M. Quenza, the Maire of Porto Vecchio, to whom I have forwarded a letter from M. Galloni d'Istria, comes to visit me—a genial and intelligent person, who offers me his company, to show me some of the best points for making drawings of the town, and who talks of the great pine forests of Spedale, which M. Merimée had particularly recommended me to visit; they are within a few hours' drive, and a good road of the second-class, or

FOREST OF BAVELLA

LA PIANA

Route Forestière, leads to them, so that this fact begins to tempt me to remain a second day here for the sake of making the excursion. M. Quenza departs, and Mdme Gianelli, bringing coffee in a tumbler, asks if I will dine at five-thirty with the 'Continentali'?—'*Tutti monshieu*,' is her expression—government employés here, the director of the telegraph, the agent of salt works, etc.; but I decline tying myself to return at a certain hour, for there may be work to do till sunset.

Next follows a return visit to M. le Maire. M. Quenza lives in a large house, with an unpleasant entrance, and all but impossible stairs, landing you in a very large and lofty room altogether out of character with the approach to it. M. Quenza, however, was out, and finding only Madame, a baby, and the room very much in déshabillé, I apologise, and retreat to a height outside this sad and ruinous-looking village—in better days a comparatively flourishing town. Here, overlooking the flat shore and the salt pans at the foot of the hill, the calm gulf, and the generally unhealthy look of crowded vegetation characterising the neighbourhood, I make a drawing, until joined by M. Quenza, who has been delayed by having to preside as Maire at a civil marriage. Porto Vecchio must be a warm place during winter; sheltered from all cold westerly winds, its climate is vaunted, and I should think justly, as the warmest in Corsica; the conditions which make it so unfit as a residence in summer rendering it precisely the reverse in winter.

The Maire takes me up to a knoll on the north-west side of the town, and there I pass most of the rest of the day, for it commands the best view of the town and gulf. A tone of sadness broods over the scene, owing to the aged and forsaken look of the thinly populated Porto Vecchio, and to the absence of dwellings round it; but the quiet gulf, like a lake, nearly landlocked by the low hills, the beautiful colour and texture given to the landscape by its extensive cork forests and olive woods, communicate to this scenery a great charm of calm softness, and though possessed of no magnificence, it has great attractions for a painter through a certain mournful wildness and an air of antiquity. Somewhat it reminds me of Santa Maura, especially as to its extent of desolate flat ground near the salt works by the sea.

Later I passed an hour at the Maire's house, where I made the acquaintance of Mdme Quenza, a ladylike and good-looking woman, and and a small Quenza, a sharp little fellow, with Napoleonic eyes. I was shown a large collection of letters, written by the first Emperor Napoleon, and by General Paoli, to the great-grandfather of M. Quenza. Those of the former are on coarse paper and coarsely written, chiefly, I think, in the year 1794 or 1795. There is an orderly-book, too, with enough signatures of Buonaparte to make the fortune of an autograph seller; heaps, and bundles, too, of Paoli's correspondence, whether ever used or not as materials for his life I am ignorant.

Lastly, as the sun set, I came again to the great rocks whence I had made my drawing, and sat in a world of grey silence. Thus far in my Corsican tour several things surprise me. First, the excellence of the roads; secondly, the sense of extreme security in town and country; thirdly, the good breeding of the lower class of people, who are, without any exception, respectful and obliging, and always leave me undisturbed to my artistic devices; fourthly, the decent accommodation and good fare at these small country inns, which are far better relatively to the larger or town hotels than I have known to be the case in other countries, Italy, Sicily, etc. All this I was unprepared for; and I confess that Corsica, to which I came without any great interest, gives me daily a desire to see more of itself.

Mdme Gianelli, whose face would make a wonderful, if not beautiful study, sends in for supper some soup and *manzo*, or boiled beef, capital fish (*denticé*), and lobster, a steak, with potatoes and salad, and broccio; at many large Italian towns you would not fare better.

M. Quenza tells me that there is literally no winter here; and I believe that for purposes of study and climate this half-dead verdant place might well serve for a painter's home through the winter. It might be wished, however, that the neglected and dirty state of the exterior of Porto Vecchio did not extend to the interior of its dwellings, as it undoubtedly does.

I have decided to start at five tomorrow to the forests, and Mdme Q. guarantees the early appearance of her husband.

APRIL 24

At 5 A.M., Peter the coachman, trap and ponies, G. with folio, cloaks, and provision for the day, are ready; and presently M. Quenza joining me, also with a full basket, we start for the mountain, soon leaving the main road and passing through an extensive cork forest, around which the soft pleasant character of the Porto Vecchio scenery is very charming. These cork woods, too, are beautiful in colour and in the texture of their thickly clustering foliage, and from their deep red stems where the bark has been removed. M. Quenza tells me that he possesses 4,000 trees in this wood, each averaging a produce of ten sous annually.

Reaching the foot of the hills, at present covered with mist, we now begin to ascend towards the forests, and the road, one of the second class, called in Corsica, Routes Forestières, is henceforth carried, curving and winding with a steep ascent, up the face of the mountain; and though it is a good one, yet it has no parapet, and the fact of seeing mules pulling up a cart, the wheels of which are not more than an inch from the precipice's edge, by no means makes me more at ease in the carriage, from which I dismount, and thenceforth walk. My companion, the Maire, is full of cheery fun, and stories innumerable. Presently we pass a wild and singular-looking individual tending two or three goats, who waves his hand to M. Quenza with an air of lordly patronage, quite unlike the respectful obeisance I observe paid to him by other peasants. 'But this poor fellow,' says M. Quenza, 'is a harmless lunatic, and his present delusion is that he is King of Sardinia, which explains his magnificent manner.' A short time since the poor fellow was persuaded of a far less agreeable fact, for he believed that he had swallowed two gendarmes, and that the only remedy for this mishap was to eat nothing, in order to starve the intruders, which resolution he rigidly adhered to, till his own life was nearly sacrificed. When all but gone, however, he exclaimed, '*Ecco, tutti due son morti di fame!*—Both of them have died of hunger!'—and thereupon he resumed eating and work with joy.

M. Quenza also tells many stories of the too-famous Colomba,[1] who was his aunt by marriage; she died only four years ago, and one of her sisters is still living. Among his anecdotes of that surprising female, he recounts that at one time the family who were in Vendetta with her own in their town Fozzano wished to build a tower, which would have commanded that of their antagonists. Colomba, therefore, improvised a

[1] This lady was a celebrated leader in the Vendetta wars at Fozzano, and is supposed to be the heroine of M. Merimée's beautiful tale of the same name.—E.L.

party of her own people, who sat down to play at cards on the ground opposite the tower, and when they were settled she went out and joined them, as if observing the game, always dancing and dandling her baby at the same time. But in the dress of the child she had concealed a loaded pistol, and, watching her opportunity, suddenly shot one of the masons on the tower, replacing the pistol in the child's girdle under a shawl. The wildest confusion ensued; but the card players had their hands full of cards, and their guns all lying by their sides, while Mdme Colomba, with both hands, was pacifying the screaming child, so that the party seemed guiltless, and a false direction was given to suspicion. This feat Columba is said to have performed on two more of the builders, till the raising of the tower was deferred *sine die*.

M. Quenza says that there are pheasants on the eastern side of the island; and, speaking of the immense multitude of blackbirds produced by the *maquis*, he says that those of Sari (of Fiumorbo) are esteemed before all others on account of some peculiarity in their food.

At six-thirty the mists begin to lift, but it is not a day for clearness of distance; the road, now that we are fairly high on the mountain, winds along deep gullies, whence far-stretching ilex woods are seen on all sides; a few cantonniers, or road-menders, and now and then wood-cutters, are met from time to time. Crags half lost in clouds, and pines growing as it were in air, or groups of evergreen oak, often tempted me to stop and draw, but I postponed doing so until the distance should be more distinct, now that on this lofty ascent all the Gulf of Porto Vecchio with Sardinia beyond was widening out at each zigzag turn. We pass Spedale, a house inhabited by cantonniers, that has been long in sight, as well as a ruined chapel close to it, and some of the masses of rock and wood near here are wonderfully beautiful, yet the feeling that two or three hours' study is necessary to do them any justice in a drawing, besides the necessity of getting up to the top, prevents my lingering. At the twenty-first kilometre from Porto Vecchio the plateau, or summit of the mountain, is reached.

Here there is a new world, one all of pines, and, to my thinking, a gloomy one, for just now the clouds are low on these lofty regions, and the vistas of grey stems towering up to masses of darker foliage seem rather monotonous than cheerful.

A little onwards much of the ground is cleared, and in a bare space encircled by lofty trees stands a large double dwelling, with gardens adjoining; here the families of two foresters or guardiani live, by one of whom I am taken a little distance off to see some of the largest pine trees—giants of twenty-five metres in height and upwards. But these forests are on level ground, and command no distance of any sort, and, except on account of their magnitude, fail to interest me; gladly would I exchange all the magnificent monotony of these tall straight mountain trees for one glimpse of the beautiful *Pinus maritima* bending over the rocks by the sea at Kakiskali or Mount Athos, which places, indeed, the poetical sighing of these vast woods of Spedale in some measure recalls. And so I go to the guardiano's house, doubting if, after all, I shall get much drawing today, and glad meantime of a thick cloak, on account of the cold, and to attack M. Quenza's substantial breakfast and not unwelcome wine gourds.

The only memorandum I could procure of this part of the mountain was by going a little later with the forester to a *massif*, as they term the groups of trees, growing among great rocks on the plateau; these are of great size, and stand up majestically against the mountain-side. To the forester, a grim tall fellow, who watched the progress of my sketch, I offer one of my pencils, on the nature of which he made some remarks; whereupon he only says, 'There are enough in my house, but I will take it—*ne ho basta in casa, ma lo prendo*'—which was not gracious on the part of Don Guglielmo di Roccaserra, for so they called him; then, leaving M. Quenza, who was tired, to follow in the carriage, I came away from the level recesses of the forest, and began to descend the mountain. At 1.30 P.M., as I come down the zigzags above the house named Spedale, the distance and Sardinia on the horizon are hidden by mist; the groups of immense ilex, with pines and crags, are all shadeless —opposite the afternoon sun—so that in the end I walked down the mountain without getting another record of its scenery. As a pictorial gain, the excursion of today has certainly been a failure; had I walked up alone, many effects of light and shade at different points in these beautiful woods could have been secured; whereas, fearing to incon- venience M. Quenza by a succession of fidgety halts, I did nothing at all, beyond illustrating my theory that study is next to impossible if you join a companion. Nor have I felt very enthusiastic admiration during this my first visit to a Corsican forest; perhaps others I may see will have finer qualities, and the day may be less cloudy and cold. At four-thirty, M. Quenza, who does not appear fully to understand my mania for walking, picks me up; we drive across the cork woods, golden in the afternoon sun, and reach Porto Vecchio by 6 P.M.

A visit to the Maire's house closed the day's work. The sharp-eyed small Quenza, a little fellow not six years old, exhibits a curiously retentive memory, and should turn out a naturalist, for he knew the name of every animal depicted in Buffon, though showing most partiality for the monkey tribe. Every one of those apes, which nearly half a century ago I used to copy so carefully from the well-known volumes at home, this little man knew at sight, shouting out, '*c'est le Talapoin*', '*c'est le Carcajou*', etc. These would be pleasant people to know, should one ever take a fit of wintering in Corsica, and make Porto Vecchio headquarters. I am told, too, that the country round is so famed for the variety of its entomology, especially of Lepidoptera, that many naturalists from France and Germany pass some time here on that account, and that one of these, a M. Reveillier, whose acquaintance I was sorry not to have had the pleasure of making, has resided here for several years; moreover, two diligences to and from Ajaccio pass in every twenty-four hours, so one would not be quite shut out from the outer world.

After dinner at the hotel, supplied as usual with that wish to oblige which I begin to recognise as an eminent Corsican trait, the friendly M. Quenza comes, bringing me a lot of pine-cones which I had asked for, and a letter to one of his relatives at Quenza, in case I should go there, that being the name of the village high up towards the plain of Coscione, near Mount Incudine, to which the whole population of Porto Vecchio migrate in summer. During the vintage they come to and fro, but as a rule the town is entirely deserted after the end of May until November.

Today I am grieved to have worked so little; possibly I may see finer forest scenery in Corsica, but hardly any that can look down on so fair a scene of sea and distance as is commanded by the south-eastern side of the mountain I ascended, towards the wooded plain, the old town of Porto Vecchio and its olives, the gulf, and the Island of Sardinia beyond. Some of the groups of rock and foliage, too, were striking and beautiful, and yet I have not found it possible to bring away more than a few jottings.

April 25

Either Solenzaro, or Ghisonaccio, or Migliacciara, is to be my halting-place for tonight, but it is not easy to decide this question beforehand, or to obtain very clear information as to the distances; from what I gather it may be forty kilometres to the first-named place, and some twenty beyond to either of the others.

Leaving forlorn Porto Vecchio at 6 A.M., the road on the eastern side of the island runs a good way inland, and seldom approaches the sea. The scenery partakes of the grave character of Corsican landscape; yet in this district I observe some qualities not noticed hitherto, owing to the mists which seem to linger about these wooded regions, and over the low grounds near the gulf. For a time, in passing through the cork wood, the varied line of the gulf hills gives the landscape great interest; the lovely morning light falling on the dark red and silvery-grey cork stems, and the changefully clouded mountains inland are full of beauty; while, on the right, gleams of bright water are seen through rich un-dulations of wild green forest.

At seven, low hills shut out the gulf, *maquis* and cork woods are on each side, and on the left an amphitheatre of far mountains, all soberly green, with a world of detached granite masses. Two or three sets of wayside houses enliven the scene, some plots of corn, some goats, and a few people.

The torrent dell' Oso is passed, a trivial stream at present, but two long bridges over which the road is carried show that water is not always so scarce as now. And a sort of feverish chill appears to me to prevail in these low marshy tracts, however lovely to look at the jungle or underwood hereabouts may be, so rich in variety of vegetation—laurustinum and arbutus, wild olive and sloe-tree, hawthorn, hemlock, bramble and bryony, ilex and cork, myrtle, broom, high heath, clematis, cystus, and reeds, with here and there a fine pine glittering with a silvery dotting of *Processionary Bombyx* sacs. And only where there is a break in this wilderness, or where a carpet of red and white cystus occurs, does the pale asphodel peep above this many-foliaged confusion. Long tracts of such vegetation succeed each other with little change as we drive along a level road; and there is little to be done except drowsily writing up notes, while Peter the coachman hums faintly, like a drowning fly.

Wondrous to say, at 7.30 A.M. there is a road-side village, perhaps containing twenty houses: it is Santa Lucia di Porta Vecchio; beyond it the road crosses a clear and pretty river of the same name, flowing to the sea near the Gulf of Pinarello; and then we relapse into cork and *maquis*, *maquis* and cork.

After eight o'clock there is more variety in the drive, nearing the sea by the tower and Punto della Fautea; after passing which, and another stream and good bridge, the road becomes a cornice, running above the shore, where the exquisite vegetation is delightful—the superb yellow hemlock, brown and purple lavender, rose and white cystus, in gorgeous masses of colour, wild olive draped with festoons of wild vine, and now and then patches of blue flax, and silver spots of tall white amaryllis. The sameness of these parts of the coast of Corsica is atoned for by such banks and dells, full of glazing colour, and crowded with warbling birds, besides an occasional hoopoe, or bee-eater. Nowhere do I remember to have seen such slopes of splendid tints, so complete and lively a clothing of flowers. At nine the Tarco is crossed by a three-arched bridge, and, beyond that, the loftier summits of the southern portion of the great snowy mountains, or central chain, begin to be seen.

All at once (nine-thirty) a pretty little bay—the Porto Favone—opens, and is irresistible to the landscape painter, who halts to draw it. The compact Cala or Marina is a perfect picture, its background the mountain range near the Incudine, towering high above the velvet *maquis*-covered hills, and clear as glass; its foreground a few small houses edging the white sandy shore, drawn up on which are two or three boats, and beyond them a river and its bridge. A dozen or so of goats, and one or two raging dogs, are all the life vouchsafed to this spot, besides an ancient and crusty Corsican, who proclaims from an upper window to the inquiring Peter that these dwellings contain no barley or horse food of any sort. Peter the coachman has been given of late to disagreeable ways; almost mute for the first days of this tour, he has latterly taken to swear at his horses with a frightful volubility and a selection of oaths which denote, if nothing else, an inventive imagination of great power; this habit, and that of beating the animals on their heads, I object to and rebuke, and for the time the evil is stopped.

After passing along more cornice road and wild gardens, it is eleven-thirty before Solenzaro appears ahead on the coast, and we reach it at noon, the last part of the way being along hill-sides covered with vine-yards; it is a village consisting of one long straggling street, with some outlying, large, tall-chimneyed buildings, a French metallurgic estab-lishment, and a good many more extensive dwellings or warehouses, and on the whole presenting a more general appearance of life than Corsican villages are wont to display.

I am directed to a poor little house as the best hotel, kept, according to what seems frequent custom in Corsica, by yet another widow—la Vedova Orsola. But, although I may have the pleasure of inhabiting her house on my return here two days hence, it is not requisite to do so now, as I have prudently provided breakfast at Porto Vecchio, and there is nothing to be done at Solenzaro but to rest the horses and become acquainted with the distances and halting-places of the onward road; for I am anxious, if possible, to get to Casabianda and to see the site of Aleria, the ancient colony of Sylla, in this trip; because, should I be prevented from going there till late in my stay in the island, the eastern plain is said to be then so rife with malaria that one risks fever by sleep-ing in it. If, therefore, I can manage to accomplish this now, I may return here and cross the forests of Bavella, according to M. Vico's itinerary, and so rejoin the road to Ajaccio at Sartène.

What information I require is soon gained from a party who are sitting at breakfast at the door of a house opposite, magnificently labelled, and with a prophetic boldness, Hotel de Chemin de Fer. All these persons very good-naturedly volunteer particulars about the road, especially one, Signor Poli, who says Migliacciara is sixteen kilometres from this place, that it stands a little way off the main Bastia road upon that leading to the baths at Pietrapola, and that I shall find a good inn there; that Casabianda, the great Penitencier Agricole, is sixteen kilo-metres farther beyond Migliacciara, and close to Aleria; and that from Solenzaro—to which I must of necessity return—it is thirty kilometres to the top of the Bavella pass, and the village of Zonza again is eighteen other kilometres beyond it. Just then there comes up another Con-tinental, who says M. Vico, the Sous-inspecteur of Forests, has written to him to say I am on my way here; this gentleman is M. Mathieu, the agent or head manager connected with part of the great Bavella forests, and he tells me that he is shortly about to go there himself, and that meantime he has directed the guardiano at the Casa Forestière to house and feed me, 'for you may get some bread', he says, 'and possibly some potatoes'. All this is very obliging, and it seems I can have but little trouble throughout; on which I thank my informants, and leave them to their breakfast.

Some spot at hand, combining two qualifications, is now to be sought —namely, first, quiet; secondly, some scenery to draw during the mid-day halt—for in or near such wayside houses as there appear to be in this village, where noise and dirt are plentiful, it is by no means agreeable to eat if one can avoid doing so, and it is a great thing if a sketch can be combined with a two hours' stay at some picturesque resting-place. G., however, has already found a place, to which the Coliseum-sack is taken, where, on turning round the point of a low hill, just beyond the village, a beautiful picture is seen; a little chapel, which stands, backed by a group of pines, on the banks of a wide stream, with the snow heights near the grand Monte Incudine above, and all the middle distance of the scene composed of those deep green *maquis*-clothed velvety hills, the delight of Corsican landscape. At this river-side also nightingales abound in incredible numbers, and their exquisite music fills the air.

The halt of this morning is thus in every way a pleasure, and no slight additional satisfaction is it to recall what one has seen in the earlier part of the day, which, after the cork woods and *maquis* had been left behind, was a wonder and a delight from hour to hour—a border of glorious flowers by the still blue seaside. Now, all at once, the landscape has become noble and majestic, and I cannot help feeling, even after seeing so little as I yet have of this island, that it would be an endless field of study to a painter resident in it.

Afterwards I draw upon the bridge above the river, whence the stream and its picturesque banks, with the lofty shadowy mountains, make a beautiful scene, till it is time to send back G. for Peter and the trap. Peter has applied again here for money for the horses; but it seems that for every advance he gives them less barley and more beating, and it is dimly becoming a sort of fixed idea with me that Miss C. was right, and that I had better have hired her man and horses, even at a greater expense.

At 4 P.M., once more onward along the high road, meeting, soon after starting, the Bastia diligence which is to reach Bonifacio tomorrow morning, and Ajaccio on the succeeding day at noon—a dreary penance of shut-up shaking I am thankful to have escaped. The high central mountains, as seen from this eastern side of Corsica, stand far away beyond a wide plain, and their bases are hidden by low hills; yet, as a snowy range, they are truly a splendid sight; and the change from the spiky promontories of the west coast, the ins and outs, and curves and corners of the sea wall, or the close vales of *maquis* shut out from all distance, to this broad landscape, is most marked and delightful.

Give me the beauty and glory of open plains, with a distance of hill or sea! Here they are both; and yet the lines of this mountain wall are not easy to draw, and rather require a morning light; nor are the undulations of rich dwarf foliage, thus crested by snowy Alpine heights, without their difficulties. The wide level of unvaried rich green which stretches from the shore to the very foot of these heights is something the like of which I have never before seen, nor have I met with any representation of it. Nearly at five the River Travo is passed by a long and fine bridge, and looking up this broad and beautiful stream the landscape is wonderfully fine, but time does not allow of stopping to draw it. At the fiftieth kilometre from Porto Vecchio the plain is really unique in beauty, and more resembling some parts of Thessaly than any place I can compare it to, but that Thessaly wants the deep full green of the Corsican *maquis* clothing.

A few roadside houses grouped together near the River Travo are all the habitations seen on this extended campagna, till after passing another bridge (Ponte Palo or Londano?) over the Vabolesco, a broad and clear river, we reached the road to Pietrapola at six-thirty. Before this, the dark green verdure of the plain had given way to plains of asphodel and half-cultivated tracts of ground, latterly to fields of corn, and as the sun goes down behind the long western mountain wall Peter drives up to a single large dwelling by the road-side, and says, '*Ecco l'Hotel di Migliacciara.*'

The hotel, indeed (built originally, I imagine, by the French Agricultural Company mentioned by Valery), is in itself the whole of the village of Migliacciara, excepting a large group of farm-like buildings on the opposite side of the road, the whole appearing what in the Roman campagna one would call a tenuta. And at this season and hour the position of this place seems delightful, when the scent of the hawthorn, the song of the nightingale, the voices of sheep and cattle, the greenness of the country round, and the grandeur of the mountain range, but a short distance away, all seem to fill it with rural charms—it is hard to believe that in a month or two hence the whole district becomes pestilential.

The interior of the so-called 'hotel' is unlike any I have yet seen in Corsica; the large building has rambling corridors and chambers, like those in many a wayside inn in the Neapolitan states of old days, or those of anti-Italian-Rome of these, and I was surprised as well as glad to secure a lofty and quiet apartment. Presently the Bastia diligence arrived; supper or dinner was suddenly announced, and the company—to wit, the conductor and one passenger, myself and servant—sat down to a meal of which it may be said that better as well as worse might be essayed.

The conductor, who is a Continental, and was a soldier in the Crimea, speaks highly of the baths of Pietrapola not far from here, and says that rheumatic complaints are completely removed by the use of their waters. He himself, he adds, after the Russian war, had rheumatic fever to a degree that lost him the use of both his arms, until, through the means of the Pietrapola hot baths, he was restored to health.

It would be pleasant to see these baths of Pietrapola; they are in a neighbouring valley; and perhaps after Aleria has been visited, time may yet allow of my reaching them.

CHAPTER IV

April 26

At 5.30 A.M. I start for Aleria; the more delay in going there, the greater
risk of fever; so once more I am on the Bastia road. How like is this to
the old days of Roman campagna life, its early hours, the fresh air, and
the outspread plain and distant mountains! To me this is the most
delightful of Corsican scenery; perhaps, indeed, partly from old associations; and none the less so that it is unexpectedly beautiful. The River
Fiumorbo, which gives its name to the canton, is soon passed, and at six
Ghisonaccio is reached—a sprinkling of tall houses by the road-side,
many of them unfinished, all ugly and forlorn to look at—children
abound, mingled with pigs, and men sit in idleness on the walls and
door-steps. Nor does anyone take notice of the passers-by, except one
man, who holding a live hare, says, 'Achetez, M'sieu?' Ghisonaccio is not
a prepossessing place. Just beyond it, on the left of the road, is a tomb
of classical shape, in memory of an overseer of roadworks, murdered
here some years back. On the right the plain is lost in marsh and great
étangs or salt pools, while towards the snowy mountains it seems one
immense green carpet of fern and lentisk up to their very base, varied
only in a few places by lines of purple or almost of black, marking the
place where the maquis has been burned. And as clouds are rising, I fear
to lose my mountain outline, and devote some time to a drawing of
these wild fern plains and green levels. Peter the coachman about this
time, I being on foot, and he somewhat ahead, gets himself into disgrace,
by reason of beating one of his horses unmercifully when it stumbled, I
and my man being unable to prevent him, far less to moderate the
astonishing current of oaths with which, in these paroxysms of fury, he
accompanies his blows. But on overtaking him I tell him that patience
may have an end, and that if he persists in disorderly behaviour, I will
telegraph to Ajaccio for a new coachman, and leave him here. Whereon
he says, 'Una cosa certa é che l'uomo deve sempre aver pazienza; quest' é una
delle prime regole della vita—One thing is certain, that a man should

93

always be patient; and this, indeed, is one of the first rules of life!'

The plain becomes much more undulating as Casabianda is approached; it stands on high ground, not far from the site of ancient Aleria—both places overlooking the Tavignano and the whole eastern plain, and consists in a group of large new buildings, not overpicturesque, notwithstanding that at a distance it has something of the air of Castel Guibilei, or similar places on the Roman campagna. In the vicinity of this important establishment, fern, myrtle, and cystus disappear, and give way to corn, lupines, and other vegetables more useful if not so poetical; labour takes the place of neglect; and, instead of a green desert, there is flourishing cultivation. Carts and cattle are met, and groups of the convicts (of which there are about a thousand in the Penitencier) going out to work. A road strikes off on the right to the reclaimed ground, near the great marshes now undergoing drainage, close to the sea, and to the left it is continued to the principal buildings of the establishment, which I reach at nine.

Fortunately for me (for, not having expected to come here when I left Ajaccio, I had had no note or recommendation from M. Galloni d'Istria), M. Benielli, the young clerk who, at Bonifacio, had volunteered to show me the lions of Aleria, happened to be at that moment at the entrance of the open space before the prisons, otherwise I could have made but little progress, owing to the sentinels and gendarmes, who naturally are on all sides in a place devoted to convict labour. M. Benielli greeted me heartily, and offered, conjointly with several other young employés, to show me all over Aleria. I was to see the new drainage, the prisons, the remains—here of a wall, there of an amphitheatre; in a word, nothing was to be left unseen. My object, however, being to procure one or two good views of the place, and to avoid giving up much time to what was not of immediate interest to my topographical work, I had little inclination to take long walks in the heat of the day; and, moreover, I had already discerned the point from which the plain of the Tavignano must be best represented. It requires all a man's available tact and politeness to intimate to fourteen or fifteen amiable individuals, without giving them offence, that you do not want their company, and would far rather be alone; but it is necessary for me to choose on the one hand between companionship and time lost, and the chance of making a good drawing on the other.

> Let us alone; time driveth onward fast,
> And in a little while our lips are dumb

and our hands useless; so I beg my new acquaintances to allow me to go my own way, to which they most good-naturedly assent, being only hospitably obstinate on the point of my returning to breakfast with them at eleven. Then, having accepted the offer of an obliging M. Liberati (who was on the point of going to the fort and village of Aleria) to show me a short cut across some fields towards the site of the old city, I set off, not without fear that the clouds, which are rapidly covering the snowy range, may prevent my getting their outline.

It was at Aleria that Theodore, afterwards King of Corsica, first landed—a character so remarkable, that I subjoin some account of his most romantic life, one intimately connected with the history of Corsicans during their rebellion against Genoa in the early part of the last century.[1]

Several pieces of Roman brickwork, clearly denoting the antiquity of the spot, are scattered about the bluff or headland to which I went, and which may have been an outpost or fort of the old Roman colony, or even the citadel of Sylla's city, the site of which is evidently well chosen, and commanding a very glorious view on all sides—northward, along the flat plain which melts into the horizon near Cervione; westward, towards Monte Rotondo, the gorge of the Tavignano, and the course of that river to the foot of the Alerian hills; eastward, over the plain, and the broad marshes, and salt lakes, or *étangs*, to the sea; and, southward, to the whole chain of snowy heights, from Mont Renoso to Mont Incudine, with its remarkable outline, and the hills which at Solenzaro close the view in that direction. The long line of white snow against the blue sky is not unlike that of the Alps as seen from Turin; and, while I remained on this eminence, I wished to make another drawing, combining the buildings of Casabianda with the mountain wall beyond the plain; but clouds gradually blot out all their forms, and finally oblige me to give up the attempt. While I am drawing, G. brings me two specimens of the Mygale, or trap-spider, so common in Corfù, called there the Κεφαλάμια, and apparently abundant hereabouts.

At eleven, return to Casabianda, where M. Benielli meets me, and a good breakfast is most welcome after the morning's work, for even

[1] See Additional Notes, page 250, for text of Lear's original footnote, quoting Boswell.

now the heat is great in these exposed plains. Whatever may be the privations of modern, compared with those of ancient, Aleria, the want of a good table is certainly not one, as sea-fish of several sorts, fresh river trout, wild-boar steaks and stew, hare and partridge amply testified; though the foreign visitor, however willing and able to appreciate such variety, could hardly help putting the friendly and simple hospitality of his French acquaintance as the highest item in the bill of fare. It seems that wild boars are very numerous here in the low underwood about the marshy districts near the sea, and the pursuit of them is a favourite amusement. M. Benielli tells me that from here to Corte is a ride only of six hours, and that on the way they pass Ghisoni, and near that place he says there is a gorge or chasm in the hills, called the *Inseca*, which he strongly urges me to see, as well as the forest of Marmano in that neighbourhood, where there exists a summer station for the Penitencier establishment. But how can I see '*all* Corsica' in ten weeks? At noon I took leave of my kindly entertainers, who, besides all the morning's attentions, pressed me warmly to stay with them two or three days.

Alas for the tops of the mountains! they are invisible; nevertheless, the one great peculiarity of this plain is ever before me; namely, that it spreads darkly green to the very roots of the hill-range rising directly out of it—a single pale blue wall, silver tipped. Meanwhile the day is hot, and progress slow, which is no evil at all, compared with my hard task in preventing Peter from beating his horses, and from swearing after a fashion which becomes unendurable when you must needs sit still and hear it.

Even in a carriage drive 'to see all Corsica' there is still room for some variety, and such may be counted the frequent walking of red-legged partridges across the road, and the sitting of bee-eaters on the telegraph wires. If possible, I shall revisit Casabianda on my way to Bastia, for not only is the spot historically interesting in more than one way, but the scenery of the east side of Corsica can be illustrated from it more advantageously than from any other point; perhaps on a second visit the distance may be less clouded, and if I cannot return, it will at least be something to have seen this side of the island, which is less easy to become acquainted with than the western.

The untidy Ghisonaccio is repassed, and the bridge over the Fiumorbo

River, at 2.15 P.M.; and at four the road to Pietrapola is reached, when I send on Peter to the inn, and take a short cut across the fields towards the entrance of the gorge in the hills, at the head of which are the village and the baths of Pietrapola, which perhaps there may yet be time to reach. In this walk, low down by the River Vabolesco, all is delightful, and strongly contrasted with the hot unsheltered Aleria; great chestnut trees, here nearly in leaf, stand on grassy levels, or among fern four or five feet in height; all along the pleasant valley the hawthorn blooms, the blackbird and nightingale sing, and gravelly paths lead on by the side of the clear running stream, between clumps of lentisk and cool verdure. Rejoining the road—a Route Forestière—which leads to the baths, it enters the pass of Pietrapola, a winding woody valley scene almost exactly like one in Derbyshire or Devonshire. The road runs at a considerable height above the beautifully clear rivulet that foams and dashes over rocks and white boulders, and only the presence of large ilex instead of ash or oak forbids an Englishman to suppose he is in his own country. But there is not time to pursue this leafy valley very far, for it is 5.30 P.M., and I turn back towards Migliacciara without having reached the baths, though the walk even so far up the picturesque and narrowing vale in the enjoyable quiet of this cool evening has its agreeable memories.

On the way back to Migliacciara by the upper road, glimpses of the plain are caught now and then from pleasant lanes, where the hedges are alive with bird-melody. There are a few fine cattle (not an ordinary sight in Corsica) here and there, some scattered cottages, all with an accompaniment of pigs, which seem more common on this than on the other side of the island, and now and then a few peasants are met, on their return home to their villages, black and brown garmented as usual, their horses carrying double. But the event of the evening lay in meeting an equestrian party, two of whom, good-looking damsels, were running a race, and others with their male friends all following in a body and encouraging the bold and fair, the like of which departure from the gravities I had not before seen in this island. Near the Migliacciara farm are immense flocks of black sheep, soon, I am told, to leave the plains for the upper mountain pastures.

The Bastia diligence had just arrived at the hotel, and as it was pretty full the party at supper were numerous; the repast, more remarkable for the rapidity with which it was consumed than for the quality of the food, was chiefly distinguished by the large supplies of capital asparagus, and for a pyramid of oysters from the *étang*, or salt-water lake, at Aleria; these are of immense size, but, to my taste, wanting in delicacy. The diligence company included some who were very amusing; the conductor, who constantly reminded his charge that time was precious, and urged fast eating; a young and merry priest, a Continental, who joked and smoked; two naturalists, one a lively youth from Dresden, the other an elderly Austrian savant, who had met by chance at Bastia on their way to collect entomological novelties at Porto Vecchio; and three or four others. In these round-table meetings there is a good deal of hurry and noise; the Migliacciara Hebe—she is like an Arab girl, with her head so muffled up as to allow as little as possible of her very brown face to be seen—sets the various dishes, or rather throws them, with great vigour and audacity at no particular point on the table, and snatches up the plates, with clashing and no small tumult, from those who have accomplished the disappearance of a portion of food; everybody helps everybody else to wine, and himself to food; and conversation becomes general and loud.

Tonight it happens to be full of amusement, till M. le conducteur, having several times vainly essayed to move the party, rises, and saying with authority, '*Messieurs! soyez raisonnables! Il faut que vous partiez*', breaks up the sitting.

APRIL 27

Off at six from the wide-meadowed and rural Migliacciara—a place that calls up many a memory of farms on the Campagna di Roma—and along the Bastia and Bonifacio road back to Solenzaro; this is my only plan, for there is no possibility of getting to Bavella in one day from here, and, moreover, the weather is cloudy and threatens rain, ill prospect for high mountain passes. And now the whole beautiful line of snowy heights, so great a compensation for the long straight high road, is altogether invisible, and the drive has but slender charms; soon even the rarely occurring houses, the lazy people and the pigs, the fields of asphodel and carpet of fern, are all shut out by hard rain for a couple of hours.

At eight the weather clears as I reach the bridge over the Travo; and since the chief necessity of this day consists in keeping clear of the village inn at Solenzaro as long as possible, I determine to make what studies I can about the river, and anyhow to stay out of doors till near sunset. G., besides breakfast and folio, has a plentiful supply of cloaks, so come rain or sunshine, Peter is sent on, and the horses, who may perhaps have a hard day's work at Bavella tomorrow, will have a long rest today.

Drawing thrives ill, for the day is sunless and heavy, yet I venture by snatches to secure the nearer parts of this beautiful river scene; and when rain falls, sitting below a thick myrtle and lentisk grove and writing up journal notes ekes out the hours. Days of Cumberland and of Devonshire Lydford seem to return as I sit by the clear and noisy river. At intervals the snowy heights appear, and then again are hidden in the most tantalising fashion, happily beaming out brightly for an hour later in the day, so that, in the end, I can procure their outline correctly.

One human being only is seen through all the morning, to wit, a half-frightened little boy, to whom I give the empty wine-bottle after breakfast; but he supposes I want it filled with water, and although on his return to the place where I was sitting he finds me no longer there, I meet him, seeking for me everywhere, a full hour afterwards, and still carrying the full water-bottle—a degree of patient virtue meriting all that remains of the unfinished breakfast.

The rest of the day's work consists in slowly walking to Solenzaro, getting one or two memoranda of the positive black-purple line of burnt *maquis* all across the plain, and watching the vast crags of the Incudine range gradually glooming out through mist and thunder-cloud as I reach the village at 7 P.M.

A very queer little hotel indeed seems this of the Widow Orsola; from its ground floor a ladder leads to an upper set of apartments, including three small rooms, all occupied, besides an open platform landing or common passage, the only place in Solenzaro where a night's rest can be got. 'Διὰ μίαν νύκτα—Only for one night'—says the Suliot, as he puts up my camp-bed in a corner, gets the room swept, and gradually contrives to change the confusion of the place into something like order. I decline the offer of one of the French employés, who good-naturedly begs to vacate his own room for me; and finally two tables are

99

introduced, one to serve for supper, the other for my man to sleep on, and the evening meal is set forth in such space as has been cleared of boxes, barrels, and sacks.

The dinner, with a curious inconsistency that I am now beginning to recognise as a regular part of Corsican travel, is quite a contrast to the rude discomfort of the room—good soup and boiled meat, trout which might do credit to a table at Ambleside, capital roast mutton and salad, with the red Tallano wine, famous in these parts. Moreover, the quiet and obliging ways of the Corsicans who administer these rustic road-side inns is beyond praise, and after two weeks' sojourn in the island I am coming to think that a more unpretendingly civil and attentive set of people to a stranger who brings them very little profit can hardly be found.

Meanwhile, in the opposite room beyond the ladder-entrance, various people employed in the metal or wood interests are supping, among them the young Dresden naturalist, who had broken down in the long diligence journey, and is going on to Porto Vecchio by slow instalments. Later, I converse with some of the Continentals, and learn the details of what I hope is to be my tomorrow's journey to the Bavella forest. The Maison de l'Alza (or Maison Forestière), the principal forest lodge, is, says M. Mathieu, twenty-three kilometres from Solenzaro, and thence it is five or six more up to the Bocca di Bavella, or head of the pass, beyond which there are twelve or fourteen more kilometres to Zonza. Provisions must be taken for the whole route, as none are likely to be found on it. Some to whom I speak say boldly that they think there is no chance of my trap, owing to its weight and the smallness of its horses, ever arriving even at the top of the first pass, for there are two; others opine that the ascent may be accomplished with care, and as I and G. shall always walk, I do not doubt that I may get there. Today, however, I shall only endeavour to reach the Maison de l'Alza, drawing as much as I can by the way. And it has rained so hard in the mountains all day that a clear morrow may, I think, be hoped for.

April 28

At 5 A.M. the weather is cloudy, but yet giving sufficient promise of clearing to allow of a start on this cross-country expedition. The oblig-ing Widow Orsola, besides recommending thin slices of toast with the morning cup of coffee, superintends the arrangements for carrying food for at least two days, in the shape of bread and cheese, a large piece of meat, twenty-five eggs, cold trout, and three bottles of wine, for all which, besides yesterday's lodging and supper, ten francs is the charge.

We are off at six, and ascending immediately behind the little chapel I had drawn three days ago, turn out of the main road into the Route Forestière, which, like that on the hills of Spedale, is broad and in good order, but without parapets. The views become finer at every turn in the steep ascent; immense tracts of wood and *maquis* stretch away to the north; before me, towards the south-west, rise the huge crags of the Bavella Pass, their summits hidden in mist, and far below rolls the river through underwood and among rocks, with pines growing close to the water's edge.

At seven-thirty a stoppage occurs from meeting the first timber carts I have seen in these lands, loaded each with a single tree-trunk a hundred feet or upwards in length, and drawn by from ten to fifteen mules. From a distance, these cars seem like giant serpents or megalosauri slowly winding down the mountain, and it is as well to perceive their coming beforehand, so as to draw up by the inner side of the road; for, although guided behind by two men with a sort of helm, they are dangerously unwieldy neighbours if encountered unexpectedly at any of the sharp turns of the road, the mules when going downhill being stopped with difficulty.

About eight a small white house of refuge in time of snow or storm is passed; outside it is a forno, or oven for baking bread. A long string of mules comes down the mountain laden with wine from Tallano; and, later, M. Mathieu, the agent or head forester, passes on horseback, and says that he shall be at the Maison de l'Alza to receive me—we are a long way off that yet, however. The pass here is very grand, and I obtain many a memorandum of it as the carriage goes slowly up the hill. The pines are much larger than those lower down, and grow wildly among the detached masses of granite, among which the river foams and dashes.

At nine forty-five, being at the eleventh kilometre, half the way is accomplished, and hitherto I see no reason to despair of getting in good time to the desired halt, if only Peter can be induced to leave his horses alone; while they toil up slowly and regularly, stopping from time to time, things go on well, but when he bursts into one of his vicious paroxysms, he beats them—if I or my man are not near enough to prevent him—till they back nearly to the edge of the precipice; once or twice a very ugly sight.

Meanwhile the pass becomes constantly finer and more interesting; the immense crags in front—the highest of this part of the lofty central range, and very close to the Mont Incudine—are wrapped in cloud, and are awfully mysterious, and somewhat resembling the great pillars of Gebel Serbal, in the peninsular of Sinai. The pines are exquisitely beautiful, and unlike any I have ever seen; perfectly bare and straight to a great height, they seem to rise like giant needles from the 'deep blue gloom' of the abyss below. Granite rocks of splendid forms are on every side, the spaces between them cushioned with fern, and the tall spires of the *Pinus maritima* shooting out from their sides and crevices. Springs by the road-side are frequent and welcome, for the way is exceedingly steep, and Giorgio has to work hard in pushing the carriage behind, which the poor little horses, willing, but ill fed and ill treated, find it difficult to pull up.

11 A.M.—At the fourteenth kilometre, where there is another little forest house or refuge (the spot is called Rocca Pinsuta, a wondrous scene of fine crags and pines), we halt for breakfast and to remain at least till one o'clock. May the heavy clouds now gathering and throwing a deeper gloom over the depths and tremendous heights around not turn to violent storm and rain! for there are still three kilometres (two miles) to the bocca, or top of the pass; two gendarmes, however, who come down the hills, say that the road ahead is less worn and not quite so steep as along the part we have come up.

Leaving G. to oversee Peter and the horses, I wander on alone with my note-book and pencil. The colour here is more beautiful than in most mountain passes I have seen, owing to the great variety of underwood foliage and the thick clothing of herbs; forms, too, of granite rocks seem to me more individually interesting than those of other formations; and the singular grace and beauty of the pine trees has a peculiar charm—their tall stems apparently so slender, and so delicate the proportions of the tuft of foliage crowning them. The whole of this profound gorge, at the very edge of which the road runs, is full of moun-

102

tain scenes of the utmost splendour, and would furnish pictures by the score to a painter who could remain for a lengthened sojourn. Sometimes ivory-white, needle-spiry pine stems, dead and leafless, break the dark yawning chasm of some black abyss far below with a line as of a silver thread; now a great space of grey mist in the distant hollow depth is crossed by lines of black-burned stems; anon the high trunk of a solitary tufted tree looks like a kind of giant flower on a tall stalk; and ever above are delicate myriads of far pines 'pluming the craggy ledge', their stems drawn like fine hair against the sky.

At three the top of the pass, or Bocca di Larone, is reached; and here the real forest of Bavella commences, lying in a deep cup-like hollow between this and the opposite ridge, the north and south side of the valley being formed by the tremendous columns and peaks of granite (or porphyry?), the summits of which are seen above the hills from Sartène, and which stand up like two gigantic portions of a vast amphitheatre, the whole centre of which is filled with a thick forest of pine. These crags, often as I have drawn their upper outline from the pass I have been ascending today, are doubly awful and magnificent now that one is close to them, and, excepting the heights of Serbal and Sinai, they exceed in grandeur anything of the kind I have ever seen, the more so that at present the distance is half hidden with dark cloud, heavily curtaining all this singular valley; and the tops of the huge rock buttresses being hidden, they seem as if they connected heaven and earth. At times the mist is suddenly lifted like a veil, and discloses the whole forest—as it were in the pit of an immense theatre confined between towering rock-wall, and filling up with its thousands of pines all the great hollow (for it is hardly to be called a valley in the ordinary sense of the term) between those two screens of stupendous precipices. As I contemplate the glory of this astonishing amphitheatre, I decide to stay at least another day within its limits, and I confess that a journey to Corsica is worth any amount of expense and trouble, if but to look on this scene alone. At length I have seen that of which I have heard so much—a Corsican forest.

The road leads down from the Bocca di Larone to the bottom of the hollow, and, crossing it, mounts the farther side, half-way up which, a small white speck, is the Maison de l'Alza, and the end of my day's journey. All along the descent there are no words for the majesty and wonder of this scenery; the tremendous mystery of those cloud-piercing

103

towers and pillars, their sides riven and wrinkled in thousands of chasms, with pines growing in all their crevices and on all their ledges and pinnacles; the waves of the forest, so to speak, stretching from side to side of the vale; the groups of ilex, mixed with pine, in innumerable pictures, massive or slender, bare-stemmed or creeper-hung, flourishing in life, or dead glittering and white.

At the end of the descent stand two small foresters' houses on the short space of level ground between the four sides of this vale of Bavella; but here, at the twentieth kilometre from Solenzaro, the clouds burst, and violent torrents of rain make shelter welcome. Yet when the storm ceases for a time, and the sun gleams out through cloud, the whole scene is lighted up in a thousand splendid ways, and becomes more than ever astonishing, a changeful golden haze illumes the tops of the mighty peaks, a vast gloom below, resulting from the masses of black solemn pines standing out in deepest shadow from pale granite cliffs dazzling in the sunlight, torrents of water streaming down between walls and gates of granite, giant forms of trees in dusky recesses below perpendicular crags; no frenzy of the wildest dreams of a landscape painter could shape out ideal scenes of more magnificence and wonder.

From the twenty-first kilometre the road again begins to wind steeply upwards between tall walls of spectre pines, half seen through a dim mist and thickly falling rain; and at times I am glad to take shelter below some of the rocks, till complete wet-throughness renders any further care unnecessary. There is now no longer any fear of precipices, for the road here has a natural parapet of rock; and G. has worked hard in superintending the progress of the carriage from behind, while the tired horses creep slowly up; for in this last stage of their discomfort, Peter the merciless is not to be suffered to beat them—a shutting up of one valve which only occasions his anger to escape more violently by another. So that when there is a pause of a few minutes he occupies them in the most ferocious cursing, often so ridiculous that it ceases even to be shocking, as he introduces into his maledictions a multitude of novel and definite detail quite surprising. Once, when the horses had stopped, and I prohibited their being touched, Peter's volubility ceased from sheer want of power to continue; 'for', said he, 'I have no more breath, and besides I have sworn at everything, and there's nothing left to *bestem-miare*—to curse.' But at that moment the upraised voice of several cuckoos, who seemed rather than not to rejoice in the rain, was heard, and gave him a fresh impetus, for, with a poetical ingenuity worthy a better cause, he exclaimed, 'May all the parliament of heaven be so full of these nasty cuckoo birds that the saints and apostles will not be able to hear themselves or each other speak; and may every drop of rain turn into a million of snakes on its way from the sky downwards!' Assuredly Peter is a most unpleasant coachman.

The Maison de l'Alza, close to the twenty-fourth kilometre, was reached at 5.30 P.M.; a neat tidy house of two stories, standing in a space cleared from trees and looking directly across the valley to the Bocca di Larone. Here M. Mathieu came out, and received me most amiably, giving me and my servant rooms; and, after putting on dry clothes, most welcome were a good fire and a hot basin of soup, not to speak of trout, pork and potatoes, and an omelette with morelles—a production of my host's—with plenty of good wine. A double-kerchiefed old woman and an old guardiano waited at table, and the house in the woods was a treasure after the day's work and walk. So also was a sound sleep in the camp-bed; but, before that happened, I had already resolved to remain here all tomorrow.

April 29

4.45 A.M.—Wake with a strong impression that it is needful to work extra hard all day, in order to secure as many records as possible of the scenery I walked through in the afternoon of yesterday, anything approaching to the magnificence of which, as forest landscape, I have never seen; yet, owing to the perfect clearness of today, there cannot be that wealth of effect produced yesterday by the passing and lifting of clouds across the enormous crags—sublime and continually changing—and that infinite variety of light and shadow thrown over the pines and all the foliage of the deep hollow valley.

The sun rises cloudlessly over the world of pines, and presently forms new and glorious pictures, as point after point of the western side of the valley is lighted up, while all the eastern part of the forest is as yet in dark and solemn shadow, below the giant crags—long streams of gold

and bronze widening out gradually into masses of luminous green, and
a flood of glory spreading slowly up the immense granite buttresses. I
set off at 5.30 A.M. down to the bottom of the valley, and crossing it,
go up as far as the Bocca di Larone, M. Mathieu, on his return to
Solenzaro, overtaking me by the way, of whom I took leave, with
thanks, for his good-naturedly hospitality.

Thenceforth, all the rest of the day went in hard work, only interrupted at eleven, after Giorgio's announcement, 'ἕτοιμον τὸ πρόγευμα,
κύριε—Sir, breakfast is ready'—and by walking from one part to another
of this never-to-be-forgotten beautiful forest, not the least of its charms
being the profound silence, broken only by the cuckoo's notes echoing
from the crags, and from the fullness of melody chanted by thousands of
blackbirds. Other forests in Corsica are much larger than this, but
surely none can surpass it in certain qualities. For, remarkable as the
valley of Bavella undoubtedly is as a whole, by reason of its intense
solemnity, and for the double range of apparently perpendicular barriers
which close it entirely from the outer world, and admit no prospect
whatever beyond its limits, it is not less so for the exquisite detail of
its scenery, the brushwood or *maquis*—particularly the arbutus and great
heath—being throughout of the most perfect beauty. In some spots,
too, groups of large evergreen oaks standing on slopes of green sward
or fresh fern, and at others, masses of isolated granite, form pictures
hardly to be exceeded in grandeur.

A slowly moving black and orange lizard is a noticeable inhabitant of
the forest; he waddles gravely across the road, and frequently gets
crushed by the wheels of the great timber carts. For, above the Maison
de l'Alza great havoc goes on amongst the stately pines, and these
enormous trees, peeled and cut angularly, are carried down to the
valley depth, and thence up to the Bocca di Larone, and all the way to
the shore at Solenzaro—often, as I have before observed, very unpleasant loads if met at sharp turns of the road. Some of these giant
trees are six feet in diameter, and require fourteen or sixteen mules to
drag them up to the Bocca.

After a hard day's drawing I come up to the Maison de l'Alza before
sunset. Although the wrapping mists of yesterday's cloud and storm are
blown away, and what seemed the fathomless hollows and immeasure-
able summits are now plainly understood; yet, in spite of this, parts of

the forest are still truly extraordinary, the greatest novelty of the scenery being that the great granite columns are so near to you that here and there some of them appear literally overhead, while every imaginable beauty of detail adorns their surface; and, again, one remarks how, sometimes, multitudes of tall needle-like pine stems shine brightly off the deep-shadowed chasms in the crags, or clusters in lines of jetty black against the pallid granite.

Some of the scenes at the foot of the ascent to the Maison de l'Alza, and close to the great precipices, occupy me two or three hours—one, a narrow gorge with a perspective of spires, leading, as it were, into the very inmost heart of the mountain; another, of bold crags, dark against the sunset sky, and rising out of the most profuse vegetation—both scenes grand beyond expression in words. Nor, indeed, except by very careful study, could many of the greatest and wildest beauties of this forest be represented in a sketch, and to attempt to do so seems like endeavouring in one day to make satisfactory notes from the contents of a whole library, full of all sorts of literature. Nevertheless, I have succeeded in obtaining a few striking points of this wonderful landscape.

The wife of the guardiano did her best to procure us a dinner, though the materials of it were only potatoes in various forms; happily the Solenzaro larder was far from exhausted. A painter, however, might and should endure anything short of starvation, to see what I have seen of Bavella.

APRIL 30

Before the red sun glows over the eastern sea, and while yet the grand forest is in deep shade, I have risen, and having paid the expenses of Madame Guardiano, and secured a lot of pine-cones and seeds for Stratton and various other English places, I leave G. to follow with disagreeable Peter and the trap, and walk on alone; strict injunctions previously given that the horses are to take their own time, since there are but six more kilometres to the top, and we shall there make a long halt.

The silence and majesty of these pine forests at this hour! the deep obscurity of dim untrodden dells! the touches of gold high up on the loftiest branches and foliage!—And as the road mounts steeply upward, how beautiful are the cushions of green, the topmost verdure of the thousands of trees on which, far below, you look down!—Generally speaking, the Corsican pine has but little lateral foliage, but sometimes on the outskirts of the forest you meet with trees that have broad arms and dark lines of flat spreading leafage, exactly resembling some in Martin's pictures. To make small memoranda as I walk up is all I can do, though in reality there are great pictures on every side, but such as require a long time to portray.

At 9 A.M., a little beyond the twenty-ninth kilometre, the last forest house, called Maison de Bavella, is reached, and here is to be the two hours' halt. The position of this little building is bewitching, for it overlooks every part of the valley, and being considerably higher than the opposite Bocca di Larone, has a most extended horizon in that direction; some of the tallest and finest-formed trees stand near, serving as frames for the scene below, and between their stems, far away on the eastern sea, appears the island of Elba (so at least say the people at the forest house, though by its situation I should have thought it Monte Cristo); and beyond that the Italian coast appears perfectly clear. An hour or more is passed in drawing at some distance from the high road. How pure at this height is the air! what stately trees around! how perfect and beautiful are these scenes! and yet, though the last two days have considerably altered my opinion about pine-forest scenery, I would rather live among palms than pines.

After breakfast, by the side of a delicious spring, on the last of the food prudently secured at Solenzaro, I wander on still upwards. All about the slopes above and around the Bavella forest-house stand numerous little houses, or rather huts of stone; these, says the woman at the Maison Forestière, are all occupied in the summer by the people of Zonza, the next village westward; the whole of the inhabitants of that place coming, as it were, upstairs, and passing three months in the forest. 'Everybody comes,' says the guardianessa, 'the maire, the doctor, the priest'; but how they exist in such miserable dwellings it is not easy to understand, the rude buildings being made of masses of granite put together in the most cyclopean fashion, with wooden roofs, and heavy stones to keep the planks in their places. Inside there are shelves to do duty as beds, and in some there are tables, all of the roughest description. I counted more than eighty of these mountain homes; as many more are fallen down, and are simply heaps of stones, while others are very unsafe and ready to collapse with the next heavy snow or violent wind. The turf-slopes and whispering tall pines about this high eastern ridge of Bavella are delightful; and, doubtless, in the summer, when the temperature is always settled, an outdoor life on this mountain-top must have charms that atone for the want of comfort these unsatisfactory domiciles must present. By noon I reach the Bocca di Bavella, or top of the pass, where pines flattened and bent tell of the fury of the south-west tempests; and here I look back for the last time on one of the most beautiful and wonderful dream-scenes of forest land-scape it has beén my lot to see. Farewell, Bavella!

After a short space of level, the road winds downward still through forests, which on this side of the mountain belong to the commune of Zonza, and are in many parts very magnificent, unfolding views of great extent and grandeur; but in no wise comparable to that in the centre or valley of Bavella, inasmuch as the accompaniment of the perpendicular crags which wall in the hollow forest there is wanting. After 1 P.M. the road passes another Maison Forestière, and now again for a space there are tall, majestic trees, and folds of innumerable pines stretch around the western sides of the mountain range, the higher points of which increase in picturesqueness as they are more remote. Farther down the trees are more mixed in species—a tangled wood of ilex and oak—and the scene is enlivened by a greater amount of animal life—orioles, chaffinches, and robins; birds, of which in the depths of the forest but few are seen. By degrees the pine ceases, and opener views succeed, gradually breaking up into plots of turf with the familiar detached masses of granite; then, little by little, groups of chestnut trees and cultivation of corn follow, and presently I halt to draw the Incudine heights towering on the eastern side of the landscape and ribbed with snow.

3 P.M.—Zonza is reached unexpectedly, for, till a close approach, it is hidden by trees—a picturesque village, with a snow-white new campanile; and, to give the horses a rest, I order Peter to pick me up later at a spot where, among vast boulders of granite, the village com-poses prettily with the near rocks and far mountain, and masses of fine though still leafless chestnut. Below Zonza the road passes much

beautiful landscape, some, indeed, of the most graceful I have seen in Corsica, very unlike the stern wild splendour of the Bavella scenery, but full of delicate and lovely Claude-like views, bosky dells, and a curving river, wooded distances, and good lines of far hill, among which I would there were more time to linger. Ever descending, the road at three forty-five passes another village, San Gavino: except as they combine with other objects, these Corsican dwellings are rarely attractive, either from their form or colour; but, adjoining this group of hamlets, there are very beautiful pastures and chestnut groves. After San Gavino is left, there is less of the picturesque and more of cultivation.

At 5 P.M. I reach Levié, the road being always carried high up on the northern side of the great valley that runs in a south-westerly direction from the Incudine range; and had I found the scenery remarkable for beauty, I had thought of stopping here for the night, since, although there is no sort of inn in the place, I have a letter of introduction from Signor Galloni d'Istria to the maire. But Levié, a large village, with detached houses along both sides of the main road, presents no inducement to remain, the buildings being ugly, separately and collectively, and in a situation commanding no views remarkable for beauty. Gardens abound in the neighbourhood, and in no place in Corsica have I seen greater abundance of fruit trees of various kinds—almond, cherry, pear, etc.; these, and the ilex and oak interspersed among the dwellings, remind me of Mezzovo, in Albania, though here, in the street and on doorsteps, are groups of idlers such as industrious Mezzovo containeth not.

5.30 P.M.—A tedious ascent follows; the road crossing the ridge that divides this deep and long valley from that of Santa Lucia di Tallono, a group of communes, which I have heard spoken of as famous for the production of some of the best wines in the island, and for its advancement in agriculture. All this part of today's journey has but little beauty to recommend it, nor, until the road dips into the next valley, is the scenery interesting, either as to general outline or nearer detail; one village only (Mera) appears to me in passing to offer any attraction for the pencil. All down these long hill drives, and from village to village, but few people are met with; three or four drivers, two timber-carts from the forest, with their long team of mules, besides half a dozen peasants, are the utmost signs of human life seen throughout this day's journey.

On approaching Santa Lucia di Tallano the landscape becomes every minute more pleasing; the principal village is compactly built on a little hill, and is picturesque from the presence of a good campanile and an old convent close by. Everywhere there is foliage and abundant streams of water, and below—for Santa Lucia stands very high—you see the valley of Tallano, almost a little plain, and full of cultivated undulating ground; a long range of hills separates this—the valley of the Tavaria— from that of Olmeto or the Boraccik which runs into the gulf of Valinco. There seem to be some very large and good houses in Santa Lucia di Tallano, and I rejoice at not having stopped at Levié.

Sometimes, however, a man may be thankful too soon; for, on driving into the little town, and inquiring of a gendarme for the 'best hotel', I am directed to a house the entrance and interior of which is so unclean and uncomfortable that, with reluctance I decide on not risking a sleepless night there. Other hotel, they assure me, there is none; and, as I have an introductory letter to Don Giacomo Giacomone, the principal proprietor of the place, I cause myself to be shown to his dwelling—a spacious house beyond the piazza. Unfortunately, Don Giacomo is from home, and, although the Signora, his wife, sends down a message begging me to remain, I do not like, at the late hour it now is, to intrude suddenly as claimant of a night's lodging; and, consequently, return to the hotel with small prospect of comfort. Luckily, meanwhile, the landlord has had the offer of a room in another building, where it is possible to get housed; this has, at least, the negative merit of being less dirty than his own, and is, before long, by Giorgio's arrangements, made tolerably available. It is but just to say that the innkeeper did all in his power to oblige, bringing in some supper—such as it was—from the hotel, and making apologies without end for being so taken by surprise as to be unable to procure any eatables except eggs, salad, and pickled tunny. In no instance as yet have I met in Corsica anything but civility; and when a traveller encounters discomfort it seems to be to these worthy people a cause of real regret.

After supper, Don Giacomo Giacomone came in, much distressed at not having been at home when I called at his house, to which he even now proposes I should go. Eventually it is arranged that at sunrise I should be shown all that is to be seen in and around Santa Lucia di Tallano, and that I should breakfast with him at ten.

111

It seems that Dr. Bennet, of Mentône, has been staying with M. Giacomone for three days, and only left this morning.

MAY 1

Waking, a vivid impression of Bavella and its wondrous trees and precipices—that strange oasis of glory, which is yet fresh and bright to memory—haunts the landscape painter, who, since days passed in the pine woods in Eubœa, has seen nothing of the sort so beautiful.

At 5 A.M. I get coffee at the 'hotel'—alas, for the state of the floors thereof!—and then meet Don Giacomo Giacomone, who awaits me with a cousin in the piazza, a square, neither small nor of undistinguished appearance, for it contains several good houses, and it seems strange that so well looking a town should be so ill off for accommodation. My first occupation is to get a drawing of Santa Lucia, from a point to which Don Giacomo takes me, whence the view, though wanting in variety, is very pleasing; and this is followed by a walk along a new road my guide is making (to join that leading to Zicavo), traced along the higher part of the valley, and commanding views up and down it both extensive and beautiful, towards Zicavo on one side, and on the other towards Sartène, a portion of which is just visible from one point of it. Don Giacomo, who is a great landowner here, and a most energetic improver of his property, is full of enthusiasm, and justly so, concerning the valley of Tallano, a canton or district containing several communes. The cultivation of the vine is one of its principal interests; the fertility of the soil, the richness of vegetation, abundance of fruit, and facility of transport by road to Sartène and Ajaccio, justify the eulogies of my wealthy companion, who is as free from ostentation as he is full of hospitality.

Our next move, after returning to Santa Lucia, is to visit the two old churches mentioned by Valery, and the ancient convent of Pisan times, now abandoned, and belonging, apparently, like everything else here, to M. Giacomone, who is evidently the Marquis de Carabas of Santa Lucia di Tillano. This convent, my guide suggests, might be made into an hotel for the use of such English visitors to Ajaccio as having wintered there do not wish to return for the summer to England or Switzerland;

GULF OF PORTO

FOREST OF VALDONIELLO

but if this design be ever carried out in Corsica, it seems to me that a more lofty situation would be preferable.

M. Giacomone proposes at nine to go to his house, which, after the fashion of houses in Corsica, is better than its entrance or exterior promises, and contains a good suite of well-furnished rooms on the second floor; the little bedroom which was shown me as that where I was to have slept had I arrived sufficiently early was perfect in its arrangement and cleanliness, and might have been in Paris.

In the reception-room were Madame Giacomone and her eldest daughter—more like sisters than parent and child—dressed plainly in black, both good-looking, and singularly graceful and pleasant. Unlike some days in former travels through Abruzzo and Calabria, when the difficulty of discourse used to be wellnigh unconquerable, conversation is here easy and agreeable, for both these ladies, though they have never been out of their native island, are well educated, and full of information about their own country, as well as of interest regarding others.

Then we all went downstairs, where a table was laid for eight or ten, exhibiting an aspect of great plenty and propriety. To each person's plate there were not less than six glasses, so that the Scotch minister—of whom it is recorded that he adapted his form of grace to what he thought the probable conditions of the banquet—commencing, when there were only beer glasses on the table, with 'Bless the food of these puir miserable creatures!' and, on the contrary, if champagne glasses were visible, beginning in a loud and joyful tone with 'Bountifully shower down all Thy blessings on these thy excellent servants!'—might have appropriately asked the latter benediction on my hosts at Tallano, even though their wines were of home growth. For, starting with bread and butter of the first quality, olives, and other etcetera, and proceeding with eels and trout, through a course of stews and *ragouts*, to plain roast fowl and mutton, and ending in creams and *broccio*; all these, with many kinds of vegetables and fruits, were simply excellent, and, moreover, all derived from the possessions of these wealthy and hospitable people. As for the wines, they were supplied rather more bountifully than I liked: this, a white vintage, was to be tried; that of red must not be neglected; and, had I any previous doubt on the subject, I should have been convinced by the experience of this morning of the eminently good qualities of the Corsican wines. Several of these are not unlike Burgundy and, unless mixed with a large portion of water, are too strong for ordinary use; the very best are made largely by M. Giacomone, and '*vino di Tallano*' is proverbial on the west side of the island for its excellence.

Two younger children, Amalia and Catarina, were of the family party, which is really pleasant and friendly; the two ladies are sensible and well bred, and Don Giacomo, fluent on the topic of his possessions, and on the prospective commercial value of Tallano to England, is hearty and jovial.

Coffee was given upstairs, and an hour passed in drawing pictures for the children. *Barrabattoli*, as they called butterflies, were most in favour; but their glee was immense at all the nonsense I scribbled for them in the shape of birds carrying parasols, fishes smoking pipes, etc.

Act the last was to ascend a tower or belvedere, thence to contemplate the whole of the village and my host's property. Santa Lucia is in all respects well placed; yet, as a landscape painter, I should prefer to live amid the ruder but more picturesque scenery of Sartène, in spite of the reputation Tallano is said to have of excelling all other valleys in Corsica for its cultivation.

At noon, after vain attempts to resist polite offers to accompany me to the hotel, I took leave of the friendly M. Giacomone and his family, and set off for Sartène. Notwithstanding the elevation at which Santa Luccia is placed, it is not very picturesque from any point except that from which I drew it this morning. Scattered hamlets, fertile slopes, gay with the pleasant green of corn and vineyard, fields of blooming flax —which seen from above have the beautiful effect of sheets of water reflecting the blue sky—chestnut groves, and general woody richness, these are the characteristics of the Tallano valley, walled in on each side by rather monotonous hill forms, unbroken by detail, and somewhat wanting in interest.

For an hour and a half the winding road descends towards the River Tavaria, by whose banks are large flocks of diminutive black sheep, and broad fields of pearly-bloomed asphodel. At 2 P.M. the valley is left, the high road to Ajaccio reached, and once more I am going slowly up the well-known ascent to Sartène.

The beauty of foreground as well as of distance, in this part of Corsica, appear to me more remarkable than ever now that I revisit it; and I gladly walk up the hill to enjoy the variety of picturesqueness on all sides, as well as to avoid hearing the cursing of the unpleasant Peter, who shall certainly go no farther with me than the next two days' journeys. Even my taciturn servant Giorgio is moved, in one of P.'s frightful paroxysms, to say, 'If you swear so and never stop, you should provide some cotton for my master's ears and mine', to which Peter says, '*Vero è: l'uomo deve esser sempre paziente; ci vuol sempre pazienza*—It is true: man should be always patient; patience is necessary.'

There yet remained time before going into Sartène to make a drawing from above the Capuchin convent, and another by the bridge, of the wide view westward that takes in all the landscape from the snow-white Incudine heights, in gradations of wood and hill down to the sea; afterwards I made visits to M. le Sous-Préfet and M. Vico, and then went to the Hotel d'Italia.

Fatima of Sartène, out of respect to my suggestion about cleanliness, has actually had the whole of her room floors coloured red, and wax polished; and is delighted with my commendation of her experiments in the way of progress. Nor, in this, my second visit here, was other fault to be found than in the overabundance of her dinner—soup, trout, and lobster, boiled beef and artichokes, stewed veal, mutton, and olives, roast lamb and salad, cucumbers, butter, etc.—an oppressive amount of good things, sending away any of which untouched sorely vexed the good landlady. My return to her hotel instead of going to the other inn greatly pleases poor Fatima, and she volunteers conversation and confidence to a degree at once surprising and mournful.

'Did you not,' said she, enumerating one by one the hotels I had been to, 'at Grosseto, at Olmeto, at Bonifacio, Porto Vecchio, and Solenzaro, find that all the hotels were kept by widows?'

'Yes,' said I.

'Have you written down this fact?'

'I have.'

'Then,' said the unhappy Fatima, 'write me down, too, a widow, and not only a widow, but *mille volte più infelice che tutte vedove*—a thousand times more unhappy than all widows!'

Whereon there followed a tremendous burst of tragic eloquence in the highest tones, and with gestures to match, telling how, after seventeen years of marriage, in which she had never given her husband the smallest cause for discontent—*la minima cagione di scontento*—he had forsaken her, faithlessly carrying off her servant girl, and settling in Sardinia under a changed name in a new hotel, had left the unfortunate Fatima, like the Ossianic heroine before alluded to, 'alone, upon the hill of storms.'

Fatima's opinion about the state of the culinary science in the other hotel at Sartène was sufficiently sweeping, the cook there being, according to her, '*un disgraziato vecchio, chi forse settanta anni fà, sapeva far una frittura,—mai più di ciò; ed ora nemmeno tanto*—a miserable old man, who perhaps seventy years ago knew how to make an omelette, never anything more; and now not even that.'

May 2

At sunrise the completion of the drawing above the town occupied me till 7 A.M., when I joined the trap at the bridge, and left beautiful Sartène with regret.

Today's journey will be over no new ground. Passing the charming river scenes, where I spent the 18th and 19th of April, I reached the unhealthy village of Propriano at eight, and having made the ascent from the shore to Olmeto on foot, reached that place at ten fifteen. The walk up from the sea, six and a half kilometres—a steep and hot pull—is pleasant from the extreme beauty of the landscape—much of which cloud and bad weather had prevented my seeing on the 16th ultimo— where graceful olives and luxuriant green vegetation, flowers now in greater profusion than ever, and the universal melody of nightingales filling the hill-sides and deep valley, are all truly delightful. The horses have a long day's work today, but though I and my servant almost always walk, it is not certain that they are better off on account of having less weight to pull, for when I am in the carriage I can prevent Peter from beating them, which he never neglects to do, if I give him an opportunity by lingering behind. At present he is to rest at least two hours at Olmeto, a place that seems fuller of idle people than at my first visit.

On inquiring for Mr. B., I found that he had become much worse than when I was here on the 17th of April, and I went up to see him. It does not seem to me possible that he can live much longer, and this, by a message he begged me to take to his father in England, is evidently his own impression. Although he has with him an attendant who takes every care of him, and although he appears to have made friends among the people of Olmeto, yet nothing could be more sad than to see so young a man dying in so lonely and desolate a manner in this remote Corsican village.

At eleven-thirty, after a walk nearly to the top of the hill above Olmeto, where groups of large trees, seldom lacking in Corsica, are plentiful, a spot is easily found—favourable alike as a place for a sketch and for the dispatch of poor Fatima's bountiful breakfast—surrounded by bushes peopled with nightingales, robins, and blackbirds, and infinitely lovely with wild flowers.

At 12.45 P.M. I go on, and at Casalabriva await the trap and the ever-swearing Peter. All the landscape, hidden by rain and cloud at the time I first passed here, is now a grand outspread of *maquis*-covered hills, green down to the very last point and deepest dell of the valley of the Taravo, and up to the high wall of snow and long lines of Mont Renoso in the north and east; but in all this extent there is no particular spot tempting me to linger and draw.

Just beyond the village of Casalabriva a wonderful spectacle strikes the eye, namely, a carriage with two horses, a lady and her maid therein, going, like the landscape painter, to 'see all Corsica'. It is Miss C., who is on her way to Sartène and Bonifacio. We stop and discourse, the cheery nature of this pleasant lady being a happy set-off to the sad scene I had left at the sick man's house in Olmeto. I recommended the lonely Fatima to Miss C.'s notice, but, unluckily, she has already written to secure rooms at the other inn; and so, as in the words of the song—

> Too soon we part with pain,
> To drive o'er dusty roads again,—

Miss C. continuing to profess herself incredulous as to the safety of my luggage, and still predicting that some indefinite woe will befall me on account of my employing Peter, of whom, now that I am experienced as to his character, certainly very little good may be expected.

The descent of Bicchisano follows, and that village is reached at two-forty. Some of the ilex-grown dells on the way are indeed beautiful, but in the great valley of the Taravo, though it is full of innumerable studies, few views of general interest can be selected, and the landscape is of a nature exacting long term of study for individual detail. Towards the bridge over the Taravo there are many lovely pictures which would delight the eye, and give work for the pencil of Creswick, who (so it seems to me) is the best portrayer (after Turner) of river and wood scenery combined. A walk along this stream is one succession of park landscapes, and the thick-foliaged white-armed ilex trees, so mingled with granite rocks, and the foaming river, would even be more beautiful were there snow on the hills to form a contrast with the dark bosky hollows.

Once only during the afternoon, at a place where two or three houses (called by Peter, Bagni di Surbalaconi) combine with the fine bridge and the high road to indicate the vicinity of man, do I see any human life; here there is a little boy tending some goats. Peter, who is somewhat ahead, having dropped the apron of the carriage, the small boy picks it up, runs after the trap to give it to him, and returns to his goats; whereon I offer him the superfluity of Fatima's breakfast—to wit, two loaves of bread. But these are rejected with a solemn and decided shake of the head by the child; who, however, on my telling him that though white, they are really good bread, takes them after a time gravely, and thenceforth appears to think that he ought to do something in return. 'Perhaps,' says he, 'you might be pleased to know the names of my goats: one is Black-nose, another Silver-spot, that is Grey-foot, and this is Cippo. Cippo is quite the best goat in these parts, and likes to be talked to—*come un Cristiano*—just like a Christian—perhaps even, if you stand still, she may let you scratch the end of her nose and I will call her at once if you choose to try.' After which gratifying information the small boy prattles about the state of the corn, and the good it has gained from the last rains, with a quiet intelligence, and at the same time with a want of vivacity peculiar to Corsican life; until at a by-lane he says, 'The goats must go down here; so addio!'—and exit.

At 6.30 P.M. I am once more at the little Hotel des Amis, kept by the Widow Lionardi, at Grosseto; the village, with its houses half hidden among large trees, has a quiet, rural character that greatly charms me, and the inn is by no means an unwelcome place of rest. Just after I arrive a sudden confusion takes place, which, thirty years ago, would doubtless have occasioned a Vendetta; a little boy throws a large stone at a little girl with whom he quarrels, and knocks out her two front teeth, besides disfiguring her face; screams resound, the mother of the girl pursues the boy; the neighbours join in the clamour, and there is every prospect of a fight (worthy of the Henrietta Street colony at the back of my London rooms), when gendarmes interfere, and forcibly wind up the commotion; as a 'moral' or finale to which, the mother of the injured girl inflicts a violent chastisement on her small daughter, either to teach her a better choice of companions, or to impress her with the fact that the saying, 'misfortunes never come single', is a solemn truth.

The Widow Lionardi, to her dinner of stewed veal, trout, and roast lamb, adds a dish of *fiardoni* or cakes made of pastry and *broccio*—in other words, cheesecakes, or as they are called in Crete, Κρητικὰ Μισιθρόπιτε.

CHAPTER V

May 3

THE Hotel des Amis, Widow Lionardi's unpretending little inn, is so good and comfortable that it would be a capital central headquarters for study to a landscape painter. Leaving it at sunrise, and sending on Peter to the Bocco, or Col San Giorgio, I made a drawing of the village from a little way up the hill; the top of the church tower is golden in the rising sun, and all the brown and shadowy depths of ilex—as beautiful a feature in the foreground of this valley as are the green splendour and softness of the distance below the farthest range of the hills near Bicchisano—are particularly delightful at this calm, early hour; a world of quiet, save for the song of nightingales and the fresh sound of running streamlets.

By 7.40 A.M. the top of the col San Giorgio is reached, and the wayside inn at Cauro by eight-thirty where three hours are allotted for baiting the horses and breakfast. After I have been down the hill as far as Barraconi to make a drawing there, which I could not get on the cloudy evening of April 15th, I shall go on to Bastelica for the night, and back to Ajaccio tomorrow.

At nine-thirty, having terminated my Barraconi drawing, I am once again at Mdme Angela Paoloni's hotel, where there are still some of the party of officials who were here at the time of my first visit; I have now, however, been long enough in Corsica to avoid mistakes. These gentlemen give me several valuable hints as to parts of the island to which I have not yet been. M. Chauton, a Continental, has, they say, a great establishment for cutting and transport of trees at Valdoniello, and they recommend me to procure an introduction to him in order to see what they affirm is the most magnificent of all Corsican forests (though secretly I believe there can be none so fine as Bavella). A carriage road, I am told, leads to Aitone and Valdoniello from Evisa, either by way of Porto or Vico.

Mdme Paoloni's breakfast of trout and beefsteak, brains and caper sauce, Irish stew, broccio, etc., good in quality and profuse in quantity, is, as usual, a curious contrast to the stairs and entry of her hotel, and is accompanied by the usual careful and obliging manners of Corsican inn-keepers. When I leave the house, the hostess says, 'Do not pay me now, but stop as you return, and pay then.'

'But, not so,' I reply, 'for who can tell what may happen? Suppose I should die at Bastelica; you would then lose your money.'

'In that case,' says Mdme Paoloni, 'although we are poor, and should miss your money, we should not feel the loss so much, because our sorrow for your death would be greater.'

Shortly after noon I went on towards Bastelica, which is twenty kilometres distant. Peter the oathful, who this morning has had some very bad fits of swearing and beating, but who is at present in a comparatively placid mood, says, 'At these villages I am very often asked who you are, and I always say you are the Ministro delle Finanze—the Finance Minister of England.'

'But why,' said I, 'do you say such a thing?'

'Oh, partly because you wear spectacles and have an air of extreme wisdom, and partly because one must say something or other.'

A Minister of Finance seems to be grim Peter's *beau idéal* of earthly grandeur, and he has frequently spoken of having accompanied the illustrious M. Abbattucci, late Minister of Finance, to the country residence of that personage at Zicavo. Now, as I was particularly in want of information concerning the road thither, I asked him one day, 'Did M. Abbattucci make the journey by Sta. Maria Zicché, or by the village of Bicchisano?'

'He went by Grosseto to Sta. Maria,' was the reply.

'But,' said I, 'as the way from Ajaccio to Zicavo is long, where did the minister stop, at Grosseto, or is there any other midway inn?'

'By no means,' said Peter, '*non si fermò punto, andava a giorno e notte*——he stopped nowhere, but travelled day and night. *Era mortissimo*—he was quite dead—that Minister of Finance—*e non era che sue cenere che si portava*—it was only his ashes that I took to Zicavo.'

Long ascents, varied by portions of level ground, lead along the hill-sides; the road is good and broad, but like other Routes Forestières, without a parapet on the sides towards the valley, up which, clothed luxuriantly with *maquis* and larger trees, the eye looks to the snowy

121

heights at the end of it, immediately above the village of Bastelica; as a whole, the picture is grand and beautiful, but possessing no particular beauty in detail. I walk up the ascent, to give the brutal Peter as little excuse as possible for maltreating his horses, who go on slowly, but regularly, if left to themselves. It is a pleasure to think that tomorrow I shall get rid of this man, and, meanwhile, though I or my servant are generally able to prevent his inhuman treatment, this is not always possible, as, accompanying the act with torrents of maledictions, he will sometimes, quite unexpectedly, strike the horses so fiercely as to make them back three or four paces.

About one-forty the valley grows somewhat narrower; bright streams of water fall from the hill-side to join the river below, the tall heath, full of white blossom, reminds me of the shores of Albania, near Porto Tre Scoglie, and all along the route the clothing of these Corsican mountains never ceases to be a charm and a wonder, for there are spreading woods of ilex, and a thick carpet of *maquis* right and left. The top of the first ascent is reached about three, at the tenth kilometre, when a level bit of road succeeds. The only life seen since leaving Cauro is in a group of charcoal burners, not to speak of twenty pigs revelling in a shallow pool of water. The charcoal burners talk with a vivacity very singular for Corsicans; but forthwith I find them to be Italians from the neighbourhood of Lucca.

At kilometre eleven and a half is a neat little forest-house and a mill. The guardiano and his family, sitting outside their dwelling, make a picture, combined with groups of trees and the beautiful river, here close below the highway, and dashing foamily over its worn stones. Beyond this point the road makes a sharp turn, and for the moment Peter is lost sight of. Latterly his swearing has been so horrible, and his cruelty so odious, that I have thought at times that he is not quite sane; consequently, I have walked nearer the carriage, and it was only by the accident of my having stopped a little while at the forest-house, to make some inquiries about the distance, that he had got considerably ahead, for here the ascent is not steep.

But on turning the corner of the road just mentioned there was a shocking sight, and one that became more so at each moment. Taking this opportunity of being alone Peter had given way to a burst of rage and violent blows with his whip handle on the poor beasts' heads. In vain did both I and Giorgio shout, running forward. Even then the carriage stood at right-angles to the side of the road, and not far from the edge of it, above the river, while at every blow the poor horses backed nearer to the ravine.

One more blow—carriage and horses are quite at the side of the precipice!—

Yet one more blow, struck with an infernal scream from bad Peter, and the horses back for the last time! And then——

Down, down, go all into the ravine!

Nothing was left on the road but the abominable old fellow, kneeling, and wailing to the Madonna and all the saints, whom a minute before he had been blaspheming.

I ran back to the corner of the road, whence I could see the forest-house, to alarm the inhabitants; and, directly, they set off on the way up to help. Meanwhile, the Suliot was already down the steep. Happily, the hillside at this spot, the twelfth kilometre, is not nearly so precipitous as it is at a few yards distance either way, and a cluster of large chestnut trees had stopped the carriage and horses from rolling downward to the stream. One of the poor beasts was, notwithstanding, killed on the spot; the other, which G. had managed to extricate, was dreadfully lacerated by a sharp rock. The carriage, as may be supposed, was broken in pieces, and the luggage—literally fulfilling Miss C.'s prediction—had rolled farther down, among the rocks and fern.

The zeal with which the forester, his son, and friends, worked to get up the *roba* and the remaining horse, was most praiseworthy; and seeing so much energy where I had expected apathy, I internally resolved to be less hasty in future in characterising Corsicans as lazy, on account of their being undemonstrative. By four all the *roba* had been carried up, and was in a pile by the road-side, as were the splintered portions of the vehicle; but what was now to be done? At Bastelica, still eight kilometres ahead, they say that a car may be got; and to send on the forester's son (a lad of sixteen or seventeen) at once seems the best plan, so that he may bring a car—or, if none can be obtained, mules—that I may then either go on to Bastelica, or back to Cauro, as circumstances may direct. The youth, Domenico Casanova, therefore sets off running; and later I resolve to walk on to Bastelica, for if that should not prove a place in which there is much work for my pencil, then I can return here with the mule-cart, or, if otherwise, pass the night there; the luggage, meanwhile, and the ruins of the carriage, will be well cared for by Giorgi, and by the good people who have been helping me so energetically.

From the thirteenth kilometre, which I passed at four-fifteen, the road up the valley commands views of a fine solitude of pine woods and far snowy heights, and at the eighteenth kilometre I am able to make a sketch of the village, which stands very high, and is seen from the midst of luxuriant chestnut groves. Bastelica, in the summer time must, indeed, be a delightful place, embosomed, as it is, in foliage below its lofty mountain amphitheatre.

On reaching the village before six, by a steep ascent at the nineteenth and a half kilometre from Cauro, I found three mules being put to one of the long carts used by the peasantry, and the forester's son actively hastening the operation. And as I had ascertained that I could do little so far as regards making a view of the very straggling village of Bastelica beyond what I had already done, and as a clear full moon is shining, I decide on returning in the jolting-car to the forest-house, and perhaps to get on as far as Cauro tonight, which place the diligence passes at 7 A.M. tomorrow. Bastelica, I perceive, should be seen when the chestnut tree is in full leaf, for without that its principal characteristic is wanting.

While Domenico went to get some eggs and wine (as it is by no means certain that his father's house contains eatables), I talk with the villagers, a large number of whom crowded round me. The propriety of conduct in these rustics strikes me very forcibly; the absence of all clamour and rudeness, and the good sense of their observations on my replying to their questions concerning the accident, are as remarkable as the intelligence which is in all their countenances. Every one of the children, too, of whom there are many, is well conducted. I find they are taught French as well as Italian, and that the more advanced could read and write in both languages; so grave and well bred a lot of little fellows one would not expect to find in such a remote place.

Pasquale, the driver of the mule-cart, was ready to start at six-thirty, but I walked down the hill as far as a cottage, where there was a halt, 'in order,' said the man of Bastelica, 'to take up something he had to convey to Cauro'. This something proved to be two immense bags, which, when lifted on to the narrow car, occupied more than half its space, though that was not of such importance as the fact that they tainted the air with the most horrible odours, proceeding, as I soon found, from the contents, which were old rags. This episode occasioned some delay, for I would neither have the rags nor the owner, and I was compelled, before the matter was settled, to tell the driver that our bargain was at an end, unless I could have the car to myself. And when the rag-bags were finally ejected, the anger of the rag-man was exceedingly funny. 'It is plain,' he said, 'that you know nothing of Corsica. Probably you never heard that Napoleon Buonaparte, the greatest man in all the world, was born here. The oldest and dirtiest rags are honourable here, and you should be grateful for smelling and touching them!'

This delay made it 7 P.M. before we were off, but the car jolted rapidly down the hill, and the moon gave a light like day; by eight we were at the ill-fated twelfth kilometre, where there was nothing now left but splinters of the carriage, and shortly afterwards arrived at the forest lodge, to which all the *roba* had been removed. Here, for I had had enough of jolting and walking for one day, I decided on remaining the night, and to go on as early as I could tomorrow to Ajaccio; so the camp-bed was put up, and the eggs, and bread and wine were the dinner, to which the good-natured forester added some onions and broccio, after frying the eggs with alacrity.

The guardiano, Stefano Casanova, is a civil and pleasant fellow, and his wife a good, bustling, tidy body; they are from Evisa, about which place they give me various information, and declare that the pines of Aitone are the most surprising in the world. 'So much so,' says M. Casanova, by a powerful metaphor, 'that the only possible way to see their tops is to lie down flat on your back and look up into the sky.' More obliging people I could not have chanced to meet with; how hard they worked with G. to get up the *roba* and horse! How quickly their son Domenico had gone to Bastelica, and how busily, while constantly worrying the slow Pasquale to bestir himself, he had managed to get the car and mules ready!

I should be glad, were it possible, to return to Bastelica before leaving Corsica; its position, in a kind of cul-de-sac, below some of the highest mountains, is fine, and although, owing to its form—being a very scattered village—it does not appear to contain many houses, it is in reality one of the largest in the island.

125

MAY 4

4.30 A.M.—The rushing river below this little forest-house reminds me of many nights' lodgings in Switzerland, particularly of one by the falls of the Aar; and, doubtless, had I not had my invaluable camp-bed here, other and livelier objects of similarity would not be wanting.

I went up the hill to the scene of yesterday's catastrophe; except the trampled bushes and splinters of broken wheels, etc., there is little sign of what took place—the last struggle of the poor falling horses will not be so easily effaced from my memory. As I returned to the forest-house the odious Peter, who has hitherto carefully kept out of my way, accidentally met me, and to him I delivered a short moral discourse on the general impropriety of anger, and the particular evil of profane swearing, in reply to which that impish individual only said, '*Oh, mi lasci! mi lasci! ci vuol sempre la pazienza; la più buona cosa è la pazienza*— Leave me! leave me! patience is always necessary; the best of all things is patience.' So I did leave him, and I truly hope I may never again see his unpleasant face.

At five-thirty Pasquale and the jolt-car were ready, and G. had packed all the *roba* on it, so, having given the worthy Casanova couple some money for their boy Domenico to buy what he liked with, jolting began forthwith, and in two hours Cauro was reached, Mdme Angela Paoloni gazing from her window in extreme surprise at my third appearance, as I passed her door in a travelling guise so different to that of my two former visits. At Barraconi there was a halt of half an hour to bait the mules, a time I employed in looking about the beautiful valley of Suarella, so historically interesting as the scene of the death of Sampiero. The Campo di Loro, clouded and obscured when I had passed it on April 15, seemed to me now most beautiful, the broad green meadows and tall poplars harmonising well with the distant snowy range beyond. By eleven Ajaccio was reached, the ungainly mule-car and its driver paid and dismissed, and Ottavi's hotel once more made headquarters. And thus ends the first 'fytte' of Corsican travel.

There were letters to read and to write, and in the afternoon a drawing to finish on the delightful hill beyond the grotto. Now that all the ridges and hollows on the southern part of those opposite mountains are familiar to me, with what a different interest is this scene, so charming even before, invested! There, high up the hill, is Cauro, there to the left of it is the pass to Col San Giorgio, and there, across the ridge, are the high snow hills beyond Grosseto; there, too, are the heights of Bastelica.

May 5

Soon after sunrise I am drawing at the grotto hill, overlooking garden and shrubbery, down to the calm gulf and silver-topped mountains; and on so lovely a morning as this it seems to me that imagination could picture no scene more beautiful.

Later, on calling at Dr. Ribton's, I find that my friends the J.S.s are not only gone, but that they have been heard of from Pisa; their transit from this side of the island to the other having been of the unluckiest, in a fierce storm of rain and wind, and with the addition of their carriage having been upset before reaching Corte.

Nor are the chances very favourable for my own progress in seeing the rest of Corsica; for, first, M. Galloni d'Istria, who had so ably and kindly helped me with introductions in my first tour, has gone to Italy; and secondly, although the Préfet, M. Géry, has returned from France, he has met with a bad accident in leaving the steamer, and is laid up; and, thirdly, my servant Giorgio has a fit of fever, possibly owing to chill after the hard work in the Bastelica ravine two days ago. As a set-off against all this, I make the acquaintance of M. Lambert (the commandant of gendarmerie in the arrondissement of Ajaccio), who dines in the rooms of the Ottavi hotel. This gentleman most ably enters into my plans of seeing more of the island, and offers me letters should I go to the western side—to Carghese, and to the agent of M. Chauton at the great forests of Aitone and Valdoniello; or, if I go to Bastia, to Bocognano and other places. This may remedy my two first grievances, the absence of M. Galloni, and of the Préfet; patience and quinine may bring back the Suliot to working condition. Nor do I myself neglect to take some preventive and precautionary quinine, for after the air of the high mountains, this of Ajaccio seems warm and relaxing.

Writing letters filled up the rest of the day.

MAY 6

An early walk along the shore to the cemetery. In spite of all the beauty of colour, and the gaiety of flowers, broom, honeysuckle, and rose cystus, and of the immense luxuriance of vegetation and elegance of foliage, a grave melancholy seems to me to be ever the character of Ajaccio scenery. Those circling snow-topped hills at the head of the gulf, that long barrier line on its southern side, and the absence of much life or movement either on land or water, all contribute to this impression, and tinge the landscape, lovely as beyond doubt it is, with somewhat of the mournful.

At midday, on calling at the Préfecture to learn how M. Géry is going on, his daughter, a most fascinating little girl—who speaks English well, owing to having been under the care of an English lady, her governess, from a child—comes into the hall to say that her father, though suffering much and unable to leave a sofa, wishes to see me. Had I expected to find the Governor of the island—of the Departement de la Corse—a formidable official, I should have been much deceived; but I had previously heard of M. Géry as a person not less known for his ability and for the high positions he has filled than for the kindness of his disposition and for the charm of his conversation. He enters with warmth into all the details concerning that portion of the island I have already seen, sketches out a second and third tour for me, promises me abundance of letters to places guiltless of inns, and finally invites me to dine at the Préfecture tomorrow. Thus, I return to the hotel with a new source of thanks to M. Merimée, whose good nature procured me an introduction of such value.

In the course of today Miss C. returns from her southern trip to Sartène and Bonifacio, and triumphs, though far from ill-naturedly, at the fulfilment of her predictions about my carriage. We quite agree about the fine qualities of the scenery we have both visited; Miss C. has been up to Zicavo, and through the forests of Marmano and Sorba, whereas, although I have not seen these, I have been to Bavella, which she has not, and I steadfastly declare that, Bavella unseen, she has seen nothing—less than nothing.

G.'s fever is not much better today; but as I have long been an expert

128

MONTE D'ORO

BOCOGNANO

fever-doctor, I believe that two or three days will bring him round. Miss C. and Dr. R. stop their ears when I venture to speak of fever; yet sickness is a fact, and there are moments when my servant's illness, added to the difficulty I find in procuring another carriage and horses for my next start, makes a gloomy side to the picture, and half inclines me to return by next Saturday's boat to Nice, leaving the remainder of Corsica to be portrayed in that far-off indefinite time when I may wind up my journeys in Crete, Palestine, Syria, and other only-in-part-visited places.

MAY 7

All the morning is rainy—propitious time for letter-writing—and the day is passed in making calls, and in searching for a carriage and horses, etc., till at 6 P.M. dining at the Préfecture adds another to the pleasant memories already afforded me by Corsica. Miss C. was there, as well as several other persons, and the excellence of M. le Préfet's table is as distinguished as the friendly and social character of the party and the pleasant conversation of the guests. Afterwards, other persons, mostly in official positions, came in, and a collection of photographs of the chief or most interesting places of Corsica was exhibited. Some of these photographs were of the finest I have seen; but it is not easy to procure copies of them, as only three perfect sets, for the Emperor, Prince Napoleon, and the Préfet, were struck off, when the photographer, owing to some pique, withdrew the whole from public circulation.

MAY 8

The mountains here have taken to invisible ways, and refuse to appear.

The search for a carriage continues, and Giovanni Carburo the Vaudois, who lets out vehicles, and is recommended by Miss C., shows me, besides other traps heavier and more expensive, a sort of double-seated car for two horses, which I may have for seventeen francs a day, and am to try later in the morning. It proves, however, far too shaky, and is rejected, so that the matter of vehicles is once more in *nubibus*.

Passed the afternoon on the hill near the grotto drawing cactus; the warbling of nightingales is truly delightful, till gendarme target practice, with infantry bugling and drumming, commence—then

> The nightingale said, 'I have sung many songs,
> But never'—

will I sing any more if this horrid hubbub continues—and thenceforth the voices of birds were hushed. My work, too, is stopped by rain, and the landscape painter becomes indisposed for further Corsican travel, and resolves at length to leave further decision till tomorrow. One thing is certain, that a good trap and horses are a *sine qua non* if I am to visit the rest of the island. 'Νὰ κάμῃς ὄνειρον, Κύριε,' says the Suliot, whose fever is departing—'Decide by dreaming, sir.'

In the evening the pleasant M. Lambert, who has many remembrances of Zante and Cerigo, Milo and Cyprus, brings a letter of introduction which he has written for me to a friend at Casabianda; but I think it will be best to visit all the western side of Corsica first, and M. Lambert promises letters tomorrow, should I procure a carriage, to facilitate my visit to the great forests, where, without some personal recommendation, little can be done. If I succeed in completing my tours in the west of the island I can proceed across it to Bastia, and go back to Nice from that port, if time does not allow of a third visit to Ajaccio.

MAY 9

The morning is hot and misty, and the mountains hidden in clouds prophetic of rain.

The first thing to be attended to today is an examination of such carriages as are on hire, as I have fully resolved to go if possible to the great forests of Aitone and Valdoniello, and Vico, a tour which I hear can be very well managed in a week, the longest space of time I can give to it. And after looking at several vehicles, all more or less unsuitable, and the owners of which manifest a great carelessness as to whether they are employed or not, I hire the only one left, belonging to the Vaudois

Jean, a roomy, good trap, which I am to have at twenty francs a day, all expenses of the driver included.

Next, I call on M. Lambert, who, in spite of all his busy occupation, has found time to write a note to the Chef de Gendarmerie at Carghese. M. Chauton, the lessee of part of the great government forest of Valdoniello, who has an establishment both there and near the coast at Porto, is unluckily away from Ajaccio at present, but, says M. Lambert, a nephew of one of the gendarmes at Carghese is M. Chauton's agent at Porto, and will send me on to the upper station.

At 9 A.M. Jean Vaudois comes to see that all is in order for my new start; the ponies seem good and the carriage comfortable, the luggage well fastened behind and carefully covered, only, the box-seat being now filled up with sacks of barley—an improvement which Miss C. does not fail to remark, and which at least indicates more care for the horses than was shown by swearing Peter—my man has to sit inside. The new driver is a Corsican youth named Domenico, of Napoleonic and grave aspect, and the party is completed by a small spotty dog of amiable and watchful deportment, called Flora, who examines the carriage and luggage with an evident expression of certainty that she is the head and moving spring of the whole arrangement. Miss C. who is looking out of Ottavi's window, begs me to send word as to progress or success, and as we set off, Giovanni Vaudois suggests that if I do not care to go as far as Cargedse tonight I may sleep at Sagona.

The way lies through Ajaccio and past the Villa Bacciocchi as far as the southern road to Sartène and Bonifacio, when the highway to Corte and Bastia is followed to the fifth kilometre, there the road to Vico strikes off to the left, and shortly beyond it another way to that place leads on the right hand through Sari. Almost up to the commencement of the Vico road, where a fine many-arched aqueduct is a picturesque addition to the landscape, the neighbourhood of Ajaccio is a continued garden of cherry and mulberry plantations, but afterwards such cultivation becomes more rare as the road winds away among pleasant, rounded, low hills, where the familiar fern, white-blossomed cystus, and asphodel, gradually take the place of fruit trees and corn-fields. The great precipitous heights which show so finely from the end of the Gulf of Ajaccio are passed on the right as you climb a hill range, and after a dip down to a green valley, a long and steep ascent follows to

Bocca San Sebastiano, which is reached at noon, the road thither being carried very high along the side of the lofty hills, which are cultivated in patches, and not remarkable for beauty of form.

At the Bocca, or summit, where there is a single roadside house, nothing is to be seen today, owing to the thick misty weather, except a vast indication of mountains mostly hidden by rolling clouds, and it seems to me that even had the landscape been visible, its extent would have been too great to allow of its being drawn as a whole. Lower down, however, on the other side of the pass, the Gulf of Sagona, with abundance of those long points and capes so characteristic of Corsican west coast scenery, would have been worth a halt had the morning been fine; on one of these promontories Carghese, already seen from the sea on April 9, is pointed out.

The winding descent towards the gulf from Bocca San Sebastiano is beautiful, all the more so from some showers of rain and effects of cloud shadows. The village of Calcatoggio stands above the road, and from it all is vineyard and garden, fig, pear, and cherry orchard, nearly down to the sea, where against the rocks of white granite that border the little bay of Liscia the quiet waves beat lazily along the lonely shore. Here, 1.15 P.M., about the twenty-ninth kilometre from Ajaccio, at a small wayside house, is to be the midday halt for two hours, for the not over-clean *Repos des Voyageurs*, as the hut is labelled, is avoided for a spot more fitted for drawing and breakfast among the boulders and cystus-growth a little way up the hill, whence the view of the gulf, widespread towards the west, is grand and solitary.

Beyond the little bay of Liscia and the tower-crowned promontory on its northern side, whence Carghese is now clearly seen, the road descends into the valley or small plain of the River Liamone, a considerable stream, flowing from the western base of Monte Rotondo and the neighbourhood of Guagno. The valley of the Liamone is a level of green corn as far as eye can see to the foot of the hills; and the river, crossed by a good bridge, reaches the sea through marshes gay with yellow iris. Beyond it the road leads through what resemble 'cuttings' of wrinkled cretaceous rock, crowned with wind-bent lentisk or schinos, now and then passing quiet coves of pure sand edged with granite rocks, whence you look down on to the wide solemn gulf beyond, till one more Genoese tower is left behind, and Sagona, the port of Vico, is reached at

4 p.m. Whatever may have been the condition of this place in the days when it was the seat of a bishopric, and possessed a cathedral, few traces of its former state remain now, some six or eight square buildings, like warehouses, and one boat on the bay, being all its present signs of life.

The highway, now a winding road, follows the shore from point to point, till it climbs the last hills before you reach the promontory of the Greek colony. Here cultivation increases, and the view over the broad placid gulf of Sagona is very fine; so I send on Domenico to the village hotel, and stop for an hour to draw. The hills around, of no great height, are well formed, and covered with corn and olive growth quite to the sea. Over all this Carghese coast broods a kind of lonely classic grandeur, which the usual scarcity of life in Corsica gives full leisure for contemplating—the promontory and little bay, with coves of white sand, and 'curving lines of creamy spray', then the broad gulf, and beyond that, the long line of hills forming the northern side of the gulf of Ajaccio, 'all barred with long white clouds the scornful crags', at half their height throughout.

Carghese, which you come upon all at once by a sudden turn of the road, is a larger place than I had expected to see, and is built with regular streets at right-angles to each other. Several scattered houses, among them the hotel and the old Greek church, are by the side of the high road, which here crosses the cape of Carghese; but the chief part of the village stands lower down, facing the south; the Latin church, and a second Greek building, large and unfinished, are in the farther part of the settlement, nearer the end of the promontory, and the whole forms a singular and picturesque scene, greatly interesting to me from what I had heard of the migration of these Greek settlers from the Morea, and of the persecution which had at one time made their adopted land little less undesirable than their own.

I had told my Suliot servant not to speak Greek at first, by way of having some merriment when our knowledge of their language came to be suddenly known; but this plan fell through by my own inattention; for from a window of one of the first houses I pass, there looks out a Greek priest with a venerable beard and the well-known cap, who makes me a bow and waves his hand, to which salute I unthinkingly reply, 'Καλὴ σας ἡμέρα!—Good morning!' and naturally elicit 'Πῶς! ὁμιλειτε Ρωμαϊκὰ?—What! do you speak Romaic?' for in the days when these Greeks came to Corsica, 'η 'Ελληνικὴ γλῶσσα was unknown as such.

The hotel at Carghese is a homely and tolerably comfortable second-floor apartment, with a certain appearance of cleanliness about its staircase and rooms, the latter having dark raftered ceilings; an elderly woman and her very good-looking daughter, with a second young woman, also pretty, receives me, and are greatly amused and pleased by my speaking Greek, which the landlady both understands and speaks well; of the two young damsels one only knew the commonest Romaic words, and the other none at all, for, said the daughter, '*questa è Franca—She is a Frank*'. After a visit from the long-bearded Papa who had spoken to me from the window, and who promises to come in again in the evening, there is still time for a ramble in the village, the right-angled streets of which, and an air of care and cleanliness about the houses, give it a novel interest to a Corsican tourist. All round the village the *Cactus opuntia* is largely grown, and (as says Valery) there is a briskness and order here contrasting not a little with the apathy I had seen in other parts of the island. It was very amusing to talk Romaic with the people here and there—that is, with the elders, for they alone seemed to understand it; one woman at a fountain spoke as if an Athenian, and with characteristic Greek curiosity inquired Ἀλλὰ διατί ἦλθ' ἡ Εὐγενέια σας ἐδῶ—*Why* did your honour come here?'

On returning to the hotel an excellent dinner was provided—soup, a dish of pilaf (the first seen in Corsica), roast lamb, etc., and very tolerable wine, but the priest, who came to pay his promised visit, brought a bottle of far better quality. The colony, according to him, came to Corsica under Genoese protection, about 1626, and consisted of 600 or 700 Greeks from Vittolo in Maina, and he says that now the population of the village is 1,200, but much crossed by marriage with the islanders, and that even some Corsicans by descent are counted in that number. He describes the site of Paomia—the first settlement of these Spartan Moreotes, and burned some thirty years after their coming—as being distant about an hour's walk from here. After its destruction the colonies took refuge in Ajaccio for fifty years. They preserve their old ritual, but are all 'united Greeks', or, in other words, Papists. The priests, he says, may marry, and at first did so, but do not now. Long since they have disused all national costume, and very generally the use of the Greek language, which intermarriage and the settling of the islanders amongst them are fast obliterating, and it is evident that they seek to separate themselves as little as possible from Corsicans. Thus, in two or three more generations their family names will be the only remaining proof of their nationality. My acquaintance, Papa Michele, seems to have been superseded, unjustly, according to his own account, by the Bishop of Ajaccio, who has given his place to a curate from the Piana de' Greci, in Sicily. 'Perhaps,' says he, 'the Préfet may one day do me justice—νομίζω αὐτὸν, ἔπειτα τὸν Θεὸν, ἦναι ὁ Πατήρ μου καὶ πρῶτος ἀνθρώπων—He, after the Lord, is (in my opinion) my father, and the first of men.'

MAY 10

At 5 A.M., coffee-au-tumbler having been obligingly brought at a still earlier hour, I am busy drawing the village of the Mainotes from a height on its east side, whence the whole locality is visible, besides a broad expanse of Mediterranean; but thick mists cover all the farther distance, and at times descend even lower than the little chapel close above the village. Below me are groves of fruit trees, resounding with hundreds of nightingales, and looking either towards the shore, or inland to the hills, all the land is cultivated, and unites with clouds above and cloud shadows far away on the sea, to make a pretty picture enough.

Descending, I draw on the other side of the village till ten-thirty. There is a look of cheerfulness about Carghese not observable in any of the places I have hitherto seen in Corsica; the scattered and rural Grosseto; the wooded and secluded Olmeto; Sartène, the grand and solemn; Bonifacio, walled and isolated; Porto Vecchio, the decayed; all have their special characteristic, but among them cheerfulness is not. Here, on the contrary, the entire openness of the position of the village is in itself a cheery feature; standing, as it does, away from rocks or trees, or overhanging height, at the end of a promontory with sea on all sides but one, so that from the southern face of the hill you overlook the whole settlement at once. The light colour of the stone of which the houses are built, in regular lines, and the gardens that surround many of them, have none of the usual gloomy Corsican aspect, and there is a

135

novelty in the wide extent of the Indian fig or cactus which stretches below the village on the north side, and along the edge of which pigs are tied to stakes, leading a life of order and propriety, instead of dirtily rambling all over the settlement. Many a trim village scene of industrious and lively Greece is recalled by Carghese. And had the shores of the opposite side of the Gulf of Sagona been clear, the view looking that way must needs be of great beauty; the indentations of the coast line and the lower hills show thus much, though the higher summits are just now hopelessly hidden by mist.

11 A.M.—Return to the inn, passing the large building which is so conspicuous in all the views of Carghese, and which they tell me is the new Greek church; it is a mere shell, standing unfinished for want of funds, and I suppose is the same edifice towards the completion of which M. Valery was so amusingly entreated to subscribe in 1835. The original chapel used by the Greeks stands on the main road. I could linger willingly in Carghese for two or three days, but, according to the scale which my limited stay in Corsica compels me to adopt, more than this one morning cannot be spared for the Mainote village, and I shall reach my next halting-place, La Piana, this evening. Meanwhile the people of the inn tell me some of the names of the Carghese families—Stephanópoulos, Papaláki, Pietroláki, Dhrimaláki, Frangoláki, Zannitáki; the priest is Michele Mendouráki; and, oddly enough, that of the landlord of the hotel Polyméros Korfiótti.

After breakfast, which, though very good, was, excepting its conclusion of roast lamb, quite marine in its character—to wit, lobster soup, fried mullet, lobster boiled, and lobster salad—I went out to see the Greek church, so called; it is very small, and differing only from similar places of worship in its having a crucifix above the altar; a fact sufficiently demonstrating that the Catholic had superseded the Orthodox in the religious system of Carghese.

After this there was a visit to pay, for on my arrival last night I had sent M. Lambert's letter to the Chef de gendarmerie, who had called, begging I would take coffee with him next day, when he would give me a letter to the agent of M. Chauton, at the forest of Valdoniello; and so, after some very good tumbler-coffee and biscuits, in the neat clean room of M. Ceccaldi and his colleague, whose daughter is married to the agent at Porto, I gained much information as to my onward route.

From Carghese to La Piana, they say are twenty kilometres, and beyond it twelve more to Porto, along a coast road cited as wonderful for precipices and fine scenery; from Porto up to the mountain to Evisa are twenty kilometres farther; but as to the forests higher up my informants are not sure—seven or eight kilometres of a bad and steep road they believe to be about the distance. From Evisa to Vico there are twenty kilometres, and thence down to Sagona on the main Ajaccio road other fourteen. At Evisa they recommend the Maison Carrara as a halting-place.

The trap is ordered at 2.30 P.M., so there is yet time to add somewhat to my sketch of the distant mountains, which are gradually clearing. Looking across the Gulf of Sagona, and away from the wide western sea, how clearly much of the history of Corsica is explained; of days when the people in its valleys, closed in by their own barrier mountain walls—hardly even in much communication with that next to them, and quite divided from the rest of the island—spent their energies in quarrels with their neighbours.

Either there is little curiosity or much good breeding in Carghese, for no one comes near or otherwise molests me while drawing, which is as pleasant as singular. Children in Corsica, as far as I have seen, are a race unique for good behaviour; no throwing of stones, as at Naples or in Greece; no shouting or teasing, and yet never is there any sign of timidity; in fact, for the sake of their quiet intelligence, I have already quite forgiven all Corsican children their habits of swarming up Ajaccio stairs.

Papa Mendoúrias Michéle Stephanópoulos comes to pay me a parting visit, and writes me down a Greek song from memory, promising me others if I will send him some from Fauriel's book; at present I can only repeat him the single verse of one sent me by M. Merimée—

'Εδῶ ἡμεῖς δὲν ἤλθαμεν
Καλὸ κρασὶ νὰ πιῶμεν.

He says that when M. Merimée was here, about 1843, a Greek costume, now quite disused, was pretty generally worn by the elder women. My clerical acquaintance imputes many changes at Carghese to a '*fuggasco*' Latin priest from Syra, in the time of Leo XII. Papa Michéle is not, however, wholly to be relied on, for in maintaining that their religious ritual is unaltered, he declares that the Athanasian Creed is used in the

Orthodox Oriental churches, which most certainly and happily is not the case. He also says there exists a MS., date 1650, written by one of their priests, detailing all their early tribulations, but does not inform me where it is.

2.45 P.M.—Flora, Domenico and Company are ready, and so farewell to the Greek colony of Carghese; a wind is rising, and a clearing of all hill-tops ensues. Soon, leaving the shore of the little Gulf di Pero and that of Chiomi, the road runs inland among pleasant green fields, up a bright vale joyous with corn; there are poplars by a stream, dazzling yellow blooming rape, and eastward a wall of mountains at the valley head, with corn everywhere, up to the very tops of the nearer hills. But as the way begins to wind up a long and steep ascent in a narrowing gorge, the well-known *maquis* encroaches gradually on the merry foodfields, gay with sunlight, and striped with cloud shades—for

> A light wind blew from the gates of the sun,
> And waves of shadow went over the corn.

4.20—Beautiful views of the far-away Carghese promontory and a clear fountain are good excuses for five minutes' rest. Henceforth the road is tolerably level, as leaving the valley of Chiomi it takes a more northerly direction, parallel to the craggy-fronted barriers, towards which I have been climbing, not without observing the good driving of the new Jehu Domenico, and the eminent qualities of his two ponies. Coasting the mountains, as it were, the head of another seaward valley is passed, woodier and more beautiful than the last, and with more picturesque mountain outlines; then succeed bosky ilex-woods at intervals, and some enclosures of cherry trees, while not unfrequently a couple of red-legged partridges trot leisurely across the road.

Shortly the ridge terminating in Capo Rosso is crossed, and at a sharp turn of the road, a vast and striking picture of mountain, cliff, sea, and the village of La Piana, starts suddenly, as it were, into life: never again shall I say, as I have said more than once, that there is no remarkable coast scenery in Corsica, for, doubtless, this may claim comparison with that of most countries for grandeur. Indeed, I cannot remember any view of the kind so magnificent, except that of Assos in Cephalonia and the coast near Amalfi, but in both those places a high snowy range like that of the Corsican Alps is wanting. Below that silver range of peaks, the great heights opposite are, at this hour, covered with the loveliest velvety grey-green, furrowed and fretted with infinite lines, and beautifully mysterious with floating clouds and misty 'scrumblings'; in the middle distance is a line of pink granite or porphyry rocks, and nearer still a crest of immense crags above the village of La Piana, in itself more picturesque than most I have seen in Corsica; placed among slopes of green gardens and groups of chestnut trees, and looking seaward to a stretch of exceedingly grand coast cliffs, running, from what I suppose is the bay or gulf of Porto, to Punt 'alla Scopa and Rossa.

Sending on Flora and Co., I worked hard till 6.30 P.M. to get a drawing of this scene—a task that seemed to have no end, as higher snow peaks were suddenly unfolded from wreaths of cloud, and the crimsoning lights and purple shades on the mountains rapidly varied as the sun set.

7.15—Reach La Piana, a pleasant-looking country village, loftily placed among this glorious scenery, and possessing a Piazza or Place, where Domenico is waiting to point out the hotel, a little house with ladder-staircases, cleaner than usual, leading to two tiny rooms unexpectedly snug and clean. The landlord, with that obliging manner and homely good breeding so constantly observable in this island, after a short apology for 'our poor and rustic dwelling, where you must not expect much', prepares the little table for dinner, which is served up by a bustling country girl; and in this remote village inn, where the slenderest accommodation might have been looked for, not only were the clean cloth and napkins and silver spoons such as you might expect at town hotels, but the fare was all good, and well cooked. Corsican country inns are, it is evident, surprisingly satisfactory by comparison with those of the towns.

The short journey of today, as well as the morning passed at Carghese, have left plenty of pleasant memories; and the air here is so fresh and bracing that G., who, thanks to quinine, has had no fresh attack of fever, will now, I think, escape that enemy. Altogether this second 'fytte' of Corsican travel seems to have commenced prosperously.

139

CHAPTER VI

MAY 11

I T is necessary to rise early to get an outline of the topmost peaks of the mountains above La Piana, about which the clouds soon gather and hide them; but this does not prevent the good folk of the house from getting coffee ready before 4 A.M., so that I could complete a drawing near the village by six. Sky, earth, and sea are all clear as crystal, and this view of La Piana and the west coast of Corsica is alone worth coming a long way to see.

Leaving G. to pay, and to follow with Flora and Company, I take leave of the tidy and obliging people at the little hotel, and walk on alone. And shortly are reached the great precipices that form so prominent a part of the view I had drawn of La Piana, standing apparently immediately behind the village, but in reality distant some half-mile, sloping down in jagged and dreadful array to the sea. What beautiful variety of form and colouring in these granite—or are they porphyry?—pillars and crags, so brilliant and gay in comparison with the sober pallid hues of limestone rocks! The carriage road—a very good one, and with a parapet throughout on the side towards the sea—is cut for a considerable distance through the heart of these crags and peaks, along the edge of this savage coast, parts of which are truly splendid. Groups of lofty spires, like cypresses turned into stone, shoot up from the shadowy depths of terrible abysses, or overhang the highway, in one place half blocked up by a mass lately fallen from the heights above, and as you wind among these strange and wild pinnacles, you look between their clusters of rugged columns to the placid gulf of Porto and the beautiful hill forms on its farther side, forming a succession of pictures, framed by the grim foreground above and below you. This part of Corsican coast scenery somewhat resembles the cornice road, near Capo di Noli; but though the mountain wall is much higher there, the Piana and Porto rocks are far more beautiful on account of their colour, in some places almost rosy, and reminding me not a little of portions of Petra.

140

At seven-thirty I walk on, having made fewer memoranda that I could wish of these remarkable coast scenes, partly that there is a long day's work ahead, partly from there being more coldness than is agreeable among the shadows of this weird region of peakedness, and its gulfs of dim gloom, strange and silent as death.

As in the song of the autumn garden of Alfred Tennyson, one may imagine that a spirit haunts the place, and 'listening earnestly', one may hear him say 'Enough that you have destroyed the solitude and quiet of my mountain fastnesses by a high road: pass on, nor linger among my stony palaces!'[1]

Broad and beautiful views open out after the last of the precipices is passed, when the descent commences to the gulf and tower of Porto, at the entrance of the valley leading up to Aitone. From the great height at which this fine road is carried through the pass from La Piana, it winds snakily down the hill-side to the sea, with a series of curves at the edge of precipices, by no means conveying pleasure to those who dislike giddy heights; Domenico, however, drives well and steadily the whole way down, allowing time to observe some of the finest scenes I have yet seen in this island. At every turn there are new and fine combinations of beauty—round-headed pines rising above the dense vegetation that clothes the whole of the middle distance, backed by immense mountains above, and with the deep green gulf lying like a mirror below.

On reaching the shore the road leaves the sea and turns up the valley of Otta, and at 8.30 A.M. I am at the timber works or establishment of M. Chauton, a large group of wooden houses, with mills, chimneys, bridges, etc., pine trunks in great piles, sawpits, mules, men and women, and abundant children—a busy spot, appearing to contain more life than one has seen on the whole route from Ajaccio, Carghese and La Piana excepted. The buildings stand not far from the mouth of the river, a torrent which flows from the high mountains above Evisa into the Gulf of Porto, the lower part of its course being through what is now nearly a dry channel, with marshy ground on each side, unhealthy in appearance, as, according to all accounts, it is in reality.

M. Martin Ceccaldi, the resident agent, to whom his cousin the

[1] This is the finest portion of coast scenery I saw in Corsica. What must the pathway from Porto to La Piana have been in the days of M. Valery?—E.L.

gendarme at Carghese had given me an introduction, received me with the gravity so characteristic of Corsicans, who, it seems to me, are little given to compliment or gaiety, and with his wife, an extremely pretty person, genial in manners, ask me to stay breakfast, promising a letter to M. Ruelle, M. Chauton's principal agent at Valdoniello. The establishment there is about twenty-three kilometres from Evisa, and that place is about as many from Porto, a steep uphill drive all the way, whereby, says Domenico, I ought to start hence at midday.

There is little employment for the pencil at Porto besides the Genoese tower at the mouth of the valley and a sketch of the bridge and mountains; moreover, there was a sensation of feverish damp, which instinctively led me to prefer sitting in M. Ceccaldi's house. Within doors, however, time passed pleasantly, not only in discussing a breakfast doubly welcome from its excellence and from the kindliness of my hosts, but in conversation on various subjects. Much is said about the Hon. Mrs. A.B., who, with the Duc de B. and others, have lately been here; her beauty seems to have struck my host and hostess with extreme admiration. We discourse, too, on the goodness of Corsican roads; on the perfect security now existing in all parts of the island; and of the contrast in this respect between its present condition and that of even thirty years ago; of Otta, the native village of M. Ceccaldi, a place four kilometres ahead, and which I am to observe as I go up to the forests; of the fertile subject of Vendetta; and of how Ceccaldi's own father was assassinated at Otta, because, when Maire, he had asked a doctor to examine the hands of a man who had been drawn as a conscript, but who shammed having lame fingers; of silkworms, and of how Madame Ceccaldi, when at school, kept so many with the *élèves* at Ajaccio, that they were able to buy a harmonium with the proceeds of the silk; and of the wrongs inflicted on Corsica by the Genoese, etc. All this, playing withal with little Leo, the elder of two small Ceccaldi children, passed the morning easily.

Domenico, says Giorgio, having volunteered that this house is 'ὡσὰν ξενοδοχεῖον—all the same as an inn', I endeavour to settle the account, but find I have made a mistake, and that I can no wise induce my entertainer to accept any money. Nor can I without difficulty find an opportunity of giving a trifling sum to the female servant, whose face speaks bitterly of fever suffered, and reminds me of many I used to see in days of Pontine Marsh malarious wanderings. So, Flora and Company being ready, I promise to send a *Book of Nonsense* to Leo, and take leave of my good hosts at eleven-thirty, with a pleasant recollection of this visit to Porto.

Recrossing the torrent by the bridge I had passed in coming from La Piana, the road leads up the great valley which ascends towards the heights of Mount Artica, and the lofty ridges west of the Niolo, keeping near the bed of the stream where masses of granite are worn by the water into most grotesque forms. The north side of this vast gorge, on which lies the property of the village of Otta, is much cultivated, olives, corn, and vineyards hanging on its steep terraced declivities;[1] on the opposite side of the pass, that along which the Route Forestière is carried, another and wilder world prevails; depths and groves of chestnuts, now full of young leaf in all the green beauty of spring, and waving above fern and foxglove and patches of cyclamen, where 'here and there a milky-belled amaryllis blew.' As you proceed to the ascent, the views into the heart of the great mountains through some of the lateral openings from this valley of Otta are exceedingly remarkable, the more that the lower part of the gorge is not particularly distinguished from many similar fine mountain scenes; some of these bursts of stupendously fine landscapes higher up in the pass are really startling, and unlike any I have seen elsewhere. Huge pyramidal crags stand above you, isolated, and rising from rich green groves of great chestnut trees; their riven peaks and towering masses magnified by floating mists pierce the clear sky, and it is difficult to exaggerate the extraordinary grandeur of their effect, though varied as they are every moment by passing clouds at times hiding or displaying them, it is not easy to seize distinct records of such fleeting magic day-dreams. The whole pass is thickly covered with wood, chestnut, and ilex, and no part of it is more romantic than about the fourth kilometre, where the village of Otta is seen perched up on the opposite side of the gorge, below tremendous heights, which seem to threaten it with destruction, especially one enormous mass of rock poised, apparently, immediately above the village.

[1] The pigs in this part of Corsica, in order to prevent them from straying in garden or vineyard, are furnished with an extraordinary apparatus of two long pieces of wood fastened above and below their heads, and having the appearance of huge horns; at a distance they look like vast grasshoppers.—E.L.

Still higher up, the gorge is more contracted, and seems to close in with immense heights and a terrible wildness of dusky grey granite and depths of awful gloom; grand as are the scenes, the great scale of their proportions hardly allow them to be favourably represented. 3 P.M.— The road skirts hollows in the hill-side, and runs disagreeably by the edge of parapetless precipices, then crosses to the opposite face of the valley, high up at the head of which you see Cristinaccie and other villages, while fruit gardens mark the vicinity of habitations; finally, at four, the top of the pass being nearly reached, I send on Flora and Company to Evisa, and linger on the edge of the great gorge for the sake of getting some memoranda of its sublime scenery, here visible down the whole of the valley of Otta to the gulf of Porto. It would take, however, far longer than the half-hour I can spare for it to portray the infinitesimal detail of its wild and gloomy precipices.

At 5.15 P.M. reach Evisa, one of the highest villages in Corsica, apparently a considerable place, stretching on the east side down to groves of chestnut not yet fully in leaf, while seaward are the great mountain crags in the valley of Otta. Although there seem to be several very tolerable houses in the village, that at the door of which Domenico is cleaning the ponies is not at all prepossessing, and betokens no pleasant night's rest. 'Is there no better hotel?' No, he knows of none; has already placed the *roba* inside, and has bespoken dinner, so, as the Suliot says, 'δὲν εἶναι ἰατρικὰ—there is no help for it.' A room opening from the road—there is here at least no ladderstair to complain of— seems used as a common *osteria* as well as kitchen and family dwelling; beyond it is the tiniest of squalid chambers, in which G. with difficulty makes up my camp-bed, himself being promised a mattress on the table in the osteria when—an unknown future—that establishment may be empty. The host and his wife—he is a Milanese, who tells me he came from Italy hither on account of *circonstanze* many years back—are obliging, and do their best to provide a supper, though that best is very feeble. Nor did it prove to be eatable, even after a long walk; one of the items, an astonishingly nasty compound of eggs, parsley, sugar, and garlic, was indeed wholly otherwise, a matter, however, soon remedied by G.'s taking the culinary department into his own hands, and turning out a dish of plain fried eggs, which, with bread and cheese and good wine, did well enough.

CORTE

VESCOVATO

This day, however, though not ending pleasantly as to lodgings, has its own valuable memories; in the morning, those of the strange rock scenery of La Piana, and later of the pass from Porto, where the vast and sublime masses of precipitous rock made new dream landscapes at every step, with magnificent alternations of light and shadow.

MAY 12

5 A.M.—The morning is delightfully fine and the air exquisite; nor, among other good things, should an excellent tumbler of coffee be forgotten, such as one would hardly have expected to find on the top of a mountain in remote Corsica; here, as elsewhere, the good people exhibit great anxiety to compensate for what they know to be their deficiencies.

While Flora and Company are getting ready I discourse with Casanova, a brother of the guardiano at the forest-house near the twelfth kilometre on the Bastelica road—scene of the memorable downfall of the carriage and horses of Peter the profane—and then set off to make a drawing of Evisa, looking towards the crags of the Porto pass. Notwithstanding M. Valery's raptures, and the '*bondants collines de la Sainte Ecriture*—Why hop ye so ye hills?' to which he likens this scenery, I had not found it so attractive as I had expected on entering Evisa by the west side; but from the east the view is far more beautiful, and as you go up the hill from the village the Porto crags are immensely majestic.

Just beyond the twenty-third kilometre from the sea, the road—a Route Forestière—divides; one branch to the right leads by Cristinaccie to Vico, the other through the forest of Aitone, up the great valley or basin of that name, to the ridge which separates it from the district or canton of Niolo, and then down the other side, through the forest of Valdoniello, as far as the establishment of M. Chauton.

In a short time the skirts of the forest are reached, and as far as eye can see is a world of pines, filling up the depths of the wide vale, and clothing the sides of it far up the mountains on either hand, a space greatly exceeding the hollow of Bavella in size, but less novel and beautiful in its aspect, owing to the unbroken wall-like character of the heights here, and the absence of the detached and varied forms of rock which are the glory of the Bavella scenery. The trees near the entrance of the forest are not of great height, and for some distance inward are mostly more or less covered with a multitude of the bright white sacs or nests of the larvæ of that remarkable insect, the *Bombyx processionalis*(?), my first acquaintance with which I had made in the woods round Cannes. Here, in Aitone, the smooth satin-like surface of these nests, shining like silver among the tall dark green pines, has a most curious effect; and not less strange, from time to time, are the long strings or processions—some of them ten or fifteen feet in length—of this extraordinary caterpillar crawling along the road, now parallel with its edge, now crossing it in unbroken file. In other parts, below trees more than commonly full of their nests, are great heaps, some of them as large as a half-bushel basket, of these creatures, apparently in a state of torpor, or only in motion towards the point from which their 'follow my leader' institution is about to take place. Now and then, in passing under trees loaded with these bombyx bags, the thought that one may plump into one's face is not agreeable, for the hairs which come from these animals on the slightest touch occasion excessive and even dangerous irritation.

But the questions arise, on seeing such myriads of these wonderful little brutes—do the nests fall down by their own weight, owing to the increasing size of the caterpillars? Or do the inmates at a certain time open their nests and fall down 'spontaneous' to commence their linear expeditions? Do they, as some maintain, migrate in order to procure fresh food? It seems to me not so from what I have noticed of their habits; for though I have continually discovered them coming *down* the trunk of a pine tree, I have never seen any going *up*. Rather is not all this movement preliminary to burrowing in the earth (as, indeed, the peasants about Cannes say they do) previously to their transformation into chrysalides? Anyhow, they are a singularly curious, though not a pleasant lot of creatures, and their most strange habits are well worth observing.

The walk through the forest of Aitone, one of the largest in Corsica, is full of interest. The carriage road which winds along the southern side of the basin or valley is not very steep, and generally in good condition; but at present, on account of the deep ruts made by the heavy timber cars, I send on Flora and Company with the letter to M. Ruelle, and prefer doing the day's work on foot. Having passed beyond a tract,

partially cleared for charcoal burning, and where there are other buildings belonging to M. Chauton, the forest becomes excessively dense,
and although it is always more and more apparent as you proceed, that
in subjects of pictorial beauty the immense expanse of these woods is
inferior to those of Bavella, owing to the want of the unique background
of crags that completes the scenery there, yet Aitone may boast of a
greater variety in its foliage—beech, spruce fir, and, high up in the pass,
birch, being mingled in the most exquisite luxuriance with the *Pinus
maritima* and *Pinus lariccio*—so that at every step you are struck by fresh
bits for study, though, so to speak, the sea of forest baffles any attempt to
portray it as a whole. All the way up the pass numberless charms arrest
your attention—the sunlight twinkling and glittering through the young
yellow leaves of the great beech trees, or glancing on their tall silvery
stems, here black with moss, there with long floating tresses of pale
green lichen waving from their branches. You look up to the highest
summits above the pass, where masses of pine contrast darkly with cushions of gold-green beech-wood; lingering in shady hollows you mark the
chequered lights on the road, or on the pure white snow, which higher
up is lying in wreaths along the banks by the wayside. Nowhere is there
any lack of the beautiful throughout.

Halting here and there to make memoranda, or to rest by the delicious streams which are frequent in these high mountains, it is ten before
I reach the *bocca* or level space that at the top of the pass divides the two
great forests, and where that of Aitone abruptly ceases as you leave the
hollow basin in which it grows. Here, among the last pines crowning
the topmost edge of the valley, I sit and look down on the vast scene, the
deep and broad gulf between two mountain walls, thousands of pine and
beech trees filling up all the intervening space, stretching down in
shadowy blue gradations towards the sea, and climbing up the barrier
ridges on each side; the sense of magnitude and solitude is profoundly
impressive, and all I have heard of Corsican forest scenery seems little
compared with the plenitude of reality before me, a scene wanting
possibly in elegance of form, but in splendour of extent and variety of
colour certainly far beyond what I had expected to find.

A few minutes' walk suffices to cross the ridge, and to bring me on
the opposite side of it to the descent leading through the forest of Valdoniello, into the great basin of the Niolo, which, from the point I now

147

stand on, is seen below in its whole breadth and length to the north-east —Niolo, the heart of Corsican romance and liberty—its long lines of hill fading away into palest blue on the horizon. All the landscape here is on greater scale than that I have left; the lofty Monte Artica on the south, and Monte Cinto (the highest summit in the island) on the north, tower above the head of this deep and wide valley of the Golo in snowy magnificence, enclosing it as it were with gigantic wings; and less lofty heights bar the outer world from this compactly delineated canton throughout its whole extent.

The great forest of Valdoniello, commencing immediately from the *bocca* or ridge I have crossed, clothes the slopes of the mountains on its eastern, as that of Aitone does its western side; but the proportions of the surrounding scenery are here so much more vast that the space covered by the pines seems less at a first glance than that in the pass from Porto; it is only when you begin the descent through Valdoniello that you perceive how widely in each direction the limits of this grand forest stretch out, and that the trees here are of the greatest size, though dwarfed by the huge mountain forms above them into apparently less importance. Two or three woodmen point out a direct path down the hill to M. Chauton's great establishment; but I prefer descending by the longer carriage route, first breakfasting—for it is now nearly noon—and then making a drawing of this magnificent scene, where, until Bavella, there is no mystery, but all is spread out in one broad picture, from the high snowy Artica and the long lines of dark pines feathering its sides, down to the farthest limits of the Niolo, a valley that may indeed rather be called a small plain, the features of which, however dear to the memory of Corsican days of liberty, do not make me regret that I shall not have time to visit it; at least, from this height it has a somewhat bare and bleak aspect.

Much of the upper part of this forest is beginning to show the ravages of M. Chauton's hatchets; here and there on the hillside are pale patches of cleared ground, with pieces of cut and barked pines; and you pass at times a spot where giant trees lie prostrate; or you see a car with many mules drawing up its ponderous burden to the bocca, whence it is carried down to Porto or to Sagona.

> They came, they cut away my tallest pines,
> My dark tall pines, that plumed the craggy ledge.

148

As I descend slowly, commencing drawings which are to be returned to on the morrow, my first impressions as to the difficulty of procuring subjects in Valdoniello are a good deal modified. At Bavella, I had said the precipices are absolutely close at hand; while here the great heights are far away; vast slopes of pines in masses, with a bare valley, Niolo, beyond—a scene too large to be reducible to a drawing. Yet, on advancing, I perceive that here the pines are larger and more spreading, and more apt by their detached manner of growth to combine gracefully and grandly with the mountains above; and it must be confessed that the very thinning of Valdoniello, which is preluding its downfall, has its advantages in providing space for light and shadow, for which there was no room in the close dense masses of wood before the work of destruction began.

Heavy showers of rain fall as I get farther down the hill, an inconvenience atoned for by the beautiful effects which follow; folds of mist are drawn like gauze curtains across parts of the forest, while others are black in cloud shade; the more open portion, where trees have been cut away, disclose vistas and depths of inner scenery, and multitudes of stately pillar-like stems; and within these recesses, deeper and farther away from daylight, all, as well as their lateral branches relieved, light off the solid wall of pines behind. None of these beautiful effects were to be seen in Bavella, nor was there there, as here, an undergrowth of silvery birch, suddenly recalling Coolhurst or Cumberland.

At 4 P.M., always descending, I reach the cleared level space in which stands the principal establishment of M. Chauton—a busy little world, in great contrast with the scenery around it, and reminding me of Robinson Crusoe's settlement as represented in beautiful Stothard drawings, those exquisite creations of landscape which first made me, when a child, long to see similar realities. A large building made of bright pale pine-wood—the house of M. Ruelle, the agent—is encircled by grounds divided from the forest by palisades, and containing gardens and houses for workmen, and stables for mules. One hundred and fifty men are employed on the spot, mostly from Lucca or Modena, and in many instances accompanied by their families—in fact, one sees a small village in the centre of a forest, the appearance of the whole betokening extreme order and cleanliness.

The demure Domenico—little Flora having long since espied and come to meet me—shows me the way through a formidable array of dogs to M. Ruelle's door, where that gentleman receives me with the greatest cordiality—'rooms for me and my servant are all ready, would I have some refreshment now?' No; for as the weather is once more clear and fine, I will go out, and return later. 'Then you must be here punctually at six, for at that hour I and my wife dine, whether you return or not, because directly afterwards I have to see to the men's supper.' M. Ruelle is a Continental, and adds to friendliness and hospitality that vivacity which is so pleasant in the cheery Frenchman.

I drew on among those tall trees till five-thirty; the whispering of their foliage, so high in air, is heard but faintly. Go ever so little away from the cleared space, and you may fancy yourself miles distant in the heart of this sadly grand forest—silent, silent; darkening, darkening, as the sun sinks lower; a lonely and majestic phase of nature, and one by no means painless or free from a strange melancholy.

5.30—In the wooden palace of Valdoniello, M. Ruelle is ready to show me a spacious room and comfortable bed upstairs, everything above and around being odorous of fresh pine-wood; and then, after a glass of absinthe, dinner was served in the neatest of rooms, clean and well furnished, after a pinewood log-house fashion. Mdme Ruelle, a pleasant, homely little lady, joined us, and a tame pigeon and a cat were all the party besides; my man G., whom they kindly ask to join it, having again a fit of fever. The dinner is excellent, and, as I remark to my hosts, the effect of the whole house and entertainment is as if Robinson Crusoe had found the Trois Frères Restaurant on his desolate island; nor, I think, in any place, can the contrasts of life be stronger, or events more inverted, than in Corsica; here, for instance, in the heart of a remote mountain forest, where the most ordinary fare would have been thankfully met with, is a small palace and a first-rate cuisine; while at cities like Bonifacio or Sartène your comfort is doubtful. My lively and intelligent acquaintance are full of pleasant conversation; they have lived four years at Moscow and Novgorod, and after dinner show me an interesting collection of Russian photographs; of their stay in Russia and of the people they knew there they speak with regret and affection. As to my praise of Valdoniello, there seems to be to that, as to all questions, two sides; for in winter they are sometimes quite blocked up by snow for two or three months; nor is the responsibility of managing so large a number of operatives in so lonely a place without its cares.

My plan of going down to Evisa tomorrow afternoon is first heard with dismay, and then utterly repudiated; and their request that I will stay another day with them is urged with so much warmth and heartiness that I accept the invitation, the rather that doing so will enable me to complete much more work than I could accomplish otherwise. So we pass a pleasant evening, talking chiefly of Corsica and Russia; nor do my two French riddles fail to secure their usual brilliant popularity— '*Quand est ce que vos souliers font vingt-cinq?—Quand ils sont neuf et treize et trois (neufs et très étroits)*'; and '*Pourquoi dois tu cherir la chicorée?—Parceque c'est amère (ta mère).*'

At nine to sleep in the wooden room of the wooden house, a perfectly comfortable chamber, and where one may fancy one's self in an Australian or backwood loghouse.

MAY 13

4.30 A.M.—Looking from the window, the red sunlight glancing on the thousands of pine stems of the forest, recalls the crimson lights on the palms in many a Nile sunrise. At five I am on my way up the hill, G. carrying a particularly abundant load for breakfast, for it had been arranged by my hospitable host and hostess that I was to pass the day in the forest, so as not to lose time by returning; and, said M. Ruelle, who busied himself in seeing the eatables packed, '*Voilà un gigot d'agneau, des truites, du pain, et du fromage et du vin; est-ce qu'on mange bien au milieu d'un forêt?*'

The day passed in hard work about the two forests, until towards 3 P.M., when the clouds, which, as yesterday, had added much to the beauty of the scenery, ceased to be either pleasant or useful, and dissolved in rain, so that it became difficult to make any more drawings requiring continued attention. While in Aitone I was convinced, as on my first passing through that forest, of the impracticability of giving an idea of the whole scene. Several of those groups of gigantic trees were, however, wonderful to look at, and especially some which, dead, and white as ivory, shot up out of the purply gloom of the deep forest, their antler-like heads looking like silver as they caught gleams of sunshine.

In Valdoniello, where at eleven breakfast was arranged by a clear stream—possibly one of the sources of the Golo—no portion of this sublime forest landscape is more striking than the flat tops of some of the singularly Turneresque or Martinesque pines, relieving almost positively black against the great distance beyond, an effect which is not seen among the more crowded trees; and, moreover, I should say that these Valdoniello pines exceed any I have seen both in girth and height. Unlike Bavella, so delightfully full of birds, the forest here seems very destitute of animal life, hardly a note being heard from hour to hour, a deficiency with which probably the constant sound of the hatcher and frequent passage of timber-carts may have somewhat to do.

While at breakfast, two gendarmes passing asked me why, at Evisa, I had gone to the inn of Constantino Colombi, an Italian refugee, instead of the Hotel Carrara; so that it seems after all there is really some better abode at the village than that I was taken to by coachman Domenico; and now that the name is mentioned it recalls to me that the gendarme at Carghese spoke to me about the Carrara house.

Late in the afternoon rain showers prevented all work, except rapidly noting down flying effects of cloud and mist, or making memoranda of the fine masses of pines mixed with groups of birch trees; and as a little book sufficed for this, I sent G., still suffering more or less from fever, down to the house. After all, at this great elevation, and so early in the summer, it is a matter of congratulation that I have not had more bad weather to hinder my tour; nor, in quite clear days can this broad open forest be nearly so beautiful as now, when it is varied by cloud and light.

At the hospitable Maison Ruelle the evening passed cheerfully with these amiable and sensible people. Before dinner we visited the little gardens, bordered neatly with wooden palings. Assuredly, 'Lo, we found it in the wood', if a scriptural motto were desired, would be the one most suitable for this Valdoniello palace.

MAY 14

The morning is glorious. M. Ruelle, followed by great watchdogs and innumerable puppydom, greets me at sunrise with coffee. At five-thirty I send Flora and Company to wait at the foot of the Aitone pass near Evisa. The passage of the heavy timber-carts along these roads after rain makes them far from pleasant to drive over, besides that on foot I can better study the immense hollow of Aitone forest, with its multitudinous glories, chaos of pine below, and gold-cushioned beech woods above. I take leave of the hospitable M. Ruelle, and begin to ascend the ridge by the short steep winding path among the pines; G., who by dint of quinine is better, follows, but Flora, who knows that her primary sphere of obedience is to stick to the carriage, and yet who has now come to believe that she should not lose sight of me, is puzzled, and sees before her a divided duty, finally rushing to the road to resume her old habits of life. Perhaps the finest scene of all here is about half-way up the ridge, whence you look down on a stern line of giant pines standing out sharply and wall-like against the clear distance and voluminous folds of forest which fringe the edges of snowy Mount Artica; this morning, bright and cloudless, would not, however, have admitted of my making any drawing opposite the sunrise, so that I have been lucky in the clouds of yesterday.

At eight, having rejoined the trap, Flora and Company, M. Chauton's charcoal station is passed, and thenceforth is Bombyx-land, the white caterpillar sacs high upon the trees shining like silvery Abou-Jerdánns on Nile palms. All the pines that I observe so infested are thin and not strong looking; whether being diseased they attract settlements of Bombyx, or whether the insects are the origin of the decay of the tree, I know not, but, certainly, in the interior of the forest, where the trees are so magnificent, the Bombyx prevails not. At Valdoniello I scarcely saw an instance of it. At nine the forest is fairly left; the careful Domenico, who, unlike swearing Peter, never loses an opportunity of well-treating his horses, stops for some minutes at a fountain; and then on to Evisa by 9.30 A.M.

Here the Hotel Carrara, on the second floor of a very tidy little house, is a surprise, from its absolute cleanliness and neatness. Domenico's excuse for not having gone there on our way from Porto is that the mistress does not receive anyone unless they bring a recommendation from some known person, and this may be really the case, because the taciturn landlady, on my saying, 'You must have many guests with such a nice clean house', replies, '*Si riceve pochi; commandanti, colonelli, gente chi come voi conoscono Mons. Chauton; gli altri si mand' à basso*—Few are received here; officers and such as, like yourself, know M. Chauton; the rest are sent down'—'*basso*' meaning the dirty pothouse where I slept two nights ago, and which is nearly opposite, lower in the road.

The perfect propriety of the two little bedrooms here, and of the plain well-furnished sitting-room, could not be surpassed in even a Dutch country inn; nor could the most fastidious have found fault with the breakfast of omelette, supported by ham and olives, mutton with *Lazagne-pasta*, first-rate trout—generally, they say, to be had here all through the year—*broccio*, walnuts, Vico raisins, and excellent wine, served, as they were, by the neat mistress of the house and her daughter, the prettiest girl I have seen in these Corsican travels, with light blue eyes and long black eyelashes. Both mother and daughter are dressed in the short black silk spencer and coloured cotton gown, and the double head handkerchief worn in this part of the island. They tell me that in the winter there are frequently three or four feet of snow here for months together. Who, in a remote mountain village of Corsica, would have looked for such a locanda—faultless in point of cleanliness, good fare, and homely civility, and with a charge, too, of only two and a half francs a head for breakfast? It is something at least to have seen life in Evista from two distinct points of view.

Off at eleven, and soon leaving the forest road to Aitone on the left, drive to the village of Cristinaccie, a small hamlet containing some tolerably good houses, at the head of the valley; thence crossing by a good and large bridge the torrent which runs by the pass of Otta to Porto, the road commences a steep ascent, occupying more than an hour. The first part of it is very interesting and beautiful, from the noble ilex groves through which it passes, and from the fine woods of mixed ilex and chestnut you look down on in the deep vale above which you are rising. Sheets of white mayflower contrast with bright green or yellow-brown foliage of the two sorts of trees, and glitter among the bare grey arms and moss-grown trunks of the dark evergreen oaks, immense in size, and feathering the mountain-sides down into far depths of shade. Farther up, these woods are left behind, as loftier heights are neared, where there are crowns and cushions of brilliant beech among granite cliffs, and dusky-hued smooth rocks shining and sparkling with streaks of white snow and streams of running water.

At twelve-thirty, winding along the edge of precipices, guarded here by good parapets, three or four of the monstrous timber-laden carriages are passed. Quite across the valley, Evisa is seen, compact above its massive chestnut groves; far below is the little village of Cristinaccie. Coachman Domenico, who never hastens his horses uphill—they obey with a word—'*fate osservazione, Signore, come ubbidiscono!*'—seizes on these opportunities to indulge in ebullitions assumed to be of a vocal character, if that may be so called which is rather a succession of mildly dismal moans in a minor key, sadly slow and monotonous. No cheerful air have I yet heard hummed or whistled by any Corsican, male or female; the women, instead of singing those far-sounding and beautiful melodies so often listened to in days of Italian life, walk mutely. Corsican gravity is continually noticeable. '*Tout est grave,*' says M. Merimée, '*en Corse.*'

At 1 P.M., after rest for the horses at a fountain, the *bocca* or top of the pass is reached. A perspective of road succeeds to the hill-climb, descending always towards the valley of Vico, and offering, as it recedes from the higher mountains, finer views in the direction of the great ranges towards Monte Artica and Monte Rotondo, where darkening clouds tell that rain storms, as yesterday, are in full play. All the drive is remarkable for beauty, and of that kind so characteristic of woody Corsica; extreme greenness, ilex trees in detached groups or crowded into dells, slopes of fern and asphodel, distances of pure blue towards the sea, and snow-topped hills lost in cloud inland, where a road leads to Guagno and its baths at the foot of Monte Rotondo.

At one-thirty the town of Vico is visible among vineyards and cultivation, in the hollow of a deep valley; and not far off on the right stands its detached convent, greatly praised for its position. So I send on Flora and Company to the hotel, of which Domenico somewhat proudly reports, '*E' all 'uso d'Ajaccio; Vico è città*—The inn is after the fashion of Ajaccio, for Vico is a city', and I walk on, taking, at a junction of three roads, that which leads to Ajaccio through Sari, the other two being those to Sagona and to Guagno, by Vico.

It is hardly possible to visit a more beautiful scene of mixed cultivation and wild distance than that which opens from the Vico convent,

155

where, after passing through a small ancient-looking hamlet, with very dark black-brown houses, I soon arrived. Leafiness is the general characteristic of Corsica, but here it is more observable than ever, so completely clothed is every part of the landscape with luxuriant foliage, except at the very tops of the mountains. Everywhere a profusion of olives and walnut and fig trees, with much vineyard and corn, give a cheery air to the nearer scenery, while all the parts less cultivated are carpeted with fern and shaded by noble chestnut groves, and though the valley is quite surrounded by mountains, yet it is sufficiently spacious to be free from any look of confinement or gloom. In the middle of all this basin of tufted greenery stands the town of Vico, a compact cluster of dwellings, backed by a tall and not unpicturesque campanile, completing the picture, doubtless one of the most beautiful in Corsica.

It was 6 P.M. before—having finished the drawings I had commenced on the convent side of the town—I went on to Vico. But I regret to say that the place was much lessened in my esteem by becoming more nearly acquainted with it; the particularly unclean streets, the appalling odours on all sides, and the hotel '*all' uso d'Ajaccio*', not appearing at all prepossessing after the perfect little inn at Evisa, or even those of Carghese and La Piana, albeit those are comparatively unfrequented localities, while Vico is a place to which a diligence runs daily from the capital, and which at one time was a Sous-préfecture.

Before dusk there is still time to see the farther side of the town, but a walk through it, and for some way along the Guagno road, shows me —luckily, since my time is limited—that there will be no necessity to make drawings in that direction, and I return to the hotel as the grey hues of evening are falling on all this beautiful valley scenery.

Meanwhile, on the arrival of the diligence, dinner is announced—a table d'hôte meal, hastily and ill served, though of tolerable quality. Three travellers by the vehicle assist at the function, besides the conducteur, myself and servant; and the courteous and pleasant manners of the Corsicans soon went far to atone for the impressions made by the rough service d'hôtel, unwashed and offensively smelling floors, and other disagreeable etcetera. Of the three travellers, two seem government employés; they discourse chiefly on local matters. also on fevers, and on the principal places in Corsica infested by malaria. The east side of Ajaccio, in summer-time, they unite in condemning.

MAY 15

I leave the hotel at Vico before 5 A.M., but carry with me no pleasant memories. Till seven I draw the town once more, and then go to the Evisa road junction, or *Τρίοδος*, to wait for the trap, D., G., and Flora. As I sit by a little chapel conspicuous for its singularly ugly architecture —the absence in Corsica of the numerous pretty chapels and shrines that so adorn Italian landscapes is to be regretted—the view all around is very beautiful; the convent hill-side is absolutely one dense mass of chestnut foliage, and everywhere the extreme greenness is delightful. The blue mountain heights and parts of the foreground remind me a good deal of Subiaco; here, however, all is richer in covering, and the scenery of a more open character. Most charming and complete are the valley of Vico and its fresh verdure, and the recollections of their great beauty are a good set-off to those of its town and hotel.

The diligence road down to Sagona, broad and furnished with para-pets, runs along the side of a valley, gradually descending to the shore, and the drive occupies little more than an hour from the junction of the Evisa and Sari roads. In the upper part of the vale there is much cultiva-tion, particularly of the vine—the village of Balogna, close to Vico, being famous for its vintage—but the hills are not remarkable for beauty, nor does the rest of the way present any novelty; fern, red and white cystus, foxglove, and other wild flowers are plentiful and lovely near the road; chestnut and ilex groves below it—all constant accompaniments in Corsican journeying. Certain objects, which look like wheel-less and bottomless cars, or decayed wheelbarrows of large dimensions, puzzle me by their frequent occurrence by Corsican waysides, and are ex-plained by Domenico to be measures for broken stone used for road-mending by cantonniers, and are called *casci di roccaglie*. The stone-breakers and road-menders in the island, unlike the woodmen and cultivators, are all natives.

Towards the sea the valley broadens, and the familiar *maquis* resumes its place in the landscape; the few forlorn houses representing the ancient Sagona and the Porte de Sagone are reached shortly after 8 A.M. Then follows the pleasant shore drive, and the beautiful vale of the Liamone with its fields of corn and its gay yellow iris marshes, after which there is nothing more worth noting, except the number of bee-eaters on the telegraph wires, and that a large snake crosses the road at the Liamone mouth. And thus Teucchia, and the wayside Repos des Voyageurs, is reached at 9 A.M. Here they tell me Miss C. is expected on her way to the forests of Aitone and Valdoniello; the untiring zeal of this lady may be of great use to many hereafter, if she will publish her observations, which are sure to be many and shrewd.

It is too soon yet for breakfast, but there are many very calm and 'shadowed coves by a sunny shore' hereabouts, and a sketch of the granite rocks and the distant gulf hills well passes the time. Long points —*à la Corse*—stretch out and form a tranquil little bay, where scarcely a plash of sea is heard. Later, G. presents a breakfast of cold hare and snow-white cheese, assuring me, as the head of the former is wanting, that he had previously examined it at the hotel, and that its long ears precluded any fear of its belonging to the genus *felis*. The judicious Flora comes to assist at the polishing of bones, running every other minute to inspect the carriage and luggage, and to bark at imaginary marauders. She returns, when breakfast is over, to her post at the trap, I to my drawing, the Suliot to the gathering of marine *bobiloa*, and the examination of blue jelly-fish, which, as he truly says, abound here as they do on the long breezy sands of storm-beaten Askalon, or on the shore at Eleutheropolis, opposite Saloniki, where I was once detained in idleness and semi-starvation for three days on account of contrary winds. But the white amaryllis of these lands was wanting there.

At eleven Domenico, who has been investing in crawfish and other marine edibles, is ready with his capital little ponies, always well kept and well driven, and away I go back to Ajaccio. I pass the fig gardens and vineyards of the village of Calcatoggio at noon, stopping now and then to take a look, or a memorandum, of Carghese, the Mainote settlement, on its long and solitary promontory; or admiring the sheets of rose-coloured cystus-bloom amongst the wide tracts of *maquis*; and thus, by a walk up the hill, reach the the Bocca di S. Sebastiano (*vide* page 132) by 12.30 P.M. Miss C. not having been met with, Domenico opines that the lady has gone round to Vico by Sari, and with Corsican shrewdness remarks, '*Quella vuol veder tutta l'Isola e quando vi sono due strade andar e ritornar, non si contenta con una*—That lady wishes to see all Corsica, and when there are two roads to come and go by, she uses both.'

The way back is well and rapidly got over, the rather that, as is its custom of an afternoon, it begins to rain. How invariably, on perceiving some little white building a long way ahead, does one find it, on drawing near, to be no Italian shrine, no picturesque Greek chapel, but a mere box-like house. In Corsica one must not look for architectural graces, except, perhaps, among the tombs.

2.30 P.M.—At Ajaccio once more. Letters and papers, and a pleasant welcome at the Ottavi hotel, and from M. le Commandant Lambert. And, as usual, the high slanting wall by the barracks is blackened with swarming children.

This, the second tour in Corsica, has been all that could be desired as to carriage, horses, and driver, the young man Domenico being a careful whip and kind master to his cattle. But he wants to know if I can certainly start for Corte on Monday morning, a decision which as yet I cannot arrive at, as it must depend on weather, among other things.

CHAPTER VII

May 16

RAIN has fallen in torrents through the whole day, holding up only towards evening, in timely allowance for a walk by the seaside. Before this walk becomes as much frequented by those flocks of English, whom hope—that springs eternal in the human breast—forcibly pictures to certain minds as making a new Promenade des Anglais on these shores, may the drainage be remodelled! for at present the nasal sense is much disturbed by its condition.

But the hours bring plenty of work—abundant writing of letters, among others one to Olmeto, from which place I hear by a note that Mr. B. continues to get worse; a call at the Préfecture, where I find the amiable Préfet recovering slowly from the effects of his accident. Taking great interest in my journeys through the island, he promises letters of introduction for various places on the eastern and northern sides, where hotels do not always exist. Zicavo, Ghisoni, and the forests of Sorba and Marmáno, are among the places he recommends me to see, but I doubt my being able to accomplish the whole programme he draws up for my next and last tour. After all, counting the chances of bad weather, and other possible causes of interruption, a tour of two months, let an artist work as hard as he may, very barely suffices to give an idea of the scenery of so large an island as this—one hundred and fifteen miles long, by fifty or sixty broad; nevertheless some twenty or more views of the most strikingly characteristic portions of its landscape may serve to give home-stayers a tolerably correct notion of Corsica, perhaps even to induce some of the migratory to visit it.

The unlucky Miss C. is supposed to have only succeeded in getting as far as Vico, and to be there imprisoned, because the violent rains will without doubt have made the mountain roads impassable. Meanwhile, my good fortune in seeing the forests so easily is a matter of congratulation.

The Ottavi talk to me of the larger hotel they hope to establish next

160

BASTIA

winter; and I hope they may do so, for they are sure to prosper. Mdme Ottavi's coffee—she learned to make it in Algeria—is alone worth much, not to speak of care and obliging ways, cleanliness, and good cookery, besides the assiduous sweepings of the waiter Bonifazio.

Tomorrow I hope to see Mellili, formerly the country house of the Buonapartes; to get a drawing of the St. Antoine scenery; and on the following day to start for Corte and Bastia.

Late in the day comes a budget of letters-introductory from M. Géry. M. Prosper Merimée, who promised little, did much in being the cause of my receiving these letters, which will be extremely useful.

MAY 17

The day, cloudy and wet early, clears at noon; the trap and ponies come, driven by their master Jean the Vaudois, Jehu Domenico and Flora having set off yesterday to Corte, where there is some particular fête. Jean discourses on the great security of the Corsican roads in our days, and of the vice versa-ness of those in Sardinia; also on the advantages of climate here, which had restored him to health, after he had been getting worse year by year at his native Luzerna in the Vaudois hills.

The drive is a pleasant one, and all things are brighter than when I was here on April 14; the vines out in full leaf, and all the verdure of cultivation—now the characteristic of these hills, which but a few years back were so bare—fresh and vivid, and resounding with the voices of multitudes of quails. There are two large penal establishments of penitenciers on these hills; the lower, whence a road (*see* page 44) goes on to St. Antonio and some villages beyond, is used as a farming depot for cattle, horses, sheep, etc.; the land around both this and the building higher up the hill is being brought into cultivation by the convicts, who are all French, and mostly youths, sentenced for venial offences to various terms of imprisonment. All wear a prison costume, and are attended by armed guardiani.

A steep pull leads to Castelluccio, the upper or chief penitencier, which stands very high, and commands a magnificent lake-like view over the head of the gulf of Ajaccio and the central mountains. The place gives an impression of that order and good administration for which the French are so justly credited, and the convicts, who, I am told, really like their life here, have, or seem to have, a look of comfort and cheerfulness, while turning the wilderness into a garden. In the grounds about the establishment I observe specimens of the Australian Eucalyptus or gum tree, now so frequently planted and flourishing at Cannes and Golfe Juan.

Beyond the Penitencier, the road, skirting the hill-sides towards the east among slopes of rich 'olives hoary to the wind', dives downward, and ends among several villas half hidden in foliage, and as Jean Vaudois has no idea of the position of Mellili, it is some time before I find the path to it; there exists, however, a short cut leading directly down to the house from Castelluccio, not far below which is the site of this very interesting spot.

Mellili is one of the places that has left with me a stronger impression than most I have visited. The house, always inhabited in the early days of Napoleon by his father and Mdme Letitia Buonaparte, is now neglected. Bequeathed by Cardinal Fesch to the municipality of Ajaccio, it is let to peasants, who keep sheep and pigs in the once probably well-cared-for grounds. The building, apparently an ordinary farmhouse or villa, tall, small-windowed, and with a forlorn look presents nothing remarkable to the observer; many large grey rounded granite rocks are scattered near it; great growth of cactus, and long-armed thin-foliaged olive trees with moss-grown stems. You pass beyond the house through a wilderness of vegetation, and find a level space covered with a tangle of cystus mixed with long grass and lupines, among which a few sheep are feeding; and at the edge of this sort of platform stands the great ilex tree—truly, as Valery says, '*un arbre historique*', for its shade was the favourite retreat of Napoleon the First.

This celebrated ilex tree—a large portion of which has been broken off by time or storms—is of great size, and stretches its venerable branches droopingly above the verdure and the stone seat it overshadows. Its tufted and thick foliage, almost yellow in colour, contrasts strongly with the green below and with the grey olives on every side; beyond its dark black-brown stem and deep grey branches the blue gulf and hills gleam; and there is no sound to break the sad quiet of this once gay spot but the voice of the wild pigeon and the sweet harmony of many nightingales. Yet the undying spirit of the past seems to pierce the dim veil of years and neglect, to colour with life all this impressive and solitary place, and to people Mellili with visions of beauty and history connected with the family who, as children, played here unnoticed, but who grew up to be the most prominent objects in the sight of a wondering world. Mdme Letitia, her five sons, four of them to sit in after years on thrones; and her three daughters, two of them to be queens. The boy Napoleon reading below the great oak, or pacing about what was then the garden, looking to those majestic mountains beyond the sea; in after days (1790) meditating on the fierce Buttafuoco letter (it is dated from Mellili), or on the whirlwind of change so soon to astonish Europe;[1] ten years later, visiting once more, and for the last time, his favourite haunts, when the fortunes of Corsica were beginning to seem insignificant among those of so many states, and mainly of France.

Like the talking oak of the poet, could the aged tree but answer our questions, and be

—— garrulously given,
A babbler in the land,

what might he not tell us of the days when Elise, Caroline, and Pauline Buonaparte sported in its shade, undreaming of the crowns of Tuscany and Naples and the princely Borghese halls; when Joseph, Lucien, Louis, and Jerome played, and Napoleon paced and meditated below its branches. Melancholy Mellili, well does the repose of the neglected garden and the beautiful scenery around suit such memories!

After making some studies of the great tree, I left the place and climbed up the short steep path to Castelluccio; from thence you look over the great slope of olive grounds down almost to the gulf, and mark where a good way beyond the old house, and conspicuous by its greenness in the midst of the sea of grey foliage stands the vast evergreen oak of Mellili—a mournful place, and one which cannot fail to engrave on some minds its outline and beauty in fixed characters.

At 3 P.M., having driven down to the lower penitencier, I walked to the rocks of St. Antoine, and, until five, made a drawing of that wild, strange scene; the multitude of granite masses, piled up and thrown

[1] The letter to Count Buttafuoco is given in full at page 370 of Gregorovius. It is dated 'From my cabinet of Mellili, January 23, Year Two.'—E.L.

thither, make a fine contrast with the delicate South Down-like turf below, dotted with patches of cystus and lentisk; but the scene is by no means an easy one to represent.

At six-thirty back to Ajaccio. Poor Miss C. has returned from Vico, having seen nothing of the forests she has taken so much trouble to visit; for, as was foreseen, the roads through them are quite impassable, owing to the late rains.

All things are arranged for a start tomorrow on my third and last journey in Corsica.

MAY 18

There are heavy clouds on the mountains; but, as in Cretan travels in May 1864, what avails it to wait for clear weather? Just twenty days remain to June 6, when the fortnightly steamer leaves Ajaccio for Nice, and as that must be the date of my exit from Corsica, this journey to the centre and north of the island must be put in practice at once—even at the risk of bad weather preventing the pass of Vivario being visible—or not at all. Off, therefore, once more at 6.30 A.M., with the same carriage and first-rate ponies, but minus Flora and Domenico, one Vincenzo being the new driver until Corte is reached.

Freshness of gardens and mulberry plantations near Ajaccio, with melody of nightingales, are the accompaniments of morning on each side of the road (which, as far as the turning to Vico, I have already gone over), and the extensive views as one advances nearer to the mountains must be very fine in clear weather; now, however, ever-thickening clouds hide the pass to Vivario and Corte, so well seen from above Ajaccio, and by degrees efface all the distant landscape. Observation, therefore, is strictly limited to the foreground, to sheets of white cystus, and here and there to a few peasants, whose dark dresses subtract nothing from the grey gloom of the scene.

At the twelfth kilometre—to me an ominous number in Corsican carriage life—an incident occurs to break the monotony of a drive; the seat by the driver being occupied by sacks of barley, G. is obliged to sit in the carriage, and, consequently, the proceedings of the new Jehu cannot be watched with satisfactory caution, nor did we know that he had gone fast asleep, and that the reins had fallen from his hand, until the ponies suddenly turned off at right-angles to the road into a path which led straight to a sort of quarry, over the edge of which, in ten paces more, we should have executed a second Bastelica somersault, had not Jehu awoke in time.

8 A.M.—The river Gravona, coming from the high ridge between the Monti Renoso and d'Oro, runs between the sides of a great basin or gorge, afterwards widening out into a spacious valley to the little plain to the east of Ajaccio, where it falls into the sea.

Up this valley lies the road to Corte. The way to Vico by Sariola and Sari is on the left, that to Corte keeps always in the valley of the Gravone through a green and beautiful country, much cultivated with corn, and with groups of olives growing among detached masses of granite. Beyond a single wayside house—where there are two mounted gendarmes, and two on foot, with a captured deserter from Castelluccio—the road enters the hills, and the valley narrows considerably, near what is, if I remember rightly, the Ponte d'Ucciani, the village of that name, as well as Tavaro and others, peering through clouds high up on the wooded hills far above. Vincenzo points out Ucciani thus: 'In that village lives the father of the other coachman, Domenico', and thereby plainly shows that he is not a Corsican, for a native would first have related that it was at Ucciani that the first Napoleon was sheltered when he so narrowly escaped being destroyed at Bocognano. The Gravona, here a foaming and clear broad river, runs between fringes of foliage; the wild hills around are covered with cystus growth and *maquis*; and granite heights, now deeply purple with cloud shade, all combine to show that this would be fine scenery for walking excursions in propitious weather. At a turn of the road here-abouts two of the great timber-carts are suddenly encountered—no pleasant neighbours when you are driving near a precipice-edge to which there is no parapet, for where the descent is steep it is not easy to stop the mules.

Gardens, corn-fields, and chestnuts now vary the wilder scenery, and at nine-fifteen the hamlet of Castellano (?) with a road-side diligence-house is reached; here is to be the midday halt, a pleasant quiet spot near the river, below chestnut trees which grow among grass and fern, and close to a stream abounding in watercresses, serving well for breakfast. High up on the north side of the valley, a black and desolate tract—

165

the forest of Vero, burned not long since—stretches away like a dark curtain; and it matters little that showers of rain prevent drawing, for the grim sad skeleton trees of the burned forest would make but a mournful landscape. At ten forty-five it is time to move on.

All the scenery of the valley of the Gravona seems of a fine and picturesque character, but increasing mists hid much of it towards noon. The good and broad Route Impériale constantly ascends, and in parts steeply, at a considerable height above the river; fields of green fern and gleaming spaces of blooming asphodel, their pale bright flowers shining starrily off dark foliage; large masses of chestnut wood; these are what I see; but the opposite side of the picture, the Monte d'Oro, which must give so much character to the pass, is lost in thick cloud, and always unseen. After 1 P.M. I send on the trap to Bocognano, a rash act soon repented of, as hard rain begins in earnest, and tree shelter is often necessary; from time to time there are glimpses of the Gravona through the world of chestnut trees along which I pass, and at three, when the steepest part of the ascent is overcome, the road, now level, reaches the great hollow or semicircle below Monte Renoso, on the side of which the villages of Bocognano are situated among the folds of thick wood, almost entirely chestnut, which clothe all this region. Bocognano is not, as I had imagined, a single town or village, but a collection of several hamlets scattered among the woods, some of them being only discoverable by the curling smoke from their houses. One tall campanile alone is seen: in Corsica churches are not very numerous.

The chief hamlet of Bocognano, the first reached from Ajaccio, from which it is distant forty kilometres, is not in itself picturesque. The main road forms the high street, the houses of which it consists being nearly all of an ordinary kind, whitewashed, with dark wooden window shutters and roofs, very rustic, and with much of that sombre dull look common to most Corsician buildings. Detached buildings are built above and below the village, as well as beyond it on the road to Corte, all more or less hidden by the luxuriant chestnut trees which grow on every side. Half-way through the hamlet, on the left hand, is a humble *locanda*, called Café des Amis, and here, again, the interior, as is so frequently noticeable in this island, is far better than the outside promises, the 'hotel' consisting of two very decent and clean bedrooms, and a rather bare sitting-room, the latter adorned with representations

166

of the life of Napoleon I, the former with a few prints of a religious character. Of the two dormitories I choose the least and worst furnished, because it looks out over the magnificent valley of chestnut woods towards Monte d'Oro, so that if tomorrow's sunrise should prove fine I have my work immediately before me. Meanwhile, pouring rain continuing to fall, a change of clothes, rest, and writing up journal till 5 P.M. are the order of the day for the present.

5.30 P.M.—M. Berlandi calls—the Maréchal de Logis de Gendarmerie—to whom M. le Commandant Lambert has given me a note which I had forwarded on arriving; a polite and pleasant fellow, who offers me any assistance I may require. I beg that tomorrow he will show me the house from which the first Napoleon escaped, but require nothing else now that I have found a lodging—about my doing which M. Lambert was in doubt, since sometimes in these places the only inn happens to be full, and then your letter to anyone in authority is of great use. M. Berlandi tells me that he was away when I arrived, searching, with nearly all the people of the Bocognano villages, for a poor half-witted youth who has now been missing for four days. He says that every year deaths occur in these mountains from children or old persons losing their way in the thick *maquis*, or from being caught, high up in the hills, by snow storms. Last autumn two little girls strayed from their home, only to be found (or rather their skeletons) when the snow melted, a month or two ago.

Dinner follows, and by no means a bad one for a little road-side inn; very decent soup, eggs and ham, good stewed mutton, a dish of excellent trout, broccio, and good wine. Might not a man live here very tolerably for ever so long a summer?

This evening a fire is welcome, for Bocognano stands at a great height above the sea, and the weather is damp and chilly. At 6 P.M. the mist clears somewhat, and as it sails away shows, as if by a curtain being partly drawn up, vast depths and breadths of grand gloom.

Later, the sky clears suddenly and completely, and most astonishing is the spectacle of the immense Monte d'Oro, all at once, as if by magic, unveiled from base to summit in all its magnificence of rock and snow; and where a minute before nothing was to be seen but a pale white mist, now rises a vast mountain, purple in the last shades of evening. I drew till seven-thirty, when darkness stopped me. I think no mountain scene has ever so much impressed me, except the view of the Jungfrau from the Wengen Alp, which this of Monte d'Oro, from its proximity and position, somewhat resembles. Here, however, there are few pastures, but everywhere grand forests of chestnut.

MAY 19

Up by earliest daylight to draw the sublime scene from my window, Monte d'Oro and the villages of this singular place, so beautifully nestled among the wide chestnut woods. The weather seems to have become perfectly fine, which in these high mountains is more than I had looked for.

5.30 A.M.—I go out to obtain, if possible, a general view of the village. Fresh and pleasant as is the air, and charming the glistening chestnut foliage, it is yet a trifle too damp by the road-side below the trees, where, in order to draw, I am obliged to take up my position. This Bocognano scenery is quite a change from what I have seen in Corsica hitherto. The great extent of chestnut woods, mistily or distinctly seen through the blue filmy smoke rising from the distant hamlets, lit up by the sun, or overshadowed by cloud; then the village, not very interesting in its forms, but having a tolerable variety of tints, brown, ochre, and grey, or its older houses, which have rich brown-madder roofs and white chimneys; and lastly, above village and woods, the vast heights of Monte Renoso—streaked with snow, and appearing or vanishing as driving clouds pass over them—form hundreds of beautiful pictures. Bocognano, to those who wish to represent such scenes of mountain grandeur, with few accessories of distance, or, to such as desire to become thoroughly acquainted with the characteristics of chestnut foliage, would be a first-rate place for summer study.

As I sit close to the village, I have at least the advantage of seeing all who come out of it on this side; but, alas, for the joyous singing of Italy! and for the gay dresses and beautiful laughing faces of Italian mountain girls as they leave the town for their work in the country! here all things are triste and mute; mopy men in black, their hands in their pockets, lead out a single black goat to some pasture, the rope fastened to their arm; women in black dresses, and black kerchiefed, and with grave though not unpleasing faces, and grave manners, also lead forth one goat apiece. Slowly and lazily walk the men, slowly the women— mournful Corsican mountain homes and inhabitants. But on the other hand I am allowed to draw quite unmolested; two or three boys on their way to school stop to look at my work, and make intelligent remarks on it, but avoid giving me the least annoyance, some of them rebuking others if they stand ever so little in my way; and when, on more of them gathering round me, I suggest that it would be better they should go to school, one of the children says, quietly, '*E vero, sarebbe meglio, andiam*—It is true, it *would* be better, let us go'—and away they all walk. I never was in any country where so little trouble was given me by bystanders.

A walk through and beyond the village next occupied me; on the whole an air of neatness and tranquillity pervades it. Children are numerous but not idle, for one and all carry books, and are on their way to school. There are many pigs, too, for it is a land of chestnuts, and the hams and sausages of the chestnut-fed are famous. As I returned, M. Berlandi joined me, and took me to see the house from which Napoleon I so narrowly escaped with life in 1780, when pursued by his enemies of the Pozzo di Borgo faction. The building is now the caserne of the gendarmerie, and near one of the windows there formerly grew a tree, by the aid of whose branches the young Napoleon was enabled to leave the house at night and to fly to Ucciani, a village not far off, where the family Poggiani protected him. My informants state that at the death of the first emperor several persons of Ucciani received legacies of 5,000 and 6,000 francs, and that their descendants are still much favoured by Napoleon III.

7.15—It is time to begin the day's journey, which is to be as far as Vivario at least. Of Paolo Mufraggi, landlord of the little Café des Amis, at Bocognano, it may be noted that his charges for yesterday's board and lodging and a substantial breakfast for today are extremely moderate, and that he himself is most civil and obliging.

As you pass out of the woody amphitheatre which half circles Bocognano there are beautiful views looking back to the church and villages. After passing the last hamlet the ascent is steep, the road winding up always in fact of the huge Monte d'Oro, divided from it by

169

a deep hollow, narrower and clothed less with chestnut and more with *maquis* as you mount higher. The scenery of this wild pass is of a vast impressive character, but not very drawable, at least without longer time for study; on the left, the heights of Monte d'Oro are bleak and savage; on the right through a lateral gorge are seen grand glimpses of the snowy Renoso; looking westward down the pass there are beautiful views of the valley of the Gravona, intricate folds of hill, and windings of river. And now, at 9 A.M., great beech-woods are reached—green, shady, delightful, silver-stemmed, their feathering foliage contrasting beautifully with the pearly lilac hills of Ajaccio. And down the pass from the Bocca comes a long train of six of the huge timber-carts, each drawn by ten or twelve mules, descending at a pace that would not be without risk to a carriage happening to meet them abruptly at one of the many sharp turns of the pass before there was time to halt the animals.

At nine-fifteen reach the top of the pass or *bocco* (at the forty-ninth kilometre from Ajaccio), a ridge, from which on one side the water flows westward to the gulf of Ajaccio, and on the other into the Tavignano to Aleria on the east coast. At this height the air is sufficiently cold to make a cloak welcome. I linger to make a drawing below a ruined house or tower, and then, sending on Vincenzo and the trap to Vivario, twelve or thirteen kilometres ahead, commence the descent through the great forest of Vizzavona.

The scenery of the whole of this walk does not, it seems to me, rival that of the three forests I have previously seen; the upper part of it is all beech of great beauty, but the distance is much hidden by the trees, and this is the case also on reaching the pines, of which, at least near the road, I see no specimens equalling those of Bavella, Aitone, or Valdoniello. And, after having stopped at noon to breakfast by a streamlet, at a grassy space purpled with violets, the lower part of this great Vizzavona forest is extremely disappointing in its appearance, for it was ravaged a few years ago by a very destructive conflagration. The black charred trunks of the tall pines make but a melancholy foreground to the distance, which now opens out more widely towards the range of Monte Rotondo and remoter blue hills beyond a deep valley, above which the eastern side of Monte d'Oro is clothed with fine forest; and in all the descent I find neither scope for the pencil nor great subject for admiration. The forest of Vizzavona, lying on the direct road from Bastia to Ajaccio, is more known and talked of than any other in the island, so that my expectations had been, perhaps, unreasonable as to its magnificence; moreover, it has been the scene of many of the stories of bandits, of whom but four years ago some of the last were hunted from these wild and dark heights, where, if report speaks truly, some, harmless to the traveller, are still living, the precise locality of their abode known but to a faithful few.

At 1 P.M. I come to the end of the burned forest, and gladly, for it only presents the deplorable spectacle of a harsh dead world of naked pine trunks and bristling brown branches. An old cantonnier—the only living being I have seen since leaving Bocognano, except the muleteers who accompanied the timber-carts—says the fire here took place in 1866, and burned for three days, and that all the Vizzavona forest would have been destroyed had not the population of the surrounding villages worked hard to prevent its spread by cutting down trees beyond its limits.

Two carriages now appear—strange sight in these lonely woods! One contains the Bishop of Ajaccio returning from the fête at Corte; the second is that I came in to Bocognano; at Vivario (says Vincenzo) Flora and Company are waiting for me. At three the house roofs of that village are seen, deep and far below the step zigzags which I am descending; little, however, am I tempted to stop for drawing, so vast and so full of multitudinous detail are the great mountain buttresses of Monte d'Oro and Monte Rotondo, filling up all the picture, and defying any attempt to give an idea of their bulky magnificence. Small were the hills, Latin or Sabine, edging the Roman campagna—small the delicate distances of Argos or Bassæ; but all were refined and beautiful. To me these Corsican Alps, like their Swiss brethren, seem generally more awful than lovely.

Vivario, situated at the foot of these great mountains, is a compact little village, and a picturesque scene might be made of it with ample time for studying the gigantic details around it; today, however, the heights are quite cloud-capped on all sides, and as in any case I must return thus far on my way back to Ajaccio, it is a question whether getting on to Serraggio for tonight is not my best policy for the present. The latter village is seen clearly from here, as well as much of the road to Corte, running along the flanks of Monte Rotondo, and ascending to the woods of Santa Maria di Venaco.

Flora, espying me from a long way off, comes to greet me at the entrance of Vivario. This village, which is distant sixty-two kilometres from Ajaccio, is not so prepossessing in its interior as externally. In the piazza is a fountain with a statue, but the rustic houses are not in very exact keeping with this embellishment. Domenico shows me the hotel of Vivario, standing in a queer little alley, but some people, of whom there are plenty lounging about, inform me that it is quite full; and this, combined with increasing cloud and the prospect of passing the afternoon here to no purpose, finally decides me on going on now, and taking the chance of better fortune on my return.

3.30 P.M.—Off to Serraggio, and perhaps even on as far as Corte; it is impossible in this kind of journey to be sure as to one's halting-place beforehand. The road runs immediately below the great Monte Rotondo and at certain points passes some magnificent scenes, especially one at the bridge over the River Vecchio—it runs from the forest of Vizzavona to the Tavignano—which I must return to draw. So far from Vivario the way is level or downhill, but beyond the bridge the ascent commences that continues to S. Pietro di Venaco. The scenery is more cheerful than that of the great passes in the centre of the island; the hills on the right hand which shut in the valley of Ghisoni gradually opening out into views of the more distant and smiling valleys towards the Tavignano and the sea.

Unusual liveliness, too, for Corsica, is added to the road by a good many cars being met with, containing people returning from the Corte fête, though hardly any colour brightens their dark and gloomy costume.

By four-twenty we have rattled up the hill at a great rate, and Serraggio is reached—a considerable village, standing among chestnut groves under the great heights of Monte Rotondo, and with beautiful views looking back to Vivario, and eastward towards the sea. There is, says Domenico, an hotel here; but as Corte is now so near I resolve to go on at once to Paoli's former capital, and leave whatever is to be done hereabouts till my return. Only I halt to inquire for the moufflon, of which Miss C. tells me they have a very fine living specimen, taken in the course of last winter, now in the village. That animal, however, I find, has been taken to be exhibited at Corte.

172

A little beyond Serraggio is a smaller village, Lugo, at which the abundance of children seemed the most observable characteristic; thence the road winds steeply up to Sta. Maria de Venaco, a village on the highest point of the road between Vivario and Corte. All the scenery about here is doubtless beautiful; the chestnut woods are noble, and at times a sunny gleam lights up the farther hills towards the coast, but heavy rain begins to fall, and forthwith clouds blot out the landscape, which, nevertheless, it has been easy to perceive is among the most interesting in the island.

The rain ceases during the descent to the valley of the Tavignano, so that the approach to the old Corsican stronghold is well seen. There, backed by the lofty mountains which divide this district and its fortress city from all the western side of the island, stands Corte—Corte so rich in associations of the history of Corsica, its capital under the rule of General Paoli, and the focus of all the national liberty for centuries. Even from the distance at which I now stand from it, it is evidently an imposingly situated and highly picturesque place, and stands—a pyramid of buildings crowned by a citadel—but a short way from the base of the high mountain wall, whence, from the heights Mounts Artica and Rotondo[1] issue forth the Rivers Restonica and Tavignano by two gorges, uniting just below the city, to flow through what is thenceforth called the valley of the Tavignano, but which is, in the vicinity of Corte, almost a little plain, with a boundary of low hills stretching towards the eastern sea.

All round this interesting city the ground is cultivated mostly in vineyards or corn-fields, and it would be difficult to imagine a town more finely placed, at least for pictorial purposes, than Corte. Sending on Domenico to the Hotel de l'Europe, I draw till nearly six, from a part of the descent commanding good views of the town and spacious valley, and not far from the celebrated convent where Paoli lived, now in process of restoration, and then go onward, diverging for a little while

---

[1] According to M. Arago, Monte Rotondo is 2,762 metres—about 8,976 feet— above the level of the sea, and there are seven others exceeding 2,000 metres (6,500 feet); among them, Monte d'Oro, 2,653 metres (8,622 feet). Forester says that at the end of October none but these two peaks were covered with snow, and he inclines to assign the height of 7,500 or 8,000 feet above the level of the Mediterranean as the line of perpetual snow in Corsica.—E.L.

to a sort of platform or promenade on the banks of the Tavignano, where a grove of chestnut trees bordering the stream forms a wonderfully good foreground to the city and mountains, and where I perceive plenty of work for tomorrow.

Corte is approached from the side of Ajaccio by two fine bridges, built above the two torrents, and is placed on a high rock, on the upper parts of which houses are perched and wedged in every possible vantage-ground and corner, its lower space being occupied by rows of great houses, not wholly divested of the magnified domino or warehouse likeness, but far more picturesque in their combined groups than those of most Corsican towns. Altogether, Corte must be acknowledged to be a grand place as to the general aspect of its exterior.

It was nearly dusk when I entered the city. Long ranges of many-windowed and very lofty houses form one side of the main road, which rises steeply to the centre and more level part of the town, and no lack is there here of bustle and life compared with the quiet of Ajaccio; even the swarms of children seem still more abundant. Suddenly, at the opening of the high street, running at right-angles to this first approach, transparencies and illuminations, bands of music, crowds of people, and universal movement greet my astonished senses. I had thought the bitterness and noise of fêtes was over with Sunday, but, on the contrary, this, the last of the three days, is the most violent and fuss-ful of the whole time allotted to rejoicing on this occasion, that of unveiling a statue of Marshal the Duc de Padoue,[1] one of the first Napoleon's generals, and a native of Corte.

Every place was thronged, and it was with difficulty I could get through the crowd to the Piazza, and thence to the Hotel de l'Europe. Here all was bustle and confusion. There were no vacant rooms; and as to where Domenico and my luggage might be found, no answer could be got; the general festivity seemed to have turned the heads of the good people of Corte. Group after group of people to whom I applied shrugged their ignorance on the subject. Nor were the efforts of Giorgio to find our driver and *roba* more fortunate, and we were meditating—as at Montenegro in 1866—on the possible chance of passing the night

[1] Jean Toussaint Arrighi de Casanova, 1778 to 1853. Born at Corte in Corsica, of a family related to that of Bonaparte. Fought throughout the Napoleonic campaigns and was created Duke of Padua.

in the street, when I remembered that M. Merimée had procured me an introduction to Signor Corteggiani, President of the Tribunals, and residing in Corte. In such a difficulty, application to one of the gendarmerie is usually the best proceeding, and had I asked M. Lambert for a letter, I could have been saved all trouble, though Corte is not in his district; as it was, a gendarme took me to the Judge's house, though this was a step but little in advance, for M. Corteggiani was giving a dinner to the Duke, the General, and others, and the servants would not deliver my letter until next day. Meanwhile, as I remained on the staircase with the gendarme and others, that functionary, who had evidently entered fully into the festal hilarities of the day, made an absurd scene by shouting 'Proclaim your rank! call aloud your title! We gendarmes are the heart and beginning of all justice! we will see everything done for you!' till a domestic, thinking it would be wiser to end the matter at once, rushed upstairs with the letter, and shortly brought down the Judge's secretary, with directions to show me a lodging, and to apologise for his not being able to receive me at the moment.

Accordingly, I was taken to a tiny house, with a very dirty entrance, but containing one available decent bedroom, and a sort of public chamber, where they promised some supper. G. shortly joined me, with two wild-looking individuals bringing up the *roba*; but these men, being in a festive and elated state, asked fabulous sums for each article and on G. refusing to pay so much, a row ensued. The most outrageous of the savage men kicked a saddle-bag downstairs, and was proceeding to further violence, when a compromise was come to by aid of the gendarme, and peace was finally restored. I had previously been told that the people of Corte had the reputation of being dirtier and more turbulent than any in the island, and, however unwilling to harbour unfavourable impressions, my first hour in this place tends to make me think the character is not undeserved.

Throughout all this hullabaloo, the people of the house—Andrei, a man and his two daughters—took no part in it, and after the savage porters had gone, were civil and kindly after their fashion, and provided a tolerable supper. G. puts up my camp-bed in the next room to the public one; but has a less chance of a night's rest than even mine, on a chair in the saloon. Already these small apartments are more than full, and others are flocking into the house. Sleep, at least during the fête of the Duc de Padoue's statue, is not to be looked for in the capital of Paoli's Corsica.[1]

[1] It is but justice to say that on the morrow the landlord of the Hotel de l'Europe, for whom the excitement and possibly the good cheer of the three days' fete necessitate some allowance, apologised very fully for his inattention, not to say rudeness; and as I have heard his hotel well spoken of, I am willing to think that the nineteenth of May 1868, was an exceptional day in his history.

CHAPTER VIII

MAY 20

No sleep, for there was noise all night long; this, together with having been more or less unwell yesterday, make it difficult for me to rise, but the bare prospect of passing an hour more than is absolutely necessary in this dwelling gives me energy to set off at five-fifteen to the Restonica Bridge, near which I draw till seven.

Why does it seem a law established by destiny that the best points for making landscape drawings are so frequently in dangerous, uncomfortable, or filthy spots? If your drawing is to be made in the country, why are you compelled to sit in a narrow and frequented mule-track, at the edge of a precipice, or below a crumbling rock, simply on account of the distance of a foot right or left preventing your seeing your subject owing to some intervening obstacle? If in a town, why for a similar cause does the top of a wall, the centre of a thronged street, or the vicinity of an *immondezzaio*, become your inevitable seat? And oh, painter, if you go to Corte ever beware of 'studying' below the houses thereof, lest the sudden opening of windows cause you eternal regret! These bitter reflections are prompted by the drawing I am making from the river bank, where my only possible position in order to see what I want is on a narrow strip of ground between the torrent and a wall, and as every five minutes there comes a vexatious mule along with a wide load of wood, I am as often obliged, for fear of a concussion, to mount the wall suddenly, while G. gathers up my folio and materials. But the view is beautifully picturesque; the rugged simplicity of Corte architecture agrees well with the proud and strong position of the citadel rock, standing out from a mountain background of the sternest sort.

Hardly able to bear up against warnings of fever, I next go to the chestnut grove beyond the junction of the two rivers, where a sort of esplanade has some benches at its borders. Few town pictures can be more interesting than that of Corte from this spot; the large trees grow on a slope quite down to the clear rushing water, and form a delightfully shady walk, particularly grateful now that the sun's heat is daily getting more powerful. I cannot as yet, however, from what I have seen of Corte, understand why some have thought of it as a place suited for the summer abode of invalids. Its position must be one of great heat during the summer months, as it is exposed to the sun from its first rising, and notwithstanding that the chestnut grove where I now am is pleasantly shady, yet a long and hot walk has to be accomplished to reach it; and, excepting the public *allée* or avenue on the further side of the town, there is no other shelter. In winter, from its situation close to great mountains immediately above it, and the two windy ravines behind the town, Corte must be as subject to extreme cold as to heat in summer.

At nine I return to the high street, and, finding that M. le Président Corteggiani has twice called on me, lose no time in returning his visit. At first, his nephew, a pleasant fellow, receives me, and then the Judge, a kindly gentleman, very profuse of apologies, no wise needed by me, regarding his inability to receive me last night—how he had gone to the landlord of the Europe Hotel, and had made '*des sévères reproches*', and how that person had acknowledged the justice of his reproof. I decline with thanks his offer of a room in his house, but accept, though very far from well, an invitation to dine with him at six this evening, and in the meantime M. Corteggiani promises to send someone at noon who is to show me the principal lions of Corte, such as Gaffori's house, etc. So I return to my 'hotel', and devote the next three hours to quinine, and to the endeavour to get some rest—the last an unattainable blessing in this noisy little den, where some twenty people are breakfasting on one side of my room, and on the other a family of screaming children wake the echoes of all the walls.

At noon I go up the steep and narrow paved streets with a cicerone who is very Corsican and ultra-liberal in his views of things in general. He shows me the house of Gaffori, the front riddled with the balls of the Genoese (there are still members of the Gaffori family residing in it), and that of General Paoli; but as I am too unwell to go into these, or to mount higher towards the citadel, I return to the inn by a lower route, pausing only below the rock to make a drawing of that part of the castle from which, in 1745, the famous escape of the Gaffori prisoners took place—all which lionising is effected with no slight difficulty.

One more effort is to be made to complete the drawing I commenced yesterday afternoon on the road leading down from Sta. Maria di Venaco; thither, therefore, I go, and return to the hotel by four-thirty. In Corte the little girls are almost all pretty, and nearly without exception fair, with pale or yellow hair like English children; they grow up darker, and get a coarser look, though on the whole there seems a good deal of female beauty in Corte, albeit, perhaps, of a stern rather than a genial expression. As for the boys, who are legion, they are sturdy but ugly little fellows.

At 6 P.M., much against my inclination, I go to M. Corteggiani's, making a strong effort to do so, rather than send an excuse, which my last night's misadventures might cause to be imputed to touchiness. I find M. le Président a plain, pleasant gentleman; the only persons at the table besides himself and me were two nephews, one of them, M. Antonio Gatta, a lively and intelligent young man, who, residing at Bastia, is well acquainted with that part of the island, and who gave me much information about distances in Cap Corse, the Balagna, etc. This last district, as well as the valley of Luri, I am counselled by no means to omit visiting. He also gives me a list of published memoirs of Paoli, and of other books on Corsica, etc., etc., which I shall probably find of use. The dinner was plentiful, good and well served, and I thought it amiable of President Corteggiani, who had been dining or dined for four days past in all the fatigues of a noisy fête, to have invited me. The wine from his own estate, a good *ordinaire*, seemed to me some of the best I have tasted in Corsica. At eight-thirty I took leave, one of the nephews accompanying me to the hotel door, and now, notwithstanding the incessant noise in the next room, am glad to get to my camp-bed, which is ready for my early return.

MAY 21

4 A.M.—Early rising, were it pleasant nowhere else, would be so in this hotel, where noise and other indescribable objections make egress very desirable. At a café good coffee is obtained at twenty-five centimes a head, and the sun was only rising when I was down at the esplanade

drawing the picturesque town above, the cool river gleaming between the dark chestnut foliage, and standing out on its bold rock away from any overhanging mountains. Indeed, the front, so to speak, of Corte catches the whole glare of day from the moment of the sun's rising till late in the afternoon, and it is only for about an hour after sunrise (at this season) that the shadows of the buildings and rock relieve so beautifully off the fine background; soon all is shadeless till afternoon, when the whole is in broad shade unbroken by lights. The upper part of the rock is of a dark grey-brown colour, cactus-covered at its points and crevices, and all the upper houses are similarly of dark brown or grey material, the windows bordered with white. One church only I have seen in the town, and that not at all remarkable in its appearance.

7.30—I return through the town; from the ascent to it the eastward view down the valley of the Tavignano has much that is graceful and pretty. Prettiness, however, is far from being the characteristic one should seek to express here, at the stern capital of Paoli, where the rugged and positive lines of scenery harmonise well with the history of the fierce struggles and bitter revenges of Corsican life. Not a part of this rock-pyramid but must have been fought over, and blood-covered; no precipitous wall of either of the two ravines, no pinnacle of the granite heights above, but must have echoed the wild cries of victory and defeat from the Pisan and Genoese wars down to the last battle with the men of Genoa in Gaffori's time.

Before going to the inn I stroll into the Piazza, where stands a statue of Pasquale Paoli; a tame hornless deer is walking about, and some persons assure me that it is a small red deer of a kind peculiar to Corsica. As for Miss C.'s moufflon, I again make earnest endeavours to see that remarkable beast, who is evidently exclusive in his habits and difficult of acquaintance—three days ago he again started on his travels to be exhibited at Bastia.

G., in wandering about yesterday, when I was too unwell to go out, discovered what he says is a good view of Corte on the Bastia road, so I go thither, and finding it to be so, draw there till nine. The whole city is beautifully seen from this side, and has, from its northern approach, the most commanding and grand character of any town, I imagine, in Corsica; its large houses cluster in well-composed lines up to the barracks and citadel apex, and the noble outline of the double mountain background makes a magnificent finish to the picture. From Bastia the entrance to Corte is by an avenue of trees, but this *boulevard* is so frequented that it can hardly be called a country walk. On one side of it, in a little piazza, is the brand-new statue of Arrighi, Duc de Padoue.

At nine-thirty breakfast at Pietro Giovanni Andrei's inn; its proprietors, a father and two gentle and graceful daughters, are pleasant and obliging, and their charges very moderate; but as their tiny house is merely a *locanda* of the commonest sort, and chiefly frequented by the gendarmerie and country people, it should not be a matter of complaint that it does not come up to the standard of comfort we northern travellers desire.

At ten all is ready (a taking of quinine pills not excepted) for the start to my next halt at Casabianda—that place so eminently full of fever-danger as the summer advances, yet to which I am determined to risk another visit for the sake of getting better drawings there than I obtained on April 26. Adieu, Corte! a crowd of whose inhabitants gaze on my departure from windows, and a multitude of whose children collect round the trap, Flora and Company. Adieu, Corte! you are picturesque, venerable, historic, liberty-loving; nevertheless, until your drainage is overhauled and remodelled, and until cleanliness is in a greater degree recognised as a virtue by your population, I should not wish to make any of your houses my home.

Domenico says there are seventy kilometres to Casabianda, but I doubt if it can be so far. I propose to go from that place to Bastia in two days, if this can be easily done, as I think it may be, because the whole distance is on comparatively level road, and the ponies will have a whole day's rest at Bastia. Of the beautiful district Catinca I fear I shall see but little, if anything, for there are Cap Corse and the Balagna to visit before returning to Ajaccio; perhaps I may succeed in getting to see Cervione and Vescovato. Meanwhile, it is a relief to have left the small and dirty rooms, the bad smells, and the noise of Corte.

On the road, which for a short distance is that to Vivario, several parties are leaving the town in cars for their country abodes (after all, it must be remembered that I have seen Corte under a very exceptional state of things); among these there are hardly anyone who does not carry a white umbrella—a sign that the heat, even now very considerable, is not thought lightly of by the natives.

The road to the coast soon leaves that to Ajaccio, and, following the course of the Tavignano as it winds among low hills, Corte is soon lost to sight; scattered cork and ilex groves are passed; and after a little while granite rocks, flowering cystus, and a line of snowy heights behind and to the right, are the features of the landscape. Presently the valley becomes deeper and narrower, and all horizon is shut out; we rattle rapidly down the good broad road, running not far above the river between low hills, covered with wild verdure, or here and there with patches of grain. One might be in Devonshire, and not in the prettiest part either.

11.30 A.M.—At the seventeenth kilometre from Corte (we get over about twelve kilometres the hour on the downhill journey) the Tavignano is crossed by a three-arched bridge; near it is a little church which seems to be a structure of Pisan times, and not to sketch it occasions a moment of regret; but the day's work may be long, so we hurry on—as the poet says, 'What time have I to be sad?'

Ever the road winds along the green valley, now at the edge of high cliffs, where the somewhat too rapid course of Domenico has now and then to be checked, now, at the twenty-second kilometre, passing a wayside house or two, a few olive trees, and scanty shreds of cultivation, dovetailed into the green *maquis* and white cystus. Below flows the river, deep and fast, often fringed with large trees, and always through a continuance of lonely but pretty scenery.

Towards the thirty-fifth kilometre the descent becomes more gradual, and the valley, though still winding among undulations of low green hills, begins to open out on wider spaces; the Tavignano flows on a broader and shallower stream between broken banks of red earth (for the region of granite is left behind) and waving fields of corn; and after a halt at 1 P.M. to rest the thirsty ponies, behold once more the rich and beautiful plains of the east side of Corsica, with Casabianda on its hill. There, stretched out in long lines, beyond the last undulations of the hills as they sink towards the coast, is the wide campagna of ancient Aleria, with its many pictures and varied interest, the vast growth of *maquis* and brilliant bloom of cystus, the river and the smooth corn-fields, and the blue remote forms of the crags of Mont' Incudine—how much of all this recalls the descent to the Roman campagna from the Sabine hills, or to some bright plain of Sicily or Greece!

All along the way the flitting of gay-hued bee-eaters, who make the telegraph wires their resting-place, is a pretty sight enough. At 2.15 P.M. the road from Bonifacio to Bastia, and the long bridge over the Tavignano (at the forty-seventh kilometre from Corte) below the fort of Aleria is reached; a few warehouse-like buildings stand near it. Here, till three, I stop to make a drawing of the fort and village, and the curve of the broad river, soon to be lost in the great Étang de Diane; the work of art I have undertaken being much abridged and hastened by the discovery that my position, in strict accordance with certain rules of destiny not long since alluded to, is close to a nest of a species of hornet, magnificent fellows of purple and burnished gold, but unpleasant as near companions. At three I start again, passing below the fort of Aleria, which is very picturesque from this side, and thoroughly Roman campagna-like; the road to Casabianda is but two or three kilometres farther, and here, sending on Domenico to the establishment with M. le Préfet's letter to M. le Directeur du Penitencier Agricole de Casa-bianda, I make a sacrifice to duty by trudging over ploughed fields in the hot sun to complete my unfinished drawing of April 26, adding thereto the mountain chain, which is now perfectly clear.[1]

No reception could be more kindly than that I met with an hour later from M. Beurville, all the more so that Mme Beurville was only recover-ing from illness, nor is it easy to describe, particularly after having so recently left the roughnesses of Corte, how delightful were the pleasant and clean apartments allotted to me; all at once, thanks to M. Merimée, it seems that I am in Paris, or, according to the Suliot's phrase, 'φαίνεται παράδεισος—it appears to be paradise'. The Director, as well as another officer of the establishment, M. de Lahitolle, a Breton gentle-man, to whom I have a letter from M. Lambert, enter at once into my plans, which they soon perceive relate rather to the far-away outlines of the beautiful mountain ranges than to the internal arrangements or exterior cultivation of the establishment. Not that the most indifferent could fail to be struck with the order and good administration of this large penal settlement—which contains nearly 1,000 convicts—and with the great change that in a short time has so visibly been wrought, a wide cultivation having replaced what only a few years back was totally a

[1] From the spurs of the chain between Aleria and Cervione some magnificent views must be obtainable.—E.L.

wilderness. But the view from the terrace below the Director's house, taking in the great central mountains of Corsica, from the Incudine to Monte Rotondo, and northward to nearly as far as the plains of ancient Mariana, is the object of greatest interest to the wandering landscape painter, whose only desire is that he may have coffee earlier than day-light, in order to be at work before the sun rises, lest vapours obscure the clear mountain outline. Then, as well as now, it is necessary, as my new acquaintances do not fail to warn me, to put on an extra coat, as the air of Aleria is, even at this season, dangerous at early morning and towards sunset, the chill from the great marshes on the coast contrasting forcibly with the heat of the day.

At dinner-time, six o'clock, the table of my host and hostess was without ceremony, but there was an exceedingly hearty welcome, and very good cheer; their little girl, an intelligent and darling child, was one of the party, and though not six years old, for good behaviour might have been twenty. On my arrival, the great size of my spectacles had attracted the observant little lady, who had whispered to her mother, '*Comme il est charmant ce monsieur avec ses beaux yeux de verre!*—What a delightful gentleman with beautiful glass eyes!'—an admiration which was at least more gracious than that of a little girl at Chamonix some years back, who, after a long stare at me, exclaimed, '*Ah, que vos grandes lunettes vous donnent tout à fait l'air d'un gros hibou!*—How exactly your great spectacles make you look like a big owl!'

Later, M. de Lahitolle, who has been for many years in Algeria, joined us, and there was much discourse about Corsica, and especially about this part of it, now in so transitional a state, owing to the treat-ment of it by the Emperor Napoleon III's government. Only a certain portion of the plain of Aleria belongs to the state; the family Frances-chetti of Vescovato and others possess much of the adjacent land, and that is all allowed to remain in its desert condition, while drainage and other agricultural labour are doing their work of civilisation at Casa-bianda. And it appears that by a great many Corsicans these improve-ments are not looked upon with very loving eyes, though there are, of course, many enlightened men among them who approve of, and per-haps have suggested, the measures of utility put in practice by the Emperor's government. As for the convicts, they naturally prefer labour in the open air, with comparative freedom, to a life within prison walls in France. In June nearly the whole establishment migrates to a Sanatorium, or mountain settlement, near Ghisoni, in the pine forest of Marmáno, which I hope to visit on my return to Ajaccio early next month.

The evening passes in making drawings for little Terése, not unenlivened by snatches of merriment; for although I labour under the disadvantage of speaking French very ill, I nevertheless always find French acquaintance ready to help all deficiencies, and with the pleasant liveliness of their nature, to seize on any opportunity of amusement. My riddle of '*Quand est ce*', etc. (*see* page 151), delights my cheerful hosts; and, apropos to the appearance of potatoes at dinner, when the question is asked, '*On en mange beaucoup en Angleterre, n'est ce pas, monsieur?*' they are charmed by my telling them the Irishman's saying, 'Only two things in this world are too serious to be jested on—to wit, potatoes and matrimony.' The beauty of the Hon. Mrs. A. B. (their party was here not long since), was again, as at Porto, a theme of admiration.

At nine M. and Mdme Beurville, knowing my early hour of rising, allowed me to wish them good night. In the sitting-room and bedroom upstairs I seem to be transported to some English country house, and neither the memories of ancient Aleria nor of modern Casabianda interfere with immediate sleep.

MAY 22

Before 4 A.M. coffee had been brought me by one of the convict-servants of the Penitencier, and as it is not easy to move about in this necessarily much be-sentinelled and be-locked-up place, MM. Beurville and de Lahitolle were soon at hand to facilitate matters, and I was speedily down on the terrace, drawing the long chain of Corsican Alps, clear as amethyst and tipped with silver as the sun rose.

The Romans were right in making a city at Aleria, in a site so majestic in itself, so well placed for communication with the outer world, and situated in the widest and most fertile territory in the whole east coast of the island, looking, on one side, to the lofty range of snowy summits, on the other to the sea, and to the River Tavignano winding through the broad plain, this part of which is so happily awakening from its long sleep of desolation. I am well rewarded for my trouble in coming here a second time, in thus seeing one of the finest parts of Corsica in cloudless weather, and in being able to procure an accurate drawing of its distant landscape. And having completed this, there remains but one more duty here—to visit some parts of the establishment which M. Beurville wishes to show me, and which, to my eye, inexperienced in such matters, appear in all the perfection of working order; the spacious kitchen, the storehouse for food, the warehouses for clothing, etc.—nearly everything is made by the convicts on the spot, from the produce of the territory—and all seems arranged and overlooked with the greatest care. A detailed account of the condition and results of this establishment for 1,000 *condamnés* would be interesting.

7 A.M.—I take leave of my amiable hosts, and of M. Lahitolle, and set off with Flora and Company along the road to Bastia, hoping to divide the journey thither by halting for the night at Vescovato.

Before passing the bridge over the Tavignano I stop to make a drawing of the fort of Aleria, with a distance of green plain and far mountain. If anything were wanting to complete the exact resemblance of this part of Corsica to the well-beloved Campagna of Rome, it is supplied just here by portions of the polygonally paved ancient road, which formerly led from Mariana to Aleria. So vividly Romanesque is the scene, and so exactly reproduced are such spots as Gabii, or similar places, that it is hard to believe the 'days that are no more' are not returned, particularly when a flock of goats passes leisurely and sneezingly, after their manner, across the long-enduring memorials of Roman dominion, wandering about the dark grey fragments of pavement as they might upon the old Via Appia—but here the parallel halts. There is no goatherd with pointed hat and peacock's feather and Malvolio-like cross-gartered gaiters; no little girl with scarlet bodice, spindle and wool in hand, and with her bright black eyes shaded by the white squared tovaglia, as—if you never saw the reality—you may see in the pictures of Penry Williams. Here, the model for the *Corsican Goatherd* might be safely selected from Holborn or Whitechapel indiscriminately.

Onward at eight. There are sixty-seven kilometres to Bastia, on the direct road from Aleria, and one hundred from Bonifacio, so say the

kilometrical milestones. Although this eastern side of Corsica is called
and seems 'a plain', it is by no means flat, any more than is the Roman
Campagna, which equally appears so from any height. A good but
straight road runs along it, mostly over undulating ground, and rarely
level. Sandy or cretaceous banks border the highway; and in so clear
and charming a morning as this there is enough of interest to prevent the
drive being a weary one, which in dull weather it would assuredly prove.
In the depressions or shallow dells the variety of flowers and the richness of the *maquis* are constant sources of pleasure; from the top of each
rise in the road you may look back at the snowy heights to the south,
gradually fading away, or forward to the green hills which approach the
coast at Cervione; to the right is the sea, with Monte Cristo and Elba on
the horizon, and all around stretches the apparent plain over which you
are passing. Rarely a human being is met; once or twice only I remarked
a hut or two, and now and then great herds of black goats filled up the
road, migrating with the goatherds and their families to higher regions,
above the reach of malaria. Everywhere there are characteristic and
picturesque bits of Campagna-like landscape; everywhere the cheerful
bee-eater abounds, sitting by pairs on the telegraph wires, and sometimes
not stirring as the carriage drives by.

9 A.M.—Since leaving Aleria—thirteen kilometres—scarcely any
cultivation has been passed; but now, as the hill-range, at the end or
corner of which Cervione stands, is approached, the scenery begins to
change, and has a less deserted look; there are a few roadside houses,
with plots of grain more or less extended, and scattered patches of alder
trees or of cork wood vary the *maquis* that clothes the flat ground to the
sea-side. The snow-topped hills to the south recede, and are seen no
more, while those ahead are of a rich velvety blue green, covered with
foliage from foot to summit, one of the lower heights being crowned
with a conspicuous lighthouse—the Faro d'Alistro. Beyond this, cultivation and signs of life become more frequent; and at ten we stop for a
rest, for the day is particularly hot, and Domenico never fails when there
is water to avail himself of it for the ponies. Here there is a fresh pool
and a stream, shaded by alders and a single willow—'one willow over
the river hung'—add also, in the interest of zoology, a very large snake,
which, as I wander about the thick vegetation, glides over my feet
towards the water. When first I came to Corsica I was told, 'There are

187

no snakes here'; but having pointed out four to Domenico, he now says, 'There are only harmless snakes'; which may be true or not.

Off again at ten-thirty and in five minutes leave the main Bastia road for a Route Forestière on the right, leading up to Cervione, where very willingly would I pass the night, could I by so doing leave time enough to see Bastia and Cap Corse, besides the Balagna, before my return to Ajaccio; well I know that from Cervione through the Casinca district exists some of Corsica's best scenery and points of greatest interest; and it is a matter of vexation that so much of this beautiful island must be glanced at thus slightly—so much left quite unseen.[1]

A very pleasant lane is the pretty steep ascent from the coast road to Cervione, shaded by chestnut and ilex, bordered with fern, and ever and anon with peeps into dells full of vineyard and walnut and cherry trees; as you mount higher the views are increasingly beautiful, over-looking all the wide plain of Aleria southward, and with Elba and the bright sea on the east. Extreme richness of foliage is the characteristic of the nearer part of the prospect down to the shore, and I am fre-quently reminded of the views from Massa Carrara and Pietra Santa, with the plain of Via Reggio below. Sending on Flora and Company, I stop to draw for a time, and then proceed to Cervione, which stands at about seven kilometres distant from the Bastia road on that leading to the west side of the island, or rather to the central point of Ponte della Leccia.

Cervione is a good-sized town (it was for a short time a Sous-préfecture), and has an imposing appearance from its high position, its lofty church tower, and massive many-windowed houses, like those of Sartène, all of which, added to some great rocks immediately above it, make a picturesque scene in combination with the rich foliage—what cherry, chestnut, and walnut trees!— on every side, and with the grand view of the plain and sea afar. Its street, too, possesses a certain air of activity and life, and on the piazza fronting the south is the very toler-ably clean little house by way of an hotel, containing a billiard-room and café below stairs, and a large and not ill-kept apartment above, arrived at by one of the ladders that do duty for staircases in these parts.

---

[1] I regret extremely not having been able to see these districts of the chestnut country, called the Casinca, or Castagniccia, since they are described as among the most beautiful and interesting of the island by all who have visited them.—E.L.

For all this, unless it could be made headquarters for several days' study, Cervione does not in itself present enough of interest to induce me to shorten the time allotted to places so important as Bastia and the Balagna, which I must needs visit, so I decide on going for the night, if it is possible to do so easily, to Vescovato, a place I much wish to see, owing to its many associations, as well as for its reputed beauty.

Quoth Domenico, who having unexpectedly fallen in with some Ajaccio acquaintance, is moved to demur to farther progress today— 'Vescovato is much too far.' Nevertheless, on hearing some gendarmes certify the way as seven kilometres to the high Bastia road, twenty along it, and five up to Vescovato, he acquiesces readily, and the trap is ordered to be ready at 3 P.M. The gendarmes say there is no regular hotel at Vescovato, but they name one M. Gravie, an old Continental and formerly in the gendarmerie, as having a decent lodging-house.

Meanwhile, the people of the little inn here, full of obliging civility— now the well-known type of Corsican manner—produce as good a breakfast as they can on so short a notice, for, as they truly say, it is impossible to kill meat and get fish in a spirit of prophecy for persons whom they have no reason to expect. The Cervione district has a high reputation for its wine, but there was none particularly good at this locanda. As to female costume, there is this change for the worse, that the women here only wear—instead of the two handkerchiefs so gracefully worn all over the west side of the island—a single one, and that simply tied round the head and knotted behind.

Once more I have to record that the small country inns of Corsica are cleaner and better than those of the towns, generally speaking. Meanwhile, I cannot bring myself to make any drawing of Cervione, though I know I ought to do so from the farthest side of the deep hollow over against the town, where, combined with the chestnut woods, the sea, and Elba, a picture might be made—but then, the houses are so commonplace!—and it is so far to go down there and up again!—and so hot!—and so late!—and thus I do nothing at all but wander a little way on the road leading to Orezza, a land of chestnut woods, not alas! by me to be explored.

Starting at 3.10 P.M., the Bastia road, very straight and unpleasant to look at, is reached at three-forty; and we drive on until at about the twenty-sixth kilometre from Bastia it is time to inquire for a road said to turn off on the left hand to Vescovato; but as there are many such lanes, the directions are not very satisfactory; and Domenico is in a land new to him. From the junction of the Cervione road the landscape has been full of cheerfulness—everywhere with much cultivation, and very little of the wild Corsican vegetation, except arbutus hedges, white and red cystus. On the left is a line of mountains, of no great height, but of good form, with a nearer and lower range of hills entirely covered with wood—here and there a house or two is passed, with corn-fields and great walnut trees. At five-thirty, a town not far from the road stands on a gentle elevation crowded with foliage, and with a beautiful picturesque campanile; this place I suppose at first to be Vescovato, but it is (I believe) Venzolasca; some people—there are in this district plenty on the road— say there is a way from it to Vescovato, but difficult for carriages.

6 P.M.—At the twenty-third kilometre from Bastia the real lane is reached, so I send on Domenico to secure what rooms M. Gravie may have, and prefer, after the long and hot drive, walking up slowly to the town of Filippini and Buttafuoco, the refuge that should have been of J. J. Rousseau, and that was so to Joachim Murat, King of Naples.

Few prettier walks could be taken anywhere—at first through open country, always approaching the hills, which are throughout completely wooded and exceedingly beautiful, the sinking sun now edging their graceful outlines with long streams of gold, green, and yellow, like the plumage of a peacock or a trogon. Then, as the narrow valley of Vescovato is entered, the way is more and more closed in by thick olive trees growing above rocky banks, and hedges where a profusion of blossoming honeysuckles scent the evening air deliciously; no town, however, is to be seen; and this leafy approach, reminding me of the lanes near Virò in Corfu, is quite unlike any I have yet seen in Corsica. And not less novel are the accompaniments of the ascent; quite a crowd is moving up to Vescovato from the plains and cultivated territory nearer the sea, with a stir and show of population altogether different from the lonely and thinly peopled western side of the island. Long strings of carts laden with hay; horses and asses, with groups of peasants carrying baskets, instruments of labour, etc.—one seems to have come to a new world—and scarcely one of all these people—I counted some hundreds—passed without touching their hats and saying, as did also the women, '*Bonsoir*'.

All at once the town of Vescovato is visible, than which I never saw any more curiously befoliaged and hidden place; nor is it till within half an hour of reaching it that it is to be seen at all, so high and so thick are the olive trees, and above them the chestnut, over the winding road that leads up to it. First you see two or three temple-like tombs, placed in striking and beautiful spots, Corsica fashion, and then suddenly the whole town is perceived, high up among the woods in which it is embedded, and looking down on a clear stream brawling onward over rocks to a little bridge, and dark haunts of shady leafiness.

Nor is Vescovato a featureless array of ugly and commonplace build-ings of the domino-warehouse type, but a most picturesque place both in form and colour, so much resembling such towns as Corchiano, or similar places in central Italy, that one seems to have been transported thither, there is even a sort of palace, as a 'roof or crown of things'—though, of course, not such as at Genazzano or Valmontone—at the highest part of the town. A multitude of unequal windows, and all sorts of angular oddities of architecture, are crowded together, to the delight of the artistic eye, the brown, grey, and yellow tints making each of the houses a picture; and on the whole, no place in all these Corsican journeys has so delighted me at first sight as Vescovato, which its historical associations alone would make worth a visit.

A smart ascent leads up to the town, and all along the way there are beautiful combinations of foliage and building. At the top, in a little piazza, surrounded by children, stand the trap and ponies, the luggage unpacked, and Flora looking as if all was not right, while Domenico comes forward to say that there is no possible lodging to be found. The Maire to whom I have a letter, is ill, and I send Giorgio to find the house of M. Gravie, when two gendarmes, who are always a civil set, come and offer their assistance; at the same time G. returns, having dis-covered the house which Domenico could not find, from being unable to leave the ponies. During G.'s search I was surrounded by seventy or eighty boys, who stared at me diligently, and in silence; and I was struck by the quiet manner in which all these children dispersed on my saying to them, 'Have you never before seen a stranger? and do you think it is right to look at him as if he were a wild beast and not a man like your own people?' '*Dite vero, è vero*—True, true,' said many of the little fellows, as they walked away, without a single instance of rude words or a grimace from any one of them; and this behaviour from a large number of common children in a remote mountain village impressed me—who remember various odious and howling juvenile crowds in other countries—as not a little remarkable.

Crooked narrow flights of super-odorous and slippery stairs—dark, too, for daylight is waning—cut in the rock, lead up to the queer little house of M. Gravie. As usual, the interior of the tiny rooms is far better than was to have been expected from the very rude approach, and the old landlord and two daughters are full of civilities and apologies. But as I have been very far from well all day, G. makes up my camp-bed at once, and I get rest till supper is announced, at which I only 'assist', for fear my not doing so may be construed as a slight to what these good people, in their anxiety to give satisfaction, have prepared—to wit, pease-soup, an omelette, stewed lamb, and a roast fowl, killed on my arrival, all good and well dressed. The supper is served by the two daughters, both of them agreeable in face and manner, and I beg the master of the house, a well-bred old French gendarme, to sit down in the room—which he will not do without a positive invitation more than once given—in order that I may have some talk with him, as I shall be off so early tomorrow. M. Gravie tells me he has been in Corsica forty years, and in this place twenty, having married a Corsican wife; I am the only Englishman he has ever seen at Vescovato, with the exception that once the English Vice-consul at Bastia slept here. The life of a gendarme in this island forty years ago was, he says, indeed, one of danger, when banditism and vendetta were flourishing institutions, and if one could but have stayed here some days, unlimited stores of romance might have been taken down from this old ex-official's recital.

Seeing how much pains these good folk took to please me, I was vexed that I could not eat, and therefore sat the longer to talk with this pleasant old man, in whose conversation there was something sad as well as interesting, particularly when he spoke of France. I should much like to linger here some days, but it cannot be done; I must see Corscia hastily or not at all. Meanwhile I only just hope to escape fever while I am in the island, not at all on account of the prevalence of malaria, but because fatigue always awakes the old slumberings of an illness to which I have for years been liable.

It is past nine-thirty before I get to the camp-bed.

SAINT FLORENT

ILE ROUSSE

CHAPTER IX

MAY 23

QUININE and a good night's rest in a quiet house are great things; by mistake I have risen at three-thirty, an hour earlier than was necessary, when—

Morn broadened on the borders of the dark.

Would that I could have got some notes and ideas of that chestnut scenery along the last few kilometres along the Bastia road! especially of the town I believe to have been Venzolasca, about which the beautiful effects of light and shade were delightful; but owing to hurry, and that the sun was low and directly opposite the eye, drawing was not possible.

Vescovato, closely shut in between densely wooded heights, with few distant glimpses of the shining eastern sea, might, it seems to me, have suited Jean-Jacques, had he accepted the Buttafuoco invitation, from its peaceful and remote position. Murat in the Franceschetti house, and Filippini in his own, must have found the place fitted to their wants; but it may be doubted if Count Buttafuoco, after the celebrated letter of Napoleon Buonaparte, did so. All these, and other names remarkable in history, stamp Vescovato as a town of peculiar interest.

After coffee, I took leave of my landlord, M. Gravie, who said, '*Je ne crois pas, monsieur, que nous nous reverrons.*' On my asking him last night if he had ever revisited France, the poor old fellow said, '*Non, monsieur, je n'ai jamais vul la France depuis que je l'ai quittée, et maintenant je ne la reverrai plus.*' I do not think my worthy host was convinced that I was not a political agent of some sort, partly because it has always been a characteristic of Vescovato to mix itself up in or initiate surprising political events; and partly that, after all, it is very difficult for these people to reconcile the popular notion of a painter laboriously working his way from place to place with that of an elderly traveller speaking four languages, and going about with a carriage, luggage, and a servant. It is of no use to attempt explanations—*qui s'excuse s'accuse*—and, therefore, silence is golden is the best rule of the traveller's life in these lands.

So at 5 A.M. I came down, leaving Domenico and Company to follow by the shady lanes where Jean-Jacques Rousseau should have loitered; and, till six-thirty, I draw below the town, by the side of the road, which is, as last night, all alive with peasants, now going to their work in the fields, many of them in cars or on horseback, and all giving me a civil '*Bonjour*'. Of costume there is literally none hereabouts, any more than in other parts of Corsica, unless the universal wearing of one or sometimes two gourds, many of them very large and flat, be considered as such. As the territory of Vescovato is all about the low lands near the sea-shore, where it is not easy to find good water, the villagers here take a large supply with them for their day's need.

In making a painting of Vescovato, as I hope one day to do, the luxuriantly leafy aspect of the place should be well attended to, and the rich broken colours of the houses, so unlike most in Corsica; especially when the stream below the town is fuller of water than it now is, few more beautiful subjects could be chosen. By 7 A.M. I am once more driving along the Bastia road, Flora having politely come up the Viscovato lane to meet me, lest I should miss seeing the carriage. At this hour the richly wooded and almost unbroken line of hills on the left of the highway are shadeless and glaring in the full eastern sunshine; the time of their great beauty was that of evening, when they were varied and lighted up by the long shadows and gold gleams of western sunset.

The valley of the River Golo and its bridge is soon passed, and already Bastia, the northern capital of Corsica, is seen, beyond what seems an interminable straight wide road. On the right hand, stretching to the sea, lie the great marsh and plain of ancient Mariana, and the wide Étang de Biguglia, so pestilentially malarious as summer draws on. I could well have liked to get a drawing of the site of the old city, but at 8 A.M. it begins to be too hot to indulge in wanderings over a marshy district of most suspiciously unhealthy aspect. Not much of the old city, I believe, remains above ground, but there might be picturesque masses of Roman brickwork, and vegetation; and the far hills, did circumstances allow, would combine to make a good illustration of the ruins. Borgo, Furiani, Lucciani, all villages on the left as you approach Bastia, would well have been worth a visit had it been possible to compass it.

Meanwhile, signs of life and cultivation continue to increase as I go on; wide corn-fields, lupines, and great plantations of almond trees stretch on both sides of the road; there are hay-fields, too, with vulgar domestic hay-cocks, dear to the memories of tumbling childhood; even the wayside accompaniments are different from those of West Corsica, inasmuch as here there are lines of great aloes, while, instead of fern, asphodel, arbutus and its blackbirds, the road is edged with thistles, tipped with the familiar goldfinch. Peasants, on foot or in cars, are numerous; and two diligences—to Cervione and Bonifacio—a sprinkling of wayside houses, and a very dusty road, all unite to exhibit a different and livelier condition of things in the neighbourhood of Bastia than is found elsewhere in Corsica. Nor is the drive without interest of association, apart from that of the destroyed Mariana, since, on the hills to the left hereabouts, took place some of the greatest events in the island history—to wit, at Borgo, Biguglia, and Furiani, villages all perched at some height above the plain, and apparently worth a painter's visit.

For the last hour the road has been quite near the sea, and now, at eight-thirty, walled gardens, a large cemetery, and villas on the hill-sides, announce the approach to Bastia, which is reached by 9 A.M., through a populous and not overclean suburb, just previously to entering which there is a picturesque view of the city, to which I shall have to return.

Bastia, a city containing about 20,000 inhabitants, is a complete contrast to its quiet, not to say slow, co-capital Ajaccio, where, comparatively speaking, few and far between are the walkers about. Here all is bustle and life, and a broad street, paved in a first-rate manner with flags after the Tuscan fashion, and with many new and large buildings, gives one an impression of having suddenly arrived at Leghorn or Naples. At the Hotel de France I get a spacious quiet room, and among the good things of a well-served breakfast in the trattoria on the ground floor, let not the fresh anchovies—for which this coast is famous—be forgotten, nor the cherries and strawberries of the Cap Corse gardens.

The afternoon passed in exploring the town, as well as in making a drawing of it from near the new pier or breakwater, now in course of construction; but there is not much to be got out of Bastia in a picturesque sense. A drawing might, indeed, be made of the old port, by way of displaying shipping, etc.; but to portray all its tall narrow houses, backed by high green hills, would take a longer time than I can afford it. Somewhat of Genoa memories revives as you walk along the lanes in the lower part of the city (the wide streets and new quarter—where there are blocks of stone-built, handsome, and solid houses—are all in the upper part of it), shop windows exhibiting gourds prettily set with stoppers and chains of silver, small silver and coral models of Corsican daggers, miniature remembrances of bygone days of Vendetta; but there is little novelty or beauty of any sort to detain a traveller long in a place, the most striking characteristic of which is its industrious and bustling character.

MAY 24

After ascertaining times and distances as accurately as I can, the best way of disposing of the ten or eleven days of my remaining stay in Corsica seems as follows: to employ two at Cap Corse, starting thither early tomorrow; three for the lower Balagna, and two for the upper part of it; and from Corte (which I must pass through once more) the remaining time may perhaps admit of my returning to Ajaccio by Ghisoni, Marnano, and Zicavo, if the above plan can be carried out without hindrance from weather or otherwise. Meanwhile, what little there is for me to do at Bastia on its south side can be easily dispatched today, leaving leisure withal for letter writing in some country nook, for this city doth not possess the charm of quiet, nor is a return through its streets desirable at broiling midday. So I make an early start before 5 A.M., G. carrying an overnight-bespoken breakfast as well as folios, etc., and getting coffee in a café by the way, walk on some four miles; the view of the city looking eastward cannot be executed till later, the sun rising fully opposite me; and instead of attempting it I make a drawing from a high point near the road, close to the spot I fix on for the day's halt.

In the latter part of summer the great extent of marshy flat between this and the sea—a tract then totally deserted—must be as dreary to look at as dangerous to remain near; but just now the high road and the seaward paths among the fields are lively with peasants working at the hay-harvest; the bright sun, though extremely hot, is tempered by a pleasant breeze, and the pale aloes are beautiful in broad light and shadow. Beyond the white city of Bastia you see a long way up the coast of Cap Corse, but the single and tame line of the hills seems to contain no scenery to be put in comparison with that of Western or Southern Corsica.

From 8 A.M. till 4 P.M. I pass the time in a hay-field below the friendly shade of olive trees, writing letters; a blazing fringe of scarlet poppies and the blueness of sea beyond and sky above are all day long a charm of glorious colour. A hoopoe or two comes near now and then, and except these, no other bird but one, who sits in a companionable way on the topmost bare bough of an almond tree a few yards off, hour after hour, chattering with a soft multitudinous kind of note, as if he were four or five birds instead of one, chibbly-wibbly-twitter-witter unceasingly, unless when he darts down to the ground to seize a beetle. This shrike—such at least he seems to me—is a restless little fellow, flitting at times from tree to tree, but always returning to his favourite broad branch opposite where I lie. He gives me no little amusement; sometimes, besides his continuous small chatter, he warbles with a good deal of pleasing delicate variety.

Slowly returning at five by the dusty road to Bastia, I make a drawing of the city from the entrance, at a spot where, by the usual destiny of discomfort, the only available site was not only close to the cliff, but exposed to the throng of carts and loaded mules, which at this hour fill all the public road. The Suliot, however, did good service, by warding off the latter, and by signing to the drivers of the former to give me a little more room, as well as by cajoling and conversing with the many children who crowded round, and I was enabled to get through an elaborate drawing successfully. Bastia from this point is picturesque, though not beautiful; no charm of architecture commends it in any way; yet the large masses of building on the edges of cliffs, with caves and coves, slips of sand, and clear water, in deep shadow, and all alive with dabbling and swimming children, make a good picture; though the houses are so full of very elaborate detail, and so crowded with peculiarities characteristic of Corsican buildings, that the view is one requiring much patience to complete.

By sunset, passing through the narrow suburban streets and the broader handsome portion of the newer town, I return to dine at the comfortable Hotel de France.

MAY 25

The daily life of cities begins late; nor in nor out of this hotel can coffee be procured before 5.30 A.M., when I set off with trap, Flora and Company, to Cap Corse, to get as far as Luri, Macinaggio, or Rogliano, as may happen. Mountains, richly wooded, and dotted with villas, rise directly above Bastia, and are prolonged to the northernmost point of the island; along their base runs the road, ever close to the sea, a sort of cornice, which follows all the indentations and sinuosities of the coast. This highway, besides the hot, dusty, and shelterless road to Bonifacio, and a third, a steep ascent, leading over the hills to the canton of Nebbio, seem the only drives about Bastia; and from what I have observed of its position, I cannot think it well adapted to be the residence of those who set their lines in pleasant places. Rambles to the villages high up on the hills there must needs be, and doubtless many pleasant ones; but for invalids, the city—noisy, though cheerful, and exposed to violent winds in winter, and to excessive heat in summer— cannot, I fancy, be attractive. Yet, in so short a stay, and with so little scope for observation, a man may overlook much, and easily jump at wrong conclusions.

The way onward has plenty of interest; here the view is never impeded by high walls, as in the neighbourhood of the northern lakes or the southern towns of Italy. To the right is the bright calm sea, with Elba on its horizon, and, looking to the left you seem always in a garden of almond, walnut, fig, and cherry trees (the diligence I meet is piled up high with cherry baskets for the Bastia market), corn, potatoes, and flax, varied at times by olive groves, while in the roadside hedges pink convolvulus, scarlet pea, and honeysuckle are blooming in gay and fragrant wreaths.

Brando, with one or two other villages, is passed; there is a celebrated grotto here—'*mais nous en avons tant vu*—We have seen so many', and I will not stop at the grotto.

But Erbalunga, a good-sized and most picturesque place, some nine or ten kilometres from Bastia, cannot be left so hastily. Standing on a little promontory, with a dark castle in ruin at its point, and with Elba beyond, this is one of the very prettiest of scenes, and detains me drawing it till 7 A.M. The still sea, palest of the pale, and more like liquid opal, and the equally pale sky of early morning, are beautifully contrasted with the dark grey of the rocks and houses, at this time in deepest shadow, and with the luxuriant foreground of fig trees and other foliage.

Beyond Erbalunga, this northern Corsican cornice becomes more wild, and resembles that on the southern or Bonifacio district (*see* page 87), except that here there is a frequent growth of aloes, wanting in the south. In both the road runs at times close to picturesque cliffs, or descends sharply inland to the marina (or 'port', of some village), which you may see high up on the hill, a half-moon of sand, with a few fishermen's houses, leaving which you again mount up to follow the cliff-cornice, with rocks and *maquis* above you, rocks and sea below.

Sisco is one of the largest of these sea-wall villages or marinas beyond Cap Sagro (its church is famous for the relics it contains); that of Pietra Corbara is a second; of Porticciuolo or Cognano a third; and from the head of each of these little bays you look up a valley wholly green, closed in by the wall of Cap Corse hills, that shut out by their direct north and south course all the western side of the cape. There is but little variety in the drive; but the oily-calm deep blue breadth of sea, and the beautiful flower-spangled *maquis*—for there is little cultivation hereabouts except in the lateral valleys—with every now and then peeps of the high backbone of Cap Corse, prevent the drive being tedious.

Porticciuolo is the last of these poor little sea-shore fishing hamlets, with its crescent of sand, its flat of grain, and its inland amphitheatre of heights, before you reach, at the twenty-seventh kilometre from Bastia, Santa Severa, the Marina di Luri, a forlorn and unpromising cluster of cottages. Here there is a road which turns inland to the valley of Luri, so enthusiastically described to me by Miss C., who advised me by all means to visit it.

So little remarkable, however, is the first opening of the vale that I feel undecided as to staying here, or rather whether I should not go on to Macinaggio, and return to Erbalunga to sleep. But farther on the thick growth of very fine old olives, lemon groves, walnut, and many varieties of fruit trees give a new character to the scenery, which improves at every minute. All the way along, a tower on a high and remarkable peaked rock, is a landmark on the hills, at the farthest end of the vale—this is 'Seneca's tower'—and now that I have advanced to its widest part, I am ready to confess that the valley of Luri is a most lovely place, crowded from end to end with profuse vegetation, shut in by beautiful hills forms with scattered hamlets on their sides, and seeming altogether like a veritable happy valley of Rasselas.

By ten the principal village, Piazza di Luri, is reached (collectively all the hamlets are called Luri, but each has its own name), and one cannot help being struck by an aspect of activity and industry in this place widely differing from what is to be observed in south and west Corsican villages. I have forgotten to ask for a letter to the Maire or to some proprietor in the valley, and the people about, all of whom seem busy, say there is no regular hotel here; but they direct me to a Casa Cervoni, in the upper part of the two or three streets forming the village, just off the main road, at which the opinion seems general that I may be able to find a lodging.

Mdme Cervoni, a very tidy bustling little body, comes out of the general shop, or store in the lower part of her house, and is at first rather difficult as to my request—'they are *occupati* just now; the silk-worms—of which their two adjoining houses are full—are about to change, and require all their attention', etc. etc.—but after a little time she relents, and pleasantly declares she will receive me on condition of my kindly adapting myself to the *circonstanze*. And then—yet another marvel of humble lodgings in remote country parts of Corsica—she shows me into a perfectly neat and clean sitting-room upstairs, with small bedrooms so completely good in all ways that I resolve at once—especially that I am now well persuaded of the beautiful character of Luri scenery—to remain here for the night. There will be fully enough work in the valley, and at Seneca's tower, to occupy me this afternoon and a part of tomorrow; and, finally, since I find on inquiry, that to go on to Tonino or Rogliano would be a journey of hurry and fatigue, not reckoning the way back by the sea-wall to Bastia, I definitely settle that Luri is to be the farthest point I can visit in the north of Corsica. (It is seventeen kilometres from the marina of Luri to Macinaggio, and this doubled, with the addition of five hence to the sea, and twenty-seven of return to Bastia, are in all sixty-six, a distance which would allow of no leisure, even if there are subjects to draw, which is doubtful.)

The breakfast which my hostess, or rather the host's sister, brings up, is a frugal one; but the nice tidy little woman apologises for its scarcity, on the usual ground that it is not possible to get either fish or meat on so short a notice; the extreme cleanliness of everything might have done credit to a Dutch inn, and was the counterpart of the hotel at Evisa. As novelties I remark a plate of preserved citron,[1] and that the wine is unlike any known to my Corsican experience, white, and not unlike an inferior Chablis, but stronger. The master of the house, too, comes, and sits down—a plain straightforward man, full of zeal for agricultural progress, and singularly unlike the more apathetic Corsican, so generally typical of the race on the farther side of the island. Not being a regular innkeeper, M. Cervoni says, 'I beg you to make as much, and as long a use of my house as you please; this room and the bedroom are at your disposal, and one upstairs for your man; and whatever other assistance or information I can give you, pray let me know.'

He talks of silkworms, which, he says, do not as yet succeed particularly well in the valley, but believes that this arises from want of knowledge and care; of the different sorts of wines made in Cap Corse; of general cultivation; and of the Maire, M. Estella, who died in 1841, and whose portrait hangs in the room, the founder of all prosperity in Luri. And I remark his Italian to be of the best I have heard spoken in Corsica; possibly the nearness of Tuscany influences the dialect of this northern part of the island, though throughout all this Corsican tour I have been agreeably surprised at finding no difficulty in understanding the people; even the peasants talk a sort of south Italian or Neapolitan dialect, which was long ago familiar to me.

M. Cervoni, as well as M. Tommei, the Maire (who comes to visit me on hearing that a stranger has arrived), tells me that I can go up in the carriage towards Seneca's tower as far as just below the Capuchin convent at its base, by the road which leads to Pino; and that from the convent the ascent on foot is easy. Both host and visitor dissuade me from going there till sunrise tomorrow, at which hour, they say, the coast of Italy is clearly visible. Miss C. seems to have been a great favourite here, and to have delighted all the people by her resolute activity and genial ways.

---

[1] The valley of Luri, and all Cap Corse is famous for the cultivation of the citron. According to M. Tommei, the Maire of Luri, the Cape produces 1,600 kilogrammes of this fruit.

Later I went with my pleasant intelligent landlord to see his silk-worms—two houses full, in every open-windowed room, on stages from floor to ceiling, and so placed as to admit of constantly cleaning the 'vermi'—a sight which recalled to me some nights of Cretan discomfort, when the said 'vermi', or caterpillars, were not in possession of a home of their own, but occupied, very unpleasantly, every inhabitable corner of the dwelling. Here everything connected with the culture was faultlessly clean.

At 3 P.M. I go out, intending to get drawings of this beautiful valley, though its position, directly east and west, make it no easy place to study in; all the views, from the nature of the place, require you to sit directly opposite the sun, and the blaze of light at this hour tries the sight extremely. Some time, therefore, is well spent below a large wych elm, close to the church, until near sunset, where the school-master gives me some information respecting the valley. There are fourteen hamlets in it, the combined population of which is 2,011. Piazza is the name of the principal village; Poggio, where the Maire resides, that of the next largest; Santa Severa is the marina.

Close to where I sit is the stream which runs through the whole length of this vale to the sea; at present but a gentle streamlet, it is a fierce torrent in winter, only kept in bounds by the causeway which M. Estella was the first to commence. Growing above the stream are mulberry and massive walnut trees, ilex, olive, fig, and alder, the great variety of the vegetation in this valley being one of its first charms, and filling it with exquisite scenery of the quietest and most delightful kind. No loiterers, who at Olmeto, Vico, or elsewhere, are so conspicuous an ingredient of Corsican village life, are to be seen here; everyone is occupied in agriculture, and the only sounds near are from the school close by, whence there comes a hum of studious children, and from the low underwood by the water, every bush of which resounds with the voices of countless nightingales; and when, later in the day, I make a drawing above the valley from close to a tufted grove of chestnuts, the multitude of warblers there is most delightful.

But, unable to encounter drawing for any length of time in face of the setting sun, I am obliged to desist, not before my eyes have suffered. Everybody, I observe, as they come up the road to the villages at the west end of the valley, protect their sight by umbrellas from the direct rays so exactly opposite. There was little to be done, therefore, but to seek out spots below the long-armed olives (they are like those at the monastery of S. Procopius in Corfu), whence I may make a drawing to-morrow; and so, by degrees, I go back to the village, never in any way molested by anyone in this Rasselas's 'happy valley'.

A dinner, more respected in its commencement of soup and boiled fowl, than in its conclusion of citron and raw peas, concludes the day. It should not be overlooked that in these places it is expedient to eat up the contents of the first dishes presented to you, lest no others so good, or even lest none at all, should follow.

Now that the sun is down, the rich full greenness of this little valley is delicious; but if it is so hot now, what must its temperature be in August? There is a good breeze, however, and no feverish feeling whatever.

Remembering Olmeto and Sartène, Bonifacio, Tallano, and Vico, how grateful is the cleanliness of this pleasant little house! Talk with my landlord and his intelligent and agreeable sister passed away the rest of the evening.

MAY 26

The most restless or fastidious might sleep well in the little bedroom of the Maison Cervoni at Luri, the cleanliness of which was so evident that I did not even have my camp-bed set up. The obliging people of the house had risen, purposely to get me coffee, at a very early hour, and at 4 A.M. Domenico and the trap were ready—Flora, perceiving that no luggage was to be taken, wisely preferring to remain behind.

The carriage road leading from Luri to Pino on the west side of Cap Corse, is one of the more recently made Routes Forestières of Corsica; it soon ascends the hills at the end of the valley, winding up the Cap Corse backbone, as it were, by beautiful woods of chestnut and ilex above Poggio and other hamlets—every turn bringing to view fresh charms, either in the combinations of the convent and the rock of Seneca's tower, or in the long vista of the vale of Luri, still all in shadow as far as the faint blue sea-line.

By five the top of the ascent is reached, one which it would not be a pleasure to drive down unless with a careful driver, by reason of frequent sharp turns on the edge of steep precipices, and of the absence of parapets. In a narrow cutting of the rock through which the road is carried at its highest point of elevation, a white marble tablet is fixed, at the height of six or seven feet above the ground, and on it is the following inscription:

Dernière pensée d'un Corse, mourant à 2000 lieues de sa patrie—
'Ecrivez à nos compatriotes d'ouvrir une route de Pino à Sainte Lucie-sous-Seneque.
Si l'argent venait à manquer, quelqu'un y pourvoira.'
23 Decembre, 1846.[1]

A dying thought, it seems to me, better worth commemoration than many less unselfish which it has been considered right to preserve.

A few steps beyond this cutting you come on the wide expanse of the sea to the west of Corsica, and I should have liked much to have followed the descending road to Pino and other villages, on this side of Cap Corse, especially to Pino, having an introductory letter to M. Piccioni the Maire of Bastia, who resides there; but of this time would not allow, and I regret extremely to be able to see so little of this Cape, one of the most interesting parts of the island.

From the top of the ascent I now send back Domenico and the trap, and following the footpath which leads up from immediately above the tablet rock, through aromatic *maquis*, to the old Capuchin convent, I continue to mount the path, here broken and narrow, to the tower, so-called, of Seneca. But after toiling a good way up I abandon the pilgrimage, because a thick mist covers the sea, and not a symptom of the shores of Italy can be discovered; the coast of Cap Corse is on this side thoroughly wild and rugged, but does not seem to me to possess any particular interest; moreover, I am disinclined to encounter any extra fatigue. The latter part of the climb to this old tower—so G. informs me, who went to the top—is very steep and difficult. The building itself, though of early date, does not appear to have anything of Roman

[1] 'Last thought of a Corsican, dying at a distance of 2,000 leagues from his country—"Write to our compatriots to open a road from Pino to St. Lucie-sous-Seneque. If money should be wanting, somebody will provide it." 23 December, 1846.' This modest tablet, I hear, was placed where it now stands by M. Piccioni, the present Maire of Bastia, and relates, I am told, to his father, Signor Piccioni, of St. Thomas's in the West Indies.—E.L.

times in its composition; rather it has been erected by the Pisans, or by the Signori di Mare, who ruled this part of the island about the tenth century. This theory, however, is treason in the estimation of the good people of Luri, who firmly adhere to their opinion that Seneca, the philosopher, was shut up in it. '*My* father,' said one of the inhabitants of the valley to me, 'told me that this was told to him by *his* father, and back from father to son for eighteen centuries; you see, therefore, that the story cannot be otherwise than true'—a position I did not attempt to combat. What is more to the purpose, so far as a painter is concerned, is that this rock and tower of Seneca are most picturesque; thick groups of ilex grow at the base of the pinnacle, and all the upper part of it is a bright bare rock.

From the very forlorn and ill-kept garden of the Capuchin convent there are beautiful views from the valley; but still more so are those from points a little below and beyond the monastery. There is something peculiarly finished and delicate in the succession of slope after slope, all clothed in green, spreading away gradually and more faintly, and diminishing into aerial distance, till the picture is closed by the sea, with Elba, floating as it were—so pale and indistinct is the sea-line—in the filmy atmosphere above it, like Gulliver's island of Laputa.

Walking down the hill, I am hailed by someone who is superintending the mending of part of the road, and the agreeable Maire of Luri, M. Tommei, joins me. It would have been a pleasure to have accepted his friendly invitation to visit him at Poggio in this charming valley, and to have explored it more thoroughly with one who knows it so well. M. Tommei thinks that the old Lurinum stood below the village of Mercurie, and he points out to me some distant old towers (not, however, to my thinking) of Roman fabrication, which he believes to mark its limits. As we arrived at his village, the Maire presses me to have some refreshment at his house, but when I tell him I dare not lose a minute of working time, now that the sun is so rapidly mounting, and that the great heat and absence of shadow in the valley would soon stop my morning's labours, he leaves me with great good breeding to my own devices.

These consisted in hard work to get such drawings as may recall as much as possible the dense vegetation of this lovely valley, and in returning higher up the road to make some fresh memoranda, a task as irksome, now that I have to look east to a dazzling sun, as that of my western drawing was yesterday evening. My foreground might at least have been embellished by the largest snake I have seen in the island, and, truth to say, it is one of five I have seen in Luri, and of these three were dead, so that it is plain their reputed harmlessness brings them no immunity from persecution.

After this there only remains the completion of drawings commenced yesterday; and by ten-thirty I returned to Mdme Cervoni's breakfast, which, today, in its excellent stewed fowl and ivory-white broccio, shows greater research than on the first essay. The Maire and the village doctor came in afterwards; and the landlord brings samples of Cap Corse vintage; a conversazione prolongs itself till Flora and Company are ready, and I leave these plain and friendly people and the happy valley with regret. Before starting I make inquiries as to the road in the Balagna near the Ponte dell' Asco, Miss C. having very kindly written to me at Bastia warning me that the bridge has been carried away by the river; the doctor says that from Belgodere there is a road to Moltifao and thence to Corte without the necessity of passing the Asco at the broken bridge, but my host and the Maire doubt if that way be practicable for my carriage, light one though it be, and advise me to ascertain distinctly well at Belgodere whether it will not be better for me to return to Bastia, and thence to Corte—a caution to which, after the Bastelica incident of May 3rd, I am inclined favourably to listen.

At 2 P.M. I leave Piazza di Luri, and passing through the groves of aged white and grey-armed olives, and the rich abundance of fig, lemon, and walnut, soon arrive at the Marina of Sta. Severa by the sea. Far beyond my expectations have been the interest and beauty of the valley of Luri, and long shall I remember its pleasant and industrious people, its quiet and shady gardens and woody hill slopes, and its lofty traditional beacon tower, with its tales of the Roman philosopher.

Very beautiful are some of the mouths of the little valleys of Cap Corse on such a day as this, the pure emerald green water close inshore rippling over the milk-white sand; the mountains south of Bastia pearl clear on the horizon, and looking seaward—'blue were the waters, blue the sky'—to the hill of island Elba on the line between them. The coast road—red-legged partridges now and then trot briskly across it—is accomplished as far as Brando, where again I reject Domenico's suggestion that the Grotto should be seen, and shortly afterwards, sending on the trap, I pass an hour, spite of the great heat, in making a drawing of the white city on its promontory, seen between graceful olives bending over the sea. By six-thirty I have walked on to Bastia. Alas for the exclusive and evanescent moufflon! After having resided here a week, he has gone back to his home at Serraggio.

CHAPTER X

May 27

6 A.M.—Off from the Hotel de France, a very fair inn, with a good cook and very obliging master.

The road to la Balagna—the two divisions of which, upper and lower, I have just four days to 'do'—climbs the steep hill immediately behind Bastia as soon as you leave it, and zigzags among villas and fruit gardens, with a view of the city ever at your feet, and more and more of a bird's-eye nature as you go slowly up the stiff ascent. In many of the gardens I remark a profusion of tall white lilies; cypresses, too, which are not common in Corsica; and, for the first time in the island, Japan medlars.

Towards the south, the plain of Mariana and the unhealthy marsh and lake of Biguglia are spread out as if in an unrolled map; no breeze is stirring, and looking eastward there is not a single ruffle or ripple on the calm water from shore to horizon. So delicately smooth is it, as perfectly to resemble the palest blue-grey satin, with a broad and lovely shimmer of light eastward of Elba—

A light upon the shining sea.

Higher up, city and cultivation left behind, the now well-known Corsican world of cystus and *maquis* commences, with here and there groups of ilex and grey rocks draped with wild vine, honeysuckle, and purple vetch, with a wondrous affluence of vegetable beauty. Still the road—a capital Route Impériale—ascends, and at 7 A.M. and onwards the Casinca hills begin to be hidden by the nearer Nebbio range of rounded green heights; at eight there is a space of level road and a good fountain, and soon afterwards the top of the *bocca* or pass is reached at, I think, about the eleventh kilometre from Bastia. Beyond this all eastern Corsica wholly disappears, and you look down on the Gulf of St. Florent on the north coast of the island, and on a new world of mountains—mountains are never wanting in Corsican landscape; and nowhere, except in the eastern plain of Aleria and near Bonifacio on the

CALVI

AVADESSA

west, has the lover of any other kind of view the faintest chance of being gratified.

The descent to the shore is in steep zigzags, but at every turn of the road the scenery becomes more interesting, from the richness of olive growth—the trees now loaded with blossom—and other fruit trees, and from the gradually widening prospect of 'mountain and of cape' northward to Cap Corse, along the south-west corner of which the road to St. Florent in this upper part of its course may be said to be traced. Three or four villages, the most conspicuous of which is Patrimonio, are in sight, among slopes of green and olives in this cheerful landscape.

9 A.M.—At the seventeenth kilometre from Bastia, the road being now nearly level with the shore and passing through a broad green vale and scattered olives, turns westward to the mountains which here descend to the sea, leaving only a narrow pass through a rocky screen—the natural boundary on this side of the once warlike canton of Nebbio. This pass of picturesquely overhanging rocks, with immense hollows or caves below them, is very fine; the dark openings of their gloomy recesses are perfectly fitted for backgrounds of 'brigand subjects' and remind me of the great caverns near Eleutheropolis on the road from Gaza to Jerusalem, and by their colour and striped surface, of several similar grottoes near Corpo di Cava of Naples. In face of these caves—where the oleander grows abundantly by a slow streamlet—I halt to draw until ten, and then drive on to St. Florent, which is but a short way beyond this striking rock barrier.

The town of St. Florent appears even smaller than I expected, considering how important a part it has always played in Corsican history, and looks almost too tiny (it has but 750 inhabitants) to have had any history at all. Its one short and narrow street leads to a little piazza, where there is a little country inn—already favourably known to me by Miss C.'s report—and quite delightful for cleanliness and comfort; this is the Hotel des Passageurs, kept by Pietro Giuseppe Donzella, and, like other inns I have had occasion to mention, is a most strange contrast for its excellence to those in some of the larger towns.

A short glance at St. Florent, which stands quite at the water's edge, and is backed by what may be called fortified heights, though of no great elevation, shows me that whatever work there may be for the pencil here will all lie in the direction of the farther side of the gulf, and that the one day I have allotted for this part of the island will abundantly suffice for all I required. M. Donzella provides at noon a capital breakfast; his inn contains several rooms besides those allotted to me, all clean and decent, the walls newly whitewashed, and profusely hung with little prints, several of them views of Naples, Vesuvius, etc.

Meanwhile this small place has been, since my arrival, a prey to amazement and curiosity, by reason of a war steamer which has suddenly appeared, and having steamed as far as nearly opposite St. Florent, has gone back and disappeared behind the point on the west side of the gulf, making no sign. But at noon she returns, in company with the squadron of French ironclads, which in all the fullness of power and ugliness, are ranged opposite the town, and boats soon coming off, these events communicate to St. Florent as much agitation and life as it is perhaps capable of receiving.

It was 2 P.M. before I went out to draw; the heat was great, and the environs of St. Florent shadeless. A more compact little gulf can hardly be imagined than this, nor one more tranquilly shut out from the world; formerly the capital of the Nebbio district, it can only be approached by sea, or by crossing mountain passes; and on realising its position, the old conditions of its existence, when ironclads and high roads were unknown, can easily be understood—days when the Bishops of Nebbio used to read mass sword in hand. And were anyone desirous of living a life of great retirement and quiet (barring the near and head-splitting sound of church bells), St. Florent might be well recommended as a fit place, especially that its little hotel is so good—always supposing that the winter climate is a pleasant one, about which I have my doubts, as this side of the gulf is not a little exposed to the north-west winds.

A feeling of extreme loneliness pervades the neighbourhood of the town; extensive shallows teeming with myriads of fish, and wide marshes communicate a desolate air to the place, though much of the marshy ground has been drained of late years. The ugly iron ships alone break the spell of solitude which seems to hang over sea and land; excepting that below the eastern hills is a hamlet and an ancient church, formerly the Cathedral of Nebbio, which I had intended, but had not time to visit. Of course (see rules of destiny, page 177), the only possible spot whence it was practicable to make a drawing of the town and gulf was on a roastingly bare slope of tilled ground, which I contemplated with dread, although preparing to sacrifice myself to an hour's broiling; but on arriving there, I found the Suliot had placed my folio and seat high up below a single lentisk (or schinos) tree of great size, which for the sake of its shade was worth a stiff climb to reach over some rocks—G. meanwhile, who, remembering how Admiral Yelverton at Malta used to take his ironclads to fire at the rock of Silsifla, continually pretends to forbode that the French admiral may suddenly happen to order this big lentisk tree to become the mark for all his squadron to shoot at. No such calamity, however, occurs, and I am able to complete my drawing of a place singularly full of individual character and beauty.

At 5 P.M., returning towards the town, I work again near it; the houses of St. Florent are not à la domino-warehouse, but are aged, irregular, picturesquely grey, and discoloured, and many beautiful little bits may be gathered on the edges of the tiny city, reflected clearly in the water from which it rises.

At the Hotel des Passageurs, lobster-eating and other festivities are being carried out on a large scale by the sailors of the squadron; but though the house is quite full, that does not prevent M. Donzella giving me a good dinner of soup and stewed veal, pease, cutlets, and olives, cream-cheese (*broccio* is out of season or does not exist hereabouts), and the Chablis-like wine of these parts, as good as the cookery. My host, who is so like a Neapolitan in dialect and manner that, coupled with the many views of Vesuvius in his rooms, I made sure of his being so, is, on the contrary, so completely a Corsican, that he has never been as far as Calvi, or even out of the Nebbio farther than Ile Rousse, of which he says, '*C'est plus belle que Calvi, mais à Calvi il y a plus de seigneurie*—Ile Rousse is prettier, but Calvi more *genteel*.'

My sleeping-room looks out on the sea, now 'a sheet of summer glass', with the line of great ships dark against the last gleaming of the pale western sky. So clean is this house that for a second time in this journey I shall try the hotel bed instead of my own. The past day has been a thoroughly pleasant one, and now there remain but nine more of Corsican wanderings.

MAY 28

There is little wisdom in trying new beds if you can avoid doing so; this one is perfectly clean, as was that of Luri, but each had its peculiarities, arising from some springs or wires of its inner constitution, which led it to make noises of the most surprising and unexpected kind; it was impossible to prepare the mind sufficiently for the sudden sounds which occurred even on your moving your head, far more when it was a question of turning round. At Luri a spring in the mattress was loose, and at times made a most remarkable humming; while in the present instance lengthened and mouse-like squeakinesses come from some incoherence of the irons; as the invalid says in Wilkie Collins's *Woman in White*, 'Take it away, something about it creaks; take it away!' and henceforth, therefore, I forsake not the old camp folding-bed. For all that, I must record that a nicer little inn, with more obliging owner and better fare, it would be hard to fall in with, in whatever part of the world you may travel, than the Hotel des Passageurs, at St. Florent.

At sunrise the gulf resounds with a reveille of bugles, and a single gun from the eight ironclads: the squadron goes to Bastia today. At 5.30 A.M. I set off to Ile Rousse with Flora and Company; the first part of the day's journey is to wind round and across the sides of Monte Ruva, the spurs of which form the western side of the Gulf of St. Florent, and separate Nebbio from Balagna. We leave on the left the road to Oletta, by the direction of the only human being in sight, an old woman whom Domenico, with scrupulous politeness, addresses as 'Madame', and then leaving the coast, ascend the hill by what the landlord at St. Florent calls a *salituccia*, along a broad Route Impériale. The view of the gulf and the little city are very beautiful from here; an extremely simple prospect— St. Florent and the whole of Cap Corse, unbroken by detail, like a single piece of opal, lie reflected in the calm transparent bay, and this view, spite of the dazzling opposite sun, claims a halt for drawing.

6.15 A.M.—For some way onward the ascent overlooks portions of the inner land of Nebbio—rounded mountainous distances and a good deal of cultivation; then, threading a lonely and narrow pass by the side of a ravine thickly clothed with underwood, the road leads along tracts of wild country, where once more cystus and asphodel still in bloom, isolated granite rocks and wild olive, are the characteristics of the scenery, and a feeling that one is in a wild unpeopled part of the world prevails, till at 7 A.M. a landscape of more cheerful character is approached, looking towards the St. Florent gulf, with beautiful views of Cap Corse, beyond slopes of pastures and innumerable olives down to the sea. This scenery, charming in colour and varied in outline, is greatly like that about Girgenti in Sicily, and to get some memorandum of it, a halt is ordered till seven forty-five.

Here and there, though seldom, a wayside house is passed, and for another hour wild *maquis* and rock are the only ingredients in the landscape, as the road, gradually ascending, skirts a vast and savage hollow or amphitheatre, walled in on the south by lofty bare rocks. This rugged scenery, without culture or inhabitants, continues till about 9 A.M., when the top of the ascent is reached and the views east towards the Nebbio and the long line of Cap Corse are exchanged for a truly magnificent panorama of snowy mountains, the great heights above the Balagna and the district of Calvi.

From this point the road rapidly descends in zigzags to the foot of the hills which divide Nebbio and Balagna, and in half an hour the small plain through which the stream of the Ostricone flows is reached, and here, at nine-thirty, after passing a few more scattered houses, is the midday halt to be made. Neither for horse or man, for landscape or for shade, is this a favourable spot; there is a fountain close by, but it is dry; a very meagre olive gives but little shelter from the great heat, and even that little is not wanted long, because a colony of ants make the ground below it an undesirable place of repose. On all sides there is a total lack of pretty landscape, and only a few birds give any interest to the locality by their voices, the quit-quit-quit of quails in the corn-field near, the turtle dove's note, and that of the cuckoo. Breakfast, therefore, is, on the whole, uncomfortable, and in half an hour after noon the journey towards Ile Rousse is gladly resumed.

In passing along this northern coast of Corsica, how clearly once more is the history of the island commented on and explained by these distinct natural divisions!—this district of Balagna is as much cut off from Nebbio as Spain from France, or Switzerland from Italy, by mountain ranges. The road, now comparatively level (with good parapets, as, indeed, there have been through all today's journey), leads close along the shore, and wonderfully lovely is the pale blue, merging into green of the sea below—moveless, oily-calm lengths of bright sapphire, traced on the space of far dark blue—'Cobalt,' says the practical artist, 'with pale passages sponged or washed out, or dragged light with a half-wet brush.' And after passing increasing cultivation, especially of larger and more numerous olive grounds, and more long points—I had fancied this part of Corsica might be rounded, but there is only the long eastern plain in all this island that is not beset by points—Ile Rousse is seen afar off, low down at the very edge of the sea on a slender rocky promontory. Arriving nearer to the town, I send on Flora and Company, and at two stop to draw what might well be called Paoliopolis, for the place owes its creation to General Paoli and hardly existed before 1760.

At 3 P.M. I make a drawing on the beach—whence the town, though not in itself possessing any beauty of detail, combines on the whole very picturesquely with its rocky harbour, and the foreground of masses of black granite scattered on the white sandy beach; the duties of the day, also, are varied by a pleasant bathe, for it is not often that hard white sand, gleaming below clear and not too deep water, presents so favourable an opportunity to anyone who is ignorant of swimming. Then onward to the town.

Ile Rousse possesses several large and substantial houses, especially some in the outskirts, near a piazza where there are some fountains—one ornamented with a bust of Paoli. There is a colonnade-bordered market-place, and a broad, well-paved street, and altogether the little town shows more activity and importance than I had been aware existed in Balagna, except in Calvi. The country immediately in the neighbourhood is full of olive slopes—

——realms of upland prodigal of oil,
And hoary to the wind—

and on the hills inland are many villages, Monticelli, Santa Reparata, etc., giving much life to the landscape, which is completed by a glorious serrated snow-topped mountain range far above all. A painter lingering some time at Ile Rousse would find that many delightful excursions might be made to the hills on the south of it, but none such are practicable for me, the limited time now at my disposal obliging me to adhere to the coast road.

So I ramble through the town and on to the pier, beyond which there are works in progress connected with a small fort—for there is a little garrison at Ile Rousse—but finding no work to do in the city of Pasquale Paoli, I go to the Hotel de Giovanni, to which the landlord at St. Florent had directed me. The inn is large, and in an airy situation, and the rooms are clean, though not as much so as at the last place; as for the people, it is the same thing everywhere—simple in manner and thoroughly obliging; anxious to please the traveller, yet free from compliment and servility.

At six-thirty dinner was ready, served by a brisk damsel of no pretensions to beauty, but with a look of *espièglerie* and intelligence; always she held a flower in her mouth; at the beginning of dinner it was a rose, latterly a pink. She waited also at a table where seven or eight Continentals—employés—were dining. The dinner was good and some Balagna cherries and cheese excellent.

Later, when the damsel—who greatly resembled a lady on a Japanese teacup—brought some coffee, I said, 'May I venture to ask, without offence, why you continually carry a flower in your mouth?' 'And,' retorted the Japanese, 'may I venture to ask, without offence, why you, a stranger, inquire about matters which are not your affairs, but mine?' '*Perdoni*', said I, 'do not be angry; I only had an idea that there might be a meaning in your doing so.' Quoth she, '*Che cosa potrebbe mai significare?*—What could it possibly mean?' 'I thought,' said I, humbly, 'it might mean you were not to be spoken to; for how, with a flower in your mouth, could you answer?' Whereat the Corsican gravity gave way, and the hotel resounded with long peals of laughter from the Japanese.

MAY 29

5.30 A.M.—Flora and Company are ready to start from the Hotel de Giovanni, which will be remembered as very comfortable; not only, however, are the high mountains clouded, but some rain falls, and a wet day is threatened. Ile Rousse has a look of being larger than it need be for its population—its Piazza is grass-grown in parts, and the houses on its outskirts are scattered about rather vaguely; yet it is said to be a

215

flourishing and increasing place. The outlines of the hills in its neighbourhood are varied and pleasing, while the long lines of Cap Corse
and the hills forming the western side of the Gulf of St. Florent, shut
in the sea like a lake; and did it possess any buildings of a shapely form, a
pretty picture might be made of Ile Rousse from the high ground to the
west of it.

The road to Calvi runs coastwise along hill-sides entirely covered
with corn and olives—these last are in thick groves, large and full trees
loaded with bloom, down to the sea-shore; great masses of grey granite
cropping out of the soil here and there. The scenery is full of beauty,
even on a day so gloomy as this continues to be; Corbara and other
villages are seen on the hills; and when the clouds are propitious,
snow peeps out on the higher mountains; everywhere there is a richness of cultivation exceptional in Corsica.

About the seventh kilometre from Ile Rousse is a small bay, on the
shore of which stands a town or village almost all in ruins; fallen and
falling walls, and roofless houses, make the few buildings which are still
habitable—perhaps a score or two in number—more melancholy by
contrast. This sad place, which has an air of having seen better days, is
indeed no other than Algayola, a town of importance under the rule of
the Genoese, but deserted towards the end of the last century, owing
chiefly to the rise of Ile Rousse, and to the fact that Calvi, during the
wars of the patriot party, was a better place of refuge. Rain prevented
my making as complete a drawing as I could have wished of the now
forlorn but picturesque condition of Algayola.

Fortunately for me, after some heavy showers, the weather became
brilliant once more, in good time to array in its fullest beauty what is
doubtless one of the finest portions of Corsican scenery, and not a little
Sicilian in character, the drive from the ruined and dreary Algayola to
Calvi, the long cape and lighthouse near which are now visible. A
succession of pictures of exquisite interest delights the eye as the road
passes along new basins or crescents at the foot of high hills, bare at
their tops, then terraced into corn-fields all the way down from those
rocky heights to the shore; the grain all ripe, and the fields full of busy
reapers, dotted with grand old olive trees, standing, not in continuous
groves, but singly, or in massive and picturesque groups, some of the
trees being quite the finest I have seen in the island. Farther on a ruined

castle crowns one of the highest points, as you continue to drive through this beautiful scenery, with the wide sea ever on your right hand, until after leaving the coast by an ascent of short duration, the road comes suddenly in full view of the bay of Calvi, that town and citadel on its farther side shining out like a gem above the purple water, by the side of a plain running up to the foot of magnificent mountain ranges, some of them the highest in Corsica. Assuredly the Genoese were wise to cling so long and so fondly to this, as it seems to me, fairest part of the island.

Perhaps even the landscape becomes still finer as you turn the sharp corner of the high point you have been ascending (about the tenth kilometre from Calvi), and come down towards the large valleys, which from the coast stretch away to Calenzana and the base of Monte Cinto and the great central Corsican Alps. Few more striking and beautiful places can be seen than Lumio, close below which the road now runs—a large village with white and brown flat-topped houses, very like those of Bethlehem or other places in Palestine, except in their wanting domes—and buried among olive trees such as I have hardly seen out of Corfu. Below Lumio are groves of cork and phyllarea, cactus in great quantity, and an inexhaustibly profuse vegetation, of which it is difficult to give an idea, filling up every corner and slope not already cultivated, till lower down is a spread of ripe and broad corn-fields, with here and there a flat-topped house, just like those in the 'country' of Malta round Valetta, or sometimes surrounded by a walled courtyard, resembling those round road-side khans in Albania.

10.30 A.M.—From the bottom of the hill—I had sent on Flora and Company to wait till I had done drawing at Lumio—the drive is less interesting. The road crosses the Calenzana River, a broad torrent, and later a still larger river-bed, half lost in the tract of marshy ground near the sea, which, whether or not its creation was the direct result of the imprudent bishop's conduct,[1] is very pernicious to the atmosphere of his diocese of Calvi. The approach to that Genoese stronghold is very

[1] This refers to the Bishop of Sagona, then resident at Calvi; a popular tradition relates that he was led astray by the fascinations of a young girl, who teased the prelate to place the episcopal ring on her finger, but at the moment when the reverend man gave way to her entreaty the ring rolled away and was found no more. On the next morning the Bishop returned to search for the ring, but the vineyard had sunk in the earth and in its place was a marsh. According to M. Valery, there is evidence that vines were formerly grown on this marshy ground.

fine; the rock on which the citadel stands, with the chief part of the city, and the cathedral, together with a church and a line of houses, close to the edge of the sea, are all reflected in the bay, and at a distance the whole has an imposing effect. On approaching nearer, however, you soon perceive that the present condition of Calvi is nowise in harmony with the proud fortress above it, and you are struck with the thinly peopled village-like nature of the place, and the feeling of loneliness haunting the formidable heights and forts, whose history is concluded, and is only that of the past; for the beauty of Calvi is that of decay, and its prosperity is departed, though few places are finer in situation, or would make a more beautiful picture.

11 A.M.—I go to the Hotel de la Marina, the best here; it stands on the sea side of the single street leading up to the citadel. The civil, but rather mournful proprietors, made their tolerably clean and very spacious rooms pleasant by that courtesy and active wish to oblige so universally met with—a repetition monotonous, but just and neces-sary—throughout Corsica. A very good breakfast of fresh fish, lobster, and macaroni, is served before noon, although the landlord apologises for the difficulty of getting what is wanted for travellers who come without warning; few people, indeed, come to this out-of-the-way place—which is a *cul de sac*, and beyond it no road leads—except those on business connected with Government, for Calvi still enjoys the honour of being a Sous-préfecture.

This morning's drive has been one of great interest, and full of novelty; the Balagna has always had the reputation of being the garden of Corsica, and, indeed, the completely cultivated look of this district contrasts greatly with that of other parts of the island. The upper Balagna, through which I must pass tomorrow on my way back to Corte, is said to be even more remarkable for beauty, and Miss C. describes it, in some notes she has sent me, as one long succession of pictures. Of the road through it, M. Francesco Orsoni, the landlord of the Hotel de la Marina, who is very intelligent and communicative, gives me informa-tion which is valuable, as Domenico does not know the distances. From Lumio (ten kilometres from here) to Muro, the half-way halt for the day's journey, are twelve kilometres, and beyond that twenty-two more to Belgodere; at the latter place he names the *locanda* of a Mdme Saëtta as the only lodging he knows of. From Belgodere to Ponte della Leccia are thirty-six kilometres, and on to Corte twenty-four more—a longer journey than that of tomorrow, but, excepting an hour or two of ascent from Belgodere to Sta. Columbana, the whole is downhill; by all which it is clear that I can carry out my plans pretty exactly, provided there be no delay at the broken bridge over the Asco. M. Orsoni tells me that year by year this city—Calvi—becomes more deserted; even the villagers from places close by do not resort to it, as they are more sure to dispose of their produce either by exchange, or for money, at Ile Rousse, and flock thither accordingly.

After noon it rained pretty heavily until between three and four, when I was able to make drawings of the grand and picturesque fortress town from the rocks above it; from immediately behind the town the noble mountain-range beyond the bay forms a magnificent background, and all the scene is characterised by a wild and lonely splendour that is extremely impressive—earth and sea, once, in the days of republican Genoa, so crowded and noisy, now by comparison so desolate and tenantless. The citadel—its walls of an even pallid grey tone of colour— stands beautifully forward in vivid light from the screen of mountains, just now almost black under piles of thunder-cloud, and I doubt if many finer subjects of the sort can be seen. Later, I draw on the opposite side of the town until warned off by the chill from stagnant ditches and low frog-frequented pools below flourishing tamarisk, when I go up to the citadel; the street leading to it is cleanly kept and well paved, and had it not been so late in the day I could well have liked to see the upper part of the city, beyond the gate over which the celebrated inscription—

CIVITAS CALVI

SEMPER FIDELIS—[1]

still remains.

I made little progress up the steep narrow lanes between the fortress walls, for the heat of the day and climbing about the rocks had pretty well tired me, and I soon returned to the hotel, the sounds of a piano-

[1] Calvi was besieged three times in the sixteenth century, and in each case successfully held out. The inscription commemorates these events. When, in 1794, the French Republican General Casabianca surrendered to Admiral Hood, it was one of the articles of capitulation that the old inscription above the gate should not be touched.

forte and the cry of a peacock being—for I saw no living creature—my only memories connected with life in upper Calvi.

It is strange how the proprietors of these inns, who appear to have no regular customers, are able to provide so well as they do for chance comers. Yet the dinner at the Hotel de la Marina admitted of no complaint, for there was good soup, preceding a dish of lamprey, followed by boiled meat and potatoes, steaks, and a lobster salad, a pudding, cheese, and cherries.

Late in the evening the storm-clouds pass away, and the mountains on the other side of the bay become clear; they are very majestic, though more wall-like and less interesting than when partly hidden by mysterious cloud.

CHAPTER XI

MAY 30

4 A.M.—A fine day is presaged by the clear line of mountain standing out, purple and dark, with silver-snow outline against the sky; the good people of the Hotel de la Marina, whose charges are as moderate as their fare is good, make no difficulty in getting coffee for me by sunrise, and thus I can obtain some more memoranda of this *Ultima Thule* of Corsica before starting. The stately mournfulness of the forsaken Calvi cannot easily be forgotten by a painter who has seen it; but, however good for the pencil, I cannot suppose it, from its unsheltered position, and from its marshy vicinities, pleasant as a residence, at any rate in summer.

At five-thirty Flora and Company pick me up, and we proceed; her master, Domenico, whistling, in harmony with the scenery, a dismal minor air. Soon, the Bishop's vineyard and the unhealthy flat ground are left behind by the fast-trotting ponies, and then, from the dark olive plantations below the lofty Lumio, I walk up slowly to the top of the hill, unwilling to lose anything of the beautiful landscape its ascent and summit command.

A little way beyond Lumio the road divides, and the lower, by which I came, is exchanged for that to the right, leading to la haute Balagne; gradually ascending, it skirts at a great height the large Basin or amphitheatre, the streams from which unite in one running into the sea half-way between Ile Rousse and the Nebbio hills, near Torre Losari; towering granite rocks form a wall to the right; while on the left are terraces of corn and olive trees down to the sea, and at intervals a flat-roofed box-like house, à-la-Maltese, stands in the expanse of ripening grain.

Turning more inland, and advancing beyond the first spurs of hill— from which you see Corbara, Aregno, and Sant' Antonino on your left— the great semicircle or principal Basin of this beautiful canton is entered, and at once you become aware that those who visit Corsica without going through upper Balagna remain ignorant of one of its finest divisions. For the next hour and a half's drive (as far as Muro, or Murato, at the twenty-first kilometre from Calvi, and half-way thence to Belgodere) no description can exaggerate the beauty of this remarkable tract of mountain background and deep valley, which, for richness of foreground, cheerful fertility, and elegance of distance, may compete with most Italian landscapes.

On all the more elevated parts of the district, below the topmost wooded heights and snow-capped mountains, stand numerous villages (there are thirty-six communes in all), and the form of this great semi-circular theatre—at the upper edge of which, as it were, these hamlets stand—allows nearly all of them to be seen at one time; most, unlike the generality of Corsican villages, possess extremely picturesque and tall campanili, and often there are detached chapels away from the hamlets, recalling somewhat of the grace of those in southern Italy. Each of these *paesi* is placed amid a profusion of wood and garden, and below them the hill-side—entirely cultivated in every part—slopes down more or less steeply from rock, oak, chestnut, olive, fig tree, and cactus, to a small plain that stretches away to the hills of the Nebbio and the sea. Beyond all this the landscape (really resembling many of Claude's) is finished by the blue sea to the east of Ile Rousse, and by the gulf of St. Florent hills, and the long line of Cap Corse delicately traced on the farthest horizon.

There is a life and cheeriness, too, in this canton that well harmonises with the brilliant and plentiful look of the landscape; many peasants are met—the women as usual not riding sidewise—on finer mules than I have yet seen in the island; and now and then some *signori* with tall black hats, which, for their shiny newness of look, might have come this very morning straight from Lincoln and Bennett's. And besides every other charm of this beautiful Balagna, there are those of never-failing civility and complete security.

Lavatoggio, Cattari, Avapessa—still new villages are passed, and still the eye delights in fresh and enchanting views; here you pause to look at a particularly graceful hamlet with its tall church spire and cluster of brown flat-roofed houses; a little way on you are arrested by park-like tracts of oak and corn-fields, dipping down to a broad plain-like flat edged with Ithome-like hills and promontories, with interlacings of cultivated levels to the shining sea and pale Cap Corse.

Near Muro the midday halt is ordained by Flora and Company, and breakfast hastily dispatched below a friendly oak, to allow of my walking back three kilometres in order to make a difficult drawing of the lovely scene near Avapessa, as well as of one or two more near Muro; for having now seen one side, or wing, so to speak, of this theatre, I have selected these two out of a multitude of almost equally beautiful subjects. Indeed, a theatre is no bad simile as applied to this great basin, by far the most industriously cultivated, the most cheerful and beautiful in all Corsica—the oak woods and the great cliffs above may represent the galleries; and, next in order, the villages, gardens, and terraces stand for tiers of boxes; the flat level of olives and corn for the pit; the sea and remote hills for the stage and scenery.

At one Flora and Company start anew; the village of Muro, at the twenty-second kilometre from Calvi, in a corner of one of the great hollows or recesses formed by a projection of the hill, with its high white campanile and combinations of arches among its houses, would be an elegant subject even on the Amalfi or Positano coast. The road (as usual, excellent) is a regular cornice, running at a great height along the mountain-side, and generally close to the villages, of which there is a succession—frequently hidden till you are close upon them—peeping out of little bays of foliage as you wind round the buttresses or spurs of the lofty heights. Feliceto and Nessa are the next hamlets; Speloncato, Villa, Costa, Occhiatona, are farther on, each with its own characterstic beauty, and forming a continuance of mountain-village scenes, such as can hardly be imagined.

It is two-thirty when, always by a gradual ascent, Belgodere is approached; it is the highest and last of all the communes in this remarkable horse-shoe valley, or rather collection of valleys, which unite in the cultivated level area below. As one looks back to the west from about the thirtieth kilometre from Bastia, there are perhaps the best views of the whole scene; yet it is on a scale so extensive and varied, that it would be very difficult to convey any idea of it with the pencil; separately, the hamlets are full of picturesque beauty, but such morsels would not represent the character of the whole landscape; while the great size of the mountains, together with the tiny proportions the villages bear to them, would prevent it being successfully transferred to paper as a whole.

223

Along this beautiful drive the great variety of foliage and the evidences of industrious labour are the unvarying characteristics of the scenery—here there are finer oaks, there the chestnut grows more abundantly, now the gardens of cherry trees seem to have no end, or the walnut and fig tree hide the houses and walls, and the olive glimmers lightly against the sky or dapples with thick groves the long level of corn that spreads northward to lines of distance rivalling Grecian landscape; anon there are bright streams of water sparkling among the foliage, or broad carpets of fern clothing the sloping hill-sides; extreme richness and fertility are everywhere seen; nor in all this interesting and beautiful canton have I met with a single beggar.

Now that I see Belgodere, which I reach at 3 P.M., I regret not having spent more time in drawing one or two of the villages I passed earlier in the day, for I soon perceive, long before reaching the village, that it contains little or no work for my pencil. Placed quite at the farthest and highest limits of upper Balagna, Belgodere looks down over an immense bird's-eye view of the whole district, wooded and olive-dotted to the shore, but though commanding the most comprehensive prospect of the canton, and one conveying the completest idea of its nature, it is, for all pictorial purposes, nearly impracticable.

Flora and Company had been sent on before, but Domenico coming to meet me, says that the *locanda* Saëtta '*non esiste più*—exists no more', and that two other lodging-houses in Belgodere—a village considerably larger than any hereabouts—are full; there is yet a third, which has two rooms, but on going to inspect them I find them by no means tolerable or to be endured; and as in this instance my going to a private house can involve no loss of time, since there is nothing to do by way of drawing. I resolve to avail myself of an introductory letter given to me by the Préfet to the Maire, M. Malaspina.

From this gentleman a most friendly welcome is forthcoming; with Corsicans—as in days I well knew of old, with Calabrians and Abruzzese —there is very little compliment and much sincerity. 'I am only too glad the inns are full, and that you are thus obliged to give me the plea-sure of receiving you, although it so happens that my family are away for the day, and therefore you will not fare particularly well'—was said gravely and evidently in earnest, as M. Malaspina took me to his house—one of the largest in the place—and told Flora and Company where were his stables.

The first floor is that resided in by the family, and that above it contains what may be called the guest rooms, and which are so well and handsomely fitted up that one seems in Paris. A more perfectly comfortable little bedroom than that allotted to me could not be found, and—for the day has been hot, and the landscape painter far from well— I am glad to get some rest in it till 6 P.M., when I join the Maire and his uncle, both intelligent and gentlemanly men, the latter an elderly person who has passed many years in differents parts of Italy.

Landscape being my main object in coming to this island, I have throughout avoided all arrangements by which delays to my work could be occasioned, and thus have allowed myself to see but little of the Corsicans, a circumstance I in some senses regret, for whenever I have done so, the making their acquaintance has been invariably a source of pleasure, and on the present occasion particularly so. At seven dinner was announced, and we descended to the family dining-room, where were the wife of the Maire's son (he himself is a widower) and his two daughters. I was carried forcibly back to days of Abruzzo travelling by the friendly ways and hospitable anxieties of these amiable people, who live in a plentiful and patriarchal style, and whose dinner, profuse and of excellent quality, gave ample evidence of a well-managed household. They insisted on the Suliot sitting at the same table, spite of his appeal to me, and as the service was limited, I thought it best to acquiesce.

What though there were dishes of hare, roast fowl, creams, and many other good things, only my host the Maire partook of animal food, the rest of the family eating snails or vegetables only, as it was a vigil or fast day; none the less, however, was their attention to their guest unremitting. Their home-made wine was thoroughly good, but they had two other sorts of Corsican vintage; altogether the entertainment was a very pleasant oasis in these days of doubtful *locande*, and well it is for me that M. Géry gave me this introduction. Later, accompanied by the three ladies, who were all unaffected and well bred, we adjourned to the well-furnished drawing-room, to which coffee was brought, and here we talked till nine-thirty, when this kindly family wished me good night.

These people are quite *au fait* regarding all European intelligence; and their remarks on Turkey, Italy, and other subjects, were free from the prejudice and violence so frequently met with in proportion to the ignorance of the speakers. Of their own island they are acquainted with the minutest details of both present and past condition, physical or political; and the wide interest shown upon European and cosmopolitan topics in so remote a mountain district contrasts curiously with the apathy and black ignorance noticeable in many similar positions. There is however, this difference respecting the Corsican's broad intelligence regarding contemporary history: his own island and people have been for so long a time actors in the principal European events, that it is but natural he should become acquainted with facts which are, so to speak, a part of his own interests, whereas to all other countries they are only outside occurrences.

Concerning the bridge of the Asco torrent, M. Jean André Malaspina tells me he has inquired, and finds that though the bridge is not yet repaired, yet the waters of the river having subsided, a carriage can easily ford them.

MAY 31

M. le Maire joins me at sunrise with coffee, and at 5.30 A.M. walks with me a good distance out of the village on my way. Provokingly watchful, my host does not allow me the least chance of conveying a tip to the female domestic, a point not easily attained in such houses. I am sorry to take leave of M. Jean André Malaspina. Nothing could be kinder than the behaviour of these amiable people, to whom a stranger and servant coming thus *all' improviso* might well have been somewhat a cause of difficulty.

A long and steep ascent leads eastward from Belgodere; this, the outpost of Balagna, being the last of its villages but one small hamlet, Palasca; and half an hour having been given to making a last drawing of the 'garden of Corsica', the fertile olive-dotted and yellowing plains soon disappear as the shoulder of the mountain is turned, and the line of blue and green Nebbio hills takes the place of more varied and cheerful scenery. A wild uninhabited space, contrasting strongly with the gay landscape of yesterday is now looked down on as the road winds upwards, and as at this height the heat of the day is not felt, I walk on to the top of the pass, or Bocca di Santa Columbana, reaching it at eight-thirty (at seven and a half kilometres from Belgodere, and fifty and a half from Calvi). Little is there to be remarked on the way up—a road to the right towards the top leads to the forest of Tartagine, to Olmi, and other villages; to the left, far below, is a wide expanse of sea, and a scrap of Ile Rousse and its rocks; and all else, excepting some groups of cattle at a fountain, is a breadth of *maquis*-covered hill-tops.

On the southern side of the Bocca di Santa Columbana, the great snowy summits of the highest mountains near Asco and the Niolo are seen, but their bases are cut off by a range of lower hills, among which a very steep descent, which occupies, at a rattling pace, from 8.30 to 10 A.M., leads southward to Corte, mostly by the stony bed of a nearly dry torrent. Ever and anon above the rounded and cystus-covered sides of this narrowing gorge peer the jagged and snowy Alp tops, but it is not to be denied that this part of the day's journey possesses very slender interest, and the observer is reduced to the contemplation of perverse stray cattle, who on no account will allow the carriage to pass them, but keep ever foolishly running on for miles ahead of the horses; and of the groups, few and far between, of Corsicans on mules, all in black cloth, but all carrying beaming white umbrellas. Here and there this closely shut-in valley is enlivened by a plot of corn, or two or three walnut trees, and at intervals a spread of scarlet-blossomed poppies adds a short-lived gleam of gaiety to the winding dullness of this, the least interesting of any part of Corsica I have seen, and the passage through which is not made more cheerful by Domenico's mournful melody of minor moan-ings, at which, after long continuance, it is clear that only Flora's extreme sense of dignity and what is right prevents her from howling aloud.

It is a relief when the valley opens out and admits some grand moun-tain distance with groups of ilex and lentisk for foreground, and shortly the bridge is reached which should span the torrent that descends from Monte Padro through the valley below Olmi and Castifao; this bridge, though not that of the dreaded Asco River, has also been broken by the heavy winter rains, but a road has been made down to the water—now much lessened, by which Flora and Company pass over. At ten-thirty (seventy-two kilometres from Calvi) is the real difficulty; here the Asco, which descends from Monte Cinto, and is in the rainy season a formidable torrent, has devastated the whole of the valley, and swept

away the greater part of the long bridge built across it. In Corsica, however, these rapid rivers soon exhaust their force, and there is at present
but little water in the river bed, so that while Flora and Company go
down by the temporary road and ford the river, a system of planks
placed at a giddy and uncomfortable height on the broken bridge piers,
enable the foot-passengers to cross it.

Here I remain till 11 A.M., for there are few views of the kind
better worth drawing. Looking up the great valley of Asco, the peaks
and crags of what I suppose to be the summits of Monte Traunato and
Monte Cinto fill the whole of the picture with an array of giant pinnacles, finer in its way than anything I have seen, except Gebel Serbal
from Wadi Es Sheikh, near Mount Sinai. A small bridge over a tributary
stream remains intact, as if to form a foreground with the trees and
lower hills above which the long range of delicately pencilled spires
rise so majestically.

Two more kilometres are passed, and Ponte della Leccia[1] is reached
—a forlorn and dreary-looking cluster of houses by the bridge over the
Golo. Here is the junction of the main road from Ajaccio and Corte to
Bastia with the Routes Forestière from Calvi and the Balagna, and that
from the country about Orezza; and so important is this spot considered
as a centre of communication in the island that it has been more than
once suggested that a city should be founded here. When those plans
are carried out, there may perhaps be better cheer for the passing
traveller than he finds at present, for, in spite of the '*che cosa volege
mangiare?*—what will you have to eat?' asked by the apathetic inmates
of the sorry and very dirty house doing duty for a wayside 'hotel',
nothing but eggs can be obtained, and those eaten with difficulty, on
account of the plague of flies which abounded, owing to the unclean
state of the floors

Nor could much be done in the way of drawing at Ponte della Leccia,
by reason of the high wind blowing; and, indeed, standing as it does in
the centre of gorges below high mountains, the thought humbly presents
itself that the climate of the future city here may not prove of the most
delightful kind. I could make only a few memoranda of the large fine
bridge and of the great flocks of black sheep arriving from the plains on

[1] Ponte della Leccia should have been, had time permitted it, my starting-point
to see the country of Paoli.—E.L.

their way to the high mountain pastures. Somehow, whether it be that the day is overcast and cloudy, or from the great contrast of the scenery here to that of the gay and beautiful Balagna, Ponte della Leccia seems to me the gloomiest place I have visited in Corsica. Nor do the few people about it enliven it—a grave and solemn set, all dressed in black velveteen; their dialect, however, is perfectly easy to understand, and their civility unfailing.

There are intervals when the most enthusiastic tire of travel, and I confess that the two hours I pass at Ponte della Leccia are of such a kind; I am vexed, too, that I have not time to visit Morosaglia and Ponte Nuovo, and other places. And today even the head of the travelling establishment, the little dog Flora, in spite of all her valuable and amiable qualities, is out of favour, for in these unclean places she contracts so large an amount of the only vivacity they possess, in the shape of lively insects, that her propinquity is shunned, to avoid contagion, so that when she enters a room she has to be ejected, an indignity she bears with touching meekness and grace.

2.30 P.M.—Off from Ponte della Leccia; the road running below distant dark-cragged mountains, where stormy effects and gleams of light on snow and granite create many a grand picture, but none of so distinctive a nature as to induce me to halt to make drawings. Many carts, containing great numbers of Italians—Lucchesi as they call them here, on account of their coming chiefly from that part of Italy—are met. These industrious people are returning to Bastia, to embark for Leghorn.

At Ponte Francardo, where the River Golo, which descends here from the Niolo, is left, the road proceeds between a pass of narrow rocks, where a drawing might well have been made had the landscape painter been in an industrious mood; but it was otherwise, and Corte—the approach to it from this side (*see* page 180) is assuredly most majestic— was reached by 4.30 P.M., Domenico driving at a great pace, to have as much leisure as possible for the enjoyment of city life.

On arriving at the little inn I had stayed at during my first visit, I find that the house is full, and as Domenico recommends another, which he says is '*Bello e grande, e ci vanno tutti i alti signori*—Fine and large, and frequented by the greatest persons of Corsica', I go thither, as it is situated at that end of the town from which I have to start tomorrow.

But so disgusting is the room I am shown into that it is not possible to remain in it, and I am at my wits' end, for should I go to the only remaining inn, the Hotel de l'Europe, that also might happen to be full, and then I should have no chance of shelter, for here they would hardly take me in if I returned, and the President, M. Corteggiani, I had already ascertained, was absent from Corte. Fortunately for me, some people at this moment are leaving the hotel, and Giorgio seizing on their room, and giving it a thorough cleaning, it becomes habitable for the few hours I need it. A very tolerable dinner is provided, and the people—let me say what I can of good—are all thoroughly civil.

But oh! for the nice clean little rooms of Evisa, Luri, and St. Florent! or even of Grosseto, Carghese, or Piana! From all these villages the proud city of Corte may well take long and deep lessons of cleanliness and decency.

CHAPTER XII

JUNE 1

AT 5 A.M. I leave Corte—nor can I add with regret—once more. Happy are they for whose noses much suffering is not decreed! but let those whose sense of smell is delicate avoid Corte until it be blessed with better drainage and cleaner habits.

It is a clear morning, and the drive up to the beautiful chestnut woods of Santa Maria di Venaco is delightful. To me this place is one of the most charming as a summer dwelling, of all I have seen in Corsica, excepting parts of Paradise-Balagna; besides its high and open position, it has the advantages of a plentiful supply of water, and of lovely walks among walnut and chestnut groves in every direction. From here I send on Flora and Company to Vivario, where tonight must be passed, intending to walk thither, the distance being but fifteen kilometres.

At Lugo, the first village through which the road passes, there are triumphal arches and flags, and other unexpected indications of excitement, with a large inscription of *Hommage à Mariani*—from all which I learn that the Baron Mariani of Corte is expected here today to visit his estates, and a fête has been promoted in consequence. Inquiring after that very exclusive beast, the transitory moufflon, I hear he is really returned to his mountain home at Serraggio, and on reaching that place at 8 A.M. I proceed to ascertain the dwelling of his moufflonship[1]

[1] Moufflon, or Musmon.

Found in wild and uncultured parts of Greece, Sardinia, Corsica, and in the deserts of Tartary.

Kamschatkans pass the latter part of summer in pursuit of these animals. Sometimes their horns grow two yards long. Ten men can hardly hold one of these Kamschatkan moufflons. Their horns are often so large that foxes shelter themselves in those which fall off by accident.

Moufflon or musmon, animal neither sheep nor goat; hair, no wool; horns like those of a ram; some grow to an amazing size, measuring above two yards long; general colour of hair, reddish brown; found in the uncultivated parts of Greece, Sardinia, Corsica, and Tartary. Form, strong and muscular; fearful of mankind, and when old seldom taken alive. Frequents the highest summits of mountains. The old rams have furious battles with each other.—Bewick's *History of Quadrupeds*.

231

'*L'animale,*' however, as the twenty or thirty youthful Serraggians who collect round me, call him, is even now not easily seen, his master being in the fields, and it was 9 A.M. before his owner came up to the village with the key of his stable, and introduced me to this long-sought-for and respected quadruped. Doubtless he is a magnificent fellow, with a prodigious pair of horns, and he has already lost the savage shyness which marked his disposition when he was first captured at the beginning of last winter, when the snow lay low on the mountains, and he had come down in search of food to the enclosed grounds, into one of which he fell from some rocks, and was captured.

After getting such a sketch of the moufflon as I was able to accomplish by reason of the crowding of intelligent but vexatious villagers, whose natural curiosity, I confess, was well atoned for by their good nature and civility, I go onward down the road as far as the tenth kilometre from Vivario, and there, below huge trees, establish myself for the mid-day halt and breakfast brought from Corte; making studies of cystus flowers—are they not a part of all Corsican foreground?—and writing letters among the shadowed fern, quickly passing the hours away. No fairer resting-place can indeed be found than this—the high arching chestnut trees with the far blue eastern hills seen through them; turf, fern, and cystus all around, a stream of fresh water gurgling close by; and a delightfully sociable blackbird sitting on a rock a little way off, and singing from time to time, for whom the lines—

> Take warning! he that will not sing
> While yon sun prospers in the blue,
> Shall sing for want, ere leaves are new,
> Caught in the frozen palms of Spring—

were never intended.

At Serraggio a 'Madame' had asked me, with loud accents, to visit her 'hotel' for refreshment, but there are many and good reasons for preferring breakfast in the open air to one in the village inns, few of which can be expected to equal those of Evisa and Luri—those, indeed, were rather private lodging-houses than inns at all—here one has fresh air, quiet—excepting the song of blackbirds and nightingales—flowers, and a beautiful prospect; while in those sad little houses you have none of these blessings, but on the contrary, are likely to find noise, flies, and dirt.

The day becomes clouded, and above the mighty heights of Monte Rotondo, on whose sides I am resting, clouds gather, and low growlings of thunder are heard, preluding, perhaps, the ordinary afternoon storm in these parts. And as all at once a blinding flash of lightning comes simultaneously with a peal of crackling thunder, as if fifty pistols had been fired off close to one's ear, warning me that the vicinity of tall chestnut trees is undesirable—to which many of their split and blackened tops bear witness—I move on towards the Ponte del Vecchio. Rain, however, now sets in, and I can only commence a drawing of this magnificent scene, which I thus pass for the second time without securing, before I am obliged to go on towards Vivario, which I reach at 4.15 P.M., after a not very satisfactory day's work. Now that the fêtes of Corte are over, this road is as unfrequented as any; two mounted gendarmes, accompanying two prisoners tied with a long rope, are the only individuals I have seen since I left Serraggio.

The hotel in the little back alley at Vivario, is, as when I came through here on the 20th, quite full, but I get two rooms in an adjoining house. The ladder entrance to the public eating-room at the inn is not prepossessing, nor is the appearance of the room itself without need of a balance of compensation, which some opine to be a universal law of nature. Such there certainly was at the hotel of Vivario, where it came in the form of a very jovial and pleasant landlady and of two surprising daughters, the sudden appearance of whom from an inner chamber was most astonishing. For not only were these two girls of extreme beauty, both in face and figure, but they were dressed in the best Parisian taste, their coiffure arranged with the utmost care, and altogether they were a very unexpected sight in so rude a mountain village; these damsels, however, take no part in the hotel ménage, but only beam forth at occasional intervals.

Of Miss C. the landlady here speaks with the greatest enthusiasm, and adds, '*C'est si remarquable qu'elle soit si gaie, parceque toutes les autres Anglaises qu'on voit sont tristes et froides et superbes*', a general accusation of my countrywomen I very positively oppose as untrue. My hostess, however, it is but just to say, excepts the Hon. Mrs. A. B., who it seems has lately been here, from this sweeping condemnation, and, like all the rest who have seen that lady, goes into raptures about her beauty.

The Ajaccio diligence arrives at 6 P.M., when the conducteur, three

233

or four passengers, myself and man, sit down to dinner, at which there are plenty of fine trout and other food of less good quality—but as the good woman says, '*Siamo in Corsica, in un villaggio*', and at short notice little can be got. While at table the storm-clouds roll away, and the mountains all at once become so perfectly clear that I resolve to go down once more to the Ponte del Vecchio, and, late as it is, to make a third and last trial to draw it. So, sending G. to the lodging for a light folio and a single sheet of paper, the diligence picks me up as I walk on, and rattling quickly down the hill, drops me close to the bridge by 7 P.M., a help forward cheaply paid for by a franc to the conducteur. Here I draw, as rapidly as possible, till seven forty-five: the great snowy summit of Monte Rotondo—if that be it which appears to the left up this wild ravine—the line of crags and dark pine woods all along the centre of the gorge, the immense granite precipices hanging just above the rapid stream, its profound shadow and narrow depths here and there lighted up with gleams and flashes of brightness, make at this hour a sublime piece of mountain scenery. There is also this association with the scene, that General Paoli, after the battle of Ponte Nuovo, took leave of his friends at the bridge here—not the solid structure now existing, but one of wood—previous to embarking at Porto Vecchio for his long exile in England.

It was eight-thirty before I had walked back to Vivario; but the magnificent bridge scene was worth this, and even more trouble.

JUNE 2

This day is to be allotted to forest journeying—by Sorba to Ghisoni, and thence to Marmano. The people of Vivario seem of the true idler stamp, so typical of many Corsican villagers, and so great a contrast to those of Cap Corse and La Balagna. The *roba* has to be brought from the lodging to the Piazza whence Flora and Company are to start; but, though there are some twenty men standing with their hands in their pockets—Domenico says they are all 'landed proprietors'—not one will lend a helping hand. It is, therefore, as late as 5.45 A.M. before we get off; for, with Flora and Company, a long time passes before luggage is properly fastened on; yet, though slow, we are sure, and none has ever come loose or fallen off.

The great mountains Rotondo and d'Oro are perfectly cloudless, the morning delightful. The road for two kilometres is the same as that to Ajaccio by Bocognano; and from the heights up which it is carried there are good views of Vivario, but so extensive and full of detail as to require more time than I dare give at the beginning of a long day's journey. Then a Route Forestière, leading to Ghisoni, turns off from the Ajaccio road, and after three more kilometres, enters the forest of Sorba, which covers the mountain—part, I think, of the great Monte Renoso—on the south of Vivario, and winds with steep and sharp curves, guiltless of parapets, to a great height through the pines, the bocca or summit being at the ninth kilometre from Vivario. Sorba, one of the smallest forests of Corsica, has naturally no pretensions to rank with those I have previously seen as to extent, but is nevertheless remarkable for the great beauty of its splendid foliage and the great size of its cushion-topped trees, and for their picturesque growth among great rocks and precipices. Moreover, through the whole ascent you have Monte d'Oro and Monte Rotondo in full view, forming the very grandest compositions when combined with the depths of pine, at this early hour all in shadow. All the route to Corte, too, as far as Santa Maria di Venaco, is mapped out below your feet.

The steep descent on the other side from the Col di Sorba—the road in such bad condition from the constant passage of heavy timber-cars that I send on Flora and Company to the valley below—is wanting in interest and beauty. High up, one glimpse of the eastern plain (not far from Migliacciara), and of the Etang d'Urbino is seen, and, for a short space, this gives somewhat of a new character to the scenery; but the greater part of the walk down to Ghisoni is through a tract, once all forest, but now in a process of 'exploitation', and completely marred and spoiled. Lower down in the valley—through which, coming from Monte Giovanni (the mountain on whose western face stands Bastelica), the stream of Fiumorbo flows to the sea near Ghisonaccio (*see* page 93) —stands Ghisoni, approached through chestnut woods, and apparently, as one looks down on its roofs, a tolerably large and stirring place; for it is the point to which the pines are brought from the forests both of Marmano and that through which I have just passed, as well as the half-way halt between the Casabianda settlement and Corte; and also it is the nearest place to the branch penal establishment of Marmano, where I intend to pass the night. But, as the midday storm comes on, with pouring rain, just as I reach the Ghisoni 'hotel', I hurry on too quickly to allow of much observation along the latter part of the road before I arrive there. The scenery from the Col de Sorba is, however, of a commonplace character by comparison with much I have seen in the island.

The hotel is a clean, nay, a spruce and tidy *locanda*, the stairs and rooms splendid when contrasted with those of Vivario; the walls and ceilings are painted with landscapes, and groups of fish, game, etc., and there are scarlet curtains to all the windows. As usual, a good dish of trout for breakfast was not wanting.

Having a letter of introduction to M. le Maire of Ghisoni, and being anxious to know something of the distances of tomorrow's journey, I send it to M. Michele Mattei, who is good enough to call, and give me much information, as well as a letter to the doctor residing at Marmano, in case no notice of my coming should have been forwarded by M. Beurville, the directeur at Casabianda. There are five kilometres, says M. Mattei, from the Marmano establishment to the Bocca or Col de Verde at the summit of the forest, and nineteen thence down to Cozzano; to Bagni di Guitera there are seven more, and to Zicavo five out of the main road and five back, so that the whole distance may be safely reckoned as being under forty-five kilometres. The great precipices called the '*Insecca*', of which I have heard so frequently as being some of the most remarkable in Corsica, are as much as eleven kilometres from here on the road to Casabianda, so that although I much wished to see them, all idea of doing so must be given up, as twenty-two extra kilometres would destroy all chance of my getting to Ajaccio on Thursday.

It was nearly 3 P.M. before the violent thunder and rain ceased, and I left the inn of Giorgio Santi, which is one of the cleanest in these parts. Ghisoni is placed among such narrow valleys and high overhanging mountains that it has an air of gloom from whichever side you see it.

The road to Marmano goes up the valley immediately below Monte Renoso, the great snowy lines of which stretch away on the right hand, while on the left towers a remarkable ridge of stupendous precipices, called by the people here Monte Kyrie Eleison, but marked in my map

as Serra del Prato; these rise out of thick woods of ilex, and are some of
the grandest and most noble rocks I have seen. As you proceed, always
ascending, the valley narrows, and at each bend round one of the spurs
of Monte Renoso, you advance amongst scenery of gloomier grandeur,
and at length see the end of the valley of Marmano, and its dense forests
closed in by the wall of Col de Verde, over which lies tomorrow's road.

Eight kilometres from Ghisoni the scenery is exceedingly wild:
woods of chestnut trees of immense size, with oak and ilex, fill up the
hollow of the valley; above these are great rocks and splendid pines, the
narrowing triangle at the head of the gorge being one mass of forest,
except a single small clearing, where a few buildings point out the site
of the summer convict establishment. The pines clothe the lofty heights
to the very summit, and the vast multitude of stems of these gigantic
trees, rising tier above tier in the dark forest, on what seems almost a
perpendicular screen of cliff, have a very striking effect. Beautiful, too,
though in miniature, are the crimson foxgloves that edge and overhang
the precipices, along which the road runs, glowing and gleaming above
the dark abyss below.

By the time I reach the end of this second part of today's journey—
the scenery of which is throughout of a severe and gloomy character—
it is 6 P.M. At the eleventh kilometre from Ghisoni you suddenly come
on a series of barracks, standing on terraces one above another, and
these, which are for the convicts, are the only dwellings in this grim
solitude, the house of the doctor, the pavillon of M. le Directeur, and
some other offices excepted. Here—for I had sent on by Flora and
Company my letter from M. Mattei—the doctor of the establishment,
M. Casanova, comes out to meet me, having already heard from M. le
Directeur at Casabianda that I should be here today.

Dr. Casanova is most polite and hospitable, but as the pavillon
occupied by M. Beureville when here is being enlarged, I am sorry that
I am the cause of putting the worthy doctor and his family to some inconvenience. He and Madame, however, make me and my servant share
their evening meal pleasantly enough, and their small children are an
intelligent and nice little lot.

The arrangements for the night are not so easy; in vain I assure these
good people that my camp-bed is sufficient for me anywhere, and that
my servant would be content with a blanket on the floor. A friendly

quarrel takes place on the subject, and ultimately nothing can prevent their turning out of a small room, or rather closet, and giving it up for my use, the whole family crowding themselves into the remaining two chambers the house contains. There is just space to insert my camp-bed, when put up in one corner, between piles of boxes, groceries, etc., any of which I positively refuse to allow of being moved, and the Suliot occupies a shelf on the other side of the room.

At night the little house is closely barred and watched by the armed guardiani of this prison in a forest.

June 3

A strange and romantic place is the forest penitencier of Marmano; during the winter the number of convicts remaining here is small; but if Valdoniello through months of deep snow be a dreary spot, what must be this remote and solitary place, with no one but condemned criminals as neighbours through long nights of gloom? From half June till October, Marmano is enlivened by the migration from the coast of the whole Casabianda establishment, but at the approach of the cold weather all return to the plain. Meanwhile labour goes on always—gardens are made, pines cut down and cut up, and if the heart of the desert does not sing for joy, at least it resounds with the blows of the hatchet.

At 5.30 A.M. I take leave of the merry and hospitable Dr. Casanova, and walk up the steep zigzags through the forest of Marmano—occasionally visited by Flora to see if I am all safe—to the top of the Col de Verde. The road is carried across and across the face of the great heights which close in the Marmano valley, always among these columnar pine stems—some of them here of extreme size—and in many parts some of the groups of rock and verdure are truly magnificent. Tall beech woods form the upper part of this forest, which, beautiful as it is, is of limited extent compared with those of Aitone or Valdoniello. How beautiful in early morning are these great woods! how deep and solemn are the shadows! how unbroken the silence, except by the cuckoo's note! nor do I see any live thing all the way but the black and orange lizards which here and there cross the good road.

The Col de Verde, or summit of the forest of Marmano, is reached at seven-fifteen (eighty-three kilometres from Ajaccio), and then follows the long descent into the great valley of the River Taravo, which (*see* p. 50) runs below Bicchisano to the gulf of Valinco at Porto Pollo. For five or six kilometres the downward-winding road continues to lead through sublime forest scenes, but about 8 A.M. the last pines of the Col de Verde forest are passed, and the valley becomes wider, opening out into glades of fern and asphodel, with woods of ilex at intervals, and an uninterrupted view of verdure and snow-capped heights as far as eye can reach—scenes of far too vast a character to be reduced or condensed into a picture. Towards the west, the mountains sink down in the direction of Bicchisano, and far away in the centre of this green landscape is a village I suppose to be Cozzano, but since the Col was passed there is no one at hand to give information as I am walking on, ahead of the trap, from curve to curve of this serpent-like road.

The hill-sides become less precipitous and the valley more spacious as I proceed, and at 9 A.M., after descending through beautiful woody scenery to about the sixteenth kilometre, I wait by a roadside house until Flora and Company come up, which at length they do, at a pace so slow that something is evidently wrong. One of the ponies has lost a shoe, and Domenico having left his bag of nails at Vivario orders a halt, and leaving the trap and one pony in the care of myself and G., goes with the other and Flora across the valley to Commanaccie, on a nail-procuring expedition.

While waiting for the driver's return, some cantonniers come and beg me to enter and rest in their little wayside house; these good people do not perceive how much more agreeable it is to sit or lie beneath a chestnut tree contemplating the wide and beautiful landscape than to encounter the disagreeables of a close room; the more so, in the present case, that besides the cantonniers there is a party of charcoal burners, who do not seem to be either of the apathetic, or civil and well-bred nature, so characteristic generally of these islanders, two or three of them having been closely examining the luggage for some time past, and having made themselves not a little disagreeable. Towards ten o'clock, however, Domenico returns, and proceeds to shoe the pony, by no means assisted in his work by the riotous group about him, most of these being 'elevated' by drink, and one of them apparently an idiot. These fellows profess to help my driver by holding up the pony's foot, but in the middle of the shoeing they purposely give it a jerk, and every time the shoe comes off again by this manœuvre they dance round the carriage roaring with drunken laughter; which game goes on in a very irritating fashion, in spite of the cantonniers' interference, so that I fear a serious quarrel may ensue. When Domenico's patience is nearly exhausted by these practical jokes, it is thought better to drive off with the shoe only partly nailed on; a sign of defeat on our part greeted by loud shouts of derision, and especially by the idiot, with the wildest shrieks and gestures. I confess I should not have been pleased to have been obliged to pass the night with the society I have just left; nevertheless, this is the one and only instance, in two months of Corsican touring, of my having received the least molestation, even in the most out-of-the-way places. This vast valley, scantily populated above Guitera and Zicavo, leads only to Ghisoni by the forests of Verde and Marmano, seems very little frequented, and thus far in it I have not seen a single mounted gendarme, who are generally met with in pairs from time to time on all the roads.

At the sixty-sixth kilometre from Ajaccio the road passes through Cozzano, a village of no especial interest; all the way thither from the scene of the horse-shoeing being through a succession of fair landscapes, of beautiful woods, and wide spaces of fern with groups of chestnut, oak, and ilex; and then follows a descent for six more kilometres through more cultivated tracts, till the River Taravo is crossed, and the road to Zicavo is passed on the left; throughout the latter part of this distance the foliage is most delightful, and the scenery about the Taravo bridge might be in the very richest Derbyshire or Devonshire valley; the hills nearer Guitera are to the full as beautifully wooded as those above the Thames at Clifden.

At noon, in the midst of this lovely wood and river scenery, I come to ten or twelve houses by the roadside, one of which is what Domenico has previously described as the '*bellissimo Hôtel de' Bagni di Guitera,*' a rustic but cleanly house, at the back of which are the mineral springs so frequented in summer by invalids from all parts of Corsica. This place is about thirty-two kilometres from Marmano, and twenty-six from Grosseto; Zicavo is twelve distant. I decide therefore on remaining at these baths tonight, the onward road to Grosseto, which crosses a spur

240

of the mountains, being, according to Domenico, a steep one; he, moreover, volunteers if I sleep here to bring me to Ajaccio early tomorrow
afternoon. Thus Zicavo can well be visited from here later in the day,
by taking Flora and Company without luggage up the hill, and walking
back.

While breakfast is being prepared, I go to see the mineral springs at
the back of the hotel, which are very remarkable. A large circular basin
boils over with the hot water, and the overflow is conducted by pipes
to a row of log barracks or huts used as private baths; for one of these
you pay five soldi twenty-five centesimi; but if you are economically inclined, you may bathe gratis in an open public reservoir close to the
main springs. To me, this water, which resembles that of Harrogate,
and has an ancient decayed-egg flavour, was disgusting; but I am assured
that you come to like it very much if you will only persevere in drinking
it; and, certainly, some persons whom I saw, quaffed whole tumblers
of it with great apparent relish.

The people of the inn—at the risk of repetition, I must state that they
were thoroughly obliging folk—gave me an exceptionally good breakfast, served by a damsel very different to those who usually attend on
the diligence passengers in the Corsican inns, and whose face, without
being abolsutely handsome, was very pretty and full of expression, of
intelligence and sweetness. When breakfast was ready, there was a
stew, which I observed my servant regarding uneasily, for it did not seem
to be hare, and was certainly not fowl—'Scusate,' said the polite waitress, apologetically, '*questo piatto à—o scusate!—di quell' animale nero—
scusate!*—Please to excuse—this dish is—oh please excuse!—that black
animal—excuse!'[1] More could not be said had the object been a cat,
whereas it was sucking-pig; and on bringing a dish of roast meat to
table, there were renewed apologies—'*Vostro perdono davvero! bisogna
scusare si sa—quest' è il parte di dietro della stessa piccola bestia nera!*—
Really I beg pardon—excuse it, you know—this is the hinder part of the
same little black beast!' Notwithstanding all these apologies, none were
needed, for the little black beast was excellent both stewed and roasted;
some apple fritters also were admirable; and, though the good cheese
of Balagna is not found in these parts, the wine was excellent; about

[1] Pig (porco) is never mentioned in Italy by polite folk without an apology, and
as all, or nearly all, Italian pigs are black, it is called '*animale nero*'.—E.L.

which, when I had inquired if they had any good here, the polite reply had been, 'Not any worthy of your merit, but some we hope you may find drinkable.'

This very rustic hotel has many rooms above the ground floor; you ascend by ladder-staircases to the upper chambers; all coarsely white-washed and as nearly unfurnished as may be; yet there is a respect for cleanliness everywhere visible about the house, the floors and passages are clean, and the whole rural establishment prepossessing, though humble. Round the house—now that one is no longer at Cap Corse or Balagna—loiterers, clad in the usual black velveteen, are not lacking, and stare in at the window fixedly. And, as usual, when the carriage stops at such houses, a small crowd of children swarm into and take possession of the empty vehicle.

The usual afternoon storm and rain having come on, it is 3.30 P.M. before I can start off from Zicavo, the 'woody places' of this lovely valley being all fresh and odorous of clematis and honeysuckle. At four, having retraced the road of this morning for a few kilometres, a Route Forestière leaves the Ajaccio highway and winds up the side of a deep gorge, where great chestnut and ilex woods are the chief characteristic, and the villages or communes of Zicavo are thereafter constantly in sight. They may be described as standing in a vast wooded amphi-theatre or hollow in the great Incudine mountain range, the plain or plateau of Coscione being immediately beyond the highest summits which tower over the villages, below more distant crags and precipices also partially wooded.

The wide space of rich foliage is brightened by scattered houses gleaming among the woods on the hill-side; and in the principal hamlet there seem some good houses as well as a rather picturesque white church; there, too, Domenico points out the Casa Abbatucci. The great ravine and river far below are full of beauty, and all the rocky descent to the roaring stream is clothed with a growth of magnificent chestnut and ilex; yet on so large a scale is the scenery that it would be by no means easy to portray Zicavo as a whole, notwithstanding the great beauty of its position. All this, however, I scarcely saw more of than in my approach to the villages, for, unfortunately, violent rain and thunder recommenced after I had sent back Flora and Company to Guitera; so that after part of the afternoon had been passed in shelter below some rocks, it became too late in the day to advance farther, and I had to make the best of my way back to the Bagni di Guitera.

As I returned to the hotel after the failure of my Zicavo exploit, the beautiful landscape round it was alive with flocks of sheep and goats (all, of course, black) going up to the mountains for the summer; some of the shepherds and their families were as picturesque as Corsican peasants can be—which in these our days is not saying much, since their old costume, the pointed cap, gaiters, etc., has ceased out of the land. Many scenes in the deep hollows of the Taravo continually remind me of leafy-glen scenery in Yorkshire or Devonshire; perhaps the bridge near Guitera, with its hanging fern and drooping alders, its rocks and foaming river, is one of the loveliest points in this picturesque neighbourhood.

Flora, this being the last day of dining in Corsican rural inns, is invited to dinner—most amiable and intelligent of small spotty dogs. Afterwards, the rest of the evening was passed in describing the cities of Europe to the pretty daughter of the house, who, notwithstanding her mother's summons, lingered to listen to details of outer-world novelties until the call had been thrice repeated.

JUNE 4

I rise at 4 A.M., and Flora and Company are off by five from the clean little humble hotel, whose managers are the civillest of people. The Hotel Guitera, kept by Ventura Bozzi, is worth a longer visit, for it is a pleasant and quiet halting-place in the midst of exquisite scenery.

The drive from the baths to the main Ajaccio and Bonifacio road, by Santa Maria Zicché d'Ornano, is one of the most enchanting in all Corsica. There is a second road along the southern side of this great valley, terminating at Bicchisano; but that can scarcely be so beautiful, since it does not include the variety of crossing the mountain spurs that form one of the most charming parts of the northern line of route. The Route Forestière to Grosseto soon turns off to the right, and rises gradually by pleasant lanes among wooded and *maquis*-covered tracts, through landscape which at this hour is indescribably lovely, and constantly recalls the best and fairest distances of Claude Lorraine's paintings. After yesterday's rain, every dark chestnut leaf sparkles with moisture, and it is impossible to conceive more beautiful spots than there are at every turn of this road, either looking back eastward to the heights of Monte Incudine above Zicavo, or westward to the long long lines of the valley of the Taravo, fading away into the hills near Sollacarò on the horizon.

Corrà is the first village passed, and one where a landscape painter might pass a summer with delight. Then another hamlet (Frasseto) with slopes of immense fern-shading chestnut trees, ilex of astonishing beauty, and vast walnut trees; and after this follows a long and steep ascent—Domenico was quite right in dissuading me from attempting it late yesterday afternoon—the top of which was reached at 8 A.M. Then the road dips down into a deep recess of mountains, and, circling round spur after spur, gradually descends to Santa Maria through a succession of villages—Sevato, Quasquara, and others—all full of picturesque beauty, not so much owing to any charm of architecture, as to the combination of the houses with foliage and distance. At about three kilometres before reaching the main Ajaccio Route Impériale, at the foot of the ascent to Col S. Giorgio, a branch road turns off to the village of Santa Maria Zicche, where there is a church with an extremely picturesque campanile; and thus, a short distance farther, always passing through beautiful scenes of graceful woody landscape, I come for the third time to Grosseto, at the seventeenth kilometre from Ajaccio, by 9.30 A.M., and once more go to the pleasant little village inn of Madame Lionardi. Undoubtedly the drive hither from Guitera ranks among the first for lovely scenery in all this beautiful island.

The little village of Grosseto is all astir, and something is happening, for the roadside is full of groups of gendarmes. Mdme Lionardi explains, with many apologies for not being able to give me breakfast in the sitting-room, that all the house is taken for the General commanding the troops in the arrondissement of Ajaccio, and for other officials, whose luggage is momentarily arriving, on account of a review of gendarmierie, a conscription, etc. But the obliging family of the hotel soon clear out another room, and I occupy an hour till breakfast comes, by drawing some of the grand ilex trees close to the house. This place, and indeed all the valley of Grosseto, and of the Taravo, is truly one for a painter to sojourn in who desires to study the evergreen oak in its most luxuriant growth and finest form. After this, a fine dish of trout, good cutlets, and superb broccio, add one more to the pleasant memories already registered of the Hotel des Amis.

The son of Madame Lionardi tells me that a brother of Mr. B. arrived at Olmeto about a week ago, and that the dying man was then removed to Ajaccio, where he died on the following day, and that the day before yesterday his body was embarked for Marseilles; news which, after what I had seen of the poor invalid's condition when I was last in Olmeto, was to me no surprise.

I give an hour to a walk to Santa Maria Zicche, to obtain a drawing (of the picturesque campanile there), probably the last I shall make in Corsica. (An old woman by the roadside asks me for '*qual cosa*', and this is only the third instance of begging I have known in my eight weeks' tour.) All along this part of the valley there have of late been very violent hail-storms, and the vines, they tell me, have been greatly damaged.

Returning to Grosseto by 1 P.M., Flora and Company are ready, and I leave the village as the arrivals of gendarmes, walking, riding, and driving, continually increase the hubbub; soon we have trotted up the Col St. Giorgio, from which I take a last look at these beautiful scenes. How lovely and green is the wide space of hill and dale! Addio, for the third time, noble and verdant valleys of the Taravo!

Soon the *maquis*-grown crescent of hills beyond the Col is passed; then the familiar village of Cauro, and the far view of Ajaccio is seen on the horizon; the run down to the Piana dell' Oro follows; and I am soon once more in Ajaccio, where the squadron of ironclads enliven the the bay, if, indeed, any place may be said to be enlivened by those speci-mens of naval architecture. My journeys in Corsica are ended; much more there is to see, but time is up, and the glass of Corsican travel is run out; close, therefore, the notebook of research, and lock it up in the closet of resignation.

After the fresh mountain air how hot does Ajaccio now seem! and above all the small rooms of the Ottavi Hotel!

Flora and Company are dismissed with esteem. No better nor more careful coachman could be found anywhere than the youth Domenico, who, by the by, is an amateur, having, as he told my servant, property

245

to the amount of 20,000 francs, and who drives about to see the world by choice—'*per piacer di veder il mondo, fuori di Corsica no—ma tutta l'isola.*' Farewell, spotty little beast of excellent qualities—Flora, best of dogs!

JUNE 5

This day has passed—first, in finishing drawings of the town at sunrise; secondly, in packing my 350 drawings and in purchasing gourds and photographs; thirdly, in making p.p.c. calls at the Préfecture and elsewhere, and in wandering among the beautiful wild olive and cactusgrown dells beyond the Cours Grandval. In the evening I dine at M. le Préfet's. Admiral Jurien de la Gravière and others are there.

Among other matters I hear that the L.K.s were in Corsica last winter, and that my old Abruzzo companion in 1843, C.A.K., was also here.

JUNE 6

A day of last packings. In the afternoon, at 4.30 P.M., I left the worthy Ottavis and the Hotel de Londres, and came on board the *Insulaire* steamer, getting the identical berth I came in two months ago. The two trotting poodles were also performing as in times past.

At six I make a last drawing of the head of the gulf; beautifully clear and rosily coloured at sunset were the cliffs above Sari, and the snows of Monte d'Oro; gorgeous beyond description the hues on the sea as the sun went down behind the rocky islet gates of the gulf. At six-thirty Miss C. and other returning travellers had come on board, and at seven-thirty we started, and soon, beyond the Iles Sanguinaires, lost sight of the gulf of Ajaccio and the wild mountain ranges.

As night came on the headlands about the gulf of Sagona were the last I could trace of Corsica, and next morning by nine we were in the harbour of Nice. Soon I was once more at Cannes, and looking at the ever-beautiful Esterelles, than which there are many grander forms, but few more delicately perfect and lovely.

ADDITIONAL NOTES

History

A colony of Phocæans from Asia Minor are the first inhabitants of Corsica whom history mentions; these, or the Carthaginians who succeeded them, founded Alalia, or Aleria. Carthage conquered by Rome, Corsica became Roman, and new cities were built by Marius at Mariana, and by Sulla at Aleria.

On the division of the Roman power, Corsica was attached to the eastern empire, and so continued till A.D. 460, when the Vandals conquered it under Genseric; after their expulsion by Belisarius and Narses, it continued a dependency of the Greek empire, as part of the Exarchate of Ravenna, until 750, when it was taken by the Saracens. These were finally defeated early in the ninth century under Charlemagne, and Corsica was granted to Boniface, Count of Tuscany, whose descendants for some time governed the island.

About the year 1000 a succession of feudal lords became the rulers of Corsica; but in 1077 these were opposed by the people, who rose against them, and gave themselves to the Popes, who, in 1081 (Urban II), transferred the sovereignty of the island to the Bishop of Pisa. The Republic of Genoa protested against this act, and in 1133 Innocent II divided the Corsican bishoprics equally between Pisa and Genoa, an arrangement which by no means pacified the island, and the two Republics continued to make it their field of battle until, in 1347, the contest was ended by the capture of Giudice della Rocca and the defeat of the Pisans, when Corsica fell under the yoke of the Genoese, who thenceforth held it for 400 years.

The government of the Pisans in Corsica was mild and just; that of the Genoese is, on the contrary, accused of having been always the opposite, nor do they appear ever to have been regarded by the Corsicans with any feelings but those of hatred.

Early in the fifteenth century, Alfonso of Arragon claimed the island as having been granted to Spain by Pope Boniface VIII, but the Spaniards were defeated in 1541, and the French, who had intervened, evacuated the island in 1559, leaving Genoa its sole mistress.

The oppression and cruelty of the Genoese was such that the islanders revolted from them in 1564, under Sampiero of Bastelica, and after this rebellion was put down, the Republic governed Corsica with unchanged severity until 1729, when, under Ceccaldi and Giafferi, an insurrection broke out, which led ultimately to the defeat of the Genoese and their final withdrawal from the island.

Genoa then solicited aid from the Emperor Charles VI, and the troops he sent were defeated by the islanders; and in 1732 a peace was signed between the two parties, of no long duration, since war again broke out in 1736, when the Corsicans chose themselves a king in Theodore, Baron von Neuhoff. In 1737 the Genoese were again obliged to call for assistance, this time from the French, and the war, on the part of the Corsicans against them and the Republic of Genoa combined, continued until 1741, when the island submitted once more to the Genoese, and the French quitted it.

Soon, however, under Gaffori and Matra, and later under the great Pasquale Paoli, the Corsicans once more rose against their oppressors, and succeeded in nearly wresting the island from their hands, except some of the fortresses, which at that time Genoa made over to the French.

Paoli, meanwhile, who ruled the interior of the island from 1755 to 1769, continued to make war on the Genoese, and by degrees dispossessed them of their hold in all parts of the island, when the Republic at length, finding itself everywhere completely beaten, entered into a secret treaty with M. Choiseul, minister of Louis XV, by which all Genoese rights over Corsica were formally transferred to the French nation.

This was in 1768, and thenceforward the French fought with Paoli and the Corsicans on their own account alone. Ultimately, after several reverses, they completed the final subversion of Corsican liberty at the battle of Ponte Nuovo, May 9, 1769.

From that time the French supremacy has been acknowledged in Corsica, with the exception of the short period, 1794–1796, when, after some troubles, during the period of the French Revolution, George III of England was proclaimed King of Corsica, a sovereignty which lasted for two years only.

Since 1796 the dominion of the French has not been disturbed; and from that date the peaceful progress of the island and its population, once so divided and harassed, has been ensured and gradually developed.

The Abbé Galletti, speaking of the allegorical figure of Corsica represented, by order of Sixtus V., in the Vatican (above the battle of Constantine and Maxentius), speaks of that Pope as Corsican by origin, and of his forming a regiment of Corsican guards, &c.

And it was by the care of this Pontiff that a number of Corsican families, oppressed by the Genoese, combined to form a colony, and established themselves in a spot which is still called Vallecorsa. This place, in the Rio di Vallefratta, near Anagni and Frosinone, is now a little town of 3,500 inhabitants. [Compiled by Lear from the works of Benson, Fries, Gregorovius, Grandchamps and others.]

GENERAL PAOLI

'Born at Rostino, on April 25, 1725, Pasquale Paoli was second son of Giacinto Paoli, one of the leaders of the Corsican people in their last great struggle against the tyranny of the Genoese. Compelled by the course of events to retire to Naples in 1739, Giacinto Paoli was accompanied by his son Pasquale, who, inheriting his father's talents and patriotism, there received a finished education, both civil and military. Being much about the court, the young Corsican acquired, with high accomplishments, those polished manners for which he was afterwards distinguished, &c. Recalled to Corsica in 1755 to take the supreme command of affairs, in consequence of the divisions prevailing among the patriot leaders, the expulsion of the Genoese became his first duty; and he soon succeeded in freeing the interior of the island, and confining their occupation to the narrow limits of the fortified towns on the coast. His next step was to remodel, or rather to create, the civil government; and in so doing he introduced an admirable form of a representative constitution, founded, as far as possible, on old Corsican institutions. It was, in fact, a Republic, of which Pasquale Paoli was the chief magistrate and commander of the forces. One of the earliest acts of his administration was a severe law for the suppression of the bloody practice of Vendetta, followed in course of time by measures for the encouragement of agriculture, and by the foundation of a university at Corte. With a small squadron of ships, which he got together and equipped, he succeeded, after repulsing the Genoese fleet, in wresting the island of Capraja from the Republic. Intestine divisions having always been the bane of Corsican independence, the party of Matra opposed to Paoli rose in insurrection, and calling in the Genoese to their aid, it was only after a long and bloody struggle that Paoli and the nationals became firmly settled in power, and grew in strength, until the Genoese found themselves unable to cope with a brave and united people. After some further ineffectual attempts, they applied once more to France for succour, and that power, by the treaty of Compiègne, 1764, limited the occupation of the strong forts of the island to a term of four years. In this position they preserved a strict neutrality, the patriots having entire possession of the country, excepting the fortified places, and thus, under the firm and active administration of its wise chief, the commonwealth flourished, and the Genoese power in Corsica shrunk to nothing. It was at this time that Boswell visited the island, &c. The time for the evacuation of Corsica by the French having arrived, they had withdrawn from Ajaccio and Calvi, when the Genoese, finding themselves incapable of retaining possession of the island, offered to cede their rights to the King of France. In 1768, the Duc de Choiseul resolved on annexing Corsica to France, and crossed the neutral lines on the eastern side of the island.

'Pasquale Paoli and his brother Clement led the people *en masse* against the threatened tyranny, and the French troops were signally defeated at Borgo. But Chauvelin being recalled, Comte de Vaux became general, and ultimately 40,000 Frenchmen decided the fate of Corsica at Ponte Nuovo in 1769. Pasquale Paoli and Clement Paoli, with 300 followers, embarked at Porto Vecchio for England.

'Pasquale Paoli was, and ever will be, the popular hero of the Corsicans. He fought their last battles for the national independence; moulded their wild aspirations for liberty and self-government into a constitutional form; administered affairs unselfishly, purely, justly; encouraged industry, and checked outrage. He was a man of the people, one of themselves, and he never forgot it, nor have they.'—*Forester: Rambles in the Islands of Corsica and Sardinia.*

KING THEODORE

'J. Baron Newhoff, in the county of La Marc, in Westphalia, was the personage who aspired to the sovereignty of Corsica. He had his education in the French service. He afterwards went to Spain, where he received some marks of regard from the Duke of Riperda, and Cardinal Alberoni. But being of a strange, unsettled, projecting disposition, he quitted Spain, and went and travelled into Italy, England, and Holland, ever in search of some new adventure. He at last fixed his attention on Corsica, and formed a scheme of making himself a king.

'He was a man of considerable abilities and address; and after having fully informed himself of everything relating to the island, he went to Tunis, where he fell upon means to procure some money and arms; and then came to Leghorn, from whence he wrote a letter to the Corsican chiefs, Giafferi and Hyacinth Paoli, offering considerable assistance to the nation if they would elect him as their sovereign. This letter was addressed to Count Domenico Rivarola, who acted as Corsican plenipotentiary in Tuscany, and he gave for answer, that if Theodore brought the assistance he promised to the Corsicans, they would very willingly make him their king. Upon this, without loss of time, he set sail, and landed in the spring of 1736. He was a man of very stately appearance, and the Turkish dress which he wore added to the dignity of his mien. He had a few attendants with him. His manners were so engaging, and his offers so plausible, that he was proclaimed king of Corsica before Count Rivarola's despatches arrived to inform the chiefs of the terms upon which he had agreed. He brought with him about 1,000 zechins of Tunis, besides some arms and ammunition, and made magnificent promises of foreign assistance, so that the Corsicans, who were glad of any support, willingly gave in to his schemes. Theodore assumed every mark of royal dignity. He had his guards and his officers of state. He conferred titles of honour, and he struck money, both of silver and copper. The silver pieces were few in number, and can now hardly be met with. I have one of his copper coins; on one side of it is 'T. R. (Theodorus Rex), King Theodore', with a double branch crossed, and round it this inscription, 'Pro bono publico Re. Co. (Regni Corsicæ), For the public good of the Kingdom of Corsica'. On the other side is the value of the piece, 'cinque soldi, five sous'. There was such a curiosity over all Europe to have King Theodore's coins, that his silver pieces were sold at four zechins each; and when the genuine ones were exhausted, imitations of them were made at Naples, and, like the imitations of antiques, were bought up at a high price, and carefully preserved in the cabinets of the virtuosi. Theodore immediately blocked up the Genoese fortified towns; and he used to be sometimes at one siege, sometimes at another, standing with a telescope in his hand, as if he spied the assistance which he said he expected. He used also the artifice of making large packets be continually brought to him from the continent, which he gave out to be from the different sovereigns of Europe, acknowledging his authority, and promising to befriend him. The Genoese were not a little confounded with this unexpected adventurer. They published a violent manifesto against Theodore, treating him with great contempt, but at the same time showing that they were alarmed at his appearance. Theodore replied in a manifesto with all the calmness and dignity of a monarch, expressed his indifference as to the injurious treatment of the republic, and appeared firm in the hopes of victory. . . . After having been about eight months in Corsica, Theodore perceived that the people began to cool in their affections towards him, and did not act with the same resolution as before. He therefore wisely determined to leave them for a little, and try his fortune again upon the continent. So, after having laid down a plan of administration to be observed in his absence, he quitted the island in the month of November. He went to Holland, and there he was successful enough to get credit to a great extent from several rich merchants, particularly Jews, who trusted him with cannon and other warlike stores to a great value, under the charge of a supercargo. With these he returned to Corsica, in 1739, and on his arrival he put to death the supercargo, that he might not have any trouble from demands being made upon him.

'By this time the French had become so powerful in the island, that, although Theodore threw in his supply of warlike stores, he did not incline to venture his person, the Genoese having set a high price upon his head. He therefore chose to relinquish his throne, and give up his views of ambition for safety, &c., &c. . . . The Corsicans now talk differently of King Theodore. Some of them, who had most faith in his fine speeches, still extol him to the skies, to support their own judgment; others, who looked upon him as an impostor, and never joined heartily in his measures, represent him as a kind of Wat Tyler—a king of a rabble; but the most knowing and judicious, and the General (Paoli) himself, consider him in the moderate light in which he has now been represented, and own that he was of great service in reviving the spirit of the nation, which after a good many years of constant war, was beginning to droop, but which Theodore restored, while he rekindled the sacred fire of liberty. They, indeed, are sensible that his wretched fate has thrown a sort of ridicule on the nation, since their king was confined in a jail at London, which was actually the case of poor Theodore; who, after experiencing the most extraordinary vicissitudes of fortune, chose to end his days in our island of liberty; but was reduced to the wretched state of a prisoner for debt. Mr. Horace Walpole generously exerted himself for Theodore. He wrote a paper in the *World*, with great elegance and humour, soliciting a contribution for the monarch in distress, to be paid to Mr. Robert Dodsley, bookseller, as lord high treasurer. This brought him a very handsome sum. He was allowed to get out of prison. Mr. Walpole has the original deed by which Theodore made over the kingdom of Corsica in security to his creditors. He has also the great seal of his kingdom. . . . He died very soon after he got out of prison, and was buried in St. Anne's churchyard, Westminster.—*Boswell: An Account of Corsica.*

CUSTOMS, ETC.

'During Paoli's administration, there have been few laws made in Corsica. He mentioned one which he has found very efficacious in curbing the vindictive spirit of the Corsicans. . . . There was among them a most dreadful species of revenge, called *Vendetta trasversa*, collateral revenge, which Petrus Cyrnæus candidly acknowledges. It was this: If a man had received an injury, and could not find a proper opportunity to be revenged on his enemy personally, he revenged himself on one of his enemy's relations. So barbarous a practice was the source of innumerable assassinations. Paoli, knowing that the point of honour was everything to the Corsicans, opposed it to the progress of the blackest of crimes, fortified by long habits. He made a law, by which it was provided that this collateral revenge should not only be punished with death, as ordinary murther, but the memory of the offender should be disgraced for ever by a pillar of infamy. He also had it enacted that the same statute should extend to the violations of an oath of reconciliation, once made.'—*Boswell: An Account of Corsica.*

'Mothers of families, whose husbands have been assassinated, preserve the dress of the deceased until their children grow up to manhood, and then show them the clothes tinged with the blood of their fathers, and exhort them to vengeance; and in dispute with others the latter taunt them if they have not revenged themselves. Thus these unhappy children have no alternative than to live dishonoured, or to destroy the murderers of their parents, and they rush headlong into crime.'—*Benson: Sketches of Corsica.*

Many interesting particulars relating to criminal trials in Corsica are related by Benson; but none more extraordinary than that of Signor Viterbi, who, himself a judge, was condemned to death in 1821 on an accusation of occasioning the assassination of some of the Frediani family, between which and his own an implacable animosity existed. Continually professing his innocence, and resolved not to suffer the disgrace of a public execution, Viterbi starved himself to death, and during the eighteen days which intervened between his first abstinence from food and his death, actually registered every change in his physical system with the utmost exactness, till, unable to write, he dictated minutely every sign of his approach to death, until his decease occurred. 'I am about to conclude my days with the peaceful death of the just,' were among his last words. 'The few moments which I have to live are passing away placidly. . . . The lamp is nearly extinguished.' This was signed by his own hand, but he lingered two days longer, till the 20 December, 1821. His wishes regarding his burial are set forth minutely in a letter addressed to his wife a few days before he died; in his singular document, Viterbi strictly charges his family to swear 'eternal hatred to his persecutors' over his grave, while kneeling.

'The Corsican *bandit* was not a thief or ''brigand'', but, as his name implied, one banned or banished by the law. In the ancient statutes of the island all those are originally called banditti who are banished from the island because justice has failed to get them into her grasp. The bandit often led a life of many years in the wild fastnesses of the mountains over the Niolo and other pathless regions, and innumerable stories are told of their exploits. Many of these, as well of the vendetta, have been worked up into tales; among them none more charming than that of "Colomba", by M. Prosper Merimée. Others are Teodoro Poli, Gallocchio, Bracciomozzo; renowned also are Giammarchi, who kept his ground in the bush for sixteen years; Camillo Ornano, who maintained himself in the mountains for fourteen years; and Joseph Antommarchi, who was bandit for seventeen years. The tales of the bandit life of Serafino, Arrighi, and Masoni, illustrate terribly and picturesquely the state of things so recently existing in Corsica. One can scarcely believe what the historian Filippini relates, that in his day, in thirty years 28,000 Corsicans were murdered in revenge!'

' "Besides their ignorance," says Filippini, "one cannot find words to express how great is the idleness of the islanders in tilling the ground. Even the finest plain in the world, of Aleria and Mariana, is desert, and they do not even chase the wild birds. But if they chance to become masters of a single Carlino, they imagine they shall never be in want again, and so they sink down into idleness and doing nothing," which (adds Gregorovius) strikingly describes the nature of the Corsican of the present day. "Why do they not graft the countless wild oleasters? —why not the chestnut? But they do nothing, and therefore are they all poor. . . . Their hostilities and their hate, their want of good faith and love, are almost eternal; hence that proverb becomes true which people are wont to say, 'the Corsican never forgives'."

'Filippini's book became nearly extinct, being suppressed as far as possible by the Genoese, of whom he had said in it many bitter truths; but it must be allowed "bitter truths" were not wanting relating to his own countrymen. On the other hand, he gives them the praise for hospitality. "I can truly say that there is no nation in the world by which foreigners are more cherished, nor where they can travel more securely; for in every part of Corsica they find the choicest hospitality, without having to disburse a single quattrino for their sustenance." '— *Gregorovius: Corsica in its Picturesque, Social and Historical Aspects.*

'The insurmountable difficulty met with by those who govern in Corsica has arisen from the character of the people—their exaggeration of all things, their fanaticism in devotion, in their implacable revenge, and in their modes of thought. The most futile motives suffice to light up secular enmity. To the most susceptible self-love is joined the constancy of friendship and most exclusive family affection. To the aid of their passions and enterprises they bring a tenacious will, a remarkable quickness of intelligence, and the endless resources of a dexterity of design never at fault. The richest inhabitants of each locality are at the head of rival and inimical parties; all seek public places, which offer them the double advantage of protecting friends or relations and humiliating enemies—intrigues without end. There were numerous edicts of Genoese governors and French kings, but always ineffectual, more or less; edicts against carrying arms, and against banditism in 1560; and against collateral revenge in the years 1548, 1560, 1569, 1573, 1768, 1769, 1770, 1778, and 1811, laws—all of the severest nature—were made against carrying arms and against banditism. It results from these documents that successive administrations in Corsica have many times endeavoured to disarm the people, and to put an end to the murders which have filled this unhappy country with blood; yet, spite of the rigour of the edicts, the same crimes are reproduced for three centuries with more or less intensity, according to the degree of power and energy of the governments. The number of murders for between 1821 and 1850 was 4,319.

'The Duc d'Orleans, after a tour in Corsica, thus expressed himself on the character and faults of the Corsicans, in a letter addressed to M. Dupin, Nov. 18, 1835: "In Corsica my task has been an easy one. The remedy for the social misfortune which torments this country is apparent at the first glance. Perseverance and firmness . . . will result in overcoming those qualities, which are the only obstacle to all amelioration. Let the Corsican be no longer armed; let the lower grade of functionaries be chosen from Continentals; cease to encourage civil war and contempt of the laws; let the lazy, sluggish, but not idle population learn wants, which will force it to work more than it does at present, when chestnuts picked up in the woods are all that is necessary to existence, and the shade of trees for shelter. Let all this be accomplished by degrees, and the condition of Corsica will be changed." '— *Grandchamps: La Corse*

Edward Lear in Greece

Uniform with this volume

EDWARD LEAR IN SOUTHERN ITALY

EDWARD LEAR IN GREECE

Journals of a Landscape Painter in
Greece and Albania

WILLIAM KIMBER
46 WILTON PLACE, LONDON, S.W.1

This Edition
first published in 1965 by
WILLIAM KIMBER & CO. LIMITED
46 Wilton Place, London, S.W.1

© William Kimber & Co. Limited 1965

MADE AND PRINTED IN GREAT BRITAIN BY
W. & J. MACKAY & CO LTD, CHATHAM, KENT

Illustrations

Publishers' Note

In 1847, Edward Lear undertook a most successful expedition to Southern Calabria, completing a series of drawings and a journal, which he later published. In the following year, he decided to explore Northern Greece and Albania, most of which was at that time 'Turkey in Europe', and governed by local pashas. It is not always easy to identify the places Lear visited, either because Lear himself never found out their names, or because his spelling is highly erratic. The more obvious names—Yannina, Salonica, Corfu and so on—have been 'translated' for this edition to give the reader some landmarks. Lear's original map is reproduced on page 8 and facing it is a modern map showing the present frontiers and the location of most of the places visited by Lear, with their more normal spellings.

The original edition of this book was published in 1851 and was entitled *Journals of a Landscape Painter in Albania*, etc. The twenty lithograph plates from the original edition have all been reproduced in the present volume.

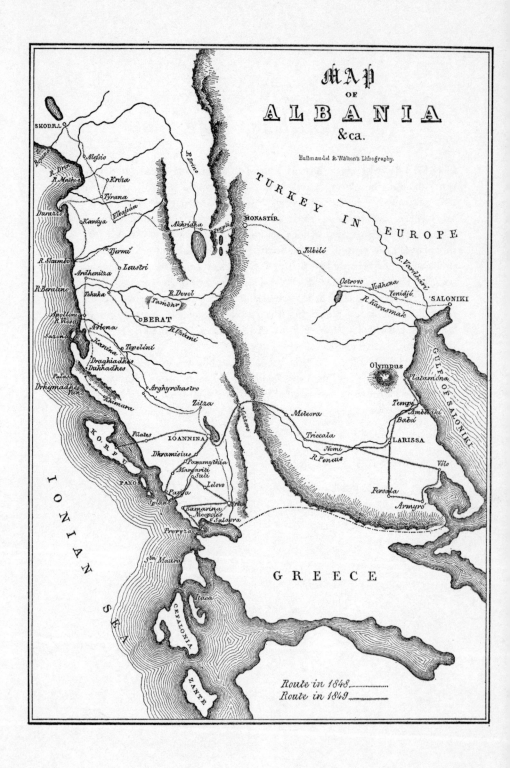

MAP
OF
ALBANIA
&ca.

Hullmandel & Walton's Lithography.

TURKEY IN EUROPE

SKODRA

Alessio

R. Drin

R. Mathis

Krộa

Tirana

Durazzo

Kaváya

Elbassán

Akhridha

zeglí

MONASTIR

R. Drino

Tjermí

Leustri

Filbelé

R. Slcumbi

Ardhenitza

Ostrovo

Vodhena

R. Vonthéori

R. Berâlino

Tshuka

R. Devol

Tamohr

R. Karasmak

Yenidjé.

SALONIKI

Apollonia

R. Wossi

Avlona

BERAT

Kanina

R. Uzúmi

Tepeléni

Sazo

Draghiadhes

Dakhadhes

Arghyrokastro

Khimara

Olympus

Platamóna

Tempi

Ambelaki

Babá

GULF OF SALONIKI

Drhigmadhes

Pass.

Zitza

Meteora

LARISSA

Palasa

Triccala

Nomi

Vélo

KORFU

Filats

IOANNINA

Dhramisius

Fanari

R. Penws

Fersala

Armyró

PAXOS

Pragamythia

Margariti

Suli

Lelovo

Parga

Splantza

Nicopoles

Tamarina

Salaora

Preryza

Sta. Maura

I O N I A N   S E A

Itaca

CEFALONIA

ZANTE

G R E E C E

Route in 1848 ....
Route in 1849 _____

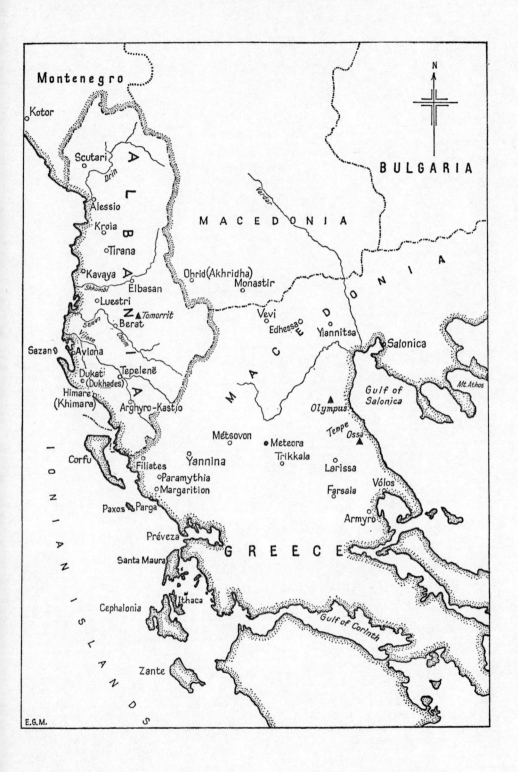

N

Montenegro

Kotor

Scutari

Drin

Alessio

Kroia

Tirana

Kavaya

Shkumbi

Elbasan

Luestri

Berat ▲*Tomorrit*

Seman

Sazan

Vijose

Avlona

Osum

Dukati
(Dukhades)

Tepelenë

Himare
(Khimara)

Arghyro-Kastjo

Corfu

Filiates

Yannina

Paramythia

Margarition

Paxos ● Parga

Préveza

Santa Maura

Cephalonia

Ithaca

Zante

A L B A N I A
Z

BULGARIA

M A C E D O N I A

Vardar

Ohrid(Akhridha)

Monastir

Vevi

Edhessa

Yiannitsa

Salonica

M A C E D O N I A

Gulf of
Salonica

Mt. Athos

▲
Olympus

Tempe

Ossa

▲

Larissa

Métsovon

● Meteora

Trikkala

Vólos

Farsala

Armyró

G R E E C E

Gulf of Corinth

I O N I A N   I S L A N D S

E.G.M.

Introduction

THE following Notes were written during two journeys through part of Turkey in Europe: the first from Salonica in a north-western direction through ancient Macedonia, to Illyrian Albania, and by the western coast through Epirus to the northern boundary of modern Greece at the Gulf of Arta; the second in Epirus and Thessaly.

Since the days of Gibbon, who wrote of Albania, 'a country within sight of Italy less known than the interior of America', much has been done for the topography of these regions; and those who wish for a clear insight into their ancient and modern definitions are referred to the authors who, in the present century, have so admirably investigated and so admirably illustrated the subject. For neither the ability of the writer of these journals, nor their scope, permit of any attempt on his part to follow in the track of those learned travellers: enough if he may avail himself of their labours by quotation where such aid is necessary throughout his memoranda of an artist's mere tour of search among the riches of far-away Landscape.

To the unlearned tourist, indeed, Albania is a puzzle of the highest order. Whatever he may already know of ancient nomenclature—Epirus, Molossia, Thesprotia, etc.—is thwarted and confused by Turkish divisions and Pashaliks; beyond these, wheel within wheel, a third set of names distract him in the shape of native tribes and districts—Tjamourià, Dibra, etc. And no sooner does he begin to understand the motley crowd which inhabits these provinces—Greeks, Slavonians, Albanians, Bulgarians, or Vlachi—than he is anew bewildered by a fresh list of distinctive sub-splittings, Liape, Mereditti, Khimáriotes, and Tóskidhes. Races, religions, and national denominations seem so ill defined, or so entangled, that he would give up the perplexing study in despair were it not for the assistance of many excellent books already published on the subject. Of these, the works of Colonel Leake stand highest, as conveying by far the greatest mass of minutely accurate information regarding these magnificent and interesting countries. Invaluable and remarkable as is the amount of erudition set forth in these volumes, the untiring research by means of which it has been obtained is not less extraordinary, and can only be fully appreciated by those who are aware of the impediments with which travelling in all seasons in those countries must, at that period, have fettered the writer.

Geographer, antiquarian, classic, and politician, having done all in their power for a region demanding great efforts of health and energy to examine it, there is but little opportunity left for the gleanings of the landscape painter. Yet of parts of Acroceraunia—of Króia (the city of Scanderbeg), and of scenes in the neighbourhood of Akhridha—the Lake Lychnitis, the Author believes himself to be the only Englishman who has published any account; and scanty and slight as his may be, it is something in these days to be able to add the smallest mite of novelty to the travellers' world of information and interest.

The general and most striking character of Albanian landscape is its display of objects, in themselves beautiful and interesting—rarely to be met with in combination. You have the simple and exquisite mountain forms of Greece, so perfect in outline and proportion—the lake, the river, and the wide plain; and withal you have the charm of architecture, the picturesque mosque, the minaret, the fort, and the serai—which you have not in modern Greece, for war and change have deprived her of them; you have that which is found neither in Greece nor in Italy, a profusion everywhere of the most magnificent foliage recalling the greenness of our own island—clustering plane and chestnut, growth abundant of forest oak and beech, and dark tracts of pine. You have majestic cliff-girt shores; castle-crowned heights, and gloomy fortresses; palaces glittering with gilding and paint; mountain passes such as you encounter in the snowy regions of Switzerland; deep bays and blue seas with bright, calm isles resting on the horizon; meadows and grassy knolls; convents and villages; olive-clothed slopes and snow-capped mountain peaks—and with all this a crowded variety of costume and pictorial incident such as bewilders and delights an artist at each step he takes.

Let us add besides that Olympus, Pindus, Pharsalia, Actium, etc., are no common names and that every scene has its own link with some historic or poetic association, and we cannot but perceive that these parts of Turkey in Europe are singularly rich in a combination of qualities hardly to be found in any other land.

These remarks apply more strictly to the southern parts of Albania

than to the extreme north (or Ghegheria); for nearer the confines of
Bosnia the mountains are on too gigantic a scale and the features of the
landscape too extensive and diffuse to be easily represented by the pencil.
There is, however, abundance of grandeur and sublimity through the
whole country; though the farther you wander north of Epirus the less
you find of that grace and detail which is so attractive in southern
Greece, and more especially in Attica and the Peloponesus.

Regarding the best mode of travelling, it is almost superfluous to
write, as the *Hand-book for travellers in the Ionian Islands, Greece, Turkey
etc.*, supplies excellent information on that head; yet the leading points
of a traveller's personal experience are frequently worth knowing. A
good dragoman, or interpreter, is absolutely necessary, however many
languages you may be acquainted with: French, German, and Italian are
useless, and modern Greek nearly as much if you travel higher than
Macedonia: Bulgarian, Albanian, Turkish, and Slavonic are your
requisites in this Babel. Those who dislike account-books and the
minutiæ thereof, may find it a good plan to pay their dragoman a certain
sum per diem—as C.M.C. and I did last year in Greece, where for one
pound five, including their own pay, the guides are accustomed to
provide for all your daily wants—food, lodging, and conveyance, that is,
if you travel singly—or for one pound from each person, if your party
be two or more. In the present case I gave the man who accompanied
me one dollar daily, and settled for all the expenses of food, horses, etc.,
at fixed times; the result of which plan, at the end of the journey, was
about the same, namely, that one pound five a day covered the whole of
my expenditure.

Previously to starting a certain supply of cooking utensils, tin plates,
knives and forks, a basin, etc., must absolutely be purchased, the
stronger and plainer the better; for you go into lands where pots and
pans are unknown, and all culinary processes are to be performed in
strange localities, innocent of artificial means. A light mattress, some
sheets and blankets, and a good supply of capotes and plaids should not
be neglected; two or three books; some rice, curry powder, and cay-
enne; a world of drawing materials—if you be a hard sketcher; as little
dress as possible, though you must have two sets of outer clothing—one
for visiting consuls, pashás, and dignitaries, the other for rough, every-
day work; some quinine made into pills (rather leave all behind than

this); a Boyourldí, or general order of introduction to governors or pashás; and your Teskeré, or provincial passport for yourself and guide. All these are absolutely indispensable, and beyond these, the less you augment your impedimenta by luxuries the better; though a long strap with a pair of ordinary stirrups, to throw over the Turkish saddles, may be recommended to save you the cramp caused by the awkward shovel stirrups of the country. Arms and ammunition, fine raiment, presents for natives, are all nonsense; simplicity should be your aim. When all these things, so generically termed *Roba* by Italians, are in order, stow them into two Brobdignagian saddle-bags, united by a cord (if you can get leather bags so much the better, if not, goats'-hair sacks); and by these hanging on each side of the baggage-horse's saddle, no trouble will ever be given from seceding bits of luggage escaping at unexpected intervals. Until you adopt this plan (the simplest of any) you will lose much time daily by the constant necessity of putting the baggage in order.

Journeys in Albania vary in length according to your will, for there are usually roadside khans at from two to four hours' distance. Ten hours' riding is as much as you can manage, if any sketching is to be secured; but I generally found eight sufficient.

A khan is a species of public-house rented by the keeper or Khanjí from the Government, and is open to all comers. You find food in it sometimes—sometimes not, when you fall back on your own rice and curry powder. In large towns, the khan is a three-sided building enclosed in a courtyard, and consisting of two floors, the lower a stable, the upper divided into chambers, opening into a wooden gallery which runs all round the building, and to which you ascend outside by stairs. In unfrequented districts the khan is a single room, or barn, with a raised floor at one end for humanity, and all the rest devoted to cattle—sometimes quadrupeds and bipeds are all mixed up together. First come, first served, is the rule in these establishments; and as any person who can pay the trifle required by the Khanjí for lodging may sleep in them, your company is oftentimes not select; but of this, as of the kind of khan you stop at, you must take your chance.

The best way of taking money is by procuring letters on consular agents, or merchants from town to town, so as to carry as little coin as possible with you; and your bag of piastres you pack in your carpet bag by day, and use as a pillow by night.

PART I

9 September to 12 November 1848

Journals of
a Landscape Painter

AFTER severe illness in Greece and repeated subsequent attacks of that persevering enemy, fever, six weeks of repose in the house of the British Embassy, on the banks of the Bosporus, under the care of the kindest of families, have at length restored energy, if not perfect health; and as the summer flies and the time for travelling is shortened, a long-anticipated plan of visiting parts of ancient Greece, Albania, etc., must be put into effect now, or not at all. To see the classic vale of Tempe, the sacred mountain of Athos and the romantic Yannina have always been among my wishes; and I had long ago determined on making, previously to returning to England, a large collection of sketches illustrative of the landscape of Greece. So, now that change of air and place is desirable as a matter of health, my motives for making this journey are more powerful than ever and overcome even the fear of renewed illness on the way. C.M.C.[1] is already gone before me to the Troad, and from thence will meet me in the peninsula of Athos, whence we shall pursue our travels together as heretofore.

3 P.M.—Came on board the *Ferdinando*, an Austrian steamer running between Constantinople and Salonica; and a pretty place does it seem to pass two or three days in! Every point of the lower deck—all of it—is crammed with Turks, Jews, Greeks, Bulgarians, wedged together with a density compared to which a crowded Gravesend steamer is emptiness: a section of a fig-drum, or of a herring-barrel is the only apt simile for this extraordinary crowd of recumbent human beings, who are all going to Salonica, as a starting-point for Thessaly, Bosnia, Wallachia, or any part of Northern Turkey. This motley cargo is not of ordinary occur-

[1] Charles Church, Greek scholar and linguist.

rence; but the second Salonica steamer, which should have started today, has fallen indisposed in its wheels or boiler; so we have a double load for our share.

Walking carefully over my fellow passengers, I reached the first-class part of the deck—a small, raised triangle, railed off from the throng below, half of which is allotted to Christians (the Austrian Consul at Salonica and his family being the only Christians besides myself), and the other half tabooed for the use of a harem of Turkish females, who entirely cover the floor with a diversity of robes, pink, blue, chocolate, and amber; pea, sea, olive, bottle, pale, and dark green; above which parterre of colours are numerous heads, all wrapped in white muslin, excepting as many pairs of eyes undistinguishably similar. There is a good cabin below; but owing to a row of obstructive Mussulmen who choose to cover up the grated opening with shutters, that they may sit quietly upon them to smoke, it is quite dark, so I remain on deck. We are a silent community: the smoking Turks are silent, and so is the strange harem. The Consul and his wife, and their two pretty daughters, are silent, because they fear cholera at Salonica—which the young ladies declare is '*un pessimo esilio*'[1]—and because they are regretting northern friends. I am silent, from much thought and some weakness consequent on long illness: and the extra cargo in the lower deck are silent also— perhaps because they have not room to talk. At four, the anchor is weighed and we begin to paddle away from the many domed mosques and bright minarets of Constantinople and the gay sides of the Golden Horn, with its caïques and its cypresses towering against the deepening blue sky, when lo! we do not turn towards the sea, but proceed igno-miniously to tow a great coal-ship all the way to Buyúkdere, so there is a moving panorama of all the Bosporus bestowed on us gratis—Kandilí, Baltalimán, Bebék, Yenikoi, Therapia, with its well-known walks and pines and planes, and lastly Buyúkdere, where we leave our dingy charge and return, evening darkening over the Giant's Hill, Unkiar Skelessi, and Anatóli Hissár, till we sail forth into the broad Sea of Marmora, leaving Scútari and the towers of wonderful Stamboul first pale and distinct in the light of the rising moon, and then glittering and lessening on the calm horizon, till they, and the memory that I have been among them for seven weeks, seem alike part of the world of dreams.

[1] An odious banishment

September 10

Half the morning we lie off Gallípoli, taking in merchandise and indulging in eccentric casualties—demolishing the bowsprit of one vessel and injuring divers others, for which we are condemned to three hours of clamour and arrangement of compensation. In the afternoon we wait off the Dardanelles, not an inviting town as beheld from the sea; C.M.C. (says the Consul's son) sets off for Athos in two days to meet me. Again we move, and day wears away amid perplexing twinges foreshadowing fever (for your Greek fever when once he has fairly secured you is your Old Man of the Sea for a weary while; you tremble—and fly to quinine as your only chance of escape). Towards four or five the mountains of the Troad fade away in the distance; later we pass near the isles of Imbros and Samothrace; and later yet, when the unclouded sun has sunk down, a mountain pile of awful form looms sublimely in the west—rising from the glassy calm waters against the clear amber western sky: it is Mount Athos.

September 11

At sunrise the highest peaks of Athos were still visible above the long, low line of Cape Drépano, and at noon we were making way up the Gulf of Salonica, Ossa and Olympus on our left—lines of noble mountain grandeur, but becoming rapidly indistinct as a thick sirocco-like vapour gradually shrouded over all the features of the western shore of the gulf. *N'importe*—the Vale of Tempe, so long a dim expectation, is now a near reality; and Olympus is indubitably at hand, though invisible for the present. There were wearily long flat points of land to pass (all, however, full of interest as parts of the once flourishing Chalcidice) ere Salonica was visible, a triangle enclosed in a border of white walls on the hill at the head of the gulf; and it was nearly 6 P.M. before we reached the harbour and anchored.

Instantly the wildest confusion seized all the passive human freight. The polychromatic harem arose and moved like a bed of tulips in a breeze; the packed Wallachians and Bosniacs and Jews started cramp-

19

fully from the deck and disentangled themselves into numerous boats; the Consular Esiliati departed; and lastly, I and my dragoman prepared to go, and were soon at shore, though it was not so easy to be upon it. Salonica is inhabited by a very great proportion of Jews; nearly all the porters in the city are of that nation, and now that the cholera had rendered employment scarce there were literally crowds of black-turbaned Hebrews at the water's edge, speculating on the possible share of each in the conveyance of luggage from the steamer. The enthusiastic Israelites rushed into the water and, seizing my arms and legs, tore me out of the boat and up a narrow board with the most unsatisfactory zeal; immediately after which they fell upon my enraged dragoman in the same mode, and finally throwing themselves on my luggage each portion of it was claimed by ten or twelve frenzied agitators who pulled this way and that way till I who stood apart, resigned to whatever might happen confidently awaited the total destruction of my *roba*. From yells and pullings to and fro, the scene changed in a few minutes to a real fight, and the whole community fell to the most furious hair-pulling, turban-clenching, and robe-tearing, till the luggage was forgotten and all the party was involved in one terrific combat. How this exhibition would have ended I cannot tell, for in the heat of the conflict my man came running with a half-score of Government Kawási, or police; and the way in which they fell to belabouring the enraged Hebrews was a thing never to be forgotten. These took a deal of severe beating from sticks and whips before they gave way, and eventually some six or eight were selected to carry the packages of the Ingliz, which I followed into the city, not unvexed at being the indirect cause of so much strife.[1]

In Salonica there is a Locanda—a kind of hotel—the last dim shadow of European 'accommodation' between Stamboul and Cáttaro [Kotor]: it is kept by the politest of Tuscans, and the hostess is the most corpulent and blackest of negresses. Thither we went; but I observed, with pain, that the state of the city was far more melancholy than I had had reason to suppose: all the bazaars (long lines of shops) were closed and tenant-less: the gloom and deserted air of the streets was most sad, and I needed not to be told that the cholera, or whatever were the complaint so generally raging, had broken out with fresh virulence since the last

[1] The Jews in Salonica are descended from those expelled from Spain in the fifteenth century: they are said to amount in number to four thousand.

20

accounts received at Constantinople, and nearly three-fourths of the living population had fled from their houses into the adjacent country. And no sooner was I settled in a room at the inn than, sending Giorgio to the British Consulate, I awaited his return and report with some anxiety.

Presently in came Giorgio with the dreariest of faces, and the bearer of what to me were, in truth, seriously vexatious news.

The cholera, contrary to the intelligence received in Stamboul, which represented the disease as on the decline, had indeed broken out afresh and was spreading or—what is the same thing as to results, if a panic be once rife—was supposed to be spreading on all sides. The surrounding villages had taken alarm and had drawn a strict *cordon sanitaire* between themselves and the enemy; and, worse than all, the monks of Mount Athos had utterly prohibited all communication between their peninsula and the infected city; so that any attempt on my part to join C.M.C. would be useless, no person being allowed to proceed beyond a few miles outside the eastern gate of Salonica. No one could tell how long this state of things would last; for, although the epidemic was perhaps actually decreasing in violence, yet the fear of contagion was by no means so. Multitudes of the inhabitants of the suburbs and adjacent villages had fled to the plains, and to pass them would be an impossibility. On the south-western road to Greece or Epirus, the difficulty was the same: even at Katerina, or Platamona, the peasants would allow no one to land.[1]

Here was a dilemma!—a pleasant fix!—yet it was one that required the remedy of resolve, rather than of patience. To remain in a city full of epidemic disease (and those only who have seen an Oriental provincial town under such circumstances can estimate their horror), myself but convalescent, was literally to court the risk of renewed illness, or at best compulsory detention by quarantine. Therefore, after weighing the matter well, I decided that my first step must be to leave Salonica at the very earliest opportunity. But whither to go? Mount Athos was shut; the west coast of the gulf was tabooed. There were but two plans open: the first was to return by the next steamer to Constantinople; but this involved a fortnight's waiting, at least, in the place of pestilence, with

[1] Such were the representations made to me at the time, and which naturally deterred me from attempting to reach Mount Athos; but I have since had reason to believe that the state of alarm and panic was greatly exaggerated.

the chance of being disabled before the time of departure came; and even could I adopt such means of escape, the expense and mortification of going back was, if possible, to be shunned.

The second *modus operandi* was to set off directly, by the north-west road, through Macedonia to Illyrian Albania, by the ancient Via Egnatia, and so rejoin C.M.C. at Yannina. This plan, though not without weighty objection—of which the being compelled to go alone and the great distance of the journey were prominent—appeared to me the only safe and feasible one; and after much reflection I finally determined to adopt it. After all, looking at things on their brightest side, when once they were discovered to be inevitable—though I was unable to meet my friend I had a good servant accustomed to travel with Englishmen: health would certainly improve in the air of the mountain country, and professional objects, long in view, would not be sacrificed. As for the risk run by thus rushing into strange places and among unknown people, when a man has walked all over the wildest parts of Italy he does not prognosticate danger. Possibly one may get only as far as Monastír—the capital of Macedonia—and then make southward, having seen Yiannitsa and Edéssa—places all full of beauty and interest; or, beyond Monastír, lies Akhridha and its lake, and farther yet Elbassán, or even Skódra— highest in the wilds of Ghéghe Albania. Make, thought I to myself, no definite arrangement beyond that of escape from Salonica; put yourself, as a predestinarian might say, calmly into the dice-box of small events, and be shaken out whenever circumstances may ordain: only go, and as soon as you can. So, Giorgio, have horses and all minor matters in complete readiness at sunrise the day after tomorrow.

SEPTEMBER 12

This intervening day before my start 'somewhere or other' tomorrow I set apart for lionising Salonica with a cicerone.

Whatever the past of Salonica, its present seems gloomy enough. The woe, the dolefulness of this city!—its narrow, ill-paved streets (evil awaits the man who tries to walk with nailed boots on the rounded, slippery stones of a Turkish pavement!); the very few people I met in

22

them carefully avoiding contact; the closed houses; the ominous silence; the sultry, oppressive heat of the day; all contributed to impress the mind with a feeling of heavy melancholy. A few Jews in dark dresses and turbans; Jewesses, their hair tied up in long, caterpillar-like green silk bags, three feet in length; Greek porters, aged blacks, of whom— freed slaves from Stamboul—there are many in Salonica; these were the only human beings I encountered in threading a labyrinth of lanes in the lower town, ascending towards the upper part of this formerly extensive city. Once, a bier with a corpse on it, borne by some six or eight of the most wretched creatures, crossed my path; and when I arrived at the beautiful ruin called the Incantada two women, I was told, had just expired within the courtyard, and, said the ghastly-looking Greek on the threshold, 'You may come in and examine what you please, and welcome; but once in you are in quarantine, and may not go out', an invitation I declined as politely as I could and passed onward. From the convent at the summit of the town, just within its white walls, the view should be most glorious, as one ought to see the whole of the gulf and all the range of Olympus; but, alas! beyond the silvery minarets reliev- ing the monotonous surface of roofs below and the delicately indented shore and the blue gulf, all else was blotted out, as it were, by a curtain of hot purple haze, telling tales to my fancy of miasma and cholera, fever and death.

Willing to exercise the mind as much as possible in a place so full of melancholy influences, I examined, in order, every ruin and record of old Thessalonica—the mosques in the lower town, and in the courtyard of one of these the pulpit said to be St. Paul's, the Roman arch, with its *bassi rilievi*, and the Hippodrome; and, although there was no one of these I particularly regretted that I could not draw, yet I saw an infinity of picturesque bits, cypresses and minarets and latticed houses; and doubtless, under more cheering circumstances, a week in Salonica might be well spent. But the fear of fever deterred me from great exertion, and sent me home long ere noon. Sad, gloomy, and confused memories of Salonica are all I shall carry away with me. In the afternoon, Mr. C. Blunt, our Consul, came to me, and strongly recommended my own decision as the best, his account of Athos and the west coast being con- firmatory of that I had previously heard. The evening was passed with his agreeable family, long resident here.

SEPTEMBER 13

By 7 A.M. the four post-horses and the Soorudji are ready. In these parts of Turkey, blessed with a post-road, you have no choice as to your mode of travelling, nor can you stop where you will, so easily as you may with horses hired from private owners. Yiannitsa being the next post from Salonica (reckoned ten hours), thither must I go. The Soorudji or post-boy, always rides first, leading the baggage-horse, and is almost always fair food for the pencil, for he wears a drab jacket with strange sky-blue embroideries, a short kilt, and other arrangements highly artistical.

The morning was sultry and uninviting. We left the ill-paved, gloomy Salonica by the Vardhári gate, which at that early hour was crowded with groups of the utmost picturesqueness, bringing goods to market in carts drawn by white-eyed buffali : immense heaps of melons appeared to be the principal article of trade ; but their sale being pro-hibited within the walls of the city, on account of the cholera, the remain-ing inhabitants came outside to buy them, taking them in *nascostamente*.[1]

The broad, sandy road, enlivened for a time by these peasants, soon grew tiresome, as it stretched over a plain, whose extent and beauty were altogether hidden by the thick haze which clung close to the hori-zon. Hardly were the bright white walls of Salonica long distinguishable ; and as for the mountains and Olympus, they were all as if they were not, —a colourless, desert 'pianura'—such seemed my day's task to over-come. Nevertheless, though the picture was a failure as a whole, its details kept me awake and pleased, varieties of zoology attracting obser-vation on all sides. Countless kestrels hovering in the air or rocking on tall thistles ; hoopoes, rollers, myriads of jackdaws, great broad-winged falcons soaring above, and beautiful grey-headed ones sitting composedly close to the roadside as we passed—so striking in these regions is the effect of the general system of kindness towards animals prevalent throughout Turkey—the small black-and-white vulture was there too, and now and then a graceful milk-white egret, slowly stalking in search-ful meditation.

The usual pace of the Menzil[2] is a very quick trot, and the great distance accomplished by Tatars[3] in their journeys is well authenticated ;

[1] Secretly.   [2] Menzil, the Turkish post.   [3] Tatar, a courier.

but not being up to hard work, I rode slowly: besides, the short shovel stirrups and peaked saddle are troubles you by no means get used to in a first lesson. At half past eleven we reached the Vardas, a broad river (the apple of discord between Greek and Turk, as a boundary question), and here crossed by a long structure of wood, bristling with props and prongs: near its left bank stands a khan—destined to be our midday resting-place.[1]

A sort of raised wooden dais, or platform, extends before the road-side Turkish khan: here mats are spread, and day wayfarers repose, the roof, prolonged on poles, serving as shelter from sun or rain. Three Albanian guards—each a picture—were smoking on one side, and while Giorgio was preparing my dinner of cold fowl and an omelette on the other I sketch the bridge and watch the infinite novelty of the moving parts of the scene which make this wild, simple picture alive with interest, for the bridge and a few willows are foreground and middle distance: remote view there is none. Herds of slow, bare-hided buffali, each with a white spot on the forehead and with eyes of bright white— surrounded by juvenile buffalini, only less awkward than themselves; flocks of milk-white sheep, drinking in the river; here and there a passing Mohammedan on horseback, one of whom, I observed, carried a hooded falcon, with bells on his turban; how I wished all these things could be portrayed satisfactorily, and how I looked forward to increasing beauty of costume and scenery when among the wilder parts of the country.

1 P.M. Again in travelling trim and crossing the rickety bridge; we trotted, or galloped for three hours across a continuous, wide, undulating bare plain, only enlivened by zoological appearances as before, all the distant landscape being hidden still. Near the road many great tumuli were observable on either side during the day, and a large portion of the plain near the Vardar was white with salt, a kind of saline mist appearing to fall for more than an hour. At the eighth hour we had approached so near the mountains that their forms came out clearly through the hazy atmosphere and one needle-like white column, the minaret of the chief mosque of Yiannitsa was visible, the town itself being nearly reached at the ninth hour, an event which, with a stumbling horse and fatigued limbs, I gladly hailed.

1 Vardar, anciently the Axius: the bridge is eighteen hundred feet in length.

25

It would not do to let a day pass without making a large drawing, so I waited outside the town or village, to work until sunset. Yiannitsa[1] is near the site of ancient Pella, the birthplace of Alexander the Great; in our days it is a beautiful specimen of Macedonian town scenery, situated in groves of rich foliage, overtopped by shining white minarets, with here and there one or two mosque domes and a few tall dark cypresses; these are the most prominent features; all the little dirty houses, which a nearer acquaintance makes you too familiar with, are hidden by the trees, so that the difference between that which seems and that which is is vastly wide. Yet as (my drawing done) I entered the place nothing can be more striking and characteristic than the interior of the village, though the poetry and grandeur vanish. Lanes, rich in vegetation, and broken ground, animated by every variety of costume, surround the entrance and conduct you to streets, narrow and flanked with wooden, two-storied houses, galleried and raftered, with broad-tiled eaves over-shadowing groups of Turks or Greeks, recumbent and smoking in the upper floor, while loiterers stand at the shop doors below: in the kennel are geese in crowds, and the remainder of the street is as fully occupied by goats and buffaloes as by Turks or Christians. Beyond all this are mountains of grandest form, appearing over the high, dark trees, so that altogether no artist need complain of this as a subject.

Curious to know how one would be off for lodgings in Macedonia, I found Giorgio at the postmaster's house, where, in one of the above-noticed wooden galleries (six or eight silent Turks sat puffing around), I was glad of a basin of tea. But it is most difficult to adopt the Oriental mode of sitting; cross-leggism from first to last was insupportable to me and, as chairs exist not, everything must needs be done at full length. Yet it is a great charm of Turkish character that they never stare or wonder at anything; you are not bored by any questions, and I am satisfied that if you chose to take your tea while suspended by your feet from the ceiling not a word would be said or a sign of amazement betrayed; in consequence you soon lose the sense of the absurd so nearly akin to shame, on which you are forced to dwell if constantly reminded of your awkwardness by observation or interrogation.

Whatever may be said of the wretchedly 'bare' state of a Turkish

---

[1] Apostolus, a village at a small distance, is the nearest place to the actual site of Pella.

house, or khan, that, in my estimation, is its chief virtue. The closet (literally a closet, being about six feet six inches by four and perfectly guiltless of furniture) in which my mattress was placed was floored with new deal and whitewashed all over, so that a few minutes' sweeping made it a clean, respectable habitation, such as you would find but seldom in Italian Locande of greater pretension. One may not, however, always be so lucky; but if all the route has accommodations like this, there will be no great hardship to encounter.

SEPTEMBER 14

To make sure of as long a day as possible, the elaborate northern meal of breakfast may be well omitted; a good basin of coffee and some toast is always enough and is soon over, and until starting-time there are always stray minutes for sketching. The inhabitants of Yiannitsa seem to know little of the *malattia*[1] (though but nine hours distant) at Salonica and ask few questions about it; but Turks are such imperturbable people that it is not easy to discover their thoughts. The outskirts of this quiet town are most peaceful and rural and the picturesque odds and ends within might occupy the man of the pencil pleasantly and profitably.

While taking a parting cup of coffee with the postmaster I unluckily set my foot on a handsome pipe-bowl (pipe-bowls are always snares to near-sighted people moving over Turkish floors, as they are scattered in places quite remote from the smokers, who live at the farther end of prodigiously long pipe-sticks)—crash; but nobody moved; only on apologising through Giorgio, the polite Mohammedan said: 'The breaking such a pipe-bowl would indeed, under ordinary circumstances, be disagreeable; but in a friend every action has its charm!'—a speech which recalled the injunction of the Italian to his son on leaving home, 'Whenever anybody treads upon your foot in company, and says, "*Scusatemi*", only reply: "*Anzi—mi ha fatto un piacere!*" '[2]

The morning seemed lowering and a drizzling rain soon fell. This perpetual haze must end in some one or two days' hard rain before the

[1] Illness.
[2] I beg pardon. On the contrary, you have done me a pleasure.

weather clears, and I speculate where the durance is to be borne the while. Avoiding the grass-grown raised pavement, which is the post-road in Turkey, wherever mud or water prevent your using the broad track parallel to which it leads, we advanced by well-worn paths over a plain somewhat similar to that of yesterday, but which became more marshy, and in parts more cultivated, as we approached the hills of [Edhessa], backed by the dark cloudy mountains beyond. From time to time we pass herds of buffaloes; falcons are numerous on all sides, and, added to yesterday's ornithology, there are hooded crows, rooks, coots, quails, and plovers. At eleven we arrive at Arnaoutlík, a village of Greek and Bulgarian Christian peasants.

Of Giorgio, dragoman, cook, valet, interpreter, and guide, I have had as yet nothing to complain; he is at home in all kinds of tongues, speaking ten fluently, an accomplishment common to many of the travelling Oriental Greeks, for he is a Smyrniote by birth. In countenance my attendant is somewhat like one of those strange faces, lion or griffin, which we see on door-knockers or urn-handles, and a grim twist of his under-jaw gives an idea that it would not be safe to try his temper too much. In the morning he is diffuse and dilates on past journeys; after noon his remarks become short and sententious—not to say surly. Any appearance of indecision evidently moves him to anger speedily. It is necessary to watch the disposition of a servant on whom so much of one's personal comfort depends, and it is equally necessary to give as little trouble as possible, for a good dragoman has always enough to do without extra whims or worryings from his employer.

At Arnaoutlík the horses rest and the fire of the khan is in request, for rain has fallen all the morning, though capotes and plaids kept it off pretty well. The village, composed of scattered wooden houses, is full of prettiness; but fierce dogs, when the rain ceases, prevent my going near any of the buildings as much as a multitude of wasps do my eating a peaceful dinner on the khan platform. Yet, spite of dogs, wasps, and wet, distances veiled over by cloud, and all other hindrances, there is opportunity to remark in the scene before me a subject somewhat ready-made to the pencil of a painter, which is marvellous: it is not easy to say why it is so, but a picture it is. Copy what you see before you, and you have a picture full of good qualities, in its way—a small way, we grant—a mere village landscape in a classic land. Blocks of old stone—squared

and cut long ago in other ages—overgrown with very long grass, clustering lentisk, and glossy leaves of arum, form your nearest foreground;
among them sit and lie three Soorudgís, white-kilted, red, brown and
orange-jacketed, red-capped, piped, moustached, blue-gaitered, barefooted. Your next distance is a flat bit of sandy ground, with a winding
road, and on it one white-capoted shepherd: beyond, yet still near the
eye, is a tract of grey earth, something between common and quarry,
broken into miniature ravines and tufted with short herbage: here lie
some fifty white and black sheep and a pair of slumbering dogs, while
near them two shepherd-boys are playing on a simple reed-like flute,
such as Praxiteles might have put in a statue's hands. A little farther on
you see two pale stone and wooden houses, with tiled roofs, mud walls,
and long galleries hung with many a coloured bit of carpet. Close by,
in gardens, dark-cloaked women are gathering gourds and placing them
on the roofs to dry. Grey, tall willows and spreading planes overshade
these houses, and between the trees you catch a line of pale lilac plain,
with faint blue hills of exquisite shapes—the last link in the landscape
betwixt earth and heaven.

At half past one P.M. a restart. Sky clearing and high mountains
peeping forth. Cultivation increases and fields of gran-turco or Indian
corn are frequent as we approach the valley of the Karasmák,[1] which we
cross by a bridge, and the country becomes more and more thickly
studded with groups of planes and various trees. At half past three we
are in sight of Vodhená,[2] and a more beautifully situated place can hardly
be imagined, even shorn as it is just now by cloud and mist of its mountain background. It stands on a long ridge of wooded cliff, with mosques
sparkling above and waterfalls glittering down the hillside, not unlike
the Cascatelli of Tivoli, the whole screen of rock seeming to close up the
valley as a natural wall.

The air began to freshen as the road ascended from the plain through
prodigiously large walnut and plane trees shading the winding paths, and
as the valley narrowed the rushing of many streams below the waving
branches was most delicious; between the fine groups of dense foliage
the dark mass of the woody rock of Vodhená is irresistibly beautiful, and
before we reached the dreary scattered walls and suburb lanes, by

[1] Karasmák or Mavronéri—anciently the River Lydias.
[2] Ægæ or Edhessa, the capital of ancient Macedonia.

29

climbing for half an hour up a winding pass between high rocks, I was more than once tempted to linger and draw. From the proud height on which this ancient city stood the combination of green wood, yellow plain, and distant mountain was most lovely, and I can conceive that when the atmosphere is clear and all the majesty of Olympus, with the gulf of Salonica (and perhaps Athos), also are visible, few scenes in Greece can surpass the splendour of this.

After six we arrived at the postmaster's house in the centre of the town—one of those strange, wide-eaved, double-bodied, painted and galleried Turkish abodes which strike the stranger with wonder; but the whole place was full of the retinue of some travelling pashá—guards above and horses below—a small outhouse abounding with cats and cobwebs being also full of a large party of Bulgarian merchants. So Giorgio set out to seek a lodging in some Greek tradesman's house, and I wound up the evening by a prowl through the streets of the town, in which, to all the varieties of Yiannitsa is added a profusion of fountains of running water and numerous streams half the width of its sloping streets. Tea and lodging (so-called) I found prepared over a large stable—a great falling off from last night's accommodation—the floor of the barn being of that vague nature that one contemplated the horses below through various large cavities, by means of some of which one might, by any too hasty movement, descend unwittingly among them ere morning.

SEPTEMBER 15

By five I was out on the road to Yiannitsa, at a dervish's tomb, not far from the town, a spot which I had remarked yesterday as promising, if weather permitted, a good view eastward. All the plain below is bright yellow as the sun rises gloriously, and Olympus is for once in perfect splendour, with all its snowy peaks; but the daily perplexity of mist and cloud rapidly soars upward and hardly leaves time for a sketch ere all is once more shrouded away.

The dervish's or saint's tomb is such as you remark frequently on the outskirts of Mohammedan towns in the midst of wide cemeteries of humble sepulchres—a quadrangular structure three or four feet high, with pillars at the corners supporting a dome of varying height; beneath its centre is usually the carved emblem of the saint's rank, his turban, or high-crowned hat. As these tombs are often shaded by trees, their effect is very pleasing, the more so that the cemeteries are mostly frequented by the contemplative faithful. Often, in their vicinity, especially if the position of the tombs commands a fine view or is near a running stream, you may notice one of those raised platforms with a cage-like palisade and supporting a roof in the shade of which the Mohammedan delights to squat and smoke. There is one close by me now in which a solitary elder sits, in the enjoyment of tobacco and serenity, and looking in his blue and yellow robes very like an encaged macaw.

A quick run down the rocky pass of last evening brought me to the great plane trees and the bright stream whence Vodhená, on its hill, is so lovely—a scene difficult to match in beauty. I met many peasants and long strings of laden mules, but no one took the faintest notice of me—a negative civility highly gratifying after all one hears of the ferocity of the aborigines of these regions. That the road as far as Vodhená is considered carriageable was proved to me by the strange spectacle which passed me on my way up to the town—eight horses pulling up the steep ascent with a carriage full of masked ladies, the beloved of some Mohammedan dignitary. Eight armed outriders preceded this apparition and a troop of guards followed the precious charge.

Before an early *déjeûner* at ten there was yet time to draw a street scene, though the curiosity of half the people of Vodhená obliged me to stand on a stone in the midst of the kennel to draw. Their shouts of laughter as I represented the houses were electrifying: '*Scroo! scroo! scroo!*' (He writes it down! he writes! he writes!) they shouted. But it was all good nature: no wilful annoyance of any kind.

Before eleven I had quitted this beautiful place and was once more on the road to Monastír, not that one hoped to get there ere nightfall, but only to some midway khan or village. Rain began to fall as I turned away from woody Vodhená and its streams, and heavier showers fell in the narrow cultivated valley through which our route lay, on the left bank of the Karasmák. Having crossed it, we ascended towards the higher mountains, their heads hidden in mist, and as the road rose rapidly among their steep sides many a lofty summit, towering above screens fringed with hanging wood, was more and more magnificent,

31

while, looking back over Vodhená, the plain of Yiannitsa and the hills of Salonica were visible afar off. But as we scaled the highest part of the pass and I saw the last glimpse of the eastern sea the rain fell in tremendous torrents, and we urged the horses to the full speed of Tatar trot and gallop. A vale and marshy lake lying at the foot of chestnut-clothed hills and a world of purple rock and waterfall reminding me of Borrowdale— high peaks frowning through the driving clouds, stony lanes, paths through overhanging oakwoods, rivulets, clay ravines, slippery rocks— all flitted by in rapid succession as we galloped on, without a halt, till the drenching tempest ceased about half-past one and I found myself looking down on the Lake of Ostrovo, whose dark grey bosom stretched dimly into worlds of clouded heights on either side of its extent. The whole of the pass from Vodhená to Ostrovo, I doubt not, is full of great beauty and I lost it with regret.

At Ostrovo I decided to remain,[1] too fearful of returning fever to hazard the seven hours' journey between it and the next village— Tilbelí; and on descending a steep path to the lake the little town and mosque shone out brightly against the lead-coloured waters and cloud-swept mountains, a scene of grandeur reminding me in its hues of Wastwater and Keswick, while the snow peaks, dark cypresses, and gay white minarets stamped the whole as truly Moslem-Macedonian. But, notwithstanding all these ecstasies, what a place is Ostrovo for a night's abode! This most wretched little village contains but one small khan, with two tiny rooms on the ground floor, in one of which, half suffocated by the smoke of a wood fire, I was too glad to change dripping garments and don dry ones; let the traveller in these countries be never forgetful of so wrapping up his *roba* that he may have dry changes of raiment when needful. Happily the weather cleared after the storm, and I drew till dusk, none the worse for the morning's wetting and feeling hourly the benefit of the elastic mountain air.

Broiled and boiled salmon trout, rice soup, and onions awaited me in the Mivart's of Ostrovo—and, let me say, that is by no means a bad supper to find in a Macedonian khan. The evening passed in the intellectual diversion of drying one's wet clothes by little bits of firewood and in packing one's self so as to sleep tolerably, spite of there being no bolt to the door. But, in truth, in so forlorn a spot as this no precautions

[1] Counted as four hours from Vodhená.

YIANNITSA

VODHENÁ

could ensure safety against force, were robbery intended. Never, in the wildest of countries, have I met with any robber adventure, and not being troubled by suspicions of danger I have come to believe that carelessness as to attack is the best safeguard against any. Mats hung to the roof and window keep out some of the air (for an unglazed hole in the wall, and a series of apertures in the roof add to the charms of this hotel), but the wood smoke is the worst enemy and I am glad to seek refuge from it in slumber.

SEPTEMBER 16

Bitter cold saluted me at rising—if that may be called rising which, in this chair-less land, consists in a perpetual scramble on the floor, reminding the performer of such creatures as swallows and bats, of whom naturalists relate that their difficulty of leaving the ground, when once there, is extreme. Brightly silvered with snow were all the great mountains round the lake, and till half past seven I drew, charmed with the grandeur and beauty of this noble scene. However miserable the village of Ostrovo (it bears marks of greater size and prosperity), its position is magnificent; the people also seem thoroughly quiet and civil.

The route to Monastír lies round the head of the lake, where, on the marshy tract, stalk numbers of ivory-white herons, and after leaving the shores we mount high above their level, by zigzag paths, whence there is many a wide and brilliant view over all the waters of Ostrovo.

For two hours we proceed by brushwood-covered hills, possessing small share of beauty or interest, to some bleak downs, where on our left stands a village, half an hour beyond which is a magnificent view of another lake (which I somewhat believe to be that of Kastoriá, the ancient Celetrum), the shores of which were beautifully indented and varied with promontories and bays, and the lines of hills on all sides graceful and striking. But beyond this oasis two hours and a half of weariness followed, treeless, bare hillsides, unbroken by the least variety of interest, and I began to repent heartily of ever having come to Macedonia, the more that rain again began to fall as I approached Tilbelí, still three hours and a half from Monastír. But it was necessary to rest the horses here, the roads of the morning having been unusually stony and fatiguing, and after such halt it would be too late to start afresh, as another tempest was evidently gathering. So at Tilbelí I remain for the night, much against my will, for this straggling village in a wide green valley presents little for the pencil. By way of compensation the khan is very decent, and my lodging is in a little chamber like a pigeon-house, over the gate of the courtyard, the ascent to which is by a ladder, which being removed the dweller above remains suspended in air. This comfortless weather is very dispiriting, for it is bitterly cold and the pigeon-loft trembles spasmodically in every gust of wind. Yet writing letters on the floor and drinking tea out of a plate (for the basin is broken) wear away the evening quickly after all.

September 17

The ornithological attractions of the village of Tilbelí seem divided between jackdaws and geese; it is difficult to imagine the numbers of these feathered musicians in every lane and on every roof; their noise is perfectly stunning. Off by six and a dreary commencement is prolonged for three hours in a bitter cold wind, over hideous hill-plains, stony and shrubless, and recalling the melancholy Murgie of Altamura in South Italy. Descending about half past nine to the great plain of Bitola, or Monastír (the military centre and capital of modern Macedonia and Northern Albania), white minarets, extensive buildings, and gardens were a pleasant sight, as the city seemed to expand on our approaching the high mountains at the foot of which it is built.

Had it not been for the caprices of our guide, a wild gipsy Soorudgí, we should sooner have arrived at our destination than we did; that worthy having met with a fellow gipsy on horseback, the twain indulged in convivial draughts of rakhee at two roadside khans to so great an extent that their merriment became boundless, and having loosened the baggage and led horses, they drove them facetiously in and out of fields of maize and corn—for we were now near the city—till their sport terminated in the lively new-comer subsiding into a quagmire, where his horse, anxious to make a good meal in the next field of gran-turco, left him to his fate. This catastrophe rather pleased me than not, till, on entering Monastír, our own Soorudgí suddenly gave way to pangs of conscience, and neither threats nor entreaties could prevent his returning for his lost friend, which meritorious act caused us an hour's delay ere we reached the barrier of the city.

Here we were interrogated by an official who, in the matter of passports, was soon satisfied by the αντός μιλόζδος Ινγλίς of Giorgio —('this English Milord', all English travellers being so termed in the East)—and we passed onward. Close to the town, on the eastern side, stretches a wide common, used as a cemetery, and forming the unmolested abode of troops of dogs, who lie in groups of ten or twenty till the town scavengers bring them their morning and evening meal.

Monastír (or Bitóla) contains not less than fourteen or fifteen thousand inhabitants, and is the metropolis of these remote provinces, a pre-eminence evidently justified by its activity and prosperity. It is also a place of the greatest importance, as commanding the direct entrance from Illyria into Macedonia by the passes of the River Drilon or Drin, and as a military centre from which Epirus and Thessaly are equally accessible.

Anticipating—as in every previous case during this journey—that the glitter and beauty of outward appearance would be exchanged on entering the city for squalor and dreariness, I was agreeably surprised at the great extent of public buildings, barracks, and offices at the entrance of the town, and, within it, at the width and good pavement of the streets, the cleanliness and neatness of the houses. The bazaars are exceedingly handsome, some entirely roofed over and lighted from above with windows, others only partially sheltered or semi-roofed with matting on poles. Great numbers of vendors and buyers throng these resorts, the principal part of the former being merchants—Greek or Bulgarian Christians—and of the latter Christian peasantry from the neighbouring villages and country. The Turks resident in Monastír are for the most part either military or officials: Greeks and Bulgarians form the majority of the inhabitants. Albanians there are few, excepting guards or exiles (Monastír is a frequent place of banishment for rebel Beys): of Jews a vast number. Being the central situation for all military operations relating to North and South Albania, Thessaly, Macedonia, and Bosnia, the bustle and brilliancy of Monastír is remarkable, and its effect appeared particularly striking coming to it, as I did, after passing through a wild and thinly peopled region. You are bewildered by the sudden reappearance of a civilisation which you had apparently left for ever: reviews, guards, bands of music, pashás, palaces, and sentry-boxes, bustling scenes and heaps of merchandise await you at every turn.

The natural beauties of Monastír are abundant. The city is built at the western edge of a noble plain, surrounded by the most exquisitely shaped hills, in a recess or bay formed by two very high mountains, between which magnificent snow-capped barriers is the pass to Akhridha. A river runs through the town, a broad and shifting torrent crossed by numerous bridges, mostly of wood, on some of which two rows of shops stand, forming a broad covered bazaar. At present three of these bridges are in ruins, or under repair after the winter's floods. The stream, deep and narrow throughout the quarter of private houses and palaces, is spanned by two good stone bridges and confined by strong walls; but in the lower or Jew's quarter, where the torrent is much wider and shallower, the houses cluster down to the water's edge with surprising picturesqueness. Either looking up or down the river, the intermixture of minarets and mosques with cypress and willow foliage, forms subjects of the most admirable beauty.

We went to the largest and best khan of Monastír—Yeni khan—an extensive building surrounding three sides of a courtyard which was full of Greek merchants in blue tunics or white-coated Albanians with laden horses, etc., and luckily I obtained a corner room overlooking all this moving scene, amongst which I mean to halt two days, as I shall hardly see a more beautiful place. A clean, whitewashed cell, with glazed windows and new mats, betokens the comparative luxury of this little metropolis.

Late in the day I devote an hour or two to reconnoitring and choosing sites for tomorrow's work. The bazaars with groups of figures in them are endless kaleidoscopes of pictures. The houses are mostly of un-painted wood, though the larger palaces are whitewashed and orna-mented, and some are as gay as red and white paint can make them: the neatness and cleanliness of the place is delightful.

At sunset I find myself at the edge of the cemetery-common, and pass the last half-hour of day in watching the effects of light and shade on the noble plain, glittering like gold in its frame of purple mountains.

SEPTEMBER 18

The wind blows keenly off the snowy mountains on the west of the town, but the sun rises brightly as I begin the day by sketching in the suburbs. Greek peasantry from the hills are entering the town with market wares. The costume of the women is a black outer capote with red borderings, worked petticoats, dresses, gaiters, and handkerchiefs; scarlet-striped aprons, and enormously thick, long bunches of black silk tied to their hair, tail-fashion. But my wanderings are soon stopped by an ancient Turk, who yells forth: '*Teskeré—Teskeré*', namely, a passport; and, as I had it not about me, the unbending policeman would not listen to any explanations from Greek passers-by, but hurried me—somewhat as I was once served on a similar occasion in the kingdom of Naples—before the bar of a judge who unluckily lived a long way off, so that half my morning was wasted by this foolish adventure, the end of which was a horrible scolding from the dignitary to the old Mahomedan—who, after all, was not in fault.

When at length I endeavoured to draw in the streets of Monastír I found it impossible to work, so great was the crowd which collected to see my operations, and I was fairly mobbed to the khan, resolving that I would use my Boyourldí to procure me a guard forthwith—for one does not come to Macedonia every day and time and opportunity are not to be thrown away. But the great man here—the Seraskíer Pashá, or commander of the forces—is unwell, so I passed my afternoon in saunter-ing warily to distant points of the surrounding hills to obtain some general view of the city, dodging about to avoid lurking companies of dogs, and shunning sentinels and passport-hunters.

Marking a dervish's tomb on the northern side of the city, I threaded my way through narrow lanes to the river, at this season a scanty stream, and crossing it where the broken bridges and the long strings of laden mules, four or five hundred together, their loads covered with white and brown striped cloths, made the most perfectly picturesque scene, I arrived at the cemetery on the hills whence all Monastír is visible. A more magnificently placed city it is hardly possible to imagine, and the great quantity of cypress and plane setting off its delicate white and pink mosques is wonderfully beautiful. But the evening began to draw on, and fearful of being massacred for a ghoul, I left the home of the dead and made my way to the khans, passing over the common near the Barracks, that '*Piazza de' Cani*', where from eighty to a hundred wolfish dogs were snarling and howling over a dead horse. Meanwhile His Highness Emím Seraskíer Pashá had sent, requesting me to come to him tomorrow.

SEPTEMBER 19

Sunrise: and I am drawing the plain and hills from the '*Piazza de' Cani*'; lines of convicts are passing from the Barracks, carrying offal in tubs to the ghouly burying-grounds and followed by some hundreds of dogs, who every now and then give way to their feelings and indulge in a general battle among themselves. It is no easy matter to pursue the fine arts in Monastír, and I cannot but think—will matters grow worse as I advance into Albania? For all the passers-by, having inspected my sketching, frown or look ugly, and many say, '*Shaitán*', which means, Devil; at length one quietly wrenches my book away and shutting it up returns it to me, saying, '*Yok, Yok!*'[1]—so as numbers are against me, I bow and retire. Next, I essay to draw on one of the bridges, but a gloomy sentinel comes and bullies me off directly, indicating by signs that my profane occupation is by no manner of means to be tolerated; and farther on, when I thought I had escaped all observation behind a friendly buttress, out rush legions of odious hounds (all bare-hided and very like jackals), and raise such a din that, although by means of a pocket full of stones I keep them at bay, yet they fairly beat me at last, and gave me chase open-mouthed, augmenting their detestable pack by fresh recruits at each street corner. So I gave up this pursuit of knowledge under difficulties and returned to the khan.

Giorgio was waiting to take me to the Pashá; so dressing in my 'best', thither I went, to pay my first visit to an Oriental dignitary. All one's gathered and hoarded memories, from books or personal relations, came so clearly to my mind as I was shown into the great palace or serai of the Governor that I seemed somehow to have seen it all before; the ante-room full of attendants, the second state-room with secretaries and

[1] No, no!

officers, and, finally, the large square hall, where—in a corner and smoking the longest nargilleh, the serpentine foldings of which formed all the furniture of the chamber save the carpets and sofas—sat the Seraskíer Pashá himself—one of the highest grandees of the Ottoman empire. Emím Seraskíer Pashá was educated at Cambridge, and speaks English fluently. He conversed for some time agreeably and intelligently, and after having promised me a Kawás, the interview was over, and I returned to the khan, impatient to attack the street scenery of Monastir forthwith under the auspices of my guard. These availed me much, and I sketched in the dry part of the river-bed with impunity—aye, and even in the Jews' quarter, though immense crowds collected to witness the strange Frank and his doings; and the word, '*Scroo, Scroo*', resounded from hundreds of voices above and around. But a clear space was kept around me by the formidable baton of the Kawás, and I contrived thus to carry off some of the best views of the town ere it grew dark. How picturesque are those parts of the crowded city in the Jews' quarter, where the elaborately detailed wooden houses overhang the torrent, shaded by grand plane, cypress, and poplar! How the sunset lights up the fire-tinged clouds—floating over the snow-capped eastern hills! How striking are the stately groups of armed guards clearing the road through the thronged streets of the bazaars for some glittering Bey or mounted Pashá! Interest and beauty in profusion, O ye artists! are to be found in the city of Monastír.

The Seraskíer's letter to the principal Bey of Akhridha awaits my return to the khan, together with a large basket of pears for which a deal of backsheesh is required. Tea and packing for a start tomorrow fill up the evening. Giorgio seems by no means to like the idea of committing himself to Albanians, Gheghes, and Mereditti, and avoids all speech about Albanians in general or particularly. Three of these men occupy part of the gallery near me, and seem to pass life in strutting up and down, in grinding and drinking coffee, or in making a diminutive sort of humming to the twanging of an immensely long guitar. Sitting on their crossed legs, they bend backwards and forwards and from side to side, shaking their long hay-coloured hair or screwing their enormous moustaches; now and then they rise, whirl their vast capotes about them, flounce out their full skirts, and then bounce up and down the gallery like so many Richard the Thirds in search of Richmonds. But Giorgio by no art can be induced to say more of them than '*Sono tutti disperati*';[1] and by all, this race seems disliked and mistrusted most markedly.

SEPTEMBER 20

At Monastír the Muezzéens, or callers to public prayer from the mina-rets, are delightfully musical: none of the nasal Stamboul monotony is heard, but real bits of melody, echoing at night or early morn from the still city to the cloud-veiled hills.

Good horses are ready before sunrise, though it was past six ere we escape from the full bazaars and narrow suburban streets; carts, oxen, laden, buffali in herds

'Choked up each roaring gate;

and when we had a little cleared these obstacles, all the luggage sud-denly lopsided, and after fruitless attempts to balance it with stones, all had to be finally readjusted. I had not yet adopted the bi-sack principle.

The morning's journey was not interesting, the less so that its monotonous features were gloomy with dark and lowering clouds, making the snow above look unnecessarily cold and shading the vale below, where large herds of goats browsingly wandered among the stunted herbage under the guarding care of ferocious dogs. About five hours were consumed in winding through two valleys or passes shut in between lofty hills, in all which expenditure of time and patience no object of beauty or interest presented itself. But in these regions such a cause for complaint is of no long duration, and about noon the road—a wide, dishevelled, stony track—emerged from the pass into a valley which opened into a plain, disclosing at its southern extremity a bright lake, walled in by high, snowy mountains.[2] Westward, a charming village, embosomed in plane and chesnut and spangled with two or three glittering minarets, enlivened the scene with all the characteristic loveliness of Albanian landscape, and surrounded, except on the southern side, by most richly wooded heights.

[1] They are all miserable creatures.
[2] I believe, the lake of Peupli—but neither my guide nor Soorudgí knew; and I foolishly omitted to ask at the place itself.

40

But, as usual, all the charm is outside. The village of Peupli possesses only the filthiest of khans, and it was difficult to find a spot to cook the midday meal. Wandering meanwhile, I succeeded, between heavy showers, in making a drawing from a rising ground, whence village, lake and hills formed a most beautiful scene; dark purple mountains delicately and sharply delineated against sweeping rain-clouds; a foreground of massy chesnut trunks; foliage in gloomy, forcible masses against the silver lake and light parts of the sky; and in the plain below, the village, with its tufts of shade. Spite of threatening, no more rain fell, so I resolved that it was wisdom to go on to Akhridha, where lodgings could hardly be worse than at Peupli and scenery probably more valuable.

At half past two left Peupli. Its inhabitants are a different order of beings to those I have yet seen, a wilder and more savage race than the inhabitants of Macedonian plains; there are fewer Greeks and Bulgarians apparently, and more Turks and Albanians; the Bulgarian language is also on the decrease.

If the morning's ride were all valley, this of the afternoon is all mountain. Straightway out of the valley of Peupli went we up the steepest of heights, climbing it by a constantly winding staircase-road, though a better one than might be expected in these parts. Beautiful was the afternoon and rejoicing in all sorts of cloud effect. As we ascended towards magnificent hanging beech-woods the plain and mountains behind, with the blue lake of Peupli, its southern side fringed with pale hills fading into the distance, were a scene of the most gorgeous description. At the summit of the pass is a guard-house (a hut containing two armed Albanians, and an irritable dog, who watch over the interests of passers-by), and here, ere the western descent begins, the view is one of the loveliest eye can see. From this great height one looked over all the lake of Peupli, to plains beyond plains, and hills, and blue Olympus beyond all; the whole seen through a frame, as it were, of the gnarled branches of silver-trunked beeches crowning the ridges of the hill, whose sides feathered down to the lake in folds of innumerable wood screens: it was difficult to leave the scene, and I resolved, at any hazard, to revisit it.

Less than half an hour was occupied in crossing the height we had been scaling—a narrow rocky plain, interspersed with stunted beeches —and here, properly speaking, begins my tour in Albania, for all I have passed through is Macedonia, nor is the Albanian tongue in much use eastward of Akhridha.

Soon a new world charmed the eye, and on arriving at the edge of the western face of this high ridge the beautiful plain and lake of Akhridha burst, as it were, into existence; gilded in the setting sun and slumbering below hills, forest and snow, piled up and mingled with cloud midway in heaven. It is scarcely possible to dream of finer scenes than these, their beauty perhaps enhanced by grand storm effects, which gave them more than ordinary magic of colour and variety of interest. Bright, broad, and long lay the great sheet of water—the first of Grecian lakes—and on its edge the fortress and town of Akhridha (in form singularly resembling the castle rock of Nice, in the Sardinian States), commanding the cultivated plain which stretches from the mountains to the shores of the lake. Such sublime scenery obliterated from the memory all annoyances of travel, and astonished and delighted at every step, I already repented of my repentance that I had undertaken this journey.

The descent to the plain of Akhridha is exceedingly steep, and one watches the lake, as one slowly reaches its level, diminishing most beautifully in perspective. Nor was time wanting to observe it, for the downward passage was uncomfortably obstructed by numerous mules laden with long planks of wood, which, as their bearers jolted down the sharp turns of the mountain path, were apt to smite incautious foot passengers who approached them. Pictures without end might be made among the majestic groups of tall beech which clothe these heights, combining with the aerial effects of sky, earth, and water. On the southern side of the lake the hills are not of so fine a form, but the general effect is good, and strongly reminded me of Celáno or Fúcino, in the Abruzzi. Towards the last turns of this steep path a strange edifice—a convent—stands in a nook of the rocks, adhering, as it were, to the brown face of the mountain, and consisting of some twenty detached cells, each like the box of Punch and Judy. Beyond this, we came to a village on the level plain, and through its vistas of walnut trees the Castle of Akhridha appears now and then charmingly. Hence, over a fertile tract of garden and pasture studded with flocks—a perfect picture of peaceful quiet—we arrived at the town of Akhridha about half-past six.

A territory more naturally defined than that of Akhridha[1] it is not

[1] The ancient Achris, on the Lake Lychnitis.

easy to conceive. The whole lake is surrounded by hills, allowing small space between their base and the water, excepting on the northern side, where they recede some three miles and leave a plain which the position of the Castle of Akhridha, on its isolated rock, entirely commands. The city lies on three sides of the castle hill; and extends east and west of the fortress along the water's edge, the rock itself being a perpendicular precipice towards the south. The unvarying characteristics of these scenes were not wanting, in the white minarets and thickly grouped planes studded over the environs of the town; and as I advanced into the streets some pretty mosques attracted my attention, and here and there a broad bazaar, or market-place, shaded by plane trees of immense magnitude.

In this, the first town I had seen in Northern Albania, the novelty of the costumes is striking; for, rich as is the clothing of all these people, the tribes of Ghegheria (a district comprising all the territory north of the River Apsus, generally termed Illyrian Albania, and of which Skodra [Shkodër] may be said to be the capital and Akhridha the most western limit) surpass all their neighbours in gorgeousness of raiment, by adding to their ordinary vestments a long surtout of purple, crimson, or scarlet, trimmed with fur, or bordered with gold thread, or braiding. Their jackets and waistcoats are usually black, and their whole outer man contrasts strongly with that of their white neighbours of Berát, or many-hued brethren of Epirus. Other proofs were not wanting of my being in a new land; for as we advanced slowly through the geese-frequented kennels (a running stream with *trottoirs* on each side and crossed by stepping-stones is a characteristic of this place) my head was continually saluted by small stones and bits of dirt, the infidel air of my white hat courting the notice and condemnation of the orthodox Akhridhani. 'And,' quoth Giorgio, 'unless you take to a fez, Vossignoria will have no peace and possibly lose an eye in a day or two.

Moving on through picturesque streets, we at last reached the most considerable khan the town possessed, a building of the same description as almost all public resting-places in this part of the world. It stood around three sides of a courtyard, with the lower part appropriated to stables, the upper to some twenty chambers, communicating with a broad gallery. Glass windows are unknown here, and paper as a substitute is rare; the rooms are little dark dens—their emptiness and facility of being swept out forming their highest claim to praise. With a mat spread in a corner and bed thereon, one soon feels at home, and after a cup of tea sleep needs little waiting for.

Of many days passed in many lands, in wandering amid noble scenery, I can recall none more variously delightful and impressive than this has been.

SEPTEMBER 21

An early walk in the town, which is full of exquisite street scenes (the castle hill or the mountains always forming a background), would have been more agreeable had I not been pelted most unsparingly by women and children from unexpected corners. Escaping to the outskirts, I sketched the town and castle from a rising ground, when a shepherd ventured to approach and look at my doings; but no sooner did he discover the form of the castle on the paper than shrieking out '*Shaitán!*' he fled rapidly from me, as from a profane magician. A mizzling rain began to fall and when—avoiding herds of buffali, and flocks of sheep, with large dogs on the look-out—I made for the lake through some by-lanes, several of these wild and shy people espied me afar off and rushed screaming into their houses, drawing bolts and banging doors with the most emphatic resolve against the wandering apparition. Returning to the khan, I prepared to visit Sheréeff Bey, the Governor and principal grandee of Akhridha, to whom the Seraskíer Pashá's letter was addressed.

The fortress, towering over all the town of Akhridha and commanding an equally good view of lake, plain, and mountain, contains the serái or palace of the Governor; its overhanging, ornamented roof, lattices, and bow-windows, and the groups of wild, strange creatures peering and lounging about the narrow stairs and wooden galleries, were all objects of curiosity to one who had seen but little of barbaric pomp and circumstance, for in Monastir the dignitaries are like great officials in any other great town; and were a traveller to go to that city after visiting the wilder parts of Albania, its effect would be unprofitably flat and civilised, though to those coming from Stamboul it is striking enough.

44

The room in which Sheréef Bey was sitting—a square chamber of no very great size—was full enough of characters and costumes to set up a dozen painters for life. The Bey[1] himself, in a snuff-coloured robe trimmed with fur, the white-turbaned Cogia,[2] the scarlet-vested Gheghes, the purple-and-gold-brocaded Greek secretary, the troops of long-haired, full-skirted, glittering Albanian domestics, armed and belted—one and all looking at me with an imperturbable fixed glare (for your nonchalant Turkish good breeding is not known here)—all this formed a picture I greatly wished I could have had on paper. The Bey, after the ceremonies of pipes and coffee, offered a letter to Tirana, a town on the road to Skodra [Shkodër], and expressed his willingness to send guards with me to the end of the world, if I pleased, declaring at the same time that the roads, however unfrequented, were perfectly safe. Mindful also of missiles, I begged for a Kawás to protect me while drawing in the town of Akhridha, and then returned to the khan to dine, and afterwards passed the afternoon in sketching about the town with my Mohammedan guard, unannoyed by any sticks or stones from the hands of true believers.

At sunset the view from the portal of the fortress becomes a scene of placid spendour one can never tire of contemplating, and both in mass and in detail Akhridha has already far surpassed my expectation. They talk of the Monastery of St. Naum at the far or southern end of the lake as the great lion of the district; but I rather postpone the wish to see it until I am in the neighbourhood of Berát, as a visit thither at present must involve a return here and occupy two days.

The certainty of night rest is not among the good things of Akhridha; in the small cell I inhabit a constant clawing and squalling of cats on one side of my pillow and quacking of ducks on the other is not favourable to sleep.

SEPTEMBER 22

A cloudless morning, fresh and brilliant, induces me to put in execution my plan of retracing the route to the mountain pass by which I came

[1] Bey, a person of superior rank, frequently governor of a town.
[2] Cogia, a priest.

hither, for the purpose of sketching the Lake of Peupli; wherefore my armed Kawás and horses were ready at 7 A.M. At the foot of the hills the little monastery was exquisitely pretty in the clear shadows of early morning, and an outline of it occupied me some time; after which I began the steep ascent to the beech forests, and in the course of the upward progress, many were my pauses to contemplate the wide silver lake and its castled rock. A Government *avant-courier*, blazing in scarlet and white, his robe trimmed with fur and his kilt and gilt belt looking afar off like the plumage of some tropical bird among the dark-green foliage, met us when half-way up the mountain, and shortly afterwards the Bey-Governor of Tirana, with a long string of laden mules and glittering retainers, added interest to the novel and beautiful scene. By half past ten we had passed the little plain at the mountain's summit and had reached the solitary guardhouse.

I was glad to have devoted a day to revisiting this most noble scene. Soothing and beautiful is that vision of the Lake of Peupli, so dreamy and delicately azure, as it lies below ranges of finely formed mountains, all distinct, though lessening and becoming more faint, till the outline of Olympus closes the remote view. Then the nearer hills, with their russet smoothness and pard-like spots of clustering forest groups—and closer, the dark masses of feathery beech glowing with every autumnal hue! It is long since I have tasted hours of such quiet, and all the roughnesses of travel are forgotten in the enjoyment of scenery so calm and lovely. Many a day—month—summer passed among the beautiful forests of Monte Casale, amid the steep ravines and oak-tufted rocks of Civitella di Subiaco, in the sheltered convent and the gleaming village of the woody Apennines—many a recollection of the far plains of Latium and the Volscians—of the brightness of Italian mornings—the still freshness of its mountain noon—the serenity of its eventide, when laden villagers wind up the stony paths to aerial homes, chanting their vesper chorus—all this and a great deal more flashed strongly on my memory as I sat hour after hour on this glorious hill summit, when the present, by one of those involuntary actions of thought which all must have experienced, was thus linking itself with places and persons of the once familiar past, with all the decision and vivacity of reality.

At half past two, after a rural dinner of excellent cold fish (the trout

of the Lake of Akhridha are surpassingly fine), I retraced my way westward and was once more at the khan before dusk.

SEPTEMBER 23

One more day in Akhridha and then westward and northward. There
is a street scene below the castle, where a majestic plane shades bazaars
rich with every sort of gay-coloured raiment. Through its drooping
foliage gleams the bright top of a minaret and below it are grouped every
variety of picturesque human beings. To carry away a sketch of this was
the work of half the morning; the rest was occupied in a walk on the
eastern shore of the lake, an excursion I was obliged to make alone, as the
protecting Kawás was sent to procure horses for tomorrow's journey.
Beautiful was the castle on its rock reflected in the clear bright water;
but what most amused me was the infinite number of birds which, all
unsuspectingly sociable, enlivened the scene; thousands of coots frater-
nising with the domestic ducks and geese—white egrets performing
stately tours of observation among the reeds—magpies (a bird remarkably abundant in the vicinity of Akhridha), hooded crows and daws—a
world of ornithology. Far away at the end of the lake[1] glitters a solitary
white speck, which they tell me is the monastery of St. Naum, but that
is out of my track for the present; so I sauntered back to the khan,
lingering now and then to look at the Greek women who, with embroidered handkerchiefs on their heads and dressed in scarlet and black
capotes, were washing linen in the lake, when, having watched their
opportunity, and seeing me unescorted, a crowd of the faithful took
aim from behind walls and rocks, discharging unceasing showers of
stones, sticks, and mud. May my spectacles survive the attack!
thought I, as forced into an ignominious retreat I arrived at the khan
considerably damaged about the nose and ears and not a little out of
humour.

In the afternoon, with my guide, I was able to laugh at my enemies
while I drew a fine old Greek church, now turned into a mosque, and
obtained lastly an extensive view from the clock tower on the castle hill,

[1] They count six hours' journey from Akhridha to the southern end of the lake.

whence the town tranquilly lying among tufted planes and tall cypresses
recalls the lines of Child Harold—

> And the pale crescent sparkles in the glen
> Through many a cypress grove within each city's ken.

Certainly Akhridha is a beautiful place. All the hillside below the
fortress is thickly studded with Mohammedan tombs—little wedges of
rough stone growing out of the soil, as it were, like natural geological
excrescences—by thousands. From the streets below parties of women
clad in dark blue and masked in white wrappers wander forth to take the
air, and near me several crimson-and-purple-coated Gheghes smoke
abstractedly on scattered bits of rock; when the sun throws his last
red rays from the high western mountains up the side of the castle hill
long trains of black buffaloes poke hither and thither, grunting and
creaking forth their strange semi-bark, which sounds like the cracking
of old furniture. On the whole, the zoological living world of Akhridha
is very oppressive; what with dogs, geese, buffali, asses, mules, and
horses, jackdaws, goats, and sheep, the streets are a great deal too full of
animated nature to be comfortable, however confiding and amiable the
several species may be. As for the white-eyed buffali, they are lazy and
serene brutes, very opposite in character to their relatives in the
marshes of Terracina and Pesto. You may bully them, either by pushing
their noses or tugging at their horns as much as you please when they
are in your way, and they never resent the indignity.

The khan was swarming with magnificence when I returned to it, the
Bey of Tirana and all his train having arrived. Simplicity is the rule of
life with Albanian grandees; they sit silently on a mat and smoke, but
their retinue bounce and tear about with a perfectly fearful energy, and
after supper indulge in music according to their fashion until a late hour,
then throwing themselves down to sleep in their capotes, and at early
morning going through the slightest possible form of facial ablution—
for cleanliness is not the most shining national virtue. These at Akhridha
seem a wild and savage set and are not easy to catch by drawing. Yet
tomorrow I enter the wildest parts of Ghegheria and must expect to see
'a rugged set of men' indeed. In preparation, the Frangistán 'wide-
awakes' are packed up, as having a peculiar attraction for missiles, on
account of their typically infidel appearance. Henceforth I adopt the fez,

MONASTIR

ÁKHRIDHA

for with that Mohammedan sign on the head it matters not how you adorn the rest of your person.

September 24

The wind which whistles through the planks and holes of my 'bedroom' here is conducive to cold in the head, and seems to prevent my neighbours, the ducks, from sleeping any more quietly than myself. Why these domestic animals inhabit the 'first floor' I cannot divine. Some fifteen of them thrust their heads through the lower crevices of the wall, and resting them on my mattress and pillow, look at me with one eye in the most comical manner, and seem to wish I was made of barley or duckweed. Although we were ready at 5 A.M., yet our guard was not, and it was six ere he joined us, flaunting in crimson drapery, and we made for the land of the '*poveretti, paurosi, desperati, spaventati, fuor di loro, fuor di tutti*',[1] as Giorgio distinguishes the Albanesi.

On leaving the suburbs large parties of Zingari or gipsies, employed by Sheréef Bey in various agricultural works, were setting out to their labour. These people are very numerous in Albania, and their peculiar physiognomy and dark complexion at once distinguishes them from the natives, who are mostly light-faced and yellow-haired. Our route lay westward by the shore of the silver lake, now enchantingly quiet and bright in the cloudless morning sun. High in air was a large falcon—possibly an eagle—hovering over a great colony of jet-black coots, who were swarming together in dismay, every one drawn up in a long straight line, and all performing simultaneous dives whenever the spoiler made a downward swoop. I saw three sets of these battles, waged by one against many, but could not observe that the persevering watchers gained aught by their warfare.

By eight we reached Istruga, a picturesque village not far from the egress of the River Drino, and as all the women here (with that caprice or love of variety which characterises the costume of every Greek province), wore white and pink capotes instead of black and crimson, there was a pleasant air of gaiety in the bazaar. From hence, the native place of Bekir, our Albanian guard (whom I had taken with me, not

[1] Poor, timid, despairing, afflicted; wanting sense; wanting everything.

knowing certainly if the road were or were not unsafe), we proceeded after a short delay through pleasant groves of chestnut, until, quitting the beautiful Lake of Akhridha, we toiled for three hours up a dull pass, walled in by low hills covered with stunted oaks. The sun was hot; and a fez, if you are not used to wearing it, is an unsatisfactory substitute for a 'wide-awake' felt hat, so that, after a descent as uninteresting as the ascent and beyond that two hours of a narrow, dull valley, I was most heartily tired, and rejoiced to see a khan, never more welcome than when seven hours of sleepy riding in an abominable Turkish saddle have made a man anything but happy.

Luckily we had brought food, for at this forlorn place there was literally nothing to be procured, not even a drop of water, nor did the situation of the khan possess interest, though I contrived to pass an hour by sketching it from the shelter of an oleander bush, surrounded by scores of tame kids. At half past 2 P.M. we were again in the saddle. A most desolate and wild country does this part of Albania seem, with scarcely a single habitation visible in so great a space; stern-wrinkled hills wall in the horizon, covered midway with oak forests; but after passing another range of low hills we came to the valley of the Skumbi, and henceforth the landscape began to assume a character of grand melancholy not to be easily forgotten. About five the infinitely varied lines of the western heights were most glorious, their giant-rock forms receding into golden clouds as the sun sank down, while below stretched the deep widening valley of the Skumbi, a silvery stream winding through utterly wild scenes of crag, forest, and slope as far as eye could see. By six we crossed over the river on a high single arch, and shortly began to ascend the heights on the left bank, where, among dark clusters of trees, a straggling village was perceptible far above a solitary khan, at which we were to rest, for there is here but little choice of a night's lodging.

Until it was too dark to discern either pencil or paper I worked away at a sketch of this lonely place, half hidden among huge rocks and walnut trees, and then turned into the single room or floor of the little window-less khan, which is the first and only inn of Kukues—so is the spot named. The accomplished dragoman had swept it perfectly clean. In the middle was a bright wood fire, the smoke escaping by a hole in the roof. On one side was my bed on a mat, while six or seven of the sons of the soil were preparing their kebabs[1] at the blazing logs, squatting quietly enough, and busying themselves about their own cookery, without overmuch remarking the tea and toast Giorgio prepared for me. Scenes of this kind are most striking and picturesque, and the traveller lies down, as it were, with one eye open—the savage oddity of all around fixing itself with his last waking thoughts in the imagination. Long after all the inmates of the khan were fast asleep I lay watching the party by the dying embers. The Albanians were slumbering in their capotes, each with his bare feet turned, and closely, to the hot charcoal; and if years of shoeless walking have not hardened the said feet, they must inevitably become altogether broiled before morning.

September 25

In spite of the apparent discomforts of the place, I slept well enough. The lively race of 'F sharps' do not abound in these solitary khans half as much as in an Italian Locanda. The Albanians never stirred; and as the fire burned more or less all night their feet must have been handsomely grilled. Once only I was awakened suddenly by something falling on me —flomp—miaw—fizz!—an accidental cat had tumbled from some un-explored height and testified great surprise at having alighted on a movable body. Would that her disturbance of my slumbers had been her only fault, and that she had not carried off a whole fowl and some slices of cold mutton—the little all I had to rely on for dinner through tomorrow's journey! Our Albanian co-tenants of the khan would assuredly have been blamed for this *mancanza*,[2] had not a fierce quarrel over the fowl, between the invading robber and an original cat belonging to the establishment, betrayed the cause of evil—the bigger cat con-quering and escaping from the roof with the booty.

At half past five A.M. we were off; the red morning sky and the calm shade of that broad valley were very striking; and the line of country we were to pursue promised a hard day's work. Continuing to ascend, on the left bank of the Skumbi, towards those gigantic rocks I had drawn

---

[1] Kebabs, slices of meat cooked on wooden skewers.

[2] Loss.

yesterday evening, and once or twice pausing to make hasty memoranda sketches, we advanced by perilous paths along the mountainsides towards a village at a great height above the river. It is very difficult, on such days of travel as this, to secure anything like a finished drawing. Even let the landscape be ever so tempting, the uncertainty of meeting with any place of repose or shelter obliges the most enthusiastic artist to pass hastily through scenes equal or superior to any it may be again his lot to see. Our progress here, too, is of the very slowest: either along sharp narrow paths cut in the rock, at the very edge of formidable precipices, or by still narrower tracks running on the bare side of a perpendicular clay ravine—or winding among huge trunks of forest trees, between which the baggage-mule at one time, is wedged—at another loses her load, or her own equilibrium, by some untimely concussion; such was the order of the day for travelling ease and accommodation; so that Dragoman Giorgio, greatly desirous of reaching Elbasan ere nightfall, strongly besought me not to linger. Nevertheless, after diving by a tortuous path into the depths of an abyss (the home of a lateral stream which descended from the mountains to the Skumbi), and after mounting a zigzag staircase out of it to the village above-mentioned, I could not resist sitting down to draw when I gazed on the extraordinary scene I had passed; it combined Greek outline—Italian colour—English luxuriance of foliage—while the village, with its ivory minarets peeping from huge walnut and chestnut groves, was hanging, as it were, down the stupendous precipices to the stream below—all these formed one of the wildest and grandest of pictures.

Beyond this (to appease Giorgio I made but a slight outline of that which I should gladly have employed a day to portray), the road was perhaps more dangerous and our progress still slower; at the narrowest point we encountered some fifty laden mules and a long time was consumed in arranging the coming and going trains, lest either should jostle and pitch into the abyss beneath. At another sharp turning lay a dead ox, skinned, filling up half the track (the edge of that track a sheer precipice of sixty or eighty feet in depth), and by no measures could we cause our horses to pass the alarming object; nor till our united strength had dragged the defunct to a niche in the rock could we progress one foot's length. At a third *cattivo passo*[1] a projecting rock interfered with

[1] Bad pass.

the sumpter horses' idea of a straight line; and, lo! down went all the baggage, happily to no great distance, but far enough to occasion a half-hour's delay in readjusting it. Every stony descent and every toil-some climb up this mountain ridge side, brought us, if possible, to more vast and wondrously beautiful scenes; far below in the valley the river wound among dark dense oaks, sparkling like a silver thread, while above towered a mountain screen, whose snow-crowned, furrowed summits frowned over slopes richly clothed with hanging woods. Per-haps the extreme beauty and variety of the colour in these scenes was as attractive as their sublimity, and in some degree offered a compensation for a certain clumsiness and want of refinement in many of the larger mountain outlines; while tracts of green wood, of bright pink or lilac earth, of deep grey hollows, or silver sides of snowy barriers, fascinated the eye from hour to hour.

On approaching the midway khan (really four hours and a half from Kukues, but which it took me till eleven to reach) I drew till dinner was ready, many peasants opportunely passing on their way to a fair or bazaar at Tirana. The female costume is a blue dress and white petticoat, with white or yellow aprons, embroidered with crimson. The khan was situated, as most of these halting-places are, in a dell, whence there is no discernible object of interest; and as soon as dinner was dispatched, two old cats and an army of ducks and fowls assisting at the repast, I was again *en route* by noon.

After three hours of winding along frightful paths at the edge of clay precipices and chasms, and through scenery of the same character, but gloomier under a clouded sun, we began to descend towards the seaward plains, and were soon effecting a steep and difficult passage between trunks of oak trees to the purple vale of the Skumbi, which wound through the plain below till it was lost in a gola or chasm through which is the pass to Elbasán. We crossed the Skumbi, here a very formidable stream, by one of those lofty one-arched bridges so common in Turkey, and as the baggage-horse descended the last step down came the luggage once more, so that my sketches would have been lost, *senza rimedio*,[1] had the accident occurred two seconds sooner. Two hours were occu-pied in passing the opening between the rocks, which admitted only a narrow pathway besides the stream, and after another hour's ride

[1] Without remedy.

53

through widening uncultivated valleys, and Elbasán is in sight, lying among rich groves of olives on a beautiful plain, through which the Skumbi, an unobstructed broad torrent, flows to the Adriatic. The same deceptive beauty throws its halo over Elbasán as over other Albanian towns; and, like its fellow paesi,[1] this was as wretched and forlorn within as without it was picturesque and graceful. It was 6 P.M. ere we reached its scattered and dirty suburbs and threaded its dark narrow streets, all roofed over with mats and dry leaves and so low that one had to sit doubled over the horse to avoid coming into sharp contact with the hanging sticks, dried boughs, loose mats, and rafters. The gloomy shade cast by these awnings did not enliven the aspect of the town, nor was its dirty and comfortless appearance lightened by a morose and wild look—a settled, sullen, despairing expression which the faces of the inhabitants wore. At length, thought I, these are fairly the wilds of Albania!

Three khans did we explore in vain, their darkness and vermin being too appalling to overcome; luckily there was still a fourth, which was a palace in comparison, though its accommodations were scanty, consisting of a row of perfectly dark cells, cleanly whitewashed and empty, but without a glimmer of any light but what entered at the doors, which opened into a corridor exposed to the street; so you had your choice of living in public or in the dark.

SEPTEMBER 26

A grey, calm, pleasant morning, the air seeming doubly warm, from the contrast between the low plains and the high mountains of the last two days' journey.

I set off early, to make the most of a whole day at Elbasán—a town singularly picturesque, both in itself and as to its site. A high and massive wall, with a deep outer moat, surrounds a large quadrangle of dilapidated houses, and at the four corners are towers, as well as two at each of the four gates: all of these fortifications appear of Venetian structure. Few places can offer a greater picture of desolation than Elbasán; albeit

[1] Towns.

the views from the broad ramparts extending round the town are perfectly exquisite: weeds, brambles, and luxuriant wild fig overrun and cluster about the grey heaps of ruin, and whichever way you turn you have a middle distance of mosques and foliage, with a background of purple hills, or southward, the remarkable mountain of Tomorrit, the giant Soracte of the plains of Berát.

No sooner had I settled to draw—forgetful of Bekír the guard—than forth came the populace of Elbasán; one by one and two by two to a mighty host they grew, and there were soon from eighty to a hundred spectators collected, with earnest curiosity in every look; and when I had sketched such of the principal buildings as they could recognise a universal shout of '*Shaitán!*' burst from the crowd; and, strange to relate, the greater part of the mob put their fingers into their mouths and whistled furiously, after the manner of butcher-boys in England. Whether this was a sort of spell against my magic I do not know; but the absurdity of sitting still on a rampart to make a drawing while a great crowd of people whistled at me with all their might struck me so forcibly that, come what might of it, I could not resist going off into convulsions of laughter, an impulse the Gheghes seemed to sympathise with, as one and all shrieked with delight, and the ramparts resounded with hilarious merriment. Alas! this was of no long duration, for one of those tiresome Dervíshes—in whom, with their green turbans, Elbasán is rich—soon came up, and yelled, '*Shaitán scroo!—Shaitán!*'[1] in my ears with all his force; seizing my book also, with an awful frown, shutting it, and pointing to the sky, as intimating that heaven would not allow such impiety. It was in vain after this to attempt more; the '*Shaitán*' cry was raised in one wild chorus—and I took the consequences of having laid by my fez for comfort's sake—in the shape of a horrible shower of stones which pursued me to the covered streets, where, finding Bekír with his whip, I went to work again more successfully about the walls of the old city.

Knots of the Elbasániotes nevertheless gathered about Bekír, and pointed with angry gestures to me and my 'scroo'. 'We will not be written down,' said they. 'The Frank is a Russian, and he is sent by the Sultan to write us all down before he sells us to the Russian Emperor.' This they told also to Giorgio and murmured bitterly at their fate,

[1] The Devil draws!—the Devil.

though the inexorable Bekír told them they should not only be scroo'd, but bastinadoed, if they were not silent and obedient. Alas! it is not a wonder that Elbasán is no cheerful spot, nor that the inhabitants are gloomy. Within the last two years one of the most serious rebellions has broken out in Albania, and has been sternly put down by the Porte. Under an adventurer named Zulíki, this restless people rose in great numbers throughout the north-western districts; but they were defeated in an engagement with the late Seraskíer Pashá. Their Beys, innocent or accomplices, were exiled to Koniah or Monastír, the population was either drafted off into the Sultan's armies, slain, or condemned to the galleys at Constantinople, while the remaining miserables were and are more heavily taxed than before. Such, at least, is the general account of the present state of these provinces; and certainly their appearance speaks of ill fortune, whether merited or unmerited.

Beautiful as is the melancholy Elbasán—with its exquisite bits of mosques close to the walls—the air is most oppressive after the pure mountain atmosphere. How strange are the dark covered streets, with their old mat roofings hanging down in tattered shreds, dry leaves, long boughs, straw or thatch reeds; one phosphorus match would ignite the whole town! Each street is allotted to a separate bazaar, or particular trade, and that portion which is the dwelling of the tanners and butchers is rather revolting—dogs, blood, and carcasses filling up the whole street and sickening one's very heart.

At 3 P.M. I rode out with the scarlet-and-gold-clad Bekír to find a general view of the town. But the long walled suburbs and endless olive gardens are most tiresome, and nothing of Elbasán is seen till one reaches the Skumbi, spanned by an immensely long bridge, full of ups and downs and irregular arches. On a little brow beyond the river I drew till nearly sunset; for the exquisitely graceful lines of hill to the north present really a delightful scene—the broad, many-channelled stream washing interminable slopes of rich olives, from the midst of which peep the silver minarets of Elbasán.

The dark khan cell at tea-time was enlivened by the singing of some Gheghes in the street. These northern, or Sclavonic Albanians are greatly superior in musical taste to their Berát or Epirote neighbours, all of whom either make a feeble buzzing or humming over their tinkling guitars, like dejected flies in a window-pane, or yell forth endless stanzas of a whining, motonous song, somewhat resembling a bad imitation of Swiss yodelling. But here there is a better idea of music. The guardian Bekír indulged me throughout yesterday with divers airs, little varied, but possessing considerable charm of plaintive wild melody. The Soorudgí, also, made the passes of the Skumbi resound with more than one pretty song.

SEPTEMBER 27

Great was my alarm when two hours before sunrise the whole khan was knocked up by a Government Tatar, raging for horses to proceed towards Skódra. All that were to be found in Elbasán I had engaged for my own journey, and the fear was, that should the Khanjí yield our steeds to the new-comer, my detention in so charming a place as this might be indefinitely prolonged; but for some reason of his own the Khanjí chose to lie in the most fertile manner, saying that some of his horses were ill, some away; and so the baffled Tatar retreated; and as the fibs were not uttered by my orders I became composed and went to sleep again with a good conscience. At half past six A.M. we left Elbasán, Giorgio growling at all the inhabitants and wishing they might be sold to the Czar, according to their fears. In any case, attachment to Abdul Medjid is not the reigning characteristic of this forlorn place. It was long before we left walls and lanes (there is more cultivation, especially of the olive, in these environs, than in any part of Albania I have yet seen) or ceased to jostle in narrow places against mules laden with black wool and driven by white-garbed, black-cloaked men; but when the route began to ascend from the valley the view southward over to Skumbi, in which the giant Tomhór or Tomórit forms the one point of the scene, was remarkably grand. In the early morning's ride there was but little interest, the greater part of it being through the narrow valley of a stream tributary to the Skumbi, the winding bed of which torrent we crossed more than thirty times ere we left it; and much after-time was occupied in painfully coasting bare clay hills till we began to climb the sides of the high mountain which separates the territory of Elbasán from that of Tirana.

How glorious, in spite of the dimming sirocco haze, was the view from the summit, as my eyes wandered over the perspective of winding

57

valley and stream to the farthest edge of the horizon—a scene realising the fondest fancies of artist imagination! The wide branching oak, firmly riveted in crevices, all tangled over with fern and creepers, hung half-way down the precipices of the giant crag, while silver-white goats (which chime so picturesquely in with such landscapes as this) stood motionless as statues on the highest pinnacle, sharply defined against the clear blue sky. Here and there the broken foreground of rocks piled on rocks, was enlivened by some Albanians who toiled upwards, now shadowed by spreading beeches, now glittering in the bright sun on slopes of the greenest lawn, studded over with tufted trees, which recalled Stothard's graceful forms, so knit with my earliest ideas of land-scape. These and countless well-loved passages of auld lang syne, crowded back on my memory as I rested, while the steeds and attendants reposed under the cool plane-tree shade, and drank from the sparkling stream which bubbled from a stone fountain. It was difficult to turn away from this magnificent mountain view—from these chosen nooks and corners of a beautiful world—from sights of which no painter-soul can ever weary: even now, that fold beyond fold of wood, swelling far as the eye can reach—that vale ever parted by its serpentine river—that calm blue plain, with Tomhór in the midst, like an azure island in a boundless sea, haunt my mind's eye and vary the present with visions of the past. With regret I turned northwards to descend to the new district of Tirana, the town (and it is now past eleven) being still some hours distant.

By half past twelve we had descended into a broad undulating valley-plain, with limits melting into undistinguishable hill and sky (for the day was a sirocco with its dust-like mist and the atmosphere like an oven), and were soon at a roadside khan, where a raised platform, with matting shelter, was by no means unacceptable. The magnificent Akhridhan, Bekír, who was charged to accompany me as far as Tirana, is of very little service in any way; his first care is to secure a good place on the platform —to take off his shoes and smoke; while Giorgio's alacrity in cooking a good dinner is a strong contrast to the Albanian's idleness. There were whispering olives hanging over the khan yard; and while a simple melody was chanted by three Gheghes in the shade the warm, slumbrous midday halt brought back to memory many such scenes and siestas in Italy.

Starting at two, the scenery along the banks of a river, a noble stream enclosed between fine rocks (the name of which I know not), was fine and varied; but the fear of arriving late at Tirana urged me onward, to the omission of all drawing—though had time allowed it would not have been easy to have selected only one from so many continually changing pictures as the afternoon's ride afforded. Other things also, good and bad, were included in the day's carte, such as capital grapes at the khan and from frequent gardens as we approached Tirana—many objects of costume among the peasantry—great flocks of turkeys—and insecure wooden bridges over little streams which obliged us, for fear of the horses falling through the planks, to make detours through charming bosky oases of cultivation. At four we forded the river and hastened on, gradually descending by low brushwood undulations to the plain of Tirana, while to the east the long rugged range of the Krôia mountains became magnificently interesting from picturesqueness and historical associations.

A snake crossing the road gave Giorgio an occasion, as is his afternoon's wont, to illustrate the fact with a story.

'In Egitto,' said he, 'are lots of serpents; and once there were many Hebrews there. These Hebrews wished to become Christians, but the King Pharaoh—of whom you may have heard—would not allow any such thing. On which Moses (who was the prince of the Jews) wrote to the Patriarch of Constantinople and to the Archbishop of Jerusalem, and also to San Carlo Borromeo, all three of whom went straight to King Pharaoh and entreated him to do them this favour; to which he only replied, "No, signori."

'But one fine morning these three saints proved too strong for the King, and changed him and all his people into snakes; which,' said the learned dragoman, 'is the real reason why there are so many serpents in Egypt to this day.'

Wavy lines of olive—dark clumps of plane, and spiry cypresses marked the place of Tirana when the valley had fully expanded into a pianura, and the usual supply of white minarets lit up the beautiful tract of foliage with the wonted deceptive fascination of these towns. As I advanced to the suburbs I observed two or three mosques mostly highly ornamented, and from a brilliancy of colour and elegance of form by far the most attractive of any public building I had yet beheld in these wild places; but though it was getting dark when I entered the town (whose streets, broader than those of Elbasán, were only raftered and matted half-way across) it was at once easy to perceive that Tirana was as wretched and disgusting as its fellow city, save only that it excelled in religious architecture and spacious market-places.

Two khans, each abominable, did we try. No person would undertake to guide us to the palace of the Bey (at some distance from the town), nor at that hour would it have been to much purpose to have gone there. The sky was lowering; the crowds of gazers increasing— Albanian the only tongue; so, all these things considered, I finally fixed on a third-rate khan, reported to be the Clarendon of Tirana, and certainly better than the other two, though its horrors are not easy to describe nor imagine. Horrors I had made up my mind to bear in Albania, and here, truly, they were in earnest.

Is it necessary, says the reader, so to suffer? And when you had a Sultan's Bouyourldi could you not have commanded beys' houses? True; but had I done so, numberless arrangements become part of that mode of life, which, desirous as I was of sketching as much as possible, would have rendered the whole motives of my journey of no avail. If you lodge with beys or pashás, you must eat with them at hours incompatible with artistic pursuits, and you must lose much time in ceremony. Were you so magnificent as to claim a home in the name of the Sultan, they must needs prevent your stirring without a suitable retinue, nor could you in propriety prevent such attention; thus, travelling in Albania has, to a landscape painter, two alternatives; luxury and inconvenience on the one hand, liberty, hard living, and filth on the other; and of these two I chose the latter, as the most professionally useful, though not the most agreeable.

O the khan of Tirana! with its immense stablesfull of uproarious horses; its broken ladders, by which one climbed distrustfully up to the most uneven and dirtiest of corridors, in which a loft some twenty feet square by six in height was the best I could pick out as a home for the night. Its walls, falling in masses of mud from its osier-woven sides (leaving great holes exposed to your neighbour's view, or, worse still, to the cold night air); its thinly raftered roof, anything but proof to the cadent amenities resulting from the location of an Albanian family above it; its floor of shaking boards, so disunited that it seemed unsafe to move incautiously across it, and through the great chasms of which the horses below were open to contemplation, while the suffocating atmosphere produced thence are not to be described!

O khan of Tirana! when the Gheghe Khanji strode across the most rotten of garrets, how certainly did each step seem to foretell the downfall of the entire building; and when he whirled great bits of lighted pitch-torch hither and thither, how did the whole horrid tenement seem about to flare up suddenly and irretrievably!

O khan of Tirana! rats, mice, cockroaches, and all lesser vermin were there. Huge flimsy cobwebs, hanging in festoons above my head; big frizzly moths, bustling into my eyes and face, for the holes representing windows I could close but imperfectly with sacks and baggage: yet here I prepared to sleep, thankful that a clean mat was a partial preventive to some of this list of woes, and finding some consolation in the low crooning singing of the Gheghes above me, who, with that capacity for melody which those Northern Albanians seem to possess so essentially, were murmuring their wild airs in choral harmony.

September 28

Though the night's home was so rude, fatigue produced sound sleep. The first thing to do was to visit Machmóud Bey, Vice-Governor of Tirana, to procure a Kawás as guardian during a day's drawing, and a letter to his nephew, Alí Bey, of Króia, for to that city of Scanderbeg I am bent on going. Of the Bey's palace, nothing can be said beyond what has already been noted of the serais of similar grandees.

Returning to the khan, I gave five dollars to Bekír of Akhridha, for his five days' service, an expense I resolved in future to forgo, as the chance of robbery in these mountains seems a great deal too small to authorise it —the more, that the only assistance I really want (that of a guard while sketching in the towns) I have no difficulty in procuring.

But even with a guard it was a work of trouble to sketch in Tirana; for it was market or bazaar day, and when I was tempted to open my book in the large space before the two principal mosques (one wild scene of confusion, in which oxen, buffaloes, sheep, goats, geese, asses, dogs, and children were all running about in disorder) a great part of the natives, impelled by curiosity, pressed closely to watch my operations, in spite of the Kawás, who kept as clear a space as he could for me; the women alone, in dark feringhís, and ghostly white muslin masks, sitting unmoved by their wares. Fain would I have drawn the exquisitely pretty arabesque-covered mosques, but the crowds at last stifled my enthusiasm. Not the least annoyance was that given me by the per-severing attentions of a mad or fanatic dervísh, of most singular appear-ance as well as conduct. His note of 'Shaitán' was frequently sounded; and as he twirled about, and performed many curious antics, he fre-quently advanced to me, shaking a long hooked stick, covered with jingling ornaments, in my very face, pointing to the Kawás with menacing looks, as though he would say, 'Were it not for this protector you should be annihilated, you infidel!' The crowd looked on with awe at the holy man's proceedings, for Tirana is evidently a place of great attention to religion. In no part of Albania are there such beautiful mosques and nowhere are collected so many green-vested dervíshes. But however a wandering artist may fret at the impossibility of com-fortably exercising his vocation, he ought not to complain of the effects of a curiosity which is but natural, or even of some irritation at the open display of arts which, to their untutored apprehension, must seem at the very least diabolical.

The immediate neighbourhood of Tirana is delightful. Once outside the town and you enjoy the most charming scenes of quiet, among splendid planes and the clearest of streams. The afternoon was fully occupied on the road from Elbasán, whence the view of the town is beautiful. The long line of peasants returning to their homes from the bazaar enabled me to sketch many of their dresses in passing; most of the women wore snuff-coloured or dark vests trimmed with pink or red, their petticoats white, with an embroidered apron of chocolate or scarlet; others affected white capotes; but all bore their husband's or male relative's heavy black or purple capote, bordered with broad pink or orange, across their shoulders. Of those whose faces were visible— for a great part wore muslin wrappers (no sign hereabouts of the wearer being Mohammedan, for both Moslem and Christian females are thus bewrapped)—some few were very pretty, but the greater number had toil- and careworn faces. There were many dervíshes also, wearing high white felt steeple-crowned hats, with black shawls round them.

No sooner, after retiring to my pigsty dormitory, had I put out my candle and was preparing to sleep, than the sound of a key turning in the lock of the next door to that of my garret disturbed me, and lo! broad rays of light illumined my detestable lodging from a large hole a foot in diameter, besides from two or three others, just above my bed; at the same time a whirring, humming sound, followed by strange whizzings and mumblings, began to pervade the apartment. Desirous to know what was going on, I crawled to the smallest chink, without encountering the rays from the great hiatus, and what did I see? My friend of the morning—the maniac dervísh—performing the most wonderful evolutions and gyrations; spinning round and round for his own private diversion, first on his legs, and then pivot-wise, *sur son séant*, and indulging in numerous other pious gymnastic feats. Not quite easy at my vicinity to this very eccentric neighbour, and half anticipating a twitch from his brass-hooked stick, I sat watching the event, whatever it might be. It was simple. The old creature pulled forth some grapes and ate them, after which he gradually relaxed in his twirlings and finally fell asleep.

September 29

It was as late as half past nine A.M. when I left Tirana, and one consolation there was in quitting its horrible khan, that travel all the world over a worse could not be met with. Various delays prevented an early start; the postmaster was in the bath, and until he came out no horses could be procured (meanwhile I contrived to finish my arabesque mosques); then a dispute with the Khanjí, who, like many of these provincial people, insisted on counting the Spanish dollar as twenty-three instead of twenty-four Turkish piastres. Next followed a row with Bekír of Akhridha, who vowed he would be paid and indemnified for the loss of an imaginary amber pipe, which he declared he had lost in a fabulous ditch, while holding my horse at Elbasán; and lastly, and not the least of the list, the crowd around the khan gave way at the sound of terrific shrieks and howlings, and forth rushed my spinning neighbour, the mad dervísh, in the most foaming state of indignation. First he seized the bridles of the horses; then, by a frantic and sudden impulse, he began to prance and circulate in the most amazing manner, leaping and bounding and shouting 'Allah!' with all his might, to the sound of a number of little bells, which this morning adorned his brass-hooked weapon. After this he made an harangue for ten minutes, of the most energetic character, myself evidently the subject; at the end of it he advanced towards me with furious gestures, and bringing his hook to within two or three inches of my face, remained stationary, in a Taglioni attitude. Knowing the danger of interfering with these privileged fanatics, I thought my only and best plan was to remain unmoved, which I did, fixing my eye steadily on the ancient buffoon, but neither stirring nor uttering a word; whereon, after he had screamed and foamed at me for some minutes, the demon of anger seemed to leave him at a moment's warning; for yelling forth discordant cries and brandishing his stick and bells, away he ran, as as if he were really possessed. Wild and savage were the looks of many of my friend's excited audience, their long matted black hair and brown visage giving them an air of ferocity which existed perhaps more in the outward than the inner man; moreover, these Gheghes are all armed, whereas out of Ghegheria no Albanian is allowed to carry so much as a knife.

I was glad enough to leave Tirana, and rejoiced in the broad green paths, or roads, that lead northwards, through a wide valley below the eastern range of magnificent mountains, on one of which, at a great height from the plain, stands the once formidable Króia, so long held out against the conquering Turk, by Iskander Bey. Certain of its historical interest, I was now doubly anxious to visit it, from its situation, which promised abundance of beauty.

After four hours' ride over ground much intersected with marks of inundation we arrived at a khan where, under a sort of pergola of dry matting, I remained to dine, and to draw the sublime view before me over the plain and wide beds of torrents towards the bare, craggy, dark mountain of Króia, with the town and rocks glittering like silver aloft, below a heavy curtain of black cloud. At two we left the Skódra, or post-road—the Soorudjí growling frightfully at my so doing—and struck directly across the vale to Króia—a winding ascent through green wooded hill-buttresses or shoulders, changed ere long for a sharp climb up to the foot of the great rock round which the town clusters and hangs —at which point I arrived at half past four P.M., and where I gladly

64

TIRANA

KRÓIA

paused to sketch, rest, and enjoy the view above, below, and around. Few prospects are more stately than those of this renowned spot; and perhaps that of the crag, with its ruined castle projecting from the great rocks above and lording over the spacious plain country north and south from Skódra towards Durázzo, reminded me more of Olévano, that most lovely landscape in a land of loveliness, than any place I ever saw. At the base of this isolated rock lies the town—a covered semicircular line of bazaars; and overlooking all is the Bey's palace and a tall white minaret against the blue sky. The peasants who passed me while drawing lingered, whispering quietly while observing the sketch, all thoroughly well behaved and a great contrast to my spectators of Elbasán. But evening advanced and I was compelled to shut up my book, feeling for the hundredth time how difficult it is to portray scenery in a country where the mere daily occupation of journeying from one town to another is attended by so much labour and hurry. Ascending through the dark-roofed bazaars—the huge crags towering over which reminded me of Cánalo in Calabria—we arrived at Alí Bey's palace—a singularly picturesque pile of building, composed of two-storied, painted galleries, with irregular windows, projecting roofs, and innumerable novelties of architecture—all in a dreary courtyard, the high walls of which shut out effectually the glorious landscape below.

In the arabesqued and carved corridor, to which a broad staircase conducted me, were hosts of Albanian domestics; and on my letter of introduction being sent in to the Bey, I was almost instantly asked into his room of reception—a three-windowed, square chamber (excellent, according to the standard of Turkish ornament, taste, and proportion)— where, in a corner of the raised divan sat Ali, Bey of Króia—a lad of eighteen or nineteen, dressed in the usual blue frock-coat now adopted by Turkish nobles or officers. A file of kilted and armed retainers were soon ordered to marshal me into a room where I was to sleep, and the little Bey seemed greatly pleased with the fun of doing hospitality to so novel a creature as a Frank. My dormitory was a real Turkish chamber; and the raised cushions on three sides of it—the high, square, carved wooden ceiling—the partition screen of lofty woodwork, with long striped Brusa napkins thrown over it—the guns, horse-gear, etc., which covered the walls—the fireplace—closets—innumerable pigeonholes— green, orange, and blue stained-glass windows—all appeared so much the more in the light of luxuries and splendours when found in so remote a place as Króia. It was not easy to shake off the attentions of ten full-dressed Albanian servants, who stood in much expectation, till, finding I was about to take off my shoes, they made a rush at me as the Jews did at Salonica and showed such marks of disappointment at not being allowed to make themselves useful that I was obliged to tell Giorgio to explain that we Franks were not used to assistance every moment of our lives and that I should think it obliging of them if they would leave me in peace. After changing my dress, the Bey sent to say that supper should be served in an hour, he having eaten at sunset, and in the meantime he would be glad of my society; so I took my place on the sofa by the little gentleman's side, and Giorgio, sitting on the ground, acted as interpreter. At first Ali Bey said little, but soon became immensely loquacious, asking numerous questions about Stamboul and a few about Franks in general—the different species of whom he was not very well informed. At length, when the conversation was flagging, he was moved to discourse about ships that went without sails and coaches that were impelled without horses; and to please him I drew a steamboat and a railway carriage; on which he asked if they made any noise; and I replied by imitating both the inventions in question in the best manner I could think of—'Tik-tok, tik-tok, tik-tok, tokka, tokka, tokka, tokka, tokka—tok' (crescendo), and 'Squish-squash, squish-squash, squish-squash, thump-bump'—for the land and sea engines respectively—a noisy novelty, which so intensely delighted Alí Bey that he fairly threw himself back on the divan and laughed as I never saw Turk laugh before.

For my sins, this imitation became fearfully popular, and I had to repeat 'squish-squash', 'tik-tok', till I was heartily tired, the only recompense this wonderful little pashá offered me, being the sight of a small German writing-box (when new it might have cost three or four shillings), containing a lithograph of Fanny Ellsler and two small looking-glasses in the lid. This was brought in by a secretary, attended by two Palikari,[1] at the Bey's orders, and was evidently considered as something uncommonly interesting. So, when this very intellectual intercourse was over, I withdrew to my wooden room, and was glad of a light supper before sleeping.

[1] Palikari—Albanian or Greek military.

SEPTEMBER 30

But one day can be allotted to Króia, so how to make the best of that day? Little liberty do I look for, the more that while I take my café an Albanian stands at the door who shies off his slippers if I only move a finger—rushing forward to know if I want anything. However, I have caused it to be known through Giorgio, that I only require a single attendant, and that that one should be well paid. Spite of forebodings, I actually escaped from the palace, and having repassed the bazaars was at work on a drawing of the castle rock, one of the most imposing of subjects, ere yet the sun had risen over the eastern hills. Above the town the view is still more majestic, and although many of the inhabitants came and sat near me, yet no one annoyed me in the least, and I drew comparisons between these well-bred people and the rude men of Elbasán and Tirana. At eleven I returned to dine with Ali Bey, an amiable little fellow, who was evidently anxious to make my stay agreeable, though he could not long control his childish curiosity from bidding Giorgio (who could ill keep his gravity) to ask me to imitate the noises of the steamboats and coaches. So I again went through, 'Tik-tok, tokka, tokkey', and 'Squish-squash, squash, squash', to the great delight of the Bey and his retinue.

The routine of dinner was as follows: ten servants, in full Albanian dress came in at once, for all the world like in an opera ballet. One of them places a little stool on the ground, upside down, as much as to say that it is not to be sat upon; others fix thereon a large flat plate of tin, or some similar metal, with a spoon, or piece of bread, to each diner (there were two guests beside myself); then an ewer with water is handed to each person by one of the domestics, who kneels until you have used it and the Brusa towel. Soup, somewhat like sago and vinegar, was the first dish placed before us; and here my good genius basely forsook me, for endeavouring to sit cross-legged like my entertainers I somehow got my knees too far below the pewter table-top, and an ill-conditioned violent cramp seizing me at the unlucky moment in which the tureen was placed on the table, I hastily endeavoured to withdraw the limb, but unsuccessfully—gracious!—sidelong went the whole table and all the soup was wasted on the ground! Constantly as a Frank is called on to observe the unvarying good breeding and polite ease of Turkish manner, this was a most trying proof of the endurance of those qualities. Nobody spoke, or even looked, as if anything had gone amiss; one of the corps de ballet wiped up the catastrophe and others soon brought in a new bowl full of soup as if nothing had happened. Nor was my awkwardness alluded to except by Giorgio, who, by my orders, offered a strong apology for the stiffness of Frank's legs in general and of mine in particular.

But I took care not to commit myself by unexpected cramps any more, and sprawled sideways through the rest of the dinner as I best could. A piláf of fowls, full of spices and bones, kebabs, a paste of rice, onions, and pie-crust, and some round balls of chopped meat concluded the repast, some grapes excepted. Nobody drank anything, and abstemiousness was the order of the day, a virtue I was compelled to practise, even more than my companions, seeing that I was unskilled at selecting proper bits from the dishes with my fingers, and not only caught at unsatisfactory bones, but let half of what I did catch fall midway between my mouth and the single bowl into which we dipped in rotation. So ended my first Turkish dinner.

It is not easy to keep conversation going on terms so unequal as those in which my host and I communicated, so I was not sorry to be once more at work, and the outside of Alí Bey's palace, fretted and galleried and painted, occupied me an hour or two, while the castle rock, taken from the east, filled up my time till sunset. After this, I was devoted for two hours to the little Bey, during which my employment was repeating in English the names of the days of the week, and the twelve months, and the letters of the alphabet, varied by 'squish-squash, squish-squash, thump, thump, tikka-tok-katok', and by occasional contemplations of the Fanny Ellsler writing-box. Later, Alí Bey showed me the rooms of his harem (the first and last I am most probably destined to see), which he was repairing with an indistinct view to future matrimony. Very picturesque and Arabian-night-like chambers they were, with a covered gallery, looking down on the (now) still bazaars and the tall minarets, to the rocks and the oak woods sloping down, down by undulating hills to the boundless plains, moonlit sea, and far faint hills of Skódra. Imagination peopled this gallery with houri tenants, waving feringhees, and laughing faces, but the halls of Alí Bey were silent for the present.

Supper—a facsimile of the dinner, save that I did not upset the soup—concluded my day in Króia, and I took leave of good-natured little Alí Bey with the sort of half regret with which any human being, whose salt one has eaten more than once in wilds such as these, is bade a farewell for ever.

OCTOBER 1

The muezzíns' call to prayers is more delightfully musical at Króia than at any place I have yet been to—it is the wildest of singular melodies. We were off by 6 A.M. While the horses were being got ready Alí Bey desired to see me again, and accordingly we had series the last of coffee, pipes, 'squish-squash, tikka-tok', and the alphabet. He had asked Giorgio of his own accord how the Franks saluted each other, and hearing that it was by shaking hands, he seized both of mine and shook them as a London footman might a door-knocker. Long after I had left the palace he was watching me from his corner window, and doubtless will longer remember the Frank who ran about and wrote down houses and divulged to him the noises of steamships and coaches. Alí is representative of his uncles, Suleimán and Machmóud Beys, Governors of Tirana, and as their deputy, judges all disputes in Króia. Young as he is, he has a good deal of energetic character, and keeps the people in strict order. 'I took away all their guns,' said he, 'directly I was chief here: for why? they shot more men than birds.' Among other amusing questions which he asked, one was, after long and accurate observation of my dress: 'How does the Frank make the collars of his shirt stand upright?' Giorgio informed him, by means of starch, on which he inquired the nearest place where he could purchase a Frank laundress; and being told Trieste, he expressed his determination to send for one shortly.

The morning was clouded and grey, and a heavy mist over the northern plains and shore foretells rain. We began to descend from Króia through graceful olive woods and pretty scenery, above which, on the right, the tops of the high mountain range peeped out through gathering clouds. Great fragments of dark rock cumber the downward path, and on the left the distant view would have been glorious if the spreading mist had been less dense. Crossing a stream by a high-arched bridge, the route lay through ever-increasingly beautiful oak forests, stretching from hill to hill and wrapping the bald and gloomy mountains in their grey and brown robes; and had not the day become more threatening each minute, I should have enjoyed the scenery more. In the thickest of the wood down came the rain in torrents; the paths were slippery, our progress was slow; and Giorgio, who considers Albania and Albanians as the most depressing of horrors, made the morning truly melancholy by incessant croaking about robbers; besides all which evils, a most odious impish little Soorudjí, who had brought me from Tirana, and who was aggrieved at being taken, as he called it, up into the hills, delayed me out of spite in every possible way, by rushing into quagmires and leaving the path suddenly to search for imaginary pools of water in impenetrable copses, that his horses might drink thereof; these symptoms of unruliness we were at last obliged to check, by leading his horse forcibly, spite of his yell of '*Sui-sui.*'[1] In about three hours from Króia, we reached the Skódra road once more and in half an hour arrived at a khan situated in a close jungly wood, a small spot of ground being cleared around the tenement, which, says the Khanjí, is five hours from Aléssio, the place meant to be the end of my day's journey. Here I resolve to halt, as the rain cannot be more violent than it is at present. Moreover, there is a fine fowl roasting, which I seize on and purchase for two piastres. These byroad khans are infinitely preferable to the vile places in the towns of Albania; a floor and a fire are comforts, and the stable at the far end of the long building did not incommode me, whose luncheon on the fowl, with rice, was only more or less disturbed by little chickens and kittens, who continually ran over me, snatching at casual bits of fugitive food. No parasitical creatures are more worrying to a traveller in Albania than chickens; they swarm by scores in these khans, and their incessant chirp and flutter are incorrigible, nor until they have shared the picking of their ancestors' bones can they be quieted.

At eleven o'clock—the rain ceasing unexpectedly—we were off again, ever through a thick wooded tract of country, the tangled branches heavy with the rain, greatly impeding our progress, and the roads being deep in mud and water. Often, to avoid the high raised causeway (the Government post-road)—the unequal pavement of which it is

[1] Drink, drink!

misery to ride over—we went aside into quiet glades of green, returning when the too thick foliage prevented the secondary pathway being followed. At an hour's distance another khan stands on the right of the road, and beyond this the wood gives place to more open glades, until we reached the plain of the broad and rapid River Máthis, which, always a disagreeable process, was forded about 1 P.M. Hence the hills we had passed began to gleam in returning sunshine, and covered with thickest foliage, seemed like vast piles of moss; while northward, and to the west, flat ground, with occasional spots of cultivation, appeared to spread to the sea—the high rocks of the ancient Lissus rising directly in front of our route. Having passed a third khan on the left at half past one, the road enters a thick copse or jungle, a belt of underwood stretching over the low marshy grounds near the Drin. The staple productions of this region are tangled brambles and low ilexes through whose green growth tall whispering reeds shoot up, while, above all, trees scattered at intervals tower, their branches bending with the weight of vines and creepers which swing in graceful festoons, in all the luxuriant rankness that surely indicates a condition of atmosphere fatal to man but favourable to vegetable life.

In these narrow and intricate paths we met many peasants returning from the bazaars of Aléssio, the women clad in fringed and tasselled dresses, the men all armed; for the Gheghe Albanians, from not having formed any union with their brethren of Toskería and Tzamouría in the last rising against the Turkish Government, are still allowed the privilege of carrying arms, which is denied to all south of the Skumbi.

About four o'clock I reached Aléssio[1]—a miserable village representing the ancient Lissus, many remains of which exist around and upon the remarkable pointed hill (the ancient Acropolis) rising above the streets of bazaars which forms the chief part of the modern town; the rest of Aléssio consists of houses standing in gardens on the banks of the Drin— in which the Christian population chiefly dwell—or in suburban residences of the Mohammedans on the hillside. On the summit of the rock is a mosque, and here tradition says that the remains of Scanderbeg repose beneath the ruins of a Christian church.

The khan of Aléssio was too bad to think of as a lodging; so, by means of a letter from the Bey of Tirana, we proceeded to a quarter in the

[1] Or Lesh.

house of a Greek Christian residing here as agent to the Austrian Consul at Skódra; and leaving Giorgio to make the best of this refuge—a sort of loft in a courtyard, bearing all the tokens of vermin—I went forth with its master, Signor Giuseppe, and by way of finding a general view of Aléssio, crossed the river in a punt-ferry and proceeded to a Latin convent which stands on a height opposite the town. Nearly all the Christians in this part of Northern Albania (that is, on the north-western coast, where the Venetian Republic was once so powerful) are of the Latin Church, and the residents of the Greek persuasion are the minority. From this spot the views are most exquisite. Looking south, they extend towards the high mountains above Króia and Tirana; and northward they range over a beautiful river which winds down from the heights above Skódra, reflecting trees and hills in the clear water.

The sole tenant of the convent, a Capuchin Friar, came forth to meet me, when, having advanced a few yards, he set up a shout, ejaculating, 'O, possibile! Sí:—è il Signor Odoardo!' while I on my part recognised him as a monk I had fallen in with some years back when staying with some friends in the Maremma near Corneto, and afterwards had frequently seen at Ara-Coeli in Rome; but the singularity of the circumstance—that we should meet again in this remote corner of Illyria—was one of those events that we should reject if in a novel as too impossible to happen. Fra Pietro exhibited great glee at seeing a 'Christian', as he called me; and on the other side I was glad enough to hear good Roman speech. 'But,' said I, 'the people of Aléssio are Christians, are they not?'—[1]'*Cristiani si, lo sono,*' said the monk; '*ma se domani volesse il buon Dio far crescere il fiume per portargli tutti in Paradiso, ci avrei gusto!—Cristiani? Ladri! Cristiani?—porchi!—Cristiani? Lupi, animali, sciocchi, scimie, brutte bestie, Grechi, Turchi, Albanesi—che gli piglia ad uno e tutti un accidente. O che Cristiani! O che rabbia*' Seeing that a sojourn in the Latin bishopric of Lissus had by no means improved my friend Fra Pietro's disposition to suavity (he was never, in the days when I formerly knew him, of the calmest or happiest temper), I hastened to change the conversation, but during the rest of our discourse this victim of exile *in partibus* continued to growl out bitter anathemas at all his Aléssian flock. At sunset I left

---

[1] Yes, they are! But if it pleased Heaven tomorrow so to swell the river as that they might be all swept off into Paradise, I should be happy, etc. etc. May they all die of apoplexy!

the angry friar (after all, a solitary life here must be no slight *penitenza*), and, promising to visit him on my return, I recrossed the Drin to Signor Giuseppe's house, where I found bed and supper ready in the upper chamber.

An old Skódrino, who talks Italian, squats on the opposite side of the fire, and tells me a great deal about Skódra and other places hereabouts, which I ought to have remembered, but I fell fast asleep. Eight hundred Latin Christians, according to him, live at Skódra; and he says, 'there may be some twenty Greek Christian families'. The Roman Catholic Bishop of Lissus resides there. In spite of all his intelligence, the old gentleman was a bore, as he was seized with a literary fit in the middle of the night, and smoked and scribbled and coughed, to the utter driving away the little chance of sleep which mice, mosquitoes, and fleas had left me.

October 2

It is half past four A.M. and torrents of rain are falling; they may fall for two or three days, in which case I am a prisoner here, as all the rivers will be impassable, so I order the horses to proceed to Skódra at all risks, though of course the obstinate little Soorudjí would not bring them till seven.

The journey was of the wettest, and kept always along the banks of the Drino, beneath enormous abele trees, with fine forms of mountains looming through the downward mist. To a man who wears spectacles a fez is not advantageous as a covering for the head on a rainy day; the glasses are soon dimmed and little does he see of all above, below, and around. In three hours we arrived at the ferry over the Drino, having passed two or three scattered villages which were proclaimed as Christian by the fact of pigs (lean, hairy pigs they were) roaming around them. Nothing in the world could be more picturesque than the ferry and its capoted rowers; but the incessant rain forbade attempts to draw, nor did I halt again till at eleven, when we reached a khan, distant still three hours from Skódra. A small bit of salt cheese and some very bad wine was all the food I could obtain; but the loss of luncheon was compensated for by the increasing interest of the costumes of the peasantry;

73

their scarlet and crimson capotes, short coarse kilts, long black hair, dark faces, and immoderately long pistols gave them an air of romance and savageness I had not yet seen.

Half past eleven—on again, through clay and water and willowy tangles and high broken causeways. Turkish paved roads, even when in repair, are miserable ways and means of travel; but when you have twenty yards of elevated stonework and then a four-feet interval of mud, the causeway being often two or three feet in height, the alternation of ups and downs is not pleasant. Vast mountain forms are lowering remotely on all sides, till the castle of Skódra[1] appears in sight. In all the objects of this, to me, new district extreme wildness is the dominant impression. The peasantry were picturesque to an incredible degree. Flocks of sheep and goats, guarded by the most savage-looking fellows, armed to the teeth and magnificent in all the colours of Gheghe clothing, were frequently in our path, and more than once fierce dogs sprang out on our half-wild Soorudjí from hidden ambushes. Once the young pickle made as if he would pursue one of the invaders with his raised whip, but the herdsman rose from his lair and coolly pointed his long gun at the offender till he resumed his course.

Skódra is situated to the south of the lake of the same name, on a point of land between two rivers, one of which,[2] the Boyána, sweeps below the south side of the isolated ridge of hill on which the fortress stands, which ridge, shutting out the plain and lake, is, as it were, split into two by a deep hollow immediately to the eastward of the fortress wherein, and on the southern side of the hill, appears to stand the town. But this is all deception; for having crossed the Boyana—at this season a fordable stream—you arrive at the southern suburbs, only to discover that they are deserted; the walls of numerous houses, ruined in some of the late sieges of this unquiet capital of Illyrian Albania, one or two handsome mosques, and a considerable extent of garden constitute the real condition of the place; while, ascending through this scene of desolation to the long lines of bazaars which cluster below the domineering fortress and fill up the hollow pass in the ridge of hill, you are still surprised to find that you are not yet in Skódra. For these bazaars, by the oddest arrangement possible, are only tenanted by day; a busy scene throughout the forenoon, they are regularly closed an hour before

[1] Or Scutari.   [2] The other is the Drino, or Drin.

sunset; every male inhabitant coming to his warehouse early in the morning and returning as regularly to what is now really the town of Skódra (though it is sometimes called 'The Gardens'), namely, a wide collection of villages and detached houses scattered over the plain on the northern side of the castle hill and bazaars, between them and the lake. The lake, stretching far and wide to the mountains of Montenegro, is not seen except by climbing high up the rock toward the castle.

On arriving in the piazza in the centre of the bazaars, I was told that Signor Bonatti (the English Vice-Consul to whom I had letters) resided at some distance: it might be a mile, or two, or four, said the bystanders, with happy vagueness—the mercantile world of Skódra seemed unprepared to give a decided opinion. However that might be, the odious little Soorudjí of Tirana instantly vowed he would go no farther, and in spite of threats and entreaties became unmanageable. Unloading all the baggage in a rage, he threw it into the mud in the piazza and decamped with the horses, swearing at all Christians with most emphatic zeal. All the Gheghes looking on maintained a provoking composure. To have sent to the Pashá in his castle would have been an operation of an hour's length, and after all of uncertain result: the Consul's abode was far off, and so little seemed known of him that it was to be doubted if his succours would have availed anything: so, in this climax of discomfort— hard rain falling all the while—we had to wait until another horse was procured for the baggage; and with a very lame guide we left the bazaars and descended to the suburban or 'garden' part of Skódra, in the northern plain. A pretty chase ensued for the Consul's dwelling; for in this strange place your house, or your mosque, or your garden stands, independently of any other building, among walls and labyrinths of lanes intricate beyond belief. Much of this flat ground is afflicted by inundation—the communications across it being formed by very narrow raised causeways, crossing intervals of mud or water as the case may be; and a full hour was consumed in walking among these weary pavements without apparently being any nearer the object of our search. At last we arrived at a door at the end of a cul-de-sac lane, when the lame old man stopped and said: 'το σπίτι,[1] Inglíz Consul.' But this was wholly an invention of his own, for no consul lived there; and had not a friendly

[1] το σπίτι, the house.

scarlet-cloaked Christian woman volunteered acting as guide, I cannot tell when the real house might have been found.

Signore Bonatti, a native of Corfú, and British Vice-Consul in the city of Skódra, is an active and lively little man, full of kind anxiety to do the agreeable to the few passers-by in these regions; but having a large family of nine or ten children, he is unable to exercise so much hospitality as he is known formerly to have done: the more the pity, for a more amiable set of people one could not be indebted to. He recommended me to a lodging in the village-city; and after a short stay with his family, thither I went.

By sunset I was settled in the house of Signor Marco, a Venetian apothecary, whose substantial dwelling, standing in a good cortile and garden, contains two or three large rooms. Here—possibly the last place in which rest will be accessible before I arrive at Yannina—I purpose staying three days before turning southward—Skódra being the farthest point of my Albanian wanderings; even were not money becoming scarce, autumn advances, and I shall have scarcely time to reach Malta ere Christmas.

OCTOBER 3

Half the morning passed by in endeavours to find the lake—which, after all, I—who have no organ of locality—did not succeed in doing. So, after walking in a circle among lanes, houses, tombs, mosques, drains, bridges, and walled gardens, I returned to the apothecary's as wise as when I set out. Repairing to the Consul, and walking with him about the suburbs, I came to the conclusion that the most picturesque points of Skódra are to be found on the southern side of the ridge—or at least that whatever views were to be obtained in the north would occupy, from their remoteness, more time than I commanded merely to select. To an artist who could remain here for a month much noble material could be gained on the shores of the lake at the foot of the Albanian mountain boundary to the east; and greatly did I long to penetrate towards Podgorizza, and the land of the Montenegrini.

At 3 P.M. I set out with Signor Bonatti on a visit to the Pashá of

Skódra, to whom Mr. Blunt of Salonica has given me a letter; and after a visit to some of the merchants in the bazaars, we climb the steep castle hill, whence the line of the lake and mountains are surpassingly lovely. The castle occupies the whole of the summit of the hill, and by its area walls and numerous decaying forts within betokens greater extent and power in bygone days. The palace of the Pashá is a building with no pretensions to size or picturesqueness, nor is its interior otherwise than of the commonest kind. From the windows, however, the view is truly magnificent on all sides: northward, it sweeps across the village, the dotted plain, and wide blue lake to the jagged Montenegro or Tcherni-gore mountains; southward, it extends over the ruined town at the foot of the hill to the plains of the Drino; westward, along the windings of the Boyána to the Adriatic; and eastward, to the third part of this oddly arranged place—the busy bazaars.

Osmán Pashá, the dignitary who at present governs the city of Skodra and its surrounding district, is a Bosniac by birth, and is said to be in great favour with the Porte from having, while in his present command, made some successful warfare against the Montenegríni, who are ever at feud with the Mohammedan Government. His Highness is short and fat, with an intelligent and amiable expression of countenance; and spite of his Oriental attitude as he squatted in his corner, a pale frock-coat and European-made trousers gave him little of the air of a Turk. Beside him sat an individual, whose closely buttoned grey vest, clerical hat, gold chain and cross proclaimed the Roman Catholic bishop; this was Mon-signore Topicka, the diocesan of Lissus, in which is included the district of Skódra. By means of the Vice-Consular dragoman, the conversation became animated. The Pashá was remarkably affable, and asked me to dine with him on the 5th. And then came pipes and coffee—pipes, pipes, sweetmeats—pipes, sherbet, and pipes; throughout which cere-mony discourse was extremely plentiful when compared with the usual run of Turkish visits.

They call this place the Siberia or exile of Turkey in Europe; and indeed it must be little less than banishment to those who have lived in Stamboul. The Pashá made several remarks, showing that he was by no means an ill-informed man. He asked if 'Lord' Cook ('*chi girava il mondo*')[1] had left any children, and if so whether they also went *intorno*

---

[1] Who went round the world.

l'universo? Various anecdotes—some very facetious, at which His Highness laughed immoderately—were told by the Consul and Bishop; and on the whole the visit, though rather long, was a merry one. There was much talk also regarding reports of battles between the Cattarési and Montenegríni on the far side of the lake. After the departure of the Vescovo, I was invited to walk on the ramparts; and, said the Pasha, 'You may note down all the state of the fortress, if you please: you may look at everything, for your Sovereign is a friend of ours.' It would have been in vain to have said that I had no commission to report upon fortresses or that I was totally incapable of so doing: any attempt to disabuse the august mind of so natural a conception would have had no other result than that of appearing to confirm it. After this I had hoped the visit was over, and was horrified to find that we returned to the divan, when fresh pipes and rose-water ensued, and pipes—pipes—like Banquo's posterity, till I was utterly weary; by the time we had taken leave and repassed the galleries full of retainers the sun had set, and it was dark ere we reached the plain, where we fell in with long lines of Scutarini leaving the bazaars and returning home, each with his empty sack.

OCTOBER 4

All day the weather looks threatening, but the clouds add a charm of magnificence to the dark blue mountains surrounding the plain of Skódra. The Skódra merchants cross it in troops at early morn on their way to the bazaars; many of these are men of considerable property, and trade largely to the coasts of Italy, especially Venice, the dialect of which place nearly all of them speak as well as Greek, Slavonic-Albanian, and Turkish. They live in a homely style in their own town, and never adopt the fustianell or kilt, being clad in dark loose capote-vests, with blue or black linen trousers like those of Corfiotes or the population of the Greek isles; below these are scrupulously white stockings—changed daily, wonderful to say—but the Scutarini are totally different in appearance, habits, and manners to the southern Albanians. The women have their faces covered, so that when out of doors you cannot distinguish Christians from Mohammedans, and one and all dress in scarlet cloaks with square hoods. But it is in Venice or Cáttaro that the Skódra merchant unfolds himself, as it were, for at home his fear of exciting the cupidity of the Turks prevents any such display. Abroad he exhibits all the blazing richness of full Gheghe costume; while it is at home that the Skodra lady indulges in a magnificence of costume almost beyond belief. In domestic arrangements the Latin Christians of Skódra have much in common with their Mohammedan rulers, under whose power they have so long dwelt as to adopt most of their practices—such, for instance, as the marriages being fixed by the parents, the bride and bridegroom never meeting till she is brought to her betrothed's house on the day of the marriage. As in Turkey, also, the female of each family are almost close prisoners, excepting when masked, and in no case hold communion with the males of any other household.

While sketching about the village I was plentifully pelted by little Gheghe boys, until the arrival of a Kawás from the Pashá secured me from annoyance. The Skódra Albanians have the reputation of excessive ferocity and turbulence; and to say truth, their countenances do not belie the report. The Latin Christian populace, on the contrary, seem as timid as civil. By the aid of a tractable Kawás I drew throughout the whole day unremittingly, from various points below the south side of the castle, whence the view is very imposing, and near a wondrous old bridge across to Bryana, constructed of pointed arches of irregular width, and having somewhat the effect of the columns in a Gothic cathedral, suddenly resolved on spanning the stream, some with little steps, some with long. Everywhere the various groups of buffalo cars and peasants, or of scarlet-coated Gheghes sitting on the ground, were full of interest; but the thin population of a place so extensive as Skódra is very apparent, and it is a great contrast to the lively and thriving Monastír.

Perhaps the grandest of all the views of Skódra is from the rock eastward of the bazaars; the castle, the mountains above—the ruined town below—the river winding beneath its bridges into far distance, form one of the finest of pictures. As the sun was sinking low, his rays, clouded through the day, lit up the northern side of the landscape brilliantly, and from the steep castle hill—my last halt—nothing could be more splendid than the rich foliage and glittering dwellings on the one side and the dark ranges of deep blue and violet hills against the bright sky. But there

79

is far to go, and it is time to set out homeward over the ankle-twisting
paved causeways of Skódra.

OCTOBER 5

It rained hard all night and at 10 A.M. (when we should have been going
up to the Pashá's dinner) torrents descended, with violent thunder and
hail. Towards eleven it held up a little, so as the invitations of three-
tailed Pashás are not to be neglected, I set off to the Vice-Consul's,
taking Giorgio, with a supply of shoes, linen, and cloth clothes as a
remedy against the wetting there was small chance of escaping. Whereupon, fresh storms commencing, Signor Bonatti, myself, the Dragoman
Pazzini and a Kawás, all rushed desperately through the falling torrents,
by odious paved paths to the castle, arriving there in a perfect deluge.
Having changed our dress, the time till dinner was served (about noon)
passed in continual repetitions of sherbet, sweetmeats, pipes, and
coffee, the Pashá being always very lively and merry.

Osmán Pashá affects European manners, and (to my great relief) we
all sat on chairs round a table; a Bímbashi (or captain on guard) appearing about as much at ease in his new position as I had done when in that
of the natives. As for the legion dinner, it is not to be described. I
counted up thirty-seven dishes, served, as is the custom in Turkey, one
by one in succession, and then I grew tired of reckoning (supposing that
perhaps the feast was going on all day) though I think there were twelve
or fourteen more. But nothing was so surprising as the strange jumble
of irrelevant food offered: lamb, honey, fish, fruit; baked, boiled,
stewed, fried; vegetable, animal; fresh, salt, pickled; solid; oil, pepper;
fluid; sweet, sour; hot, cold—in strange variety, though the ingredients
were often very good. Nor was there any order in the course according
to European notions—the richest pastry came immediately after dressed
fish and was succeeded by beef, honey, and cakes; pears and peaches;
crabs, ham, boiled mutton, chocolate cakes, garlic, and fowl; cheese,
rice, soup, strawberries, salmon-trout, and cauliflowers—it was the very
chaos of a dinner! Of those who did justice to the repast I was not one;
and fortunately it is not considered necessary, by the rules of Turkish

SKÓDRA

DURÁZZO

etiquette, to do more than taste each dish; and although the Pashá twice or thrice helped me himself, it is sufficient to eat the smallest atom, when the attendant servant removes your plate. As for drink, there were marsala, sherry, hock, champagne, Bass's pale ale, bottled porter, rakhí, and brandy—a large show of liquor in a Mohammedan house; nor did the faithful seem to refrain particularly from any fluid; but there was no unbecoming excess, and as is remarkably the case with Turkish manners, quiet and order were observable throughout the festivity. Only the Bimbáshi, a heavy, dull man, seemed marked out for practical jokes, and they made him take an amazing mixture of porter and champagne, assuring him it was a species of Frank soup, which he seemed to like little enough. As the entertainment draws to a close it is polite to express your sense of the host's hospitality by intimating a sense of repletion, and, by pointing to your throat, the utter impossibility of eating any more; and perhaps the last delicate act of complimentary acknowledgement, which it is not easy to describe otherwise than as a series of remarkable choral ventriloquism, was the queerest and most alarming trait of the whole fête. On the whole, there was much to amuse, though I should not like to dine with Pashás often. Osmán Pashá surprised me by his questions concerning Ireland, Scotland, the game laws, etc., and appeared to have read and understood a good deal about European nations. After dinner, I amused him greatly by drawing one or two of his attendants, and should have obtained the portraits of more, had not the Mufti, or Mollah, or Cadi, in an orthodox green and white turban, been suddenly announced, a visit which put a stop to my unholy pastime. At six we came away. How disagreeable the raised pavement of Skódra is none but those who have slipped off it into deep mud and water every five minutes can tell.

OCTOBER 6

An April day of sun and showers. Early I went to the Consul's, to make a drawing of a Gheghe chief, Abdulláh Bey, who was magnificently attired in a full suit of scarlet and gold; and afterwards one of Callíope Bonatti, the Consul's second daughter, a very pretty girl, who good-naturedly sat to me in a bridal Scutarine dress which Madame Bonatti had most obligingly borrowed. No toilet can be more splendid; purple silk and velvet, elaborately embroidered in gold and silver, form the outer garment, the patterns worked by hand with the greatest taste; two or three undervests covered with embroidery, full purple trousers, innumerable chains of gold and silver coins and medals, with a long white veil, complete the costume, excepting several coloured silk handkerchiefs which are sewn inside the outer vest and have a tawdry and ill-arranged look when compared with the rest of the dress. This gay attire is only worn on great fête days, or on marked occasions, such as marriages and christenings.

The Consul and his wife are in great distress about the ways and manners of Skódra, as to face-hiding, for, since Christian as well as Mohammedan women conceal their faces, no woman can stir out unmasked without receiving some insult, as indeed to appear barefaced marks total loss of character. Consequently, Mesdemoiselles Bonatti do not like to go out under such risk of reproach, while, on the other hand, their mother will not allow them to wear the yashmak; for she says: 'Are you not Christians? And why should you be ashamed of showing your face?'

Their being one of the few families here professing the Greek form of Christianity probably makes this objection stronger; and the result of this difference of opinion is that the young ladies never leave the house at all, from one year's end to another. Bitter complaints of Skódra as a residence may be heard on all sides. The clashing of various races, religions, and castes must render it an odious abode; while alarms and feuds, risk of property and life, hatred and petty warfare, prevail among all.

At 1 p.m. dinner was served at the Vice-consular table, the only guest being Antonio Súmma the merchant, a very good specimen of his order. Of the host and hostess it would be difficult to speak too favourably. The eldest daughter alone is wedded to Skódra fashions; and the being obliged to appear in the company of men was evidently a great pain to the unfortunate girl, who with difficult refrained from crying if looked at or spoken to: so strong is the force of habit.

At four we adjourned to the house of Antonio Súmma—a substantial building in a large courtyard, all the appurtenances about which indicated opulence and comfort. The usual compliments of pipes, coffee, and lemonade were gone through, and I made a drawing of the worthy merchant in his Skódra costume; but on his younger brother coming in (both were men of about forty years of age), and requesting to be sketched also, I, for want of paper, was obliged to make a small though accurate portrait of him on the same page as that on which I had drawn his eldest brother, on a larger scale.

'O, canto cielo!' said the younger, in a fury of indignation, when he saw the drawing; 'why have you done this? It is true I am the youngest, but I am not smaller than my brother; and why should you make me so diminutive? What right have you thus to remind me of my inferior position? Why do you come into our house to act so insultingly?'

I was so amazed by this afflicting view of my innocent mistake that I could hardly apologise when the elder brother took up the tale.

'I, too,' said he, 'am vexed and hurt, O Signore! I thought you meant well; but if you think that you win my esteem by a compliment paid at the expense of the affection of my brother, you are greatly mistaken.'

What could I say? Was there ever such a lesson to unthinking artists in foreign lands? I had made two enemies by one sketch, and was obliged to take a formal addio, leaving the injured brothers bowing me out with looks of thunder.

A settling regarding horses and luggage, and the procuring a fresh supply of money in bills, on Avlóna [Vlonë] and Yannina, at the hospitable Casa Bonatti, concluded my fourth and last day in Skódra.

OCTOBER 7

The apothecary's house has been no bad resting-place in the Illyrian metropolis. It hath very few disagreeables. A large dog sits and howls at the window during the night, and a good many mice and rats course about its rooms—but that is all. Don Marco is a mysterious little man; and his household consists of one old and three young women, of whom two are very pretty, but timid to the last degree of Skódra bashfulness—

catching up towels, or saucepans, or whatever comes to hand if they are unfortunate enough to meet a man when their face is uncovered. The apothecary tells Giorgio that he came there from Venice to try his fortunes, and found this widow and family, who let him the house: 'And,' said he, 'while I hesitate as to which of the three daughters I shall marry, time passes, and we all grow old!'

All things being in readiness for starting, I went to take leave of the Vice-Consular family—the members of which I left with regret, almost the only feeling of the kind I had experienced in a month's travel. How different are these to the days of Abruzzo and Calabria! Poor Signora Bonatti with her ten children! There is something very sad in such isolation as Greek Christians are here doomed to live in. And considering the hopeless character of Skódra, '*vendette, nasconderíe, sospetti, incendie*'[1]—the extremes of revolutionary and despotic, Turk against Christian, Latin opposed to Greek—no place seems more fully fraught with the evils of life. Addio, Skódra; and here terminates the northern extent of my Albanian journey—though much novelty yet is in store in the south. I looked my last on the Illyrian city as we came round the eastern side of the castle ridge to avoid the bazaars, and were soon on the flat ground beyond the Boyána.

The day was bright; and the horses being good, we soon reached the khan I had halted at on the 2nd—the roads being far better than was to have been expected after the heavy rains. Grand in form and colour are the ranges of hills east of the Drin, and beautiful are the huge white-stemmed abele trees, their branches loaded with wild vine festooning into the water. At half past two we reached the river, and crossed it in a crowded ferry-boat. Large parties of Tóskhide Albanians, known by their white caps and grey capotes, were waiting in many a picturesque group to pass the broad stream, for there is some great bazaar at Skódra tomorrow, and a world of travelling merchants are hastening to it.

After an hour of quick trotting, below the silver-armed abeles—by the Latin villages with the hairy lean pigs and scrubby yellow goats, and beyond these, after some slow pacing over ground inundated by the rains, we entered the melancholy Aléssio at half past five. Small time, alas! was there for sketching, since I had still to recross the Drin, a feat

[1] 'Revenge, intrigue, suspicions, incendiaries', represented to me as the daily ingredients of Skódra existence.

soon accomplished by the aid of the Soorudjí (a good-natured fellow pleasantly contrasted with that wild ourang-outang who guided me from Tirana), but it was nearly dark ere I arrived at Padre Pietro's convent, and with a desperate energy I outlined the proportions of the hills as they loomed out from the grey sky, hoping that a bright morning would console me for this second failure to my attempt to sketch Aléssio.

I found the friar more energetic than ever in abuse of his Albanian flock, *'Maledetti tutti dal cielo'* being his mildest expression concerning them; the fact of a favourite servant having been that morning found murdered at a short distance from the convent being no slight excuse for his anger. The tenantless cells and large gloomy refectory of the monastery, joined to the unceasing vituperation of its sole occupant, did not add liveliness to the evening. My own stores set forth a very tolerable supper, and the monk's acid wine contributed to vary the repast. In the first part of the evening the poor man was diffuse about his own situation *'Vita d'inferno'*, etc.; and with that of his co-mates in exile, *'Sparsi siamo noi altri frati della religione vera. Sparsi quà e là ne' boschi come majali spaventati.'*[1] This subject exhausted, he fell upon Pope Pio IX, whose inaptitude to govern, he predicted, was about to bring great miseries on Rome and the Church; then he lashed out against the Turchi of the district, attributing vices by wholesale to their community in a comfortless category of bitter accusation; nor did the Christians escape. A black list of crimes, falsehood, unbelief, immorality of all kinds covered them with blots, and he summed up his maledictions by saying: *'In fine, sono tutti porchi pregiati del gran Diavolone nero.'* Poor Signor Bonatti came in for his share, too, though poverty seemed to be the only evil condition to be attributed to him; and a slight seasoning of flattery to, *'Quella nazione tanta forte che amabile, quel gran popol d'Inghilterra,'* filled up his eloquent discourse. After supper, Padre Pietro insisted on giving up his room to me, a favour I firmly resisted as long as it was possible, for I should greatly have preferred the bare corridors to a close dormitory filled with books and furniture; but the monk was inexorable, so I retired for the night to wrap myself in my plaid and endeavour to think lightly of the gnats, which are very numerous from the vicinity of the river. In the chamber hang engravings

[1] We brethren of the true religion are dispersed here and there in these woods like frightened pigs.'

of the Piazza del Popolo and San Pietro. How clearly and sharply in this remote place do they bring back the memory of years passed in Rome!

OCTOBER 8

With difficulty I contrived to obtain two views before it began to rain; and by the time horses and luggage were ferried over the river a blackening thunderstorm was fast rising in hard-edged masses of cloud from all the plains below Króia, soon to burst over the hill of Aléssio. To proceed while it lasted was impossible, so I sat in the empty, dark bazaars; it was Sunday, and no Christians were at their shops, though the few passing peasants were worth observation, the female costume covered with fringes, tassels, and embroidery, and the men wearing a capote sort of short spencer, the hood of which, square and oddly fashioned, protects the head against rain, and looks like a tuft or crest of some strange black bird. Such deluges fell that the rattling roofs seemed about to give way; but, as the sky gave token of clearing, we thought it better, towards noon, to remain for the midday meal before starting, and accordingly I adjourned to Signor Giuseppe's house once more, where the old Scutaríno still lingers on his way to Skódra.

At one we started, as I was resolved to make some progress, if possible, seeing that the roadside khan below Króia cannot be a worse abode than this, and one is farther out of the low country, which may be inundated if the bad weather lasts; but, though the soft sirocco air threatens no distant change, all is bright and clear for the present. Soon we entered the briery copse, with its tall, creeper-hung trees; the pathway which led through its tangled mazes—never very obvious—was now, from the heavy rains, which had beaten down the branches and half obliterated the narrow, winding track, wellnigh impassable. At one moment the long drooping boughs and drapery-like clematis seemed to defy all progress; at the next a tract of mud two feet deep threatened to become a stable for the night to our luckless steeds. Many were my misgivings as to the chance of ultimately passing through this hideous swamp; but thanks to patience and our very good horses, we crossed it after two hours' hard work, and were glad to rest for a short space

by the roadside khan nearest Aléssio, and then to proceed by less disre-
putable roads to the Máthis, which was much swollen, and barely fordable.

The Króia range of mountains were magnificently indistinct in a
watery haze; and as the sun sank a thousand tints were thrown over all
the wide landscape. After this, the beautiful oak wood was reached,
and the green oases, with the scattered flocks and the slippery causeway
or selciata winding beneath the fresh, tall trees seemed a perfect paradise
after the frightful copse-wilderness on the plain of Aléssio. About five
we arrived at the first khan in the forest; but as there was a moon, or
three-quarters of a moon, it was judged feasible to press on to the khan
at which we lunched on the 1st, making a better division of distance
between Aléssio and Tirana; so on we went. As the moonlight gained
strength nothing could exceed the beauty of those silent groves, where
the giant aerial stems of abeles, with their white branches loaded with
wild vine grouped together with the majestic oak and spreading beech—
it is long since I have enjoyed so exquisite a forest scene by moonlight.
Yet some drawbacks were notable by a short-sighted man; the projecting
boughs, against which I came often with great force, had more than once
wellnigh done a mischief to head and eyes. By 7 P.M. furious barking
proclaimed the neighbourhood of the 'roast fowl khan', and there we
shortly arrived. The raised part of it was already occupied by five very
unclean-looking Albanians, but one side of the fire was at liberty and
soon swept and arranged for me; and Giorgio ere long prepared tea on
the little squat stool-table, after which sleep quickly followed; not,
however, before I had leisure to meditate on the fact that I was now
actually in the very wildest phase of Albanian life.

Those five wild creatures, blowing the fire, are a scene for a tale of
the days of past centuries. When they have sipped their coffee they roll
themselves up in capotes, and stretching out their feet to the embers,
lie motionless till an hour before daybreak. The large khan is now
silent (for even the vile little fussy chickens cease to scrabble about in
the dead of night), and only the champing of the horses in the farther
part of this great stable-chamber is heard; the flickering light falls on
these outstretched sleepers, and makes a series of wonderful pictures
never to be forgotten, though I fear, also, never to be well imitated by
the pencil. That I do not speak the language, and that I had not previously studied figure-drawing, are my two great regrets in Albania.

OCTOBER 9

During the night a shrill and wild cry echoes through the forest several times and the barking of distant dogs follows it. This proceeds from shepherds who perceive the vicinity of a wolf by some movement of the flock and there-upon alarm their watch-dogs.

With morning comes the reflection that I must go to Tirana tonight, and no farther—perhaps even to that very foulest of pigsties with the circulating Dervish seen through the hole in the wall.

The day begins badly, according to Giorgio's way of regarding omens; for, firstly, as he has made an admirable basin of coffee, with toast, a perverse hen, either owing to the infirmity of a near sight or a spasmodic presentiment that she should one day become broth in a similar piece of earthenware, suddenly came down from the rafters above with a great shriek and flutter into the well-filled breakfast platter, upsetting coffee and toast together into the fire in her efforts at self-extrication. Giorgio meekly prepared to make it all over again; but, said he, a day so commenced must have other ill luck in it before sunset. Secondly (and consequently), the horses being all in starting trim— when an obese buffalo foolishly persisted in walking all among them into the centre of the khan, and when the alarmed beasts put themselves, us, and the luggage in jeopardy, amid a fearful confusion of flying fowls and barking dogs, then Giorgio saw the spell of ill luck at work, and foreboded more evil ere we reached Tirana. Thirdly, on starting, down came the rain, and for a long time we could only advance at the very slowest rate through the thick forest, athwart pendant vines and dense foliage, beaten down across the narrow pathways. The day, however, cleared and we soon entered beautiful undulating wood scenes, where paintings of Hobbima or Swanveldt start to life at every moment; such were the tall and spreading, or light fairy-like oaks, with misty grey distances of hanging foliage on the green hills below Króia, seen through opening boughs, while below were red winding paths amid a carpeting of dear old English fern: most lovely were these scenes. At half past eight the khan of Presa was passed on the right, and after two and a half more hours of riding over alternate wooded undulations or flat ground, we arrived at the khan where, on September 29th, I had

88

drawn majestic Króia, soaring high over the plain on the opposite mountainside. Poor little Alí Bey! Perhaps he is yet sitting in his corner, meditating on tik-a-tok, squish-squash, A, B, C, etc. Here I halted to dine and ruminate on cold veal—wasps—and clouds; the first I eat, the second I killed as fast as may be; the third grew hideously black and threatened the most violent of storms.

At two we were again on the road; the curtain-clouds above the hills gradually lost their outline and draw a gradual grey veil over all nature and torrents soon fall. Lucky have I been to get drawings of Króia before this wet season's commencement! Few intervals of light or of cessation of rain ensued; and long before Tirana was reached I was drenched thoroughly; it was some consolation that we had really good horses and an active, good-natured Soorudjí, so that we galloped on at a great rate. Luckily, too, a better khan was found on this than at our last visit to Tirana, since only a part of its broken roof admitted the rain and the walls were tolerably sound. Clearly it is my best plan to make for the south without delay, for the great rivers and swampy land of these Gheghe regions will shortly become totally impassable, and who can tell how long one may be detained among them? Had I remained at Alessio, this afternoon's rain must have rendered the Mathis, and the marshy copse, a bar to all further progress for the present.

OCTOBER 10

It is 4 A.M. and the Muezzins chant, so plaintively beautiful in these wild North Albanian places, awakes me. There are other symptoms too of approaching day peculiar to these places; none more so than the incessant tremulous cackle of numberless geese. At seven, spite of the threatening looks of cloud, we prepare for a start; the smallness of this smoky den—for den is the mildest term that can be applied to even this, the best khan here—prevents anything being dried and one may just as well be making progress in wet clothes as sitting still in them. Yet it is nine o'clock before horses come, by reason of the postmaster being in the bath as before—this delay is the more undesirable, inasmuch as that there is every prospect of fresh storms ere we can finish our day's journey. Durázzo is the next place in my route, as I plan to return south-ward by the coast, striking inward only to Berát, whence at Avlóna, and thence if it be possible, to Acroceraunia—the great point of novelty in the tour. Shortly after leaving Tirana, we overtook and joined com-pany with a Mohammedan Albanian of that town. He calls it but eight hours or less to Durázzo, though you pay post for nine. This Osmán, who speaks Italian, is diffuse on his domestic circumstances—he talks of how much substance he had collected during twelve years' service with a Trieste merchant—of what property speculation had since pro-cured him—*buffali*, *terre*, *cavalle*, and two wives; and hints that one grows old, and that he should shortly get a third. After two hours' riding we crossed a wide river by a fine stone bridge, built, according to our Albanian companion, by a Trieste merchant of Tirana, and shortly afterwards we rode into the river itself, the bed of which occupies all the narrow valley down which we proceeded, the broad but shallow stream winding from side to side, so that before we arrived at Diróc-chio, we had passed it eight times—always an unpleasant task. At Dirocchio, a scattered village among olive grounds, the banks advance, and the river runs between high cliffs; in another half-hour the valley widens out towards the sea, into which, as we rose over heights com-manding a broad view of the coast, the silver stream can be traced by its white torrent track. There was now a high and barren range of hills to cross, along the sides of which, deeply indented into hollows, runs a pathway so narrow, that had it rained the slippery clay soil would have prevented the surest footed beast from making progress; for in parts eight inches of slanting earth were all the foot had to depend on and I looked down the deep-shelving abyss with a conviction that I might be better acquainted with it before long, the rather, that towards the sum-mit the horses' nerves were miserably troubled by the ferocious attacks of some fourteen or fifteen dogs, who saw us from afar off and expended a most unnecessary amount of labour and breath in crossing a deep ravine before they reached us. When we arrived at length at the highest point the view was very beautiful, with a wide expanse of blue sea stretching southward to the plains of Kaváya [Kavajë], and northward to the long slender promontory of Durázzo,[1] on the point of which stands the ancient castle of that once important city; and doubtless

[1] Durázzo—Epidamnus; afterwards Dyracchium.

there was much more of extended distance now hidden by heavy cloud and mist. A rapid descent brought us to the shore; and a gallop on the smooth sand was no bad contrast to the tiresome hill-paths.

By four (a seven hours' journey after all) we reached a large khan standing in a suburban street outside the walls. The town itself has now shrunk to the dimensions of a single street running to the end of the promontory and overlooked by the massive grey towers of the castle, which are built on considerably higher ground. Towards these I speedily set out to procure a good view of Dyracchium. The castle is a building apparently Norman, though much patched and repaired, its fortifications extend down the hillside to the water's edge, where they join the town walls, and in various parts of them I observed armorial shields having owls carved on them in basso-relievo. The combinations of scenery around are very elegant and delightful and extremely unlike any Albanian view I had yet seen. At this point I thought I was safe from intruders but all the children of the town soon espied me, and climbed up to my retreat, so that I was surrounded by a host of red-capped, red-robed urchins all calling out, '*Capitagno! O capitagno! Pará! pará!*' I adopted one as guide and safeguard against the rest of his brethren, promising paras[1] on returning to the khan; whereon, armed with a little brief authority, he dealt promiscuous blows among his brethren, and kept them at a respectful distance. My sketch finished, I went down to the town, and entering the gates, walked through the single street of modern Durázzo which occupies nearly the whole of the narrow point of land projecting into the sea, and ending in a mole. The houses here are far neater than in the interior of Gheghería; and although the line of bazaars was as usual partly covered over, it was with rich pergolata of vine-trellis, not with old mats—a substitute which gave an Italian air to the scene. The tradespeople, too, seem to speak Italian—whether from commerce with the opposite coast, or from old links of former Venetian existence, I know not.

As I walked down the bazaars nearly everybody spoke to me—an odd contrast to the savage indifference of Elbasán or Tirana—and mostly with complete familiarity, as if I had been an old acquaintance. '*Ah, Signor Capitano!* (for the knowledge of foreign parts being confined at Durázzo to the medium of captains—*omne ignotum pro capitano*). *Come*

[1] A small Turkish coin.

stai, Capitano? Donde vieni, caro Capitano mio? onde sei? dove vai? Comprate qualche cosa, etc.' At the end of the bazaar-street is a fortress, through which a quay is reached, where a Turkish garrison were smoking. The Bimbáshi or Captain desired to interrogate me, merely looking at my teskéré as a matter of form, and asking sundry news about the *malattia* of Salonica—whether it was coming that way, etc.—the first I had heard of it since we left Yiannitsa. The familiar people of Durázzo nevertheless inveigled me into purchasing some of their wares before I quitted the town, of which an oke (three pounds) of walnuts and apples, though costing one penny only, was not a sample of excellence. Returning to my cell in the khan at dusk, to supper, I was greatly charmed by the singing of a man in the street (according to Giorgio, a Slavonian of Montenegro), who appeared to enthral the whole neighbourhood by his tuneful voice, and I regretted not being able to take down, otherwise than very imperfectly, the wild and strikingly beautiful airs he sang. His audience seemed to the highest degree enthusiastic, and frequently interrupted him with applause, forcing him to repeat many verses. But there is a musical atmosphere in Durázzo, and I hear many melodious hummings, of which most of Albania seems guiltless.

OCTOBER 11

Rain again!—but it subsides into drizzle, and meanwhile I prowl about Durázzo. It possesses singularly little of artistic interest, considering its former extent and grandeur, though many fine pictures might still be made in its neighbourhood, the castle being always to be introduced as the principal feature. From eight to ten, between showers, I jotted down scraps of the town and bay, but clouds obscure the line of hills towards Acroceraunia, which ought to be seen from this place, and the damp prevents steady drawing, besides which, the Gheghes came and bullied me (as it was not worth while asking for a Kawás), by shaking my sketch-book in paroxysms of orthodox piety, by secreting pencils, and asking for paper. So I gave up Dyracchium, and retreated to the khan through groups of irascible female buffaloes, which creaked and grunted as I passed, following me with their porcelain-white eyes, as if

I intended to embezzle their calves—strange little beasts, motionless except the twinkle of their ears, and lying crouched together like bits of hairy Indian rubber on the grass.

At twelve, early dinner being over, it is time to start for Kaváya, but from this place there is no more posting, and henceforth throughout Albania, the journeys must be on horses hired from place to place, and adieu to Soorudjís and leather saddles. In the present instance the horses are good, but there are only pack, or wooden saddles to be procured (I, for one, think them far more comfortable than your Turkish penance), rope stirrups and bridles made of string. The route lay at first along the shore, with a green and troubled sea breaking on the sounding sands, but in two hours we left the coast and struck inland, and after crossing some low hills, the mosques of Kaváya were already in sight standing in the flattest and widest of plains. The aspect of this part of Albania is very striking; the immense plains which reach in an almost unbroken level from Durázzo to Avlóna southward, and extending to the foot of Tomórit, and the hills of Elbasán towards the east, the sea being their western limit, may, indeed, rather be called one vast meadow.[1] Their appearance from the neighbourhood of Kaváya—perfectly green and dotted with numberless herds and flocks—is as novel as beautiful, while northward the long promontory of Durázzo resembles an island on the water's edge.

Kaváya is the most southern town of the Gheghes on the coast, and the entrance to it by a long dirty street was not prepossessing, or prophetic of a comfortable dwelling; there were two or three more than ordinarily picturesque mosques, and long bazaars matted and roofed as usual to the jeopardy of the heads of the incautious. The khan stood beyond the town, and in our way to it, I met the Governor with a suite of some twenty guards, taking that minute portion of exercise which these people call their afternoon walk. Remotely considered, the khan was not a bad khan, but on a near inspection, it proved to be a negative abode, and quite out of the question as a lodging for the night, for there were no walls to the rooms, no ceiling, no floors, no roofs, no windows, no anything, so that I was in despair as to where to go, when a Greek Papas,[2] who had followed us, came up, and in good

[1] This district is termed the Mizakía.
[2] Papas, a Greek Christian priest.

Italian offered me his house, which I gladly accepted, and after a tour of half the town, we arrived at a galleried picturesque place in a court-yard thronged with geese, and incumbered with barrels. '*Camera vostra*,' said the priest, showing me into a large and handsome room occupying one wing of the upper floor of the building, and I, with the utmost innocence, supposing that this offer was all hospitality such as one may find in dear old Abruzzi or Calabria, made fifty apologies and agreeable speeches to the reverend man, till I accidentally caught sight of Giorgio's knocker-like visage writhing itself into amazing contortions in the background, by way of expressing that I was quite wrong, and should have to pay full dearly for my place of refuge. So I settled myself for the night with Papa Andréa, the Ecónomos of Kaváya, taking occasion to sketch his house between falling showers—for there seems no chance of settled weather; and how Berát is to be reached, if these storms last, I know not. Meanwhile, at eight or nine o'clock, supper is brought in, composed of various dishes of fish, salad, beans, etc.; the Ecónomos (who resembles the statue of Moses in S. Pietro de' Vincolis —I mean as to his length of beard), with his son and two grandsons, continually waiting on me much more obsequiously than I could wish. Lastly, a bed and sheets are brought in by the clergyman and his descendants, but though very picturesque and antique, there were many objections to availing myself of them in preference to my own.

OCTOBER 12

The morning is brilliant, and I make early use of it, taking an armed Kawás as well as the priest's son, to keep off intruders. Close above Kaváya there is a rising ground, whence the view is delightful, and full of rural quiet; it consists of large olive trees spreading over paths and broken banks; of lanes, mosques, and a high clock tower; Gheghe figures, bright in black, red and white; burying grounds with sparkling tombs; garden trees anon, tower above dark red roofs and tall white chimneys; waves of blue-green groves of olive; and then vast flat meadows stretch to the sea, with 'endless flocks and herds,' while a line of pale low hills to the south-west, and the blue Adriatic with Durázzo on its promontory melts tenderly into the horizon.

At half-past eight I went with Giorgio to Achmét Bey, the Governor, whose palace, though highly picturesque, is inferior to Alí Bey's of Króia. The great man sat in his corner, in a large ancient square room, gilded and carved all over so that it resembled the inside of some gigantic toy. Blue-vested and furred Muftis, with some red and black Gheghes, composed groups of wondrous colour, and the Governor himself was all politeness. Among other matters, he wished me to see a surprisingly excellent map of London and Frangistán, in the finding of which there was much delay, and great fuss in presenting it for my inspection. Lo! it was a chart of the Japanese Seas, and a map of Java, published in Holland a century back! '*Pecche?*' said the Bey, 'is it good? Is London like?' After this morning call, I drew in the town, but with great difficulty, owing to the press of people, besides the vicinity of odoriferous slaughter-houses; for your only points for sketching in these places are sure, by infallible rules of destiny, to be close to some horror. There is a very curious burying-ground in the centre of Kaváya surrounded by numerous columns, apparently antique and mostly wanting their capitals; but I could learn nothing of whence they came (possibly from old Apollónia, or Dyracchium). While sketching this, there was a hum and hush among the crowd, '*Gynaike*[1]—*gynaike!*' said some of them to me, and all retired to the side of the street, allowing room for some twenty ghost-like females to pass, shrouded in dark feringhís with white head-wrappers. It seemed an etiquette with the world of Kaváya to look another way while the fair procession was near us.

The patriarchal family of the Ecónomos had prepared an unnecessarily sumptuous repast against my return; but the horses which his reverence had procured for us were not in harmony; all four were in evil condition, yet no others were to be had. We started at noon. Bérat I cannot hope to reach tonight, but Leustri,[2] six hours hence, is to be aimed at, and the weather seems to favour the possibility.

The great meadow-plains of Kaváya, bounded by low down-like hills, clothed with growth of olive-trees, were most pleasant to look on; and in consequence of the baggage horse falling, by which all the roba was disarranged, one had the more time to contemplate the oxen and buffali without number, and the sheep and geese that enliven the wide green surface. Throughout the extent of flat country great flocks

[1] Women.　　[2] Lushnjé.

of geese are taken out to pasture every morning by a gooseherd; they are carefully watched from sunrise to sunset, for fear of vultures by day and wolves by night; and are then driven home to their respective villages, after the fashion of goats in Italy. We met many peasants, but the gay Gheghe colours are giving place to white costume. They all furnish a bad account of the great river of Elbasán, the Skumbi, which is to be crossed, and which they say is rising rapidly in consequence of the mountain rains. About three we met a bridal party—the bride being conveyed on horseback to the future husband's house; she seemed to be a strange thing, like a large doll—so closely swaddled and wrapped up that neither face nor figure were visible, while a tall sprig of rosemary, which finished off her head-dress, gave her the appearance of some exotic plant in process of careful conveyance to a gardener's ground.

Several times we turned towards the river, but always retreated at the approach of peasants who exclaimed: '*Yok, yok!*' '*Mir ist!*'[1] said some Albanians, pointing to the sea, so on we went for two hours— the plain becoming more and more beautiful as the sun sank lower in the horizon, and the great monarch Mount Tomóhr, frowned in purple grandeur amid cloud and storm. At last we arrived at the formidable river—one too broad, deep, and rapid, to be forded, while the bridge, a long and narrow structure of a shaking and incoherent nature, pre- sented wide gaps through which you saw the rushing stream between the loose wattles that formed its floor. The transit was really not a little dangerous. I felt relieved when the last man had passed over it, each leading his horse very slowly from end to end before the next put foot on the crazy fabric, which would not have supported two parties at once; if the river continued to rise, we must assuredly have been the last who ever made use of that bridge as a medium of passage.

For half an hour we returned eastward on the left bank of the river, and then proceeded by broad lanes, deep in thick black mud, to the village, or scattered collection of hive-like thatched huts, called Tjermí. I have now left Gheghería, and am in the land of the Tóskidhes—a new tribe; the people, at least these of Tjermí, seem a poorer and more squalid race; their dress is white—even to their little skull-caps; but dirt and squalor of the outer and timid wretchedness of the inner man

[1] No, no! Yonder it is good!

seemed the characteristics of these pauper-beings, who arose from the ground in their rags as I passed, and saluted me with looks of terror—widely differing from the haughty gaze of the crimson-coated Gheghe. Here, too, the defeat of the last Albanian movement under Zuliki is recorded in the absence of arms as well as in the appearance of the peasantry.

I never saw grander landscape than that of these plains, as majestic Tomóhrit grew grey in the waning light. It was dusk when we arrived at the khan of Tjermí—a place far short of our original destination, for it is in reality only three hours distant from Kaváya, though it has taken six to reach it, owing to the long detour the swollen river has compelled us to make. Khan Tjermí is a wretched-looking den, standing all alone on the wide waste, yet its little loft to which one climbed by a ladder possessed at least a new floor, clean walls and mats and wooden window shutters.

Four Délvino Greeks, or Epirotes, had arrived before me, but there was still a corner, and the fire was by no means disagreeable, either from its heat or from calling up many pictures of light and shade so often remarked in these night scenes. Giorgio, who expected to have been unable to pass the Skumbi, or possibly to have fallen through that alarming bridge, is in great glee and makes a capital supper. They talk of nine or ten hours from here to Berát.

OCTOBER 13

A fearful night of wind and storm-rain. Doubts passed through my waking thoughts if we should not all be carried away into the river, khan, Epirotes, Frank, and Dragoman, by one of those thunderful gusts which swept over the plain at intervals with terrific force. In the pauses between the rage of the tempest all the surrounding country seemed alive with dogs, whose howling and barking added point to the furious din of the elements.

'Water—water—everywhere, but not a drop to'—wash in; for, in spite of the pouring rain, the supply of fluid within reach was of the smallest, and that little was seized for coffee—breakfast versus cleanliness. Long before sunrise the three Délviniotes should have set off, but the utter blackness of the tempest confined us all to the circle round the embers, waiting till daylight should bring better times. The Khanjí, an emigrant Acharnanian, diverted me by his scraps of polyglot discourse: '*Bavarese nichts gut*—τιποτες—*Ingliz, Franciz,* καλα, καλα, *Moscoffs nichts. Bavarese* πολυ *wein drinkt,* ολιγον *wasser,*' etc. At six the rain ceased, and the scowling clouds curtained themselves into gloomy folds, so, hoping for the best (though assuredly my Albanian journey does not prosper at present), I was again at half past six on my way towards Berát, over plains surrounded by the roots of hills, whose heads were hidden in cloud, excepting a low, bare, ill-outlined range on the left, which was ugly enough to have been obscured without any loss. Farther on, the downs on the west sink into the plain and a lake stretches out almost to the shore. Perseverance through mud and water brought us to Leustri at half past ten; but hoping to arrive at Berát I did not halt, except to rest horses at a wayside khan; its floor was occupied by a Skódra merchant, who was making himself as comfortable as circumstances permitted—considering that neither bread nor water could be obtained and that the rain came through the roof plentifully. To have lingered in such a place would have been folly, so hey for Berát once more at eleven. They said it required but five hours to reach it, so in spite of fresh falling deluges I presisted in advancing, though never was there less inducement to do so, for, apart from the vexation an artist feels who knows that he is surrounded by beautiful scenery, the only chance in his life of seeing which is so adversely destroyed by unlucky weather, the physical annoyance of sitting hour after hour in drenching rain and high wind, on a stumbling horse— advancing one half-mile per hour (at the quickest pace) through thick mud and overinundated meadows—this is no trifle, added to the loss of time and money from such unprofitable pastime, which is very trying to purse and temper. During this part of the day our late host, the Ecónomos of Kaváya, was regarded by Giorgio with the most acrid feelings of disgust (that reverend man of Ghegheria having charged us unseemly prices for steeds which were positively next to useless), and the recollection that I had so foolishly fancied the priest a hospitable man, who was offering his home for the use of me as a wanderer and foreigner, embittered the oppressed Dragoman to such a degree that at each stumble of his horse strong expressions escaped from him to the prejudice of Papa Andreas and Greek Papades in general.

After three hours of this miserable work, feeling that there might be six or eight more at the rate we advanced to Berát, and as the track became undistinguishable from the increasing rain, I gave in, the rather that Giorgio was hurt by the last fall of his horse and seemed unwilling to proceed. So having passed the fast-rising Beratino[1] by a bridge opposite to the khan Tchúka—a large building on a rising ground above the river—here we halt for the night. 'Do I lie on a bed of roses?' was the substance of my remonstrance to Giorgio, who grumbled for a while with deep groans about all this '*soffrire per niente*';[2] but the worthy Fanariote soon came to himself as we bustled to secure the two sides of the fireplace in the huge lofty-raftered khan-stable—first come first served being khan-law.

The difficulty of changing all one's wet clothes (and to escape fever this precaution is always most requisite) can only be appreciated by those who have made their toilet under similar circumstances; but this done, a good dinner of rice, pilaf, and kebabs, with coffee and a cigar, are beyond description refreshing; and the wayfarer soon forgets the inconveniences of travel while recording with pen or pencil its excitements and interests. Truly, in such weather as this of the last week there is little pleasure in travels even where better accommodation exists: so to Yannina, unless times grow better, must be my direct path.

At three the storm cleared, and then came the pleasing reflection that had I proceeded I might have reached Berát, though possibly it was more prudent to stop here. I go on to the bridge—the river rolls furiously below and heaps of purple and golden-edged clouds hang over the shaded base of Tomóhrit.

Midnight—O khans of Albania! Alas! the night is not yet worn through! I lie, barricaded by boxes and bundles from the vicinity of the stable and enduring with patience the fierce attacks of numberless fleas. All the khan sleeps, save two cats which indulge in festive boundings, and save a sleepless donkey which rolls too contiguously to my head. The wood fire, blazing up, throws red gleams on discoloured arches within whose far gloom the eye catches the form of sleeping

---

[1] The Devoli, anciently Apsus. [2] Suffering for nothing.

Albanian groups. Bulky spiders, allured by the warmth, fall thick and frequent from the raftered ceiling. All is still, except the horses champing straw within and the gurgle of the rapid river chafing without.

OCTOBER 14

The principal event of the night was the donkey's walking unexpectedly into the fireplace, thereby causing a confusion in my nocturnal arrangements only to be remedied by a complete decamping. By half past four, therefore, coffee is taken, the horses are ready, and I once more on my way to the unreachable Berát. There was a brilliant full moon, but big clouds are flitting over it and the road is now in bright light, now dark as Erebus; nor is it too warm at this early hour, the more that wet apparel is as yet barely dried. The wild Gheghe guide from Kaváya insists on loading Giorgio's tumble-down horse with the baggage, and all we can do in opposition is fruitless, as the mind of a Gheghe when once arranged is immovable. So on we advance by the strange flickering moonlight. Presently clouds gather and down comes rain as usual.

We are crossing the great plain of Berát and following a sort of track two feet deep in mire and water, when lo!—the baggage-horse falls, as I foreboded—but gets up again, which I did not look for. An old sick Albanian on his mule joins us, and we jog on slowly for an hour, when, losing the right path, that wretched baggage-horse falls plump into a ditch and no art can extract him. This is not a pleasant matter on a tempestuous moonlight night, but there is no help for the evil but the unloading the oppressed beast and transferring his burden to another. During this operation the contrast between the conduct of Giorgio, who, knee-deep in water and suffering from a fall yesterday, spake never a word, and that of the Kaváya guide, who swore himself into convulsions, is edifying. The priest of whom the horses had been hired seemed the chief object of his eloquence, as the word *prift* (Albanian for priest) was frequently heard among the clatter of strange monosyllables—dort beer, dort bloo, dort hitch, hitch beer, blue beer, beer chak, dort gatch, with other musical sounds. During this delay the sick Albanian was reposing on a knoll of turf (rather a damp bed) raised above the water; and when at length we were ready to start, in getting up he missed his footing and rolled down into the very ditch whence we had just extricated the steed; so there was a fourth halt to pull out and set up this feeble old man of the mountains.

A very breakdown procession did we make, slowly plodding through quagmire and stream, when at last we were fairly under way, and right glad was I when cocks crew, dogs barked, the moon faded, and grey day coldly and slowly came, unveiling 'vast Tomóhrit' a long way off beyond a weary expanse of plain. Yet over that have I yet to go, for Berát lies immediately at the foot of the mountain. About the third hour the journey became interesting, for Tomóhrit is a noble mountain, and the multitudes of sheep scattered over the wide, shrub-dotted meadow-plain formed beautiful features in the landscape. At length the celebrated fortress of Berát appeared—dark blue and diminutive on a pointed hill. Approaching the capital of Central Albania—a place I had so long desired to see—every step leads into grander scenes. The River Apsus or Beratíno is repassed on a stone bridge and the road winds over the plain on the banks of the wide stream, through a tract of country of the finest character, the high form of Tomóhrit, here seen from end to end, being the principal feature throughout. I do not remember to have known a finer specimen of a simple river scene than this—it combines the broad white-channelled serpent-stream, with its broken and reed-clad banks varied by sheep, goats, kine, and buffali, while above rises the giant mountain's single form, wrinkled into a thousand furrowed chasms, towering aloft over the uninterrupted and decided lines of the plain in grand simplicity.

Owing to the deep mud, it took us two long hours to ride from the bridge over the Beratíno to that in the town; and at 10 A.M. we entered this magnificently picturesque place, which, much as I had imagined of its grandeur, far surpassed my expectations.

Berát[1] is situated in a narrow gorge or pass of the Beratíno, which seems to have forced a passage through the tremendous rocks on either side, leaving merely a narrow space between the cliff and the water. The great Tomóhr fills up, as it were, all the eastern end of the pass; and to the west and south the mountains through which the vale of the

[1] Berát, anciently Antipatria.

Beratíno winds seem equally to enclose this singular place, though the fortress height looks over the plains to a great distance.

The city is placed chiefly on the right bank of the river, as also is the Acropolis or castle hill which rises immediately above the town—the houses and mosques are piled one above another on the steep ledges of rock which slope from the frowning fortress and its stupendous cliffs down to the water's edge, and constitutes a view that combines Tyrolese or Swiss grandeur with all the pretty etcetera of Turkish architecture.

Passing below the cliffs of the gorge and entering the street of bazaars which runs quite through the town, I was at once struck by the entire change of costume in this district—that of the Tóskidhes. Instead of the purple frock, scarlet vest, black waistcoat, and short kilt of Gheghería, here all is white, or spruce fluffy grey cloth, with long, many-fluted fustianells, while the majority, instead of the red fez, wear white caps. Beyond the bazaars, which are extensive and well filled, is a wide open space by the river, whence the view of the dark gorge of the Beratíno, the town, and castle are truly wondrous. On one side of this piazza or market-place is a large new khan, and here I took possession of a corner room looking out on to the busy scene that extends to the foot of the hill—a space in which hundreds of figures sat continually before me for their pictures without suspicion or restraint. This was a khan arrangement which pleased me not a little, besides the comfort of the room, which was new and clean, and had well-glazed windows. Nothing could be more amusing than the variety of life below. There was the Dervísh with high white or green caps—the Mohammedan, as well as most of the Christian women, in loose blue feringhís and closely veiled—while infinite numbers of carts drawn by coal-black buffali— Greeks, Turks, Albanians, mingled and moved in profusely changing groups.

Having a letter to the Pashá (Berát, with Skódra and Yannina, are the three existing Pasháliks of Albania), I sent Giorgio with a request for a Kawás, who shortly arrived, and after early dinner I began to sketch (there is no time to be lost in places so full of interest) on the riverside below the castle, hundreds of people pouring forth to see my operations; but all were violently repelled by the active guardian Kawás with a stick, which he threw with all his force at the legs of such unlucky individuals as pressed too closely on me or interfered with the view. When this club was ejected from the incensed authority's hand the rush to escape was frightful and the yells of those who received the blows very disagreeable to my feelings. After a time my guard got tired of his work, and sitting down calmly to smoke, delegated his power to a young pickle of a boy, who took infinite delight in using his temporary dignity to the utmost, greatly to the disgust of his elders, who durst not complain.

Towards evening I walked through the town and over the bridge to that part of Berát which is built on the left bank of the Beratíno; but the best general views are from the side on which the castle stands.

OCTOBER 15

The mountain Tomóhr is nearly clear; I draw figures from the window till eight; then putting on 'society dress', I go with Giorgio and a Kawás to make a morning call on Husséin, Pashá of Berát. A most picturesque palace is his residence; galleries and courtyard full of the pomp of attendant guards as usual, and in the reception-room is no lack of secretaries and officials, among whom a Cadi, in white turban, and long brown gold-embroidered robes, shone resplendent. The visit was much like other Turkish visits. The Pashá was agreeable in manner, and conversation, by the aid of continual pipes and coffee, dragged its slow length along. The cholera at Salonica being touched upon, Husséin Pashá asked Giorgio to inquire if I had known in that city (where he, the Pashá was educated) an English Bey called 'Jim', who resided there and used to take the Pashá out hunting, with '*cani magnifici*' and '*fucili stupendi*';[1] but I, never having heard of 'Jim', could give no information. I made a point of asking for good horses for the journey from hence to Avlóna, remembering what I had suffered by those of the Kaváya priest; and his Highness ordered the matter to be looked to instantly, for he said: 'It is a pleasure, as well as a duty, to assist an Englishman; Inghilterra, and his master the Sultan, loved each other, and so should all the subjects of both countries.' After this visit I

[1] Magnificent dogs, and stupendous guns.

103

employed two hours by sketching from the door of the khan, supported by the Kawás, the crowds gazing at a respectful distance; not that this self-restraint on their parts saved them from disgrace and evil, for a huge Bolubáshi (or head of the police), casually passing, and being seized with an extemporaneous conviction of some impropriety requiring castigation, thereupon he rushed wildly into the midst of the spectators, with the energy of a Samson, dashing his stick at their legs, heads, and backs, and finally dispersed the unresisting crowd. After this, the enraged guardian of public manners gave my Kawás a blowing up for allowing the slightest symptom of interruption, and finally committed two large staves to some lively juveniles, with a stern charge that they should use them well and frequently. This unnecessary harshness grieved me, and on finding my remonstrances were unheeded, I gave up my sketch. Of all the numerous Beratini so unceremoniously struck, I observed but one who did not exhibit great signs of fear and dismay; this man remained steadily till he was twice hit, when he picked up a stone and walked away scowlingly and muttering suppressed anger. A pleasant land to live in!

Sketching on the bridge and on the west side of the town occupied me for two or three hours. The women of Berát are all veiled. They wear a close-fitting, dark blue cloth vest, or pelisse, not at all unbecoming; and their very thin muslin 'face-cover' is so well and cleverly adjusted, particularly by the younger and pretty part of the female population—and these are numerous—that the outline of the features can easily be distinguished.

Towards evening the lines of purple Tomóhrit were exquisitely fine. Every wrinkle and chasm in its vast sides is perfectly delineated, and from the market-place (that is, in fact, at this season, the dry bed of the river, which does not rise so high until much later in the year) the broad foreground of yellow sand, covered with a never-failing succession of reposing groups, was charming. A great part of the people sit about and smoke, by tens and twenties, after the indolent fashion of the Albanians, and the community seemed to enjoy keenly the pranks of a little imp whom they called Móostafa. Long mounted lines of elderly men on asses were returning to Berát from vineyards or village gardens higher up the river; and as they passed by Móostafa teased the old-men-bearing-quadrupeds to a fearful degree, by pulling their tails, avoiding, with will-o'-the-wisp activity, all the blows aimed at him by the incensed riders. At length the furious victims dismounted, when behold little Puck was running away like lightning; and the exasperated ancients, knowing all hope of chase to be out of the question, remounted slowly and sullenly, to find their graceless persecutor at their backs in two minutes, when the same scenes occurred again, '*da capo*'. All the crowd, of four or five hundred spectators, were greatly interested at these gambols and yelled with delight at each of Móostafa's exploits, though they nearly ended by a kicking horse putting the little buffoon's head in jeopardy.

As for me, I finished the day in a cemetery eastward of the town, whence the fortress and river are extremely grand. There is an air of seclusion and sternness about the pass of Berát which makes it certainly one of the most interesting of scenes. Home to the khan early, to try if, by getting some more sleep, I can have a longer day tomorrow. But oh! the way in which cats bounce and tear about these places all night long! and then the mode of singing adopted by the Tóskidhes Albanians all through the dead hours of darkness! There is a large party of them in the next room to mine: four begin to form a sort of chorus; one makes a deep drone or bass; two more lead the air; and the remainder indulge in strange squeaking falsettos, like the whinings of uneasy sucking-pigs.

OCTOBER 16

As this day was to be passed on the banks of the Apsus, for the purpose of sketching Tomóhr, I awoke and rose at three, and by daylight the mountain sparkled like clear crystal. A sketch of the palace and a visit to Husséin Pashá's brother, Achmet Bey (an hour of pipes and coffee), and ten o'clock is arrived. A Kawás and horses were ready, for I had planned to go some miles from the city, and was soon on my way upon a white charger, most gorgeously bedecked, with my armed guide on another, trotting (for the deep mud of last week's rain is already dry) by the riverside as far as the bridge by which I had arrived on the 14th. The Kawás put up his horses at a hut and I drew very satisfactorily till it was time to return, and although a grey sirocco had thrown a cloud over all the beauty of colour, yet the form of Tomóhrit is in itself a picture, combined with the broad Beratíno in its stony channel and cliff banks and the distant fortress of Berát perched on its rocky hill. My ever-smoking guide, too, is now and then meeting a fellow rider, when the two guards greet each other by rushing forwards impetuously with drawn swords in attitudes of wrath, as if the last moments of one or both had come, firing off their pistols and closing with their hands at each other's throats as if for mortal combat. Below the fortress a company of Turkish cavalry were exercising, wheeling about, discharging fire-arms, and charging full speed into the low ground by the river. Such incidents, united with the scenery, were wildly picturesque.

I was back at Berát by four or five, and rode over the castle hill, whence there is a superb view of the mountain, with the valley of the Beratíno at its feet and the minarets of the town in the near foreground.

OCTOBER 17

Rain, hail, and thunder all night long, and at daybreak small chance of starting. Weary of this bad weather, I could half bring myself to go straight hence to Tepeléne, and thence to Yannina, giving up Avlóna and Acroceraunia. Gleams of sunshine burst forth at nine, and the arrival of the horses decides me in favour of Appollónia, which I cannot, however, reach today owing to my start being so late. So, at half past ten, declining the escort of six foot guards sent me by the polite Husséin Pashá, and taking a mounted armed Kawás, we set off. We were soon out of the gorge of Berát, and I could not help regretting having left a scene of such great magnificence; for an artist may go easily enough at any time of his life to Rome or the Rhine, Matlock, Constantinople, Jerusalem, Killarney or Calcutta, but Berát and Illyria are not easy places to revisit. The horses are good: two of them belong to the sick old man whom we call the Filosofo, by reason of his remaining so placidly in the ditch on the morning of the 14th, he being on a return journey to Avlóna; the other two belong to a man of Berát, who walks by our side (if you hired fifty horses of fifty men in this part of the world, you would have all the fifty owners for company, because in

Albania nobody lends anything to anybody). Our party is further illuminated by a Greek priest in his blue dress, black cap, and floating hair
and beard, and by a friend of his, a lean, tortoise-necked Albanian, in a
brand-new capote and white cap; these, with my Kawás, who glittered
in blue and gold, made a picturesque caravan, and we all galloped over
the plain, which, at a little distance from the first bridge (for we must
retrace our steps as far as the second bridge), was capital ground. The
plains of Berát, dotted over with infinite flocks of sheep and spotted
with clumps of dark reeds or briers, were beautifully cheerful; the sun
shone brilliantly across their wide expanse and light clouds climbed
around the highest rocks of Tomóhr.

At half past two we reached Khan Tchúka, recrossed the Beratíno,
and following its right bank quitted the road by which we had come
from Kaváya and Leustri on the right hand. The priest and his friend
advise me to go for the night to the Greek convent of Ardhénitza,
which, say they, is but three or four hours from Apollónia and stands
on a high hill commanding a view of all the world. Meanwhile he tells
me a marvellous story of his having travelled here with a party of six
friends some years back in a violent thunderstorm. The horses took
sudden fright at the lightning while passing along the narrow path we
are now upon and one and all fell into the river, swimming over to
the other bank with the seven riders holding fast, when all of them
landed safely and undamaged, excepting that one of the party became
entirely deaf and has ever since remained so. The history, if true, is
uncomfortable to hear just now, because the path is so slippery and
narrow that I contemplate the ducking, if not the deafness, as extremely
probable occurrences. At half past three we came in sight of a long,
low, isolated hill, a dark spot on the highest part of which is pointed
out to me as the convent trees; but though another hour was passed in
wading through mud in uncultivated places, where now and then,
remote from every other sign of life, a tranquil young buffalo peered
calmly out of a pool of black water, yet still Ardhénitza on its hill
seemed 'never the nearer'.

At half past four we passed Ghóurza, a village of detached thatched
houses, in gardens, and full of furious dogs; here we had intended to
stay the night had it not been resolved to go to the convent. A little
farther on is Kadipashá, our companion priest's residence, and at a

most picturesque little spot, embosomed in plane and abeles, we halted. It was the courtyard surrounding the Greek Church, and over the gateway leading to it were two rooms, the abode of our reverend comrade. And very glad was I to rest there a while, for galloping in short Turkish stirrups is not refreshing to the gasterocnemii muscles, nor is a small cup of coffee sufficient support from 4 A.M. to 4 P.M. Some capital cheese, less salt than the generality of that of Greek manufacture, and wine less savouring of resin were by no means disagreeable additions to the repose on the cushions of the hospitable priest's little room. Before we left him he showed me some old *bassi-relievi* on the walls of his church, where numerous ancient bits of material bore witness to some pre-existing building of days bygone; several twisted columns also, and a remarkably hideous St. George and the Dragon were part of this antiquarian feast, after which we set off to Ardhénitza once more.

Beautiful green meadows like those of Kaváya, stretch on all sides (indeed, from Durazzo to the Viósa is one continued meadow), unbroken by any division. Sheep, geese, and turkeys whitened these plains, the goose-herds and turkey-drivers sitting by their charge. The sheep have bells; and now and then a song, not unlike the yodelling of the Swiss, breaks the quiet of these placid meads, or a huge dog rushes to attack the Albanian *pietone*.[1] The bright sun was setting behind the hill of Ardhénitza as we arrived at its foot, and having passed another village we began to wind upward to the summit, by paths through pleasant underwood, where the monastery, a plain building, stands among cypresses and ilex. The interior of this, the first Greek convent I have seen, is picturesque; and a painter is ever sure of a group of bearded brethren in the foreground. The view, as might be supposed from the isolated position of the hill, is truly stupendous—it includes the meadow-plain to Durázzo—the far mountain ranges of Tirana and Skódra—the near majesty of Tomóhr and its dependent heights, and the plain again to Apollónia. At dusk I was taken to a most comfortable little room surrounded with sofas, where for two hours or more I awaited the reverend household's performances in cookery, though I had much rather have had a simple meal at once. But at eight the chief Papas, with five or six others, entered with dishes unnumbered; pilaf,

[1] Foot traveller.

roasts, boiled, fried—fish and fruit—honey, cheese, walnuts, and wine. As soon as I could I begged to dispense with my host's attendance, and as Giorgio and the Kawás had, like myself, fasted since sunrise (the refection at Kadípashá excepted), I was glad to hear the festivities of supper beginning in the priestly halls on the opposite side of the corridor, whence the old Protopapas' voice resounded in hearty laugh through the monastery—a cheerful noise in these days of living among Turks, who hardly ever laugh at all. After supper they paid me a visit, and inculcated Romaic sentences, το κζασι, ειναι καλῂτεζον απώ τον νεζόν,[1] with other similar moral apothegms. One old gentleman entreated, as some of the Albanians at Króia had done, to be taken to England, the protection of my signoria being all he desired for the rest of his life. Giorgio describes the supper in the refectory as '*un pranzo di paradiso*',[2] and says that the Protopapas means to accompany me to a church and school on the way to Apollónia tomorrow, there to give me a roast lamb at the archiepiscopal residence—an ecclesiastical attention not fully appreciated by me, as I want time to sketch at Apollónia.

OCTOBER 18

The clear and glorious sunrise from Ardhénitza was a sight never to be forgotten. I drew for an hour or two. '*Scroo, scroo, scroo*,' I heard the Albanian servants saying, and well they may wonder what I write down so much. The Económo or Protopapas also, Papa Lazus, was a magnificent subject for a sketch, and in return for his likeness he begged me to give him a little memorandum recording my reception at the convent, that he might show it to Husséin Pashá, to prove how devoted a servant of his Highness he delighted to be: poor people! naturally enough they seek to win golden opinions from anyone having the least communication with their rulers.

The Protopapas and his servant accompanied me, at half past ten, down the pleasant hill of Ardhénitza, and in an hour we arrived at the ferry over the Beratíno, to cross which was a work of time, as the boat was small and the horses having to be unloaded could go but one at

---

[1] Wine is better than water.　　　　[2] A dinner of Paradise.

once. The day was warm, but sirocco wind began to rise, dimming the colour of the beautiful prospect, which from a little height above the river greatly resembles that from Richmond Hill; olives (for hereabouts there is much cultivation, under the auspices of the monastery) being placed in the picture instead of elms. On the southern side of the Beratíno we at first crossed a marshy flat tract, with scattered shrubs, throughout which concealed dogs rushed out with unpleasant abruptness from innocent-looking bushes. There are few peasants to be seen, saving here and there some women laden with implements of husbandry, for throughout the whole of Albania females are a hardworked race. We now advanced towards a group of low hills—the site of ancient Apollónia—once more over rich, smooth meadow land, and about twelve reached a little wood of plane trees, with exquisite creepers falling in long festoons from their branches and overshadowing a convent and church built by that arch-dodger, Alí Pashá, in the days when it suited him to buoy up the hopes of the Greek Christians, as well as to support those individuals among them from whose care and cultivation of all these rich plains more advantages accrued to his interests than could have arisen had they been dispossessed of their lands for the sake of less-industrious Mohammedans.

This Greek church, forming one side of a quadrangle, the remaining three being composed of a convent and stables, with two lines of cloistered arches, the whole shaded by the high trees which hung over them, bending with wild vine, is as pretty a picture as may be found.[1] A little village is scattered in the heart of this quiet wood scene; and a school, a rural building, supported by a long row of arches and shaded by feathery trees, stands by the church; some thirty or forty children were sitting in a row learning to read or chanting in a low tone. Many of these are the children of Papades resident in the villages of these plains, and others the offspring of well-to-do peasants; they were a bright-eyed, cheerful set of little ones, and added much to the interest of this new scene. The ground below the trees is perfectly carpeted with that beautiful little flower—the cyclamen—in full bloom. While I am sketching, Papa Zacaría who resides at this village, comes to inform me that the fathers of Ardhénitza are roasting a turkey, a duck, and a

[1] Intent on my sketching, I carelessly omitted to ask and note down the name of this place, though I have an imperfect recollection of its being Kosmá.

110

fowl for my lunch, and that the repast will (like that of Beau Tibbs in
'the Citizen of the World') be ready in two hours at farthest. This, to
me, is not agreeable news, as I fear to lose daylight for drawing Apollónia by the delay; but, as the compliment is well meant, I cannot
refuse it, and so I wait patiently till the dishes are served, Papades
Lázus and Zacaría keeping me company during the entertainment. The
former is one of the Vláchi—a tribe which in this part of Albania is
generally found wandering as shepherds, but in the recesses of Pindus
exists in several large settlements. Papa Zacaría is a Khimáriote by
birth, and gives me a good deal of information about Acroceraunia,
which, if it be possible I am resolved to visit. About half past two P.M.
I left these courteous people and their establishment in the wood and
set off through deep mud surrounding the village (for the flocks of
sheep and herds of buffali efface all vestige of a road), and thence
over a wilder and less mead-like tract of flat ground, towards the hill
of Apollónia; but the sirocco wind which is making earth and sky of
one uniform grey, is now blowing so furiously that the afternoon ride
is anything but agreeable. At the foot of the hills—which give no
prospect of beauty, so dreary and dull do they seem—we halted at the
little village of Póllina, which, with the convent above, is all the
representative left of the old city. It was desirable to re-establish the
baggage, shaken by the terrific wind, and to allow the old Filosofo
to have some wine, but for this, when Giorgio offered a small coin as
payment, the proposal was received by the villagers with an unanimous
groan, and a small child who made a snatch at the lucre was buffeted
and snubbed severely. A short ascent led us to the monastery of
Apollónia, enclosed within walls, and standing on the highest part of
the hill—the inconsiderable height of which does not prevent its
command of a most extensive view, owing to its isolated position in so
level a country. The exterior of the building offers nothing picturesque
—but inside the walls the large courtyard, strewn with ruin and overgrown with grass, is very striking—everywhere evidences of past ages
meet the eye—a strange mixture of ancient Greek stones, Roman
columns, medieval cornices and capitals, later Greek brickwork, and
Turkish galleries. The church, in a ruinous condition, occupies the
centre of the quadrangle, and the rooms of the convent form one of the
sides—if those can be called rooms which are merely two half-roofed

111

barns over a great stable, the abode of numberless goats. Meanwhile the wind continues to rise, and it is well if the 'rooms' do not take flight altogether; to hold a sketch-book becomes impossible, and after I have with difficulty drawn the church I stroll out on to the hill among extensive remains of what seem the walls of the great Illyrian city. From this spot I perceive the solitary column on the low rising ground to the south, of which a drawing is given in Dr. Holland's work. But the sun sinks into a red bank of cloud beyond the western sea and I return with the goats to the convent.

One of the barn-apartments is allotted to me, the other to Giorgio, and what he dignifies by the name of my '*seguita*'[1] (namely, the Filosofo, the Pietone, and the Kawás) share with two very poor Greek monks. Certainly, the night's lodgings are not obtrusively luxurious, though there is a romance in these solitudes and their want of accommodation which contrasts pleasantly with the annoyances of the populous Gheghe towns, whose appearance led to infer greater expectations of comfort; here one anticipates none, and consequently is not disappointed. The loft is wide and dark; the planked floor is full of holes, through which comes up a perpetual jingling of goats' bells, and their sneezings and coughings—they are very asthmatic goats; and it is difficult to keep a lamp burning owing to the blasts which circulate on all sides; verily these are not cheerful phases of existence; and what is worse, I fear rain for tomorrow. However, from seven to ten, the lay friars of the Apollónian establishment were most musical, and together with my *seguita* did all they could to enliven the dullness of an Illyrian city in the nineteenth century by singing their monotonous wild airs; the melody indeed was little varied, but the harmony of the voices taking different parts was pretty.

OCTOBER 19

In spite of all those superfluous goats below, not a drop of milk is to be had; but this I have long observed to be a general rule in Italy, as well as in Greece. The more goats, the less milk.

1 Suite.

BERÁT

KHIMÁRA

Taking a peasant from the convent as guide, I went at sunrise to the single Doric column—the only remaining token of Apollónia above ground. It stands on a dreary little hill, covered with long grass and brambly thorn, and a more lonely and forlorn record of old times cannot well be contemplated. The pillar is of coarse sandstone, and all the marks and dimensions of cella and temple are distinct, though the remaining columns have been transported by some Pashá to adorn Berát. On every side of this single relic of grandeur how noble are the objects in the distance. Eastward and northward, the mighty Tomóhr, the convent of Apollónia, and the hills of Durázzo; and southward, the smooth green plains, stretching to the very foot of the Acroceraunian range. Descending from this interesting spot about nine, I was joined by Giorgio and the Kawás, and for two hours rode over the greenest of pasture land, without a single undulation. The morning became perfectly fine (contrary to expectation), and the clang of our shovel stirrups resounded merrily as we galloped over the plain.

The great flocks on these beautiful quiet tracts would inspire the stranger with a complete idea of peace, were they not always attended by huge guardian dogs, who rush out like enraged demons at the horses, and threaten the riders' legs. One company of these angry brutes was particularly outrageous; and although the Kawás repeatedly shouted to the wild shepherd, as he lay on his shaggy cloak, he merely looked up, and neither checked his hounds by voice or gesture. The neglect cost him dear; for as the horse on which the Kawás rode became unruly, from the persevering attacks of some eight or ten of the dogs (who gather, at the sound of battle, from all parts of the plain), the man of arms lost patience, and galloping straight to the peasant, thundered over his shoulders with his kourbatch[1] till he yelled. This, however, did not mend the matter; for the beaten man showed signs of fight, by setting on all the dogs at once, and threatening the Kawás with an immense club, so that I momentarily expected to see my Berát escort suffer the end of Actæon, when suddenly he changed weapons, and pointing his gun at the enemy, reduced him to terms. The dogs were called off and the club thrown away: and the shepherd was left to reflect that resistance to armed Turks and setting dogs upon travellers is an unprofitable pastime.

[1] Whip.

At 11 A.M. we reached the Viosa,[1] here very broad and rapid, ere it joins the sea; and as current and wind were both against us, it was some time before we reached the opposite side, both men and horses were stowed away in a ferry-boat, resembling a magnified washing-tub. Hence we went on again, over plains, sometimes marshy, sometimes greensward, and alive with still greater multitudes of sheep. Thirty or forty immense flocks were frequently in sight at once and all guarded by lion-like dogs; and by degrees the plain became gradually bare and white with salt; and the sea-view as we neared the hills of Avlóna was shut out by the long island of Sázona. A most beautiful amphitheatre of olive-covered heights surrounds Avlóna, whose silvery mosques peep out from deep green foliage, while Kánina, a town majestically placed upon an eminence beyond, finishes one of the prettiest of pictures. Full of artistic incident is the town itself (where I arrive before four); you have mosques and bazaars, storks' nests,[2] and picturesque desolation; for Avlóna is but a poor place now, and having suffered in the latest Albanian (or Zulíki's) rebellion, exhibits a mournful air of decay.

Passing through the town, I made my way to the residence of a merchant, Herr J——, who, with Herr S——, a doctor of quarantine in these coasts, lives in a two-storied wooden house overlooking town, plain, and sea; and by means of a walled courtyard, a broad veranda, a gallery, and some inner rooms, has made himself a very comfortable place for such an out-of-the-way part of the world. I was received, on presenting a letter from Signor Bonatti of Skódra, with courtesy, though with an eternity of fuss and compliment I would have dispensed with. A good room, used as an office, was given me to abide in, but the difficulty of attaining the usual degree of travelling cleanliness was greater here than at the houses of either Greeks or Turks, seeing that the masters of this continually came in and out, and scrutinised with infantine curiosity all their guests' acts and property. Having read with avidity some German papers conveying the latest intelligence of the past six weeks (news of the most extraordinary events occurring throughout all Europe), I sat with my hosts till their supper-time, conversing about

[1] Viosa, the ancient Aous.
[2] The storks arrive at Avlóna from the 15th to the 20th of May and depart before 15th August.

parts of Albania, especially Acroceraunia or Khimára, with which the doctor is well acquainted. They advise me to visit that coast and its unknown villages, and offer their servant as guide—a trustworthy Khimáriote, who speaks Italian well and is known throughout his native territory. At supper-time Herr S——— held forth on German and European politics with alarming enthusiasm. Prophecy succeeded prophecy, as to all the royal and noble heads to be cut off; and the plates and salt-cellars jingled to the thumps which accompanied each denunciation of tyrants and each appeal to liberty. Not thinking it well-bred to expostulate with my host on the length of his monologue, and not quite agreeing with all his sentiments, I wished he was a silent Turk, and entreated to retire to sleep.

OCTOBER 20

The perfection of an autumnal clear day! After early coffee, I went out with Anastásio, the Khimáriote domestic—or rather Kawás (for as a servant of Government he carries arms). He says I can go through 'his country', weather permitting, in five or six days, and that, as he is of one of the best families in Vunó, everybody knows him and he knows everybody. This seems an opportunity of seeing Acroceraunia not to be lost; and I shall undertake the adventure—leaving Giorgio Kozzáchi at Avlóna until I return from those unexplored lands.

Avlóna lies in a recess or bay of the mountains, which here leave a level space of two miles or more between their base and the sea. The town is built for the most part at the foot of a crescent of rock, but the sides are dotted with houses; and at the two horns of this natural amphitheatre stand many conspicuous Dervísh tombs of pretty architecture, surrounded by groves of cypress. From hence the eye looks down on Avlóna in its garden of plane and olive-trees, its principal buildings, the fine palace of its late Bey, and some good mosques, which stand out in beautiful relief from the wide salt plain and gulf beyond. The gulf—shut in on one side by the long point of mountain called La Linguetta, and on the other by the island of Sázona (Sazan)— has exactly the appearance of a lake; so that the effect of the whole

115

picture is most complete and charming. Having drawn assiduously till twelve, I returned to the Casa J——, where the renewed vehemence of my host's political ebullitions, joined to the attacks of numberless flies infesting their room, made me rejoice when the midday meal was over.

In the afternoon we are to ride somewhere—Herr S—— being well acquainted with all the ins and outs of the neighbouring landscape, and in the meantime I draw the portraits of two Mohammedan Gheghes of Elbasán, who come to visit my hosts. No sooner were these good people squatted in the little wooden gallery, with their garments, faces, and pipes in complete arrangement for my drawing, than a bit of india-rubber fell from my book, and making two small hops upon the ground, as is the wont with that useful vegetable substance when dropped accidentally, caused indescribable alarm to the two orthodox Gheghes, who jumped up and hissed at it, saying, '*Shaitán! shaitán!*' and trembling with horror as the little imp remained close to their feet. Nor did my taking it up calm their fears; and when I put it in my pocket their disgust was increased at such ostentatious truckling to the comforts of a familiar demon. So as I found they could not be again induced to remain tranquil enough to be sketched, I seized a moment when they were not looking at me, and bounced the offending caoutchouc on the planked floor, when up it flew to such a degree that the unhappy and tormented Mohammedans screamed aloud, and shrieking out '*Shaitán! shaitán!*' jumped off the accursed platform and fled away.

At four, horses being brought, we set off in quest of the picturesque, attended by a black slave Margiánn in full-armed costume. Paths such as none but very sure-footed horses could climb, narrow slippery ridges along the brink of deep ravines, ascend from Avlóna, through groves of large thick olives like the slopes of Tivoli. At a distance of two or three miles we reached the top of an eminence whence, looking down on the valley of the Viosa on the one side, the great mountain of Kúdhesi near at hand, and Tomóhr ever towering in the distance, with the ruined fortress town of Kánina, forming the opposite interest of the picture, I confessed the taste of my host in matters of landscape, and passed an hour gladly in sketching those views. By sunset we returned to Avlóna.

OCTOBER 21

A bright sun and clear sky seem to foretell prosperity in the beginning of my Khimáriot journey, the most romantic as well as the most novel of my own (or anybody else's) Albanian wanderings. I shall have six days for the excursion: longer than that I must not stay, for by the 30th I should be at Arghyró Kastro, or at least, Tepeléne; and on the 7th of November at Yannina, a plan of arrangement necessary by way of timing steamers for Malta.

Messrs. J. and S. having politely volunteered to accompany me as far as Kánina, I waited for them till past ten, grieving over the loss of what I always consider the best part of the day; hours, moreover, are valuable in a tour of this kind, apart from the loss of mountain shadows when the sun is high. After unpleasant potterings and fussings, horses brought without saddles, etc. etc., we at length moved off, attended by Anastásio, my Khimáriot guide, and the black Margiánn whose employment was to supply his masters with pipes unlimited. After having passed a ruined fort by the sea-side and the outskirt olive-grounds south of Avlóna, a strong and steep pull brought us over evil ledges of precipitous ascent to Kánina: but the journey was not rendered more pleasant by my hosts, for Herr J——, being very slow, stopped every ten minutes for tobacco, and entreated Herr S——, who was of the liveliest, not to be so rapid; thereby arose contentions betwixt the two, and the effect of the constant jarring was to make me reflect on friends who do not dwell in unity. By degrees we reached the fortress, one of the most commanding positions I have seen in Albania. On the one hand, you have the wide sea beyond Avlóna, its bay, and the Island Sázona; on the other, Tomóhr and Kúdhesi, with inland torrents and woods, and gorges infinite. This crowning fort of Kánina[1] occupies the highest point of the hill, and has long since been a heap of ruins, though the area of its walls still remain; below stands the modern town with its two or three mosques and scattered little houses. Some of the lower parts of the wall seem of very ancient workmanship, but I grew tired of poking into all the corners of the old citadel, the brothers

---

[1] Kánina, Bullis Maritima.

117

being full of weary tales and surmises concerning its downfall. Among other matters, they say it was long the residence of the widow of Manfred of Sicily.

At eleven we went down to the town, and therein to the gallery of a Dervísh's house, where two Cogias brought us coffee and pipes, after which our sitting broke up, and my late hosts returned to Avlóna, leaving me in charge of the Khimáriote, who, with a Pietone, sent with me by the Turkish police, formed my whole retinue. Down the opposite side of the hill of Kánina we rode. A small knapsack contained all my property (the fewest articles of toilet ever known to have been taken by a Milordos Ingliz)—a plaid and greatcoat (for there are snowy mountains to cross) and a large stock of drawings materials. I had arranged about payment of expenses by giving Anastásio, who is a trustworthy servant of the Casa J——, a sum of money, from which he is to defray all the outlay and account to me for the same, though I anticipate no great prodigality, as I am to live at the houses of the natives and go from village to village experiencing the full measure of Khimáriote hospitality.

Before 1 P.M. we reached the shore and made for a little cove (there are many like it on the coast east of Plymouth) where a spring of pure and icy fresh water gushes from the foot of a rock into the sea and offers a natural halting-place for all who travel between Khimára and Avlóna. Kría Néra is the name of this sea-side station, and it was pleasant to rest on a carpet thrown down on the smooth sand beneath the high rocks which shut in this little nook. Several peasants with their horses are resting here, and Anastásio and the policeman join them in a lunch of bread and cheese; beyond them are grey cliffs and green dun heights—a strip of white sand and the long promontory of Linguetta stretching out into the gulf; the clear splashing sea at my feet and above all the bright streaked sky. A quiet half-hour in such a scene crowds many a reflection into the tablets of thought, but such can have no place in journals.

Of the peasants halting at this natural khan with my own party, most are Khimáriots, going to Berát or other mid-districts of Albania; others are Beratíni. These wild and rugged men have in general a forlorn and anxious look, and are clad in blanket-like capotes, their caps mostly white. 'Some,' saith Anastásio, 'two years ago, were

118

"*roba fina de' ladri*",[1] but now Albania is purged of danger and romance, thieves and rebellion, from end to end.

But it is past one, and time to set off once more, for there are four long hours to Draghiádhes, the first Khimáriot village. The pathway is ever along the side of the gulf, and rises far above the blue, blue water. Anything more frightful than these (so-called) paths along the iron rocks of Acroceraunia it is not easy to imagine: as if to baffle invaders, the ledges along which one went slowly now wound inward, skirting ravines full of lentisk and arbutus, now projected over the bald sides of precipices, so that, at certain unexpected angles, the rider's outer leg hung sheer over the deep sea below. To the first of these surprising bits of horror-samples of the highways of Khimára I had come all unknowingly, my horse turning round a sharp rocky point and proceeding leisurely thence down a kind of bad staircase without balustrades; I declined, however, trying a second similar pass on his back and at the first spot where there was safe footing dismounted. Meanwhile the Khimáriote, who ever and anon kept shouting, '*Kakos dromos, Signore,*'[2] fired off his pistol at intervals, partly, as he said, from '*allegria*'[3] and partly to prevent anyone meeting us in this dire and narrow way. When we had overcome the last of the Kakos dromos—lo! a beautiful scene opened at the narrow end of the gulf, which lay like a still and dark lake below the high wall of Khimára territory. Draghiádhes, the door, as it were, of Acroceraunia, stands on a height immediately in front, while the majestic snowy peak of Tchika (the lofty point so conspicuous from Corfú, and on the southern side of which stand the real Khimáriot villages), towers over all the scene, than which one more sublime, or more shut out from the world, I do not recollect often to have noticed. At the sea-side I stole time for a short sketch, and then remounting, our party rode on over the sands to nearly the end of the gulf, whence we turned off to the left, and gradually ascended to Draghiádhes. Flocks of sheep, and most ferocious dogs abounded as we climbed higher; and Anastásio never wearied of injunctions as to the awful character of the dogs of Khimára, especially of the two first villages. 'It is true,' said he, 'I am responsible for your life, but at the same time you must do just as I bid you; for if you look at a dog of

[1] The cleverest of robbers.
[2] A bad road, Sir.   [3] Mirth.

Khimára, there will hardly be anything but some of your largest bones left ten minutes afterwards!' which unfettered poetical flight seemed about to become a fact in the case of the Pietone, who shortly had to defend himself from some ten of these outrageous beasts; they assailed him spite of all manner of missiles, and the battle's issue was waxing doubtful when some shepherds called off the enemy. As we advanced nearer to the town Anastásio's cheerfulness seemed to increase. '*Mi conoscono tutti*,'[1] said he, as each peasant hailed him by the title of '*Capitagno*'. With some he stopped to laugh and converse; others he saluted after the fashion of Albanian mock-skirmishes, drawing pistols or yataghan from his girdle and seizing their throats with many yells, and between whiles he kept up a running accompaniment of a Greek air, sung at the top of an immense voice and varied by pistol shots at irregular intervals. We passed the village of Rádima high above us, and after I had contrived to make another sketch the scene momentarily grew finer as the descending sun flung hues of crimson over the lonely, sparkling town of Draghiádhes and the bright peaks of the huge Tchíka.

Presently we came to the oak-clad hills immediately below the town, where narrow winding paths led upwards among great rocks and spreading trees worthy of Salvator Rosa and not unlike the beautiful serpentára of Olévano. I have never seen more impressively savage scenery since I was in Calabria. Evening or early morn are the times to study these wild southern places to advantage; they are then alive with the inhabitants of the town or village gathering to or issuing from it; here were sheep crowding up the narrow rock-stairs—now lost in the shade of the foliage—now bounding in light through the short lentisk— huge morose dogs, like wolves, walking sullenly behind—shepherds carrying lambs or sick sheep, and a crowd of figures clad in thick large trousers and short jackets and bearing immense burdens of sticks or other rustic materials. These last are the women of Draghiádhes, for here, and at the next village (Dukádhes), the fair sex adopt male attire, and are assuredly about the oddest-looking creatures I ever beheld. Worn and brown by hard labour in the sun, they have yet something pensive and pleasing in the expression of the eye, but all the rest is unfeminine and disagreeable. They are, as far as I can learn, the only Mohammedan women in these regions who do not conceal their faces—

[1] Everybody knows me.

whether it be that their ancestors were Christians and turning to the faith of the Prophet did not think it worth while in so remote a place as Khimára to adopt articles of such extra expense as veils, I know not—but such is the fact, and they are the only females of their creed whose faces I ever saw. 'But,' said Anastásio, 'when we have passed Tchika, and are in true Khimára, out of the way of these Turks, then you will see women like women and not like pigs. Ah, Signor mio! these are not women!—these are pigs, pigs—Turks—pigs, I say! For all that, they are very good people, and all of them my intimate friends. But, Signore, you could not travel here alone.' And, although Anastásio certainly made the most patronising use of his position as interpreter, guide, and guard, I am inclined to believe that he was, in this, pretty near the truth, for I doubt if a stranger could safely venture through Acroceraunia unattended. Assuredly also all the world hereabouts seemed his friends, as he boasted, for the remotest and almost invisible people on far-away rocks shouted out '*Capitagno*' as we passed, proving to me that I was in company with a widely known individual.

At length we reached Draghiádhes, the houses of which were by no means pretty, being one and all like the figures of 'H was a House' in a child's spelling-book. Alas! for the baronial castle or the palazzo of Italy! the whole place had the appearance of a gigantic heap of dominoes just thrown down by the Titans. Sunset had given place to shadowy dusk as we passed below two of the very largest plane trees I ever beheld, where, in the centre of the village, the trouser-wearing damsels of Draghiádhes were drawing water at a fountain—a strange, wild scene. Many came out to greet Anastásio and all saluted me in a friendly manner, nor was there the least ill-bred annoyance, though I was evidently an object of great curiosity. Sending on the horses to the house we were to sleep at, we first went to one of Anastásio's friends, who would take it as a '*dispetto*' if he did not visit him. I sat on the steps outside and sketched: the rocks of Calabria, with figures such as are to be seen only in Albania, gathered all around—how did I lament my little skill in figure drawing and regret having so much neglected it! The long matted hair and moustache—the unstudied and free attitude— the simple folds of drapery—the expression of the individual—the grouping of the masses—all heighten the inconceivable originality of these scenes. Let a painter visit Acroceraunia—until he does so he

121

will not be aware of the grandest phases of savage, yet classic, pictures-queness—whether Illyrian or Epirote—men or mountains; but let him go with a good guide or he may not come back again. Acroceraunia is untravelled ground and might not be satisfactory to a solitary tourist.

It was dark when we returned to the upper part of the town and I was ushered into my host's house for the night—a large room on the ground floor—all rafters above and planks below, with a fireplace and fire in the middle of one end and with carpets and cushions (of no very inviting appearance) on either side of the hearth. On to one of these I threw myself and waited patiently for all further occurrences. Presently our host (whose name is Achmét Zináni and who is a tall, thin, ancient Mohammedan, clad all in red save a white kilt), having made me a speech profuse of compliments through Anastásio, brings two cups of coffee, and supper is supposed to be about to follow. Dirty and queer and wild, as this place is, it is far better than those Gheghe-holes, Tirana and Elbasán—at least the novelty and fine subjects for painting all about one, and the friendly relation in which the stranger stands with regard to the natives, makes him prefer Khimára, even at the outset. Previously to supper Achmét Zináni prayed abundantly, going through the numerous genuflexions and prostrations of Moham-medan devotion in the centre of the room. After this the meal com-menced.

The plan of Khimáriot hospitality is this: the guest buys a fowl or two and his hosts cook it and help him to eat it. We all sat round the dish and I, propping myself sideways on cushions, made shift to partake of it as well as I could; but a small candle being the only light allotted to the operation, I was not so adroit as my co-partners, who fished out the most interesting parts of the excellent fowl *ragout* with astonishing dexterity and success. The low round plate of tin was a perpetual shelter for eight or nine little cats, whom we pulled out from beneath by their tails at momentary intervals, when they wailed aloud, and rushed back again, pleased even by feeling the hot fowl through the table, as they could not otherwise enjoy it. After the *ragout* had nearly all been devoured and its remains consigned to the afflicted cats, there came on a fearful species of cheese soup, with butter, perfectly fabulous as to filthiness; and after this, there was the usual washing of hands, *à la turque*, and the evening meal was done. Supper over, we all sat in a semicircle about the fire. Some six or eight of the townsmen came in—a sort of soirée—and drinking cups of coffee was the occupation for some hours. Albanian only is spoken and very little Greek understood here. About ten or eleven all but the family gradually withdrew; the old gentleman, Achmét, and the rest of the Albanians rolled themselves up in capotes and slept, Anastásio placed himself across my feet, with his pistols by his side; and as for me, with my head on my knapsack I managed to get an hour or two of early sleep, though the army of fleas, which assailed me as a new-comer, not to speak of the excursion cats, who played at bo-peep behind my head, made the rest of the night a time of real suffering, the more so that the great fire nearly roasted me, and was odious to the eyes, as a wood fire must needs be. Such are the penalties paid for the picturesque. But one does not come to Acroceraunia for food, sleep, or cleanliness.

OCTOBER 22

Before daylight all were on foot and Anastásio had made a capital basin of coffee and toast, an accomplishment he had learned of Giorgio. Anxious to see the bright sun after the night's penance, I ran to the door; but hardly had I gone three steps from it when I felt myself violently pulled by the collar and dragged backwards before I had time to resist; a friendly assault on the part of Achmét and Anastásio, the motion of which was adequately explained by a simultaneous charge of some thirty immense dogs, who bounced out from the most secluded corners and would straightway have breakfasted on me had I not been so aptly rescued; certainly the dogs of Khimára are the most formidable brutes I haveyet seen, and every wall and lane here seems alive with them.

'*O Signore!*' said Anastásio, in a tone between anger and vexation, '*tanto sciocco vuoi essere! Ti dico—sarai mangiato—amazzato—e se non vuoi far a modo mio, e tutto cio che ti dico di far quì in Khimára, sei morto; non voglio andar più in avante così; non andrai mai più fuor di vista mia!*'[1]

---

[1] O, Sir, why will you be such a fool? I tell you you will be eaten, murdered, and if you won't do as I bid you, you are a dead man. I will not go farther with you in this manner; henceforth you shall not stir out of my sight.

So I promised I would in future be obedient, for after all it was plain that the Khimáriote was in the right.

I decided on making a drawing at Draghiádhes before starting for Dukádhes, the next village, where I am to sleep tonight; for beyond that is the great pass of the Tchíka mountain, which shuts in the Khimára coast, and to arrive at the further side of it would require more time than could be found today without hurrying. So I sat above the huge planes and drew the view towards the gulf, very Poussinesque and fine, some twenty picturesque fellows sitting smoking round me, all infinitely polite. One of them who speaks Italian volunteers a list of the Khimáriote villages in their consecutive order, from Draghiádhes. All of these I cannot hope to see; but I would fain get as far as Khimára, which gives its name to the whole district.

About nine we left Draghiádhes and began to ascend towards the hill of Dukádhes, first through a tract of low wood and then by an uninteresting gorge, down which the wind came with frightful force, making it very difficult to keep a footing on the loose stones of the watercourse, which was our road. Higher up in the pass the violence of this sudden and furious mountain storm was such that both Anastásio and myself were knocked down more than once, and towards the summit we could only advance by clinging from rock to rock.

At the highest part of the pass a most singular scene opens. The spectator seems on the edge of a high wall, from the brink of which giddy elevation he looks down into a fearfully profound basin at the roots of the mountain. Above its eastern and southern enclosures rises the giant snow-clad Tchíka in all its immensity, while at his very feet, in a deep, dark green pit of wood and garden, lies the town or village of Dukádhes, its houses scattered like milk-white dice along the banks of a wide torrent, which finds its way to the gulf between the hill he stands on and the high western ridge dividing the valley from the sea.

To this strange place, perhaps one of the most secluded in Europe, I began to descend, and as we slowly proceeded halted more than once to sketch and contemplate. Shut out as it stood by iron walls of mountain, surrounded by sternest features of savage scenery, rock and chasm, precipice and torrent, a more fearful prospect and more chilling to the very blood I never beheld—so gloomy and severe—so unredeemed by any beauty or cheerfulness. After a weary ride over rugged

124

places in the bottom of this hollow land of gloom, we stopped at length at one of the houses of the village—standing, like every dwelling of Dukádhes, in the midst of a little garden or courtyard. Its general appearance was very like my last night's abode, only that we had to climb up a very odious ladder to the family 'reception-room'—which, besides being several shades dirtier than that of Achmét Zinani, had not the advantage of being on the first floor. Most of these houses consist of two stories, the upper floor, divided into two or three chambers, being allotted to the women of the family, the lower being a single large room serving for general purposes. It was half past one when we arrived, and before I go out to sketch Anastásio cooks a lunch of eggs roasted and fried in butter, of which he partakes with the Pietone. This last accomplished person does not indulge in shoes, and I observe that when his hands are occupied he holds his pipe in his toes and does any other little office with those, to us, useless members. Throughout the whole of the day's journey I have seen numbers of women carrying burdens of incredible size and weight—from one hundred and fifty to one hundred and eighty pounds, I am assured, is no unusual loading. These poor creatures are indeed little like women in appearance, for their faces are worn into lines and furrows of masculine hardness by excessive and early toil; and as they labour pitifully up the rocky paths, steadying their steps with a staff, or cross the stony torrent beds, bent nearly double beneath their loads, they seem less like human beings than quadrupeds. A man's blood boils to see them accompanied by a beast of a husband or brother, generally on horseback, carrying—what?—nothing but a pipe! And when he is tired of smoking, or finds himself overclad, he gives the women his pipe to hold, or throws his capote over her load! The ponderous packages of wool, grain, sticks, etc., borne by these hard-worked creatures are hung to their neck by two strong straps; the dress is dark blue, with a blue handkerchief on the head—dark full trousers—no petticoat or apron—and red worked woollen gaiters. They are short and strongly made in person, with very light hair; their eyes are almost universally soft grey, and very pretty, but the rest of the face, apart from the worn and ground-down expression, is too broad and square in form to be prepossessing.

In the afternoon I made drawings of Dukádhes, a gloomy sky and threatening storm adding to the inherent melancholy of the landscape.

The lines around the town are on too gigantic a scale, and its houses too destitute of the picturesque to supply much employment for the pencil; and the chilling sullenness of this dreary abyss of terror did not incline me to devote much time to its ungracious qualities. I was accompanied in my researches by Súlio, the Pietone, Anastásio being engaged in finding mules for the morrow's ascent, since horses go no farther than this place—the threshold of Khimára; and I give the last hour of daylight to delineating a tree full of Albanian idlers who sit smoking tranquilly on the gnarled wide-spreading branches of a huge ilex which hangs over a precipice—as wild a piece of poetical painting as Salvator might wish for.

At sunset the indescribable dark terror of this strange place was at its full; yet, unwilling to retreat to my night's prison till the last moment, I lingered on a rock in the middle of the ravine, while crowds gathered round me, saying, '*Scroo, scroo, scroo,*' after their fashion, and were greatly pleased at my drawing them. At length it became quite dusk and I went reluctantly to my second night-home in Khimára. The loft had a more comfortable appearance by firelight than by day, inasmuch as its mysterious and suggestive gloom was more prepossessing than its bare walls. A rug was, as before, laid for me on the farther corner, fitting in between the wall and the wood fire, which is always made on a square sort of hearth projecting into the room. Two pillows, also, were in readiness; but mistrusting these adjuncts of luxury, I wrapped myself in plaids and coats, with my knapsack under my head. It is needless to say the traveller reposes by night in the same dress he wears by day, for it is by no means possible to change it on all occasions. Vunó, however, Anastásio's native town, is held out to me, with what degree of truth or poetry I know not, as a sort of metropolitan abode of the luxuries and graces which are to atone for all privations endured previously to reaching that favoured spot. Meanwhile he informs me that, supposing I am desirous of seeing as much of Khimáriote manners and society as is possible, he has asked two gipsies (!) to pass the evening with us, they being great performers on the guitar, which they accompany with the voice, and as not improbably we might have a dance also he had invited a Christian—one of his own friends (from Arghyró Kastro) staying at present in Dukádhes—to dine with us, a gentleman whose long dishevelled hair fell most dramatically over his

126

shoulders and who, like the rest of the 'society', rejoiced in bare feet and gaiters. In fact, my arrival at Dukádhes seemed the signal for a sort of universal soirée; and I was to promote the general hilarity by the gift of an unlimited quantity of wine—an arrangement I willingly acceded to for the sake of witnessing 'life in Khimára'.

In an hour or two came in the usual round tin table, preceded by napkin and water, precursors of a good dish of hashed mutton and a plain roast fowl which, with tolerable wine, made no bad supper. After the repast is done a process of sweeping always goes on, a mere form, but never neglected by these people; unwilling to incommode me, they swept all round me carefully, and now there was nothing to do but to announce the visitors.

Presently the company came, and queer enough it was! The two Messieurs Zingari, or gipsies, are blacksmiths by profession and are clad in dark-coloured garments, once white, now grey-brown; the contrast between them and the Albanians round them, nearly all of whom have light hair and florid complexions, is very striking. The gipsy, all grin and sharpness, who plays second fiddle is continually bowing and ducking to me ere he squats down; but the elder, or first performer, is absolutely one of the most remarkable-looking creatures I ever beheld; his great black eyes, peering below immensely thick arched brows, have the most singular expression of cunning and ferocity, and his black moustache and beard enclose a mouth which, when shut, argues all sorts of tragic obstinacies, but on opening discloses a grin of brilliant ivory from ear to ear. Take him for all in all, anything so like a diabolical South Sea idol I never yet saw living.

At first the entertainment was rather slow. The gipsies had two guitars, but they only tinkled them with a preparatory coquettishness, till, another friend dropping in with a third mandolino, a pleasing discord was by degrees created and increased to a pitch of excitement that seemed to promise brilliant things for the evening's festivities. Anastásio, also, catching the melodious infection, led the performers by his own everlasting Greek refrain—sung at the full power of a tremendous voice and joined in by all present in the first circle—for now many more than the chorus had entered the room, remaining seated or standing behind, and the whole formed, in the flickering light of the wood torches, one of the most strange scenes imaginable. Among the

127

auditors were the padrona of the house (a large lady in extensive trousers), her daughter (a nice-looking woman), and two pretty little girls, her grandchildren—all unveiled, as is the mode in Dukádhes. As the musical excitement increased, so did the audience begin to keep time with their bodies, which this people, even when squatted, move with the most curious flexibility. An Albanian, in sitting on the ground, goes plump down on his knees, and then bending back crosses his legs in a manner wholly impracticable to us who sit on chairs from infancy. While thus seated he can turn his body half round on each side as if on a pivot, the knees remaining immovable; and of all the gifted people in this way that I ever saw, the gipsy guitarist was pre-eminently endowed with gyratory powers equal almost to the American owl, which, it is said, continues to look round and round at the fowler as he circles about him till his head twists off.

Presently the fun grew fast and furious, and at length the father of song—the hideous idol-gipsy—became animated in the grandest degree; he sang and shrieked the strangest minor airs with incredible accompaniments, tearing and twangling the guitar with great skill and energy enough to break it into bits. Everything he sang seemed to delight his audience, which at times was moved to shouts of laughter, at others almost to tears. He bowed backwards and forwards till his head nearly touched the ground and waved from side to side like a poplar in a gale. He screamed—he howled—he went through long recitatives and spoke prose with inconceivable rapidity; and all the while his auditors bowed and rocked to and fro as if participating in every idea and expression. I never saw a more decided instance of enthusiastic appreciation of song, if song it could be called, where the only melody was a wild repetition of a minor chorus—except at intervals, when one or two of the Toskidhes' characteristic airs varied the musical treat.

The last performance I can remember to have attended to appeared to be received as a *capo d'opera*: each verse ended by spinning itself out into a chain of rapid little Bos, ending in chorus thus: 'Bo, bo-bo-bo, BO!—bo, bobobo, BO!'—and every verse was more loudly joined in than its predecessor, till at the conclusion of the last verse, when the unearthly idol-gipsy snatched off and waved his cap in the air—his shining head was closely shaved, except one glossy raven tress at least three feet in length—the very rafters rang again to the frantic harmony:

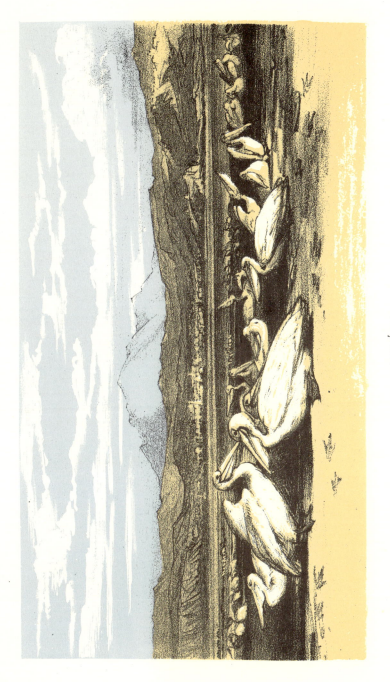

AVLÓNA

TEPELÉNE

'Bo, bo-bo-bo, bo-bo-bo, bo-bo-bo, bobobo, BO!'—the last 'BO!'
uttered like a pistol-shot and followed by a unanimous yell.

Fatigue is so good a preparation for rest that after this savage mirth
had gone on for two or three hours I fell fast asleep and heard no more
that night.

OCTOBER 23

I am awaked an hour before daylight by the most piercing screams.
Hark!—they are the loud cries of a woman's voice, and they come
nearer—nearer—close to the house. For a moment the remembrance
of last night's orgies, the strange place I was lying in and the horrid
sound by which I was so suddenly awakened made a confusion of ideas
in my mind which I could hardly disentangle, till, lighting a phosphorus
match and candle, I saw all the Albanians in the room sitting bolt
upright and listening with ugly countenances to the terrible cries
below. In vain I ask the cause of them; no one replies; but one by one,
and Anastásio the last, all descend the ladder, leaving me in a mystery
which does not make the state of things more agreeable; for though I
have not 'supped full of horror' like Macbeth, yet my senses are
nevertheless 'cooled to hear so dismal a night shriek'.

I do not remember ever to have heard so horrid and deadly a sound
as that long shriek, perpetually repeated with a force and sharpness not
to be recalled without pain; and what made it more horrible was the
distinct echo to each cry from the lonely rocks around this hideous
place. The cries, too, were exactly similar and studiedly monotonous
in measured wild grief. After a short time Anastásio and the others
returned, but at first I could elicit no cause for this startling the night
from its propriety. At length I suppose they thought that, as I was now
irretrievably afloat in Khimára life, I might as well know the worst as
not; so they informed me that the wailings proceeded from a woman
of the place whose husband had just been murdered. He had had some
feud with an inhabitant of a neighbouring village (near Kúdhesi) nor
had he returned to his house as was expected last night; and just now,
by means of the Khimáriot dogs, whose uproar is unimaginable, the

head of the slain man was found on one side of the ravine, immediately below the house I am in, his murderers having tossed it over from the opposite bank, where the body still lay. This horrid intelligence had been taken (with her husband's head) to his wife, and she instantly began the public shrieking and wailing usual with all people in this singular region on the death of relatives. They tell me this screaming tragedy is universal throughout Khimára, and is continued during nine days, commonly in the house of mourning, or when the performers are engaged in their domestic affairs. In the present instance, however, the distressed woman, unable to control her feelings to the regular routine of grief, is walking all over the town, tearing her hair and abandoning herself to the most frantic wretchedness. These news, added to the information that it is raining, and that the weather may probably prevent my leaving this delightful abode throughout this or who knows how many more days, are no cheerful beginning for the morning, for one may be fixed here for some time, since the Tchíka pass is impracticable in stormy weather. But towards eight the rain ceased; and although a drizzling mist still continued to fall the roba was packed under lots of covers and we started on mules, with bad saddles and packthread stirrups. Bidding adieu to the harem until my return, I was soon out of Dukádhes, spite of the multitude of dogs ready to devour me at every garden and wall. A rude track leads across the valley, ascending gradually, now over undulations of uncultivated turf or rich fern, and now dipping by rough ledges and slanting paths into tremendous chasms, which convey torrents from the northern face of Tchíka to the river of Dukádhes, west of the valley.

Advancing nearer to the pass, the giant Tchíka appeared more formidable at each approach—its pine-clad sides black in the sullen misty cloud; but as we descended the last cliff-walled abyss at the foot of the ridge or spur of the mountain which closes eastward the valley-plain of Dukádhes, driving clouds came furiously down, and thenceforth, to my great vexation, no more of the pass was visible. Toilfully we wound upwards, for an hour or more, among rocks and superb pines, now and then a cloud rolling away to disclose vistas of cedar-like firs deep below or high above in air. It would be difficult to see a finer pass even for foreground objects: such variety of crag and shrub—such huge pine trunks slanting over precipices, or lying along the side of the

130

path like ante-mundane caterpillars crawling out of the way of the deluge. At the top of the pass the driving fog became thinner, the 'shrubless crags seen through the mist' assumed their distinct shapes, and we entered magnificent forests of beautiful pine and undergrowth of grey oak, with here and there a space of green turf and box trees, where great black and orange lizards were plentifully crawling.

At half past ten we began to descend, and soon emerged from the clouds into bright sunlight, which lit up all the difficulties of what is called the Strada Bianca or Aspri Ruga—a zigzag path on the side of the steepest of precipices, yet the only communication between Khimára and Avlóna towards the north. The track is a perfect staircase, and were you to attempt to ride down it you would seem at each angle as if about to shoot off into the blue sea below you; even when walking down one comes to an intimate knowledge of what a fly must feel in traversing a ceiling or perpendicular wall. Half-way down the descent the long flat island of Fanó, north of Corfú, is visible, and soon after-wards the end of Monte St. Salvador in Corfú itself—a merry sight, and something of a foreshadowing of England in this far-away land. Immediately below the Strada Bianca lies a long tract of land between sea and mountain, showing the position of nearly all the Khimáriote villages, the whole territory between the Adriatic and the western wall of hill being known generally as 'Khimára'. Lower down in the descent a migration of Khimáriotes—the most restless of people—met us; some eighty or one hundred women laden as never women were else-where—their male relations taking it easy up the mountain—the ladies carrying the capotes as well as babies and packages.

'Heavens!' said I, surprised out of my wonted philosophy of travel, which ought not to exclaim at anything, 'how can you make your women such slaves?' 'O Signore,' said Anastásio, 'to you, as a stranger, it must seem extraordinary; but the fact is we have no mules in Khimára—that is the reason why we employ a creature so inferior in strength as a woman is (*un animale tanto poco capace*); but there is no remedy, for mules there are none and women are next best to mules. *Vi assicuro, Signore*, although certainly far inferior to mules, they are really better than asses, or even horses.' That was all I got for my interference.

These Khimáriote women were of all ages, and many of them very

131

pretty; their dress was a full white petticoat, with an embroidered woollen apron (worn behind, and not before!) The men were white-capoted, strong-looking fellows, walking with all that nonchalance and air of superiority so characteristic of Albanians; almost all the individuals spoke to Anastásio as a general acquaintance. The whole party is on the way to Avlóna to work in the olive grounds there through the winter.

After having cleared the descent of Strada Bianca—a weary penance, the last part of it a little shortened by a steep flight of stairs cut in the perpendicular rock—we arrived at that extraordinary torrent which, descending in one unbroken white bed from the very mountain-top down its seaward face, is known by mariners as '*il fiume di* Strada Bianca' or Aspri Ruga. Without doubt this is a very remarkable scene of sheer mountain terror; it presents a simple front of rock—awful from its immense magnitude—crowned at its summit with snow and pines and riven into a thousand lines all uniting in the tremendous ravine below—which, though now nearly dry, is in winter a torrent of destructive magnitude.

Crossing this great watercourse, our route lay at the foot of the hills, through ground more and more cultivated and cheerful, and about 1 p.m. we reached the village of Palása.[1] Here we halted, after a good morning's work, in a sort of piazza near a disreputable-looking church, sadly out of repair.

A few Khimáriotes were idling below the shady trees, and Anastásio was soon surrounded and welcomed back to his native haunts, though I perceived that some bad news was communicated to him, as he changed colour during the recital of the intelligence and clasping his hands exclaimed aloud with every appearance of real sorrow. The cause of this grief was, he presently informed me, the tidings of the death of one of his cousins at Vunó, his native place, a girl of eighteen whose extreme beauty and good qualities had made her a sort of queen of the village, which, said Anastásio, I shall find a changed place owing to her decease. 'I loved her,' said he, 'with all my heart, and had we been married, as we ought to have been, our lives might have been most thoroughly happy.' Having said thus much, and begging me to excuse his grief, he sat down with his head on his hand, in a mood of woe befitting such a bereavement. Meanwhile I reposed till the moment

1 Palása, anciently Palæste.

came for a fresh move onwards, when lo! with the quickness of light the afflicted Anastásio arose and ran to a group of women advancing towards the olive trees, among whom one seemed to interest him not a little, and as she drew nearer I perceived that she was equally affected by the chance meeting; finally they sat down together and conversed with an earnestness which convinced me that the newcomer was a friend, at least, if not a sister, to the departed and lamented cousin of Vunó. It was now time to start, and as the mules were loading the Khimáriote girl lingered, and I never saw a more exquisitely handsome face than hers: each feature was perfectly faultless in form, but the general expression of the countenance had a tinge of sternness, with somewhat of traces of suffering; her raven tresses fell loose over her beautiful shoulders and neck and her form from head to foot was majestic and graceful to perfection; her dress, too, the short, open Greek jacket or spencer, ornamented with red patterns, the many-folded petticoat and the scarlet embroidered apron, admirably became her. She was a perfect model of beauty, as she stood knitting, hardly bending beneath the burden she was carrying—her fine face half in shade from a snowy handkerchief thrown negligently over her head. She vanished when we were leaving Palása, but reappeared below the village and accompanied Anastásio for a mile or more through the surrounding olive grounds, and leaving him at last with a bitter expression of melancholy which it was impossible not to sympathise with. 'Ah, Signore,' said Anastásio, 'she was to have been my wife, but now she is married to a horrid old man of Avlóna, who hates her, and she hates him, and so they will be wretched all their lives.' 'Corpo di Bacco! Anastásio, why you told me just now you were to be married to the girl who has just died at Vunó!' 'So I was, Signore; but her parents would not let me marry her, so I have not thought about her any more—only now that she is dead I cannot help being very sorry; but Fortína, the girl who has just gone back, was the woman I loved better than anybody.' 'Then why didn't you marry her?' '*Perchè, perchè,*' said the afflicted Anastásio, '*perchè,* I have a wife already, Signore, in Vunó, and a little girl six years old. *Si signor, si.*'

So much for the comfortable arrangement prevalent throughout this country[1]—of marriages being arranged beforehand by the parents of

[1] See page 79, Skódra.

the parties, independently of the individuals most concerned in the matter, for the refusal of a bride by the bridegroom, if the lady be once brought so far as his house, is strongly resented by her family—notwithstanding which, Anastásio, by his own account, greatly rebelled against orthodox Greek rules and told his parents that if his bride (a girl of Arghyró-Kastro and a relative of his mother's kinsmen) were not sufficiently agreeable or good-looking he would not have her at all; and therefore they were obliged to connive at their wilful son's seeing his betrothed ere they set out, lest the chief of the bride's house should be outraged by a refusal at the eleventh hour. This occurred at Délvino; and his account of being permitted to look at the lady through the opening of a door was amusing—how she was sitting down, and how he said, *O, Signora, camminate! Camminate, per l'amour del cielo;— perchè voleva vedere se non zoppicasse.*[1]

From Palása to Dhrymádhes (the next in the line of Khimára villages) the route is comparatively uninteresting, except inasmuch as the great features of the Khimára country—the bright blue sea on one hand and the high mountain-wall on the other—were always attractive.

About half past two we arrived at another deep fissure or torrent-chasm, cloven from the heart of the mountains to the sea, and here, perched and thrust in all possible positions among the rocks of the ravine, stands Dhrymádhes, more magnificent in its situation than any of the places I had hitherto seen in Acroceraunia, and not a little resembling Atráni, or Amálfi, or Cánalo in Calabria, though the beauty of architecture in those Italian places is ill supplied by the scattered and formless collection of houses that hangs on the brink of the craggy gorge, through whose narrow sides remote peeps of the lofty summits of Tchíka are visible.

Sending on Anastásio and the mules to a house he indicated on the farther side of the ravine, I remained behind to sketch, and was soon surrounded by curious observers; all, however, treated me with the greatest good breeding, and one old gentleman begged me, in Italian, to favour him by taking some coffee in his house. The Khimáriotes are in the habit of using the Italian tongue more than any natives of Albania, a practice induced by their wandering lives and frequent intercourse with Corfú, Naples, etc.

[1] O Madam, get up and walk for the love of Heaven! (For I wanted to see if she did not limp.)

134

To sketch Dhrymádhes hastily was impossible; so, trusting to draw it on my return, I hurried onward round the head of the gorge, and found Anastásio at the house of one of his uncles—a quiet, unpretending dwelling, reminding me of many at Sorrento or other Italian places. The civilisation of this part of Albania seems indeed (speaking of the indoor enjoyments of life) far beyond what I have yet seen; and my surprise was great on observing the clean whitewashed walls of the rooms I was taken to—the rows of jugs, plates, etc., on shelves—the chairs and four-post bedstead, with tidy furniture, and every other comfort in proportion.

'*Zia mia!*'[1] said Anastásio, of a nice-looking, middle-aged woman—and 'my uncle' was a fine specimen of a Palikar, in appearance venerable, perfectly gentlemanlike in manner, and speaking Italian fluently. All Khimáriotes have great store of adventures to tell you and one might collect a good book of anecdotes from these roving people. 'My uncle' was one of the Khimáriotes taken by Alí Pashá as hostages, and was long imprisoned at Yannina; he was also in the French-Neapolitan service, and more lately one of Lord Byron's suite at Missolónghi; so that he had seen a variety of life. Promising if possible to stay with these good-natured people on my return, and having partaken of some very tolerable wine, I left them, and as the mules were to go back hence to Dukádhes the little roba I had with me was strapped on the backs of two women (according to Anastásio, the best mode of conveyance in default of better) and sent onward to Vunó.

Rapidly as a traveller but glances at a country in this mode of journeying, the pencil conveys a far better idea of it, and in a few lines, than an inexperienced pen can hope to do with any amount of description; it is sufficient, therefore, to say that all Khimára is full of picturesqueness well worthy the study of a landscape painter. A wild tract of rugged nature succeeds to Drymádhes, and in one hour I reached Lliátes, the third village; it consisted of a little knot of houses standing in gardens of olives, an oasis of cultivation which seems a rare exception to the general barrenness of this part of Khimára, though closer to the sea there appears to be a considerable portion of more fertile land.

After a halt of ten minutes at Lliáttes, where some of Anastásio's invisible friends brought us some fresh water at his call, I am again

[1] My aunt.

walking over rock and plains of lentisk, till I reach the last ravine, previously to arriving at Vunó, a deep chasm between red cliffs, much like those in the neighbourhood of beautiful Civita Castellana, and which, according to Anastásio, runs widening to the sea, and renders all progress by land impossible, except by the track we are now pursuing, at the very root of the mountains. The view of Corfú above this long perspective of ravines is exceedingly beautiful and tempted me to linger till the setting sun warned me to hasten.

The bright orb went down like a globe of red crystal into the pale sea and the fiery-hued wall of jagged Acroceraunian mountains above us on our left grew purple and lead-coloured, yet there was still half an hour's hard walking to be accomplished; and before I turned the angle of the little ravine of Vunó there was only light enough to allow of a vague impression of a considerable town filling up the end of the gorge, without being able to discern the numerous excellencies of a place of which Anastásio was constantly remarking in a triumphant tone, '*Ma, Signore, quando si vede Vunó!*' as if Paris or Stambúl were nothing to it. We passed what seemed a large building, which my guide said was 'Casa di Bábba', the house of his uncle, who was head of the family (his father having been a second son), and soon came to the paternal roof, now the property of his own eldest brother; for Anastásio is a secondo-genito and obliged to get his living á la Khimáriote as he can: his mother still resides in her deceased husband's house, as do Anastásio's wife and child, besides Kyr Kostantíno Kasnétzi, the eldest brother, with his children, he being a widower. All this domestic crowd, joined to a great variety of nephews and cousins, were waiting to receive us as we entered a courtyard, from whence we ascended to a spacious kitchen, where the females of the family saluted me with an air of timidity natural to persons who live in such Oriental seclusion. The manners of Anastásio towards this part of the community appeared to me to savour a good deal of the relation between master and slave; and now that my guide is at home he walks about with a dignified and haughty nonchalance very different from the subdued demeanour of the domestic in the Casa J—— at Avlóna.

I was led again up stairs, to a large octagonal room, panelled and closeted and fitted up with sofas, etc., in the usual Turkish style; but the presence of many et cetera announces a people of very different habits to those of the wild Gheghe or rude inhabitants of Dukhádhes. A small four-post bedstead stands in one corner; half a dozen side tables adorn the sides of the room, with intervening chairs; the walls are whitewashed; there are chests of drawers; the centre of the ceiling is tastefully ornamented with dried grapes, hung in patterns; and round four of the sides of the chamber shelves, thickly covered with jugs and other crockery-ware, complete the list of domestic small comforts. The windows are very small, and several loopholes in the exceedingly thick walls allude distinctly to the days of predatory warfare, when people shot their enemies out of the first-floor window. No sooner was I settled, glad enough to rest on the low sofa, than Anastásio's little girl, an exquisitely pretty child of three years of age, with eyes like black beads, came into the room, very cleanly and nicely dressed; down she sat, and taking my hand in hers began to sing in the prettiest manner possible, with as little shyness as if she had known me all through her short life. Next came the Capo di Casa, the eldest brother, Kostantíno, a rough but prepossessing fellow, with moustache enough for ten. He spoke no Italian, so our converse was confined to Greek commonplaces, while Anastásio talks in his stead, and assures me that his brother is a man of extreme wisdom and attainments, and by profession a doctor. 'O Signore! *è un uomo chè sa assai—per Bacco! sa tutto! E medico.* Two years ago there was a boy of Vunó who threw a stone at another little boy; he broke his head and filled it full of bones: full, I say! *pieno, pieno, dico, di osse; osse grande ed osse piccole, pieno, pieno*; but the learned man (*tanto dotto è*) pulled them all out—*tutte, tutte—si, Signore*—every one! and the little boy lived for ever afterwards in great health and prosperity.'

After the usual preliminary coffee, two or three Vuniote cousins came in, and among them one who had been at Corfú and Vido, where he had picked up some very lively and energetic samples of the English language more surprising than proper, with which he seasoned his broken Italian oddly enough. His stories were numberless, and there was no help but to hear them. One of the least comprehensible was of a lord, a *grandissimo mylordos*, who had a *cootter—con tanti marinari: e con questo cootter il gran lordos sempre girava il mondo ogni anno—e sempre aveva un vescovo dentro il cootter*; but the name of this circumvoyaging lord, or that of the marine bishop, I could not learn.

Supper, consisting of a fowl excellently boiled and stewed, was brought in by Anastásio and his brother, and they waited while I ate; but I gave them decidedly to understand that I would take my meals with the family while in their house, for as I had been hail fellow well met with all the gipsies and dirty people of Draghiádhes and Dukádhes, I did not see why I should be more magnificent in Vunó, especially as I had here a chance of seeing somewhat of decent Khimáriote ways.

OCTOBER 24

The comparative luxuries of Vunó, the clean bed and quiet room, etc., can only be duly valued by those who have passed such nights as my last two in Albanian villages. Soon after sunrise I set off with book and pencil, accompanied by ten or fifteen of Anastásio's cousins, and soon found enough below the town to occupy me for three or four hours. Like the village of Dhrymádhes, Vunó is placed fronting the sea at the base of the mountains, in a sort of horse-shoe-formed hollow at the head of a ravine. A series of rock terraces support the houses, behind which the hills rise magnificently in a bay or semicircle, and towards the sea the land slopes rapidly to the level tract of ground, which is, perhaps, broader below Vunó than at any part of the Khimára country I have passed. I was surprised at the extent and character of the buildings at Vunó, some of which, those of the Kasnétzi family in particular, were more like palazzi in many Italian provincial towns than dwellings in Albania; and the whole village has an air of neatness and regularity for which I was quite unprepared. The spot where I sit is bright in the morning sun; groves of thin olives and small oak throw a pleasant shade over the meadow; several of the picturesque people of the village are playing at quoits near me, and the quiet repose of the scene is a great treat after the unrest of the last few days. Close by stands the only apparent church in the place, and that is a very small one; indeed, the state ecclesiastical does not seem very flourishing at Vunó, for on my inquiring of Anastásio how many priests there are in his village he answers: '*Due: uno x'è ammalato: e l' altro non si sa dov' è.*'[1]

[1] Two; one is sick, and the other is gone, no one knows where.

At eleven I returned to the Casa Kasnétzi; and it is worth remarking that one of the most pleasant points of civilisation in Vunó consists of the possibility of walking about this compact town where the stranger pleases, without fear of being torn to pieces by rabid mountain dogs, as he infallibly must be in Dukádhes and Draghiádhes, where the dwellings are scattered in gardens, and where flocks are the great commodity of life, instead of wine and corn—not that there seems too much of that—produced by the Khimára strip of plain.

Anastásio's warbling little girl came and amused me till noon, when dinner was served on the usual tin table, in the shape of a good substantial meal of rice soup, boiled and stewed mutton, with the best wine I had tasted in Albania. It would be most interesting for a person well versed in Romaic (which nearly all here speak, or at least understand) to travel through Khimára and by remaining there for some time glean detailed accounts of the habits of life among these primitive people; as for me, I could only arrive at snatches of information by means of Italian, which many of the Vuniote men speak. On my asking Anastásio if his wife and mother were not coming to dinner, he replied that the women never eat with the men, but that his wife, Marína, would come and wait on us at supper, as by that time she would have less '*vergogna*'[1] of a stranger, an uncommon sight to Khimáriote females.

Since the days of Alí Pashá, the great pullerdown of all high persons and places in Khimára (for up to his time it had existed as a set of little republics, nominally dependent on the Porte, but willing at any time to join its enemies), the villages of the Khimáriote district pay certain taxes to the Turkish Government through the Pashá of Delvinë, in whose pashalík their territories are included; but no Turk, or rather, no Mohammedan, resides in any of the towns (I do not include Draghiádhes, Rádima, or Dukádhes, as within Khimára), and they may be said still to enjoy a negative sort of independence, though their power of union in resistance, as a body of Greek Christians, is virtually as much gone as that of Parguinote or Suliote, whose habitations, and almost names, have passed away.

Anastásio relates that two years back a Turkish Bey, with troops, came on a recruiting tour through this territory, and quartered one hundred men in the house of his father and uncle, during whose stay,

---

[1] Shyness—fear.

the '*spavento*'[1] of the Khimáriote women and the '*rabbia*'[2] of the men
was unbounded. For four days the women were shut up under lock and
key in closets and cellars, and the Bey nightly intoxicated himself
with rakhee, making a horrible row, and amusing himself by firing off
pistols all about the room and through the ceiling, the damage done
by which facetious diversion is visible enough to this day as proof.
One of these pistol-balls nearly killed the wife of Kostantíno Kasnétzi,
and he and Anastásio thereupon confronted the Bey, who finding his
own men disposed to take part against him, consented to evacuate
Vunó on the morrow. But, with the exception of such rare visits, or
the passing through of the Pashá of Délvinë's guards in search of some
criminal, Khimára is a tranquil place, though its inhabitants are forbidden
to bear arms; and in consequence of various modes of depopulation—
such as wandering abroad, enlisting in the Sultan's armies, etc.,—they
are now but a thinly scattered and broken people.

While this conversation was proceeding there arose the wail for the
poor girl, the cousin of the Kasnétzi, who died three days ago. It was,
as at Dukhádhes, a woman's cry, but more mournful and prolonged,
with sobs between nearly each cry; and when the first wail was over a
second female took it up in the same strain. Nothing can be more
mournful than this lament for the dead; yet there seems to be a sort of
pride in executing the performance well and loudly, for when I spoke
of the sadness of the sound—'*Ah, Signore!*' said Anastásio, '*ci sono altre
chi piangono assai meglio di quella!*'[3] The death of this cousin led the
eldest brother to apologise much for the curtailed hospitality which
iron custom compelled them to show to me under the circumstances:
they should have killed a sheep—they would have had a dance, and all
sorts of fêtes, etc. etc., but on the decease of near relatives no allegria
is ever permitted for nine days.

There was much animated conversation at dinner-time relating to
the domestic affairs of an uncle and aunt of the Kasnétzi: the latter is
lately remarried to a Khimáriote, and he is already tired of his bride
and inclines to leave her. '*E perchè?*' said Anastásio; '*E divenuta sorda!
ed eccovi tutto!*'[4] But although the party agree that the *povera donna* has

---

[1] Terror.   [2] Rage.
[3] Ah, sir, there are others who cry ever so much better!
[4] And why? She has become deaf, that is the only reason.

no other fault but a growing deafness, still they are equally of accord that the uncle may purchase a separation from the bishop of the diocese by means of so many dollars, even for no sufficient reason. Anastásio concludes the discourse by saying that if his aunt is forsaken, legally or not, he shall '*amazzare*'[1] the zio forthwith. The Khimáriotes appear to have a code of some very severe laws, and all tell me that they know no instance of their ever having been broken through. Those, for instance, for the punishment of conjugal infidelity insist on the death of the woman and the cutting off ears and nose of the other offending party. Two or three instances have occurred among the various towns in the memory of my informers, and one gentleman whose head is unadorned with ears or proboscis, I have myself seen. Another was pointed out to me today, as a man who made a great disturbance in Vunó by destroying the peace of one of its best families: the wife was instantly put to death, but her paramour escaped and remained abroad for two years, when he returned and is now settled here. 'But,' said I, 'how did he remain unpunished?' 'Because he escaped.' 'But why, since your severity in these cases is so extreme, why was he allowed to return?' 'Because we killed his father instead of him!' '*O, cielo*, but what had his father done?' '*Niente! Ma sempre ci vuol qualcheduno ammazzato in queste circonstanze; e così, abbiam preso il padre.* Somebody must have been killed. *E lo stesso—basta così*'[2]—an obliquity of justice alarming to parents with unruly offspring.

After drawing some of the innumerable cousins of the house of Kasnétzl—each of them a picture (though from their sense of mourning I could not get sketches of any of the females)—I went out, and drew Vunó from the north, until sunset, surrounded by groups of Khimáriotes, a naturally well-behaved set of people whose conversation is intelligent and various and whose interest in my drawing reminds me of Abruzzi and Calabria.

At supper, when a dish of beef fried in batter was placed on the table, Marína, the wife, waited with water and towel; we were a select party of her husband and his brother and three cousins—so that she was able to overcome her *vergogna* sufficiently to remain in the room.

[1] Murder.

[2] Nothing at all; but somebody must be killed under these circumstances, so we killed the father; it is all one.

It is not surprising that Anastásio locked her up while the Turks were in the house—for a more lovely creature it is impossible to imagine : her face was perfectly Greek in outline and form, and her eyes of the softest dark blue imaginable—her figure was thoroughly graceful and her expression so simple and pure as to resemble that of a saint drawn by one of the early masters; at present being in mourning, her dress was dark grey, unornamented in any manner, but on a festal day I could have liked to see her in full Greek splendour of costume.

Tchibouques and conversation made the hour of rest a late one. Even now, after the lapse of so many years, a foreigner perceives that the awful name of Alí Pashá is hardly pronounced without a feeling akin to terror. I am most curious to see the places where his great genius and power were so conspicuous.

OCTOBER 25

Long before day two women at once had begun their mournful wail for the dead in the house immediately adjoining this. The sun is not yet up, and Corfú, like an island of opal, seems to float on the pale grey sea at the cloudless pink horizon. At half past seven, I set out for Khimára : the town so called is considered as the capital of this district, to which it gives its name—although Vunó is now by far the most flourishing of all the villages. Anastásio, and a '*Germano*,'[1] with a *mosca*—which, Albanitically speaking, means a mule—are my suite; but I prefer walking to jolting on those wooden quadrupeds, over such break-neck places as our track passes.

For more than an hour after we left Vunó we followed paths crossing sandy chasms; we then approached a most savage pass in the mountains, which here advance close to the sea. Above, in clouds and air, hangs one of the Khimáriote villages, Pílieri, and on all sides are inaccessible precipices—inaccessible at least to any but Khimáriote women, who, in their daily avocation of gathering sticks and brushwood for firing, climb to the most fabulous spots. I watched some who were throwing down great bundles to their companions in the ravine below from sheer

[1] Cousin.

142

rocks of stupendous height; and ever as we walked on numbers of these Vuniote females emerged from chasm and cliff, appearing like animated trees or great balls of black-wood—all crouching beneath portentous burdens of boughs or green brushwood, and each answering to Margarítas or Marínas as my guides called to them from incredible distances. The acuteness of sight and hearing in Albanian mountaineers is beyond description prodigious, and their faculty of conversing at great distances almost supernatural; the ordinary obstacles which under such circumstances mortals find to communication seem in their case entirely removed.

The whole of this pass was of a thoroughly wild character, and the paths through it worse than any which I had seen in Khimára, and consist of mere shelves or ledges of crumbling earth half-way down perpendicular rocks or fallen masses of stone. The broad watercourse, or ravine, in which the pass terminated widened out gradually between lower hills, and shortly opened in a view of the formidable Khimára itself—perched on a high isolated rock, the torrent running below it to the sea, with Corfú forming the background of the picture. Khimára is now a ruined place, since its capture by the overwhelming Alí Pashá, but it still retains its qualities of convenient asylum for doubtful or fugitive characters: for what force can penetrate the fastnesses by which the rock is surrounded without time being given to the pursued to escape beyond the possibility of capture?

At the foot of this celebrated Acroceraunian stronghold I sat down to sketch, before scaling the height. Several Khimáriotes descended to speak with Anastásio, among others the priest of the town, in a tattered blue robe, flowing black beard and red fez. There came also two old women, with the hope of selling some fowls, which they incautiously left on a ledge of rock a short way above us while they discussed the terms of the purchase with Anastásio; but behold! two superb eagles suddenly floated over the abyss—and—pounce—carried off each his hen, the unlucky gallinaceæ screaming vainly as they were transported by unwelcome wings to the inaccessible crags on the far side of the ravine, where young eagles and destiny awaited them. Hereupon the two old ladies set up a screeching wail, almost as loud as that in use for the departed relations, and were only to be quieted by being presented with the price of the hens (about twopence each) which had

143

been carried off so unsatisfactorily to all parties excepting the inmates of the eagles' nests. The sketch done, I began to ascend the rock, which is only easily accessible on the eastern or mountain side, and numbers of the inhabitants came down to salute and examine so novel a creature as a Frank, for by the accounts of the people—how true I know not— I am the second Englishman who has been here. From Avlóna hither I do not find that any English traveller has yet penetrated; no great wonder, considering the nature of the country.

The houses of Khimára are all of dark stone, and bear signs of having seen better days; on every side are heaps of ruin, and a great extent of rubbish, with walls of different dates, proclaims this remarkable Acropolis to have been once a considerable place.[1] The people of Khimára are all of Greek origin, and speak Romaic, though those of the towns I have passed on my way, although Christian, are all Albanian with the exception of a few families such as the Kasnétzi. The Khimáriotes of this place declare that the town contains vestiges of sixty-two churches. There are some remains of fifteen or sixteen on the lower part of the rock, but all in a state of total ruin, and the appearance of the Ecónomo of Khimára is in complete accordance with that of his native ecclesiastical edifices.

As I walked slowly up the zigzag path to the entrance of the town, I had leisure to examine my numerous new acquaintance, whom I thought by far the most wild and most typical of Albanian character that I had yet seen; the men wear their hair extremely long, and walk with the complete strut of Albanian dignity—the loftiest and most sovereign expression of pride and independence in every gesture. As for the females, I saw none, except a few of the heavy stick-laden, who were toiling up the hill, clad in dark blue dresses with red aprons (worn behind), and red-worked hose. Guided by Anastásio, who seemed here, as elsewhere, a general acquaintance and was greeted with excessive hilarity, we proceeded to a house where, in a dark room of great size, a mat and cushions were spread for me and there was no lack of company. A very aged man, more than a century old, occupied a bed in one corner; a screaming baby in a cradle on the opposite side illustrated another extreme point of the seven ages of the family; two or three women, retiring into the obscurest shade, seemed to be

[1] Khimára, anciently Chimæra.

ARGHYRÓ KASTRO

YANNINA

knitting, while circles of long-haired Khimáriotes thronged the floor.

Many of these, both outside and in the house, extended their hands for mine to shake, I supposed from being aware of Frank modes of salutation; but among them three or four gave me so peculiar a twist or crack of my fingers that I was struck by its singularity; though it was not until my hand had been held firmly for a repetition of this manœuvre, accompanied by a look of interrogation from the holder, that the thought flashed on my mind, that what I observed was a concerted signal. I shortly became fully aware that I was among people who, from some cause or other, had fled from justice in other lands.

Of these was one who, with his face entirely muffled excepting one eye, kept aloof in the darker part of the chamber, until having thoroughly scrutinized me he came forward, and dropping his capote discovered to my horror and amazement features which, though disguised by an enormous growth of hair, I could not fail to recognize. 'The world is my city now,' said he; 'I am become a savage like those with whom I dwell. What is life to me?' And covering his face again, he wept with a heart-breaking bitterness only life-exiles can know.

Alas! henceforth this wild Alsatia of the mountains—this strange and fearful Khimára—wore to my thoughts a tenfold garb of melancholy, when I considered it as the refuge during the remainder of a weary life of men whose early years had been passed in far other abodes and society.

This specimen of 'life in Khimára' had taken away my appetite; and when the dinner, long preparing, was set before us, in the shape of a substitute for the eagle-devoured hen, I could not eat what would otherwise have been a welcome refreshment. Accordingly I originated a move to visit the western or seaward side of the town, glad to shake off mournful feelings in the gay sunlight; nor was it to be forgotten that the same daylight was wearing away and it was yet far to Vunó.

Papa Néstore led the way, up narrow, dirty, shattered streets to what he called the fortezza, three or four tiers of regular Hellenic architecture, mixed at intervals with superadded structures of modern times; the lower part of these ancient fortifications is extremely massive and strong. We then went down, on the west side, to a platform overlooking all the territory belonging to the town, from the foot of the rock to the sea, including apparently a good tract of cultivated land. Hence the view of Khimára, backed by the mountains, forms a most magnificent scene, and I sat down to '*scroo*' it, with some thirty or forty wild Khimáriotes crowded around me; after which, resisting the importunity of our morning's host to return to his house, I set out on my retreat to Vunó, followed by adieux in several languages shouted to me from this home of the homeless. I would fain visit the farther villages in the line of the Khimára coast, but if I am able to do so the journey must be made from Délvinë. We hurried on to the entrance of the gorge leading inwards to the hills and soon were shut out by the pitiless rocks from all sight of Khimára.

Far up the ravine there is a detached rock, covered with Greek inscriptions; I mean modern names, inscribed in Romaic. '*Tutti scrivono*,' said Anastásio, '*scrivete anche voi!*'[1] so as I defaced nothing by the act I added my name to the visitors' book of the Pass of Khimára, the only Englishman's there, and it will be long before there are many more. Much time must elapse ere Khimára becomes a fashionable watering-place, and before puffing advertisements of 'salubrious situation, unbroken retirement, select society, and easy access from Italy', meet the eye in the daily papers of England.

In the stony river-bed we fell in with three armed Albanians, of Délvinë, and they instantly commenced a sham fight with Anastásio, as did the Kawás of Berát, by seizing throats, firing pistols, laughing and screeching uproariously. I left them at this pastime, and wound up the path of the ravine, whence, looking down, I perceived the men of war examining my three-legged sketching-stool, carried by Anastásio, with every kind of experimental sitting. The sun was low by the time all the precipices and chasms were past; and as we entered Vunó, it seemed, by comparison with Khimára, a city of palaces. Coffee and pipes, administered by the charming Marína, were well earned after a hard day's walk; and after little Alessándra Kasnétzi had sung her usual melodies, supper and conversation ensued—Costantíno, the brother, eating nothing because it was a fast day, which Anastásio heeded not, saying he was on a journey. All the family looked over my drawings until bed-time and were delighted with the people delineated.

The poor woman next door is still wailing, filling the air with her monotonous cry.

[1] Everybody writes—write your name also.

OCTOBER 26

Daybreak and wailing; wailing at night, wailing at morn. Shrieks and Khimára will ever be united in my memory.

Some clouds are gathering over the sea, but the hills are as clear as they have been for two days of cloudless sunshine. I would we could pass that formidable Tchíka today, but we must halt for the night at Palása. About eight I left Vunó, on my return to Avlóna. All the Kasnétzi family assembled to take leave of me, and I shook hands with the mother and Marína, a proceeding greatly diverting to the whole household. A more agreeable and respectable set of people, as far as I have seen during my short stay among them, it is long since I met with. So, Anastásio fired off his pistol at the last point of the rock where the town was visible, and I went on my way to dine and draw at Dhrymádhes, which I reached at half past ten. After making a polite call on the Zia, the sister of Dhimítri Kasnétzi, of Vunó, and wife of the gentlemanly one-eyed Palikár, I drew constantly till noon, the magnificence of this place being inexhaustible. Several of the villagers squatted round me; and while Anastásio was gone away for a time some of them asked me 'If I had an order from the Sultan to write down this town?' so constantly, and not very unnaturally, is the idea of political espionage ever associated with the act of topographical drawing.

The Dhrymádhiotes also inform me that snow is sent in great quantities hence to Corfú, and that it is gathered from the summit of Tchíka, now glittering above me, by women of the village. There are but few good houses in Dhrymádhes and it seems far below Vunó in the scale of general comfort and civilisation.

At one, dinner was served at the aunt's, in the same manner as throughout all these villages—plain boiled fowl, bread and cheese, being the principal articles of food. The Zio relates that up to Ali Pashá's time the Kasnétzi family were not only the first in Vunó, but in all Khimára; but the Vizír took all their plate and goods and thoroughly ruined them, with all the other proprietors of the district—a statement quite consistent with his known levelling policy and the extent of his genius for grinding and oppression. The golden age of Khimára's liberty seems to have been in the days of the Pashás of Avlóna, before Alí had

147

swallowed up all Albania; but since his reign this restless race are withered and broken. 'We serve the Sultan,' say they; but if asked whether they are Albanians, Christians, or Turks, they say—'Neither; we are Khimáriotes.'

We had left the clean and comfortable dwelling of the aunt and uncle and were threading a little lane, before we had turned the end of the deep ravine which divides Dhrymádhes into two portions, when a frightful shrieking burst forth from the upper room of a house immediately over us. Anastásio became fixed as a statue as another house took up the cry, and then another, and so on till the echoing chasm of Dhrymádhes, with its scattered dwellings above and below, resolved itself into one dismal howl.

'It is my uncle's brother,' said Anastásio, the man of many relatives; 'I heard he was ill, but did not know he was in such danger. That is his house, and he has died there just this very minute. That was his daughter who first began the death-shriek, and as all Dhrymádhes are more or less nearly related to his family, you see, Signore, the wailing is general. *Ringraziamo Dio*,' he went on to say—'let us thank Heaven that we have dined! for if this old gentleman had died ever so little earlier—*una mezz'ora piu presto*—we could not have had anything to eat, for the Khimáriotes dress no food on the day a near relative dies. *Dunque, Signore mio, ringraziamo Dio che abbiamo giù pranzato!*' After this novel reflection on the death of his aunt's brother in-law, we passed over to the further side of the ravine, and I had time for a large sketch of this surprisingly grand place. '*Sentite! O sentite, Signore!*' said Anastásio, '*quella è la mia Zia che piange!*—my aunt has now heard of her brother-in-law's death, and that loud cry is hers! *Piange davvero, come piange bene!*'[1] as if this fearful shrieking, so characteristic of Khimára, were the most charming of accomplishments, any excellence in the performance of which was greatly appreciated.

There was a group sitting near me all the time I was drawing—formed of an aged man, weeping plenteously, who appeared with much energy to oppose a host of reasoners and advisers of all ages, and among them a pretty girl, who might be his granddaughter, that were sympathising with and trying to console him by caresses. Unluckily they

[1] Listen, Sir! That is my aunt who is crying; she cries properly! How well she cries!

talked Albanian, so the tragedy was a riddle to me, until Anastásio explained to me that the old man's son had just been seized, by mistake, at Berát, for a robbery; and although the real culprit had been subsequently captured, yet by some error of the judicíal authorities the innocent victim was not yet liberated. The old man's friends were advising him to bribe some of the grandees of Berát, but he, setting forth his poverty, became at last so angry with his Job's comforters that he stamped and raved in fury and finally strode away with an air like that of a distraught seer.

We reached Palása just as the sun was setting and went to one of the few detached houses of the place—a long, low boarded loft of one story in height belonging to one Dhimitri, who had once been a policeman in Corfú. I was soon established for the night on the usual mat by the fireside. Our party was increased from Vunó by the addition of one of Anastásio's interminable nephews on his way to see life at Avlóna; and after supper the priest of the village, in blue gown and black beard,[1] came in, when we sat talking and smoking until late. But the night was so lovely that I was glad to sit on the outside of the hut and exchange its atmosphere of tobacco for cool freshness, while I gazed on the clear sky spangled with myriad stars and on the solemn mountains calm in silence.

OCTOBER 27

A more bright and cloudless morning could not be desired; so at least this time the Pass of Tchíka may be visible throughout. We were off soon after sunrise and had not gone far from Palása when behold once more the beautiful Fortína carrying my knapsack and the capote of Anastásio, who had been suddenly seized by a great compassion for the mules and thought fit to diminish their luggage; and since so it was to be, there was Fortína (by the merest chance in the world), perfectly unoccupied, and too glad to have the means of gaining a few piastres by this division of labour. So the fair Khimáriote, with the small nephew and the mosca, went round by the horse-track to the Strada Bianca,

[1] The priests alone wear beards among the Christians and Albanians.

while I, after making a drawing of the great ravine and ascending by the steps or scortatura, rejoined them during the ascent.

Slight mists began to gather as we toiled up the Strada Bianca. Anastásio and Fortína, during a halt we made on the sides of this great mountain, held rather a prolonged discourse with two women, so they said, very high up in the gorge on the Palása side; they might have been talking to anyone in the air for aught I could see or hear, yet, at so immense a distance can these people communicate with each other, that it was no wonder I could not discern the other half of the conversationists, since even Anastásio said, '*Appena si può sentirle.*'[1] At the summit of the Strada Bianca the mists cleared away and the Pass of Tchíka[2] commenced in all its unhidden majesty. The huge sides of the mountain are wrapped in pine forests and the bare snowy peaks above stood forth in the utmost magnificence. The groups of trees are most beautiful and resemble feathery cedars; indeed, the whole Pass throughout is a noble scene of mountain beauty.

About eleven we had reached the little fountain in that world of dark pines; and the beauty of the place was increased at this moment by the arrival of fifty or sixty Khimáriotes, on the way to find work during the winter about Avlóna and the Berát district. All rested to drink at the pure stream and sat in parties at the foot of the clustering pines, or on the top of the rocks, in varied groups which I could not resist trying to sketch, though there was little chance of fixing any, for they soon rose and in their sweeping style of progress rushed through the forest.

We also soon followed down the steep-clothed sides of the Tchíka towards the gloomy Dukádhes, and after one of the most beautiful walks I have ever enjoyed, arrived there an hour before daylight, not without a regular fight with the troops of dogs which hastened to attack us.

The family at whose house I had spent so festive an evening on the 22nd were away at a farm, or vigna, on the hills, and it was some time ere it was certain where I was to pass the night; but by the time I had 'scroo'd' a few figures the key of the lower part of the house we last lodged in was found and we took possession of that vast barn with its earthen floor; and by the time the fire was lighted in its centre the

---

[1] They can hardly be heard.

[2] I am uncertain as to the true name of this mountain; possibly Gika would be nearer the truth.

daughter of my late host, with his wives (numbers two and three) had arrived, and preparations for supper began. After the evening meal entertainment appeared in the shape of the Idol-Gipsy and his guitar (his follower, from having committed himself by drinking too much at the last soirée, having been forbidden polite society), and the singing and swinging to and fro were as energetic as on my first visit. About midnight we dismissed the performers, and became a more select circle, though for my own part I was writhing under the attack of myriads of ants, (not at the time supposed to be such innocent creatures). They infest every part of the mud floor; indeed, from being a constantly inhabited part of the dwelling, entomology would have been a thriving study. Sleep was impossible, and I watched the strange scene by the dying embers. The daughter of the house (who had a new pair of grey trousers on) chose to sit up all night and was particularly animated and loquacious, devoting herself to my instruction in Greek and Albanian phraseology. '*Ah! quella porca turca!*' said Anastásio irreverently, '*non vuol lasciarici dormire?*'[1] On the other side of me sat the sad Fortína.

OCTOBER 28

Long before daylight the wail for the man murdered on the day of my last visit commenced; while crowing cocks and howling dogs added their mites also to the morning melodies of Dukádhes. The 'upper chamber' where I abode on the night of the 22nd was the perfection of repose compared with this usual home of the family, which seemed to abound in every parasitical enemy to humanity.

Before sunrise, as they were baking their large flat cakes of bread by the fire, Fortína came in and stood for awhile, with the red light shining on her most beautiful features, saddened with the keenest expression of sorrow. She took leave of Anastásio in a very few words, and turning to me, wished me, with a half-broken voice, 'many happy years of life', and then wrapping her handkerchief closely over her head, went out rapidly, and by the time the sun rose must have been already far on her journey towards Palása.

[1] O, that Turkish pig! Will she not let us sleep?

Long also ere the sun had risen above the frowning cold walls of the gloomy mountains circling Dukádhes we also had recommenced our journey. I had hired two diminutive mules, with a Pietone to take us back to Avlóna, all the good beasts being away at vintage or harvest in the Campagna.

Avoiding the gorge of Draghiádhes, we descended the bed of the Dukádhes River, which, after passing through the deep basin where the town stands, emerges from its narrow boundaries and flows through a widening vale to the gulf. The journey by its banks, between high-wooded hills, possesses nothing of remarkable interest, though the cool, broad shadows of morning, and the groups of Dukádhes' peasants returning to the town, added variety to the scene; the women were all clad in immensely clumsy capotes and large breeches and were driving mules laden with Indian corn.

Below Draghiádhes the stony white river channel was our tedious route, and heartily glad was I to regain the little stream where, on the evening of the 22nd, I had stopped to draw, and farther on to arrive at the bright gulf, into whose waters I eagerly rushed, recovering in their coolness from the tortures of last night's dormitory.

To this succeeded the ugly crag-paths and lentisk and myrtle-covered precipices below Rádima, and at noon we had regained the quiet little cove of Cría Néra, where we halted to lunch. At two we began to ascend towards Kánina; turning the corner of the path, I came suddenly upon a most magnificent eagle, sitting majestically not four feet from me, on a rock, whence he soared away deliberately to higher points. There was time to make two drawings of Kánina ere the sun was sinking low and we left it by the descent to Avlóna. One view of it has a striking background: the great sea-level of the Avlóna plain, with a curious peninsula, shaped like a forceps; the pincers holding, as it were, the island of Aghia Marína, in an enclosed space of water, all but a perfect lake. Anastásio's nephew, a boy who had never before been out of Khimára, was horribly alarmed at the sight of the Kánina women, who were all masked 'à la turque'. '*O! Aghio Jánni! O! Aghio Dhimítri!*' said he, and crossed himself at each goblin face we met.

One hour after sunset saw me again in Avlóna at the Casa J——, having made one of the pleasantest of excursions, and rejoicing in my good fortune as to weather, and in the number of new ideas and sketches I had obtained.

152

OCTOBER 29

Alas! for the integrity of Khimára! A new coarse waistcoat and trousers which I had taken in my knapsack have disappeared; whether by the hands of the Dukádhes' muleteer while I was bathing, or by those of the fair, forsaken Fortína, with or without the connivance of Anastásio, can never be learned. I had rather impute the theft to the former of the two; but the clothes were gone and there was no remedy. I said nothing about the loss, for one hates to make odious memories of squabbles. On the whole, the trip through Acroceraunia has greatly rewarded me, and I have been particularly satisfied and pleased with the constant good humour and attention of the Khimáriote Anastásio. As for Giorgio Kozzáchi, my hosts were full of complaints against that luckless Dragoman, who they declared was '*immer besoffen*'—always intoxicated from morning to night; though with me he had hitherto shown no signs of intemperance. On the other side, Giorgio thanked his fate that he was not to remain at Avlóna, where he vowed the usage of the domestics was worse than that of any slaves he had known in his wide travels.

At sunrise I went down into the plain with the Black Margiánn, and drew Avlóna from the level ground near the sea, returning to dinner before noon. At this meal, the overbearing and violent political thunderings of Herr S—— against all monarchs, tyrants, kings, autocrats, etc.(they had received new gazettes from Austria) was so profoundly disagreeable, that I was rejoiced to know that two horses had arrived, with which, the Black being my guide, I was to visit the monastery of Aghia Marína di Svernéz, in a little island about two miles from Avlóna.

We had soon passed the border of olives that surround the town and were trotting over the wide plain, almost impassable with mud when I had arrived, but now hard and dry; and beyond this, always making for a little woody peninsula which projects into the sea, we came to the salt works. Here they take a sort of mullet, from which is prepared the roe called *bottarga*, for which Avlóna is famous. As we skirted these salt lagunes I observed an infinite number of what appeared to be large white stones, arranged in rows with great regularity, though yet with something odd in their form not easily to be described. The more I looked at them, the more I felt they were not what they seemed to be, so I appealed to Blackey, who instantly plunged into a variety of explanations, verbal and active, the chief of which consisted in flapping his arms and hands, puffing and blowing with most uncouth noises, and putting his head under one arm, with his eyes shut; as for his language, it was so mixed a jargon of Turkish, Italian, Greek and Nubian that little more could be extracted from it than that the objects in question ate fish and flew away afterwards; so I resolved to examine these mysterious white stones forthwith, and off we went, when—lo! on my near approach, one and all put forth legs, long necks, and great wings, and 'stood confessed' so many great pelicans, which, with croakings expressive of great disgust at all such ill-timed interruptions, rose up into the air in a body of five or six hundred and soared slowly away to the cliffs north of the gulf.

These birds frequent the coast around Avlóna in great numbers, breeding in the rocky inlets beyond the bay and living on fish and refuse in the salt lagunes. Pleased with these ornithological novelties, hitherto only seen in zoological gardens or at Knowsley,[1] I followed the faithful Margiánn (who nearly fell off his horse with laughter at my surprise at the transmutation of the white stones) through levels of deep sand, by tracts of sedge and rushes and groups of salt-kilns, till we reached the foot of the low hills beyond the isthmus which I had drawn yesterday from the hill of Kánina. Here a pleasant fountain, glades of green, and tufts of thick olives contrasted delightfully with the sand I had passed. At the top of the hill is a small scattered village, and beyond it the track descends through a perfect little park slope to the shore of the lake, in the centre of which stands the monastery, half hidden in its island by cypress and plane foliage. A charming object is that solitary building in its quiet isle; beyond, Sázan and the great summits of Tchíka add to the beauty of the scene; but the sun was setting and I was desirous of making a drawing of Avlóna from the salt works, with a foreground of pelicans, wherefore, as Aghia Marína contained in itself nothing remarkable, and as a long time would have been occupied in ferrying thereto and back again, I turned my horse and on my way over the sandy plain, obtained three sketches of that singular scene; the last when the sun was throwing its latest red ray over the beautiful form of lofty Kúdhesi and the glens of Avlóna. Then we galloped across to marshy sand waste,

---

[1] The 13th Earl of Derby, who became a close friend and patron of Lear, had formed a unique private menagerie at Knowsley Hall, his country house.

pursued now and then by ravenous howling dogs, and by half an hour after dark were at the gate.

The party there was increased by a Vúniote who had been one of Lord Byron's guards at Missolonghi. He told me some anecdotes of the poet, but on such slight authority, I write them not down. As for my hosts, the news of the Emperor's flight from Vienna had made them more full of political excitement than ever; between their pipes they thumped their table destructively, predicting with sinister glee all sorts of bloodshed and downfall of tyrants. In vain did I attempt to change the current of discourse; but when they proceeded to some long and violent tirades against 'England and the English', I broke through my role of passive listener, and having much the advantage of my hosts in fluency of Italian, took the liberty of telling them what I thought of their illbreeding in thus victimizing a guest who might by possibility not quite agree with all their opinions—requesting earnestly that we might henceforth talk about pelicans, or red mullet, or whatever they pleased, so that we eschewed politics.

Tomorrow I intend to start for Tepeléne, and hope to sleep at Kúdhesi; but as yet it seems no horses have been procured, so early starting appears out of the question.

OCTOBER 30

To Kúdhesi—to Tepeléne, and Yannina! But the horses? Seven, eight, nine, ten o'clock came, and none arrive. At eleven, after frequent messages from Giorgio, they are driven into the yard, and saddles and luggage are about to be fastened on when a dire dispute arises, the owners insisting on being paid the whole of their bargain (i.e. as far as Arghyró-Kastro, three days' journey) before starting, and Giorgio very properly refusing to do what would probably prevent our moving at all. He offered half the money; but all or none was the word; and anxious as I was to start, I could not interfere with the experienced Dragoman, who said that if they received all their payment there would be no hold on their fears and they would in all probability desert us at Kúdhesi tonight. He never had paid all beforehand, in fifteen years' dragomanship; and so help him Saint Dhimítri! he never would. The Casa J——

interfered on the side of the men of Avlóna, and said they always paid the whole sum for horses before leaving home; but this, as Giorgio replied, was no precedent for us, who were not known in the land, and who would cut but a miserable figure if left in the lurch tonight or tomorrow. So, as neither party would yield, off went the owner of the horses with his steeds, and Giorgio repaired to the police, leaving me aghast and disconsolate, and moreover exposed to the triumphant consolations of my hosts, who assured me I should now probably remain there for an indefinite period—'it might be years, and it might be for ever'.

In half an hour Giorgio returned in fierce anger. The police had procured two weasels, quoth he; horses?—mice, starved mice; so as a last resource, and in spite of Herr J——'s crowings, he rummaged out the Sultan's Bouyourldí (never yet used in my behalf), and declaring that we would and should go to Kúdhesi this night, rushed forth in a frenzy, my hosts still professing to doubt the probability of my ultimate departure. But the inflexible Dragoman knew his business, and presently returned, saying that he had been to the Bey of Avlóna, and had terrified him horribly with the sight of the Bouyourldí, by virtue of which he had demanded instant attention, and had left him, vowing that if horses—and good ones—were not forthwith supplied, a message should be sent off to the Pashá Kaimakán of Berát, the results of which step he would not like to contemplate.

Immediately, all Avlóna was in a hubbub; and shortly after horses and mules of all kinds came rushing into the courtyard of the Casa J—— in the most ludicrous numbers, driven by frantic emissaries of the alarmed Bey, who had seized and imprisoned various dodging natives who had sworn to having no quadrupeds. Of this confused assemblage of beasts we chose three, and by twelve were off, with a Zaftí, or armed footguard.

As I left the courtyard the black Margiánn took my hand and kissed it after slave-fashion, and surprised me by suddenly sobbing and crying as if his heart would break. Poor fellow! he had told Giorgio that he would go away with me if he could, and was greatly vexed by being informed that I could take no more servants, even though he offered to go all over the world for no wages. What a suite one might be travelling with if all the offers of service so lavishly made had been accepted!

From the olive hills above Avlóna I went on my way to the birthplace of the wondrous Alí Pashá. The day's journey was not at first very interesting, though bright sun and fresh air made it pleasant: there was a long, winding, narrow vale, and a stream to cross, then an interminable hill, from the top of which one looked over the broad Viósa hurrying to the sea, between cultivated hills on whose sides frequent villages glittered—Grádista, Karbonára, etc. (scenery not unlike that of Abruzzo Citeriore), while towering over all rose the great Tomóhr. By four we had crossed a level tract at the summit of this hill, and descending thence towards the north-east the view was strikingly magnificent. The Viósa pours through a narrow gorge in the rocks at the foot of Mount Kúdhesi, and above this dark outlet rise the detached and finely formed mountains of Trebushín and Khórmovo. Immediately below the spectator is the great extent of stony river course, along which the Viósa, no longer confined in its straitened limits—its dark waters sparkling like so many winding threads on a dazzling white ground—rushes in broad freedom, and many-channelled, to the sea.

Numerous scattered hamlets cluster round the sides of Kúdhesi and are all called by the mountain's name. To one of these, on the banks of the Viósa, we descended, after I had made a drawing, as there was a little khan there where a night's lodging might be hoped for; and reaching it before sunset, found, by great luck, two little rooms unoccupied, and clean. Supper, and journal written by the light of a tiny Albanian lamp hung to a nail, complete my day.

In the stable below, the Zaftí and his two friends sung half 'the livelong night'.

OCTOBER 31

It is yet half an hour before sunrise. Breakfast is over and all things are packed for starting. The pure, cloudless sky is of the palest amber hue over the eastern mountains, whose outlines are dimmed by a few filmy vapours; and all is still except the formidable Viósa murmuring in its white stony channel. It was too chilly to ride, even had the mule-tracks' rudely marked ledges or broken paths by the side of precipices—tempted me to do so. The route ascends the Viósa to the dark gorge—which is so narrow as to allow only of the passage of the river—and when that is swollen it must close this communication altogether; but though grand and gloomy, I did not think the scenery so fine as others of the sort I have seen (for instance, the pass of the Sagittaria at Anversa in Abruzzo Ulteriore), although, in one or two spots, where the cliffs rise perpendicularly to a great height above the stream, or where the path mounts by a corkscrew ascent over the rocks and the eye looks down on the abyss below, the effect is very imposing. The whole morning passed in threading the winding vale of the Viósa, through scenes of wild grandeur, but possessing no particular quality of novelty or beauty: the mountain of Khórmovo, ever in view, gave the chief character to the walk, delightful as it was from the exquisite autumnal weather.

Nearer Tepeléne we met many peasants, all in white caps and kilts and of a more squalid and wretched appearance than any I had yet seen; the whole of this part of Albania is indeed most desolate and its inhabitants broken and dejected. Their rebellion under Zulíki seems to have been the last convulsive struggle of this scattered and disarmed people, and the once proud territory of Alí Pashá is now ground down into a melancholy insignificance, and wellnigh deprived of its identity.

It was nearly 3 P.M. ere the last tedious windings of the valley disclosed the great mountain Trebushín and its neighbour of Khórmovo, visible now from base to summit—each calmly towering in bright purple below peaks of glittering snow. Beneath them the junction of the two rivers Viósa and Bantja forms the long promontory of Tepeléne,[1] whose ruined palace and walls and silver-toned mosque give a strange air of dreamy romance to this scene, one of the most sublime and simple in Albania and certainly one most fraught with associations ancient and modern.

My curiosity had been raised to its very utmost to see this place, for so many years full of the records of one of the most remarkable of men; yet it seemed so strange, after all one had read of the 'no common pomp' of the entertainer of Lord Byron and Sir J. C. Hobhouse, to find a dreary, blank scene of desolation, where once, and so recently, was all the rude magnificence of Oriental despotism!

Giorgio went on to find a lodging in this fallen stronghold of Albania, and I, meanwhile, sat down above the Bantja, to sketch the town, which, on its rocky peninsula seems a mere point in comparison with the

[1] Tepeléne, anciently Antigoneia.

magnificent mountain forms around. Afterwards, having forded the
river with the Zaftí and a horse, I walked up, over heaps and lines of
ruined fortifications, to the strong and high walls of Tepeléne, which still
exist, though there are but very few buildings within their enclosure.
Outside the walls is a short street of miserable bazaars, and beyond—
near a green burying-ground covered with the ordinary tombstones, and
some of those pretty Dervísh tombs—stand a khan, some barracks, and a
Bey's house; these are all now existing of the once celebrated Tepeléne!
There was still time to make a drawing within the walls, so, taking with
me the Zaftí guard I went inside the gates and through a few streets—
than which anything more sad and gloomy cannot be. Heaps of stones
and falling walls arrest your attention as you pass along the very narrow
lanes, and here and there a carved stone window, or columns at the
doorway of a deserted house, and over all an indescribably melancholy
air of ruin and destruction.

At the end of the space enclosed by the walls and overhanging the
river is a single mosque—solitary witness of the grandeur of days past;
and beyond that, all the space, as far as the battlement terrace looking
north and west is occupied by the mass of ruin which represents Alí's
ruined palace. The sun was sinking as I sat down to draw in what had
been a great chamber, below one of the many crumbling walls—perhaps
in the very spot where the dreaded Alí gave audience to his Frank guests
in 1809—when Childe Harold was but 24 years old and the Vizír in the
zenith of his power.[1] The poet is no more; the host is beheaded, and
his family nearly extinct; the palace is burned, and levelled with the
ground; war and change and time have, perhaps, left but one or two
living beings who, forty years back, were assembled in these gay and
sumptuous halls. It was impossible not to linger in such a site and brood
over such imaages, and of all the scenes I have visited the palace of Alí
Pashá at Tepeléne will continue most vividly imprinted on my recollection.

But the desert chambers and the rushing wide river below and the
majestic peaks above are grown cold and grey as the last crimson of
daylight has faded. A solitary Cogia, having cried a mournful cry from
the minaret opposite, sits motionless on the battlements—the only living
object in this most impressive scene. Of all days passed in Albania, this
has most keenly interested me.

[1] *Childe Harold.* Canto II. 56.

NOVEMBER 1

The khan of Tepeléne is a concatenation of minute cells or closets, with uncloseable doors, pervious to cats and dogs, while a perverse old goat with a bell round his neck, who infests the wooden gallery, bumps and jingles up and down it all night long; the wind also howled dismally as it swept through the hollow passes of the lofty mountains; so there was little sleep—but the feeling of the deadly cold loneliness of Tepeléne was a preventative against being harassed by such commonplace evils.

An hour after sunrise I set off to draw on the eastern side of this melancholy town; but though most majestically placed amid towering heights, Tepeléne and the lines of its landscape are not easily adaptable to art. Soon came Giorgio and the horses, when the Zaftí returned to his master the Bey of Avlóna, and I commenced walking to Arghyró Kastro, which they reckon as seven hours hence.

The whole morning was employed in making way along the valley of the River Dryno, which abounds in fine features, though not very drawable or possessing any individual characteristics. The river runs in a deep bed below the road, here both broad and good, and carried on banks high above the level of the stream; and the whole valley bears a striking resemblance to that of the Anio below Roviáno, or Cervára, on the way from Tivoli to Subiáco. One of the prettiest spots in the morning's walk was a fountain below a group of large planes. It was constructed by Alí Pashá, who was wont to halt under its shades in his progresses through this part of Albania, which it is said he used to perform in a carriage. Indeed the communication between Tepeléne and Yannina merits more the name of Strada Carrozzabile than any I have seen in his dominions.

At noon we arrived at the khan Subáshi, standing in the narrowest part of the valley, and exhibiting a guard of soldiers placed by the roadside to ask for Teskerés, or passports; the Bolubáshi, or head of which guard, was authoritative and disagreeable, declaring that the muleteers of Avlóna had no regular passes, and that he had serious thoughts of detaining me accordingly. Upon this, Giorgio thought fit to make a speech about αντος Μιλόρδος Ινγλις, which favourably impressed his auditory, inasmuch as the Bolubashí ceased his expostulations and condescended to eat some bread and cheese in my company forthwith.

160

NICÓPOLIS

ARTA

A stone bridge crosses the Dryno opposite the khan Subáshi, and I thenceforth proceeded, at half-past twelve, along the right bank of the river, which here runs through the wide valley of Derópuli. Its magnificent dimensions now opened in all their extent; the high wall of mountains on its western side displaying the city of Arghyró Kastro, yet afar off, at its foot. For two hours I advanced through the rich flat meadows of this broad vale—leaving the hills of the fatal Gardhíki[1] on the right, and speculating on the distant peaks towards Pindus and Yannina. The lines of Derópuli are, however, pictorially speaking, rather straight and monotonous, and I was less struck with the beauty of this noble valley than I expected to be, though the sensation of freedom of breathing, the delight of leaving the close river-bed and pent-up mountain gorge, made my walk through it a charming one.

All through the cultivated grounds which I have passed since I entered the vale of the Derópuli district, the costumes of the Greek female peasantry have been very pleasing and various: dark blue or red capotes, fringed and tasselled most fancifully and prettily. 'These,' quoth Giorgio, 'are Greeks!—Greeks, signore! We are not among Albanians now, Signore! let us be thankful we had gone out of the reach of those *poveri disperati! Quí siamo in Epiro, Signore! ringraziamo il cielo*, we are among Epirotes!' (For though the country opposite Corfú is distinctly known as Albanian, the innocent traveller who happens to speak of its natives to one of themselves as 'Albanians' finds himself in as wrong a position as if he should address Messrs. A. and B. and C., residents at the Cape of Good Hope, as so many Hottentots.)

At about four we arrived opposite Arghyró Kastro, at a bridge over the Dryno, one of those parapetless, high-arched constructions which rise in the most alarming manner, till a descent quite as precipitous brings you to the opposite shore.

Many of the women were washing clothes in the stream, and two or three were pouring forth lamentable yodelling wailings for departed relatives, after the manner of the Khimáriots.

Hence we crossed the plain—for so this wide valley must be called—directly to the foot of the city.

The general appearance of Arghyró Kastro is most imposing; but the glittering triangular area of houses, which from afar appears as one great

[1] The Gardhíkiotes were massacred by Alí Pasha.

pyramid of dwellings against the mountainside, is broken up, on a nearer approach, into three divisions. The whole town is built on three distinct ridges, or spurs of rock, springing from the hill at a considerable height, and widening—separated by deep ravines or channels of torrents—as they stretch out into the plain. The town stands mainly on the face or edge of these narrow spurs, but many buildings are scattered most picturesquely down their sides, mingled, as is the wont in Albanian towns, with fine trees, while the centre and highest ridge of rock, isolated from the parent mountain, and connected with it only by an aqueduct, is crowned by what forms the most striking feature of the place, a black ruined castle, that extends along its whole summit, and proudly towers, even in decay, over the scattered vassal-houses below.

Arghyró Kastro is in fact three towns; and no place could have been more beautifully contrived for the perpetuation of the family feuds which long disturbed its harmony; rival houses placed at the opposing edges of the same ravines could brave each other's anger; and while their inmates were distant only a space of a few yards in appearance, a real hour's descent and climb separated two seats of hereditary squabble; but after the inevitable Alí had seized on the town, the separate communities ceased to differ, and it was thenceforward reduced to the level of his other widely scattered dependencies.

We ascended the most northerly of the three ridges and threaded our way between thickly placed and most picturesque houses, up the dirtiest and steepest of narrow streets, to the upper part of the town, where, at the junction of the three ravines, are lines of bazaars, placed on a considerable space of level ground. The first khan we examined was 'à la Gheghe', and did no great credit to Giorgio's boastings of Epirote superiority; but the second was in all ways perfection. Speaking of khans, its galleries and stairs, of bright new deal, announced a cleanliness hardly to be looked for, while its ample new-boarded corner chamber, with large glazed windows, looking out on the castle and grand trees below it, presented a luxury beyond the reach of hope to have pictured. Violent rain began to fall by the time I was settled, and as Arghyró Kastro is a halting-place for a day or two, it is a comfort to think that detention of weather can be little annoying in a lodging so tolerable within and so picturesque without.

NOVEMBER 2

A very mistiferous morning, and this high part of Arghyró Kastro enjoys all the rolling mountain clouds. After the oft-repeated necessity of arranging pencil-drawings so as not to be obliterated, a duty known only to wandering draftsmen, I went with Giorgio to the serai of the Khimakán, Governor of the town. The houses in this singular place have a most independent air; scattered here and there, standing on crags and precipices, or on little isolated levels or platforms of ground, each adorned with whitewash and arabesque painting, which gives the whole building (itself pretty in form) the most pleasing character of colour and finish. The Governor's serai, as well as the visit to it, was of the ordinary class of similar places and visits. There was the usual narrow wooden stair and guarded gallery; the ante-room, with secretaries and Cogias, and the audience-chamber, with the great man in the corner. The real Khimakán was away; but his deputy was a gorgeous object, in a fur-trimmed yellow silk vest; and when (pipes and coffee the while) I had explained my wish for a guard, to enable me to sketch without molestation, and a refulgent Bolubáshi, glittering like a South American beetle, in purple and gold, had sent for a Kawás to wait on me, the visit drew to a close. It was prolonged only by the inquiring investigations of a half-witted old Dervísh, who was squatted on the floor, as to the nature of my three-legged camp-stool, a zeal for knowledge which led to the display of my useful travelling companion in the centre of the chamber, and the trial of it by more than thirty guards successively with the most unlimited applause. Taking leave of the dignitary clad in sulphur-coloured silk, I went off with my attendant, and drew hard while daylight lasted. But Arghyró Kastro is a place so wonderfully crowded with beautiful bits of landscape, that knowing how few can be portrayed, even with the utmost energy, an artist is angry with himself for not being able to decide where to settle at once, that no time may be lost. Indeed, to reach various parts of the town is no easy task; for though the houses seem close together, the deep fissures between the rocks separate them widely in reality. From almost any point you may select, the views of the fortress and line of broken aqueduct, backed by a sublime horizon of plain and snowy mountain, are as exquisite as indescribable. Late in the

163

the day I went into the castle, at present a shell of dark mouldering walls; it was built by Alí Pashá, to command the town after its subjection to him, but was dismantled and destroyed upon his fall, though its remains are witness to its former strength and importance. But of all surprising novelties, here or anywhere else, commend me to the costume of the Arghyró Kastro women! The quaintest monsters ever portrayed or imagined fall short of the reality of these most strange creatures in gait and apparel; and it is to be wondered at when and by whom the first garb of the kind was invented, or how human beings could submit to wear it. Suppose first a tight white linen mask fixed on the face, with two small slits cut in it for the eyes to look through. Next, a voluminous wrapper of white, with broad buff stripes, which conceals the whole upper part of the person, and is huddled in immense folds about the arms, which are carried with the elbows raised, the hands being carefully kept from sight by the heavy drapery; add to these, short, full, purple calico trousers, and canary-coloured top-boots, with rose-coloured tassels—and what more amazing incident in the history of female dress can be fancied?

November 3

A day of pouring rain: a mountain tempest continued hour after hour; thunderstorms bursting at intervals, with thick cloud driving down the ravine, or effacing the dark earth and aqueduct into so many dissolving views. Well it is that the khan is so good, and that it has such a spacious gallery, tenanted, moreover, by several Epirotes in all their plumy finery, who not being at all averse from being portrayed, gave me employment in 'scrooing' all day long.

But hark!—wailing again! The quiet of the hill city is suddenly broken and all the world of Arghyró Kastro is startled with the ill-omened cries!

Heavens! what howls! Is all the Epirote city going distraught? The cause of all this is, news has just been received that one of the principal Arghyró Kastriote merchants has died suddenly at Stamboul. The Cogia is chaunting from the mosque opposite, a few wild notes, most impressively sad as they rise above the small tumult of little cries in the lower part of the ravine. Each note is held on for an incredibly long time, and is distinctly marked with a singular power and effect. Then the immediate family of the deceased swell the chorus, yodelling and shrieking with deafening clamour, and wonderful cries, half sob, half piercing howls; house after house takes up the doleful tale, and in less than an hour the melody of grief pervades the whole place, bursting forth from crags above, and resounding from depths below—shrill and solemn, bass and treble—one general lamentation and woe. Thank goodness, none of my neighbours in the khan feel it incumbent on them to add to the wailing! for they are all travelling merchants, and share not in the three-hilled city's mourning.

From three to half-past four P.M. it was clear, and I sketched by the river at the foot of the town; but the cold-Cumberland feeling of these mountains after rain savours too much of fever to allow of sitting long to draw. It is a pleasant thing in walking about to meet Christian women, whose faces, though coarse by early toil, are always more or less pleasing; but the oddity of the Mohammedan females is beyond belief, as, half-blinded by their masks, and bungling with their awkward muffled arms, they fumble in their yellow boots among the rocks. When they perceive a man coming they instantly rush at the nearest wall, butting at it with the crown of their heads at right-angles while he passes them, staring at him, nevertheless, out of their small eye-holes, directly he is a little way from them.

A bright sunset gives hopes of a fine day for starting towards Yannina tomorrow. Wonderful luxuries of food are there in this city of Epirus! Turkeys and tongues, walnuts and good wine, with other pleasant solidities and frivolities quite out of character with Albanian travel.

NOVEMBER 4

The morning is clear, though the upper part of the town is all in mist. The tremulous and multi-vocal wailing is already in full play. The horses are here (we take three out of six, which are on the return to Yannina, having brought merchandize hither). The sun has not yet risen; but what with packing and arranging the bill at the Arghyró Kastro hotel, and a squabble with the Kawás, who gave way to the most fallacious expectations as to what I should give him for his one day's work (viz. sitting near me and smoking a pipe, for which he asked seven dollars, and I would only give him one), it was nearly nine before we crossed the head of ravine No. 1, and making a tour half round the castle or centre ridge, began to descend ravine No. 2 into the plain. The whole town was hidden from sight by dense mists, nor till we were fairly down in the great vale of Derópuli, did the mountain tops and blue sky become visible. The route lay among fields of corn and gran-turco—cultivation was on all sides; anon there were perplexing little dikes and irrigations, with irritations on finding the track suddenly cut off—then broad, grassy routes only interrupted by deep spaces of black mud, from which our horses not unfrequently extricated themselves with difficulty; such was my progress up the wide green vale of Derópuli, while always on the left hand the white clustering town of Libóchovo is in sight (the next place in importance in the district of Arghyró Kastro), and many other villages hang on the side of either range of mountains. But, in spite of having heard much of the vale of Derópuli, I did not feel inspired to draw any part of it; and I often thought of the bare valley of Aquila in Abruzzo, only that this Epirote vale is more decidedly simple in its outline. About noon we reached a solitary khan at the foot of the low hills, which concludes and shuts in the valley at the southern end, and gradually ascending, we reached the pretty little village and church of Episkopí at its summit. Hence I look back on all the great valley of Arghyró Kastro—a smiling and cultivated tract of land, but as landscape, deficient in many qualities; chiefly from lacking variety of form and detail in its hillsides, which are very bare of interest.

We halted at the khan of Episkopí, close to a little stream full of capital watercresses which I began to gather and eat with some bread and cheese, an act which provoked the Epirote bystanders of the village to ecstatic laughter and curiosity. Every portion I put into my mouth, delighted them as a most charming exhibition of foreign whim, and the more juvenile spectators instantly commenced bringing me all sorts of funny objects, with an earnest request that the Frank would amuse them by feeding thereupon forthwith. One brought a thistle, a second a collection of sticks and wood, a third some grass; a fourth presented me with a fat grasshopper—the whole scene was acted amid shouts of

166

laughter, in which I joined as loudly as any. We parted amazingly good friends, and the wits of Episkopí will long remember the Frank who fed on weeds out of the water.

So various are the accounts here as to the time required to reach Delvináki, where I ought to halt for the night, that I dared not linger to draw, though the grouping of some houses and cypresses, combined with the mountains towards Délvinë, strongly tempted me to do so. I longed also to sketch a little Greek church, exquisitely placed in a grove of trees on a platform of rock overlooking the whole vale below and certainly one of the prettiest spots in the day's journey.

After coasting a hillside commanding the last view of the region of Derópuli, a barren rocky pass succeeded, and dullness reigned for an hour, till a descent brought me, as it were, into a new land, in which the hills were broken into various forms, with wood and rock, foreground and distance, in every variety. At the foot of the pass is a khan, and a dignified Bulubáshi, with attendants, made a great rout about Teskerés and luggage, insisting upon a most minute inspection of the latter; this for a short time we resisted, until on the party in power vowing to look into all my porfolios, Giorgio told them they should do so, but that after they had exercised their authority, they should see the Bouyourldí, enjoining all the Sultan's liege subjects to let my lordship pass un-molestedly; on hearing which they were seized with uncontrollable dismay, and tying up the unloosened baggage, whipped our horses, entreating us to depart from them immediately.

Infinitely beautiful is the route beyond this khan Xerovaltó. It is full of variety of form—brushwood hills, light oak woods—bare sand rocks—lines of plain—far blue mountains—and undulating meadows; but there was no time to sketch, for it was now 2 P.M., and Delvináki is declared four hours distant; moreover, the driver of the Yannina horses says there is no place to lodge in at Delvináki, and that we must go on to a khan below it, called Tzerovína.

Few human beings are encountered in these lonely regions: you meet now and then a Greek family migrating with furniture and household—a peasant or two, near some forlorn hut—or a travelling merchant, with laden mules and armed guards. The sun was setting as we arrived at a height overlooking the valley of the Kalamá and caught sight of a little lake, immediately below my feet, surrounded by most beautiful scenery.

I walked on alone by the side of that quiet, still water, enjoying the calm glades, and the pleasant wood of brown oak. There was a carcase of a horse, with a vulture soaring above it, and many falcons on the upper boughs of the trees, and there were numerous tombstones, and two or three Dervísh sepulchres in one of those quiet solitudes.

After sunset I reached the khan of Tzerovína—a solitary, walled, dilapidated building, not promising in appearance, with a distant background of the snowy Pindus range. Alas, for accommodation! All the little space of the khan was already fully crowded by a fat Dervísh in green and white, and some sixty or eighty Albanian guards, journeying to Berát, or Arghyró Kastro, so that no shelter remained but that of the lofty and wide stable; and even this, five minutes later had been denied me, for several parties came in, and those who could not find room in the stable slept outside. '*Bisogna adattarsi*',[1] as the Romans say: the evening was bitterly cold and a bad shelter is better than none.

A huge fire is lighted on a sort of hearth on one side of the windy, half-dismantled tenement, and Giorgio seizes upon all the khanjí offers by way of supper, so that there was no danger of starvation. The travelling groups of Albanians arranged themselves in different stalls of the building, forming, with mules and horses, many a wondrous firelight scene. After their repast, they all sang furiously about Zulíki till late in the night, by which time I was fast asleep in a thick capote.

NOVEMBER 5

Aurora was saluted by some score of geese who lived in the khan yard, but there was no alacrity on her part to look pleased at the compliment, for nothing but a thick cloud could be perceived, and a mist or rain soon began to fall.

All the higher part of the landscape seems hopelessly invisible for the day, but the nearer and lower scenery clears as we proceed, and shows a rich and beautiful country through the vale of the Kalamá. All the scene appears richly wooded, and abounding in forms of dell and gentle heights with innumerable charms of broken foreground. Perhaps one of the

1 Make the best of things.

prettiest points in the morning's ride was near the falls of the Kalamá (three hours after leaving Tzeróvina), which not even the incessant drizzle of sleet, with bitter wind, could prevent my admiring. A wearily cold ascent led up the hill of Zítza—a place I had looked forward to visiting as much as to any in Albania—and it would have been the more vexatious to reflect, that I should enjoy it so little, had not its small distance from Yannina held out hopes of revisiting it. All my enthusiasm regarding 'Monastic Zítza', so long familiar in prose and poetry vanished as the rain came down in torrents and the wind blew so hard as to make sitting on horseback difficult. By the time I arrived at the door of the much celebrated convent, numbed and shivering, I had no other feeling left but that of desire for dry clothes, a fire, and luncheon.

The monastery of Zítza—a low-walled building at the highest point of the hill on which the village stands—resembles that of Ardhénitza, or most other Greek convents, as to its internal arrangement—of its cloistered courtyard, galleries, and little rooms. There are now but three or four Papades living in this retreat—a place of greatly diminished grandeur—and these monks, with the schoolmaster of the hamlets below, were my hosts. Meanwhile the outer storm increased, and the little diván-surrounded room to which the Ecónomos led me was darker than it would have been otherwise—its window and low roof allowing no great light at any time. With that pleasing and unassuming politeness so usual among these people, the priests set before me a very good meal of boiled beef, omelette, etc., during which a mixed discourse of Greek and Italian—the Didáskalos being slenderly furnished with the latter medium of communication—enlivened our intercourse. Lord Byron was of course one of the subjects—the elder of the two priests well recollecting his stay at the convent in 1809 on his way to Tepeléne. Many questions were asked to which I could not reply, and some comments were made and anecdotes told, which slight, and perhaps unfounded in strict truth, I shall not add to the list of crude absurdities too often tacked to the memories of remarkable men.

There is a pause in the rain, so I resolve to descend to Yannina, and to return hither at a more favourable opportunity—leaving a palace I had looked forward to seeing with the greatest interest, in (be it confessed) no satisfied humour. Making due allowance for the bad weather, I cannot but feel disappointed in Zítza: the surrounding scenery, though doubtless full of varied beauty, does not seem to me sufficient to call forth such raptures of admiration, even if selected as a spot where an imaginative poet, reposing quietly after foregone toils and evils, might exaggerate its charms. But after travelling through the daily-remarkable beauties of Albania, the view from Zítza, to speak plainly, disappointed me.

The route led through extensive vineyards, and across the little plain on the top of the hill of the monastery—the charms of which I had been so indifferently able to appreciate, and a tiresome, stony descent of an hour and a half in duration led to the plains of Yannina and the lake Lapsísta. Thenceforth relentless torrents poured down, and the lake Lapsísta was only dimly seen through intervals of shifting dark cloud—conveying a sensation of water and mountain, rather than an ocular conviction of their presence; and so amid rolling thunder and flashing lightning did I gallop on, across the treeless level, till the sky cleared suddenly, and in three hours and a half from leaving Zítza, I saw from a slight eminence the lake of Yannina unexpectedly spread below me.

With the keenest interest I surveyed a scene, already familiar to me from many drawings. Apart from its associations with modern and ancient records, the first feeling with which I gazed on it as a picture was nearly akin to disappointment—perhaps from the extreme bareness of the surrounding hills, and the too unbroken line of Mitzekéli, the great mountain which forms one side of the landscape.[1] There lay the peninsula stretching far into the dark grey water, with its mosque, its cypress tufts, and fortress walls; there was the city stretching far and wide along the water's edge; there was the fatal island, the closing scene of the history of the once all-powerful Alí.

The approach to Yannina through its straggling suburbs of wooden houses, walls, and gardens, Turkish burying-grounds, etc., has nothing of peculiar interest to require description, and I was soon at the British Consulate, where Signor Damaschinó, Her Britannic Majesty's Vice-Consul in Albania, received me with those amiable manners, and that hospitality, which dwell pleasantly in the recollection of all Englishmen who have passed through this part of Albania during his residence in its capital. After the khans and horrors of upper Albania, the spacious and clean rooms at the Vice-Consulate were delightful to repose in; and

[1] I learned to think far differently of the scenery of Yannina afterwards.

newspapers, letters, joined with all kinds of comfort, suddenly and amply atoned for all by-gone toils and disagreeables.

November 6

Among my letters is one from a friend asking me to accompany him to Cairo, Mount Sinai, and Palestine, an offer not to be lightly refused; yet to avail myself of it, I must go hence directly to Malta and Alexandria. But I am the more inclined to do this, by the increasing cold of the weather, and from the small chance of making further progress in drawing among Albanian scenes at this late season. I determine, then, if possible, to come back a second time to Albania to 'finish' Epirus, before I return in the summer of the following year to England; and meanwhile resolve finally to start tomorrow for Arta and Préveza, and so by the Ionian Isles to Malta with all speed. Meanwhile my friend, C. M. C——, between whom and myself the monks of Athos drew their cholera cordon, passed through Yannina but two days ago; and this chance of rejoining him at Preveza or in quarantine—not to speak of the necessity of timing one's departure by certain steamers—all contribute to my decision; thus, therefore, I arrange the final page of my tour in Albania.

The rest of the day I pass in exploring Yannina under the guardianship of a black Kawás of the Vice-Consular household—another Margiánn. From every point the beauties of this fair spot are innumerable, and increase by observation; and the difficulty would be, where to settle to draw its infinite variety of combinations with lake and mountain. The bazaars, too, are most interesting with their endless exhibition of wooden ware, national knick-knacks and embroidery; but all these things I trust to see more completely on my return to these localities next year.

November 7

I started before daylight in order to have as long a day as possible to reach Arta before dark. A Zantiote, on his way back to the islands with horses purchased at Yannina, two of his countrymen, a messenger of the Consulate, and Margiánn, the Black, joined our party; and long before sunrise we were far out of the city. Many a beautiful scene I left behind with regret, for the day's work was toilsome, and sketching could not be permitted. Beyond the long suburban street of the capital of Southern Albania, we crossed a wide plain, with the fine forms of the Epirus mountains around; but the cold was bitter, and even by hard walking it was impossible to keep warm until the sun had risen high. At about the third hour, after passing two or three khans, we began to ascend a bare hill leading to a bleak valley equally uninteresting, whence the road ascended again to the khan of Pende Pigádhia, the half-way house betwixt Yannina and Arta, each of which are six or seven hours' journey from the summit of the hill on which it stands. Nothing could be more dull and disagreeable than the walk; but the view of the Pindus range from the high ground is very noble. The khan of Five Wells is a perfect specimen of the lonely and hopeless place of refuge in these parts: it is a large, ruinous building (though once fortified) in an extensive courtyard. Here we were to halt for luncheon, but while doing so, a first-class quarrel ensued, which I thought might have ended awkwardly. A frantic, or intoxicated Albanian guard, insisted on seeing the inside of every article of luggage, to which the consular officials said no—it is 'Roba Ingliz Consul'. From words and gesticulations pistols were drawn, and the wrathful Kawás was rushing at Black Margiánn when he was seized by the Bulubáshi and others, and the struggles and yells ensuing are not to be described. Giorgio extricated the Bouyourldí from the depths of the baggage, which partly calmed the affray; but the confusion was immense; and the enraged Albanian tore his long hair and foamed in a way I never witnessed in any human creature.

From this squabble we passed to a cold collation of bread and bottarga, and starting once more at half past two, descended the hill to the plains of Arta, which, with many a blue pale line of Acharnanian hill now appeared far away; in another hour, however, we had become pent up in a weary river bed, nor did we reach the plain, over gravelly paths and good trotting ground, till the full moon rose, throwing long shadows from scattered trees. How tedious was that hour or two after sunset!—the long point of hill behind which Arta is placed seemed never fated to be reached. No sensation is more disagreeable than the inability to keep awake on horseback, and when the traveller is creeping a mile in the hour, over a paved Turkish causeway, the wearisome disgust is intolerable.

Endless lanes and gardens seemed to environ Arta; and after having passed the great bridge over the Arachthus, we wound through dark and strange places full of mud, among masses of building black against bright moonlight, till jaded, and more fevered than I had been ever since I had left Salonica, we arrived at the house of the British consular resident agent, Signor Boro, a Greek of Arta. I long earnestly to retire at once to sleep, but the hiccupping flutter of a fowl in the death-agony, announces, in spite of my entreaties, that a supper is in preparation: nevertheless, this clean large house, these good rooms, and sofas, are most welcome to a way-worn tourist.

NOVEMBER 8

More Albanian obstacles: our horses are all seized and dragged from the stables by a Turk—a nautical Turk, whose ships are at Préveza; he, with many Mohammedan 'middies' require steeds to gallop over the plains of Arta; so he takes ours, and snaps his fingers at Giorgio, and the Bouyourldí of the Sultan.

Bouyourldís are for land Turks,' quoth he; 'I am a water Turk.' Giorgo storms, the consular agent remonstrates, and both send to the Governor with an instant requisition of fresh horses for a Prince of Frangistán, desirous of going immediately to Salágora, there to embark for the country of the Franks.

Down comes the Governor, Secretaries and Muftis; and away go Kawási all over the place as they did at Avlóna, so that in less than an hour three horses are in readiness. Meanwhile, I walk with Signor Boro to the ancient walls of Arta, which are fine examples of Hellenic architecture. Nor can any place be more superbly situated than this; which, with the sweeping Arachthus below the town, and the Tzumérka range beyond the plain, forms a magnificent picture. There is a very curious old Greek church too; but trusting to return to these parts of southern Albania I gave but little time to lionising Arta, and at eleven we were again ready to start for Préveza.

Threading the incommodious streets of Arta (which streets are deep gutters, or ditches, full of mud, with a raised trottoir on each side) and once more passing the lanes, olive grounds, and orange gardens, and the lofty bridge over the broad river, we came at length to the grand open plain which stretches uninterruptedly to the gulf. No groups of mountains are lovelier than those within sight of this part of Epirus: whether the eye gazes at the Acharnanian heights beyond Vónitsa—or at those of Agrafa, Tzumérka, and Pindus—or whether it turns towards the dread Suliote hills, and terrible Zálongo, the closing scene of heroism and despair.[1]

The latter part of the journey was by a high paved road over a wide, marshy ground close to the gulf, and in four hours from leaving Arta I reached the hilly peninsula eminence sheltering a hamlet of ten or fifteen houses, known as the Scala of Salágora, or port of Arta. Here we should have embarked for Préveza, but owing to the wind, which is peculiarly perverse at the mouth of this gulf, the caique which plies between the two coasts is not come, and the khan is full. Meanwhile a Greek merchant good-naturedly gave me a lodging in a warehouse of rice till midnight, when the bark arrived, and taking our party on board, set sail to Préveza.

November 9, 10, 11

I pass these days at Préveza, a place that does not possess in itself any agreeable compensation for the vexatious detention by contrary wind, which prevents my sailing across to the quarantine of Sta. Maura.

But the kindness and hospitality of Sidney Smith Saunders, Esq., and all his family, would render any place an agreeable sojourn. It is delightful, after roaming over the most uncivilised places, to find a nook stamped with the most thoroughly English character in one of the spots where you would least expect it.

November 12

The wind has changed, and the sea is like glass; before sunrise I am in the Consul's cutter; every moment brings me nearer to Leucadia—the

[1] See Journals, May 2, 1849. Page 182.

point of Préveza, with the ruins forming part of what was once Alí
Pashá's serai, lessens into one little bright speck on the water's edge. The
snowy ranges of Tzumérka glitter palely in the early sunbeams, and
gradually fade into hazy, cloud-like forms. And so, bidding farewell to
Albania, for the present I enter a nine days' quarantine at Santa Maura.

PART II

24 April to 9 June 1849

Journals of
a Landscape Painter

APRIL 24, 1849

AFTER two months passed most pleasantly in Greece (the winter having been well defied in Cairo and at Mount Sinai), there are yet six weeks on my hands, ere, after having suffered from repeated attacks of Greek fever, it would be prudent to encounter the variable English spring. And now, if ever, I must endeavour to complete my tour in Albania; I long to visit that most romantic portion of it—the land of the Suliotes: to make careful drawings of Yannina: to see Metéora and Thessaly— even to the gulf of Volo—and once more to attempt reaching the lonely Mount Athos.

F. L., my Greek companion, is obliged to return to Malta, so I set out alone; but first, the judicious old Andréa Vríndisi'[1] who is equally at home in the wilds of Tzamouriá as in the civilised streets of modern Sparta, and whose tongue (master of ten languages) is not less valuable than his general skill and arrangement of the domestic comforts of travel, is taken by me at the usual rate of £1 5s. daily, for an indefinite period of service.

Perhaps the best way of entering Albania from Patrás would be by crossing to Missolonghi, and thence, by a journey of three or four days' length, to Vónizza and Préveza; but the desire to see some persons in Corfú who will not be seen there on my return, as well as the choice which, when the traveller is once in that island, is open to him, as to the part of the opposite coast he will first explore, these determine me on relinquishing my design of passing through Acharnania; and I have embarked in the Austrian steamer *Elleno*, which luckily arrives

[1] Andréa Vríndisi, of Patrás: an excellent guide and dragoman in every respect and worthy of high recommendation.

and starts on the very day after the conclusion of my Greek journey with L.

For the third time I watch the high Mount Voidhiá, now glittering in a snowy mantle, and contemplate the exquisite forms of the Peloponnesian and Acharnanian hills; then, as evening gradually covers the cloudless sky with duskier tints, Ithaca succeeds, and lastly Leucadia's 'rock of woe', starlit and solemn, sleeps on the bosom of the calm sea.

APRIL 25

Morn dawns, and with it stern Albania's hills,
Dark Sulí's rocks, and Pindus' inland peak:

and no lines of mountain more beautiful—none more teeming with romance and interest—can be gazed on by traveller, be he painter or poet. Fast advancing through that lovely channel, we soon reach the long-descried citadel of Corfú, and delight in again welcoming scenes, than which the world has few more charming.

During the four succeeding days time went by very pleasantly in the Government palace, where the kindness of the Lord High Commissioner and his family added one more to my many pleasant recollections of Corfú. But on the 30th, Lord Seaton offering to take me as far as Préveza, on his way to Santa Maura, I decided to recommence my Albanian researches from that point, and joined the party in the Government steamer. We were off Préveza at 4 P.M., when I once more set foot in Epirus. Signor Damaschinó, the Vice-Consul at Yannina, and my acquaintance of last year, his wife, and her brother Viani, were also of the Albanian-bound party, and we were all soon heartily welcomed at the Consulate by Mr. Saunders and his ever-hospitable family.

MAY 1

Today Andréa being employed in procuring little necessaries for the journey—I devote to visiting and making drawings of Nicópolis, which I hastily glanced at when passing through Préveza last year. The ruins of this city, founded by Augustus after the battle of Actium, lie not above three miles from Préveza, and the walk thither is very pleasant, through plantations of olive trees.

The scattered remains of Palaio-Kastro (so the peasants call the site of Nicópolis) occupy a large space of ground; and although there are here and there masses of brickwork, which forcibly recall to my memory those on the Campagna of Rome, yet the principal charm of the scene consists in its wild loneliness, and its command of noble views over the Ionian sea as well as of the Gulf of Arta and the mountains of Agrafa. My principal object was to obtain correct drawings from the great theatre, as well as from the Stadium and the lesser theatre; but at this season of the year I found many impediments which in the late autumn of 1848 had not presented themselves. Vegetation had shot up in the early spring to so great a size and luxuriance, that a choice of position was difficult to find among gigantic asphodel four or five feet high—foxgloves of prodigious size, briars and thistles of obstinate dignity. Nor was the passing from one point of the ruins to another, through the fields of beans and Indian corn which cover the cultivated portions of the soil, a light task; there were snakes too in great numbers and size, so that when the sun's heat became powerful, I found the operation of exploring the whole of the Augustan city too nearly allied with risk of fever-fits to prolong it. Great as was the destruction of Nicópolis by Alí Pashá, who carried off vast portions of it for the construction of his palace at Préveza, there is yet abundance of picturesque beauty in what remains; and the view from the upper seats of the great theatre, looking across the Gulf of Ambracia to the hills of Acharnania and Leucadia, is one of the most noble of prospects.

Returning to Préveza at noon, I sketched for the remainder of the day in the outskirts of the town. A student of landscape might well employ himself in this corner of Epirus for a summer: it abounds with pretty bits of foreground and peeps of the beautiful mountain forms around. But in itself, this frontier town of Albania contains little interest. The great palace of Alí Pashá exists no more—it is utterly destroyed—and the whole place has an air of melancholy desolation, increased possibly by one's knowledge of its past history and evil destiny.

MAY 2

It is 8 A.M. before the horses and *roba* are ready, and Andréa gives the signal for starting. He has ordered three horses to Yannina, but it is understood that I am to go thither as I please—bound to no particular route, or time of arrival. Travelling on Turkish horses has led me to adopt one improvement, namely, take with me a pair of stirrups and a strap to hang them by. These I have purchased in Patrás, and they are gilt; whereon, as I leave the town, I hear an old Greek woman remark: 'This milordos is the son of a king: even his stirrups are of gold!'

We go through the olive woods as far nearly as Nicópolis, and then, turning to the left, reach the sea, following a route by its bright blue waves at the foot of low sandy cliffs clothed and fringed with rich fern. In three hours after starting we turned inland towards the hills of Zálongo, but rain, long threatening, prevented any sketching, though the scenery became more interesting at every step. All nature was of the freshest green, and the luxuriant oakwoods, deep dells of brushwood, gentle lawns, and vales dotted with flowering thorn, formed pleasant rural landscapes on every side.

At half past one we reached the village of Kamarína, which stands high up on the hill and is a straggling hamlet of white-washed houses and reed-built cabins, placed in gardens of fruit-trees, or shaded by great forest timber, growing at the foot of overhanging rocks clothed with trailing, wild vines.

At three or four, in a pause between showers, I attempted to reach the rock of Zálongo, immediately above the village. This was the scene of one of those terrible tragedies so frequent during the Suliote war with Alí. At its summit twenty-two women of Súli took refuge after the capture of their rock by the Mohammedans, and with their children awaited the issue of a desperate combat between their husbands and brothers, and the soldiers of the Vizir of Yannina. Their cause was lost; but as the enemy scaled the rock to take the women prisoners, they dashed all their children on the crags below, and joining their hands, while they sang the songs of their own dear land, they advanced nearer and nearer to the edge of the precipice, when from the brink a victim precipitated herself into the deep below at each recurring round of the dance, until all were destroyed. When the foe arrived at the summit the heroic Suliotes were beyond his reach.

But this is only one of many such acts which, during the Suliote war, furnished some of the most extraordinary instances on record of the love of liberty.[1]

I wished much to see the actual scene of these events, as well as to visit the remains of Casópe, on the summit of the hill; but to my great vexation, such violent rain fell, that I could not even reach the rock of Zálongo, and returning to the cottage, at Kamarína, I was obliged to content myself by drawing at intervals from the door of the cottage, in which Andréa had arranged my night's lodgings. It was one of those large and long rooms, usual in Greek villages, and forming the home of a whole family, which sat at the farther end, while I occupied my own allotted portion of clay floor. The inhabitants of Kamarína are all Greek Christians, and indeed throughout the south of Epirus there are very few Mohammedans; the women of the house have a mournful air; and well may they, for many of the elders among them can still remember the terrors of those evil days, in the first years of the present century.

Outside this cottage of Kamarína all is delightful, so quiet is the foreground near at hand, so fair the prospect far below; the long point of Nicópolis and Préveza, the broad bright Gulf of Arta, the scene of the battle of Actium; and the clear hills of Greece and Sta. Maura, all spread like a map at my feet. It seems a spot marked out for peace and tranquillity, nor can I remember a village more deliciously placed as a summer's retreat; the rain has made the herbs and spring flowers around full of fresh odour, and multitudes of nightingales are singing on all sides.

MAY 3

I am off by half past five. The morning is bright, and the nightingales, who have warbled all night long, are as melodious as ever. In spite of my regret at not having been able to see Zálongo or Cassópe, I shall remember the green hill of Kamarína with pleasure.

[1] The rock of Zálongo is famous also for other combats between the Suliotes and the soldiers of the Vizír.

I descend through woodland glades, with views of the Gulf of Arta ever before me, and the peaks of its fine mountains are wrapped in rolling mist. Lower down, towards the plain, the route winds among groups of oak and walnut trees, and below them are shepherds with their flocks. In about two or three hours we reach Lúro, a scattered collection of huts, with one or two better houses at the foot of the hills, and following the track at their base, shortly arrive at clear springs, and a quiet secluded lake, fringed with luxuriant foliage, and resounding with the notes of the nightingale and the cuckoo.

All the country hereabouts resembles the most beautiful park or woodland scenery in England, excepting that the variety of underwood is greater, and the creepers and flowering shrubs are such as we have not. The tall white stems of the ash and plane shooting out of dark masses of oak foliage, and reflected in the clear water below, form charming pictures.

In the midst of this delightful bosky region, at an hour's distance from Lúro, stands Kanzá, a hamlet of a few very poor thatched huts; and from hence, keeping always through a thick and shady wood, which skirts the base of the hills, the route passes onward, till it emerges (after two hours' ride from Kanzá) on to an elevated pasture land, opposite the Castle of Rogús,[1] and here I halt for midday rest.

This fortress, standing on an ancient site, forms a part of one of those beautiful Greek scenes which a painter is never tired of contemplating. Rising on its mound above the thick woods, which here embellish the plain, it is the key of the landscape; the waters of a clear fountain are surrounded by large flocks of goats reposing. The clumps of hanging plane and spreading oak, vary the marshy plain, extending to the shores of the Gulf; while the distant blue mountains rise beyond, and the rock of Zálongo shuts in the northern end of the prospect. All these form so many parts, each beautiful in itself, that combine to make a composition, to which I regretted not being able to devote more time.

After a short repose, I pursued my journey across the plain in the direction of Arta, where I intend to pass the night. We soon cross the Lúro, on a narrow bridge, and so unstable as to allow of but one horse passing at a time, and then we follow the track across the wide level.

---

[1] Rogús—ancient Charadra. The stream of Lúro (Charadrus) runs below the walls.

During this morning's ride I have seen upwards of twenty large vultures; but now, the ornithological denizens of this wide tract of marshy ground are storks, which are walking about in great numbers, and their nests are built on the roofs of the houses, clustered here and there in the more cultivated part of the district. Snakes and tortoises also were frequent during the morning, concerning which last animals Andréa volunteers some scientific intelligence, assuring me that in Greece it is a well-known fact that they hatch their eggs by the heat of their eyes, by looking fixedly at them, until the small tortoises are matured, and break the shell.

We arrived at Arta about four. The group formed by castle, and town, and mosques, half encircled by the broad sweeping Arachthus, and the fine range of Djumérka, struck me as even more beautiful than I had thought it on my visit here last November. The house of the Consular agent, Signor Boro is now, as then, hospitably open.

MAY 4

At early morn I was finishing my drawing begun six months ago. Few places in Albania are more magnificent in aspect and situation than Arta and to an antiquarian its attractions are still greater than to the artist. Nothing can exceed the venerable grandeur of its picturesque Hellenic walls, and from the site of its ancient Acropolis, the panoramic splendour of the view is majestic in the highest degree. Before nine, I left Arta for the second time, and it was long before we escaped from its narrow, muddy streets, and endless suburban lanes; these, however, were less disagreeable now than heretofore, on account of the odoriferous orange trees, all in full bloom. Arta is surrounded by gardens, and in a great degree supplies the markets of Yannina with fruit and vegetables.

We pursued the paved post-track to Yannina for nearly two hours and as the pace over those causeways is of the slowest, I am on the look-out for incidents of all kinds, and find sufficient amusement in watching the birds which haunt these plains; there are jays and storks, and vultures, in greater numbers than I had supposed ever congregated to-gether. Even the unobservant Andréa was struck by discovering on a near approach, that multitude of what we thought sheep, were in fact vultures and on our asking some peasants as to the cause of their being so numerous, they said, that owing to a disease among the lambs, greater quantities of birds of prey had collected in the plains than the oldest inhabitant could recollect. A constant stream of these harpies was passing from the low grounds to the rocks above the plain and they soared so closely above our heads, that I could perfectly well distinguish their repulsive physiognomies. I counted one hundred and sixty of them at one spot, and must confess that they make a very grand appearance when soaring and wheeling with outstretched wings and necks. All the ground in this marshy part of the plain was covered with the most brilliant yellow iris in full bloom.

On leaving the Yannina road, we held on our course westward, and crossed the plain to the village of Strivína on the banks of the river Lúro, which we followed for more than an hour. The scenery of this part of Epirus is not unlike that of the Brathay near Ambleside, but the closely wooded sides of the hills are here and there enlivened by a Greek scattered hamlet, giving its own character to the scene. Higher up the stream the trees are of a larger size, and fringe the lower hills beautifully and when, at 1 P.M. we reached Pasheenás bridge, I thought I had never seen a more romantic bit of English-like scenery. It is delightful to rest below the fine old oaks and planes in this spot, whence as far as the eye can reach thick foliage gladdens the sight. Crossing the Charadrus, we started once more at two, and in one hour—the route always leading through glades and wild woodland—came to the little Lake Zeró, which I had been strongly recommended by Mr. Saunders not to omit seeing. And, in truth, it is well worth a visit, not that it has any character peculiar to Epirus or Greece (for it is more like Nemi than any lake I am acquainted with), but on account of the surpassing beauty of its deep and quiet waters, from whose clear surface bold red rocks rise on all sides, hung with thickest ilex, and surmounted by dense woods of oak which extend to the very summit of the hills above. There was barely time to make two sketches of Lago Zeró, ere the sinking sun warned me onward, and another hour brought us to the vale of Lélovo, a village which is built on the western side of the hills enclosing the glen; the other, as I entered the hamlet, became gloriously bright in the last rays of sunset, all the detail of rock and tree changing from red and

186

purple, and cold grey, until finally lighted up by the bright full moon.

A very comfortable lodging was obtained at the top of the village of Lélovo, in a house which, like all in these parts, stands alone in a court-yard, and is well arrayed with galleries and stairs. Its tenants were a Greek priest (Lélovo is a Christian community), and a very old nun; they allowed me to occupy for the night, one of their rooms, a clean and good one. The scenery through which I have passed today and yesterday has greatly delighted me; it is rare in Greece to find such rich foliage combined with distant lines of landscape, and this, indeed, is a beauty peculiar to the southern parts of Epirus; towards Yannina, and to the north of it, such clothing of vale and mountain is not frequent.

MAY 5

At sunrise the vale of Lélovo is full of mist, and resounding with the lowing of invisible cows, on hearing which domestic sound, I thought, of course, there would be no milk, but for a wonder, there was. How enjoyable was the walk through the meadows as we left the village on our route to Sulí. The song of birds, the fresh breeze, and all those charms of early morning which to the experienced sojourners in southern lands, marks the best hours of the day! We halted but once at a shepherd's capanna, for a bowl of fresh milk, ere we began a severe ascent, which in two hours brought us to Kragnà, a little village among noble old oaks, whence the views extended over the gulf of Arta with the Tzumérka and Yannina hills. But the people of Kragnà were cross-grained and dis-obliging, and no offers would induce them to furnish us with another horse (that which carried the baggage not being a very strong one), nor would they shew us the road to Zermí, on the way to Sulí, except for a minute's walk beyond their village. About eight we left it, and passed from dell to dell, by very difficult paths, steep, narrow and rocky, with no little fear of losing the way in places where the track was quite obliterated by torrents. We steered well, however, and finally leaving the thick oak woods, arrived at the hill of Zermí, high up on which is the scattered village of the same name, guarded by troops of angry dogs, as is the custom in these parts.

We went to the house of the Primate,[1] and found him and all his family at dinner: it was the fête of St. George, today being with them the 23rd of April. With the heartiest hospitality they insisted on our sharing the feast, which was by no means a bad one, as it consisted of roast lamb, two puddings made of Indian corn, one with milk and herbs, the other with eggs and meat, besides rakhee. The room was extremely neat and clean, and the best in all respects I had seen in Southern Albania but, sitting in a draught of air when heated by exercise, that premonitory feeling which indicates coming fever, obliged me to quit the society almost immediately. We waited for some time in expectation of another horse, but at half past twelve tidings came that it had escaped, and so we divided our baggage into two parts, in order to lessen the feebler steed's burden, and thus arranged set out again.

Descending the hill of Zermí we came in less than an hour to the vale of Tervitzianá, through which the river of Sulí flows ere, 'previously making many turns and meanders as if unwilling to enter such a gloomy passage', it plunges into the gorge of Sulí. We crossed the stream, and began the ascent on the right of the cliffs, by narrow and precipitous paths leading to a point of great height, from which the difficult pass of the Suliote glen commences. And while toiling up the hill, my thoughts were occupied less with the actual interest of the scenery, than with the extraordinary recollections connected with the struggles of the heroic people who so lately as forty years back were exterminated or banished by their tyrant enemy. Every turn in the pass I am about to enter has been distinguished by some stratagem or slaughter: every line in the annals of the last Suliote war is written in characters of blood.[2]

[1] Primate, the first or head proprietor of a Greek village.

[2] As some notice of the Suliote history may be desirable, I add as much matter as is necessary to illustrate the subject. The mountain of Sulí may be conjectured to have been occupied by Albanians about the thirteenth or fourteenth century, and when the greater part of the surrounding country lapsed to the Mohammedan faith, this race of hardy mountaineers adhered firmly to Christianity.

During the eighteenth century the Suliotes carried on a predatory warfare with the surrounding territories of Magaríti, Paramythía, etc., but when Alí Pashá, under pretext of reducing disaffected districts to the obedience due to the Sultan, had subdued all the surrounding tribes, the inhabitants of Sulí found that he was an enemy, determined either by craft or force to dispossess them of their ancestral inheritance. From 1788 to 1792 innumerable were the artifices of Ali to obtain possession of this singular stronghold; in the latter year he made an attack on it,

But my reflections were interrupted by a disagreeable incident: in a rocky and crabbed part of the narrow path, the baggage horse missed footing and fell backward; fortunately, he escaped the edge of the precipice; but the labour and loss of time in rearranging the luggage was considerable; and when we had scaled the height, and I sat looking with amazement into the dark and hollow abyss of the Acheron, a second cry and crash startled me—again the unlucky horse had stumbled, and this time, though safe himself, the baggage suffered—the basket containing the canteen was smitten by a sharp rock, and all my plates and dishes, knives, forks, and pewer pans—which F. L. had bequeathed to me at Patrás—went spinning down from crag to crag till they lodged in the infernal[1] stream below. These delays were serious, as the day was wearing on, and the 'Pass of Sulí' was yet to be threaded. This fearful gorge cannot be better described than in the words of Colonel Leake: 'A deep ravine, formed by the meeting of the two great mountains of Sulí and Tzikurátes—one of the darkest and deepest of the glens of Greece; on either side rise perpendicular rocks, in the midst of which are little intervals of scanty soil, bearing holly oaks, ilices, and other shrubs, and which admit occasionally a view of the higher summits of the two mountains covered with oaks, and at the summit of all with pines.

---

which nearly proved fatal to himself, while his army was defeated with great slaughter. In 1798, after six years of bribery and skirmishing, a portion of the territory of Sulí was gained by the Mohammedans, through treachery of some of the inhabitants, and thenceforward the accounts of the protracted siege of this devoted people is a series of remarkable exploits and resolute defence, by Suliotes of both sexes, seldom paralleled in history.

Every foot of the tremendous passes leading to Sulí was contested in blood ere the besieger gained firm footing; and after he had done so the rock held out an incredible period, until famine and treachery worked out the downfall of this unfortunate people.

Then, in 1803, many escaped by passing through the enemy's camp, many by paths unknown to their pursuers; numbers fled to the adjacent rocks of Zálongo and Seltzo; others destroyed themselves, together with the enemy, by gunpowder, or in a last struggle; or threw themselves into the Acheron or from precipices. Those of these brave people who ultimately escaped to Párga crossed over to Corfú, and thence entered the service of Russia and France. Many, since the days of Greek independence, have returned to various parts of Epirus or Greece; but they have no longer a country or a name, and the warlike tribe who, at the height of their power formed a confederacy of sixty-six villages, may now be said to be extinct.

[1] The river of Sulí is the Acheron of antiquity.

Here the road is passable only on foot, by a perilous ledge along the side of the mountain of Sulí; the river in the pass is deep and rapid and is seen at the bottom falling in many places over the rocks, though at too great a distance to be heard, and in most places inaccessible to any but the foot of a goat or a Suliote.'

I shall not soon forget the labour it cost to convey our horses through this frightful gorge. In many places the rains had carried away even what little footing there had originally been, and nothing remained but a bed of powdered rock sloping off to the frightful gulf below; and all our efforts could hardly induce or enable each horse to cross singly. The muleteer cried, and called on all the saints in the Greek calendar; and all four of us united our strength to prevent the trembling beast from rolling downwards. There were three of these passi cattivi, and the sun was setting. I prepared to make up my mind, if I escaped the Acheron, at least to repose all night in the ravine.

At sunset we reached the only approach on this side of 'the blood-stained Sulí'—an ascent of stairs winding up the sides of the great rocks below Avaríko—and very glad was I to have accomplished this last and most dangerous part of the journey. Before me is the hollow vale of Avaríko, Kiafa, and Sulí—places now existing little more than in name; and darkly looming against the clear western sky stands the dread Trypa—the hill of Thunderbolts—the last retreat of the despairing Suliotes.

Here, at the summit of the rock, Alí Pashá built a castle, and within its walls I hope to pass the night. I reach it at nearly two hours after sunset, the bright moon showing me the Albanian governor and his twenty or thirty Palikári sitting on the threshold of the gate. But as unluckily I had not procured any letter from the Turkish authorities at Préveza, the rough old gentleman was obdurate, and would not hear of my entering the fortress. '*Yok*,' said he, frowning fiercely, '*yok, yok.*' And had it not been for the good nature of a Turkish officer of engineers who had arrived from Yannina on a visit of inspection, I must have passed the night supperless and shelterless. Thanks to him, men and horses were at length admitted to the interior of the fort.

I was ushered through several dilapidated courtyards to the inner serai or governor's house—a small building with wide galleries round two sides of it. In a narrow and low room, surrounded with sofas, the military dignitary sat down with his suite of 'wild Albanians'; and to be polite, I followed their example; but the excessive smoke of the wood fire, added to that of the tchibouques, was so painful a contrast to the fresh air, that it was almost intolerable. No Greek was spoken; so Andréa was called in, and they expressed their conviction that I 'looked miserable—neither eating, nor talking, nor smoking'—an accusation I willingly acceded to, for the sake of rest and fresh air, and transferred my position with all haste to the outer gallery. There I had my mattress and capotes spread, and old Andréa brought me a capital basin of rice soup. It had been a severe day's labour for a man of his years and great size, and during the passage of the gorge, he had more than once been unable to advance for some minutes; yet, with his wonted alacrity, he had not only prepared my bed as usual, but had exercised his talent for cooking withal.

I gazed on the strange, noiseless figures about me, bright in the moonlight, which tipped with silver the solemn lofty mountains around. For years those hills had rarely ceased to echo the cries of animosity, despair, and agony; now all is silent as the actors in that dreadful drama.

Few scenes can compete in my memory with the wildness of this at the castle of Kiáfa, or Sulí-Kastro; and excepting in the deserts of the peninsula of Sinai, I have gazed on none more picturesque and strange.

MAY 6

Before sunrise everyone was on foot; but the military duties of the garrison were interrupted by the circumstance of my being obliged to wash my face in public. Unlike the Turkish Mohammedan, the Albanian prefers satisfying curiosity to the maintaining of dignity. Officers and men came hastily, on the report of the Frank's extravagance, to gaze at the extraordinary proceeding. I believe they thought it a species of water-worship.

I passed some hours on the rock of Trypa, and a more mighty scene of grandeur can hardly be conceived. On each of the jutting ends or horns of the hill, which is semicircular in shape, there was formerly a fortress. These are now destroyed; but from their ruins the view is most characteristic, and seems as it were a part of the sad Suliote history, so darkly and terribly magnificent. One little peep towards the east shows the Gulf of Arta with its hills beyond the stern precipices of the Acheron; that to the west looks on to the plain of Fanári and the Ionian Sea, while in each picture the deep, deep river rolls far below in its close and wooded gulf.[1]

At eight, the baggage having gone before, I took leave of the cross old Governor. I had distributed some coffee to his men; but he nevertheless asked for several articles for himself, begging I would send to Sulí from the next large place I came to, a mirror, a good telescope, four wine glasses, and a cut glass bottle for rakhee; pistols, scissors, and English cloth; all of which things Andréa said, in Albanian, that I would forward on the first opportunity; which lavish promises, as I did not hear them made, I did not feel bound to observe.

The descent westward to the Acheron is a difficult narrow path, in some places of extreme steepness, but of course not like the route of yesterday, which was never intended for horses. At the bottom of the ravine, they ford the deep rapid torrent, while I go on to a point beyond the junction of a stream where the Acheron is crossed by a bridge. But what a bridge! The river, confined between two very narrow perpendicular crags, boils and thunders below them, while the space between is connected by two poles, over which branches of trees are laid transversely, and over all a covering of leaves and earth, by way of pavement; an awkward structure, and one well calculated to render the approach to Sulí, even on this side, a matter of difficulty. Slowly, on hands and knees, and holding the poles, I passed this bridge over the river of Pluto, its oscillations being far from pleasant; but the huge Andréa manifested much solicitude ere he ventured his heavy frame on the slight support, throwing his shoes and most of his dress over to the other side, before he attempted to cross. On the left bank, the road thenceforward becomes a little less difficult; and after following several windings of the stream, sometimes at a great height above it, finally leaves the tremendous gorge of the Acheron for the level plain of

---

[1] From the precipices impending over this ravine, it is related that the Suliote women threw their children, when the contest for their liberty had come to an end. To such a spot the epithet given by Aristophanes, 'the rock of Acheron dropping blood,' may indeed be well applied.

192

SÚLI

PÁRGA

Fanári, on which I was once more glad to welcome the familiar lentisk and clumps of squills.

Shortly we again forded the Acheron, here, in the vicinity of the ruined church of Glyky, a broad and considerable river; the Albanians who accompanied me breasting the rapid waters on foot, hand-in-hand. At every turn of the gorge, through which the river escapes, there are views of Sulí most varied and magnificent, but from this point its general aspect is most strikingly noble.

Anxious to reach Párga ere night, I did not visit the ruins at Glyky, but pursued the route in the plain, through rice grounds, to the village of Potamiá,[1] where at midday we halt.

I could well have liked to have made many studies of these wild homes of Tzamouriá; but the difficulty of drawing during the whole of the day is great, especially at this period, when the heat begins to be oppressive, and a little neglect and idleness is excusable, though often afterwards regretted. After an hour and a half of repose, below large vine-hung willow trees, lulled by the murmur of innumerable bees, and always jealously watched by a score or two of the ferocious dogs which guard these villages, it was time to proceed once more, and we again rode on towards the sea.

A good deal of time was devoted to picking our way among the ditches and irrigations of the rice grounds, which are very extensive in this part of the marshy plain of Fanári; the paths among them form a perfect labyrinth, and much labour is lost in making useless détours. At length, however, we crossed the Vuvó[2] by a bridge, and leaving the Acherusian plains, took a course eastward towards Párga.

Another hour was wasted by the muleteer persisting in the descent of a ravine, which conducted to no place whatever. There were new cuts of mule track also, which evidently greatly puzzled poor old Andréa,

[1] The appearance of this and similar Albanian villages is well described by Mr. Hughes, at his visit in 1815, and will perfectly well serve for their illustration in 1849—the best huts consisting of hurdles were constructed formed 'only of branches of trees, half cut through, which being turned down and fastened to the ground, form a kind of tent, to which the trunk of the tree serves as a pole. Notwithstanding its apparent misery, the village has a curious and picturesque appearance, being intersected with green alleys, covered with vines, shaded by trees, and adorned with a vast quantity of flowers for the nourishment of bees, which every family seemed to cultivate.'

[2] The ancient Cocytus.

who had not been here since 1833; and by the time we arrived at the hills on the coast looking towards Paxós, the sun was very low, and there were no symptoms of Párga. It was so late, that as this new broad track seemed necessarily about to lead to some village, an experimental retrograde move was objectionable, so we went onwards, though by the winding of the path over cliffs to the south, it was evident to me that Párga was not to be my home tonight.

At length we entered a thick wood, and began to descend rapidly, when lo! once more we were in sight of the Acherusian plains, with the port of Fanári or Splántza at our feet. The route we had followed by mistake was a new one, lately made from that increasing village to Párga and Paramythía, but the discovery of his error threw poor old Andréa into great distress.

'Old age is coming upon me, and my memory is going,' said he; 'I never missed my way before, and now for the first time I perceive that I shall be unable to act as guide any longer. I, my wife, and my daughter, shall all die of starvation.'

In vain I declared, in order to comfort him, that he had done me a great service, for I particularly wished to have a drawing of the ancient port Glycys Limen, which in reality is a beautiful scene. The poor old fellow was inconsolable, so I sent him onward with the baggage, and remained until the sun had set, sketching the quiet little bay and its village, at the edge of the marshy plain, with the beautiful island of Leucadia forming the background.

It became dark ere I reached the edge of the thick wood; and in places where the track divided, the Albanian who led my horse, felt (for it was too dark to see) for the freshest traces left by the horse's shoes, on the edges of the flints in the path. I left the thicket, and on rounding the hill which overhangs the marsh, I saw Andréa and the horses far on the shore, 'lit by a large low moon'; and following the edge of the Acherusian swamp, that sparkled with myriads of fireflies, I reached the sands of the calm bay, and the hamlet of Splántza, where I found lodging provided in the large room of a Greek family, agents to the people whom I knew at Préveza, and who were glad to make any arrangement for my comfort.

Late at night I strolled on to the bright sands, and enjoyed the strange scene: air seems peopled with fireflies, earth with frogs, which roar and

194

croak from the wide Acherusian marsh; low-walled huts cluster around; Albanians are stretched on mats along the shore; huge watchdogs lie in a circle round the village; the calm sea ripples, and the faint outline of the hills of desolate Sulí, is traced against the clear and spangled sky.

MAY 7

Long before sunrise we were away from Splántza, and taking another guide to insure certainty in reaching Párga, I bade adieu once more to the plain of the Acheron and dark Sulí, as we followed the track which led us in less than two hours to the spot we had reached last afternoon, and thence for some distance along the high cliffs above the bright blue sea, through underwood of lentisk and thorn.

About nine we arrived at beautiful and extensive groves of olive, for the cultivation of which Párga is renowned; they clothe all the hills around, and hang over rock and cliff to the very sea with delightful and feathery luxuriance. At length we descended to the shore at the foot of the little promontory on which the ill-fated palace and its citadel stood; alas, what now appears a town and castle consists of old ruined walls, for Párga is desolate. A new one built since the natives abandoned the ancient site, is, however, springing up on the shore, and with its two mosques is picturesque: this, with the rock and dismantled fortress— the islands in the bay, and the rich growth of olive slopes around, form a picture of completely beautiful character, though more resembling an Italian than a Greek scene; but it is impossible fully to contemplate with pleasure a place, the history of which is so full of melancholy and painful interest.

A dark cloud hangs over the mournful spot. Would that much which has been written concerning it were never read, or that having been written it could be disbelieved!

A lodging was found me in a very decent house and shelter against the heat of midday was grateful. In the afternoon and evening I made many drawings from either side of the promontory of Párga. From every point it is lovely, very unlike Albanian landscape in general, and partaking more of the character of Calabrian or Amalfitan coast scenery. But in spite of the delightful evening, and the sparkling white buildings that crowned the rock at whose feet the waves murmured, the whispering olives above me, the convent islets, and the broad bright sea beyond, in spite of all this, I felt anxious to leave Párga. The picture, false or true, of the 10th of April 1819 was ever before me, and I wished with all my heart that I had left Párga unvisited.

MAY 8

About seven I retraced my steps to the road communicating between Paramythía and Splántza, and throughout the route leading over the hills which surround the Párguinote territory there was but little interest, excepting some Hellenic remains on the right, which I did not leave the track to examine.

Before eleven we reached Margaríti; it stands in a close valley surrounded by hills, the outline of which is not possessed of much beauty; but, as in many other instances, the frequency of interesting detail that forms, as it were, numerous small pictures, atoned for the want of general effect. Along the hillside are scattered great numbers of detached Turkish houses situated in gardens; one or two small minarets glitter above the fruit trees, and fine groups of plane shade parts of the vale below.

Margaríti, still a considerable place, was once extensive and powerful, and one of the last which held out against the power of Alí, but in the end it shared the fate of its neighbours. A cottage received me for repose and refreshment until the heat of noon was over. At half past 1 P.M. we began to ascend the range of high hills which divide the territories of Margaríti and Paramythía, and to toil over a tract of ground as barren of herbage as of interest and beauty; near the summit of the height, however, is seen the extremity of Corfú, and higher up to the south lies Santa Maura; and the day being very sultry, there was a pleasant breeze, which partly compensated for the absence of charm in the landscape. Nor was there long to wait for this worthier scene; for we shortly began to descend into the green and pleasant plains of Paramythía, the town and castle of which are situated at its northern end, backed by magnificently formed mountains. Every step across the plain of the Cocytus increases the beauty of the appearance of this fine place, without doubt one of the most grandly situated towns in Albania. The mountains which enclose the valley on every side prevent any distant view, but the interest of the hill of Paramythía is in itself sufficient to employ an artist for a long space of time. The summit of the rock, on the sides of which the houses of the town are built, is crowned with a castle, and below it are scattered the picturesquely grouped dwellings intermingled with cypress and all kinds of foliage, while streams, stone fountains, Greek churches and mosques—a second castle, that rises above what may be termed the lower town, large tufts of lofty trees in the vale, and the fir-clad mountain above, add to the charm and splendour of the scene. I lingered long on the banks of the Cocytus drawing this beautiful place. The costume of the Greek women here is one of the prettiest I have seen; and as a party passed me on its return to the town from a neighbouring wedding, I had a good opportunity of observing several of them.

On arriving in that part of Paramythía which is most thickly inhabited, the narrow and dirty streets present a strange contrast to the beauty of the town, when seen from below, and although we discovered a khan to which some of the peasants had recommended me as '*troppo polito!*' it was so dismal and filthy an abode that we tried to find a substitute in some Greek Christian's house. After some search, however, I was forced to relinquish the idea of comfort, and remain in a close and foul cell for the night (a place little better than some of my Illyrian lodgings), and listen to the wild octave-singing of the Albanians below, till the arrival of midnight, silence, and sleep.

MAY 9

In these holes, miscalled rooms, light there is none, and it is only by the sudden and simultaneous clattering of storks, twittering of swallows, bleating of goats, and jingling of mules' bells, that a man is advised of the coming day. Starting at seven, two hours of toil brought us to the top of a rocky and uninteresting pass, at a place called Eléutherokhório, one of the often-contested spots in the wars between Alí and the people of Paramythía, Margaríti, and Sulí.

Here passports were demanded by a guard of Albanians, a matter more of form than use, as Andréa hardly deigned to exhibit my Boyourldi. Hence we descended into the bed of a torrent, whence we remained making weary way among low planes, not yet in leaf, so much colder is the temperature in this district, than on the southern and western side of the mountains, where all was brilliant verdure. By 1 P.M. we had already crossed this tiresome stream forty times; rain began to fall, and the day was gloomy and cloudy, so that, growing colder every hour, I grew every moment more weary of a day's journey, in which there was little beauty, novelty, or interest.

About three we turned to the right, leaving the road to Yannina, which we had hitherto followed, and ascending the sloping base of Mount Olytzika, arrived about half past four at the village of Bagotjús, where we halted to pass the night. It was too late to visit the theatre of Dhramisiús, so after drawing some of the scenery from the door of the priest's house where I am to lodge, I pass the evening as well as I can; the ceiling of my night's home is hung with pendant Indian corn and great globes of raw cotton; outside, the view is peculiarly interesting: infinite clumps of fine trees clothe the sides of the hill, or are dispersed in the pasture land below; some of these shelter the village church in a very pleasing manner, as is the usage in these countries.

May 10

To my great disappointment, it was raining hard at sunrise, and the clouds did not give any promise of holding up. Nevertheless, resolved to see the ruins of Dhramisiús: I walked thither with a guide, as they are not above twenty minutes' distance from the village of Bagotjús. In spite of the driving cold rain, which nearly hid Mount Olytzika from view, it was impossible not to be greatly struck with the magnificent size and position of the great theatre, which ranks in dimensions with the largest ones of Greece, Sparta, Argos, Athens, Megalopolis, etc., its total diameter being four hundred and sixty feet.

It is supposed that these extensive remains belong to a hierum and place of public meeting of the Molossi: 'a place of common sacrifice and political union, for the use of all the towns of that division of Epirus'. I greatly regretted not being able to make such drawings as I wished at this interesting spot, though I did get one; but, had it been fine, the vale below the immense theatre, with the great peaks of Olytzika above, the immense clumps of trees at its base, would have tempted me to pass a day there.

On Andreá joining me with the horses, we made the best of our way to Yannina in pouring rain, which never ceased until we were near the lake, when Pindus, glittering in silvery snow, peeped forth from clouds, and all the wide meadows south of the city were flocked with number-less white storks.

Before eleven I reach Yannina, and am once more at the hospitable Vice-Consulate, where Signor Damaschinó and his family have arrived a few days back from Préveza.

MAY 11, 12, 13

Three days passed at Yannina, but with constant interruptions from showers. The mornings are brilliant, but clouds gather on Mitzikéli about nine or ten, and from noon to three or four, thunder and pouring rain ensues. The air is extremely cold, and whereas at Párga I could only bear the lightest clothing, I am here too glad to wear a double capote, and half the night am too cold to sleep.

Apart from the friendly hospitality of the Damaschinó family, a sojourn at Yannina is great pleasure, and were it possible, I would gladly pass a summer here. It is not easy to appreciate the beauty of this scenery in a hasty visit; the outlines of the mountains around are too magnificent to be readily reducible to the rules of art, and the want of foliage on the plain and hills may perhaps at first give a barren air to the landscape. It is only on becoming conversant with the groups of trees and buildings, picturesque in themselves, and which combine exquisitely with small portions of the surrounding hills, plain, or lake, that an artist perceives the inexhaustible store of really beautiful forms with which Yannina abounds.

During these days time passed rapidly away, for there was full employment for every hour; one moment I would sit on the hill which rises west of the city, whence the great mountain of Mitzikéli on the eastern side of the lake is seen most nobly: at another, I would move with delight from point to point among the southern suburbs, from which the huge ruined fortress of Litharítza, with many a silvery mosque and dark cypress, form exquisite pictures: or watch from the walls of the ruin itself, the varied effect of cloud or sunbeam passing over the blue lake, now shadowing the promontory of the kastron or citadel, now gilding the little island at the foot of majestic Mitzikéli. Then I would linger on the northern outskirts of the town, whence its long line constitutes a small part of a landscape whose sublime horizon is varied by mountain forms of the loftiest and most beautiful character, or by wandering in the lower ground near the lake, I would enjoy the placid solemnity of the dark waters reflecting the great mosque and battlements of the citadel as in a mirror. I was never tired of walking out into the spacious plain on each side the town, where immense numbers of cattle enlivened the scene, and milk-white storks paraded leisurely in quest of food: or I would take a boat and cross to the little island, and visit the monastery, where that most wondrous man Alí Pashá met his death: or sitting by the edge of the lake near the southern side of the kastron, sketch the massive, mournful ruins of his palace of Litharítza, with the peaks of Olytzika rising beyond. For hours I could loiter on the terrace of the kastron opposite the Pashá's serai, among the ruined fortifications, or near the strange gilded tomb where lies the body of the man who for so long a time made thousands tremble! It was a treat to watch the evening deepen the colours of the beautiful northern hills, or shadows creeping up the furrowed sides of Mitzikéli.

And inside this city of manifold charms the interest was as varied and as fascinating: it united the curious dresses of the Greek peasant—the splendour of those of the Albanian: the endless attractions of the bazaars, where embroidery of all kinds, fire-arms, horse-gear, wooden-ware, and numberless manufactures peculiar to Albania were exhibited—the clattering storks, whose nests are built on half the chimneys of the town, and in the great plane-trees whose drooping foliage hangs over the open spaces or squares: these and other amusing or striking novelties which the pen would tire of enumerating, occupied every moment, and caused me great regret that I could not stay longer in the capital of Epirus. And when to all these artistic beauties is added the associations of Yannina with the later years of Greek history, the power and tyranny of its extraordinary ruler, its claim to representing the ancient Dodona, and its present and utterly melancholy condition, no marvel that Yannina will always hold its place in memory as one of the first in interest of the many scenes I have known in many lands.

Of the people of Yannina I saw nothing except in the streets. I went about perfectly unmolested; nor was there any curiosity shown as to my drawing: once only some Turkish officers observing my work on grey paper, sent for an interpreter to tell me that what I was using was not good London paper, for it was not white. Margiánn, the black Kawás of the Vice-Consulate, accompanied me everywhere, and smote the little red-capped children hither and thither if they came too near me. Among the women I observed none very pretty, and several were painted (as I remarked also at Paramythía) in the coarsest manner, quite to the eyes and roots of the hair.

The unsettled state of the weather, which characterises the spring and early summer in this place, prevented my even being able to obtain such sketches of the city and its neighbourhood as I had wished; and the same cause made me very undecided as to pursuing my journey eastward; yet it seemed hard to return to England without seeing Metéora, Tempe, Olympus, and Athos; and when on the 13th the wind changed, and there were all sorts of atmospherical signs of permanently fine weather about to set in, I finally resolved on crossing the Pindus into Thessaly and ordered horses for the morrow.

May 14

The morning promises well and we start as early as half past five; it is bitterly cold at this early hour and the paved Turkish road forbids other than a very slow pace. At the southern end of the lake the passage between it, or rather a tract of marsh, and the hill of Kastrítza is merely wide enough to admit of this causeway—the high road from Yannina to Constantinople. The ancient remains on the hill I reserved for a visit on my return, when I hoped to make drawings to aid at a future day in some poetical illustration of Dodona, for with that ancient city the site of Kastrítza is considered by Colonel Leake to be identical; the fortress peninsula of the present city of Yannina he suggests as the position of the Dodonean temple. The cautious research carried on for so long a time in Epirus, and the great learning brought to the aid of such careful personal observation, offer very weighty reasons for putting faith in any of Colonel Leake's suggestions as to the sites of antiquity: but apart from these, I feel determined to believe that his arguments concerning Kastrítza are correct. And until I see a more beautiful Dodona I will believe, and it is a harmless even if an ill-founded credulity, that Dodona and the temple did stand at Kastrítza and Yannina.

Crossing the plain of Barkumádhi, where there is a roadside khan, I began to ascend Mount Dhrysko—a part of Mount Mitzikéli, or the ancient Tomarus—arriving about nine at the top of the ridge, thence looking back on the lake, peninsula, and island. Descending on the eastern side of the ridge, the prospect shows the two great branches of the Arachthus, or river of Arta; that on the west coming from the hills of Zagóri; that on the east from the mountains of Métzovo. Above, the vast forms of the Pindus range tower amid snow and forests of pine; woods in dense array clothe the hillsides and below the river winds in many a serpentine detour.

Passing a khan, not twenty minutes in descending from the ridge of Dhrysko, we continue the downward route to a second khan—near a bridge which crosses the Zagóri branch of the river. Here we made the midday halt; there is ever something pleasing in these moments of repose, if the weather permit them to be enjoyed out of doors; you have the rustling plane tree shading the galleried khan, around whose steps a host of little kids are sleeping, nightingales singing on all sides, purple-winged dragon flies gleaming in the sun, and unseen shepherds pouring forth a pleasing melody from rustic pipes; all these are matters of interest, though the actual scenery around me has rather a cumbrous air with undefined forms of hugeness not very adaptable to paper.

Half an hour after noon we again set off, and crossing the bridge begin the ascent of the Métzovo branch of the Arta. Disliking the continual necessity of fording the rapid stream, I essay to follow the road, which is carried along the right bank of the stream; but soon finding it entirely broken down by torrents, we are obliged to retreat and descend to the bed of the river.

To those who are pleased with the operation of river fording I strongly recommend the ascent of the Métzovo mountain, as ensuring a greater portion of amusement in that line than any other equal space of ground. No fewer than forty-seven times had we to cross and recross the tiresome torrent ere we reached our evening's destination.

I had hoped to lodge at Triakhánia, where there are, as the name implies, three khans; but we found on arriving there, as late as 4 P.M., that none were inhabited, and owing to last year's inundations one was carried away and the other two left roofless and dilapidated.

Meanwhile the scenery was becoming more alpine and tremendous in character as we advanced into the darker gorges of the ravine, and the picturesqueness of the pass was much enhanced (though my chances of getting a night's lodging were proportionably diminished), by the passage of a regiment of Turkish cavalry with led horses. As the route occasionally leads at a considerable height from the river, while crossing from one ford to another, the long lines of soldiers dashing through the stream added great life to the picture.

Disappointed of our resting-place at Triakhánia, there was now no alternative but to pass on to Métzovo, and after much tedious splashing through the roaring stream, we passed the military detachment and hastened onwards, hoping to secure some part of a khan before they arrived. After much labour and hurry over roads which skirt the edge of precipices overhanging the torrent, we reached Anílio, the southern half of Métzovo—a large town divided into two portions by the ravine, and presenting no very picturesque appearance. Here we arrived at half past seven o'clock, after a harder day's work than I had contemplated.

Guards were stationed at the public khans, to prevent any one taking rooms in them; so we had gained nothing by our haste. Andréa, however, soon procured a lodging in one of the houses of the village—a great contrast to those of the ordinary Greek peasants, being, although very small, perfectly neat and clean.

Métzovo is inhabited by Vlákhi or Vlákhiotes—a people of Wallachian descent, already spoken of in these journals as occupying portions of Albania. In general their employment is that of shepherds, and as such they move about with their flocks from district to district. But in certain parts of the mountains settled colonies of them exist, who possess large flocks of sheep and goats, and are distinguished for their industrious and quiet habits of life. Many of the men emigrate as labourers, artizans, etc., to Germany, Hungary, Russia, etc., and return only in the summer to their families. They retain their language. Their costume is ordinarily that of the Greek peasantry—a dark blue capote—with the head frequently bound by a handkerchief turban-wise above the fez or cap.

MAY 15

There is much that is interesting and pleasant in this elevated town. The houses stand mostly detached among gardens, rocks, beech and ilex trees, and a thousand pictures of pastoral mountain life might be chosen, though the general scenery is of too large a character for the pencil. The people also seem simple and sociable in manners: while I am drawing many of them bring me bunches of narcissus and cowslips and endeavour to converse. All have a robust and healthful appearance, very different to the people of the plains.

At half past six I begin to ascend towards the highest ridge of the Métzovo pass, called the Zygós, a formidable journey when there is any high wind or snow. At present the weather is calm, and the magnificent groups of pine at the summits of the ridge are undisguised by even a single cloud. Few mountain passes are finer in character than this part of the Pindus range. Towards the very highest point the rock, bald and rugged, is so steep that the zigzag track cannot be overcome but upon foot; and the immense space of mountain scenery which the eye rests on in looking westward is most imposing. Parent of the most remarkable rivers of Greece, and commanding the communication between Epirus and Thessaly, the Zygós of Métzovo is equally renowned for classical associations, for geographical and political position and picturesqueness.

But in this latter quality it is for the wondrous and extensive view over the plains of Thessaly that it is most celebrated—a scene I was not fated to be indulged with; for no sooner had I surmounted the last crag of the ridge, in enthusiastic expectation of the outstretched map of which I had so often heard, than lo! all was mist. Nor, till I had for some time descended through the beautiful beech-forests which cover the eastern side of the Zygós, and which are carefully preserved as a shelter from the winds which would at some seasons otherwise prevent the passage of the mountain, did the clouds disperse; but even then only so partially as to show but little of the vast Thessalian distance.

Passing a khan—the Zygós khan—shortly below the summit, we descended through woods into the more open country to a second, and in two hours and a half from the Zygós reached the third khan, that of Malakássi, on the Salympria.

At the khan of Malakássi we rested till nearly 1 P.M., when we pursued the route by the banks of the Salympria, or Peneus, often crossing and recrossing it, according as the track was more eligible on one or the other side. The scenery, confined at first and unmarked by any peculiar character, became more beautiful as we advanced farther from the mountains, whose thickly wooded slopes began to assume the blue tints of distance. Luxuriant planes grow in the greatest abundance by the riverside; and the route often wound for half an hour through fresh meadows and the richest groves, resounding with the warbling of nightingales and overshadowing rivulets which flow into the stream. We met numerous files of laden horses, journeying from Thessaly to Albania; but picturesque as they often were, there was a civilised sort of commonplace appearance about them, which to an artist's eye is infinitely less pictorial than the bearing of the wild hordes of Albania. We passed also more than one khan by the road, and usually at these places the Albanian guards asked us questions and insisted on seeing passports which they had not the slightest idea of reading. As a proof of this, on my taking out by mistake the card of a hotel-keeper at Athens, the Palíkar snatched at it hastily, and after gravely scrutinising it, gave it back to me, saying, 'Good; you may pass on!' At the next guardhouse I confess to having amused myself by showing a bill of Mrs. Dunsford's Hotel, at Malta, and at another the back of an English letter, each of which documents were received as a Teskeré. So much for the use of the Dervení guards, placed by the Turkish Government to take accurate cognisance of all passers-by.

As the day wore on and the river opened out into a wider valley the eastern horizon suddenly exhibited a strange form in the distance, which at once I felt to be one of the rocks of the Metéora. This object combines with a thousand beautiful pictures, united with the white-trunked plane trees and the rolling Peneus, ere, escaping from the woods, the route reaches the wider plain; and the inconceivably extraordinary rocks of Kalabáka, and the Metéora convents, are fully unfolded to the eye.

'Twelve sheets', says Mr. Cockerell, in a letter, Feb. 9, 1814, 'would not contain all the wonders of Metéora, nor convey to you an idea of the surprise and pleasure which I felt in beholding these curious monasteries, planted like the nest of eagles, on the summits of high and pointed rocks.' We arrived at Kastráki, a village nestled immediately below these gigantic crags, at sunset. I do not think I ever saw any scene so startling and incredible; such vast sheer perpendicular pyramids, standing out of the earth, with the tiny houses of the village clustering at the roots.

With difficulty—for it is the time when silk-worms are being bred in the houses, and the inhabitants will not allow them to be disturbed— Andréa procured a lodging for me in the upper part of a dwelling, formed as are most in the village, like a tower, the entrance to which, for the sake of defence, was by a hole three feet high. Here, after having gazed in utter astonishment at the wild scenery as long as the light lasted, I took up my abode for the night. The inhabitants of this place, as well as of Kalabáka (or Stagús),[1] are Christians, and every nook of the village was swarming with pigs and little children. 'Πολλα πιδλια,' said an old man to me, as the little creatures thronged about me, ' δια τον νερόν χαλόν.' What a contrast is there between the precipices, from five to six hundred feet high, and these atoms of life playing at their base! Strange, unearthly-looking rocks are these, full of gigantic chasms and round holes, resembling Gruyère cheese, as it were, highly magnified, their surface being otherwise perfectly smooth. Behind the village of Kastráki, the groups of rock are more crowded, and darkened with vegetation; and at this late hour a sombre mystery makes them seem like the work of some genii, or enchanter of Arabian romance. Before the dwellings, a slope covered with mulberry trees descends to the

[1] Anciently Aeginium.

river, and grand scenes of Thessalian plain and hill fill up the southern and eastern horizon.

MAY 16

I went very early with a villager to visit and sketch the monasteries. Truly they are a most wonderful spectacle; and are infinitely more picturesque than I had expected them to be. The magnificent foreground of fine oak and detached fragments of rock struck me as one of the peculiar features of the scene. The detached and massive pillars of stone, crowned with the retreats of the monks, rise perpendicularly from the sea of foliage, which at this early hour, 6 A.M., is wrapped in the deepest shade, while the bright eastern light strikes the upper part of the magic heights with brilliant force and breadth. To make any real use of the most exquisite landscape abounding throughout this marvellous spot, an artist should stay here for a month: there are both the simplest and most classic poetries of scenery at their foot looking towards the plain and mountain; and when I mounted the cliffs on a level with the summit of the great rocks of Metéora and Baarlám, the solitary and quiet tone of these most wonderful haunts appeared to me inexpressibly delightful. Silvery white goats were peeping from the edge of the rocks into the deep, black abyss below; the simple forms of the rocks rise high in air, crowned with church and convent, while the eye reaches the plains of Thessaly to the far-away hills of Agrafa. No pen or pencil can do justice to the scenery of Metéora. I did not go up to any of the monasteries. Suffering from a severe fall in the autumn of last year, I had no desire to run the risk of increasing the weakness of my right arm, the use of which I was only now beginning to regain, so the interior of these monkish habitations I left unvisited; regretting that I did so the less, as every moment of the short time I lingered among these scenes, was too little to carry away even imperfect representations of their marvels.

I had been more than half inclined to turn back after having seen the Metéora convents, but the improvement in the weather, the inducement of beholding Olympus and Tempe, and the dread of so soon re-encountering the gloomy Pass of Métzovo, prevailed to lead me forward.

Accordingly, at 9 A.M. I set off eastward once more along the valley of the Peneus, which beyond Kastráki widens rapidly into a broad plain, enlivened by cattle and sheep, and an infinite number of stocks. As we approached Tríkkala, the pastoral quiet beauty of the wide expanse increased greatly, and the view close to the town is delightful. Standing on a rising ground, the Castle of Tríkkala, with magnificent plane trees at its foot, makes a beautiful foreground to a distance, the chief ornaments of which are the chain of Othrys and distant Oeta. The scenes of life and activity, the fountain with groups of Thessalian women at its side, the little mosque with its cypresses, offer a most welcome change to me after the sullen ravines of the Pindus, and the close-wooded valley of the Upper Salympria.

We halted at midday in a café of Tríkkala, the keeper of which was a man of Trieste, who talked of '*quella Londra, e quel Parigi*' with the air of a man of travel. But the sort of mongrel appearance of every person and thing in the town are not pleasing to the eye of an artist who has been wandering much among real costume and Eastern characteristic. Blue-tailed coats worn over white Albanian fustianelles, white fleecy capotes above trousers and boots, are doubtless innocent absurdities, but they are ugly.

At half past three we again proceeded. The town of Tríkkala is large,[1] but greatly neglected, and partly in ruins; nevertheless, the bazaars seem extensive and bustling.

The plains grew wider and wider. We pass a few villages, each more widely apart from its neighbour than the preceding, and by degrees I feel that I am really in Thessaly, for width and breadth now constitute the soul and essence of all the landscape. To the north only the distant form of Olympus rears itself above a low range of hills; and to the south the hills of Agrafa and Oeta are gradually becoming less distinct. Before me all is vast, outstretched plain, which never seems to end. Agriculture and liveliness are its predominant characteristics. It is full of incident; innumerable sheep, goats, horses, buffali, and cattle, corn or pasture land, peasants' huts, hundreds of perambulating storks, give a life and variety everywhere. And then so green, so intensely green, is this immense level! and the peasant women, in their gay, fringed and tasselled capotes—how far handsomer than any Greeks I have seen!

[1] Tríkkala, ancient Tricca.

METÉORA

TÉMPE

At sunset we halt at a village (Nomí); there are plenty of villages as halting-places on all sides, but I have had enough work for today.

The Primate's house, which we go to, is newly whitewashed, and very damp, so Andréa persuades a Mohammedan agent for the Turkish proprietor of the village, Seid Efféndi, to let me have a room in his house. And a delightful house it is—the room on the upper floor is lined throughout with new wood, and adjoining a gallery, which looks over all the wide, wide plain.

With curried mutton, roast fowl, and fish from the Peneus, Andréa makes an excellent dinner. He tells me that Seid Efféndi possesses seven thousand sheep, which are kept by the shepherds of these villages, who receive the tenth lamb with the tenth of the wool of the flock as their pay.

These Thessalian plains are alive with dogs, who bark all through the night.

May 17

A lovely scene! as the sun rises over the immense extent of verdure, which soon becomes animated with rural bustle. It will be difficult at a future period to recall, even to memory, the indescribable clearness and precision of this Greek landscape, far more to place it on paper or canvas. We start early and trot quickly over green roads which cross the wide level from village to village. There are buffali ploughing; and there are strange wagons, with spokeless wheels of solid wood, drawn by oxen; and great caravans of horses carrying merchandise from Salonica to the mountains—the lading tied in sacks of striped cloth. With some there are whole families migrating, children, puppies, and fowls, mingled in large panniers. The men wear black capotes, the women white, and dress their long plaited hair outside a white hand-kerchief. There are great grey cranes, too, the first I ever saw enjoying the liberty of nature. These birds seem made for the vast plains of Thessaly: how they walk about proudly by pairs, and disdain the storks, who go in great companies! Now and then there is a vulture, but there is too much society for them generally. As for jackdaws and magpies, they congregate in clouds and hover and settle by myriads.

We come to the Peneus once more—now a great river. Giant,

white-stemmed abeles, in Claude-like groups, are reflected in its stream; herons are peering and watching on its banks; and immense flocks of brown sheep are resting in the shade of the trees.

Between nine and ten we stop for a little while at the khan below Zárcho, and after that we enter a wide valley, through which the Peneus runs; the sides of the vale are low undulations, which shut out all the distant plain. At twelve we came again to the riverside, and passing it by a ferry, halt for food and repose below large plane trees. Bee-eaters[1] with their whistling pipe flutter in numbers around the upper branches.

At 2 p.m. we are off again; the delightful character of the Thessalian plains is changed. The ground is no longer a perfect flat, but composed of undulations of such great size, that no part of even the mountain boundaries of the plain—Olympus, Ossa, Oeta, or Pindus—can be well seen; and sometimes for half an hour the traveller dips into an overgrown cornfield, beyond the limits of which he sees and knows nothing. I confess I was most heartily weary as I came in sight of the minarets of Lárissa; and although the view of all Olympus is unobstructed at its entrance to the town, from which there is a view of the river sweeping finely below it, yet it is clear that the extremely simple lines of this part of Thessaly are ill adapted for making a picture, and least of all can anything like expression of the chief character of the country, i.e. its vast level extent, be given.

The heat is great, and I have, moreover, a feeling of returning fever, so that I do not observe the environs of Lárissa so much or so carefully as I might, but entering the city, go at once to the house of Hassán Bey, the richest proprietor in Lárissa (to whom the Hon. Captain Colborne has given me a letter); and although the Bey himself is from home, his family gave orders for my being placed in a good room, where I pass the night.

MAY 18

The morning is occupied in a visit to the Governor of the Pashalík, Samí Pashá, an agreeable man, who has lived at Cairo, London, and all

---

[1] Merops Apiaster.

kinds of civilised places. He is a Greek by birth; but speaks French and Italian well.

There is a heaviness in the atmosphere here, which either producing, or combined with, a constant fear of fever fits, prevents my making the least exertion in sketching any one of the beautiful things around me. Yet to be so near Tempe and not to go there! Nay, whatever happen, I will see Tempe.

At noon I dine with two of Hassán Bey's sons, his eldest by one wife; various other sons come into the fine room in which dinner is served, but retire before the meal begins. Hassán Bey has seven wives and eleven wivelets, or concubines, and consequently is a sad polygamist; nurses and children are continually to be seen in every part of the residence; but they all appear to dwell in harmony. It is provoking to know that from a high lattice on one side of the courtyard all the eighteen pair of eyes can perfectly look at us while at dinner and yet that I can perceive none of them. The conversation of our party is not very current, as neither I nor my young hosts are very proficient in Romaic. After dinner, I amuse them by drawing camels, etc., till Andrea informs me that it is time to start for Tempe.

Promising to return to Hassán Bey's family, a well-bred and good-natured circle, I set off with Andréa, two horses and a knapsack, and a steeple-hatted Dervísh, at whose convent in Babá, at the entrance to the Pass of Tempe, my night's abode is to be.

They call the Dervísh Dédé Efféndi, and he is the head of a small hospitable establishment, founded by the family of Hassán Bey, who allows a considerable sum of money for the relief of poor persons passing along the ravine. The Dervísh is obliged to lodge and feed, during one night, as many as may apply to him for such assistance. There are many interesting views about Lárissa; but not feeling sufficiently fever-proof, I dared not halt to sketch. During two hours we crossed the level plains; and as the sun was lowering, arrived at pleasant green lanes and park scenery, below the mighty Olympus. By six we arrived at Babá, which stands at the very gate, as it were, of Tempe, and is certainly one of the loveliest little places I ever beheld. The broad Peneus flows immediately below the village, and is half hidden by the branches of beautiful abeles and plane trees, which dip their branches in the stream. A small mosque, with its minaret, amid spiry cypresses, is the Dervísh's abode; and on the opposite side of the river are high rocks and the richest foliage, rejoicing in all the green freshness of spring. In the summer-time, when this exquisite nook still preserves its delightful verdure, the hidden passage from the wide parched plains of Thessaly must doubtless be charming beyond expression.

The little square room in the Teké, or house of the Dervísh, was perfectly clean and neat, and while I ate my supper on the sofas surrounding it the well-behaved Dédé Efféndi sat smoking in an opposite corner; his son, the smallest possible Dervísh, five or six years old, dressed like his father in all points excepting his beard, squatted by his side. For the Dervísh is a married man, and his wife, he assures me, has made one or two dishes for my particular taste and is regarding me at this moment through a lattice at the top of the wall.

Towards nine many poor passengers call for lodging and are stowed away in a covered yard by the mosque, each being supplied with a ration of bread and soup.

MAY 19

The early morning at Babá is more delightful than can be told. All around is a deep shadow, and the murmuring of doves, the whistling of bee-eaters and the hum of bees fills this tranquil place.

The village of Ambeláki is situated on the side of Mount Ossa, and thither, having heard much of its beauty and interest, I went early, before pursuing the road by the Peneus, through the gorge of Tempe. I cannot say I was so much delighted with the expedition as I expected to be, but this was mainly because heavy clouds shut out all the upper portions of Olympus, partly also from not having felt well enough to seek for the best or most picturesque points. But judging from what ought to be seen if the great mountain of the Gods had been clear, and relying on the descriptions and taste of perfectly good judges, I believe Ambeláki would well repay a long visit. On returning to the route to Tempe I met a young man dressed in the usual Thessalian garb, and on my hailing him in Greek, I was surprised to find my salutation returned in good French. At the fall of the commercial community of Ambeláki, the father of Monsieur Hippolyte, one of the richest merchants of the place, fled to France, settled and married there: this was his son, who, returning to his native place, had for some years resided on the paternal property. 'Sometimes I live here,' said he, 'sometimes in Paris; but I come here principally for hunting.' Town and country—Paris and Tempe—certainly are two points of Europe in which one might easily find pleasure and occupation.

Leaving Monsieur Hippolyte, I went onward into Tempe, and soon entered this most celebrated 'vale'—of all places in Greece that which I had most desired to see. But it is not a 'vale', it is a narrow pass— and although extremely beautiful, on account of the precipitous rocks on each side, the Peneus flowing deep in the midst, between the richest overhanging plane woods, still its character is distinctly that of a ravine or gorge.

In some parts the Pass (which is five or six miles from end to end) is so narrow as merely to admit the road and the river; in others the rocks recede from the stream, and there is a little space of green meadow. The cliffs themselves are very lofty, and beautifully hung with creepers and other foliage; but from having formed a false imagination as to the character of 'Tempe's native vale', I confess to having been a little disappointed. Nevertheless, there is infinite beauty and magnificence in its scenery, and fine compositions might be made, had an artist time to wander among the great plane trees on the border of the stream: a luxuriant wooded character is that which principally distinguishes it in a pictorial scene from other passes where there may be equally fine precipices bounding a glen as narrow. Well might the ancients extol this grand defile, where the landscape is so completely different from that of any part of Thessaly, and awakes the most vivid feelings of awe and delight, from its associations with the legendary history and religious rites of Greece.

As it was my intention to pursue the route towards Platamóna as far as time would allow, and to return to Babá at evening, I left the gorge of Tempe and crossed the Peneus in a ferry-boat opposite a khan at the eastern extremity of the Pass. Hence, the scenery was precisely that of the finest English park—rich meadows and noble clumps of trees at intervals. In two hours we reached a guard-house called Kará Alí Dervení—and from a rising ground above it I halted to make a drawing

213

of the view, which is one of great beauty. The waters of the Peneus meandered sparkling in many a winding curve, through delightful meadows and woods, to the sea; beyond was the low isthmus of Pallene, and above it the lonely Athos, whose pyramid I gazed on a second time, without much hope of reaching it.

Towards Ossa and Olympus also the scenery would, doubtless, have been fine, but thick clouds provokingly hid them throughout the day.

In some meadows near a little stream flowing into the Peneus were several camels, which are frequently used about Salonica and Katerína, etc. They were very ragged and hideous creatures, and offered a great contrast to the trim and well-kept animals of our Arabs, which we had so familiarly known in our journey through the desert of Suez and Sinai. But as I returned towards Tempe I perceived a young one among the herd, and I rode a little way towards it spite of the clamorous entreaties of the Yannina muleteer. I had better have attended to his remonstrances, for the little animal (who resembled nothing so much as a large white muff upon stilts), chose to rush towards us with the most cheerful and innocent intentions, and skipping and jumping after the fashion of delighted kids, thrust himself into the way of our three horses with the most facetious perverseness. One and all took fright, and the muleteer's reared, threw him and escaped. There was much difficulty in recapturing the terrified animal, and when we had done so forth came the little muffy white beast once more, pursuing us with the most profuse antics over the plain and rendering our steeds perfectly unmanageable. To add to our discomfiture, the whole herd of camels, disapproving of the distance to which we were inveigling their young relation, began to follow us with an increasingly quick trot; and we were too glad to ford the stream as quickly as possible and leave our gaunt pursuers and their foolish offspring on the opposite side.

It was evening when, having recrossed the Peneus, I arrived at the Dervísh's house in Babá, and the little owls were piping on every side in that sweet valley.[1] Mr. Urquhart says that when he was at

---

[1] The Strix Passerina (or Scops?) which abounds in these groves, as in the olive woods of Girgenti in Sicily, and southern localities in general: its plaintive piping, so different to the screech or hoot of the larger owls, is a pleasant characteristic of the evening hours.

Tempe the Dervísh roosted in one of the cypress trees; but I cannot say that the respectable Dédé Efféndi indulged in such a bird-like system of repose. He, the female, and the miniature Dervísh, all abide in a little house attached to the mosque, and the good order and cleanliness of his whole establishment very much disarranged all my previously formed ideas of Dervíshes in his favour.

MAY 20

On my return to Larissa there is but just time to make one drawing of dark Olympus ere a frightful thunderstorm, with deluges of rain, breaks over the plain and pursues me to the city. It continues to pour all the afternoon, and I amuse myself, as best I can, in Hassán Bey's house. It is a large mansion, in the best Turkish style, and betokening the riches of its master. It occupies three sides of a walled courtyard, and one of its wings is allotted to the harem, who live concealed by a veil of close lattice work when at home, though I see them pass to and fro dressed in the usual disguise worn out of doors. I watch two storks employed in building on the roof of that part of the building. These birds are immensely numerous in Thessaly, and there is a nest on nearly every house in Lárissa. No one disturbs them; and they are considered so peculiarly in favour with the Prophet that the vulgar believe the conversion of a Christian as being certain to follow their choice of his roof for their dwelling; formerly a Christian so honoured was forced to turn Mussulman or quit his dwelling—so at least they told me in Yannina, where two pair have selected the Vice-Consul's house for their abode. It is very amusing to watch them when at work, as they take infinite pains in the construction of what after all seems a very ill-built nest. I have seen them, after twisting and bending a long bit of grass or root for an hour in all directions, throw it away altogether. That will not do after all, they say; and then flying away they return with a second piece of material, in the choice of which they are very particular; and, according to my informants at Yannina, only make use of one sort of root. When they have arranged the twig or grass in a satisfactory manner they put up their heads on their shoulders and clatter in a mysterious manner with a sound like dice shaken in a box. This clattering at early morning or evening, in this season of the year, is one certain characteristic that these towns are under Turkish government, inasmuch as the storks have all abandoned Greece (modern), for the Greeks shoot and molest them; only they still frequent Lárissa, and the plain of the Spercheius, as being so near the frontier of Turkey that they can easily escape thither if necessary. This is foolishness in the Greeks, for the stork is most useful in devouring insects, especially the larva of the locust, which I observed in myriads on the plains near the entrance of Tempe; and I counted as many as seventy storks in one society, eating them as fast as possible, and with great dignity of carriage.

That part of the roof of the harem which is not occupied by storks is covered with pigeons and jackdaws, a humane attention paid to the lower orders of creation being always one of the most striking traits of Turkish character.

The storm continues all night. The air of Lárissa is heavy and close, and so much threatens fever, that I resort to quinine in no little quantities.

MAY 21

It is fine, but with that instinctive feeling that certain air in this country infallibly brings on return of fever, I decide on leaving the capital of Thessaly without making even one sketch to recall it to memory; and I do this with great regret, for there must be many of the most beautiful and characteristic Thessalian scenes to be found in its level environs and on the banks of its broad river.

Starting about seven, we held a southward course; the plain was one unvaried green undulation. Lárissa, and even Olympus, except now and then its highest peaks, are soon lost to sight, from the comparatively uneven nature of the ground; and it is only from some eminence where a village is planted (of which there were two or three in the day's ride) that anything like a satisfactory drawing can be made.

Yet the very simplicity, the extreme exaggeration of the character of a plain, is not without its fascination; and the vast lines of Thessaly have a wild and dream-like charm of poetry about them, of which it is impossible for pen or pencil to give a fully adequate idea.

After passing some elevated ground, from which the view of the range of Mount Oeta is most magnificently fine, we halted at midday at one of these villages—the name I neglected to take (Hadjobáshi?)—and hence the charm of Mount Oeta and the hills of Pharsalus or Férsala make one of the most beautiful of landscapes, combined with the mosque and its cemetery, and the profusion of animal life usual in these Thessalian hamlets.

Having crossed the stream Férsalitis (the Enipeus), it was past 5 P.M. ere we arrived at Férsala, which is full of picturesqueness. The scattered town on the side of the rocky height and the splendid plane-tree groups delighted me extremely. I was glad to have visited a spot so famous in history as well as interesting from its beautiful situation—one, not the least, of its claims to admiration being the full view of the broad Olympus opposite. The view from the Acropolis, its ancient walls, the ruins, and the fountains below the town, with its kiosk below the white-branched planes, whose fluttering foliage shelters numerous storks and their nests, all combine to render Férsala a place worthy of a longer stay than I could make in it.

MAY 22

With a feeling of attraction towards new scenes, and with a faint hope that I might yet, if there were a fair wind, sail from Volo to Athos, I started early from Pharsalus. There was much interest, if not great beauty, in the morning's ride, and the route passed near several ancient sites.[1] But it was not until the afternoon that, crossing the low range of hills near the gulf of Volo, we came in sight of its blue waters, and looked down on the plain of Armyró, with the chain of Othrys beyond, and the Magnesian promontory to the east. Visions of Athos still float before me, and I decide on going to Volo instead of Armyró; for although it had an appearance of great prettiness, embedded as it is in green groves of wood, yet I must have devoted a whole day to it had I

[1] Thetidium, Eretria Phthiotis, Phylace?

gone thither at all, the hour being already far advanced: so, having halted for a while, I turned northward.

Many were the incidents which filled up the rest of the day: first, we lost our way among cultivated rice-grounds; and secondly, in a deep quagmire—a more serious matter, which took up much time to remedy. At length, by the sounding blue waves, we went onward towards the head of the gulf, keeping in view some white houses to the left where we trusted to find a night's lodging; but alas! when we arrived at them they were nothing but ruined, uninhabited walls. At sunset, having retraced our steps, we were climbing the lentisk-covered cliffs at the farthest head of the gulf, and many parts of it brought back scenes and pleasant journeys in Attica and Eubæa. But as it grew dark, and we were descending towards Volo, Andréa's horse fell and precipitated him from a rock some four or five feet in height. It was long before the muleteer and myself could lift the unlucky Dragoman on to his horse once more; and the great pain he was suffering obliged us to go at a very slow pace over the causeway of rough pavement which leads to the town. There we arrived at ten at night; and it was midnight before we could procure lodging within the cellar of a house—in which nevertheless it was necessary to be contented till morning.

May 23

Alas! the woes of Thessaly! It is again pouring with rain, and the wind is set in southerly, so that once and for altogether I give up all idea of sailing to Athos.

The horses are ordered, and as soon as Andréa can get about I start at length to return to Yannina.

As I ride away Volo, its gulf and the scattered villages on the hills of Magnesia seem truly beautiful; but to what purpose should I linger? Tomorrow, and tomorrow, may be equally wet. Mount Athos! Mount Athos! All my toil has been in vain, and I shall now most possibly never see you more!

All day long I rode on in hard rain, and at sunset we stopped at one of the many villages in this great green plain. No one would look at the Bouyourldí, although poor old Andréa ran about with the open document in his hand, exclaiming 'το ϵλϵπϵτϵ—look at it!' with the most dramatic emphasis. But no one would look at it. One said he was blind, another declared he had illness in his family, and all retreated into their houses from fear or obstinate resolve to have nothing to do with strangers; and if an old woman had not charitably given me a lodging, in a shed full of calves, I might have been drowned in the torrents which fell. Eventually, however, we procured a cottage floor.

May 24

The woes of Thessaly continued: once more by deep mire and incessant cornfields, through pastures full of cranes, jackdaws, and storks, and always in hard rain as before. We kept on the right bank of the Peneus, as far as the bridge near the khan of Vlokhó, and in the evening found shelter once more in the house of Seid Efféndi, at Nomí.

Towards sunset it cleared a little, and as I arrived at the night's halting-place all the village was alive with the gaieties of a wedding. Like the dance L—— and I had seen at Aráchova, the women joined hand-in-hand, measuredly footing it in a large semicircle, to a minor cadence played on two pipes: their dresses were most beautiful. Half the women wore black capotes bordered with red, their hair plaited, long crimson sashes, worked stockings and red shoes: these were the unmarried girls. The other half—matrons or betrothed—wore dazzling white capotes, worked at the collar and sleeves with scarlet, the skirts bordered with a regular pattern of beautiful effect, and the red fez nearly covered with silver coins, which hung in festoons on their necks and half-way down the crimson sash tails.

Besides this the belt, six or eight inches broad, was covered with coins, and fastened by two embossed silver plates, four inches in diameter, and gave a beautiful finish to the dress; the aprons, too, were magnificently worked. Of this lively company, most were pleasing in countenance, but few could be called beautiful. The bride, one of the prettiest of the party, came round to everyone present and kissed their hand, placing it afterwards on her head, a favour she extended to me also as one among the spectators. Fatigued and wet through, I regretted not being able to avail myself of the opportunity of drawing this pretty village festive scene.

MAY 25

The woes of Thessaly continued. In the middle of the night, the roof of Seid Efféndi's house being slight, a restless stork put one of his legs through the crevice and could not extricate it; whereon ensued much kicking and screams, and at the summons came half the storks in Thessaly, and all night long the uproar was portentous. Four very wet jackdaws also came down the chimney and hopped over me and about the room till dawn. It rained as hard as ever as we went over the plains to Tríkkala, and infinitely worse between that place and Kalabáka, so that the spectral Metéora rocks looked dim and ghastly in their gigantic mistiness. With difficulty we crossed the Peneus beyond Kastráki, and at sunset reached one of the small khans in the wood by the roadside which must be my abode till morning. This unceasing deluge is, however, a very serious affair, as should the Métzovo River be too much swollen to ford, I may be a prisoner in the Pass for an indefinite time.

MAY 26

The woes of Thessaly prolonged! Until a little after sunrise (when it began to pour again) how grand were the Metéora rocks rising above the thick dark foliage on the banks of the Salympria!

For hours we threaded the narrowing valley of the river, which at each ford grew more violent and rapid; above the next two khans parts of the road were very dangerous, and near Malakássi the streams running into the Salympria—mere rivulets on our journey hither—were now such foaming torrents that my little white pony could hardly accomplish the passage.

At noon we reached Malakássi, yet the peasants declare that it has been quite dry on the Métzovo side of the mountain. Starting at one, we made the ascent to the Zygós khan by half past four, and thence to Métzovo, finding it to be true that less rain had fallen there. (The summit of the mountain was in thick mist, as when I came, so I never saw that Thessalian view.) We passed the town, anxious to be as far advanced within the gorge as possible in case of bad weather tomorrow; and halted for the night at sunset at the little khan about a mile above Triakhánia.

MAY 27

No more Thessaly—we are in Epirus once more. We hasten down the river, now disagreeably wide and reaching in places from bank to bank; at length we reach the Lady's Khan and, ascending Mount Dhrysko, halt. Then bursts the rolling thunder and the buckets of heaven are emptied. Floods pour down from Métzovo and Zagóri, and the river will be very shortly impassable; it is therefore lucky I have crossed it. So I reach Kastrítza and the causeway by the lake and the Casa Damaschinó once more before five, most heartily delighted to have quitted Thessaly, however much I regret the little I have drawn there. But May is the wet season of Albania and an artist should avoid it.

MAY 29

Resting throughout yesterday (when, as is universally the case, rain fell after ten throughout the day), I prepare to leave Yannina this morning and take leave of the hospitable Damaschinó. Zítza, Kastrítza, Zagóri, Dhramisíus, and many other drawings I lose—so short is my time—so uncertain the weather. Addio, Yannina! which I gaze on for the last time from the height above the lake, its bright city backed by black clouds of thunder.

Soon the storm burst, but we halted ere long at Vérchista, and in the afternoon proceeded to the night's resting-place—Ravení, a village in a beautifully wooded hill district.

MAY 30

Wonderfully rich and beautiful landscapes are there between Ravení and Philátes! Perhaps some of the most lovely I have seen in Albania, both as to the form and clothing and arrangement of the hills and the disposition of the foregrounds. After descending a narrow ravine, we arrived at Philátes about twelve, a place abounding in exquisite beauty, and placed near that very remarkably formed rock which from Corfú is so effective a feature in the scene.

Much I regretted not to draw Philátes from the descent to the plain by the sea-shore, for, indeed, there are some of the very finest scenes in all Albania or its environs.

At the Scala of Sayádes I arrived at six and, hiring a boat for Corfú, was deposited safely in quarantine by noon on the 31st.

JUNE 9

I was out of quarantine on the 5th and have passed some pleasant days in the town since, though not so much so as formerly. 'All things have suffered change.' Lord Seaton's family and many others I knew are gone.

Good old Andréa Vríndisi I have paid and sent off to Patrás; and today I am on board the Malta steamer *Antelope* and am sailing through the Ionian Channel for the ninth time. Off Párga: there are the mosques, silvery-white; there, high up beyond the plain, is the dark hill of Sulí. There is the fatal hill of Zálongo—the point of Préveza.

At sunset Sappho's leap—Leucadia's rock of woe. The mountains of Tchamouriá fade away and I look my last on Albania.

At midnight the moon rises over dark Ithaca, and lights up the Bay of Samos, where we stay half an hour.

Sunrise.—Patrás once more and the pearly-tinted Mount Voidhiá. Noon.—Gay Zante, bright and bustling as ever.

And so, with the last point of Zákynthus and the dim, distant mountain of Cephalonia, ends my journey in the lands of Greece.

Edward Lear in Southern Italy

EDWARD LEAR IN SOUTHERN ITALY

Journals of a Landscape Painter in
Southern Calabria and the
Kingdom of Naples

Introduction by

PETER QUENNELL

WILLIAM KIMBER
46 WILTON PLACE, LONDON, S.W.1

First published in 1964 by

WILLIAM KIMBER & CO. LIMITED

46 Wilton Place, London, S.W.1

© William Kimber & Co. Limited 1964

LITHOGRAPH PLATES BY MACKAYS OF CHATHAM

MADE AND PRINTED IN GREAT BRITAIN BY PURNELL AND SONS, LTD.
PAULTON (SOMERSET) AND LONDON

Introduction

by

Peter Quennell

Edward Lear

1812–1888

A modern writer has described the great artist as a 'self-cured neurotic', as a man, that is to say, who through the practice of his art has found, if not a permanent remedy for his spiritual ills, at least a means of controlling and disarming them by translating his secret obsessions into vivid and harmonious imagery. Edward Lear was certainly a minor artist; but he had an exquisite individual gift; and his life, too, exemplifies an artist's struggle to solve problems and surmount inherited difficulties that might otherwise have overwhelmed him. Few gifted men have had to confront such grievous disadvantages. Not only was he short-sighted and plain, with a large oddly-shaped nose and a bulky, awkward body, but he suffered from chronic bronchitis and asthma, and from epileptic attacks—probably *le petit mal*—that often recurred three or four times a week and had darkened his existence since he was seven years old. He called his disease 'the Terrible Demon', once remarking that his persistent affliction 'would have prevented happiness under any sort of circumstances', and that it was 'a most merciful blessing that I have kept up as I have, and not gone utterly to the bad mad sad'. His attacks were followed by long spells of deep melancholy and excruciating irritability. The background of his childhood was equally unpropitious. His stern father, a London

5

stockbroker, went bankrupt and entered a debtors' prison when Edward Lear was thirteen; and, about 1827, at the age of fifteen, having discovered that he could produce saleable sketches, the boy began to draw 'for bread and cheese. . . .'

Out of these unpromising materials the artist shaped his own *persona*—an artistic second self that both protected his sensitiveness and focused his creative talents. Even his ugliness ceased to hamper him—it became a mask that won him friends—as he developed into the Mr. Lear whom it was 'pleasant to know', the bearded sage whose thick-lensed spectacles suited him so well that they seemed an essential adjunct of his face. '*Comme il est charmant*', cried an appreciative little girl, '*ce Monsieur avec ses beaux yeux de verre!*' Though seldom at his ease with adults he did not know, Edward Lear was much loved by, and always felt at home with, children; and it was the affection he felt for companionable children that encouraged him to explore his vein of wild poetic fantasy. Hence originated the famous *Nonsense Books*, which have had a far wider and more lasting appeal than his distinguished topographical series or learned zoological volumes. In his comic verses and fantastic drawings the personality behind the mask emerges under a succession of strange disguises. Lear was a highly sociable, but at heart a very lonely, character. Now and then he had passing thoughts of marriage; but 'he had an ingrained conviction (we are told) that he was too ugly for any woman to accept him'; and the transitory impulse soon subsided. He was deterred, moreover, by the fact that he was short of money, and the victim of an incurable and humiliating disease. Throughout his poems the theme of loneliness persists—in the solitary wanderings of the Dong, the self-conscious perplexities of the Pobble, the disillusionment and romantic flight of the love-lorn Yonghy-Bonghy-Bò. Among the fabulous beings he imagined and depicted, 'the Owl and the Pussey-cat', who actually celebrate their nuptials, form a rare and interesting exception. For the most part, they sail away into the sunset towards a melancholy, mysterious future.

Besides these literary images, Lear has left us many self-portraits—graphic sketches of a massive ungainly gentleman, with huge spectacles, a protuberant stomach and spindle-shanked, tight-trousered legs, sometimes accompanied by his devoted cat Foss, a stripy, bob-tailed patriarch who lived to be almost seventeen. It is thus that we usually picture the artist—as an amiable eccentric who would have been perfectly at home amid the legendary monsters he had created. In fact, he was also an extraordinarily practical person, who for over half a century earned his living as an industrious commercial draughtsman. His first book, *Illustrations of the Family of Psittacidae*, a splendid folio with over forty lithographed plates, which had been commissioned by the Royal Zoological Society, appeared in 1832; and the delicate exactitude of Lear's drawings of parrots secured him an important patron, the 13th Earl of Derby, a keen amateur zoologist, who invited the young man to Knowsley Hall, where he soon became a favoured guest. During his lifetime, Lear worked for Lord Derby's son, his grandson and his great-grandson. The whole family learned to admire him, both the grown-up Stanleys and their numerous children; and it was for the benefit of the nursery at Knowsley that he launched his series of comic limericks and began the original *Book of Nonsense*, published in 1846.

At the same time, Lear was travelling extensively and gaining renown as a topographical artist. *Views of Rome and its Environs* came out in 1841, to be followed by two series of *Illustrated Excursions in Italy*, the *Journal of a Landscape Painter in Greece and Albania*, the *Journal of a Landscape Painter in Southern Calabria*, *Views in the Seven Ionian Islands* and, finally, the *Journal of a Landscape Painter in Corsica*, produced in the year 1870. At their best, Lear's landscape paintings and the wash and pen-and-ink drawings, with which he fixed his impressions of a place, have a peculiar romantic charm. They fascinated Tennyson, who dedicated a lyrical tribute to '*T. E. L. on his travels in Greece*' that contains some memorably evocative lines:

> And trust me while I turn'd the page,
> And track'd you still on classic ground,
> I grew in gladness till I found
> My spirits in the golden age.
>
> For me the torrent ever pour'd
> And glisten'd here and there alone
> The broad-limb'd Gods at random thrown
> By fountain-urns;—and Naiads oar'd
>
> A glimmering shoulder under gloom
> Of cavern pillars; on the swell
> The silver lily heaved and fell;
> And many a slope was rich in bloom
>
> From him that on the mountain lea
> By dancing rivulets fed his flocks
> To him who sat upon the rocks
> And fluted to the morning sea.

Although Lear, being especially disturbed by noise, often railed at the miseries of foreign travel—he could scarcely believe, he wrote, that the entire population of Naples was not 'stark mad . . . they yell and shout in a manner quite superhuman'—he found that his long journeys up and down Europe provided the relief that his restless spirit needed. A 'totally unbroken application to poetical-topographical painting', he had decided, was a 'universal panacea for the ills of life'; and he pursued his chosen calling with prodigious energy. In 1865 alone he executed no less than four hundred and eighty outdoor sketches. Later, during a six-months' tour of India, he made five hundred and sixty drawings, filled nine sketch-books and completed four journals.

Introduction

Lear wrote as fluently as he drew; and the present volume is a
fine specimen of his literary-topographical method. Calabria was
then—indeed, it is still—one of Europe's strangest corners. No
doubt its melancholy appealed to Lear, the decrepitude of its
ancient cities, the desolation of its spacious prospects. Lear had
the painter's trained eye—the special delicacy and acuteness of
vision that we also detect in Constable's note-books, Benjamin
Robert Haydon's diaries and Fromentin's accounts of his North-
African adventures. Lear uses his pen as if it were a pencil or a
brush, whether he writes of the 'dry, burning, white stones' of a
river-bed, where great black swine wallow in the 'dull pools',
but the arid landscape is occasionally enlivened 'by the glittering
flight of a bright kingfisher', or of the 'interminable olive-woods
—high, grey, filmy, feathery olives' with their 'twisted mossy
trunks'. He is often poetic; but he is always delightfully exact,
at a time when artistic exactitude was more highly valued than it
is today. The draughtsman who enchanted Tennyson was no less
appreciated by Queen Victoria; and in 1846, following the
appearance of *Illustrated Excursions in Italy*, he was summoned to
Osborne where he gave his sovereign drawing-lessons and,
despite his habit of occupying the hearthrug, which court-
etiquette reserved for the Queen, made a generally good impression. Afterwards, if she admired a landscape, the Queen
would say that it 'put me so much in mind of Mr. Lear's drawings'.

But then, Lear has always had devotees; and, during the years
that elapsed between the First and Second World Wars, Tennyson
and Ruskin (who applauded the nonsense verses) were joined
by the poets and painters of the revolutionary Surrealist Movement. André Breton and his disciples have claimed the author
of the Nonsense Books as 'one of themselves'; and more recently
a learned American writer has translated 'the Owl and the
Pussey-cat' into delightful French verse. What would have been
Lear's response to some of his more unorthodox admirers? He

9

was no revolutionary himself, no spiritual iconoclast, and, though he criticised organized religion, clung to the idea of a Supreme Being. In many respects, he remained a product of his social period—a period that exalted the conventional virtues, yet tolerated, even favoured, the most surprising forms of individual eccentricity. Edward Lear was a true eccentric; for at an early age it had been revealed to him that he was not as other men, and that his only hope of personal salvation was to go his own way. His work, like the work of every artist, is the record of a continuous hard-fought struggle to find his proper place on earth. In his efforts to make some sense of the world—a world that, since his childhood, had buffeted him continually and hurt him cruelly— he invoked the aid of so-called nonsense.

Preface

To the present Volume of Journals but little preface is requisite: they were written during tours made in the autumn of 1847, throughout the southern of the three Calabrian Provinces and in that of Basilicata.

Few places visited by the author have not already been fully described in the accurate and interesting travels of the Hon. Keppel Craven.[1] Mr. Swinburne has written a notice[2] of many places in Calabria, though his observations are principally confined to the coast; and the western road by the sea has been well and amusingly treated of in a little book called *A Tour in Calabria*, by Arthur Strutt.[3] The older notices[4] of the province are so confused or so cumbrous, as to be little read or known.

While some villages in this, the most southerly portion of the beautiful kingdom of Naples, have, however, hitherto remained unexplored by Englishmen, and others, till now unillustrated by views, are for the first time made known to the public,—the general aim of the writer to make his journal a Landscape-painter's Guide-Book will stand as an apology for his having sometimes described ground already better treated of in the above-mentioned works.

The mode of travel which I and my fellow-wanderer adopted while these journals were written, was the simplest, as well as

[1] *A Tour through the Southern Provinces of the Kingdom of Naples*, by the Hon. R. Keppel Craven. 1821.

[2] *Travels in the Two Sicilies*, by Henry Swinburne, Esq. 1785.

[3] *A Pedestrian Tour in Calabria and Sicily*, by Arthur J. Strutt. 1842.

[4] Alberti (Fra Leandro), *Descrit. di tutta l'Italia*. Venetia: 1596.

P. Marafioti (Girolamo), *Antichità di Calabrià*. Padova: 1601.

Giustiniani, *Dizionario del Regno di Napoli*. 1797.

cheapest—we performed the whole tour on foot; except that in Basilicata some of the high roads were well got over in a carriage. In Calabria, a horse to carry our small amount of baggage, and a guide, cost us, altogether, six carlini daily[1]—no very heavy expenditure; but as there are no inns in that province except on the coach-road, which skirts the western coast, the traveller depends entirely on introductions to some family in each town he visits.

The tour in the more northern provinces was undertaken under somewhat different circumstances. The long journeys on the high road, or over the plains near the east coast of Italy, do not offer sufficient inducement to pedestrian exercise. In no country, perhaps, can greater contrasts be found, than between the far-stretched campagna of Apulia or the dreary ridges of part of Basilicata, and the fertile gardens, the wondrous coast scenes, or the purple gorges of the heart of Calabrian mountains.

Wishing to confine these journals strictly to the consideration of landscape, I have said as little as possible of events which occurred in 1848, and their sequel. Yet it is but right to add, that some provincial families, whose suspicions and apparent want of hospitality marked them in our eyes as unlike their compatriots, were but too well justified in keeping themselves aloof from any strangers, whose motives for visiting this country were but little understood, and whose presence might possibly have compromised them in the event of disturbances which, they may have been aware, were on the eve of occurring.

LONDON,
September 15, 1852.

---

[1] Little more than two shillings (about 10s. now).

PUBLISHER'S NOTE

The maps on pages 14 and 15 were drawn and lithographed by Edward Lear, and are reproduced as they appeared in the original edition. No attempt has been made to modernise the spelling of the place-names, since these contemporary spellings have been left in the text. It is not thought that this will present any difficulty, as the modern styles have changed very little.

The title page of the original edition reads: *Journals of a Landscape Painter in Southern Calabria*, etc. Between Chapters XV and XVI there was a second title page reading: *Journals of a Landscape Painter in the Kingdom of Naples*. This occurs at the point where Lear broke off his journey, and travelled by ship to Naples, where he resumed his travels. Lear and his companion, John Proby, had already noticed signs of unrest among the population of Calabria. When he reached Reggio, in the early days of September 1847, he met the first signs of open rebellion, the Risorgimento, which was to start in earnest early the next year, 1848. He thought it prudent to leave the remoter regions of Calabria, and he and Proby left Messina by steamer on September 5th.

Calabria was at this time part of the kingdom of Naples, as the maps indicate. The King of Naples was himself to be overthrown in the revolution.

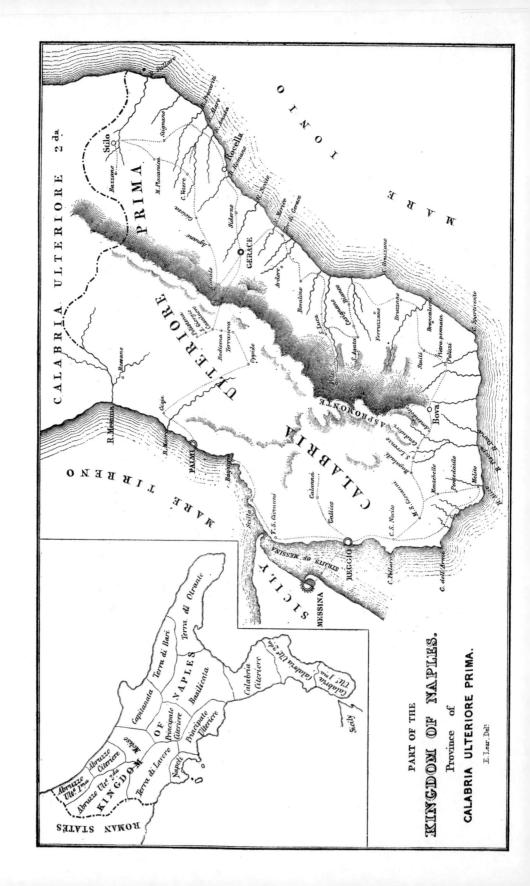

PART OF THE

KINGDOM OF NAPLES.

Province of

CALABRIA ULTERIORE PRIMA.

E. Lear. Del.ᵗ

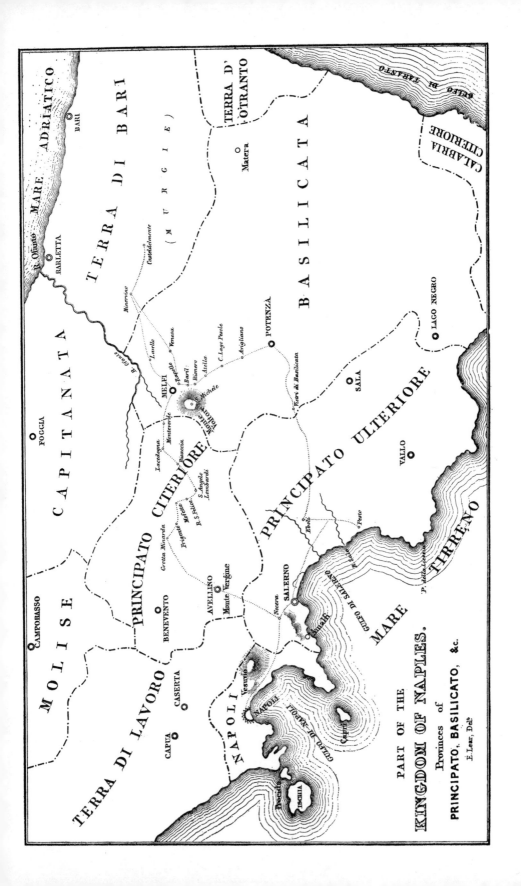

MARE ADRIATICO

GULFO DI TARANTO

TERRA D' O'TRANTO

CALABRIA CITERIORE

TERRA DI BARI

(M U R G I E)

BARI

R. Ofanto

BARLETTA

Matera

BASILICATA

CAPITANATA

Castelmonte

Monteroni

FOGGIA

Lavello

Venosa

C. Lago Paolo

Avigliano

POTENZA

LAGO NEGRO

Melfi

Barili

Atella

MELFI

Monteverde

Fiori di Basilicata

SALA

Monte Voltore S. Michele

PRINCIPATO ULTERIORE

VALLO

Lacedogna

Bisaccia

S. Angelo Lombardi

Frigento

Matese

R. S. Rise.

Gretta Minarda

Elvi

Peto

MOLISE

PRINCIPATO CITERIORE

P. della Licosa

TIRRENO

CAMPOBASSO

PRINCIPATO

BENEVENTO

AVELLINO

Monte Vergine

Nocera

SALERNO

GOLFO DI SALERNO

MARE

CASERTA

NAPOLI

Cava

CAPUA

Vesuvio

NAPOLI

GOLFO DI NAPOLI

TERRA DI LAVORO

Procida

ISCHIA

CAPRI

PART OF THE

KINGDOM OF NAPLES.

Provinces of

PRINCIPATO, BASILICATO, &c.

E. Lear, Delt.

Contents

Contents

Contents

Contents

Contents

Contents

Edward Lear's
Lithograph Drawings

MAPS

CALABRIA

Note to the Original Edition

Calabria is situated at the most southern extremity of the Kingdom of Naples. Its division into three provinces (the sub-divisions and population of which will be found below) is of very recent date. From the thirteenth down to the end of the last century the second and third provinces were included in a single one under the name of "Calabria Citeriore" was known as "Provincia Val di Cratis et Terre Jordane."

Provinces	Population in 1828	Principal Town	Districts (or Sott' Intendenze)
Calabria Citeriore (Northern Calabria, or Province of Cosenza)	406,359	Cosenza	Cosenza Castrovillari Paola Rossano
Seconda Calabria Ulteriore (Central Calabria, or Province of Catanzaro) . .	298,239	Catanzaro	Catanzaro Monteleone Nicastro Cotrone
Prima Calabria Ulteriore (Southern Calabria, or Province of Reggio) . .	260,633	Reggio	Reggio Palmi Gerace

PART I

*Journals of a Landscape Painter
in Calabria*

CHAPTER I

Anticipations of Calabrian journeying.—Arrival at Reggio;
Police, Dogana, &c.—The 'Giordano' inn.—Chances of
obtaining goat's milk.—Beautiful situation of Reggio.—Its
gardens.—The Bergamot orange.—The Villetta Musitano.—
Friendliness of the Reggiani.—Consigliere da Nava, &c.—
Introductory letters.—Plans for visiting the interior.—Search
for a guide.—Ciccio the silent.—'Díghi, dóghi, dághi, dà;
dógo.'—Absence of pointed hats.—Departure from Reggio.
—Road to Motta San Giovanni.—Don F. Marópoti's house.
—Conversazione of neighbours.—Opinions about England.—
Hospitable reception.

July 25, 1847.—The very name of Calabria has in it no little
romance. No other province of the kingdom of Naples holds
out such promise of interest, or so inspires us before we have set
foot within it,—for what do we care for Molise, or Principato?
or what visions are conjured up by the names of Terra di Lavoro,
or Capitanata? But—Calabria!——No sooner is the word
uttered than a new world arises before the mind's eye,—torrents,
fastnesses, all the prodigality of mountain scenery,—caves,
brigands, and pointed hats,—Mrs. Radcliffe and Salvator Rosa,—
costumes and character,—horrors and magnificence without
end. Even Messina derives its chief charm from the blue range
of mountains and the scattered villages on the opposite shore,
—Reggio glittering on the water's edge,—Scylla on its rock,
where the guide-books (by a metaphor) say you may hear
(large?) dogs barking across the straits,—the lofty cloud-topped
Aspromonte, and the pearl-pale cliffs of Bagnara. Yet this land of
pictorial and poetical interest has had but few explorers; fewer

29

still have published their experiences; and its scenery, excepting
that on the high road, or near it, has rarely been portrayed, at
least by our own countrymen.

In the afternoon, having hired a boat to cross the straits, P——
and I were ready to start from Messina. Leaving a portion of our
luggage there we took enough for a month or six weeks' journey
through the nearest province, or Calabria Ulteriore Prima; and,
well supplied with letters to those persons in its chief city who
would send us on our way through the interior, we set sail for
Reggio, and soon the lemon-coloured forts of Zancle were far
behind us on the deep blue sea. By degrees the furrowed hills
around Messina spread out into one long chain, the heights of
distant Taormina and cloud-capped Etna closing the scene. Yet,
near as Reggio appeared, we did not reach it until the sun had
set, an hour when the broad walk, in front of the uniform
façade of houses built along the Marina since the last earthquake,
was full of evening promenaders. There was a 'Sanità' and a
'Dogana' to encounter, of course; but having an introductory
letter to the Direttore, whose address we casually asked for in a
judiciously elevated tone of voice, no one molested us either as
to our state of health or property: we went off accordingly,
preceded by porters, to the Locanda Giordano, situated in the
high street of Reggio, which runs parallel to the coast, and
contains some very decent rooms, the largest of which we seized
on as our own for the sum of four carlini[1] daily. Having ordered
some supper, we forthwith proceeded to report ourselves to the
Polizia, the manager of which dwelt in an unsatisfactory house at
the other end of the town, and had perched himself at the top of a
totally dark and crooked staircase, the ascent of which was
disputed step by step by an animated poodle. After this we went
to deliver the Duke of ——'s letter to the Direttore, an old

---

[1] A carlino, twelve of which compose the Neapolitan dollar, is worth four-
pence farthing English money [about 1s. 10d. now]. There are ten grani in a
carlino, or Sicilian tornesi, a copper coin frequently used in Southern Calabria.

French gentleman who was playing at whist, double dummy. 'What could he do for us?—we had but to command.' We begged for letters to Bova and other out of the way places in the toe of Italy, all of which he readily promised. Another letter of introduction we delivered to Consigliere da Nava, who proved a great ally.

July 26.—If you wish for milk at breakfast-time in these parts of the world, you ought to sit in the middle of the road with a jug at early dawn, for unless you seize the critical moment of the goats passing through the town, you may wish in vain. If you have any excursion to make, and require to start early, you may as well give up the idea, for the 'Crapi' are 'not yet come;' and if you delay but a little while, you hear the tinkle of their bells, and perceive the last tails of the receding flock in vexatious perspective at the end of the street.

At sunrise I set out on an exploring expedition, and was soon dodging here and there to find the best views of Reggio among its endless cactus and aloe lanes, fig gardens, and orange groves. Reggio is indeed one vast garden, and doubtless one of the loveliest spots to be seen on earth. A half-ruined castle, beautiful in colour and picturesque in form, overlooks all the long city, the wide straits, and snow-topped Mongibello[1] beyond. Below the castle walls[2] are spread wide groves of orange, lemon, citron, bergamot, and all kinds of such fruit as are called by the Italians 'Agrumi;'[3] their thick verdure stretched from hill to shore as

[1] Mongibello, the Saracenic name of Mount Etna, is generally in use among the Sicilians and Calabresi.

[2] In an old picture of Reggio, in Pacichelli, the whole town is represented as walled.

[3] The Bergamot orange, from the peel of which the well-known perfume is extracted, is cultivated to a great extent round Reggio, and the fruit forms a considerable article of commerce. There are several notices on this subject in Swinburne's Travels.

'The spirit is extracted by paring off the rind of the fruit with a broad knife,

far as the eye can reach on either side, and only divided by the broad white lines of occasional torrent courses. All the fulness of Sicilian vegetation awaits you in your foreground; almond, olive, cactus, palm tree,[1] aloe, and fig, forming delightful combinations wherever you turn your steps.

In the afternoon we went to the Villetta, a country-house about a mile distant from the town, with a letter of introduction to its proprietor, the Cavaliere Musitano, who resides there during summer. If one were a neighbour it would be difficult not to covet that garden-home—at once the most agreeable as to its situation, and the most superior to all others in the district as to the quality, quantity, and arrangements of its botanical contents. Strange fruits are hanging on every side (though none of them particularly eatable); one magnificent palm raises its airy tuft above all the green level of shrubs; a broad vine-covered trellis shadows the court in front of the villa where, in rows of little cages, many exotic birds were rejoicing under the surveillance of a large red and blue macaw; in a word, the Villa Musitano, one of the great lions of the province, is full of agreeable materials, and the friendliness of its possessor was not among the least of the pleasant impressions left on our minds by the visit.

At Ave-Maria we returned to the city to make calls with other letters of introduction, and otherwise to prepare for our excursion into the interior of the province.

---

pressing the peel between wooden pincers against a sponge; and as soon as the sponge is saturated, the volatile liquor is squeezed into a phial and sold at fifteen carlini the ounce. . . . There is a small sort of citron set apart for the Jews of Leghorn, who come here every year to buy them for three tornesi a-piece. As they are destined for some religious ceremony, the buyers take great care not to pollute them by a touch of the naked hand.'—*Swinburne's Travels in the Two Sicilies*, p. 360.

[1] Mr. Swinburne states that in the days of Saracenic dominion at Reggio 'stately groves of palm-trees' adorned the territory, but that many were cut down when the Reggiani repossessed their town, as being memorials of infidel usurpation.

REGGIO

BOVA

July 27.—Assiduous drawing passed away the morning rapidly. Owing to the obstructions of cactus or aloe hedges, walls, &c., it is no easy matter to get a good general view of Reggio; one of the best I could obtain was from the loggia of a poor man's house, who obligingly allowed me to sit in the open doorway, although his wife was still in bed, and so close to my elbow that my drawing was accompanied by her illustrative remarks. At two we dined with the Musitano family, who kindly wrote several introductory letters for our tour. Our friend Consigliere da Nava was indefatigable in our interest, and had on our return to the town already prepared fifteen notes to the principal proprietors in towns we should pass through. Then, after the usual ices, indispensable at sunset, Don Gaetano Grisi (Cav. Musitano's nephew) took no little pains to procure us such a guide and mule as we wanted,—not always an easy task. There is this objection to taking one individual into your service for the whole of a long tour, viz., that he may not be acquainted with the remoter parts of the country to be visited; yet, on the other hand, there is this advantage, that if he be tractable he soon gets into the way of knowing your habits and plans, and thereby saves much of the trouble which a change of guide or muleteer at every fresh halting-place must necessarily occasion.

July 28.—Occupied in finishing drawings already commenced, and in procuring more letters, &c. There is one of the most beautiful views of Reggio from the north end of the 'Marine Parade'; looking towards Etna, the straits of Messina appear like a lake shut in by the giant volcano, at its southern extremity. A stroll to the Musitano Villa; a visit to Signor Capelli, who gave us introductions to the convent of Sta Maria di Polsi, situated amongst the most picturesque scenes of Southern Calabria: these, with fresh attempts at *combinazione* with a Vetturino, left little of the evening undisposed of. A man must be guided pretty much by hazard in arranging a tour through a country so little visited as this: the general rule of keeping near the mountains is perhaps the best, and if you hear of a town, or costume, or piece of antiquity anywise remarkable, to make a dash at it as inclination may devise, sometimes to be repaid for the trouble,—as often the contrary.

July 29.—We could get no guide until noon, an arrangement not ill-fitting with our plan of sleeping the first night at Motta San Giovanni, on our way to Bova: so at two we prepared to start. We had engaged a muleteer for an indefinite time: the expense for both guide and quadruped being six carlini daily; and if we sent him back from any point of our journey it was agreed that his charges should be defrayed until he reached Reggio. Our man, a grave tall fellow of more than fifty years of age, and with a good expression of countenance, was called Ciccio,[1] and we explained to him that our plan was to do always just as we pleased—going straight a-head or stopping to sketch, without reference to any law but our own pleasure; to all which he replied by a short sentence ending with—'Dógo; díghi, dóghi, dághi, dà'—a collection of sounds of frequent recurrence in Calabrese lingo, and the only definite portion of that speech we could ever perfectly master. What the 'Dógo' was we never knew, though it was an object of our keenest search throughout the tour to ascertain if it were animal, mineral, or vegetable. Afterwards, by constant habit, we arranged a sort of conversational communication with friend Ciccio, but we never got on well unless we said 'Dógo si,' or 'Dógo no' several times as an *ad libitum* appoggiatura, winding up with 'Díghi, dóghi, dághi, dà,' which seemed to set all right. Ciccio carried a gun, but alas! wore no pointed hat; nothing but a Sicilian long blue cap. Our minds had received a fearful shock by the conviction forced on them during our three days' stay at Reggio, namely, that there are NO pointed

[1] 'Ciccio' is short for 'Francesco,' in the Neapolitan kingdom States. In the Roman States it is 'Cecco.'

hats in the first or southern province of Calabria. The costume, though varying a little in different villages, is mainly the same as that throughout Sicily, and it is only in the provinces of Catan-záro and Cosenza where the real (and awful) pyramidal brigand's hat is adopted. Ciccio tied four packets (one of vestments, &c., another of drawing materials for each man), plaids, umbrellas, &c., on a quiet-looking steed, touching whose qualities its owner was wholly silent, thereby giving me, who go by contraries in these lands, great hope that it might be worth a good deal, for had it been a total failure one might have looked for a long tirade of praises: and so, all being adjusted—off we set.

The road led over the torrent-bed and by the Villa Musitano, through suburban villages for two or three miles, and for a considerable distance we passed numerous odoriferous silk factories,[1] and many detached cheerful-looking houses, with lofty pergolate[2] or vine trellises spanning and shading the whole public road from side to side. Beyond, the broad dusty highway was uninteresting in its foregrounds, but the blue straits of Messina were ever on our right, with Etna beyond, while on the left a wall of hills, with Castel San Nocito and San Vito perched on their summits, sufficed for men who were all alive for impressions of Calabrese novelty. Always in sight also was the town of Motta San Giovanni, our night's resting-place, but so high up as to promise a stout pull to reach it.

When in fullest sight of Mongibello, we turned from the coast and began to ascend the hills. For a while the path lay on the northern side, and at every turn we looked over a wider expanse of the beautiful garden-plain of Reggio, broken by the lines of its white torrents, and backed by the straits and hills of Messina; but afterwards we wound up a path closely shut in betwixt high

[1] The cultivation of silkworms is carried on to a great extent in Calabria, especially in the territory of Reggio.

[2] Pergola, or Pergolata, is the general name for any balcony or trellis covered with vine.

37

sandy banks, or placed on the edge of clay ravines looking over slopes thickly planted with dwarf vines. High winds prevented our making any drawing, and indeed it was nearly Ave-Maria[1] when we had risen above the weary sandy gorges immediately below the town, which stands at a great elevation, and overlooks earth and sea extensively. With little difficulty we found the house of Don Francesco Marópoti, who received us with hospitality, and without show of ceremony, only apologising that, owing to his being alone in this his country residence, our reception could not be in point of fare and lodging all he could wish. Indeed this worthy person's establishment was not of the most recherché kind, but I had warned my companion (hitherto untravelled in these regions) that he would probably meet with much simplicity, much cordiality, and heaps more of dirt throughout Calabria. There is always in these provincial towns a knot of neighbours who meet in the house of the great man of each little place, to discuss the occurrences of the day for an hour or two before supper; already a long perspective of such hours oppressed me, loaded with questions about Inghilterra and our own plans and circumstances. 'Cosa c'e da vedere in Bagaládi?'[2] said our host's coterie with one voice, when they heard we wanted to go there,—and one elder was fiercely incredulous, proposing that, if, as we said, we were in search of the beautiful or remarkable, we should set out directly for Montebello or Mélito, or any place but Bagaládi. He also explained the position and attributes of England to the rest of the society, assuring them that we had no fruit of any sort, and that all our bread came from Egypt and India: and as for our race, with a broad contempt for minute distinctions, he said we were 'tutti Francesi,' an assertion we faintly objected to, but were over-

---

[1] Ave-Maria is half an hour after the sun sets at all times of the year, when it is then dark in Italy, and the computation of hours, 1, 2, 3, &c., recommences.

[2] What should there be to see in Bagaládi?

ruled by—'in somma—siete sempre una razza di Francesi è lo stesso.'[1]

At last the clique departed, and we sate down with Don Francesco to supper, an unostentatious meal, accompanied by tolerable wine, but with a rural style about the service, &c., more resembling that in the remoter villages of the Abruzzi than of the towns near any of the provincial capitals of the northern Neapolitan provinces. There was, however, no want of good will or good breeding, and we were neither bored by questions nor pressed to eat, nor requested to sit up late; so we soon retired, and, on perceiving very clean beds, were not slow in congratulating ourselves on the prosperous commencement of our Calabrian tour.

[1] In a word, you are a sort of Frenchman; it's all the same.

CHAPTER II

Landscape round Motta San Giovanni.—Second day's tour.—
The 'toe' of Italy.—Extensive prospects.—Lofty mountains.
—First view of Bova.—Fiumaras, or dry torrent-beds.—
Peasants of the district; their complaints of the devastation of
the rivers.—Reach Bagaládi.—Speculation as to our hosts
there.—Don Pepino Panutti and his agreeable wife: their
cordiality.—We remain at Bagaládi and postpone Condufóri
till to-morrow.—Striking scenes in the valley.—Village of San
Lorenzo.—Cheerful comfort of our host's house.—Travels of
his wife, and the cause thereof.—Repose of night scene.

July 30.—How like a vast opal was Etna as the sun rose and
lighted up the immense prospect from our southern window!
But alas! a world of cloud rose also, and soon threatened rain.

P—— and I had a discussion as to what plan we should
pursue touching domestics in this our 'giro,'[1] and we agreed
that it would be right to offer something: but although we had
a good opportunity while our host was inditing an introductory
letter to a relative at Bagaládi, our proffered coin was decidedly
though respectfully refused.

After coffee Don Francesco lionised us over the little town,
the older part of which is half deserted and crowned by a
ruined chapel commanding a world of distant view; the lower
half of Motta San Giovanni is composed of detached houses,
forming very picturesque groups, which combine beautifully
with the severe and decided forms of the hills around; already I
begin to perceive that Calabrian scenery has a character peculiar
to itself. By six we were ready to start, our friendly host begging

[1] Tour.

us to wait on account of the inevitable rain, but we were proof against fears and entreaties.

The outskirts of Motta are beautiful, and there are many scraps of Poussinesque landscape which I would fain have lingered to draw, but a drizzling rain, augmenting rapidly, forbade delay; so we followed Díghi Dóghi Dà along lanes and paths, over the slope of bare hills, and up a long ravine, till the weather cleared and we arrived at an elevated plateau, whence the whole 'Toe of Italy' is finely discernible, a sea of undulating lines of varied forms down to the Mediterranean; a few towns glittered here and there, and towering over the most southern extremity of land, a high cluster of rocks, the wild crags of Pentedátilo, particularly arrested our attention. Before us, eastward, is the lofty chain of mountains, on the last or southernmost peak of which Bova, whither we were bound, is visible: but when we asked whether we should reach that town to-day, the silent Ciccio turned up his chin and shook his head with an air of decided negative which rendered language wholly unnecessary. The sun came out as we descended a steep mountain path towards a white fiumara or dry torrent-course, along which we toiled and broiled patiently for an hour or two. Lonely places of devastation are these fiumaras: blinding in their white or sandy brilliancy, barring all view from without their high cliff-sides, and recalling by the bare tract of ground right and left of their course how dismal and terrible the rage of their wintry watery occupant has once been throughout its destroying career. Bagaládi was yet far distant, and we were glad to meet in a garden of pear-trees some chance labourers, who gave us as much fruit as we wished. Bitterly they complained of their abodes—'We do not know what we are to reap; sow we never so much, the torrent swells and carries away all our work.' Even with the bright blue sky above, I confess to a heart-heavy feeling among these stern scenes, where nature appears independent of man, and where any attempt on his part to set up his staff permanently seems but allowed for a season, that his defeat may be the more completely observable after years of laborious cultivation.

One more ridge yet remained betwixt us and the valley of Bagaládi, and from its crown we beheld an opposite range of loftier and more thickly wooded heights, with the aerial Bova above, still, as it were, in the very clouds: then, descending to the level of another torrent, we arrived by lanes among pear-gardens at the village, which stands in two scattered portions on either side of the broad fiumara: that had, indeed, destroyed a great part of this lonely little spot of inhabited earth in the preceding autumn.

It is always a great amusement to us to speculate on the reception we are likely to meet with from our unknown hosts on arriving at any new place, and on who or what they may prove to be. In the present case, as the family Panutti had dined (it was 2 p.m.) and were all in bed, it was some time before we gained admission to a small cottage annexed to a large house in process of building; but, notwithstanding our unseasonable arrival, Don Peppino Panutti (a good hearty fellow, capourbano[1] of the district), and a very pretty little woman, his wife, received us in the most friendly manner imaginable, and soon refreshed us with a substantial meal of maccaroni, &c., good wine, and sparkling snow. Much did these good people press us to stay all night. Condufóri, the next village, was yet several hours distant; nor could we be sure of meeting with so clean a dwelling and such agreeable hosts; so we agreed to remain, and make the cloud-capped Bova our next day's journey; besides, we had footed it for more than seven hours under a hot sun and had need of rest, which we were glad to obtain after dinner.

On waking from our siesta, the sun was already low, but I rushed out to get at least one recollection of this curious Calabrian home, and though surrounded by wondering gazers, I contrived to do so before it actually grew dark. It is a wild scene; the

[1] Head of the rural or district police, established in the Neapolitan provinces.

shattered houses still hang ruinously over the shivered clay sides of the mighty torrent-track, a broad sweeping line of white stone, far, far winding through the valley below; above rise the high hills we have to cross to-morrow, half in golden light, half in purplest shadow; and among the topmost furrows and chasms sparkles the little village of San Lorenzo—atom signs of human life made more striking by their contrast with the solitude around. We returned to our humble but very clean home, and sate us down at a little table to pen out some of our sketches as comfortably as if we had lived at Bagaládi for the last five years. The evening closed with a very agreeable supper, when, in addition to our host's pretty young wife, his eldest daughter by a former helpmate made one of the party. The very superior manner of our hostess and of her household arrangements surprised us less when we found she was a Livornese by birth, and moreover had seen Malta, Constantinople, and various other parts of the world, having gone for awhile to join her father in some remote place, whither he had fled from Livorno on account of what Donna Giacinta Panutti quietly called 'Una piccola disgrazia, cioè, un' omicidio.'[1]

At night the moon was full; the wide valley was all still, save for the twitter of its myriad hosts of grasshoppers;—a solitary region, but beautifully majestic.

---

[1] A little accident; that is to say, he killed someone.

CHAPTER III

Leave Bagaládi, and set out for Condufóri.—Fatiguing hills.—
Bova once more—a long way off yet.—Woodland scenery.
—Tracts of beautiful landscape.—Cicadas.—Descent to
another fiumara.—Arrive at Condufóri.—Greek language
spoken.—House of Don Giuseppe Tropæano—repulse there-
from.—Alarm of the hostess.—Our retreat to an osteria.—
Forlorn Calabrian accommodations.—'Turchi' spectators.—
Unprepossessing Cyclopean girl.—Pursue our way.—Intense
amusement of the silent Ciccio.—Ascent to Amendolía.—
Magnificent prospect.—Laborious ascent.—Good-natured
peasants.—Bova is reached at last.—House of Don Antonio
Marzano.—Another hospitable reception.

July 31.—By sunrise, the little Livornese lady had given us our
coffee, with some orgeat and abundance of little confetti.[1]
Ciccio, who, as far as we have yet gone, seems the prince of
faultless guides and attendants, was in complete readiness, and
Don Peppino Panutti accompanied us down the fiumara on our
way. Short as had been our visit, we regretted leaving these
friendly people. A long pull up winding paths led to the hill
below San Lorenzo, and our last night's quarters looked like a
cluster of dominoes far below. From the summit, once more the
blue distant Bova soared aloft in apparently unreachable dignity;
yet we could now discern a sort of castle, and peaks of rock, and
fringes of forest. Between us and it were beautiful tracts of
woodland, groups of fine trees, tumblings of earth, and not a
few of those painful fiumaras through which we knew full well
we were doomed to toil ere we commenced our ascent to the

[1] Sugar-plums or sweetmeats.

44

Greek town; for Bova is said to be the last remnant of Magna
Græcia, still, with four adjoining villages, preserving the language
and some of the habits of its ancestral colonisers.

The morning's walk was most delicious: at every step its
scenery became grander, in vast mountainous extent of distance,
and close oak-filled vales. All my hopes of Calabrian scenery
are fulfilled. Stopping here and there to make an outline of what
most struck us (though these are landscapes not to be hastily
drawn), we arrived about ten on a sunny height, where, beneath
a spreading oak, we halted to draw a glorious seaward view,
where rock and ravine, wood and vale and water, were so
mingled as to form one of the finest of scenes. The whole
atmosphere seemed alive with cicadæ,[1] who buzzed and fizzed,
and shivered and shuddered, and ground knives on every branch
above and around. At eleven we began to descend towards
Condufóri, by paths which even the alert and accomplished
horse of Ciccio found very unsatisfactory;—beautiful are those

---

[1] The cicada (C. Plebœia), or cicala, is the most noisy of insects, and during
the heat of the day, throughout the months of July and August, the clamour
made by the infinite numbers of this small creature in Southern Italy is most
remarkable. I cannot remember ever to have heard them sing (so to speak)
before sunrise or after sunset; but as soon as the first ray of morning warmed the
tops of the olives in the glens at Tivoli, or the red rocks of Amalfi, earth and
air resounded with the lively insect armies. At the latter place the children often
catch them, and tie them by twos and threes to their ears, when the effect
produced must strongly resemble a scissor-grinder's wheels in full action on
each side of the head. While at Reggio it did not occur to us to test the truth
of the report, that, on that portion of the west side of Calabria, cicale never
make any noise, which they are said not to do by ancient authors as well as
moderns; and various causes have been assigned for the different behaviour of
these unmelodious songsters on the Reggian and Locrian territories. Marapóti
notices a popular version of the subject, that St. Paul, while preaching in
Rhegium, was so disturbed by these perverse creatures, who would not let the
congregation hear his sermon, that he anathematised all that generation of
Rhegian cicale; and their descendants have been mute ever since. 'But this,'
says the judicious Marapóti, 'I cannot believe to be true, because the cicale only
appear in June, and St. Paul was at Rhegium in the month of March.'

wild oak woods!—and at last we lost sight of the eternal Bova, and were once more threading a fiumara like a furnace between white cliffs, speculating on our reception at Condufóri, and devoutly hoping our next host might not have dinner ere we arrived. On our asking Ciccio as to the properties and characteristics of the village and its habitants, we could get nothing from him but 'Son Turchi,'[1] except that we construed into a negative testimonial his volunteering the information 'that we had done well to sleep last night at Bagaládi,—díghi, dóghi, dà.' So we thought too; for our walk of this morning would have been too much to have added to that of yesterday, not to speak of the loss of such scenery after dusk.

Condufóri, a little village, wedged in a nook between two hills, the torrent at its feet, and the mountain mass of high Apennine threateningly above it, was at length reached, and the house of Don Giuseppe Tropæano discovered. Alas! the master was away at the Marina,[2] or Scala, and our appearance threw his old sister into such a state of alarm, that we speedily perceived all hope of lodging and dinner was at an end. We stood humbly on the steps of the old lady's house, and entreated her only to read the letter we had brought—but not she! she would have nothing to say to us. 'Sono femmina,' 'Sono femmina,' she constantly declared—a fact we had never ventured to doubt, in spite of her immoderate size and ugliness—'Sono femmina, e non so niente.'[3] No persuasions could soften her, so we were actually forced to turn away in hunger and disgust. As for Ciccio, he merely took his short pipe from his lips, and said, 'Son Turchi —dóghi, dà.'

[1] They are Turks.

[2] All or most of the hill towns on the coast of Southern Italy have a sort of port, or quay, or haven on the shore, where, in default of roads, they embark and disembark goods, and the produce of their territory; this 'port' they call the Marina, or Scala di —— &c., the town to which it appertains.

[3] I am a woman, I am a woman, and know nothing about anything.

Neither man nor horse could proceed further under the broiling heat, and unrefreshed by food; so we found a most vile taverna, where, for want of better accommodation, we prepared to abide. Ciccio,—the Phœnix of guides,—stowed away the horse and baggage, and set the 'Turchi' to get lots of eggs, which, with wine and snow, made our dinner. It was more difficult to find a place to eat it in, and we truly congratulated ourselves on not having come on to Condufóri last night. The wretched hut we were in was more than half choked up by the bed of a sick man, with barrels, many calf-skins filled with wine, and a projecting stone fireplace; moreover, it was as dark as Erebus; so in the palpable obscure I sat down on a large live pig, who slid away, to my disgust, from under me, and made a portentous squeaking, to the disquiet of a horde of fowls, perched on every available spot above and below. The little light the place rejoiced in was disturbed by a crowd of thirty or forty 'Turchi,' who glared at us with the utmost curiosity, and talked in their vernacular tongue without ceasing. We had also a glimpse now and then of our Hebe handmaid, the assistant or 'waitress' in the establishment, a woman with one eye, whose countenance struck both of us as a model of a Medusa: nor was her mistress (the hostess) much better. Spite of all this, we nevertheless greatly enjoyed our roasted eggs, and were soon ready to start again; for although the heat was great out of doors, yet it was nearly as much so within; besides, Bova was a weary way off, and Díghi Dóghi Dà made signs of impatience, so he paid for our lunch, and off we went once more into the blazing fiumara.

We had not gone far, before a chuckling sound was heard to proceed from the hitherto imperturbable Ciccio, who presently went into convulsions of suppressed laughter, which continued to agitate him for more than an hour, only broken by the words, 'Sono femmina, e non so niente,—díghi, dà,' by which we were led to perceive that the rude reception given us by Mrs.

Tropæano had made a forcible impression on our quaint quiet
guide's imagination.

Leaving the dry river-bed of Condufóri, we climbed the
second ridge, and descended to another fiumara, which runs to
the sea below Amendolía,[1] a castellated, but deserted town,
half way up to the skies, as it were, and yet far below Bova. Here
we entered the Distretto de Gerace,[2] and were ordered to halt
by some gendarmes, who came from a hut and inspected our
passports, after which delay we began to climb the ascent to
Bova in earnest, and for many an hour. But still we wearily
worked on and up, Bova seemed always like the phantom bark—
never the nearer:—we had long passed the level of the Castle of
Amendolía, and were looking down into its empty courts,
yet the unattainable peak was still far above us,—and truly
magnificent was the view, looking back from the points of rock
where we frequently halted to rest, after passing the thick oak
woods which encircle Bova. With these objects below our feet,
the immense perspective of diminishing lines and torrents,
finished by the complete and simple outline of Etna beyond the
sea, is certainly one of the very finest scenes to be found even in
beautiful Italy. While drawing it, numerous groups of picturesque
peasants passed us, on their return homewards, and almost all
stopped and offered pears, in the most good-natured way
possible. After a last hard climb, we arrived at Bova, as the
evening had made all things dark and alike, and we were unable
to perceive 'what like' was the palazzo of Don Antonio Marzano,
who, with his wife, received us with the greatest hospitality, on
reading the recommendatory letter furnished us by Don Antonio
da Nava. The greatest penance of this roving life is the state of

[1] Améndolia, by some authors considered as identical with a Chalcidian city—
Peripolis, said to be the birth-place of Praxiteles, produces honey, and mushrooms, and asparagus, all the year round; spoken of by Pacichelli as a considerable place in his time; by Swinburne as a poor village.

[2] The province of Calabria Ulteriore Prima is divided into three Distretti—
Reggio, Gerace, Palmi. See page 13.

exhaustion and weariness in which you arrive at your evening abode; and as you feel very properly obliged to play the polite for a certain time to your entertainers, the wrestling between a sense of duty and an oppressive inclination to sleep is most painful. The good people, too, persist in delaying supper (in order that they may provide a good one) till you are reduced (ere it comes) to a state of torture and despair, in the protracted struggle between hunger, Morpheus, and civility.

CHAPTER IV

August 1.—Our host was ready, in expectation of showing us
some of the best points of view, which around this eagle's-nest
of a place are most extraordinary. The great characteristic of
Calabrian towns, picturesquely speaking, appears to consist in the
utter irregularity of their design, the houses being built on,
under, and among, separate masses of rock, as if it had been
intended to make them look as much like natural bits of scenery
as possible. The Marzano Palazzo is among the most prominent

PALIZZI

FOREST OF PIETRAPENNATA

of the houses here, and, homely and unornamented as it is, stands on its brown crag, looking over worlds of blue wood, and Sicily floating on the horizon's edge, with a most imposing grandeur—and just where a painter would have put it.

Our host, Don Antonio, lives entirely on his property in this remote place, though, like most of the Possidenti hereabouts, he was educated at Naples. Albeit a scholar as regards Greek and Latin authors, his knowledge of English geography and personages is limited, and he refers in rather a misty manner to our 'compatriota glorioso il grande Fox;'[1] who, he says, once came to Bova to study geology; 'ma se fosse prima o dopo che governasse l' Inghilterra insieme con Lord Pitt,'—this he did not clearly know. According to our friend, Bova (with the four casali mentioned in page 45, all of whose inhabitants speak a corrupt Greek, and are called Turchi by their neighbours,) is a real old Grecian settlement, or rather, the representative of one formerly existing at Amendolía, and dating from the time of Locris and other colonies. The Bovani are particularly anxious to impress on the minds of strangers that they have no connection with the modern emigrants from Albania, &c. (See *Illustrated Exc. in Italy*, vol. i.)[2] In no list of these settlers, as far as I can

[1] 'Our glorious compatriot, the great Fox. But whether it was before or after he governed England with Lord Pitt ——.'

I have lately learned from Edward H. Bunbury, Esq., M.P., that an uncle of his, who was nephew of the celebrated Charles James Fox, actually *did* visit Bova in 1829, and hence the not very surprising error of our host.

[2] Since the above was written, I have referred to the opinions of several authors as to the antiquity of the Greek settlements in this part of Italy. Many circumstances combine to persuade me that the following view, held by the Hon. Keppel Craven on the subject, is most probably the correct one, namely, that although the inhabitants of Bova are not to be looked upon as the lineal descendants of the Locrians or Rhegians, and that their settlements are not to be traced to a more remote era than that of the lower Greek empire,—'previous, it is true, to the invasion of the Saracens, or the settlements of the Normans, yet that they are *infinitely more ancient* than the establishment of the Epirote and Morean colonies, though as distantly removed from those which emigrated in the classic ages of ancient Greece.' [*continued overleaf*

trace, are any of these southern Greco-Italian establishments
included: their great distance from the more frequented parts
of the peninsula, and their consequently scanty intercourse with

---

1. In the laborious Dizionario, by Giustiniani, all the dates of the various
emigrations, six in number, are given, whether from Albania or the Morea;
and the places of abode are carefully enumerated to the amount of forty-five
distinct towns and villages in the various provinces of the kingdom. Among
these no mention is made of Bova, or of its adjacent casali, Affrico, Condufóri,
&c., although these places are individually detailed in the usual manner in the
body of the Dizionario.

2. I did not perceive at Bova any of those traces of costume (of the differences
of Albanian or Greek dialect I unfortunately could not judge) or manner, which
in other of the later Albanian or Moreote settlements which I have visited are so
remarkable.

3. Marapóti, who wrote in 1600, and who devoted considerable attention
to the description of the habits and manners of the Albanian and Moreote settlers,
says that their Church services are celebrated neither in Latin nor Greek, and
is very diffuse in notices concerning their wild modes of life, their abode in
'Tugurii' or caves, and their mode of dancing (evidently the same as that
practised by the modern Epirotes and Greeks), their cooking of sheep whole,
&c., which if molested they leave and burn. But he by no means confounds
these very distinct people with those around Reggio, of whom he says, 'In
questi casali (Motta Leucoptera,—the modern Motta S. Giovanni—[Pacichelli],
—Sant' Agata, &c.) comunemente si parla in lingua Greca, &c., *che anché
s'vsa nella piu gran parte del' habitationi convecine a Reggio*,' p. 61. Here is no
mention of Albanesi or Moreoti.

4. Pacichelli (1703) alludes to the Greek language as spoken in the district
of Bova, but does not mention the inhabitants having emigrated, as he does those
of Barile, &c. &c.

5. Of Rossano, Mr. Swinburne says, 'so late as the sixteenth century, the
inhabitants of this city spoke the Greek language,' &c.; but I find no mention of
the inhabitants of Rossano having emigrated from Albania or Greece. It would
be desirable to learn on what authority Mr. Swinburne remarks, that the people
of Bova 'emigrated from Albania only a few centuries ago; many of these
Albanese settlements are poor, those in the neighbourhood of Bova remarkably
so.' The observation is repeated in Sir J. Hobhouse's (Lord Broughton)
Journey through Albania.

Would it not then rather appear that the statements of Keppel Craven are
correct? Why should Bova, the largest place of all, have escaped the notice of all
Italian writers, and have been unknown by its own inhabitants to be of Albanian
origin?

their neighbours, have, according to their own account, contributed to keep their race distinct. From the same causes—the vast height at which the city is built, and its remoteness from any channels of communication with the capital, even the most ordinary traffic is of necessity tedious and difficult; but a great change seems about to be wrought in the affairs of Bova; for the present Bishop is doing all in his power to attract the inhabitants to the Marina di Bova, an increasing village by the sea-side. Hither, through the episcopal influence, the public offices and residence of the governor, &c., are already removed, and many families follow them, rather than have the present annoyance of the steep ascent. But the old possessors of property in the town thus in process of compulsory migration, cling stedfastly to the site of their ancestral homes, and oppose, as far as they dare, the innovating schemes of the go-a-head moderns. Thus, even in this Ultima Thule of Italy, domestic dissension is rife; and a severe illness having attacked the venerable Vescovo within the last month, the aspirations for his recovery on earth, or his translation to the world above, are less the impulses of abstract charity or piety, than of the feelings which actuate the parties in this Bovan feud.

Our day passed quietly away between lionizing and drawing: the Marzano family, plain, homely, well-bred people, was of the friendliest. At sunset we sauntered in what they termed, 'Il Giardino,' one of those weed-full disarranged plots of ground, so delightful to the 'dolce far niente' of Italian life, and so inducive of 'lotus-eating,' quiet and idleness;—a pergola-walk, tangled with grass below and fig-bushes hanging above over walls of gray rock, commands vistas, among the vine-branches, of the long graceful form of Etna, with clear lines of rock and river sweeping down to the far sea. Then there were hives, with wondrously good honey; for superiority in which product Bova and Amendolía contend as zealously as they dispute their several titles to be styled the birthplace of Praxiteles, the Greek sculptor. The cactus grows in immense luxuriance over every crag and mountain side hereabouts—it is the very weed of the country: the fruit, which at its best may be compared to a very insipid apricot, is greatly valued by the Calabrians, and seems to form no small proportion of the food of the poorer classes.

From the precipices which frown above the numerous fiumaras towards the shore, this extraordinary vegetable hangs downward in grotesque festoons and chains of great length, and in many places forms a thickly-matted surface, which to any fortress on the cliff above would be a complete defence. In early summer its bright yellow blossoms add a charm to **its strange** and wild appearance.

August 2.—A repetition of yesterday—was passed in drawing about the rock town of Bova. The Bovani take a great interest in our performances; and Don Antonio makes a sonnet thereon, which I append,[1] notwithstanding it is in praise of my sketches,

[1] SONETTO

Salve genio d'Albione! oh come è bello,
    Veder natura su le pinte carte
Figlie del tuo pensier, del tuo pennello
    Dal vero tratte con mirabil arte!
Io là veggo le roccie, ed il castello
    Le case, il campanile, e quasi in parte
Tutta la patria mia: e il poverello
    Che dal monte per giù vi si diparte.
E se per balze e valli, e boschi ombrosi,
    Molto questa contrada all' arte offria
Italia è bella pur nei luoghi ascosi.
    Ed ivi l' amico lasci, cui il desio
Di memoria serbar pei virtuosi
    Gli scalda il cor, perché desir di Dio.

ALL 'EGREGIO DISEGNATORE PAESISTA SIG. EDOARDO LEAR, NEL DIPINGERE
DELLE VEDUTE NELLA CITTÁ DI BOVA.

as a specimen of 'unpublished' Calabrese poetry.

Yet, in the elegancies of society, the Marzani are far behind most families of similar position in the Abruzzi provinces, how-ever their equals in every kind of hospitality and good-nature. To-morrow we start for Staíti, San Angelo di Bianco, and San Luca, on the way to Santa Maria di Polsi, one of our greatest objects of curiosity in Calabria Ulteriore I.

August 3.—Hardly could we persuade the domestics to accept of three carlini, even in remuneration for washing our linen. As we started from Bova ere the earliest sunbeams had changed Etna from a blue to pale rosy tint, the worthy Don A. Marzano bade us a hearty adieu, entreating us to write to him from whatever part of the world we might be in, generally, and from Gerace in particular.

Descending the narrow street of steep stairs,—for whosoever leaves Bova must needs so descend, unless he be a bird,—we passed the public prison, and lo! glaring through the bars was the evil countenance of the woman whom, in the tavern-hut of Condufóri, we had remarked as a species of Medusa: she had

---

A friend sends me the following translation of the foregoing verses:

> Genius of Albion, hail! what joy to see
>   The landscapes glowing on the tinted board,
> Fair children of thy thought, so wondrously
>   Drawn with thy magic brush from nature's hoard!
> I see the rocks, the frowning citadel,
>   As line by line the well-known shapes unfold,—
> The houses, and the tall tower with the bell,
>   And there a peasant wandering down the wold.
> Ah! if these glens, and vales, and shady groves,
>   Yield to the pencil matter without end,
> Among the scenes where artist seldom roves,
>   How fair is Italy! There, O my friend,
> Thou leav'st me, hoping, as a good man should,
> To live within the memory of the good.

been sent hither last night for having murdered one of her fellow Turchi or Turche. The broad dark shades of morning filled the deep valley below the mountain, as the winding pathway led us on from wood to wood throughout a delicious vale, at the lowest end of which a mill and stream, with a few cottages, added a charm to the wild scene; and still through the thick foliage magnificent peeps of overtowering Bova were seen from time to time. And having passed the fiumara at the foot of the ridge crowned by the aerial city, we began to ascend once more a brown cistus-covered hillside, with giant naked-armed oaks in the foreground, and the vast blue forest-clothed mountains of Aspromonte closing the landscape on all but the southern side. As the time for our mid-day halt came on, and the heat began to be rather troublesome, we came in sight of Palizzi, a most singular town, built round an isolated rock commanding one of the many narrow valleys opening to the sea. Coming, as we did, from the high inland ground, we arrived at the top of Palizzi, the castle of which is alone visible from the north side, so that to reach the level of the stream and lower town, it is necessary to descend a perfect ladder between houses and pergolas, clustered in true Calabrese style among the projecting cactus-covered ledges of the parent rock from which they seemed to grow. No wilder, nor more extraordinary place than Palizzi can well greet artist eye. Leaving P—— to finish a drawing I went forward to seek some shelter against the heat, and, reaching the castle, soon found myself in the midst of its ruined area, where, though full of incidental picturesqueness—namely, a cottage, a pergola, seven large pigs, a blind man, and a baby, I could get no information as to the whereabouts of the taverna; until alarmed by the lively remonstrances of the pigs, there appeared a beautifully fair girl who directed me down to the middle of the town: the light hair, and Grecian traits, like those of the women of Gaeta, seemed to recall the daughters of Magna Græcia.

The streets of Palizzi, through which no Englishman perhaps

had as yet descended, were swarming with perfectly naked, berry-brown children, and before I reached the taverna I could hardly make my way through the gathering crowd of astonished mahogany Cupids. The taverna was but a single dark room, its walls hung with portraits of little saints, and its furniture a very filthy bed with a crimson velvet gold-fringed canopy, containing an unclothed ophthalmic baby, an old cat, and a pointer dog; all the rest of the chamber being loaded with rolls of linen, guns, gourds, pears, hats, glass tumblers, puppies, jugs, sieves, &c.; still it was a better resting-place than the hut at Condufóri, inasmuch as it was free from many intruders. Until P—— came, and joined with me in despatching a feeble dinner of eggs, figs and cucumber, wine and snow, I sate exhibited and displayed for the benefit of the landlord, his wife, and family, who regarded me with unmingled amazement, saying perpetually, 'O donde siete?'—'O che fai?'—'O chi sei?'[1] And, indeed, the passage of a stranger through these outlandish places is so unusual an occurrence, that on no principle but one can the aborigines account for your appearance. 'Have you *no* rocks, *no* towns, *no* trees in your own country? Are you not rich? Then what *can* you wish *here?—here*, in this place of poverty and incommodo? What *are* you doing? Where *are* you going?' You might talk for ever; but you could not convince them you are not a political agent sent to spy out the nakedness of the land, and masking the intentions of your government under the thin veil of pourtraying scenes, in which they see no novelty, and take no delight.

Going out to explore the lower part of the town, I could not resist making a sketch of its wonderful aspect from below; the square towering rock of Palizzi seems to fill the whole scene, while the houses are piled up from the stream in a manner defying all description. But to transfer all this to paper was neither easy nor agreeable; the afternoon sun reflected from the

[1] Oh where *do* you come from?—Oh what *are* you going to do?—Oh who *can* you be?

crags of the close and narrow valley, making it like an oven, besides that every available bit of standing ground is so nearly covered with intractable cactus-bushes as to be utterly vexatious; and, add to their alarming prickles, and the frying heat, that the stream was full of soaking hemp, the poisonous stench of which was intolerable, and that all the juvenile unclothed population of the town came and sate over against me, and it may be perceived, that to sketch in Palizzi, though it be truly a wonder in its way, is indeed a pursuit of knowledge under great difficulties.

We left this town at three P.M., and made for Staíti, where we were to sleep, and, keeping always distant some miles from the sea, began to ascend the hill of Pietrapennata. From the north side, Palizzi appears totally different in form, and is one of those Poussinesque scenes so exquisite in character, and so peculiar to Italy. The village of Pietrapennata contains nothing remarkable, but from the height immediately above it, one of the most glorious landscapes bursts into view. What detached and strange crags! what overhanging ilex and oak! what middle-distance of densest wood! what remote and graceful lines, with the blue expanse of the eastern sea, and the long plains of the eastern side of Italy! The setting sun prevented our sketching, but we resolved positively to return to this most exquisite scenery, from Staíti, which now towered above us on the opposite side of a deep dark gully, filled with wondrous groups of giant ilex. As we slowly toiled up to this most strange place, wholly Calabrese in aspect, with its houses jammed and crushed among extraordinary crevices, its churches growing out of solitary rocks, and (what forms the chief character of these towns) all its dwellings standing singly—the Zampognari[1] were playing, and all the peasant population thronging upwards to their evening rest. Here, too, were the first symptoms of local colour in costume, the women wearing bright blue dresses with

[1] Peasants who play on the Zampogne, a sort of bagpipes used in Southern Italy.

broad orange borders, and all we saw gave promise of real unmixed Calabrian characteristics, unspoiled by high roads and the changes of all-fusing and assimilating civilisation.

Don Domenico Musitani, the chief man of the place, to whom the never-failing care of the Consigliere da Nava had recommended us, was sitting in the Piazza—an obese and taciturn man, who read the introductory letter, and forthwith took us to his house; which, among many unpleasing recollections, will certainly ever rank as one of the most disagreeable. Life in these regions of natural magnificence is full of vivid contrasts. The golden abstract visions of the hanging woods and crags of Pietra-pennata were suddenly opposed to the realities of Don D. Musitani's rooms, which were so full of silkworms as to be beyond measure disgusting. To the cultivation of this domestic creature all Staíti is devoted; yellow cocoons in immense heaps are piled up in every possible place, and the atmosphere may be conceived rather than described; for there is no more sickening odour than that of many thousand caterpillars confined in the closest of chambers. Almost did we repent of ever having come into these Calabrian lands! After the usual refreshment of snow and wine, we waited wearily for supper; at times replying to the interrogatories of our host on the subject of the productions of Inghilterra, and right glad when dismissed to what rest might be found in couches apparently clean, though odious from the silkworms all around them; but necessity as well as poverty makes the traveller acquainted with strange bed-fellows.

CHAPTER V

Explore Staíti.—Feeding among the silkworms.—A dinner party.—Silkworm pie, &c.—We resolve to return to forests of Pietrapennata to-morrow.—Sociable peasantry.—Discomforts of Staíti.—Return to the forests.—Extreme beauty and variety of the environs of Pietrapennata.—The Archpriest of the village, and his hospitable welcome.—Return at night to Staíti.—Uncomfortable evening.—Speculations on Sta Maria di Polsi.—We descend to the sea-shore again.—Reach Motta Bruzzano.—Cultivated grounds.—Beautiful bits of scenery.—Good wine at Bruzzano.—The silent Ciccio urges us to proceed.—Good qualities of our guide.—Extreme heat.—Ascent of the hill of Ferruzzano, and descent to the shore once more.—Fatiguing walk to the convent of Bianco. —Disappointment at the monastery.—Ascent to Carignano, and halt there.—Further ascent by beautiful woods to Sta Agata di Bianco.—The Baron's house. The usual hospitable welcome—with the addition of luxuries and refinements.— Difficulty of passing the evening hours.—The family supper party.

August 4.—Long before daylight a troop of pigeons came into our room through the ill-shut door, and after them followed fowls, then dogs; all of which visitors we rejoiced to leave, and were soon exploring the town. Staíti has its full share of Calabrian mystery in its buildings, caves, and rocks, and employed our pencils far and near till noon, when we returned to our hosts to find dinner laid out in one of our bedrooms, all among the silkworms as before. The contrast between the condition of this house of discomforts, and the cleanliness of

62

those of the more northern provincials in the Neapolitan kingdom, is very striking. Donna Angela Musitani, who had not
appeared last night, presided at the table, and our arrival
seemed the occasion of a sort of dinner-party in our honour; for
there was the Giudice of the town, besides a Canonico or two.
The former, a well-bred man, when speaking of his 'life of
exile' here, said, in the saddest of tones, 'O Dio! Signori! Fra
Napoli e Staíti! fra il Paradiso e l'Inferno!' and, indeed, barring
the out-door picturesqueness of the place, few more uninviting
abodes than the odoriferous Staíti could be pointed out. Nor did
the annoyances of a tribe of spoiled children and barking dogs add
charms to the family dinner. But the 'vermi di seta' were our
chief horror; and so completely did silkworms seem the life and
air, end and material, of all Staíti, that we felt more than half
sure, on contemplating three or four suspicious-looking dishes,
that those interesting lepidoptera formed a great part of the
groundwork of our banquet—silkworms plain boiled, stewed
chrysalis, and moth tarts.[1] Glad we were to rush out, to sit and
draw among the rocks, pondering how we should once more
revisit Pietrapennata on the morrow. Almost all the peasants
had some greeting for us as they passed homeward after sunset.
Some gave us pears, which seem the staple fruit of Southern
Calabria;[2] many asked us if we were planning and writing down
for our govérno; and one woman begged me to ask *my* king to
ask *hers* to let her have salt cheaper; while another set forth a

[1] By way of illustrating this our melancholy foreboding, and to show that
such things have been, are, and may be, I subjoin the following quotation from a
recently published work,—*The Ansayrii*, &c., by the Hon. F. Walpole. Bentley,
1851.

'A sort of sherbet is made here [Diarbekr] of the cocoon of the silkworm;
it is considered a great luxury, and is exported for a beverage for the rich all
over the surrounding country. To me it appeared very nauseous, tasting exactly
as the cocoons smell, &c.'—Vol. i. page 366.

[2] '—— Of which,' suggests a friend to me, 'they continue as prodigal to
strangers and pigs as in the days of Horace. (Ep. i. vii. 14.)'

claim to her house being re-roofed, on account of her grandfather having been killed in battle. The Archpriest of Pietrapennata also accosted us, and, finding how desirous we were of revisiting that village and its forest scenery, good-naturedly asked us to dine at his house. Lingering as late as we could, we took refuge with the Giudice, Don Antonio Morano, for an hour, whose comfortable clean room (though not free from the general taint of the town's vermicular atmosphere) was a favourable contrast to our host's home. Thither, however, we at length retreated, to endure as best we might its evils: there we endured more strange food; the children screamed, the dogs howled; and the fat hostess amused herself by catching unwary dragonflies, and holding them in the candle.

August 5.—An hour before daylight we left the Palace of Cocoons with joy. How exquisite was the sweet morning light and air—the deep ravine full of elix, the mill, and the ascent to the opposite side, where those surpassing woods fringed the park-like glades, or formed magnificent pictures with their grey trunks, and arms flung out over rock and dell! O rare woods of Pietrapennata! I do not remember to have seen a lovelier spot than the 'winged rock'—not unaptly named, feathered as it is from base to summit. None of your dense carpet-forests —your monotonies of verdure, but made up of separate combinations of pictorial effect, such as one can hardly fancy— Claude and Salvator Rosa at every step! All the morning we drew in this beautiful place, and little enough could our utmost efforts make of what would occupy a regiment of landscape-painters for years, if every one of them had as many arms and hands as Vishnoo. At noon, a constant breeze plays among these umbrageous groves, making even the heat of the day pleasant, and we moved reluctantly to the top of the hill, whose crown of foliage spread away in unmeasured lines to the north; hence the forest slopes conduct your eye eastward to Brancaleone and other villages, starry bright against the blue waves. At the hamlet of Pietrapennata we found our acquaintance the Archpriest, Don Domenico Lucianò, waiting for us in his rustic dwelling, the divine himself clad in an undress of corduroys and a shooting-jacket, the like of which was never seen in the grave Roman States. As all and everybody of the village thronged to see us, we were fain to allow our reverend host to shut us up in a small dark room, where our homely dinner of beans, eggs, and salad was soon ready, and the old gentleman not being of an interrogative turn, his simple hospitality was very agreeable; and although his wine was very abominable, yet we had had the forethought to load Ciccio with a basketful of snow, four rotoli of which, wrapped in cloth, had melted but little, and served to nullify our host's fluid.

About three we set off for Silkworm Hall, taking new paths through those most glorious scenes, but so continually distracted by fresh groups of wondrous beauty that we worked but very little, and arrived late (the later the better) at Staíti, well pleased at having once more seen a place which must always dwell in my memory as the beau-ideal of Calabrian park or forest scenery. Supper and silkworms once again: screaming children and howling dogs; the fat lady shouted and scolded, and anathematised the daddy-longlegs who flew into the candles; and mine host was savage at our having visited 'quel prete di Pietrapennata.' There may, however, be yet many Silkworm Halls in store for us; but, go where we may, we shall hardly find another Pietrapennata to compensate for their evils. What will Sta Maria di Polsi be like? On the map it is most inviting—black and deep among the horrors of Aspromonte. The variety of hope in such tours as these lightens the annoyances of the present hour.

August 6.—Half-an-hour before sunrise: addio—Don Domenico and Donna Angela Musitani!—Staíti is a considerable place, resembling in extent Celano, Magliano, or Pescina, in Abruzzo Ulteriore II; but woe is me! for the contrast between its habitants and the Tabassi or Masciarelli! Truth compels me to say, though after two days' hospitality it might be wrong so to feel, that P—— and I grew more lighthearted, step by step, as we left our late host's, and followed old Díghi Dóghi Dà and his faultless horse down the steep hill through many a lane towards the plain below. The plan of our route was to leave the hills for a space; nor until Motta di Bruzzano[1] was passed were we to turn once more towards the mountains and Sta Maria di Polsi; so we came again into a land of olives, and sandy paths, and irrigated fields of Indian corn, with the sea on one side and blue lessening hills westward. Here and there, we could not help lingering to sketch some line of Claude-like simplicity. Farther on, we glanced at Moticella, a village at the foot of the hills, but waywardly we did not think it worth a visit; and thus, by degrees, having passed through gardens and fields, and by cottages surrounded with gourds, we arrived below Bruzzano, placed as if arranged by G. Poussin for a picture, on the edge of a great rock rising out of the plain, and built with all that beauty of simple form, and that independent irregularity, so identified now in our minds with the towns of Calabria. Many charming views are there round Bruzzano, looking through pergolas to the sea and cape, with glittering Brancaleone to the south, and the blue woody hills towards the north. After making a drawing we lingered, early as it was, at the door of a wineshop, indulging, over a loaf of bread, in moderate libations of the best Calabrian wine we had yet tasted. Well for us, we afterwards found, that so we did. But the day (it was a burning and weary scirocco) advanced, and quoth Ciccio, 'If you mean to sleep at Sta Agata, so as to arrive at Polsi the following evening, you must go on—dógo.' In all the chances and changes of our tour, hitherto old Ciccio had ever been perfectly, yet judiciously, amiable. If we wished to halt, he said, 'Díghi, dóghi, si.' If we wished to go on, he said

[1] Bruzzano was the headquarters of the Saracens in 1075, according to Marapóti.

the same. We never differed, only the communication on our side was scanty; the 'Dógo' was sufficient.

So, hot as it was, we obeyed orders, and began to ascend one of those steep Apennine spurs running down from the high Aspromonte chain to the sea. At the top of it, where there was a Bivio,[1] one road leading to Feruzzano, the other to the plain again, we had to decide summarily where our night's quarters should be. Feruzzano, judging from what one saw hence, was uninteresting; and, moreover, we had no letter to any of its people. Sta Agata, on the other hand, though we *had* a letter to its principal proprietor, the Barone Franco, was a great deal farther off, nor as yet visible, and the day was of the uttermost degree of scirocco heat, without a breath of air. So, at the very top of the narrow ridge, we threw ourselves down under the only shade bestowed us by a few bushes of thick lentisk, and finally decided on this difficult question by that intellectual process of reasoning generally known as 'tossing up.' Heads?— Tails? Heads,—Sta Agata. Down, therefore, we went into a new scene—ridges and lines beyond lines of chalky-bright heights, town-crowned heights, and glaringly white fiumaras, a great tract from hill to sea of glitter and arid glare. The picking and stealing of some grapes growing near the burning sandy road seemed a light matter to our parched consciences as we pursued this hottest of walks through the plain, towards the first out-works of the steeps, high on which stood the convent of Bianco; the houses of the town of that name being dotted along a narrow ridge of the whitest of chalk—oh how white! how ultra chalky! We became very cross as we crept on in the scorching sun, and passed along the stony fiumara;—

> 'The river-bed was dusty white,
> And all the furnace of the light
> Struck up against our dazzled eyes.'

[1] A double or divided road.

The Fiume Verde, a river in winter, was now reduced to a sham of a stream, containing as many tadpoles as drops of water, and barely admitting the least face-washing refreshment; while the little shade, real or supposed, to be gained in the olive-grounds scattered around was barred from us by thick lentisk hedges. It was as much as either of us could do, aided by some water-melons, to reach that longed-for spot the convent of Bianco, beyond which we looked earnestly to ever-rising grounds with fresh woods and bluer mountains beyond, speaking of air and endurable existence once more.

At last, behold us at the monastery door. O fallacious hopes! All the monks were fast asleep, so we could only penetrate into a courtyard, where, indeed, was a well of clear water, and an iron bucket chained thereto, which neither P—— nor I shall ever forget. Let any philosopher or stoic walk from sunrise till past noon in a Calabrian August on the shadeless low grounds by the sea, and such a well with such a bucket he will remember through life! When the monks arose, we, who had taken no provision of food with us, were aghast at the two small bits of crust which they apologisingly offered us, the Superiore declaring that they were out of provisions; so off we set again. 'Coraggio, díghi, dóghi, dà,' said Ciccio; and we climbed on through vine-yards and hanging woods for another hour to a village, we fondly hoping it would be Sᵗᵃ Agata;—not at all—it was Casignano, Sᵗᵃ Agata being yet half-an-hour beyond!

From this place, where we indulged in a rest, and more snow and wine, all the rest of the afternoon's march was delightful. Smooth walks led us through rich chestnut woods (such as abound in that most beautiful place Civitella di Subiaco), or along narrow high-banked lanes of red earth, with feathery oak over head, and the eastern sea shining through the branches over the woodland tracts we had last left, and the chalk-white fiumaras and golden sandy plain far below. At length our night-halt, the little village of Sᵗᵃ Agata, was reached; a humble place,

SANTA MARIA DI POLSI

GERACE

half of which seemed merged in the Baron's huge old dirty Poussinesque Palazzo. And, as we arrived at the house, the whole baronial atmosphere seemed one of slovenly and lethargic melancholy; though there was no want of hospitable reception. The drawing-room was very untidy, and there were four very unwashed poets' heads at the four angles. The Baron's brothers and sons were dirty and sad; and the priest was sad and dirty; the doctor (a professional man of Gerace, the Capo Distretto) seemed the only lively person, and apologised for the Baron's absence; the Baroness being ill. But the will to welcome, which we have not yet found wanting in Calabria (save in Condufóri), was perfectly manifested in an unexpected display of maccaroni, eggs, olives, butter, cheese, and undeniable wine and snow, on a table covered with the whitest of linen, and sparkling with plate and glass, arrangements at variance with the outward appearance of the mansion. After this refreshment, and a half-hour's sketching, evening set in, when cards prevailed (an amusement my ignorance of which I have often lamented in these regions), and P—— and I vainly tried to look polite and sleepless till supper was announced at eleven; a dreary meal, the whole family and party, twenty in number, sitting round a plentifully loaded table in speechless solemnity.

CHAPTER VI

August 7.—We left the Baron's house before sunrise, with
many apologies from the family that no one was up and on foot to
attend to our departure, the increasing illness of the lady of the
house explaining the gloom of last night, as well as the invisi-
bility of the household this morning. Truly delightful was the
walk through the shady chestnut-groves—ahi!—those early hours
in Italy! Again we passed Casignano, but, instead of descending
towards Bianco, we held on an inland route, facing the high
Aspromonte range of mountains, in hopes to reach the sanctuary
of Sta Maria di Polsi by night. San Luca—where we were to

procure a guide to the convent,—was in view, though we had to walk for some hours up one of those eternal white fiumara-courses, full of oleander-clumps, before we arrived at it. We reached the village at ten. It stands at the termination of one of the northernmost ridges, forming the valley of the great torrent known ere it joins the sea as Fiume Buonamico. Don Domenico Stranges, the chief proprietor, was away at the Marina (for there is generally on the track along the coast some cluster of houses, or a hamlet representing the community whose chief home is in the hills), but no timid inhabitant of the Casa Stranges forbade our entrance as at Condufóri: here a most graceful and handsome barefooted girl, a local Hebe, brought us snow and wine, bidding us wait and be welcome till her masters came.

In Calabria, as in other parts of the Neapolitan kingdom (see *Excursions in Italy*), the family often continue to dwell together till each of its members marry. One of the Brothers Stranges soon arrived, and a most thoroughly hearty good fellow he was. 'You must take what you can find,' said he; 'there is no time to get anything: si signore, non vi sono qui mercati—qui non siamo in Napoli;'[1] but there were heaps of maccaroni, and cocuzzi and pomi-d'oro,[2] and a roast hare, and that is not matter for complaint in the heart of Calabria. Don Giacomo asked, as usual: 'In che cosa abbonda l'Inghilterra?'[3] and we replied, al solito, 'Vi sono belle vacche, bovi, cavalli, grano,' &c., &c.

'V' è del riso?'

[1] There are no markets here; this is not Naples.
[2] Vegetable marrows and tomatoes.
[3] In what does England abound?
In cows, oxen, horses, corn, &c.
Have you any rice?
No; we import it.
O heavens! Do you make any wine?
No.
O mercy! Then of course you have no fruit?
But indeed we have.
O that is not possible.

'Non, signore; si fa venire di fuori.'

'O cielo! Dunque—si fa del vino?'

'Non, signore.'

'O misericordia! Frutti allora di certo non vi sono?'

'Ma si.'

'O! possibile non è,' and a polite grin of incredulity closed the category.

The worthy man pressed us much to stay, to see all the hills. 'Since you *are* come to this out-of-the-way place, what difference *can* a week or two make? Stay, and hunt—stay, and make this your home!'

'Alas, good Don Giacomo! so we would gladly, but life is short, and we are trying hard to see all Calabria in three months.'

So we slept: but instead of waking at nineteen (five) o'clock, it was half-past twenty[1] before we were in order to start—leaving only three hours and a half for a journey which our Calabrian friends described as 'sommamente feroce.'[2]

So we left San Luca, our good-natured host giving us a huge water-melon to help us on our road, and the handsome girl firmly refusing to accept any 'compliment' or 'remuneration' of coin, great or little.

For three miles up a torrent bed was our path at setting out, our guide (for Ciccio did not assume knowledge of the intricate ways of Polsi), clad in the costume of brown cloth worn by the peasants hereabout, going on in advance. As we proceeded up the stream, the rocks began to close in nearer and nearer, till above the high-cliffed gorge, the towering forms of Aspromonte seemed to shut out the sky—the long furrows in the mountain-sides clothed with the densest wood. Now our route lay on this, now on that side of the torrent, sometimes at the level of the river, among blooming oleander-trees, of the largest size I ever

[1] In Southern Italy the whole number of hours contained in the day is always spoken of.

[2] Utterly terrible.

saw (not excepting even those at Sortino, in Sicily); sometimes at a great height, among the trunks of luxuriant ilex-trees, overhanging the rocks. The sentiment of these scenes and solitudes—the deep, deep solitudes of those mountains! are such as neither pen nor pencil can describe!

We were obliged to walk as fast as possible, that we might arrive at Polsi by daylight, and as we ascended, the labour was not a little severe. It was twenty-two o'clock when we reached a fountain very high up in the mountain, yet the brown-garbed guide said three hours were still requisite to bring us to our night's lodging. Clear streams, trickling down at every step to the great torrent, refreshed us, and soon we left the valley, and began to climb among oak woods, till the deep chasm, now dark in the fading daylight, was far below our feet.

A circuitous toil to the head of a second large torrent, skirting a ravine filled with magnificent ilex, brought us to the last tremendous ladder-path, that led to the 'serra,' or highest point of the route, wherefrom we were told we should perceive the monastery. Slowly old Ciccio and his horse followed us, and darker grew the hour. 'Arriveremo tardi,' quoth he, 'se non moriamo prima—díghi, dóghi, dà!'[1] But alas! when we did get at the promised height, where a cross is set up, and where, at the great festas of the convent, the pilgrims fire off guns on the first and last view of this celebrated Calabrian sanctuary—alas! it was quite dark, and only a twinkling light far and deep down, in the very bowels of the mountain, showed us our destination. Slow and hazardous was the descent, and it was nine o'clock ere we arrived before the gate of this remote and singular retreat. It was a long while before we gained admittance; and the Superiore, a most affable old man, having read our letter, offered us all the accommodation in his power, which, as he said, we must needs see was small. Wonder and curiosity overwhelmed the ancient man and his brethren, who were few in number, and

[1] We shall arrive late, if we do not die before we get there.

clad in black serge dresses. 'Why had we come to such a solitary place? No foreigner had ever done so before!' The hospitable father asked a world of questions, and made many comments upon us and upon England in general, for the benefit of his fellow-recluses. 'England,' said he, 'is a very small place, although thickly inhabited. It is altogether about the third part of the size of the city of Rome. The people are a sort of Christians, though not exactly so. Their priests, and even their bishops, marry, which is incomprehensible, and most ridiculous. The whole place is divided into two equal parts by an arm of the sea, under which there is a great tunnel, so that it is all like one piece of dry land. Ah—che celebre tunnel!' A supper of hard eggs, salad, and fruit followed in the refectory of the convent, and we were attended by two monstrous watch-dogs, named Assassino and Saraceno, throughout the rest of the evening, when the silence of the long hall, broken only by the whispers of the gliding monk, was very striking. Our bedrooms were two cells, very high up in the tower of the convent, with shutters to the unglazed windows, as a protection against the cold and wind, which were by no means pleasant at this great elevation. Very forlorn, indeed, were the sleeping apartments of Sᵗᵃ Maria di Polsi, and fearful was the howling of the wind and the roaring of a thunder-storm throughout the night!—but it was solemn and suggestive, and the very antithesis of life in our own civilised and distant home.

CHAPTER VII

August 8.—A little rain falls, and great volumes of mist are rolling up the sides of the gigantic well in which the convent seems to be placed; but after caffé with the Padre Superiore, who was again diffuse on the subject of a married priesthood, P—— and I went out to explore, in the teeth of the stormy elements.

Assuredly, Sta Maria di Polsi is one of the most remarkable scenes I ever beheld; the building is picturesque, but of no great antiquity, and with no pretensions to architectural taste; it stands on a rising ground above the great torrent, which comes down from the very summit of Aspromonte, the highest point of which—Montalto—is the 'roof and crown' of the picture. From the level of the monastery to this height rises a series of screens, covered with the grandest foliage, with green glades, and massive clumps of chestnut low down—black ilex and brown oak next in succession, and, highest of all, pines. The *perpendicular* character of the scene is singularly striking, the wooded rocks right and left closing it in like the side slips of a theatre; and as no other building is within sight, the romance and loneliness of the spot are complete. Neither is there any other, even the remotest, glimpse of contrasted landscape, as is often the case with secluded monasteries in Italy, which, from their high and solitary place, overlook a distant plain, or the sea. Here all around, above and below, is close wood and mountain—no outlet, no variety—stern solitude and the hermit sentiment reign supreme.

The monks are frequently snowed up for many of the winter months, and must lead at all periods a life of the strictest seclusion; for, except on a day early in September, when half South Calabria comes to the annual festa, no living soul but the few dependents of the monastery visit it. Some of these—woodmen and labourers—passed us as we sate on peaks of rock above the downward path, wrapped in our plaids, and hardly able to hold our books for the violence of the wind; and they gazed with breathless amazement at the novel sight—a simple, hardy race of people, with none of that ferocity of countenance which English Lavaters attach by habitual tradition to Calabrese physiognomy.

The noontide hours were employed in sketching in the cloisters, and in examining the relics and treasures of the church under the auspices of the Padre Superiore. The subjects which weigh most heavily on his mind are 'Quel tunnel,'[1] and 'Quei Preti maritati! Vescovi sposati! o cielo! Una moglie di arcivescovo; O che stravaganza!' The afternoon we passed in strolling about the fine scenes around this hermit-home; but, though containing endless material for foreground study, its general picturesque character is limited, and we decide on leaving Sta Maria di Polsi to-morrow. We must retrace our steps as far as San Luca, and then make for Gerace, sleeping either at Bovalino or Ardore, as time may allow.

[1] The tunnel, and those married priests! Married bishops—O heaven! Wife of an archbishop!—O what amazement!

August 9.—The worthy Superior presented us with a medal and a print of the Madonna di Polsi, the original picture having been discovered by a devout ox, who inveigled one of the early Norman Conquerors of Sicily all the way from Reggio to this place, for the particular purpose of inducing him to build a monastery. The excellent ox, said the monk, led on the prince from hill to hill till he reached the proper spot, when, kneeling down, he with his pious horns poked up the portrait of the Virgin Mary, which was miraculously waiting some inches below the ground for its bovine liberator. A print recording this circumstance was also given to Ciccio, who wrapped it up carefully with signs of devotion: we have never yet had a fault to find with this valuable fellow—he was, as King Charles the Second is said to have said of somebody, 'never *in*, nor ever *out* of, the way.'

Having reached the height of the cross we turned to bid a last addio to Sᵗᵃ Maria di Polsi, and thenceforth we enjoyed the magnificent landscape of distant hills now visible throughout this high part of the gorge; we descended to the depths of the torrent bed, and its gay oleander-trees by the ferny glens and ilex ravines, which we had threaded on our way up to the monastery on the afternoon of the 7th; and so we again reached the widening valley and its painful fiumara course of white stones below San Luca. Contrary to our first intention, which had been to push on for Bovalino—we returned into the little town, for our horse had lost a shoe, and the fierce heat demanded an hour or two of rest.

The party at the friendly Don Giacomo Stranges was increased by his brothers D.D. Domenico and Stefano, who were all delighted to ask questions about the 'abbondanza d' Inghilterra,' while they offered us snow and wine, and a clean cloth being spread, maccaroni, eggs, ricotta,[1] honey, and pears, soon exhibited proofs of their ready hospitality.

[1] Ricotta is a preparation of milk, usually sheep's milk, in very general use throughout Southern Italy.

It was two o'clock before the horse-shoe was adjusted, and we started once more from San Luca and its kind homely set of inhabitants, who to the last insisted on giving us letters to Stignano, Stilo, Rocella, and other places at which we might chance to halt.

Our route was a weary one, as it was ever descending straight to the sea in the midst of the stony oleander-dotted water-course—hot and tedious; near the coast we came to sandy roads for two hours, with our old friends cactus and aloe bordering cultivated grounds to the water's edge, from which our halt was hardly a mile distant. Ciccio also growled now and then, having lost one of his own shoes, and being obliged to ride: he did not like to overwork his horse—he was a good fellow that old Díghi Dóghi Dà.

It was late when we arrived below Bovalino, sparkling on its chalky height in the last sunbeams, and as we found that to go on to Ardore would have been too far and fatiguing, we turned through olive grounds from the sea, and began the long ascent to the town, which we reached at dusk. Bovalino is a place of considerable size, and we were charmed by its strongly defined Calabrese character, as we ascended the winding pathways full of homeward-bound peasants, the costume of the women being prettier here than any we had yet seen.

We went at once with an introductory letter to Count Garrolo, one of the chief proprietors of the place, and fortunately found him just returned from the country: the small rooms of his house betokened the literary man, heaps of books, maps, globes and papers, filling up all corners, and great wealth of very old-fashioned furniture, leaving small space for sitting or standing. The Conte himself was a most good-natured and fussy little man, excessively consequential and self-satisfied, but kind withal, and talking and bustling in the most breathless haste, quoting Greek and Latin, hinting at antiquities and all kinds of dim lore and obscure science, rushing about, ordering his two domestics to and fro, explaining, apologising and welcoming, without the least cessation. He had come from a villa, a villetta, a vigna— an old property of his family—Giovanni Garrolo, Gasparo Garrolo, Luca Garrolo, Stefano Garrolo,—he had come just now, this very minute: he had come on a mule, on two mules, with the Contessa, the amiable Contessa, he had come slowly— pian, pian, piano, piano, piano—for the Contessa expected to be confined shortly—perhaps to-day—he hoped not; he would like us to be acquainted with her; her name was Serafina; she was intellectual and charming; the mules had never stumbled; he had put on the crimson-velvet housings, a gilt coronet embossed, Garrolo, Garrolo, Garrolo, Garrolo, in all four corners; he had read the Contessa an ode to ancient Locris all along the road, it amused her, a Latin ode; the Contessa enjoyed Latin; the Contessa had had six children, all in Paradise, great loss, but all for the best; would we have some snow and wine? Bring some snow, bring some wine.—He would read us a page, two pages, three—Locri Opuntii, Locri Epizephyrii, Normans, Saracens— Indian figs and Indian corn—Julius Cæsar, and the Druids, Dante, Shakespeare—silkworms and mulberries—rents and taxes, ante- diluvians, American republics, astronomy and shell-fish,—like the rushing of a torrent was the volubility of the Conte Garrolo— yet one failed to receive any distinct impression from what he said, so unconnected and rapid was the jumbling together of his subjects of eloquence. Nevertheless, his liveliness diverted us to the utmost, the more from its contrast to the lethargic and monotonous conversation of most of our former hosts; and we wondered if the Contessa would talk a tenth part as much, or as loudly. Supper was ready sooner than in most of these houses, and when it was served, in came the Contessa, who was presented to us by her husband with a crash of compliments and apologies for her appearance, which put our good breeding to the severest test; in all my life I never so heartily longed to burst into merri- ment, for the poor lady, either from ill-health or long habitual deference to her loquacious spouse, said nothing in the world but 'Nirr si,' or 'Nirr no,'[1] which smallest efforts of intellectual discourse she continued to insert between the Count's sentences in the meekest way, like Pity, between the drummings of despair in Collins' Ode to the Passions.

'Scusatela, scusatela,' thundered the voluble Conte, 'scusatela —cena, cena, a cena—tavola pronta, tavola pronta'——

'*Nirr si.*'

'Subito, subito, subito, subito.'

'*Nirr si, nirr no.*'

'Sedete vi, sedete vi—(sorella sua morta quattro mesi fa).'

'*Nirr si.*'

'Mangiate! mangiate!'

'*Nirr no.*'

'Maccaroni? pollo? (madre morte, piange troppo,) alicetti si, zuppa si, ove si.'

'*Nirr no.*'

'Signori forestiere prendete vino. Contessa statevi allegra.'

'*Nirr si.*'[2]

It was a most trying and never-ending monologue, barring the choral nirr si and no, and how it was we did not go off improperly into shrieks of laughter I cannot tell, unless that the day's fatigue had made our spirits tractable. Instantly after supper the Contessa vanished, and the Conte bustled about like an armadillo in a cage, showing us our room, and bringing in a vast silver basin and jug, towels, &c., with the most surprising alacrity, and although

---

[1] Nirr si, nirr no,—the common way of assent or negation in the kingdom of Naples; meaning the last syllable of Signor si, or Signor no, or etymologicè,— 'gnor si, 'gnor no.

[2] Excuse her, excuse her, supper, supper, supper, the table is ready; the table is ready.—*Nirr si.*—Quick, quick, quick, quick. *Nirr si, nirr no.*—Sit down, sit down:—(her sister died four months ago).—*Nirr si.*—Eat, eat. *Nirr no.*—Maccaroni? fowl? (her mother is dead—she cries too much) anchovies? soups? eggs?—*Nirr no.*—Signori strangers, take some wine. Countess, be merry. *Nirr si*, &c. &c.

the ludicrous greatly predominated in these scenes, yet so much prompt and kind attention shown to the wants of two entire strangers by these worthy people was most pleasing. For all that, how did we laugh when we talked over the ways of this amazing Count Garrolo!

CHAPTER VIII

View from the heights of Bovalino.—Last words of Conte Garrolo.—Descent to the valleys of Ardore; pursue our road to the sea-shore again.—Arrive at Torre di Gerace.—Site of ancient Locris.—Ruins.—We strike inland towards Gerace.—Cross the fiumara Merico.—Long ascent to the picturesque city of Gerace.—Description of Gerace: its frequent earthquakes; its Cathedral, &c.—Norman castle.— Its inaccessible position.—Extensive prospects.—Palazzo of Don Pasquale Scaglione.—Agreeable and hospitable reception.—Large rooms and comfortable house.—High winds frequent at Gerace.—Beautiful views of Gerace.—Constant occupation for the pencil.—Vino Greco of the Calabrese.— Locrian coins.—A treatise on ancient Locris, and our appreciation thereof.—The Medico of Gerace.

August 10.—The rising sun shone brightly into the eastern loggia of Count Garrolo's house, and wide is the view therefrom: eastward, the sea and broad lines of plain; and westward, the long mountain ridges in succession, with Ardore, and Bombili, and Condajanni, and, clear in the blue distance, Gerace on its hill,—successor to old Locris, and in the present day, a Sott' intendenza, or provincial sub-governor's residence, and Capo-distretto.

The bustling Count whisked us all over the town, into the church, the castle, the lanes,—showed us the views, the walls, the towns, the villages, manuscripts, stables, the two mules, and the purple velvet saddle and crimson housings, with coronets, and Garrolo, Garrolo, Garrolo, Garrolo—tutto-tutto-tutto,—put us in charge of a peasant to show us a short cut to Ardore,—

shook hands fifteen times with each of us, and then rushed away with a frantic speed: 'Scrivere alcuni pensieri poetici, ordinare la servitú (those two servants how they must have worked!) vendere un cavallo, comprare grano, cogliere fiori, consolare la Contessa. Addio! addio!'[1] Addio, Conte Garrolo! a merry obliging little man you are as ever lived, and the funniest of created counts all over the world.

A broad valley intervenes between the ridges of Bovalino and Ardore,[2] and by pleasant lanes we descended to delightful vine-yards, cornfields, and figgeries (if there be such a word), where our peasant-guide loaded us with fruit, and left us. We decided on not going into the town of Ardore, as it had not a very pre-possessing exterior, and to see *all* the towns of Calabria would have occupied too much time; so, ascending the hill on which it stands, we crossed the narrow ridge, and descended once more towards the sea—a wide tract of cultivation now separating us from Gerace on its remarkable hill. About noon we rested at a roadside osteria, for the sake of shade and water melons, (you buy three of the largest for $2\frac{1}{2}$ grani); and, continuing to plod along the broad, dusty level road, we passed Condajanni on our left—apparently very picturesque—and shortly afterwards came to the Torre di Gerace, a single tower of the Middle Ages, standing on the edge of the sea-shore, at the spot which anti-quaries recognise as the indubitable site of ancient Locris. Foundations of antique buildings exist for a great extent in all the vineyards around, and innumerable coins are dug up by the labourers. Very pretty is that gray tower, standing all alone on the rock by the blue waves, with a background of the graceful hill of Gerace, and the many lines of more distant and loftier mountains. Round the foot of the Locrian tower, and all over the sandy spiaggia, or beach, grow abundance of the whitest amaryllis,

[1] To write down some poetical thoughts; to give orders to the servants; to sell a horse; to buy some grain; to gather some flowers; to console the Countess.

[2] 'Ardore was,' says Pacichelli, 'called Odore, from its many flowers.'

filling the air with their delightful perfume. At half-past one we left the sea-side, and, soon arriving at the broad fiumara, the river Merico, which runs below Gerace, we crossed it, and thence began the extremely long and gradual ascent leading to this grand and most picturesque place, where we arrived at half-past four, P.M.

Gerace,[1] one of the three Sott' intendenze into which Calabria Ulteriore I is divided, is a large cathedral town, full of beautifully-placed buildings, situated on a very narrow edge of rock, every part of which seems to have been dangerously afflicted by earthquakes—splits, and cracks, and chasms, horrible with abundant crookednesses of steeples, and a general appearance of instability in walls and houses. Towards the north-west, the sharp crest of rock ends abruptly in a precipice, which on three sides is perfectly perpendicular. Here are the dark and crumbling ruins of a massive Norman castle, from which, by a scrambling path, you may reach the valley below; but all other parts of the town are accessible only by two winding roads at the eastern and less precipitous approach. The great height at which this place is situated, and its isolated site, give it a command of views the most wide and beautiful in character: that towards the sea being bounded by Rocella on the north, and Capo Bruzzano to the south; while the inland mountain ranges towards the west, are sublimely interesting. In fact, Gerace is by far the grandest and proudest object in general position, and as a city, which we have yet seen in Calabria.

Consigliere da Nava had given us a letter to Don Pasquale Scaglione, who inhabits one of the largest houses in the city,

[1] Gerace, Gierazzo, (Fra Alberto,) Hieraci (Mazzella). Not a bad plate of it in Pacichelli. All antiquarians agree that it represents Locris, though it seems uncertain if the Greek city stood close to the shore, or on the slopes of the hill on which the modern town is built. Frequent mention is made by several old authors, that manna is found along the Locrian territory; Marafioti speaks of 'manna which falls from the sky,' as commonly abounding in the woods of the eastern side of Calabria, and particularly in the vicinity of Gerace and Bovalino.

ROCELLA

STILO

overlooking the whole eastern sea view from its windows. Don Pasquale, a prepossessing and gentlemanlike person, welcomed us warmly; and after we had had the usual snow and wine, and had made ourselves comfortable with some water and half-an-hour's sleep, set us down to an admirable dinner—albeit, their own was long ago finished. Nothing can be kinder nor more well-bred than the hospitable reception given us by this family, who remind me more of the Abruzzesi than any of those Calabrese I have yet seen. After dinner, we went out to the unsafe precipices of the Castle, which frowns magnificently in its decay; but the wind, for which even on clear days Gerace is notorious, was too high to allow of drawing happily, so we passed the evening at home in conversation with these new acquaintances.

August 11.—Early we wandered near the town on the ascent from the sea-side, and drew till eleven, wondering at the infinity of pictures presenting themselves on every side: each rock, shrine, and building at Gerace seems arranged and coloured on purpose for artists, and the union of lines formed by nature and art is perfectly delicious. Of costume there seems little enough, except that all the women dress in black, and wear the skirt of their outer dresses turned over the head, like those of Civita Castellana in the Roman States. At twelve we dined at the Casa Scaglione. This is a very well-bred and agreeable family in essentials, although there are certain Calabrian modes and usages less refined than those of the northern provinces among families of a similar class. Donna Peppina Scaglione, the eldest brother's wife, is very pretty and lady-like in appearance, and with agreeable manners. Then there are the brothers, Don Nicola and Don Gaetano, the canonico, and Don Abennate, a priest of Stilo, staying in the house as a guest, and little Don Cicile, the heir, of five or six years old, a quaint little Calabrian, full of joy and fun. Their family dinner consisted of soup, fish, boiled and fried meat, and potatoes, all plain and excellent.

After dinner, the last act of which was to imbibe sundry glasses of an old wine, much esteemed by the Calabresi, and called Greco, we adjourned to the great show-room, or salone, of the Palazzo, the view from which eastward is most splendid. Here Don Pasquale showed us a large collection of Locrian, Syracusan, Roman, and other coins found in the neighbourhood, after which our good host victimised us fearfully by reading aloud chapter after chapter of a work which he is writing on Locris—an 'opus magnum', which, however learned, was vastly dull. All hints about repose were vain; so when P—— fell fast asleep, and I was nearly following his example, I was about to beg we might retire, when the author himself yawned, and paused, and fell into the arms of the drowsy god, whereupon the committee of literature was broken up *nem. con.*

After siesta, drawing again. A beautiful trait of Gerace is its admirable colour; its white or delicate fawn-hued cliffs, and gray or dove-coloured buildings coming beautifully off the purple of mountains. Returning at Ave Maria, and eating ices in a café, we encountered the medico, whom we had seen at Sta Agata di Bianco: the Baroness Franco had died on the morning we left the house; so that we now fully understood the mournful silence of the family, aware of her near dissolution, but anxious that if possible any excuse to relieve them from the exercise of hospitality should be avoided. A most pleasing instance of good feeling, and well worth remembering. Supper with the Scaglione family, who are really very agreeable people: it being Wednesday, scate, prawns, and rice-risolles are the order of the day.

CHAPTER IX

We remain at Gerace, and draw constantly.—Evening visit
to the Sott' intendente.—Cathedral of Gerace.—Church of
S. Francesco.—We leave the Palazzo Scaglione, and descend
to the river Novito.—Arrangements to return to Gerace, so
as to visit all this province before proceeding to Calabria
Ulteriore II.—Town of Siderno; dress of the women.—
General civility of the peasantry and of all orders of people.—
Descent to the sea-shore.—Magnificent appearance of Rocella.
—Approach to the town.—Night comes ere we ascend the
rock.—Search in the darkness for the Casa Manni.—Hospitable reception by the family of Don Giuseppe Manni.—
Ancient palace.—Our fatigue and inaptitude at conversation.—Endless interrogatories.—The Rocellesi are decided
in their opinions as to our native productions.—Their
rejection of our fruits and vegetables as wholly fabulous.

August 12.—A day passed in drawing either on the platform
below the town, or on the open space near the old castle. The
powdery state of the architecture of Gerace is not agreeable
when under the influence of the winds usually prevailing around
the isolated rock. There is a feeling of home about the good
family Scaglione and their ways, which is most pleasing. In the
evening we all adjourned for a prima sera visit to the house of the
Sott' intendente, Don Antonio Buonafede, and there passed an
hour or two, ere the return to supper, in showing drawings to
admiring officials and their families.

August 13.—We had arranged to start after dinner for Rocella,
the next place in our line to the north-east corner of the province,

so we devoted the morning to our hosts, going with them to see the lions of their native town. The cathedral of Gerace must have been most interesting as it formerly existed; but except the great number of columns from ancient Locris, the Norman building has totally disappeared, all the upper part having been destroyed by the great earthquake of 1783,[1] which left half Gerace in ruins. There is a crypt below the cathedral, which, to architects, would prove extremely interesting, as would the mosaic altars in the upper building, as well as those of San Francesco, another church in the city.

Having made all ready before dinner, we quitted the amiable family of Scaglione soon afterwards, promising to return to them on our way back from Stilo, for I purpose to go no further northward than that town, the boundary of this province. Thence, in order to see the whole of Calabria Ulteriore I, before advancing into the next division, it appears to me that the best plan is, having gone northward by the sea-shore, to return hither by the hills (Gerace being a central point of the province), and then cross them to the western side of the peninsula.

Descending to the River Novito, whose broad fiumara runs from the mountains north of Gerace to the sea, we ascended the hill of Siderno, and passed through that town, a large, but not picturesque place. The costumes of the peasantry are, however, becoming more marked in character; the women all wear deep-blue dresses, with four-inch broad orange or pink borders, and their heads are covered with black or white panni-cloths, adjusted as in the province of Terra di Lavoro. Throughout this, and all our walks hitherto, the civility and friendliness of every person we meet is most agreeable. Hence, leaving the Marina di Siderno on the right (it is said to be a thriving place among the little ports of this coast), we descended towards the sea in a northerly direction, and after many a long lane, by olive-grounds and fig-gardens, reached the beach. Rocella, on its

[1] See Hon. K. Craven on the Cathedral of Gerace. Swinburne.

rocky cape, always a beautiful object even from Gerace, becomes more and more beautiful as one advances towards it; but the hour grew late, and so low was the sun, that it was only by hard running that I reached a spot, among aloes and olives, by the sea-side, near enough to draw the fine outline before me. When the sun had set, there were yet three miles to the town, over a flat ground, intersected with deceitful ravines, so that delays in approaching it were as unexpected as unavoidable. Troops of peasants passed us, playing the Zampogne merrily; dark grew the sky, and the stars were bright, as we arrived at the foot of the suburbs of Rocella—once a stronghold of the Caraffa family—now a collection of scattered houses below, and a knot of others on the double fortress rock. Don Giuseppe Nanni, to whom our letter directed us, we were told lived close to the castle; so up we went to the upper rock, through black arches and passages to a piazza surrounded by houses, all, as we could see, by their ragged walls against the sky, in utter ruin.

Ciccio shouted aloud, but no signs of life were given in the total darkness. We tried this turning—it was blocked up by a dead wall; that way you stumbled among sleeping horses; the next path led you to the precipice. We despaired, and remained calling forth 'ai! ai! Don Giuseppe Nanni! Oo! ooo! ai! ai!' till we were hoarse, but there was no other way of attracting attention. At last (as if there had been no steps taken at all to arouse the neighbourhood), a man came, as it were casually, forth from the dark ruins, holding a feeble light, and saying mildly, 'Cosa cercate?'[1] 'We seek Don Giuseppe Nanni's house,' said we. 'This is it,' said he. So we walked, with no small pleasure, into the very place under whose windows we had been screaming for the last hour past. It was a very old palazzo, with tiny rooms, built against a rock, and standing on the extreme edge of the precipice towards the sea. As usual, the family received us cordially—Don Giuseppe, and Don Aristide,

1 What do you want?

93

the Canonico, and Don Ferdinando; and during the doleful two
hours preceding supper, we sat alternately watching the stars, or
listening to the owl-answering-owl melody in the rocks above
our heads, or fought bravely through the *al solito* questions about
the tunnel, and the produce of Inghilterra, though I confess to
having been more than once fast asleep, and, waking up abruptly,
answered at random, in the vaguest manner, to the applied
catechetical torture. I will not say what I did not aver to be the
natural growth of England—camels, cochineal, sea-horses, or
gold-dust; and as for the *célèbre tunnel*, I fear I invested it drowsily
with all kinds of fabulous qualities. Supper was at last announced,
and an addition to our party was made in the handsome wife of
Don Ferdinando, and other females of the family, though I do not
think they shared greatly in the conversation. Vegetables and
fruit alone embellished the table. The world of Rocella particularly piques itself on the production and culture of fruit; and our
assertion that we *had* fruit in England, was received with thinly
hidden incredulity.

'You confess you have no wine—no oranges—no olives—
no figs;—how, then, *can* you have apples, pears, or plums? It
is a known fact that *no* fruit does or can grow in England, only
potatoes, and nothing else whatever—this is well known. Why,
then, do you tell us that which is not true?'

It was plain we were looked upon as vagabond impostors.

'Ma davvero,'[1] said we, humbly; 'davvero abbiamo de'
frutti—e di piu, ne abbiamo certi frutti che loro non hanno
affatto.' Suppressed laughter and supercilious sneers, when this
assertion was uttered, nettled our patriotic feelings.

[1] But indeed we *have* fruit; and, what is more, we have some fruits which
you have not got at all.

Oh what fruit can you possibly have that we have not? Oh how you are
laughing at us! Name your fruits then—these fabulous fruits!

We have currants, gooseberries, and greengages.

And what are gooseberries and greengages? There are no such things—this is
nonsense.

'O che mai frutti possono avere loro che non abbiamo noi?
O quanto ci burlano! Nominateli dunque—questi frutti vostri
favolosi!'

'Giacché volete sapere,' said we; 'abbiamo Currants—
abbiamo Gooseberries—abbiamo Greengages.'

'E che cosa sono Gooseberries e Gringhegi?' said the whole
party, in a rage; ' non ci sono queste cose—sono sogni.'

So we ate our supper in quiet, convinced almost that we had
been telling lies; that gooseberries were unreal and fictitious;
greengages a dream.

CHAPTER X

We pass the morning at Rocella.—Its magnificently picturesque character.—We leave Rocella and the sea-side.—Cross
the River Alaro.—Rich vegetation.—Ascent to Stignano.—
Vast herds of goats.—Two pointed hats from the province of
Catanzaro.—The family of Don Cicillo Caristò.—Evening in
the balcony.—Little owls.—Hospitality as usual.—Somewhat of dullness.—Prospective costumes in Northern Calabria.—Fête of the Madonna.—Drums and noise.—We grow
weary of Stignano.—The dinner.—New idea for a valentine;
Cupid among the maccaroni.—We set off to Stilo.—The River
Stillaro.—Grand character and architectural beauty of Stilo.
—Its magnificent situation.—Its well-kept streets.—House
of Don Ettore Marzano.—Agreeable host and thoroughly
cordial reception.—Difficulty of selecting views among a
multitude of fine points.—A visit to Bazzano.—Courteous
manners of peasantry.—Daily thunder-storm.—Agreeable stay
at Stilo.—Fly-flappers.—Life at Stilo.—Conversazione.—
Plans for continuing the tour.

August 14.—We politely declined Don Aristide as cicerone
through the town, as we had but the morning to choose points
to sketch from, as well as to work hard, for we had planned
to go as far towards Stilo as possible in the afternoon. Full
occupation was there in Rocella till noon, for the town and rock
is a little world of scenic splendour, and besides its various
beauties as a whole, its details are exquisite—palm-trees and all
sorts of vegetable incidents included. The Nanni family are good
hearty people, but less refined than the Scaglioni of Gerace.

At dinner they had procured dishes of the largest pears and apples
to be found in Rocella, by way of dessert, and they watched
our faces for signs of mortification thereat, evidently attributing
our non-amazement to our firm resolve not to tell truth, and
betray our country's horticultural failings.

At half-past two we left Rocella, certainly one of the very
finest coast scenes of Southern Calabria, and turning round the
end of the promontory, pursued our way northward along the
sea-shore; but so frequently were we tempted to sketch, that
there were no hopes of reaching Stilo ere night-fall. After passing
the River Alaro, too large a stream to be crossed on foot, we
struck inland, through lanes bordered with every possible kind of
shrub, and rich with the most luxurious vegetation; and as we
commenced the long ascent to the large village of Stignano, the
mountain views were more than ordinarily first-rate. In the wide
fiumara of the Alaro, we observed a flock of five or six hundred
goats among the picturesque accidents of the day; and we also
met two men with real positive pointed hats—a circumstance of
the most exciting nature. Are we then at last leaving the land
of Sicilian long blue nightcaps? But, alas, quoth the spokesman
of our two peasants, 'Siamo della provincia di Catanzaro—
siamo di Squillace.'[1] So we must wait patiently yet.

At Stignano we arrived late. It is a wild place on a steep
height, and we went with a letter to the house of Don Cicillo
Caristò, who received us heartily enough; but, in common with
all his family, overwhelmed and grieved us with bitter lamentations that they were obliged to live at Stignano. Once they lived
in Napoli, but now they were doomed to lifelong discontent
concerning all things in general, and their Stignano existence in
particular: like the people in the happy valley of Rasselas, they
said, we feel a chain around us, and would sacrifice all to go once
more into the gay world! The unexpected decease of an elder
member of the family had given the present possessor his little

---

[1] We come from the province of Catanzaro—we come from Squillace.

property in this remote village; and very ill did the gift of fortune seem appreciated.

We sate all the evening in a balcony looking towards the mountains; pleasant pastime enough, as the moon shone brightly, and we listened to the 'gufi,' or little owls, answering each other far and near; yet, for all this, we were half asleep before the supper was announced, and moreover the family of Caristò were not possessed of any conversational talents. Nothing did they care for the Thames Tunnel, and as little for the produce of England. The grandfather, the host, his children of all ages, and some old domestics, composed the party; and what was wanting in refinement was made up in good-will and heartiness to us, though among themselves the circle seemed rather to jar and spar.

The costume of the good-looking girl who waited at table was the prettiest we had seen; and say the Stignanesi, 'if costumes please you, you will find better ones at every place you go to henceforward.'

August 15.—It is not easy in this wandering life to arrange matters so as to see certain parts of the country with a view to a comfortable division of halting places. In order to have more leisure at Stilo, we agree to pass the morning here, and to go thither after dinner; and though all Stignano, on account of the day being the festival of the Madonna, seems to have formed itself into a committee of drummers, we must bear the noise as best we may.

But it must be confessed that life at Stignano is oppressive. The famiglia Caristò would never leave us alone; when they do not catechise, they stand in a row and stare at us with all their might; and the grandpaternal Caristò is a thoroughly scrutinising and insatiable bore. At dinner, also, there was a most confused assemblage of large dogs under the table who fought for casual crumbs and bones, and when they did not accidentally bite one's extremities, rushed, wildly barking, all about the little room. But the most remarkable accident during our stay was caused by a small juvenile Caristò, who, during the mid-day meal, climbed abruptly on to the table, and before he could be rescued, performed a series of struggles among the dishes, which ended by the little pickle's losing his balance and collapsing suddenly in a sitting posture into the very middle of the maccaroni dish, from which P—— and I rejoiced to think we had been previously helped. One sees in valentines Cupids on beds of roses, or on birds' nests; but a slightly-clothed Calabrese infant sitting in the midst of a hot dish of maccaroni appears to me a perfectly novel idea.

At half-past three we commenced our journey northward once more. The route from Stignano to Stilo is a mule-track threading a wild region between mountain ranges, which here shut out all view of the sea; the hills extending far eastward to the coast, so as to leave but little space for cultivation. In less than an hour we arrived at the Stillaro; which the violent rains, accompanying a thunder-storm at noon, had so swollen, that the crossing it was not to be easily performed on foot: the imperturbable Ciccio, however, carried us over on his back safely enough. Soon the town of Stilo on its height became visible, and though it was dusk before we arrived there, yet there was light enough to perceive that its general aspect was most promisingly picturesque; standing immediately below perpendicular precipices, it is built on a sort of amphitheatrical terrace, the projecting rocks at each extremity crowned with the most picturesque churches and convents. There appeared to be more evidence of care and cleanliness in the streets than in other Calabrian places we had passed through, and there was an air of orderly feeling and decent neatness, which struck us as remarkable in a place more remote from the capital than any we had yet visited. Don Ettore Marzano, to whom our introduction was addressed, seemed a thoroughly hearty, as well as polite, young man, and his large house was well kept and comfortable (speaking of things as they are in Italy), though without attempt at splendour. With ready alacrity our host put us in possession of two large rooms, and then leaving us, sent a servant to administer to our wants; a tact and attention which reminded me of my old friends of Abruzzo, whom I was continually holding up to my fellow-traveller as the models of Italian provincials. Supper, a simple and good one, was announced when ready, without any preparatory waiting or questions; our host, a bachelor, being the third of the party. The friendly and gentleman-like tone of this all' *improvviso* reception, in so remote a district, greatly delighted us.

August 16.—When a landscape painter halts for two or three days in one of the large towns of these regions, never perhaps to be revisited by him, the first morning at least is generally consumed in exploring it: four or five hours are very well spent, if they lead to the knowledge of the general forms of the surrounding scenes, and to the securing fixed choice of subject and quiet study to the artist during the rest of his stay. So many and so exquisite are the beauties of Stilo, that to settle to drawing any of them was difficult, and after having glanced at all the notabilia close to the town, I employed the rest of the morning in walking to Bazzano and Bigonzi, two villages on the farthest outskirts of Calabria Ulteriore I, in face of the mountains among whose depths lie the ruins of the famous Norman convent of Santo Stefano del Bosco. The gorge between Stilo and Bazzano is excessively grand, but the villages were not such as to tempt me to sketch them; the morning's walk, however, was delightful, if only for the opportunity it offered of observing the universally courteous and urbane manners of the peasantry. It is probable that no stranger had ever visited these wild and unfrequented nooks of a province, the great towns of which are themselves out of the route of travellers; but no one met or overtook me on the way to Bigonzi without a word or two of salutation; there were few who did not offer me pears, and parties of women laden with baskets of figs would stop and select the best for us. Nor did anybody ask a question beyond, 'What do you think of our mountains?' or 'How do you like our village?' In the town of Stilo we were sometimes followed by not less than fifty or a hundred people, but ever with the utmost good feeling and propriety. The well-bred population of Stilo we shall ever remember with pleasure.

In these high mountains, a mid-day thunder-storm frequently occurs betwixt eleven and noon; and this interruption to the labours of the pencil gave us more opportunity of conversing with our hospitable friends. There is, however, but little to note in the house or household of Don Ettore Marzano, except that all was perfectly orderly and agreeable. The only trait which was so uncommon as to be at all worth recording, was that a domestic stood at meal-time close to the table, and in order to dissipate the flies, which at this season are a legion, flapped a long flapper of feathers, Laputa-wise, close to our faces. No sooner did we begin to speak than whizz—flick—down came the flapper, so as to render conversation a rather difficult effort.

August 17.—Was passed in the usual routine of drawing, and of quiet home-life at the Casa Marzano. Crowds are attracted to see our occupation when we busy ourselves with sketching near the town; but all are merry and orderly. Employment for life might be found in the grand and novel mountain scenery round this magnificent Stilo. A walk to a garden belonging to Don A. Marzano's family amused us in the later afternoon; and in the evening we went to a 'soirée,' at one of his uncles, Don Antonio Crea. There were good rooms in his palazzo, and round them was hung a large selection of engravings, from Claude and

Poussin. Cards were the principal amusement, and ices were handed round at intervals. To-morrow we leave this place; and hope to reach Gioiosa by night, if not compelled by weather or lack of time to halt at Castel Vetere. On the 22nd we hope to be at Gerace once more, Cánalo having been visited in the interval.

CHAPTER XI

Departure from Stilo.—Early morning.—Town of Motta
Placánica.—Its extraordinary appearance.—Cross the river
Alaro.—Ascent to Castel Vetere.—Palazzo of Don Ilario
Asciutti.—The grandfather of the family; his eloquence.—
The dinner.—Discourse on flesh, fowl, and fish.—Our host is
angry at our early departure.—We appease him, and depart.
—We descend the valley of the river Meano.—Come in sight
of Rocella.—Ascend the river Romano, and reach Gioiosa at
dusk.—Reception at the house of the Baron Rivettini.—
Interview with the Baron.—Card-playing.—Doubts and
questions.—The evening meal.—'Why?'—Coming events
cast their shadows before.

August 18.—Once more upon the road.—Long before sunrise we had said addio to Don Ettore Marzano, the most pleasing
of the younger Calabrese gentry whom we had yet seen; a
thoroughly good and hospitable fellow, and well informed on
most subjects. Stilo we shall ever recollect as in all respects
agreeable.

All nature was deep gray and brown—no rock lit up by the
yet hidden sun,—as we descended to the valley of the Stillaro, and
retraced our steps as far as Stignano, the home of the querulous
Caristo family, and the scene of the maccaroni-throned infant.
Leaving the town on our left, we plunged into a deep vale between
olive-clothed slopes, and, climbing up the opposite side, were
soon in Motta Placánica, one of the most truly characteristic of
Calabrian towns. Like others of these strange settlements, this
place has no depth, but is, as it were, surface only, the houses

being built one above another, on ledges and in crevices, over
the face of a large rock rising into a peak, its highest pinnacle
being graced by a modern palazzo. The strange effect which
these towns have, even upon those long used to the irregu-
larities of South Italian village architecture, is not to be imagined;
—Motta Placánica seems constructed to be a wonder to passers-
by. Long we lingered to draw this most singular place; and,
leaving it by a steep descent, we came to the valley of the
Paganiti, crossing it and winding up the height on its farther side,
whence the rock of Motta Placánica appeared like a giant king
of nine-pins, as seen edgeways against the sky—no one of its
buildings but the crowning castle being visible. Hence, also,
the eye ranged beyond the river Alaro, which we had crossed
on our way from Rocella, to the high hill and walls of Castel
Vetere (representative of the ancient Caulon[1]), a town built
on one of those isolated hills which, to antiquarians, at once
proclaim an ancient site. By the aid of the placid Ciccio
and his horse, we crossed the swollen river, and, ascending
wearily to the town, found it, though mean in appearance from
below, full of houses of a large size and indicating wealth and
prosperity.

To that of Don Ilario Asciutti we went, narrowly escaping the
mid-day autumn thunder-storm, and found a large mansion, with
a hall and staircase, ante-room, and drawing-room very surprising as to dimensions and furniture; the walls were papered,
and hung with mirrors, prints, &c.; chiffoniers, tables, and a
book-case adorned the sides of the rooms, and there were foot-
stools, with other unwonted objects of trans-Calabrian luxury.

---

[1] Caulon, antiquaries agree in placing at or near Castel Vetere. Pacichelli
speaks of its splendid and regular fortress, and its palace belonging to the
Caraffa family. The Asciutti are named by him as an old family. The modern
town stands between the rivers Alaro and Musa, but from earthquakes or other
causes, is now in a very ruinous condition, excepting a new quarter of the town
which is in process of building.

GIOIOSA

PASS OF CANALO

The famiglia Asciutti were polite and most friendly; there were two smart sons, just come from college at Naples; a serene and silent father; and last, not least, an energetic and astute grandsire, before whose presence all the rest were as nothing. The Nonno[1] Asciutti was as voluble as Conte Garrolo; but with more connected ideas and sentences, and with an overpowering voice; an expression of 'L'état, c'est moi,' in all he said and did. The old gentleman surprised us not a little by his information on the subjects on which (apropos de bottes) he held forth—the game laws of England, and Magna Charta, the Reformation, the Revolution of 1688, Ireland, and the Reform Bill. He was becoming diffuse on European politics, having already discussed America and the Canadas, and glanced slightly at slavery, the East and West Indies and the sugar trade, when, to our great satisfaction, all this learning, so wonderful in the heart of Magna-Grecia, was put a stop to by the announcement of dinner. The silent son, and the two gay grandsons, listened to their elder relative's discourse, but took no part therein; and we, however superior the matter of the oration might be, greatly longed to exchange the orator for dear, little, fussy Conte Garrolo.

In the large dining-room were assembled many female and juvenile Asciutti, all very ugly;—hitherto we are not struck by Calabrian female beauty in the higher orders, though many of the peasant girls are pretty. The ladies spoke not during dinner, and the whole weight of the oral entertainment fell on the erudite grandfather, who harangued loftily from his place at the end of the table. It was Wednesday, and there was no meat, as is usual on that day in South Italian families. 'It would be better,' said the authoritative elder, 'if there were no such a thing as meat—nobody ought to eat any meat. The Creator never intended meat, that is the flesh of quadrupeds, to be eaten. No good Christians ought to eat flesh—and why? The quadruped works for man

---

[1] Grandfather.

while alive, and it is a shame to devour him when dead. The sheep gives wool, the ox ploughs, the cow gives milk, the goat cheese.'—'Cosa fanno per noi i lepri?'[1]—whispered one of the grandsons. 'Statevi zitt'!'[2] shouted the orator. 'But fish,' continued he—'what do *they* do for us? Does a mullet plough? Can a prawn give milk? Has a tunny any wool? No. Fish and birds also were therefore created to be eaten.' A wearisome old man was the Asciutti Nonno! but the alarming point of his character was yet to be made known to us. No sooner, dinner being over, did we make known our intention of proceeding to sleep at Gioiosa on account of our limited time, than we repented having visited Castel Vetere at all. 'O Cielo! O rabbia! O che mai sento? O chi sono? O chi siete?'[3] screamed the Nonno, in a paroxysm of rage. 'What have I done that you will not stay? How can I bear such an insult! Since Calabria was Calabria, no such affront has ever been offered to a Calabrian! Go—*why* should you go?' In vain we tried to assuage the grand-sire's fury. We had staid three days in Gerace, three in Reggio, two in Bova and in Stilo, and not one in Castel Vetere! The silent father looked mournful, the grandsons implored; but the wrathful old gentleman having considerably endangered the furniture by kicks and thumps, finally rushed down stairs in a frenzy, greatly to our discomfiture.

The rest of the family were distressed seriously at this incident, and on my sending a message to beg that he would show us a new palazzo he was constructing (himself the architect), for the increased accommodation of the family Asciutti, he relented so far as to return, and after listening favourably to our encomiastic remarks, bade us a final farewell with a less perturbed countenance and spirit.

[1] What do the hares do for us?

[2] Hold your tongue!

[3] Oh heavens! Oh rage! Oh what do I hear? Oh who am I? Oh who are you?

There are many fine views of Castel Vetere, which has some-what in it of the grandiose and classic, from whatever point regarded, but we left it with less agreeable impressions than those we had carried from most of the larger Calabrian towns, partly from the feeling that we had vexed our host's family, and partly that it was yet so far to go to Gioiosa, that old Ciccio, with more than one admonitory growl, would not allow us to pause to sketch—no, not even for a quarter of an hour. Soon—after passing over high ground, from which the last views of ancient Caulon were very noble—we entered the downward course of the Meano, which, eternally winding over white stones, shut us in between high banks, till we came, at sunset, in sight of Rocella on its double rock; this, together with the river-bed, we bid farewell to by taking a route parallel to the coast, as far as the Fiume Romano, which we ascended for an hour, till we arrived at Gioiosa, apparently a large and well-built town, on the banks of a narrow part of the stream. The house of the Baron Rivettini, to whom we had letters, was large and imposing, but the Baron was not within, and the servants, with none of that stranger-helping alacrity of hospitality, so remarkable in more northern provinces of the Regno di Napoli, appeared too much amazed at the sudden arrival of 'due forestieri,'[1] to do anything but contemplate us; and, to speak truth, neither our appearance, considering we had toiled through some rain and much dirt all the afternoon, nor our suite, consisting of a man and a horse, were very indicative of being 'comme il faut.' With difficulty we obtained leave to rest in a sort of ante-office, half stable, half kitchen, while a messenger carried our letter of introduction to the Baron Rivettini. When he returned, quoth he, 'The Baron is playing at cards, and cannot be interrupted; but, as there is no locanda in the town, you may sleep where you are.' Un-washed, hungry, and tired as we were, and seeing that there was

[1] Two strangers.

nothing but an old rug by way of furniture in this part of the Baron's premises, we did not feel particularly gratified by this permission, the more that P—— was rather unwell, and I feared he might have an attack of fever; neither did the domestics offer us caffè, or any other mitigation of our wayfaring condition. 'Is there no caffè?' 'Non c'è.'[1] 'No wine?' 'Non c'è.' 'No light?' 'Non c'è.' It was all 'Non c'è.' So said I, 'Show me the way to the house where the Baron is playing at cards.' But the proposal was met with a blank silence, wholly unpropitious to our hopes of a night's lodging; and it was not until after I had repeated my request several times, that a man could be persuaded to accompany me to a large palazzo at no great distance, the well-lighted lower story of which exhibited offices, barrels, sacks, mules, &c., all indicative of the thriving merchant. In a spacious salone on the first floor sate a party playing at cards, and one of them a minute gentleman, with a form more resembling that of a sphere than any person I ever remember to have seen, was pointed out to me as the Baron by the shrinking domestic who had thus far piloted me. But excepting by a single glance at me, the assembled company did not appear aware of my entrance, nor, when I addressed the Baron by his name, did he break off the thread of his employment, otherwise than by saying, 'Uno, due, tre,—signore, si—quattro, cinque,—servo suo,—fanno quindici.'[2]

'Has your Excellency received an introductory letter from the Cavalier da Nava?' said I.

'Cinque, sei,—si, signore,—fanno undici,'[3] said the Baron, timidly.

This, thought I, is highly mysterious.

'Can I and my travelling companion lodge in your house, Signor Baron, until to-morrow?'

[1] There is none.

[2] One, two, three,—yes, sir,—four, five,—your servant, sir,—make fifteen.
[3] Five, six,—yes, sir,—make eleven.

'Tre e sei fanno none,'[1] pursued the Baron, with renewed attention to the game. 'Ma *perchè*,[2] signore?'

'*Perchè*, there is no inn in this town; and, *perchè*, I have brought you a letter of introduction,' rejoined I.

'Ah, si si si, signore, pray favour me by remaining at my house.—Two and seven are nine—eight and eleven are nineteen.' And again the party went on with the Giuoco.

There was an anxiety, and an expression of doubt and mystery on the faces of all the party, which, however, did not escape my observation, and I felt sure, as I left the room, that something was wrong; though, like King Coal's prophet of traditional celebrity, 'I knew not what that something could be.'

When I returned to the Palazzo Rivettini, all the scene was changed. Coffee was brought to us, and a large room was assigned for our use, while all the natural impulse of Calabrese hospitality seemed, for a time at least, to overpower the mysterious spell which, from some unknown cause, appeared to oppress those inhabitants of Gioiosa with whom we were brought in contact. But the magic atmosphere of doubt and astonishment returned in full force as other persons of the town came in to the evening conversazione. Few words were said but those of half-suppressed curiosity as to where we came from; and the globose little Baron himself gradually confined his observations to the single interrogative, '*Perchè?*' which he used in a breathless manner, on the slightest possible provocation. Supper followed, every part of the entertainment arrayed with the greatest attention to plenty and comfort; but the whole circle seemed ill at ease, and regarded our looks and movements with unabated watchfulness, as if we might explode, or escape through the ceiling at any unexpected moment; so that both hosts and guests seemed but too well pleased when we returned to our room, and the incessant '*Perchè? perchè? perchè?*' was, for this evening at least, silenced.

[1] Three and six are nine.   [2] Why, what for?

By all this mystery—so very unusual to the straightforward and cordial manners of these mountaineers—there was left on my mind a distinct impression of some supposed or anticipated evil. 'Coming events cast their shadows before.'

CHAPTER XII

August 19.—As usual, we rose before sunrise, 'O Dio! *perchè?*'
said the diminutive Baron Rivettini, who was waiting outside the
door, lest perhaps we might have attempted to pass through the
keyhole. A suite of large drawing-rooms was thrown open, and
thither caffè was brought with the most punctilious ceremony.
My suspicions of last night were confirmed by the great precision
with which our passports were examined, and by the minute
manner in which every particular relating to our eyes, noses,
and chins, was written down; nor was it until after endless

interrogatories and more '*perchès*' than are imaginable, that we were released. But our usual practice of taking a small piece of bread with our coffee renewed the universal surprise and distrust of our hosts.

'Pane!' said the Baron, '*perchè* pane? O Cielo!'

'I never take sugar,' said P——, as some was offered to him.

'Sant' Antonio, non prendete zucchero? *Perchè?* O Dio! *perchè* mai non prendete zucchero?'[1]

'We want to make a drawing of your pretty little town,' said I; and, in spite of a perfect hurricane of '*perchès*,' out we rushed, followed by the globular Baron, in the most lively state of alarm, down the streets, across the river on stepping-stones, and up the opposite bank, from the steep cliffs of which, over-hung with oak foliage, there is a beautiful view of Gioiosa on its rock.

'O per carità! O Cielo! O San Pietro! cosa mai volete fare?' said the Baron, as I prepared to sit down.

'I am going to draw for half-an-hour,' said I.

'Ma—*perchè?*'

And down I sate, working hard for nearly an hour, during all which time the perplexed Baron walked round and round me, occasionally uttering a melancholy—

'O signore, ma *perchè?*'

'Signore Baron,' said I, when I had done my sketch, 'we have no towns in our country so beautifully situated as Gioiosa!'

'Ma *perchè?*' quoth he.

I walked a little way, and paused to observe the bee-eaters,[2] which were flitting through the air above me, and under the spreading oak branches.

'Per l'amor del Cielo, cosa guardate? Cosa mai osservate?'[3] said the Baron.

---

[1] Do you not take sugar? &c.

[2] Merops Apiaster.

[3] For the love of Heaven, what are you looking at? What do you perceive?

'I am looking at those beautiful blue birds.'

'*Perchè? perchè? perchè?*'

'Because they are so very pretty, and because we have none like them in England.'

'Ma *perchè? perchè?*'

It was evident that do or say what I would, some mystery was connected with each action and word; so that, in spite of the whimsical absurdity of these eternal what fors and whys, it was painful to see that, although our good little host strove to give scope to his hospitable nature, our stay caused more anxiety than pleasure. Besides, his whole demeanour so strongly reminded one of Croaker—'Do you foresee anything, child? You look as if you did. I think if anything was to be foreseen, I have as sharp a look out as another,'—that it was no easy task to preserve a proper degree of gravity.

His curiosity, however, was to be tried still further; for, having heard that Gioiosa was famous for the manufacture of sugarplums or confetti, we had resolved to take some hence to Gerace, to give to little Cicillo and Maria Scaglione; but when we asked where confetti could be purchased, the poor Baron became half breathless with astonishment and suspense, and could only utter, from time to time, 'Non è possibile! Non è possibile! O gran Cielo! Confetti? confetti? *Perchè* confetti? Non è possibile.'[1] We proved, however, that sugarplums we were determined to have, and forthwith got the direction to a confectioner's, whither we went and bought an immense quantity, the mystified Baron following us to the shop and back, saying continually '*Perchè, perchè*, confetti! O Cielo! *perchè?*' We then made all ready to start with the faithful Ciccio, and, not unwillingly, took leave of the Palazzo Rivettini, the anxious Baron thrusting his head from a window, and calling out, 'Ma *fermatevi, perchè? Perchè andatevi? Statevi a pranzo, perchè* no?

[1] It is not possible! it is not possible! O great Heaven! Sugarplums? *Why* sugarplums, &c.

Perchè ucelli? *Perchè* disegni? *Perchè* confetti? *Perchè perchè, perchè, perchè?*[1] till the last '*perchè*' was lost in distance as we passed once more round the rock, and crossed the river Romano.

Long did we indulge in merriment at the perturbation our visit had occasioned to our host, whom we shall long remember as 'Baron Wherefore.' Nevertheless, a certainty impresses me that so much timidity is occasioned by some hidden event or expectation.

Merrily we went through the long garden lanes which stretch away seaward from Gioiosa, over a rich tract of country most luxuriant in vegetables and fruit. Soon we left the coast once more, and winding round the uninteresting olive-clad hill of Siderno, ascended to Agnano, a village on the hill-side above the river Novito, the valley of which stream separates it from the rock of Gerace. From Agnano the eye looks into the very heart of the ravine of the Novito; and high above it on the west below stupendous cliffs, stands Cánalo, a village at the entrance of the Passo del Mercante, a wild route leading across the mountains to the western side of Calabria.

To Cánalo we were bound; it had been described to us by our friends in Gerace as 'Un luogo tutto orrido, ed al modo vostro pittoresco;'[2] and although Grotteria and Mammola were named in the same category, we could not devote time to all three.

We rested an hour at Agnano, with Don Nicòla Speziati, to whom we had a letter; but although there were mines of iron or copper in the neighbourhood which we ought to have gone to see under Don Nicòla's guidance—he being the agent for the works—yet we neglected to do so, preferring the search after landscapes of Cánalo to exploring scenes of utility made illustrious by the recent visit of King Ferdinand and his Queen. All

[1] But stop—*why* do you go? stay to dinner; *why* not? *why* birds? *why* drawings? *why* sugarplums, &c.
[2] A place altogether horrible; and, after your fashion, picturesque.

the Court had arrived in the preceding autumn on the coast in a steamer, and came hither from the Marina of Siderno on a vast crowd of donkeys, collected by the peasantry for the occasion. 'Maestà,' said the owner of the ass on which the royal traveller rode, 'no one else can ever ride on this donkey: it shall have a bit of ground and a stable to itself for the rest of its honourable life. I wish, nevertheless, Maestà, that I had another; for though the honour is great, yet I have no other mode of getting my livelihood.' The King, say the villagers hereabouts, gave the acute countryman all the dollars he had about him, and settled a small pension on him besides for life.

The view of Cánalo from the ravine of the Novito is extremely grand, and increased in majestic wonder as we descended to the stream through fine hanging woods. Having crossed the wide torrent-bed—an impracticable feat in winter—we gradually rose into a world of stern rocks—a wilderness of terror, such as it is not easy to describe or imagine. The village itself is crushed and squeezed into a nest of crags immediately below the vast precipices which close round the Passo del Mercante, and when on one side you gaze at this barrier of stone, and then, turning round, perceive the distant sea and undulating lines of hill, no contrast can be more striking. At the summit of Cánalo stands a large building, the Palazzo of Don Giovanni Rosa, the chief proprietor of the place, an extremely old man, whose manners were most simple and kind. 'My grandchildren,' said he, 'you are welcome to Cánalo, and all I can do for you will be too little to show you my goodwill;' and herewith he led us to the cleanest of rooms, which were to be ours during our stay, and apologised for any 'mancanza'[1] we might find. 'You must excuse a bad fare to-day, but I will get you better to-morrow,' quoth Don Giovanni Rosa. The remainder of the afternoon we employed in wandering about the town and its most extraordinary environs, where masses of Titan rock threaten to crush the atoms of life

[1] Deficiency.

that nestle beneath them. I have never seen such wondrous bits of rock scenery. Meanwhile, old careful Ciccio never lost sight of us; he was always silent, contenting himself by following our footsteps as attendant and guard, lest excess of enthusiasm might hurry us over one of the fearful precipices of Cánalo.

August 20.—Every spot around this place possesses the very greatest interest, and is full of the most magnificent foreground studies. All the morning we drew on the hill-sides, between the town and Agnano; and very delightful were those morning hours, passed among the ever-changing incidents of mountain scenery—the goats and cattle among the tall oaks, the blue woody hills beyond. At dinner-time, good old Don Giovanni Rosa amused and delighted us by his lively simplicity and good breeding. He had only once in his long life (he was eighty-two) been as far as Gerace, but never beyond. 'Why should I go?' said he; 'if, when I die, as I shall ere long, I find Paradise like Cánalo, I shall be well pleased. To me "Cánalo mio" has always seemed like Paradise—sempre mi sembra Paradiso, niente mi manca.'[1] Considering that the good old man's Paradise is cut off by heavy snow four months in the year from any external communication with the country round, and that it is altogether (however attractive to artists) about as little a convenient place as may well be imagined—the contented mind of Don Giovanni was equally novel and estimable. The only member of our host's family now living is a grandson, who was one of our party, a silent youth, who seemed never to do or say anything at any time. Our meals were remarkable, inasmuch as Paradiso cookery appeared to delight in singular experiments and materials. At one time a dish was exhibited full of roasted squirrels, adorned by funghi of wonderful shapes and colours; at another, there were relays of most surprising birds: among which my former ornithological studies caused me to recognise a few corvine mandibles, whose

[1] My Cánalo always seems Paradise to me, I am in want of nothing.

appearance was not altogether in strict accordance with the culinary arrangements of polite society.

Over all the doors which connected the suite of apartments we lived in, were rude paintings of various places, by a native artist, with their names placed below each. There were Naples and Rome, Vesuvius and Etna, London, Paris, Constantinople, and Saint Helena; but as most of these views contained three similar fuzzy trees, a lighthouse, and a sheet of water, or some such equally generic form of landscape, we were constrained to look on names below as more a matter of form than use.

The peasantry of Cánalo were perfectly quiet and well-behaved, and in nowise persecuted us in our drawing excursions. Only a poor harmless idiot followed us wherever we went, sitting below the rock or path we took for our station, and saying, without intermission, 'O Inglesini! dateci un granicello——wh——ew!'[1] the which sentence and whistle accompaniment he repeated all day long. Stern, awful scenes of Cánalo! Far, far above, along the pass to the western coast, you could discover diminutive figures threading the winding line among those fearful crags and fragments! or deep in the ravine, where torrents falling over perpendicular rocks echoed and foamed around, might be perceived parties of the women of Cánalo spreading out linen to dry, themselves like specks on the face of some enormous mass of stone; or groups of goats, clustered on some bright pinnacle, and sparkling in the yellow sunlight. Cánalo and its rocks are worth a long journey to behold.

August 21.—After dinner at noon, we made our last drawings in this singular place, and bade adieu to the Casa Rosa, with its clean, airy, neat rooms, its painted doors, its gardens, vines, and bee-hives, and its agreeable, kind, and untiringly merry master, old Don Giovanni Rosa. The pleasant and simple hospitality of

[1] O, little Englishman, give me a farthing!

Cánalo had once more restored us to our former admiration of Calabrian life and its accompaniments, which the little casualties of Gioiosa and Castel Vetere had begun to diminish.

Instead of returning to Agnano, we kept a downward route in the channel of the Novito. Throughout this valley there are interesting scenes of cultivation; the patch of gran turco or Indian corn, the shelving terraces of olives, and the cottages here and there, covered with luxuriant vine. Once opposite Gerace, we crossed the river, and gradually ascended to the town, which, with its crumbling white rock, is very grand and simple in form from the northward approach.

On arriving at the Palazzo Scaglione all the family were delighted to welcome us back, including little Cicillo and his sister, to whom the sugarplums were a source of high edification; and it was great sport for us to tell them of all our adventures since we had left them, save that we did not dilate on the facetiæ of the Baron Rivettini. All Gerace was in a fever of preparation for a great Festa, to take place on the following day; and in the evening P—— and I, with Padre Abbenate and Don Gaetano Scaglione, inspected the site of the entertainment, which was arranged at the west end of the rock, on the platform by the ruined castle. Here were Zampognari and booths, and dancing and illuminations, all like the days and doings of Tagliacozzo in the fête of 1843,[1] but on a smaller and more rustic scale. The Sottintendente, Don Antonio Buonafede, was presiding at the preliminary festivities. There was also, as in the Abruzzo, a temporary chapel erected in the open air, highly ornamented, and decked with figures of saints, &c.; but the usual accompaniments of dancing were expected to be rather a failure, as the Bishop of Gerace had published an edict prohibiting the practice of that festive amusement by any of the fairer sex whatever, so that poor Terpsichore was to be represented only by the male gender.

---

[1] See *Illustrated Excursion in Italy*, McLean.

in Calabria

August 22.—We passed all the morning, being left to our own devices by the good people of our host's family, in a quiet shade on the great rocks east of Gerace.

Parties from all sides of the country were winding up the sides of the ravine to the festa; but there was little or no costume, the black skirt, worn mantilla-wise after the fashion of the Civita-Castellanese, being the only peculiarity of dress in Gerace.

In the late afternoon we all repaired to the walls of the town to gaze at the procession of the saint's image, followed by the inmates of every one of the monasteries, and by all the ecclesiastics of the place. On the rocky platform, far below Gerace, yet elevated high above the maritime plain, are several convents, and far, far over the terraces of crags, among which they are built, the long line of the procession crept slowly, with attendant bands of music and firing of cannon—a curious scene, and not easy to pourtray. Hence, as evening was closing and the last golden streams of sunset had ceased to gild the merry scene, we came to the castle, where hundreds of peasants were dancing to the music of the Zampognari; black-hooded women ranged in tiers on the rock-terraces, sate like dark statues against the amber western sky; the gloomy and massive Norman ruins frowned over the misty gulf beneath with gloomier grandeur; the full moon rose high and formed a picturesque contrast with the festa lights, which sparkled on the dark background of the pure heaven; and all combined to create one of those scenes which must ever live in the memory, and can only be formed in imagination, because neither painting nor description can do them justice.

After supper all the Scaglione family wished us a hearty farewell—and may all good betide them! as kind a set of folk as stranger or wayfarer has met anywhere at any time. The days we passed with them will always be recollected with feelings of kindliness for their hearty welcome and friendly hospitality. Separated as Gerace is, though the chief town of a district, from the more civilised parts of Italy, its inhabitants marry chiefly among families in the immediate neighbourhood, and very rarely out of the province. Among the richer classes a few years of youth are passed away at Naples, where the sons attend schools and colleges, and the daughters are educated in nunneries; but after their return to their rocky fortress city, they seldom quit its precincts; and the changes of seasons, as they busy themselves with the agricultural produce of their sea-shore plains, and inland river vales, or the little politics of so narrow a space, alone vary the monotony or calm of Calabrian existence in these days, when mediæval party wars and the romance of brigandage are alike extinct.

SAN GIORGIO

PALMI

CHAPTER XIII

We leave the Casa Scaglione, and the east side of Calabria Ulteriore Prima.—Ascend the central ridge of mountains.—Come in sight of the Western sea.—Descent to the immense plains of Gioia, Terranova, &c.—Complete change in the character of the scenery.—Dreadful earthquake of 1783.—Descent to Castelnuovo.—Reception of Don Vincenzo Tito.—Character of the environs of Castelnuovo.—Olive-woods.—Plans for to-morrow.—Vast olive-grounds.—Town of San Giorgio.—Costume of its female inhabitants. Polístena.—Visit to the house of Morani the painter. Portraits of Sir Walter Scott and of Pio Nono.—Hospitality of Don Vincenzo Tito.—Departure from Castelnuovo.—Road through the olive-woods.—Radicena.—The destroyed town of Terranova.—Immense olive-plains from the mountains to the sea-shore.—We reach Oppido late, and find no friends there.—A disagreeable night's shelter.

August 23.—The domestics, as usual, could not be persuaded to accept anything on our leaving the Casa Scaglione, which we quitted an hour before sunrise. At the early period of our departure, Gerace was as yet undisturbed and still, and our regrets at leaving it were only broken by an unwonted torrent of loquacity on the part of Ciccio, and the burthen of which seemed a song of praise in honour of the hospitalities and of the festa of the city, and some strong comparisons in disfavour of Gioiosa —Díghi, dóghi, dà. We were soon ascending the central ridge of the mountains towards the western districts of Southern Calabria. The two coasts are here united by the 'Passo del Mercante,' and by the tremendous pass above Cánalo. Addio

Gerace! with Rocella and Siderno, Ardore, Bovalino, and all our old friends. The rock and Norman castle were long in sight ere woody hills and chestnut-clothed dells surrounded us on all sides, and shut out the eastern sea.

Our route to the west side of Italy was for a long while by a steep ascent; at its summit there is a broad green plain in the midst of beech-woods,—a calm inner hill-scene, where were cattle and shepherds; as on the higher parts of Monte Gennaro, near Rome, or many an Abruzzo altitude, we had hoped to have reached a spot whence both seas might be visible, but the east side was soon hidden by the highest peaks of Montalto, the loftiest point of the Aspromonte range, below whose woody crown lay the dark vale of Polsi, and the Hermit home, so cut off from all sympathies with the outer world. At length, the morning breeze and the fresh fern beneath our feet having made our walk truly pleasant, we came in sight of the Gulf of Gioia, and the scene changed to one of beautiful forest-groups of foliage, through which sparkled the soft western sea; descending through which we soon came to the wide tract of cultivated ground stretching from Nicótera to the hill country around Palmi and Bagnara. The heat became oppressive from the sultry scirocco, as we wound downward towards a most extensive and wondrous plain of olive-grounds—a filmy blue foliage occupying the whole wide level. We had come into a new world; no more gray and white rocks, but strange cones and points, and Vesuvian furrows, and volcanic smoothnesses; green tumuli and slopes covered with short brushwood, and everything from hill to sea suggesting something subterranean, not quite as it should be.

The mind instantly reverted to the fatal days of February, 1783, when one of the most terrible earthquakes on record utterly overwhelmed this beautiful tract of country, and when all this fair western coast of Calabria became one great sepulchre. The following graphic account of that event is extracted from the Hon. Keppel Craven's *Tour through Naples*, pp. 274–278:—

'On the 5th of February, 1783, a day indelibly stamped upon the recollection of every older native of this plain, all the towns and villages situated within its circuit were overthrown by the terrific shock, which extended far into Upper Calabria on one side, and reached to Sicily on the other. * * * * At Castelnuovo every edifice was cast to the earth. * * * * At Terranova one straight street, containing 700 inhabitants, remains in the midst of ruins, which are those of a town of 13,000 souls. * * * * Three particular days, the 5th and 7th of February, and the 28th of March, of the year 1783, are recorded as the periods of the most severe efforts of the convulsion; but six successive weeks from the first of these dates would perhaps be more correctly assigned to the continued internal fever, marked during that period by not less than a *thousand* distinct shocks: these were neither periodical, nor attended by any particular symptoms in the state of the temperature. The summer of the preceding year had been remarkably hot, and followed by violent and continued rains till the month of January. The winter was rather more severe than usual, as may be inferred by the frost on the night of the 5th and 6th of February. It has been observed, that this month and the following have in these regions been marked by the recurrence of four several earthquakes of more than ordinary violence.

'A thick fog succeeded the spring, and seemed suspended over all Calabria for some months, obscuring its shores from navigators, and only indicating their proximity by its existence, so unusual in these latitudes. It is difficult to imagine a more extraordinary picture than the appearance of this portion of Italy, during the first few months which followed this awful visitation, by which an extent of territory exceeding 140 miles was more or less laid waste, and which can only be assimilated to the dissolution of the human energies and frame, under the activity of the operation of a violent poison. Here the finest works of nature, and the improvement they had received from

127

the industry of man, were swept away by the same terrible agency which hurled mountains from their bases, and checked rivers in their speed. The convulsion extended from sea to sea, and the wreck throughout was universal. The wretched survivors fled from the few buildings which might have afforded shelter, while they only threatened destruction; and either wandered round the ruins which had overwhelmed the bodies of their friends and relations, or, mutilated and disabled, lay in hopeless apathy among their vineyards and fields, now affording neither fruit nor vegetation. These, as well as the necessaries of life, which the fertility of soil and benignity of climate render so abundant in these provinces, were involved in the general destruction; mills and magazines were annihilated: the wine and oil which could be saved had suffered such singular and offensive alterations as to render them useless; and even the water was not drinkable. All domestic animals seemed struck with an instinct of terror, which suspended their faculties; while even the wilder species were deprived of their native shyness and ferocity. The stillness of the air was remarkable, and contributed to render more appalling the deep-seated thunder which rumbled in the recesses of the earth, and every fresh throe was responded to by the apprehensive lamentations of the human, or the howls and screams of the brute creation.

'An epidemical disorder, produced by the stagnation of the water, the want or bad quality of food, and the exposure to night air, filled the measure of misery up to the very brim, and left the unfortunate victims of such accumulated calamities, no hope but that of a speedy termination of their woes in the apprehended dissolution of the world itself, which they looked upon as awfully impending.'

Far below us was Castelnuovo, one of the towns which have arisen from the scattered remnant of those ruined by that fatal period of devastation and depopulation so well described above, when the whole of the western side of Calabria was so fearfully afflicted. Standing on an elevated site above the plain, this modern and unpicturesque successor to the former city exhibits long streets flanked by low one-storied houses, with bright red-tiled roofs, and in no part of its composition does it offer any loophole for admiration, or capability of artistic picturesqueness. We at length arrived at it after a long descent from the hills, and soon found the house of Don Vincenzo Tito, to whom our letter was addressed. Don Vincenzo, who seemed a wealthy proprietor, with a dwelling full of conveniences, seemed to hesitate as to his reception of us; but after a long scrutiny, and many interrogations, he apparently decided in our favour, and, showing us some good rooms, ordered a dinner for us anew, his own being finished. But the manner of our host was abrupt, restless, and uneasy; and his frequent questions, as to whether we had heard anything from Reggio, &c. &c., gave me a stronger suspicion than ever that some political movement was about to take place. Although long accustomed to hear that some change of affairs was anticipated in the kingdom of Naples, and equally in the habit of studiously remaining as far as I could in ignorance of all political acts or expressions, I half concluded that now, as often before, the suspicious reserve of Don Vincenzo, and possibly that of Baron Rivettini also, proceeded from some false rumour afloat. Nevertheless, I confess that more than one trifling occurrence in the last two days had increased my feeling that 'something is about to happen.'

Be this as it might or not, the afternoon passed in wandering around Castelnuovo to obtain some characteristic views of its position, and of the great plain it stands on. This is not easy; studies of tall graceful olives, and Claude-like richness of distance, are innumerable, but the choice among such scenes is difficult. I sate me down by the side of a broad torrent-bed, and drew one of many landscapes; all perfectly pastoral, calm, and elegant, and essentially different in their outline and expression to the scenes of Eastern Calabria.

Before supper we were penning out our drawings in Don Vincenzo's room, and we seemed to puzzle him much by our professional labours, and obstinate ignorance, real or assumed, of political events. We have adopted this quiet mode of passing the evening hours of late, as a passive refuge from the persecution of continual interrogations; for the interest our sketches awaken in the families where we may chance to be, fully occupies their attention.

We shall devote to-morrow morning to a visit to San Giorgio, which, by a description of its castle, seems worthy of a walk; and we think of making a chance dash at Polístena, one of the numerous villages dotted over the great plain of cultivation, and to me interesting, as being the native place of one of the best Neapolitan painters—Morani—whom, years ago, I had been acquainted with in Rome.

August 24.—By long lanes, through the immensely extensive olive-grounds, and by descents into earthquake-marked ravines, —by crossing torrent-beds, and walking in irrigated gardens, we came in three hours to the foot of the hill of San Giorgio, which is an isolated ridge, running out from the central range of hills, and crowned most magnificently with a town and castle. Among the numerous grand positions of towns in this varied land, San Giorgio may bear an eminent place. Thick foliage clothes the steep sides of its pyramidal hill, and its houses are crowded together on plateaux of rock, or are piled up into spires with a beauty and abundant variety striking even in Calabria. As you rise up to its many entrance-paths, the broad blue plains of Gioia and the glittering sea are peculiarly lovely. The costume of the women is here perhaps the best we have yet seen in Calabria, and the wearers certainly the handsomest; but, excepting the interesting groups of figures, the interior of the town of San Giorgio had but little to repay a visit. We lingered awhile in the Piazza, wandered through two or three of its streets, and soon decided on bending our steps to an onward route. Descending once more by olive and chestnut shades to the plain, we arrived, by ten, at Polístena, a large town, where riven rocks, a broken bridge, shattered walls, and desolate streets, bore witness to the fatal catastrophe of 1783.[1]

We easily found the house of Morani's family—'Quel pittore famoso,'[2] as the town's-people called him, and entering it, were welcomed by his mother and sisters, who seemed pleased that any stranger should inquire after his dwelling. 'These,' said two very nice girls, throwing open the door of a small room, 'are all the works we possess done by our brother;' little supposing that to an Englishman one of the portraits possessed the highest possible interest. It was a small drawing made from Sir Walter Scott during his visit to Naples; and though neither remarkable for beauty of execution, nor pleasing as a likeness, it was highly interesting as the last record of that great man taken from life. 'Si dice questo qui essere uno scrittore famoso,'[3] said our two hostesses. There, too, was Pio Nono, a sketch just made from nature.

After this visit to Polístena, which a short sojourn at its principal café concluded, we returned to Castelnuovo by half-past twelve, the tall, thin olive-trees casting a gray veil of filmy shade over our path all the way thither. 'Tirate, tirate, magniate sempre,'[4] said old Don Vincenzo Tito, at our hospitable meal; but on my asking for a letter of introduction to Palmi, he drew back, and abruptly declined, 'Là c'è locanda,'[5] said he, which refusal, so different to the way in which the Abruzzesi used to say—'Go to our cousin this, or uncle that, but *not* to a locanda;' or, 'Che disgrazia, andare in una locanda! Non ci saranno

---

[1] Polístena is represented in Pacichelli's work as a fine city.
[2] That famous painter.
[3] They say that this was a famous author.
[4] Work away—eat always.
[5] There is an inn there.

de' parenti nostri in quel paese forse?'[1] rather revived my suspicions.

At nineteen o'clock we left Castelnuovo, with the intention of sleeping at Oppido, a town also on the plain, and the native place of Donna Rosina Scaglione's family. A delightful road through never-ending olives, with wondrous glimpses of a perfect sea of foliage, down to the Gulf of Gioia, brought us in two hours to Radicéna; everybody we met offering us grapes, peaches, and pears, with the good-natured profusion usual among these people. You see little of the towns in this great plain until you arrive at them: they are composed mostly of low and scattered houses, placed on eminences in the heart of deep ravines or hollows—like San Vittorino, Pratica, Gallicano or Galera, in the Campagna di Roma. Few buildings of more than a single story in height having been raised since 1783—and these are well-nigh hidden by cultivation; but albeit there is little strikingly or individually picturesque to be found, the whole aspect of the country, which slopes gradually to the sea, is one of rich, though monotonous beauty. At twenty-two o'clock, after passing many immense ravines and undulating earthquake-traces, where fern, and all kinds of vegetation grow most luxuriantly, we ascend to Terranova, once the largest town of this district, but utterly destroyed by the fearful event of 1783. The old city is altogether overwhelmed and buried in chasms, and below crags and dells, and its successor is a single straggling street of lowly dwellings of most melancholy appearance. All the surface of the neighbourhood seems changed and destroyed. But there were yet above three hours' walk to Oppido,[2] so we still went on over that wondrous plain, with peeps of waves of

[1]What! go to an inn? Are there then none of our relations in that town?

[2] Oppido is represented as a large walled city in Pacichelli's work; and is spoken of as a bishopric, and a large and important place by Marafioti.

The latter author describes Terranova as the greatest and most flourishing city of all that plain.

foliage—now like a sea of bronze in the setting sun, which gilded this extraordinary olive-garden. Then rose the full round moon, and all the scene became one of gray filmy light and shade, the long stems of the olive making a net-work of shadow on the deep dusty roads. At Ave Maria, we passed another village (Mesignáde) and later yet, Trisilico—hamlets faintly seen among the tremulous moonlit olives. We were well tired by the time we reached Oppido, which had the appearance of a large and tolerably well-built town; nor were we sorry to stand at the door of the house where we hoped to be entertained, but alas! Don Pasquale Zerbi, its owner, was away, and all his palazzo shut up for repairs! Our only hope and help, therefore, was in a most wretched locanda—a very horrid den: at its door we sat, and prolonged our supper of eggs till late: but the numbers of formidable vermin were so great and distressing in the sleeping apartments, that we could not contemplate the animated beds without a shudder; whereon we sat up and waited till daybreak, as best we might.

CHAPTER XIV

Olive-woods on the way to Gioia.—Fiumara, or River Marro.
—Burning heat.—Rice-grounds.—Melon-gardens and elevated look-out houses.—Malaria.—King-fishers.—Weari-
some walk.—Arrival at Gioia.—Its character for very bad air
and deadly fevers.—We set off towards Palmi.—High-road
travelling in Calabria.—Approach to the city of Palmi.—
View of the Lipari Isles.—The angry landlady and the good
inn.—Breakfast.—Beautiful situation of Palmi.—We send
Ciccio to Bagnara by the road, and go ourselves by sea.—
Fine coast scenery.—Beautiful position of Bagnara.—
Carriage-road to Scilla.—Its position.—Its rocks and castle.
—Opinion of Calabrians of our drawing.—Boat to the rock
of Scilla.—Squabble with the innkeeper.—We leave the
town: halt at Villa San Giovanni.—Retrospective glance on
our thirty days' tour, and plans for the future.—We reach
Reggio once more.—Consigliere da Nava.

August 25.—Once more on the road—hoping to repose
to-night at Palmi! and the infallible Ciccio, never yet put out by
changes or chances, advises us to go hence directly to Gioia, on
the sea-shore, and from that place to Palmi, by the carriage-
road, instead of lengthening the journey by passing through
Seminara. So, from Oppido we walked on, always downward
toward the sea, and ever through interminable olive-woods—
high, gray, filmy, feathery olives, with twisted mossy trunks.
But the pleasant freshness of early morn soon ceased; and when
we left the last flock of goats below the last great oak-tree on the
red clay banks of a huge white watercourse, we had no prospect
but that of burning heat, ever increasing through the shadeless
journey to Gioia. Gioia, forsooth! Noia it should be called; for

the whole of the lower part of its great plain is celebrated for the most deadly malaria; so that although the Scala, or port of Gioia, is the centre of business for all the produce—oil and olives—of the whole of this wide and fertile tract, yet, after early May, it is not habitable, and in July or August to sleep there is almost with the certain consequence of fever.

Lower down, towards the gulf, our route in the fiumara of the river Marro became disagreeable to the greatest degree—there were not even oleanders to vary its monotony; extensive rice-grounds, irrigated and irritating, were stretched on either side, and to these succeeded immense fields of melons, placed among which were many lofty stands here and there, made of boughs, and roofed with dry foliage, in which aerial boxes dwelled the melon-growers, enjoying a bird's-eye view of their property. This mode of protecting vineyards and other produce is frequent also throughout Sicily, and its details always abound in pictur-esque characteristics;—the bronzed faces of two or three children projecting from their airy home—the scattered clothes or house-hold utensils below—the clustering goats beneath the shade of the lofty chamber—or a thousand other accidents, all conspire to form pictures. The heat of the day grew most intense, and the passage through stagnant sheets of water or mud, and over dry, burning, white stones, was most weary. Now and then we saw large herds of black swine, of that race whose proportions are so highly esteemed—wallowing in the dull pools of the river, or tended by half-naked children on the borders of the rice-grounds, but unless by these encounters, or by the glittering flight of a bright kingfisher, our walk was unvaried by any incident. We passed and repassed the stream, till we were fairly disgusted; a thick heavy atmosphere, a sentiment of solid disease and heat, seemed to brood over all things, and we were extremely glad of even the little shade afforded us by the shelter of one of the melon-growers' towers, a two-storied leafy hut, round whose base melons were piled in prodigious quantities.

Here we reposed, if that might be called repose which consisted
of sitting on a heap of Indian corn leaves, in the very small space
to which the sun's rays did not penetrate, and in disputing with
hungry pigs the right to lunch on one of their master's melloni
d'acqua. At length, on resuming our walk, little undulating
heights covered with bosky oak and thick underwood, betokened
that we were leaving this unpropitious region, and approaching
the vicinity of the high road from Naples to Reggio; and,
crossing this, we were soon within the limits of pestiferous
Gioia,[1] a mere village, consisting of some large warehouses, and
a huge osteria, which stands close to the sea-shore.

In this public resort, a tenement containing two huge rooms,
mostly filled with the oily, but by no means odoriferous, produce of the neighbourhood, we sought food and rest, though our
prospect of the latter was small; for the wary Ciccio said, ever
and anon, 'Se dormite, siete morti, díghi dóghi dà!'[2] and if we
ever closed our eyes for a moment, all the people of the osteria
shrieked out with one voice, 'O santo cielo! svegliate vi!
svegliate vi!'[3] Gioia is, indeed, one of the most mournful of
places; for, although the trade carried on from it in oil is very
considerable, and numerous workmen are transporting barrels,
&c., on every side, these are all people of the adjacent city of
Palmi, who come hither at morn and return home at night.
There is no drinkable water in the place; and the few poor
wretches who are left in charge of the warehouses are melancholy and horrible objects—malaria-fever being written on every
line of their face and form. Here were on every side the
emaciated limbs, the skin contracted closely to the bones of the
face, the yellow complexion, the swollen stomach, the harsh
and grating voice—all unerring signs of the nature of the air in

[1] Gioia is described by Alberti as possessing a plain most abundant and fruitful
in character. Site of Metaurus (Pacichelli, Cramer, &c.). The river Metaurus
is the modern Marro.

[2] If you sleep, you are dead men!

[3] O heavens! wake up!

such localities, and too easily recognised by long sojourners in the marshes or Campagna of the Roman States.

Hot as was the afternoon, we considered that any extremity of discomfort might be a relief to that we were suffering; wherefore, with the fear of fever before our eyes, we preferred to set off as early as we could along the burning high road towards Palmi. How undeniable is the simplicity of those who think they have 'done' Calabria, by travelling in a carriage from Naples to Reggio! All the beautiful incidents of pastoral or mountain life, all the romance of a wandering artist's existence, is carefully banished from your high-road tourist's journey; and the best he can boast of is an extended view from some elevated point of road. We looked back with fond regret to the mountains of Aspromonte, or to the shady paths in the groves of the upper plain of Gioia, and voted all highways eminent nuisances and vulgarities.

Leaving a road to Seminara on the right, we toiled up the hill of Palmi, and long before arriving there, the burning sun and white dusty 'via carrozzabile' had thoroughly wearied us. Dreary walls by the road-side, enclosing gardens of villa or casino, foretold our near approach to the city; and these, in the absence of shade, were our only consolation, except that in one open warehouse we were treated to a draught of refreshing water. Palmi is one of the three sottintendenze of the province, and is placed on the high cliffs of its western coast, immediately opposite the Lipari Isles, which, in shape somewhat like a row of inverted cups and saucers, here adorn the horizon. Suburban residences surround the city to a considerable extent, but the views from it are rather remarkable for the great distance they embrace, than for possessing any first-class landscape qualities. Eastward, high cliffs overhang the town; northward, the endless plain of Gioia stretches far away; and southward, Scilla and part of Mongibello occupy the picture, with the blue sea, Stromboli and its satellites, to the west. Palmi bears in its first aspect the character of a neat, clean, and bustling place—indeed, we find we are at once and plainly come to the end of Calabrian romance and interest, and had we not been heartily wearied by our walk we might probably have regretted that we had not chosen the road hither by Seminara, where at least there were woods which in former days were among the most celebrated in the province as the haunt of robbers.

We went to a locanda which had been named to us by someone on the road, but in going thither old Ciccio twice shook his head, and said 'Non credo[1]—díghi dóghi dà,' wherefrom we did not augur any great success in our search. When we arrived at the bottom of the scala or staircase, all the upper part of it was filled up by the most Brobdingnagian of living landladies: moreover, this enormous woman was peculiarly hideous, and clad in the slightest and most extraordinary of simple costumes: true, the thermometer was at the highest, and the lady might be suffering from the great heat; but the apparition of her dishabille and globe-like form was so remarkable, that we paused at the threshold of so formidable a hostess—the rather that she had evidently been sacrificing earnestly to Bacchus, and was as unsteady on her feet as clamorous with her tongue. 'Let us try some other locanda,' said we to each other, and were turning away, when the monster landlady shouted out—'O, figli miei! venite, venite;'[2] but seeing that her invitation made no impression—'Andatevi al diavolo nero,'[3] quoth she, accompanying her words with a yell, and an abrupt ejection of a large broom from her right hand down the staircase, so that we fairly fled without further discussion, and followed the silent but grinning Ciccio to another locanda, called 'Il Plutino,' and situated in the chief piazza of the town. Here was everything in very tolerable order, and no southern Italian provincial inn can boast

[1] I doubt.
[2] O, my sons, come in, come in.
[3] Go to the black devil.

of better accommodations. In the evening we explored the town—a bustling and active scene, and contrasting strongly with many of our late homes. The solid wheeled cars used here to transport goods, and drawn by cattle, struck us as peculiarly picturesque. Of costume in dress there is little enough.

August 26.—After the unheard-of Calabrian luxury of a real breakfast, we drew in the piazza near the sea. At this spot is one of the views on which those few travellers who pass from Reggio to Naples by land are accustomed to bestow enthusiastic praise; nor is it unworthy of its reputation. A flat promenade or platform, half surrounded by seats, and a balustrade, the resort of the evening idlers of Palmi, is terminated at one end by the clustering churches and other buildings of the town; and at the other, sinks down into the blue sea, a perpendicular cactus-clothed precipice. Immediately above the town frowns a bluff point, the sides of which also shelve downward, and are lost in a world of olive and orange groves, a feathery palm-tree peering here and there over the little houses embosomed in the luxuriant foliage. Beyond is spread a wide expanse of sea, with the single town of Scilla sparkling at the foot of its cliff, while pale Etna, with its snowy point, closes this most beautiful prospect. Many are the pretty bits of landscape around this charming spot—gray rocks and olives or gay gardens, with the town of Bagnara seen afar between the graceful branches of the trees.

At mid-day, the bill of the 'Hotel' was by no means so unexceptionable as the dinner and style of the accommodation, and it was not without much dispute and combat that we succeeded in paying one-seventh of the sum asked, but which seventh was more than a sufficient remuneration.

Sending Ciccio with the horse and baggage by the road, we descended to the Scala, and embarked in a boat for Bagnara, which, placed on a peninsular rock, projects grandly into the water beyond the Bay of Palmi. The cliffs are infinitely majestic between the two towns—descending in sheer and perpendicular crags to the sea, and were it not for the absence of buildings, the coast would have often reminded me of that of Amalfi, or of Positano; as far as the motion of a boat in a very rough swell would allow me to observe them, I enjoyed these scenes extremely, but I was glad to approach the shore once more. On the north side of the rock of Bagnara we landed, glad once again to welcome our old friends the aloes and cactus, which ever love to adorn the rocky coast or beetling crag; they affect but little the smooth plains of Gioia, the olive-ground and orange-garden, nor does the stately aloe thrive among the colder mountain-heights, though the Indian fig was common, albeit not in its own full luxuriance, even on the crags of Cánalo. Bagnara rises from the water's edge in an amphitheatre of buildings, crowned by a high rock which is joined to the mountain above by a castle and aqueduct,[1] and is assuredly one of the most imposing and stately towns in appearance which we have yet seen. The arches of the aqueduct span a chasm in the rock-peninsula on which it stands, and while a castle adorns the seaward portion, the land-cliffs are studded with a glittering row of buildings, many of which nestle down to the very shore below the torn and cracked ravines into which the precipices are shivered. A smooth half-moon of sand extends at the foot of the rocks, and gives a calm and pleasant air to the whole picture.

We wound up the path which leads to the upper town, and passing through the arches of the viaduct (for it serves for a road as well as to transport water) were even more delighted by the sight of the southern side than we had been with the northern. Bagnara from this point of view is wonderfully striking, and few coast scenes of Western Calabria can rival it.

It grew late ere we finished sketching, and a courteous priest

[1] At Bagnara, Marapóti speaks of having seen considerable remains of ancient baths.

BAGNARA

SCILLA

directed us to a good inn, where we found Ciccio arrived before us.

August 27.—We had no squabble with the host of our very comfortable and quiet locanda here: few people ever stop at Bagnara, so the world is less acquainted with the modes of high-road depredation. There is a good carriage route all along the coast, which decided us on sending Díghi-dóghi-dà to Scilla, and we loitered forward, making drawings as we proceeded, until we reached that town about noon, and found (so much for 'roughing it' on this side of Calabria) another very clean inn by the sea-side, just beyond a most picturesque rock and castle.

Scilla is one of the most striking bits of coast scenery, its white buildings and massive castled crag standing out in noble relief against the dark blue waves—while the Lipari Isles and Strom-boli, with the Faro of Messina, form a beautiful background. But beyond the general appearance of the place, which from all points of view is very imposing, there is but little to note down. No hospitalities, no family incidents, fill up the wandering landscape painter's journal when he leaves the more unfre-quented regions of mountain scenery, for plain and civilised highways; and although old Alberti says that Scilla 'hath a rock shaped like a man, surrounded by caves, emitting howls of wolves and screams of other beasts,' we could not perceive even that degree of romance in our researches.[1] Exploring and drawing Scilla occupied the whole day; but at the close of it, in

[1] On the 5th of February, 1783, Scilla, in common with all the other towns on this coast, was nearly wholly overthrown at night. The aged Prince of Scilla, with 4,000 of the inhabitants, had remained on the sands of the little bay on the south side of the promontory on which the castle stood, and awaited the return of daylight in terror and suspense. Before midnight, a recurrence of shocks ensued, and vast portions of the mountains above Scilla were thrown into the Straits. One huge wave, resulting from these convulsions, swept over the strand of the bay, and engulphed in one moment the whole 4,000 human beings.

I   143

spite of the favourable appearance of our locanda, we could get nothing to eat but a very antique fowl, which baffled knives and forks, and we anticipated from such bad fare, and from the landlord's continual compliments, that the charges would be proportionally heavy.

August 28.—A throng of numerous observers crowded round us while drawing the castle this morning: 'questi,' said an old man as we were thus busily employed, 'questi sono tutti persone scelte dal governo loro per raccogliere notizie del Regno nostro,'[1]—a conceit universally ridiculed by Englishmen, but not quite so absurd as it may seem, if we reflect that the conquest of many countries by others has been preceded by individual observation and research.

In the course of the morning we took a boat to the rocks of Scilla, and very magnificent did they appear, rising above the boiling current of dark blue foamy water. But it was too rough for so bad a sailor as I am to allow of making any drawings, so we returned to our inn, where, on our departure ere noon, a great conflict was occasioned by the 'conto,'—twelve ducats being demanded for what we gradually reduced to two ere we left Scilla, and great was the outcry of feminine shrieks, and masculine maledezioni, which followed us long after we left the place.

As we neared Villa San Giovanni and were opposite to the well-known coast of the Faro, we seemed, as it were, at home, and talked over our thirty days' tour in Calabria with many pleasant memories, arranging also how we should execute the exploring of the remaining two provinces; one thing was certain—Díghi-dóghi-dá was such a capital old fellow, he must be our guide to the end of the journey.

As yet we seemed but to have trodden on the threshold of Calabrian fastnesses; the narrow neck of land between two seas

[1] These are all persons chosen by their government to gather notices of our country.

of the province of Catanzaro, the dense and fearful forests of the Sila, the pointed hats of Cosenza, and the rich Greek costumes of Calabria Citeriore, were all as yet unseen, and we looked forward to our return to the truly wild and romantic with enthusiasm and impatience.

At Villa San Giovanni, which is the centre of a knot of scattered villages covering that part of the Calabrian coast opposite to the Faro, we found a good locanda, and halted for midday rest, as well as for maccaroni, occhiali, which are a very good fish, molignani, as good a vegetable, and Lipari wine.

At four we again set out, through long lanes between villas and large silk factories, (the atmosphere reminding us of the silk-worm days of Staíti), and a little while after Ave Maria, by a road—now

'Silent in its dusty vines,'

we reached Reggio once more, which, with its lamps here and there, its broad streets, and its numerous inhabitants, seemed to us a sort of Paris in bustle and splendour, after such places as Cánalo and Gerace.

We again settled ourselves in the Locanda Giordano, and closed our day by a call on Consigliere da Nava, to thank him for the letters by which he had so ably and good-naturedly assisted us throughout our journey. Had we not indeed been furnished with these introductions, much of the interest, and nearly all the comfort, of our tour would have been denied us, and the recollections of Southern Calabria would have been far other than those we now enjoyed.

CHAPTER XV

Arrangements.—Ciccio and his pay.—Plan to see some fine forests near Reggio to-morrow; and to visit Pentedatilo before starting for the other Calabrian provinces.—Morning calls at Reggio.—Set out to Gallicó.—Ciccio's house.—The village of Calanna.—Fine views of the Straits of Messina, and Etna.—We find no fine trees on the hills of Basilicò, and return late to Reggio.—We cross to Messina, and I return to Reggio alone.—I set off by the road to Melito, and reach that town by Ave-Maria.—Wonderful views of the crags and town of Pentedatilo.—The discomforts of the house of Don P. Tropæa.—Agitation and distress of his family.—The supper. —Revelations of revolution.—Announcement of disturbances.—The supper party breaks up.—The bed-room.—The midnight adventure.—I leave Mélito.—Ciccio's foreboding silence.—The River Alice.—Amazing views of Pentedatilo— its ravine and rocks—its strange form.—I ascend to the town; surprise and alarm of its inhabitants.—Proceed to Montebello. —Indian figs.—The revolution and its shadows.—'The Pentedatilo Tragedy,' a tale of horrors.—Ascent to Motta S. Giovanni—and return to Reggio.—Commencement of the revolutionary movements of 1847-8.—Appearance of Reggio. —Absurd waiter at Giordano's hotel.—Interview with Consigliere da Nava.—Explanation of various doubts and circumstances throughout our tour.—Processions of the insurgents, &c.—An anxious morning.—I escape from Reggio, and reach Messina.—P—— and I embark for Naples in a Malta steamer.—Farewell to Calabria Ulteriore Prima!

August 29.—A day of arrangements for past and future. Ciccio received his thirty-one dollars and a half, with four more as

Buonamano;[1] whereon the ancient guide burst into tears, and said he should have thought it quite enough to have worked for such nice people as we two for his stipulated pay only: he moreover declared that we appeared to him in the light of sons and nephews, and that he would live or die for us, as, how, and when we pleased. Díghi-dóghi-dà was indeed a most meritorious fellow.

To-morrow, having one spare day, we agree to go to Melanicò, where there are said to be fine forests, and after that the programme for the next five days is as follows: we cross to Messina, and while P—— remains there for three days, I intend to return here and go to Capo d'Armi and Pentedatilo; after which I then rejoin my friend at Reggio on the 4th of September, so as to start on the 5th for Monteleone, commencing thence our *giro* in Calabria Ulteriore II.

Visits to Reggio acquaintances occupied greater part of this day: in the evening we took part in the usual carriage-drive along the Marina and high street of Reggio—a mode of passing two hours, and of seeing the neighbours or strangers as much in use in the capital of Calabria Ulteriore II, as in the Chiaja of Naples, the Corso of Rome, or Hyde Park.

August 30.—We set out for our day's expedition to the hills of Basilicò at early dawn, and retraced our steps along the high road to Naples, nearly as far as Gallicò, a village which stands at the foot of the mountains, and is exquisitely picturesque, owing to its wide streets being entirely webbed and arched over with a network of pergolate. Here, as it was Ciccio's native village, we paid a visit to his cottage, where his wife and family gave us heaps of fine figs and grapes, and did all they could to welcome us in their way.

Toiling up a fiumara we ascended hence to Calanna, a castellated village, placed in a grand rocky pass; after making a drawing of which, we continued to ascend the hills—looking back on

[1] Extra money given in token of satisfactory service.

147

ever-widening views of the Straits and Etna, and forwards
towards the heights of Basilicò, on the hills of Aspromonte. But
the forests which all the world of Reggio talked of were little
worth looking at; those who had described them to us had never
seen either Polsi, or Pietrapennata; and we were sadly disappointed with the result of our exertions. At length we reached
some few men who were at work at the 'Sega,' or sawpits,
placed on the highest part of the mountain; these laughed at our
questions about 'large oak trees,' and grinned incredulously
with odd signs which we could not make out. 'Oak trees are
all bosh,' said they, 'and you know that as well as we; but as for
the men you seek we assure you they are *not* here: but we do not
say they are not at Santo Stefano, that village you see below.' In
vain we said we sought no persons. 'You are wise to keep your
own counsel,' was the reply. So again we saw there was some
mystery we could not unravel. Therefore, voting the mountain
of Basilicò an imposture, we left it, and came straight down to
Reggio. Possibly, after all, we had not gone high enough up in
the hills to discover the gigantic oaks. We returned by a
different route, and before we reached Reggio it was dark.

August 31.—We crossed to Messina, paying twelve carlini for
a boat, which we took for ourselves. In the fine old cathedral,
and in the exquisite views from the higher parts of the city, there
is sufficient amusement for travellers, and we, besides, had
colours, paper, and wandering artist conveniences of all kinds to
look after.

September 1.—For three carlini I recrossed the Straits in one
of the public boats, leaving P—— at Messina to join me at
Reggio on the 4th. A fair wind soon placed me on the Calabrian
shore, where I found the faithful Ciccio awaiting me with
welcome, and a considerable piece of eloquence ending with
Díghi-dóghi-dà as usual.

By one o'clock all was in readiness for starting, my passport, as well as a letter from Consigliere da Nava to a proprietor in Melito, where I am to sleep to-night for the purpose of visiting Pentedatilo, that strange rock-town which we had seen from Bova, and which at all risks I had resolved to examine. So I set off in a *caratella*, for three ducats, all by the dusty pergola-covered high-road of July 29; the views of Etna increasing in magnificence as I approached Capo dell' Armi, to the extreme point of which a *strada carrozzabile* is carried, and where I found Ciccio and his horse already arrived. Leaving the carriage we then struck inland, as the sun was getting low, by mule-routes crossing the frequent fiumaras here joining the sea. On advancing, the views of the wondrous crags of Pentedatilo become astonishingly fine and wild, and as the sun set in crimson glory, displayed a truly magnificent and magical scene of romance—the vast mass of pinnacled rock rearing itself alone above its neighbour hills, and forming a landscape which is the beau-ideal of the terrible in Calabrian scenery. On the sea-shore, a few miles below Pentedatilo, stands Mélito, a large town, the most southerly in all Italy, and ere we reached it, we arrived at the house of D. Pietro Tropæa, in the outskirts, whose residence is a kind of ill-kept villa; for albeit Don Pietro gave me a most friendly welcome, it is not to be disguised that his casino was of the dirtiest; and when I contemplated the ten dogs and a very unpleasant huge tame sheep, which animated his rooms, I congratulated myself that I was not to abide long with them.

Moreover, it appeared to me that some evil, general or particular, was brooding over the household, which consisted of a wife, haggard and dirty in appearance, and agitated in a very painful degree; an only son, wild and terrified in every look; and a brother and nephew from Montebello, strange, gloomy, and mysterious in aspect and manner. The host also apologised for being ill at ease and unwell. The singular uneasiness of the whole party increased presently at the sound of two or three guns being fired, and Donna Lucia Tropæa, bursting into tears, left the room with all the family but Don Pietro, who became more and more incoherent and flurried, imparting the most astounding revelations relative to his lady and her situation, which he declared made all his family and himself most afflicted and nervous.

These excuses for so remarkable a derangement as I observed in the manner of all the individuals of the family did not deceive me, and I once more suspected, more strongly than ever, that 'something was to be foreseen.' This feeling was confirmed at supper-time when the assembled circle seemed to have agreed among themselves that it was impossible to conceal their alarm, and a rapid succession of questions was put to me as to what I knew of political changes about to take place immediately. 'Had I heard nothing? Nothing? Not even at Reggio?' 'Indeed I had not.' 'Ma che! it was folly to pretend ignorance; I must be aware that the country was on the very eve of a general revolution!' It was useless to protest, and I perceived that a sullen ill-will was the only feeling prevalent towards me from persons who seemed positive that I would give no information on a subject they persisted in declaring I fully understood. So I remained silent, when another brother from Montebello was suddenly announced, and after a few whispers a scene of alarm and horror ensued.

'È già principiata la revoluzione!'[1] shrieked aloud Don Pietro; sobs and groans and clamour followed, and the moaning hostess, after weeping frantically, fell into a violent fit, and was carried out, the party breaking up in the most admired disorder, after a display, at least so it appeared to me, of feelings in which fear and dismay greatly predominated over hope or boldness.

As for me, revolution or no revolution, here I am in the toe of Italy all alone, and I must find my way out of it as best I may; so, wrapping myself in my plaid, and extinguishing the light,

[1] The Revolution has already begun.

I lay down in the front room on the bed allotted me, whose exterior was not indicative of cleanliness or rest.

Hardly was I forgetting the supper scene in sleep, when a singular noise awoke me. After all, thought I, I am to encounter some real Calabrian romance, and as I sate up and listened the mysterious noise was again repeated. It proceeded from under my bed, and resembled a hideous gurgling sob four or five times reiterated. Feeling certain that I was not alone, I softly put out my hand for that never-to-be-omitted night companion in travelling—a phosphorus box, when before I could reach it my bed was suddenly lifted up by some incomprehensible agency below, and puffing and sobs, mingled with a tiny tinkling sound, accompanied this Calabrian mystery. There was no time to be lost, and having persevered in obtaining a light in spite of this disagreeable interruption, I jumped off the bed, and with a stick thrust hastily and hardly below the bed, to put the intruder, ghostly or bodily, on to fair fighting ground,——Baa—aa—a!—

Shade of Mrs. Radcliffe! it was the large dirty tame sheep! So I forthwith opened a door into the next room, and bolted out the domestic tormentor.

September 2.—None of the Tropæa family were moving when I started at sunrise. A letter to a proprietor of Montebello, where mid-day must be passed, was sent to me, with apologies for the non-appearance of the household. 'What is the meaning of this?' said I to Ciccio; but nothing could be extracted from that Phœnix of Muleteers but a clucking sort of glossal ejaculation; nevertheless, he seemed anxious and gloomy.

Off we set; our route followed a tiresome and tortuous road in the bed of the Alice, and then became a rugged path crossing to the Fiume della Monaca ere Pentedatilo was visible; for this strange town is so placed, that although seen from all the country around, you may pass close to it without being aware of its proximity. The ravine in which the river flows is crowded and blocked up with crags to the south of the great rock on which the town is built; so that it is necessary to cross to the western side of the stream, and ascend the heights which enclose it before finally recrossing it, in order to reach the remarkable crag itself. But having gained the high ground opposite, the appearance of Pentedatilo is perfectly magical, and repays whatever trouble the effort to reach it may so far have cost. Wild spires of stone shoot up into the air, barren and clearly defined, in the form (as its name implies) of a gigantic hand against the sky, and in the crevices and holes of this fearfully savage pyramid the houses of Pentedatilo are wedged, while darkness and terror brood over all the abyss around this, the strangest of human abodes. Again, a descent to the river, and all traces of the place are gone; and it is not till after repassing the stream, and performing a weary climb on the farther side, that the stupendous and amazing precipice is reached; the habitations on its surface now consist of little more than a small village, though the remains of a large castle and extensive ruins of buildings are marks of Pentedatilo having once seen better days.

I had left Ciccio and the horse below at the stream, and I regretted having done so, when, as I sate making a drawing of the town, the whole population bristled on wall and window, and the few women who passed me on their way to the hanging vineyards, which fringe the cliffs low down by the edge of the river, screamed aloud on seeing me, and rushed back to their rocky fastnesses. As it is hardly possible to make these people understand ordinary Italian, a stranger might, if alone, be awkwardly situated in the event of any misunderstanding. Had the Pentedatelini thought fit to roll stones on the intruder, his fate must have been hard; but they seemed filled with fear alone. I left this wonderful place with no little regret, and rejoining Ciccio, soon lost sight of Pentedatilo, pursuing my way up the stream, or bed of the Monaca, which is here very narrow and winding, and so shut in between high cliffs, that in winter-time the torrent prevents all access from this quarter. Higher up in the ravine stands the village of Montebello; its district is famous in Calabria for the excellence of its cactus, or Indian fig, all the rocks of the neighbourhood being covered with a thick coating of that strange vegetable. The town is situated high above the river, on a square rock, perpendicular on three sides, amid wide ruins of walls and houses, betokening former times of prosperity. In the centre of this wretched little place is the house of Don Pietro Amazichi, who, though receiving me with every kindness and hospitality, was as much agitated as my acquaintances at Mélito. It seems evident that coming events are casting rapidly deepening shadows, and in vain again do I try to persuade my hosts that I am not in the secret. 'It is *impossible*,' they said; 'you only left Reggio yesterday, it is true; but it is certain that the revolution broke out last night, and everyone has known for days past what would happen.' On which there was another scene. The lady of Montebello, less feeble than she of Mélito, gave way to the deepest affliction; her exclamation of 'My sons! my two sons! I have parted from them for ever in this world!' I shall not easily forget; and the husband strove to comfort her with such deep feeling, that I became truly grieved for these poor people, ignorant though I was actually of pending circumstances.

About two, Don Pietro accompanied me to the foot of the rock, and for some distance up the dreary fiumara; meanwhile he illustrated the history of Montebello and Pentedatilo by a tale-tragedy of the early ages of these towns, when their territories were governed respectively, the first by a Baron and the second by a Marquis.

For centuries the families of these two feudal possessors of the towns of Pentedatilo and Montebello had been deadly foes, and they ruled, or fought for, the adjoining country from their strongholds in persevering enmity. The Baron of Montebello, a daring and ferocious youth, was left heir in early life to his ancestral estates and rights, and fell in love with the only daughter of the Marchese Pentedatilo; but, although the young lady had contrived to acquaint her lover that her heart was his, her hand was steadfastly denied him by the Marchese, whom the memory of long injuries and wars hardened in his refusal. Opposition, however, did but increase the attachment of the young lady, and she at length consented to leave her father's house with her lover; an arrangement being made that on a certain night she should open a door in the otherwise impenetrable rock-fortress of Pentedatilo, and admit young Montebello with a sufficient force of his retainers to ensure the success of her elopement.

The Baron accordingly enters the castle, but finding that equal opportunity is presented him for vengeance on his feudal enemy, and for possessing himself of the object of his attachment, he resolves to make the most of both; he goes first to the chamber of the Marchese of Pentedatilo, and finds him sleeping by the side of the Marchesa, with a dagger at his pillow's head. Him he stabs, yet not so fatally as to prevent his placing his left hand on the wound, and with his right seizing his stiletto, and plunging it into the heart of the innocent Marchesa, suspecting her as the author of his death. The Baron Montebello repeating his blows, the Marchese falls forward on the wall, and his five blood-stained fingers leave traces, still shown, on part of the ruined hall,—a horrible memorial of the crime, strangely coincident with that of the form and name of the rock.

Immediately on the consummation of this double tragedy, the active young Baron Montebello carried off the young lady, his retainers having put all the family of the Marchese to death, except one infant grandchild, whom a nurse saved by concealing him in a crevice of the rocks; the castle was then dismantled, and the lady became Baroness of Montebello. But she never spoke more; the horror of having been indirectly the destruction of her whole race occasioned her to become insane, and she poisoned herself within a month of her departure from her native town.

In process of time, the child saved by the nurse grew up, and was introduced as a page into the Montebello family, the Baron having re-married, and being now the undisputed possessor of both territories as far as the sea; but, after many years of life, the wretched man became wild with remorse for his past iniquities, and made over all his possessions to the Church, provided only no living descendant of the Pentedatili could be found, a decent proviso, apparently made without any risk. When lo! the nurse and a small number of the old Marchese's friends proved, beyond any doubt, that the page was heir to the estates and revenge of his ancestors! And here you might suppose the story ended. Not at all. The Baron's hatred returned on finding there was really something on which to exercise it, and he ordered the torture and execution of young Pentedatilo forthwith. But now the tables were turned; the Baron's long reign of wickedness lent weapons to his adversary's cause, and, in his turn, the last scion of the murdered Marchese became a tyrant. Forthwith the whole family of the Baron Montebello were destroyed before their parents' eyes, and he himself then blinded by order of the avenger, and chained for the rest of his days in the very room where he had slain the grandsire Pentedatilo. Finally, as if it were ordered that the actors in such a wholesale domestic tragedy were unfit to remain on earth, the castle of Pentedatilo fell by the shock of an earthquake, crushing together the Baron and Marchese, with the nurse, and every other agent in this Calabrian horror!

After we had reached Fossati, ever by the tiresome fiumara—weary sad haunts are these for man to dwell among!—our route followed the hill we had descended on July 30, and passing to the right of Motta San Giovanni, turned towards the coast below San Nocito, one of the most picturesque of ruined fortresses. Hence the way was long and tedious to Reggio, the more that I was impatient to know what was really occurring, since Ciccio's philosophy was less and less proof to the task of concealing his agitation, which for one so usually tranquil was remarkable.

At the hour of one in the night we reached Reggio, and here the secret divulged itself at once.

How strange was that scene! All the quiet town was brilliantly lighted up, and every house illuminated; no women or children were visible, but troops of men, by twenties and thirties, all armed, and preceded by bands of music and banners inscribed, 'Viva Pio IX,' or 'Viva la Constituzione,' were parading the high street from end to end.

'Cosa x'è stata,[1] Ciccio?' said I.

'O non vedete,' said the unhappy muleteer, with a suppressed groan. 'O non vedete? é una rivoluzione! Díghi, dóghi, dà!'

No one took the least notice of us as we passed along, and we soon arrived at Giordano's Hotel. The doors were barred, nor could I readily gain admittance; at length the waiter appeared, but he was uproariously drunk.

'Is Signor P—— arrived by the boat from Messina?' said I.

'O che barca! O che Messina! O che bella rivoluzione! Ai! ao! Orra birra burra—ba!' was the reply.

'Fetch me the keys of my room,' said I; 'I want to get at my roba'—

'O che chiavi! O che camera! O che roba! ai, ai!'

'But where are the keys?' I repeated.

'Non ci sono più chiavi,' screamed the excited cameriere; 'non ci sono più passaporti, non ci sono più Ré—più legge—più giudici—più niente—non x'è altro che l'amore la libertà—l'amicizia, e la costituzione—eccovi le chiavi—ai! o-o-o-o-o-orra birra bà!!'[2]

Without disputing the existence of love, liberty, friendship,

[1] What has happened?

[2] There are no more keys—there are no more passports, no more kings, no more laws, no more judges, no more nothing! Nothing but love and liberty, friendship and the constitution!

or the constitution, it was easy to see that matters were all out of order, so, taking Ciccio with me, I went hastily through the strangely-altered streets to Cavaliere da Nava's house. From him, whom with his family I found in serious distress, I heard that a concerted plot had broken out on the preceding day; that all the Government officials had been seized, and the Government suspended, he (da Nava), the Intendente, and others being all confined to their houses. That the telegraph and the castle still held out, but would be attacked in a day or two; that the insurgents, consisting mostly of young men from the neighbouring towns and villages, had already marched into Reggio, and were hourly increasing in number; that on the opposite shore, Messina was also in full revolt; and that the future arrangements of the Government could only be known after time had been allowed for telegraphic communication between Reggio and Naples. The Government impiegati are all naturally dejected, as nothing of their future fate is known, except so much as may be divined from the fact that no one has hitherto been maltreated. Thus, the agitation of the people at Montebello and Mélito; the suspicions of Don Tito, and of the woodmen at Basilicò, and even those of the fat Baron Rivettini, were all fully explained and justified; for whether those persons were for or against Government, the appearance of strangers on the very eve of a preconcerted revolt was enough to make them ask questions, and put them all in a fuss.

I returned to the inn. As for what I should do, there seemed no will of my own in the matter; I might be arrested, or executed as either a rebel or a royalist—as things might turn out; so there was nothing for it but to wait patiently.

All that long night the movement increased: large bodies from Santo Stefano, and other places—most of them apparently young mountaineers—thronged into Reggio, and paraded the streets, singing or shouting 'Viva Pio Nono,' with banners, guns, swords, and musical instruments.

September 3.—No boat stirs from Messina. I watch on the beach in vain. I sit with Da Nava and his perplexed family. The telegraph works away incessantly; but there is no attempt to stop it, and no attack on the castle. If there is no movement in the northern provinces, troops will certainly march hither, and, in any case, steamers will come, and this wretched town will assuredly be bombarded into annihilation or repentance. On the other hand, Messina will as surely undergo the same fate, and the more probably, inasmuch as it is of more importance. Nevertheless, as P—— is detained there, and I cannot ascertain what extent of fighting therein prevails (owing to no boats having put off from the Messinese shore), it appears to me better to go over to him if possible.

So, by hard work, I persuaded some very reluctant boatmen to take me: and I quit the Da Nava family with regret, for a cloud of uncertainty seems to hang over all Southern Italy, and the foreshading gloom of it has earliest reached this remotest place.

After intolerable waiting for five hours with a boat-load of depressed and anxious natives, we were towed by oxen as far as Villa San Giovanni, and thence (the sea was rough and the wind contrary) came over to a point about a mile from Messina, where we landed out of reach of the guns of the fort. Here I was glad at Nobile's Hotel to rejoin P——, whose suspense had been equal to mine. The revolt at Messina has occasioned the death of fourteen or fifteen men; but the Government has firm hold of the citadel. Distress and anxiety, stagnation and terror, have taken the place of activity, prosperity, security, and peace. A steamer comes from Malta to-morrow, and I resolve to return to Naples thereby; for to resume travelling under the present circumstances of Calabria would be absurd—probably impossible.

September 4.—Two war-steamers are at Reggio, and firing is heard, though the details of action are of course unknown to us. The poor town is undergoing evil I fear, nor will it be wonderful

PENTEDATILO

SANTA MARIA DI MONTE VERGINE

that it does so; for that 400 or 500 men should seize and hope to hold permanently a distant part of a large kingdom, unless assisted by a general rising, appears to be the extreme of folly, and can only, whatever the cause of complaint, meet with ultimate ill-success and probably with severe chastisement.

No steamer comes, and we remain at Messina.

September 5.—The steamer arrives from Malta, P—— and I go on board, and at six in the evening we sail. Soon the sparkling line of Reggio ceases to glitter on the purple waters; soon we pass the Faro; and the Rock of Scilla, the headland of Nicótera, and the long point of Palmi recede into faint distance.

I leave the shores of Calabria with a grating feeling I cannot describe. The uncertainty of the fate of many kind and agreeable families—Da Nava, Scaglione, Marzano, &c.—it is not pleasant to reflect on. Gloom, gloom, overshadows the memory of a tour so agreeably begun, and which should have extended yet through two provinces. The bright morning route of the traveller overcast with cloud and storm before mid-day.

PART II

Journals of a Landscape Painter in the Kingdom of Naples

PRINCIPATO CITERIORE, BASILICATA, TERRA DI
BARI, ETC. PROVINCES OF AVELLINO, POTENZA,
BARI, ETC.

CHAPTER XVI

Return to Calabria not advisable.—A tour to Melfi and part of Apulia resolved on.—We set off to Avellino.—Travelling with the eyes open.—Beautiful character of the country round Avellino.—Convent of Monte Vergine.—Vineyards and villas.—Costume and appearance of the women.—Ascent of Monte Vergine.—Historical notices of the convent.—Extensive prospect from the mountain.—Arrangements for visiting Melfi, &c.—We leave Avellino.—Highroads and caratelle.—Uninteresting drive to the valley of the Calore, and Grotta Minarda.—Anticipations of Apulia.—Attempt to reach Frigento.—A guide hired.—We leave Grotta Minarda. —Unpicturesque approach to the hill of Frigento.—The lonely osteria.—Don Gennaro Fiammarossa and his hotel.—We return to the lonely osteria, and make the best of it.—Wheat beds, with onion curtains.—Departure from Frigento.—Barren and dreary scenery.—The Lake of Mofette; its appearance and qualities.—Dead birds.—Rocca San Felice.—Ascent to St. Angelo de' Lombardi.—No carriages nor carriage-roads.—The old man and his ass.—We seize on a roast fowl, and make ourselves as comfortable as circumstances permit.

September 11.—Days have passed; and our decision about not returning to Calabria is fixed. All that part of Italy is at present in too unsettled a state to admit of prosperous artistic tours. But as P—— has yet nearly a month before he is obliged to turn his steps northward, we resolve to see parts of Basilicata, &c.; for to various towns in that province I have some good introductory letters from one of its greatest landed proprietors, and there is much interest in that part of the Regno, particularly in the country of Horace, and some of the Norman castles of Apulia. We set off, therefore, by railroad to Nocera, and thence take a caratella (price two ducats) to Avellino, the chief town of Principato Citeriore. The Sanctuary of Monte Vergine, close to the city, is a monastery I have long wished to see.

All the bustle, so characteristic of the environs of Naples, diversifies our route; but having been up very late on the preceding night, we both of us fall fast asleep before we reach San Severino, and never once wake—so much for 'travelling with one's eyes open'—until we are driving into Avellino.

To how few spots on the map of Italy can one turn, and yet be disappointed in finding beauty and interest! Totally distinct in character as is this part of the kingdom of Naples from the stern scenery of Calabria, it yet abounds with exquisite landscape: fertile vineyards link tree to tree with rich leafy festoons; the hills clothed with olives, and the higher mountains with chestnut woods; villas and villages dotted in glittering clusters on every slope. Each part of this varied kingdom has its distinct features; and here cheerful industry and abundance light up all around.

Avellino,[1] standing on the river Sabato, itself forms part of several very noble views, and, in all of them, the most remarkable feature is the high mountain, Monte Vergine, which, thickly wooded to its summit, rears its lofty form to the west of the city. High among the clouds you may see a white spot nearly at its highest peak: that is the monastery of Monte Vergine.

Avellino possesses a tolerable inn. Here be high-roads and rattling carriages, shouting drivers, and crowded markets, and a dining-room with a smart waiter. We are in Principato Citeriore, and only a few miles from Parthenope.

[1] Avellino, the Abellinum of the Romans, is the chief town of the province of Principato Citeriore, and is one of the districts into which it is divided, the other two being Ariano, and Sant' Angelo de' Lombardi. The town contains about 5,000 inhabitants, and is 28 miles from Naples.

September 12.—A cloudy day; and as the ascent of the mountain is not a trifling matter, we postpone it till to-morrow, when the weather may permit a more distant view from the summit. From hour to hour we wander in the shady lanes, or among vineyards. They are all open, and one is never weary of looking at the beautiful outline of Avellino and Monte Vergine through the framework of hanging vines. All this part of the country has a lively appearance from the costume of the peasantry, whose dresses are mostly red, and peculiar in form. The women arrange their hair beautifully, and are almost universally good-looking, and the very picture of health and neatness.

September 13.—September is but an uncertain month for those high mountain excursions; yet, though the upper part of Monte Vergine is covered with a dark curtain of cloud, we dare the ascent. There is a carriage-road from the city to the village of Spedaletto, situated at a considerable height on the mountain, and beyond this, the path to the monastery is for more than three miles a very steep zig-zag, in overcoming which you are indulged with a fine view of Vesuvius rising from its velvet plain. Noble groups of chestnut-trees clothe the lower part of the mountain, and above their leafy heads is the craggy summit of the hill with the picturesque convent, which combine to make many a beautiful picture.

This celebrated sanctuary, built on the site of a temple of Cybele, as several inscriptions and remains attest, was founded about 1100 A.D., and on account of its possessing a particularly miraculous image of the Virgin Mary (not to speak of the bones of Shadrach, Meshach, and Abednego!) its sanctity is great. Great numbers of pilgrims[1] come hither from the surrounding

---

[1] It is said that four hundred pilgrims died here in 1611—some one of them having profanely brought up some meat for luncheon. The peasants say that eating meat near the sanctuary will bring on a thunderstorm and hurricane at any time.

parts of the country; and on the high festa days of the image there is no doubt a goodly show of costume. But, independently of the attractions held out by the relics, &c., the Monastery of Monte Vergine has little in itself which can be called interesting: the great view it enjoys from its isolated and elevated position constitutes (at least to a landscape-painter) its chief charm. Moreover, the cold was too severe at the summit of this high mountain to tempt a lengthened stay; so we descended to Mercugliano, a large village at the lower part of the hill, where stands a great monastic establishment, connected with the sanctuary, and which is the residence of its abbot. The remainder of this day, and all the following,

September 14.—Was passed in sketching among the environs of Avellino, a place of quiet walks and shady groves. How deep and dark green were the tufts of chestnuts against the lilac hills afar off! The evening went in disputing with vetturini, and arranging to be taken, as near as possible, to Melfi in Basilicata, which is the main object of our journey, though we wish to see the Mofette, or Sulphureous Lake, if it can be easily reached. At length we agree; for two dollars we are to be taken as far as Grotta Minarda, and thence pursue our route as best we may.

September 15.—After numberless irritations from the lies and subterfuges of drivers—for the race of vetturini around Naples are odious to deal with—we finally set off at 10 A.M.

The road lies through cheerful places: gardens, cottages, and numerous villages and towns are always in sight; but after leaving Prata and Pratola on the left, and Montefuscolo on a high hill beyond, the country grew more and more uninteresting as we approached the mid vertebral line of Italian mountains, here more broken and less striking in appearance than in any other part of the Regno. A tedious descent to the valley of the River Calore, with some monotonous undulations, followed, till we

reached Grotta Minarda, during our journey to which the outline of the town of Ariano on the east, and on the west that of
Monte Vergine, formed the principal, or rather the only,
features of a wide expanse of country. Picturesquely speaking we
were by no means pleased with this part of his Neapolitan
Majesty's dominions; but we trusted to find compensation for
such barrenness of interest, in Apulian plains, Norman castles,
and Horatian localities, by and by to be visited. At a tavern
below Grotta Minarda we dismissed our vetturino, and dined
on the universal and useful Italian omelette and maccaroni.

But now came the difficulty. Where should we go next? and
how should we get there? Melfi might be reached in two whole
days; but as we wished to devote an hour or so to the 'Mofette,'[1] if we could find it, Frigento appeared to us as the most
fitting place to sleep at; for although it did not seem clearly
understood whether the infernal basin was nearest to Frigento
or to Sant' Angelo de' Lombardi, yet the latter place was too far
off to be reached before night. Had we been at Gioiosa in
Calabria, the Baron Rivettini might well have said, '*Perchè!* do
you go to such a disagreeable place as the Mofette?—*Perchè!*'

Much search and earnest persuasion produced a half-witted old
man with a donkey which might carry our small quantity of
luggage, and after long hesitation he agreed to go with us to the
Mofette, the way to which he knew, though, he said, he should
not tempt Providence by going very near the spot. He also held
out indistinct views of accompanying us all the way to Melfi if
he were well paid. The more enlightened inhabitants of Grotta
Minarda also said that we should have no difficulty in finding a
delightful home at Frigento in the house of Don Gennaro
Fiammarossa, who they declared was the wealthiest and most
hospitable of living men—'È tutto denaro, è tutto cuore:

---

[1] 'Le Mofette' is the name by which the lake or pool of Amsanctus is known;
identified by Antiquarians (see Craven, Swinburne, &c.) with the description
in Virgil, 'Est locus, Italiæ medio, sub montibus altis,' &c.—*Cramer*.

possiede Frigento, possiede tutto.'[1] So we set off, resolving
to confide our destinies to the care of Don January Redflame, who
is all money and all heart, possessing Frigento in particular, and
everything else in general.

Frigento was immediately before our eyes, standing on a very
ugly clay hill, and although the grandeur of shifting clouds,
storm, and a rainbow did their best to illumine and set off the
aspect of the land, yet we were obliged to confess that our
journey lay over a most wearily monotonous country. Nor, on
arriving at the foot of the bare hill of Frigento, had we any wish
to make acquaintance with Don January Redflame for the sake of
his native place; and it was not until we had peeped into a very
unsatisfactory osteria at the high-road-side, that we reluctantly
resolved to ascend the dismal and ugly cone before us. At the
miserable little town of Frigento itself we made one more trial,
but the only taverna was so palpably disgusting, that it was not
to be thought of as a place of sojourn, even by us, tried Calabrian travellers; and thus we were at length driven to appeal to
the hospitality of the benevolent Don Gennaro, whose house is
the only large one in the town. Everything in his mansion
betokened wealth, and we contemplated with pleasure the comfortable hall with crockery and barrels, and all kinds of neatness
and luxury; and until Don Gennaro came, we were pressed to
take a glass of wine by the steward and his very nice-looking
wife.

But lo! the great January arrived, and all our hopes were
turned to chill despair! '*How* grieved he was not to be able to
have the pleasure of receiving us, none but he could tell;'—
this he said with smiles and compliments, yet so it was. He was
expecting an aunt, four cousins (anzi, cinque[2]), three old
friends, and four priests, who were to pass through Frigento on

[1] He is all money and all heart: he possesses Frigento—he possesses all
things.
[2] Nay, five.

their way to a neighbouring town; they might come and they might not, but he dared not fill his house. But what of that? There was a capital inn at Frigento, one of the very best in Italy; he would take us there himself; it was time we should be sheltered for the night. And forthwith he led the way out into the street, overwhelming us with profuse expressions of compliment—'Signori miei gentilissimi e carissimi illustrissimi padroni garbati e cortesi,—amici affezionatissimi,' &c., till, to our dismay and surprise, he stopped at the door of the very filthy osteria which we had ten minutes ago rejected with abhorrence as impracticable and disgusting.

'Viaggiatori culti, eccellentissimi Giovani, ecco qui l'albergo qui troverete tutto, tutto, tutto, tutto, tutto,'[1] said our friend; and, bowing and smiling to the very last, he retreated hastily towards his own house, leaving us very distinctly 'sold,' and not a little enraged at Don January Redflame's proficiency in the art of humbug, though we excused him for not desiring to house unknown wanderers in these days of unsettled events.

We turned away from the man 'all money and all heart,' and came indignantly down the hill wishing ourselves in Calabria, and composing our minds to the necessity of passing the night at the one-roomed osteria at the hill-foot. Here, at least, we found civility, though there was little but the bare walls of the taverna to study: a stove filled up one side of a little chamber, half of which was used as a stable; yet when our new muleteer had cooked us some poached eggs, we made ourselves tolerably comfortable by the fireside, and finally slept well in a granary on large heaps of grain, which had the advantage of cleanliness as well as novelty when considered as beds. The furniture of our dormitory was simple to the last degree: the before-named wheat-heaps, long strings of onions depending from above, and numerous round boxes of eggs below.

[1] Polished travellers—excellent young men, here is the inn; here you will find everything—everything.

September 16.—Leaving our wheaten couch ere sunrise, we prepared to start afresh. Our accommodation cost us in all two carlini each; but coffee, alas! there was none. With Antonio the foolish (who talked to himself without ceasing), we followed a route leading over most forlorn and bare hills, Frigento over-looking all from its ugly pinnacle, and in the far distance loom the forms of mountains, which appear fine in outline, but a scirocco haze makes them all indistinct as to detail and colour. After walking a mile or two we left the high road, and for another mile and a half descended by paths through a wild country, ever becoming drearier and less prepossessing, till as we neared a deep little valley, strong sulphureous odours warned us of our approach to the Mofette.

The hollow basin in which lies this strange and ugly vapour bath is fringed on one side by a wood of oaks, behind which the mountain of Chiusano forms a fine background: but on the northern approach, or that from Frigento, the sloping hill is bare, and terminates in a wide crust of sulphureous mud, cracked, dry, and hollow at some little distance from the pool, but soft, and undulating like yeast at the brink of the little lake itself. The water, if water it be, is as black as ink, and in appearance thick, bubbling and boiling up from a hundred springs which wrinkle its disastrous looking surface: but when the liquid is taken out into any vessel, it is said—for we did not make the experiment—to be perfectly clear and cold. Whether or not birds can fly across or over the enchanted pool, I cannot tell, but as we found many stiff and dead on its brink—namely, two crows, four larks, three sparrows, and eight yellow-hammers—it is but fair to conclude that the noxious vapours had something to do with stocking this well-filled ornithological necropolis; and as to ourselves, we found that to inhale the air within two or three feet of the water was a very unpleasing experiment, resulting in a catching or stupefying sensation, which in my own case did not entirely pass away for two or three days.

Possibly the strength and properties of this curious volcanic lake may differ at various seasons or states of the atmosphere;[1] as for our guide he implored us not to go near, and would not by any means be persuaded to go within a hundred yards of the 'accursed eccentricity.'[2]

After having made a drawing of the celebrated Mofette we called a council as to what decision we should come to concerning our future route. The town of Bisaccia was fifteen miles distant—hardly to be reached with ease ere evening. That of St. Angelo de' Lombardi was but six miles from us at present, and we settled to go thither, hoping to find some conveyance thence to Melfi. We journeyed on over a bare and hilly country by uninteresting paths along undulating clay slopes or cultivated valleys, till we came to a conclusion that the province of Principato Citra is one of the dullest of the kingdom of Naples. In an hour or two we reached Rocca San Felice, and passed through it. Around this little town, in itself picturesque, there seems to lie the only pretty scenery we had observed since we left Avellino; but a coming storm prevented our lingering to sketch even this single bit of character; so, after a long descent and ascent, we attained to the town of St. Angelo de' Lombardi just as rain began to fall heavily. Our fate, so far as reaching Melfi, was soon known; there is no *strada carrozzabile*, and no carriages in or from St. Angelo de' Lombardi; so, resolving to go on to-morrow towards the Norman city with the old man and his ass,

---

[1] Swinburne says—'The Mofette several times spouted as high as our heads; a large body of vapour was continually thrown out with a rumbling noise, accompanied by a nauseous smell and danger of suffocation.' Craven supposes that changes take place in the action of the lake, as he found no smell, and heard no noise, and saw nothing. In the pool of Amsanctus he finds no impediment to respiration; black clay is deposited, leaving the waters clear and tasteless, and icy cold. Raven and wood-pigeon flew over it—worn-out fable—whole ground strewed with dead butterflies—stopped his watch—and discoloured all metal, &c. Mazzella, however, speaks of 'all birds dying who fly over the pool.'

[2] 'Cosa curiosa maledetta,' as he called it.

we discovered a tolerable locanda, and adapted ourselves to pass the rest of the day there. The hostess declared she had no food of any sort in the house; but the distinct odour of a roast fowl caused us to pay but little attention to her assertions: with the energy of hungry men we forced our way into the kitchen, and laid violent hands on the detected viands, together with some eggs and *alici*—all intended for somebody else. After dinner and siesta, and when the rain had ceased, we wandered forth in quest of food for our pencils, but found little. St. Angelo de' Lombardi is one of those places (and in Italy there are but few such) having no goodly aspect or form in themselves, and placed so as to command a wide panorama below, but with no foreground, tree, or rock to set off against its abundant extent. And, unluckily, where there was really an appearance of fine mountain lines, mist and cloud prevented it from being seen distinctly. St. Angelo de' Lombardi is but a dismal place; the people of the inn, however, were obliging, though the 'accommodations' of the dormitories compelled each of us to sleep in his cloak.

CHAPTER XVII

September 17.—Glad we were, on rising before day, to find the morning beautifully clear, and the foolish old man, our guide, waiting with his ass below. There were finer mountain views, too, now that the clouds had passed away, than we had given St. Angelo de' Lombardi credit for possessing.

For two hours our advance was very agreeable; we turned from the hill on which stands our last night's home, and passing Guardia Lombardi, another town, high on a hill of its own (and whose unpicturesque appearance, we agreed with old Pacichelli, might fully merit his condemnation, 'it contains no object worthy of any praise whatever'), we began to cross monotonous grassy downs, from each undulation of which, when we looked back, the hill of Monte Vergine was still ever in sight.

The mountains on this part of the eastern side of Italy decrease by very slow gradations to the flat country near the shore; and we next traversed wide and long meadow plains, enlivened by large droves of horses, and much like parts of the Campagna around Rome; but there was great want of good form and outline, and my expectations of the Great Pianura of Apulia began to sink apace. And in spite of the appearance of Monte Voltore, which now began to adorn the horizon, and at whose base we ought to sleep to-night in the city of Melfi, these undulating downs, or plains, grew sadly wearisome, and we were glad to spy the far-off top of a tower, which the foolish old man declared was the church of Bisaccia. It was long, though, ere we arrived there, and when we did, in how odious a place did we find ourselves! So unwilling were the inhabitants to commit themselves by any attention to strangers, that, for all the civility we met with, we might have had the plague. Most of the people loitering about, to whom we spoke, shrugged their shoulders, and passed on; while a few indicated a very filthy osteria as the only place of accommodation in this uncouth wilderness. And when within the walls of the unclean locanda, no one had any edibles for sale; and all the inmates, after staring at us for awhile, went on with their occupations with the most profound indifference to us and our wants. Three exotic-looking men, with long uncombed hair and moustache, and velvet cloaks, looking much like comedians, come and observe us; they say they are Bolognese—we think them refugees. Four priests gaze at us, with the shrug ignorant, as we again ask for food. A fifth says, 'È indecente! due fores-tieri garbati, e non sanno che fare, ne come mangiar, ne

MELFI

CASTEL DEL MONTE

alloggiar;'[1] but his faint zeal is rebuked and extinguished by the others. After a long hour of persuasion and quest, we are taken to another osteria, rather less filthy than No. 1, and here we unload our ass. But lo! to our additional dismay, the foolish old guide of Grotta Minarda suddenly vows he will go no further with us. 'E come posso? con' sto ciucciarello?'[2] No animals or guide are to be procured here, and Melfi is still eighteen miles off, and there is the River Ofanto to be crossed in the way thither!

All sorts of evils seemed at once in array against us, so we took time to decide on future plans, and, sending out for eggs and wine, we made a luncheon, to the best of our ability, among the half-naked children, dogs, and dirt. All our endeavours of persuasion were now directed to induce the silly old man to go with us as far as the next town, Lacedogna, which being a possession of Prince Doria (who had given me letters to his castle at Melfi), I thought promised some better chance of assistance on the journey than the forlorn place we were now halting in; and at length, by dint of bribes and appeals to his feelings, the old man relented, the last weight in the scale of our favour being a gift of three spigole, which had been brought to us for sale, and which we had innocently purchased, the same, on being boiled, proving highly odoriferous. 'Buono per noi, non per voi,'[3] said the old gentleman, on graciously accepting the present, and tying up two of the fish in his pocket-handker-chief for 'to-morrow,' by way of waiting for the more perfect development of their flavour.

After this we set off from Bisaccia, a place, according to old Pacichelli, 'of which little can be said.' There are many very pretty bits of architecture in it, however; and the view of the

[1] It is really a shame. Two well-conditioned strangers, and they don't know what to do—what to eat, or how to lodge!

[2] How can I, with this little ass?

[3] Good for us, though not for you.

distant plains is noble from the outskirts of the town. None of
your half-and-half undulations, but real flat Apulian plains—pale
and pink, and level as a calm lake, and stretching away, as it
were, into the very clouds. The costume here, too, is pretty:
the dresses of the women are all red, the skirt plaited and
adjusted differently to the general mode. But for drawing there
was no time, neither was there any one view of surpassing or
characteristic interest; so we hurried down a steep descent,
crossed a valley, and once more ascended elevated spurs of hill,
whence Monte Voltore, on our right hand, grew more large
and distinct; and Lacedogna, a large but unpicturesque town, lay
full before us.[1]

There we arrived about 2 or 3 P.M., and made instant inquiries for a horse. One, they said, was to be hired, so we
engaged it hastily, for there was no time to be lost—Melfi is
still twelve miles off. We sate in a wine-shop, unloaded the ass,
and paid the foolish man. 'Is the horse coming?' said we to the
surrounding idlers. 'Yes, it is on the way: it will be here in
half a minute.' A quarter of an hour passes—half an hour—three
quarters, and still no horse. 'Where *is* the horse?'—'Ah,
signori, they are saddling it.' It would soon be too late to start
for Melfi, so we rushed to the stable indicated as containing the
fabulous quadruped, and lo! there it was calmly lying down, and
evidently wholly guiltless of any attempt, passive or active,
towards leaving Lacedogna. Moreover, a dark and surly woman
said, 'It never was to be hired—it never was intended to go to
Melfi—and it never shall.' So, all our hopes vanishing, we were
in a complete fix.

In great trouble, we stood resolving what to do. A man with
two mules passed. Nothing is lost by asking.

'Will you go to Melfi?' said we.

[1] Lacedogna, of which the concise Pacichelli remarks, 'It is of narrow
extent, and contains nothing either curious or beautiful fit for observation,'
belongs to the Doria family.

'No,' was the answer, 'unless for two ducats.'

'They are yours,' we replied; and seizing on the lucky moment, and the bridles, we lost no time in transferring our little luggage to the opportune *vettura*,[1] and were really, after all difficulties, once more on the way to Melfi, leaving Lacedogna, like other places in Principato Citra, with very little regret. Our route led at first by the side of a winding stream, and then by a great ascent to Monteverde, the last town in the province. Here we arrived just before sunset, and, from its elevated site, the views of Monte Voltore, with the territory called Monticchio, adjoining the isolated volcanic woody height, are most gorgeous. The sudden contrast between the uninteresting country over which we had been for three days journeying, and this novel and beautiful scenery, was delightfully animating, notwithstanding our resting-place was still far off. Monte Voltore is the Soracte of this part of the Regno di Napoli; standing alone, and graceful in form (much resembling Vesuvius), it is, though inconsiderable in height, conspicuous among the tame undulations on all sides, and its colouring is always exquisite. On its eastern and southern slopes lie the towns of Melfi, Rapollo, Barile, Rionero, and Atella; on the north it is covered with dense forests—a royal demesne, little visited by strangers; and the hollow centre of this singular hill, once its crater, contains the secluded lake and convent of San Michele, which, ere we leave Basilicata,[2] we trust to see. At sunset we crossed the Ofanto, a broad, but shallow river at this season, and the line of division between Principato Citeriore and Basilicata. Henceforward, after a short ascent, we went on apace for two long hours, which sufficed to bring us, sleepy and weary, to Melfi, a

[1] Any mode of conveyance.

[2] The province of Basilicata (part of ancient Lucania) contains 431,789 inhabitants (Del Re, 1828), and was called by its present name in the time of Frederick II. It is divided into four districts—Potenza (now the chief town), Metera, Melfi, and Lago Negro.

The old authors speak of manna being commonly found in many parts of it.

city which has given us so much trouble to reach it, that we are anxious lest our labour should not be well repaid. But on our entering the town, it is too dark to discern any of its beauties or failings. Yet the castle of Melfi, which we reach by a short ascent from the streets, is sufficiently imposing at this silent hour of night. There is a drawbridge, and sullen gates, and dismal court-yards, and massive towers, and seneschals with keys and fierce dogs,—all the requisites of the feudal fortress of romance.

Signor Vittorio Manassei, the steward and agent of Prince Doria, received us most amiably, and ushered us into magnificent halls, forming a strange contrast to our late sojourning places. Around were mirrors and gilded furniture in all the full splendour of Italian baronial style, and the perfect order and cleanness of the establishment did high credit to the Roman agent's skill and taste.

September 18.—A delightful place of sojourn is Melfi,[1] the first stronghold of Normans in Apulia. One of the towers of Roger de Hauteville still exists, but the great hall, where Normans and Popes held councils in bygone days, is now a theatre.

The present building dates from the sixteenth century, and the offices and other additions still later. The castle overlooks the whole town of Melfi, but no great extent of distant country, for one side of the horizon is wholly filled up by the near Monte Voltore, and the remainder by a range of low hills, so that the site of the town seems to have been selected as much for concealment as strength.

[1] Melfi is one of the four capi-distretti of the province of Basilicata. According to Pacichelli and others, it was originally Melphis, a Greek city. He speaks of Popes Nicolo II, and Urban II, holding councils there in 1069 and 1098. K. Craven gives the dates 1089 and 1100. The castle and town were built by the sons of Tancred de Hauteville. After the defection of the Caraccioli, to whom the castle had been given by Giovanna II, the emperor Charles V bestowed it on Andrea Doria, and the dukedom of Melfi has ever since remained in his family.

A morning's ramble made me acquainted with all the characteristic beauties of the place, which is a perfect tame oasis among much uninteresting scenery. The picturesque buildings of the city (which seems to occupy the site of some ancient place); the valley below it, with its clear stream and great walnut-trees; the numerous fountains; the innumerable caves in the rocks around, now used as stabling for goats, which cluster in swarthy multitudes on tiers of crags; the convents and shrines scattered here and there in the suburbs; the crowded houses and the lofty spires of the interior; and the perfectly Poussinesque castle, with its fine corner tower commanding the whole scene:[1] so many fine features in a circumscribed space it is not common to see, even in Italy. If one must find a fault, it is that Melfi cannot boast of a beautiful bit of remote landscape to fill up the list of its excellent qualities.

In the middle of the day we returned to the castle, and were treated most hospitably by the polite Signor Manassei and his family, consisting of his wife and two daughters; and, after we had passed the afternoon in drawing, a sort of réunion of Melfitan neighbours, guitars, singing, and cards till supper-time, closed a very agreeable day.

September 19.—There is a formidable long gallery adjoining our room, full of old oak chests, and older armour; and its windows are seized every now and then with terrible fits of rattling, so that one is apt to think old Andrea Doria's ghost may be walking about, if not that of some old Norman. We dined with the whole family to-day, and found them very agreeable, particularly one of the daughters. Signora Manassei has, in speaking of the world of Melfi, that mixture of kindness and pity which characterises the true Roman manner. Then we loitered on vine terraces and under pergolate, and ate grapes in the large vineyards behind the castle; and, along with Signor Vittorio and

[1] All this, alas! has passed away. See Postscript, page 207.

his two merry daughters, examined all the older part of the building, the prisons, and the old hall, used as a theatre in the last century.

September 20.—Another merry day—drawing out of doors—laughter within. What a home one might make of the Castle of Melfi, with its city below and its territory around—the beau ideal of old feudal possession and magnificence.

September 21.—But what shall we do when we go out once more into the wide world and its dirty osterias?—after these princely subtleties of luxury, this buttered toast and caffé for breakfast, these comfortable rooms and merry society? The ease and grandeur of the Palazzo Doria in Melfi will have spoiled us, methinks, for rough travelling.

This day, like its fellows, went by, and left no shadow on memory's path; but we had now made as many drawings as we had a right to require, and we had had four days of unvariedly pleasing reception, so we prepare to depart on the morrow for Minervino and Castel del Monte; these, with visits to Venosa, San Michele, and Castel Lago Pesole, will fill up the remainder of our time for wandering.

Before the evening réunion, a foreman or Campagna steward of the Doria family was called in by Signor Manassei. Don Sebastiano, 'il Fattore,' is a large and important person, who, knowing all roads far and near, is strictly enjoined to take charge of us as far as Rio Nero, and to see that we want for nothing in going or returning.

CHAPTER XVIII

Leave Melfi.—Regrets for old Díghi, Dóghi, Dà.—The magnificent Don Sebastiano.—Lavello.—We prefer walking to riding.—Mid-day halt.—View of Monte Voltore.—Apulian plains—their great flatness and paleness.—Approach to Minervino.—Its appearance—streets, animation, &c.—Plain of Cannæ.—Monte Gargano, &c.—Don Vincenzino Todesche: his warm and friendly reception.—The family supper. —Don Vincenzino's hospitable opinions.—Weary ride from Minervino by the stony Murgie.—Immense extent of Apulian pianura.—Remarkable beauty of Castel del Monte.—Its architectural interest.—Return to Minervino.—Tradition concerning the architect of Castel del Monte.—We leave Minervino.—Reputation for cordiality enjoyed by the south-eastern provinces of the Regno.—Halt at Monte Milone.— Oak woods.—Views of Venosa and Monte Voltore.—Picturesqueness of Venosa: its streets, &c.—Palazzo of Don Nicóla Rapolla, and agreeable reception there.—His family.— Luxuries and refinements.—The castle of Venosa: its modernised interior, prisons, stables, &c.—Agreeable stay at the Casa Rapolla.—Venosa Cathedral.—Church of La Trinità. —Ruined church and monastery of the Benedictines.— Amphitheatre.—Another day at the Casa Rapolla.—We leave Venosa.—High roads, commerce, and civilization.—Skirts of Monte Voltore.—Towns of Rapolla and Barile.—Large town of Rio Nero.—Indications of its wealth and activity.—House of Don P. Catena: its comfort and good arrangements.— Our hospitable welcome.—Signor Manassei again.—Evening musical party at Rio Nero.

September 22.—We did not start very early from the lordly gates of Melfi Castle. No luggage mule was to be found, but our little *roba*[1] was dispersed upon three horses, one of which was ridden by the corpulent Fattore. We took leave of the cheerful Manassei family, with feelings something more akin to those with which we used to part from Calabrian entertainers than we had experienced since we had entered these midland provinces. But ah! in these days of Basilicata and Principato how often did we wish for good old Díghi, Dóghi, Dà! Not but that our large guardian, Don Sebastiano, was very obliging (he was extremely like Dr. Samuel Johnson seen through a magnifying glass and dressed in a tight blue jacket and trowsers), but from having been Guardiano in the service of the King, when he was staying at the Palazzo Doria, and having then accompanied him in various hunting expeditions, the worthy man was so pompous, and so full of long stories of royal doings, that his manner rather oppressed us, the more that being seventy-three years old, he seemed too venerable to be ordered hither and thither.

About eight miles from Melfi we passed close to Lavello, rather a pretty town. Farther on we encountered a tiresome elevated plain, and the uninteresting valley of the river Bonovento, where, giving our horses to a man who accompanied us on foot, we proceeded to walk; but at this proceeding Don Sebastiano was horrified. The horses, he said, were not good, and he would return instantly to Melfi for others. In vain we assured him that Englishmen did occasionally walk as a matter of choice: this assertion he treated as wholly poetical; and he never during the journey ceased to regret his choice of steeds. After a gradual ascent from the low grounds of the Bonovento, where were abundance of buffali, and great flights of a bird which the Fattore called 'calendroni,' we arrived at the summit of the last ridge of hill on the eastern side of Italy, where, in a sort of ruined guardhouse, we halted to lunch and rest at half-past

---

[1] 'Roba' is a word of wide signification in Italian; in the present case it means 'baggage,' but it may be generally well rendered by the English 'things.'

twelve. From this spot there is a fine view of Monte Voltore, which stands alone on the western horizon; but the prospect to the south and east is one of the most surprisingly striking character, and totally unlike anything presented by other parts of Italy—portions of the Campagna of Rome near the sea perhaps excepted. Yet even those scenes fail to recall the exceeding paleness, and pinkness, and flatness of the great outstretched sheet of pianura, which spreads away from the foot of the Apennines to the sea—those wide plains of Apulia, so full of interest to the historian, and doubtless not less so to the painter.

To the south, on a spur of the hills overlooking the maritime part of the province of Basilicata and Capitanata, stands Minervino, and thither we directed our course, over undulating green meadows which descend to the plain, and we arrived about an hour before sunset at the foot of the height on which the town is situated. Minervino enjoys a noble prospect northward, over the level of Cannæ to the bay and mountain of Gargano, at which distance the outspread breadth of plain is so beautifully delicate in its infinity of clear lines, as to resemble sea more than earth. The town is a large, clean, and thriving place, with several streets flanked by loggie, and altogether different in its appearance and in its population from Abruzzese or Calabrese towns. The repose, or to speak more plainly, the stagnation of the latter, contrasts very decidedly with these communities of Apulia,—all bustle and animation—where well-paved streets, good houses, and strings of laden mules, proclaim an advance in commercial civilisation.

We encountered in the street Don Vincenzino Todeschi, who on reading a letter of introduction, given to us for him by Signor Manassei, seemed to consider our dwelling with him as a matter of course, and shaking hands with us heartily, begged us to go to his house and use it as our own; he was busy then, but would join us at supper.

In the evening there was a family gathering at that meal; there was Don Vincenzino, the host, who conversed on statistics, commercial pursuits, railroads, and increasing facilities of communication, and other practical matters. 'Send any of your friends who come this way to me,' said he: '*stendere relazioni*, to increase a connection all over the world should be the object of a liberal-minded man; knowledge and prosperity come by variety of acquaintance,' &c. &c. There were three sons also with their tutor, a gentlemanlike and well-informed abbate; and a very nice little girl, Teresa, who, her mother being dead, was evidently the family pet. The Fattore Don Sebastiano sat in silence, though before supper he had been rather loquacious concerning the family Todeschi, whom he looks down upon as 'novi ricchi,' spite of the show drawing-room, chimney mirrors, carpets, and tables full of nicknacks.

P—— and I are not a little perplexed as to what we shall do to-morrow, for, owing to time running short, we have but one day left ere we turn towards Naples. Canosa (ancient Cannæ) and Castel del Monte, are the two points, either of which we could be content to reach; but as each demands a hard day's work, we finally resolve to divide them, P—— choosing Canosa, and I the old castle of Frederick Barbarossa, of which I had heard so much as one of the wonders of Apulia.

September 23.—Before daylight each of us set off on his separate journey on horseback,—P—— with the bulky Don Sebastiano to Canosa, I to Castel del Monte, with a guardiano of Don Vincenzino Todeschi's family. Oh me! what a day of fatigue and tiresome labour! Almost immediately on leaving Minervino we came to the dullest possible country,—elevated stony plains—weariest of barren undulations stretching in unbroken ugliness towards Altamura and Gravina. Much of this hideous tract is ploughed earth, and here and there we en-countered a farm house with its fountain: no distant prospect ever relieves these dismal, shrubless, Murgie (for so is this part of the province of Bari called), and flights of 'calendroni,' with a few skylarks above, and scattered crocuses below, alone vary the sameness of the journey. At length, after nearly five hours of slow riding, we came in sight of the castle, which was the object of my journey; it is built at the edge of these plains on one of the highest, but gradually rising eminences, and looks over a prospect perfectly amazing as to its immense extent and singular character. One vast pale pink map, stretching to Monte Gargano, and the plains of Foggia, northward, is at your feet; southward, Terra di Bari, and Terra di Otranto, fade into the horizon; and eastward, the boundary of this extensive level is always the blue Adriatic, along which, or near its shore, you see, as in a chart, all the maritime towns of Puglia in succession, from Barletta southward towards Brindisi.

The barren stony hill from which you behold all this extraordinary outspread of plain, has upon it one solitary and remarkable building, the great hunting palace,[1] called Castel del Monte, erected in the twelfth century by the Emperor Barbarossa, or Frederick II. Its attractions at first sight are those of position and singularity of form, which is that of an octagon, with a tower on each of the eight corners. But to an architect, the beautiful masonry and exquisite detail of the edifice (although it was never completed, and has been robbed of its fine carvedwork for the purpose of ornamenting churches on the plain), render it an object of the highest curiosity and interest.

The interior of this ancient building is also extremely striking; the inner court-yard and great Gothic Hall, invested with the sombre mystery of partial decay, the eight rooms above, the numerous windows, all would repay a long visit from any one to whom the details of such architecture are desiderata.

Confining myself to making drawings of the general appearance

[1] Excellent descriptions of this most beautiful castle are to be found in Mr. Swinburne's and the Hon. Keppel Craven's works.

of this celebrated castle, I had hardly time to complete two careful sketches of it, when the day was so far advanced that my guardiano recommended a speedy return, and by the time I had overcome the five hours of stony 'murgie' I confess to having thought that any thing less interesting than Castel del Monte would hardly have compensated for the day's labour. I reached Minervino at one hour of the night, and found P—— just arrived from his giro to Canosa.

While riding over the Murgie, slowly pacing over those stony hills, my guide indulged me with a legend of the old castle, which is worth recording, be it authentic or imaginary. The Emperor Frederick II having resolved to build the magnificent residence on the site it now occupies, employed one of the first architects of the day to erect it; and during its progress dispatched one of his courtiers to inspect the work, and to bring him a report of its character and appearance. The courtier set out; but on passing through Melfi, halted to rest at the house of a friend, where he became enamoured of a beautiful damsel, whose eyes caused him to forget Castel del Monte and his sovereign, and induced him to linger in the Norman city until a messenger arrived there charged by the emperor to bring him immediately to the Court, then at Naples. At that period it was by no means probable that Barbarossa, engaged in different warlike schemes, would ever have leisure to visit his new castle, and the courtier, fearful of delay, resolved to hurry into the presence and risk a description of the building which he had not seen, rather than confess his neglect of duty. Accordingly he denounced the commencement of Castel del Monte as a total failure both as to beauty and utility, and the architect as an impostor; on hearing which the emperor sent immediately to the unfortunate builder, the messenger carrying an order for his disgrace, and a requisition for his instant appearance in the capital. 'Suffer me to take leave of my wife and children,' said the despairing architect, and shutting himself in one of the upper rooms, he forthwith destroyed his whole family and himself, rather than fall into the hands of a monarch notorious for his severity.

The tidings of this event was, however, brought to the emperor's ears, and with characteristic impetuosity he set off for Apulia directly, taking with him the first courtier-messenger, doubtless sufficiently ill at ease from anticipations of the results about to follow his duplicity. What was Barbarossa's indignation at beholding one of the most beautiful buildings doomed, through the falsehood of his messenger, to remain incomplete, and polluted by the blood of his most skilful subject, and that of his innocent family!

Foaming with rage, he dragged the offender by the hair of his head to the top of the highest tower, and with his own hands threw him down as a sacrifice to the memory of the architect and his family, so cruelly and wantonly destroyed.

September 24.—Having risen before sunrise, the energetic and practical Don Vincenzino gave us coffee by the aid of a spirit lamp, and we passed some hours in drawing the town of Minervino, the sparkling lights and delicate gray tints of whose buildings blended charmingly with the vast pale rosy plains of Apulia in the far distance. At nine we returned to a substantial *déjeûner*, and at half-past ten took leave of our thoroughly hospitable and good-natured host.

Basilicata, Bari, and the southern or Apulian province of Otranto, hold as high a place in the Regno di Napoli for their 'civilizazione e cordialità,' as do the Abruzzesi and Calabresi: the central provinces, either from vicinity to the capital or other causes, are less amiably depicted, and assuredly our experience of Principato Citra had borne out the truth of the legend.

Turning our faces westward, we resumed our route, which at first was not of the most agreeable kind, carrying us ever at the bottom of a narrow valley bounded by low acclivities, until, ascending the hills which skirt the Apulian plains, we came in sight of Monte Milone, and the beautiful form of Monte Voltore beyond. At Monte Milone we halted, as well to draw as for refreshment, which, in the shape of bread and grapes, and good wine, we found in the village osteria, in whose dark chamber, one sick unclothed child on a bed, and five others in similar undress perversely crawling about the floor like so many brown spiders, were the only remarkable objects. After leaving the village we entered on a track leading over a pleasant plain, through a beautiful scattered wood of young oaks, between which were noble views towards the left of Acerenza, and before us of Venosa; 'Mons Vultur' ever closing the horizon of the onward landscape. Nothing could be more agreeable than this latter part of the day's ride, barring that the horse-flies were so numerous that we were fain to shelter ourselves and steeds with gathered oak boughs. At twenty-three o'clock we arrived at the ancient town of Venosa, which, both externally and internally a most picturesque place, stands on the brink of a wide and deep ravine, its cathedral and castle overlooking the whole area of habitations. Extremely clean streets, paved from side to side with broad flags of stone, like those in Naples; numerous bits of columns or capitals, mediæval stone lions, and the machicolated and turreted towers of the old castle, gave great hopes of great employ for the pencil.

We easily found the house of Don Nicóla Rapolla, to whom Signor Manassei had addressed us, the principal proprietor of the place; it was an extremely large rambling mansion in a great court-yard, where granaries, stables, and a profusion of pigeons, and other domestic creatures, indicated the wealthy man. Two ladies of considerable beauty, and graceful exterior and manners, informed us that Don Nicóla was from home, but his brothers, DD. Peppino and Domenico, husbands of the two ladies, soon joined and heartily welcomed us. Don Peppino, dressed in the extreme of Neapolitan fashion, and Donna Maria in a riding habit and hat, appeared to our amazed senses as truly wonderful and unexpected objects in this the land of Horace. Presently, Don Nicóla, a sacerdote, but head and eldest of the house, and lord and master of all Venosa, came home, and renewed welcome followed; we were shown into very good rooms, containing four-post bedsteads, pier-glasses, wardrobes, and other luxuries which Horatian ages knew not; and after a while we prepared ourselves in 'our best clothes' for supper; for our hosts are Neapolitan grandees of the first caste, and all their household arrangements exhibit good taste and order. As for the two ladies, they talk French as well as Italian, and are infinitely agreeable and intelligent. To-morrow we are to be lionised over Venosa.

September 25.—The castle of Venosa[1] is a fine old building of the fifteenth century; it is inhabited at present by Don Peppino Rapolla and his lady. Hither, attended by Don Nicóla, whom I in vain endeavoured to detach from us, we repaired at early morn, and sate down before it to draw, our polite host lingering by our sides, until, on my telling him that we might be fixed for two or three hours, he at length withdrew. Afterwards we crossed the ravine, and drew the town of Venosa, with its old churches and picturesque houses, and the purple Monte Voltore behind,—one of the most pleasing landscapes I had seen in this part of the Regno.

At noon we paid a visit to the castle and its inmates. Don Peppino has modernised one of the great halls into a very delightful drawing-room, where a grand piano and sofas harmonise well with old carved chairs and ornamented ceilings; its pretty and ladylike mistress being the chief charm of the *salon*.

We explored the whole of this old feudal fortress: a long winding stair leads to fearsome dungeons, their sad and gloomy walls covered with inscriptions, written by the hands of despairing captives. Most of these mournful records are dated in the

[1] Erected in the fifteenth century by Perro di Balzo, Prince of Altamura and Venosa.—(Craven.)

early years of the 16th century, and a volume of ugly romances
might be gathered from the melancholy list. Then there were
four stables to see, each made to hold fifty horses; and a deep
moat round the whole castle, with other et-cetera—'quæ nunc
describere,' &c.

Returning at noon to the Casa Rapolla, we found the dinner-
hour fixed at three—woe to us for the fashionable hours of our
hospitable hosts!—through which arrangement we fear our
afternoon sketching must be relinquished. Don Peppino and his
wife were of the party, and the entertainment was excellent
in all respects. The conversation is often on English literature—
Shakespeare, Milton, &c., on whom there are various opinions;
but all agree about 'quel Autore adorabile, Valter Scott!' The
Canonico reads one of the romanzi once a month, and the
whole family delight in them; and are also equally conversant
with other known English writers. The cuisine is of a much
more recherché kind than is usually met with in the provinces,
and we are particularly directed to taste this dish of seppia or
cuttlefish, or to do justice to those mushrooms. The wines,
moreover, are superexcellent, and the little black olives the best
possible; and all things are well served and in good taste.

After dinner we move into the library—a large room well
stored with books; here we have caffè and a visit from the Giudice
and other Venusiani, after which we go out in a carriage to see
the lions of the town. And first the ancient cathedral, spoiled by
modern 'improvements,' whitewashed and dedaubed, one good
arch only remaining intact; many fragments, apparently of
Roman workmanship, are built up into the walls. Next, the
church of La Trinità, an extremely ancient low building with
pointed arches; two large stone lions guard the door, and near
it is a vestibule containing a single column, around which,
according to the local popular superstition, if you go hand in
hand with any person, the two circumambulants are certain to
remain friends for life. The interior of this most interesting

VENOSA

SAN MICHELE DI MONTE VOLTORE

church is miserably spoiled by neglect and additions: on the walls are yet visible many half-effaced frescoes of early date,—one of Pope Niccolo has suffered but little from time. There are the tombs also of Robert Guiscard, and Ademberta his wife, but so shamefully out of repairs, that the Trinità church is a disgrace to Venosa. Hence we went to a church commenced on a great scale by the Benedictines, but the progress or completion of the building was interrupted by an earthquake or want of funds; there is a fine perspective of ancient columns and capitals, but the whole edifice is now overgrown with vegetation and part of it turned into a vineyard, the vines forming a pergolata walk where the middle aisle should be: nothing of its kind can be more picturesque than this verdant ruin.[1]

Later we went to the remains of the amphitheatre, a ruin only partly excavated; and from thence we adjourned to the castle, where was a 'soirée' and some good singing, till four hours of the night, when we returned to the Casa Rapolla to supper. Such is the fashion of Venosa!

September 26.—Luxuries again! Coffee and hot buttered toast are served at sunrise, the latter food being firmly believed by Neapolitans to be as much a part of English breakfast as roast beef is of dinner. The morning, fresh and delightful, we passed quietly on the banks of the ravine, or in the church of the Benedictines; the wild air of by-gone times characteristic of Venosa is mournfully charming. Our mid-day and early afternoon was passed at the Casa Rapolla, always pleasurably; the intelligence and affable cordiality of our host is very agreeable. Towards evening we walk out. The grandeur of these great men of Venosa is observable at every moment, in the obsequious

[1] The church and monastery of della Trinità was erected about 942, on the site of a temple of Hymen, by Gisulphus, Prince of Salerno; repaired one hundred years afterwards by Robert Guiscard. In the thirteenth century the Benedictines used up the great Roman amphitheatre to mend it, but it was never completed. (Craven.)

demeanour of all the people we meet: as for the peasantry, they doff their hats a long way off, and crossing over to the opposite side of the street stand like statues as we pass.

After seeing the golden sun sink down behind Monte Voltore, we passed two or three hours in music, chess, and drawing, at Don Peppino's, returning to the evening meal at our host's. We set off to-morrow for Barile, Rio Nero, and S. Michele.

September 27.—With great regret I left Venosa, and the pleasant family we had staid with—the only people one has greatly cared for in all this tour. Our route led us over an un-interrupted series of undulations to the foot of Monte Voltore, and but that the early morning was very lovely, we should have voted the walk tiresome. The bulky Don Sebastiano had left us, and a guide with a donkey was our escort. An oak-fringed slope and lanes between vineyards brought us to Rapollo, a town which stands on the base of the mountain close to Melfi, and hencefor-ward we are once more (save for the digression we shall make to the Convent of San Michele) in the high carrozzabile road of civilisation, and commerce. Rapollo is a picturesque place, but we sketched it hastily, and left it at noon, expecting better things at Barile and Rio Nero. In this hope we were disappointed. A broad high way gradually ascends and skirts the base of Monte Voltore, but although at every turn a greater extent of Apulian plain is unfolded, yet the lines of foreground and middle distance are awkward and bad. Barile (four miles from Rapollo) possesses no beauty worth a moment's delay, although it is one of the Greek or Albanian settlements of the Regno, and I had expected to see somewhat of costume. A vain hope! The inhabitants still speak their own language, but they have entirely dropped all distinction of dress.

Another mile brought us to the large and populous town of Rio Nero, standing at a considerable elevation on the base of Monte Voltore, which rises above it not unlike Vesuvius above

Pompeii, and overlooking the plain southward towards Atella and Lago Pésole. If the provincial splendours of the Casa Rapolla had surprised us, what were they in comparison to the rich mansion of Don Pasqualuccio Catena, whither we had been directed by Signor Manassei, whom we found awaiting us with his son Pirrho. Here were halls and anterooms, and a whole suite of apartments for ourselves fitted up as well as those of any of the first palazzi of the capital. When dinner was over (the least pleasing accompaniment of which was the presence of a great Barbary ape, who made convulsive flings and bounces to his chain's length, and shrieked amain), P—— and I took an hour's walk about the environs of this increasing and prospering place; but vainly did we search for any view to draw. Rio Nero is not beautiful to the eye; so we adjourned, with the family of Don Pasqualuccio, to the house of his brother Don Tommas 'Antonio—a palazzo still finer than his own. Here were long galleries and large rooms, empty of all but a circle of sofas, and glittering in all the novelty and magnificence of blue and gold papers, pedestals and busts, cornices and mirrors; and at the end of these apartments was one of still larger dimensions and super-eminent splendour, where a grand pianoforte stood the centre of the scene. The lady of the house sang and played fifteen songs with terrible energy, and the master played four solos on the flute; after which they performed three extensive duets, till the night wore, and it was time to depart; but as it began to rain a little, these extremely obliging people ordered out their carriage and horses, and we were driven back to our host's two streets off. Such are the quasi-metropolitan 'finezze' of Rio Nero,[1] a place full of thriving merchants and possidenti, and rapidly rising as a commercial community by the production and manufacture of silk, and other articles of luxury.

[1] See note, p. 210.

CHAPTER XIX

September 28.—To-morrow being the great Fêsta of San
Michele, all the population of the surrounding country usually
flock to the monastery, and if we should be fortunate enough to
have fine weather, all the world says it is one of the prettiest
sights in southern Italy.

We set off early, with a guardiano and a man on foot, and at
first the road, winding round the volcanic mountain, was not
interesting: but when we had reached the western side of the
hill, we entered most beautiful beechwoods, which continued
increasing in thickness and size as we advanced. The path
through these shady forests turns inward to a deep dell or hollow,
formerly the principal crater of the volcano; and soon through
the branches of the tall trees we saw the sparkling Lake of
Monticchio, and the Monastery of San Michele reflected in its
waters. A more exquisite specimen of monastic solitude cannot

be imagined. Built against great masses of rock which project over and seem to threaten the edifice; the convent (itself a picture) stands immediately above a steep slope of turf, which, descending to the lake, is adorned by groups of immense walnut-trees. High over the rocks above the convent the highest peak of Monte Voltore rises into air, clad entirely with thick wood: dense wood also clothes the slopes of the hill, which spread as it were into wings on each side of the lakes. The larger sheet of water is not very unlike Nemi, on a small scale—only that the absence of any but the one solitary building, and the entire shutting out of all distance, makes the quiet romance of S. Michele and its lake complete. Great numbers of peasants were arriving and encamping below the tall walnut-trees, forming a Fair, after the usual mode of Italians at their Fête; the costumes individually were not very striking, but the general effect of the scene, every part of it being clearly reflected in the water, was as perfectly beautiful as any I ever saw. We visited the chapel and the dark grotto of the patron saint (but the crowd of pilgrims in these cases makes this no pleasing part of Fêsta duty), and at noon, after drawing until rain began to fall, we came in to our two cells, which were already well cleaned out by the care of Don Pasqualuccio Catena, and arranged for our comfort with the addition of a large dinner sent ready cooked from Rio Nero.

Alas! there was heavy rain all the afternoon, quite deranging the peasant-encampment and Fair: all those, and they were many, who could not be accommodated within the walls of the monastery, returned ere the daylight faded away to their respective homes, and no others supplied their places, so that the numerous body of pilgrims who should have been the chief charm of the scene was wanting. Neither could we do more than sketch hastily between the showers: but we wandered about the neighbourhood of this most beautiful of places, enjoying its variety of aspects with infinite pleasure.

The long passage or gallery adjoining our rooms was full of peasants, sheltered from the weather by the monks of the convent, and during half the night, their jovial festivities were very noisy, not to speak of the proximity to our chamber door of asses and mules, which frequently brayed and outnoised the clamour of an improvisatore, and four or five zampognari in full practice, as well as some large choral parties employed in singing, in a very terrestrial manner, spiritual songs concerning the miracles of S. Michele.

September 29.—It rained all night, and chillingly damp were the woods of Monte Voltore at sunrise—yet as the day wore on, the sun brightened everything, and numbers of peasants arrived ere midday was passed.

In the afternoon we left San Michele. As we returned by the beech-woods of the great dell, nothing could be prettier than the view of the convent through the foliage, the blue smoke from the peasant-fires on the green glades rising filmily among the high woody hills,—the hundreds of people in many-coloured dresses on the green sward beneath, and the numerously windowed monastery beneath the great rocks—all clearly reflected in the watery mirror below.

We reached Rio Nero by sunset, where our good hosts were as usual hospitable and attentive, and appeared greatly charmed by our expressions of pleasure at the result of our visit to the convent—the great lion of the northern part of Basilicata.

September 30.—At sunrise we were ready to start in our entertainer's own carriage, accompanied by the good-natured Don Pasqualuccio on our way as far as Atella (two or three miles distant from Rio Nero), a picturesque but melancholy town, lying lowest of all those placed on the slope of Monte Voltore, and indeed almost on the plain. Here we found a guardiano with horses waiting to take us on to Castel del Lago Pèsole[1], the last of Prince Doria Pamfili's possessions in this part of Italy which we had arranged to visit.

The castle on its elevated hill was soon in sight, and perhaps from a considerable distance it is better worth the trouble of drawing than on a nearer approach. It was a favourite resort of the Emperor Frederick II as a hunting-seat (its surrounding territory is still famous for game), and in later days inhabited by Queen Joan; but this ancient place has no pretensions to beauty, nor, excepting from the south whence it combines as part of the landscape with the plain and Monte Voltore beyond, is it in any way picturesque: the lines around are desolate and bare of interest, and the lake (or rather marsh) from which it derives its name lies altogether hidden in the wooden tract below the castle hill.

We found our Melfi friend, Signor Manassei, and his son, staying at the castle, which in its interior is modernised and comfortable, but so little is there of interest either outside or in, that for once we could not find wherewithal to employ our pencils during the afternoon. Below the castle is a small village of cottages, increasing under the care of the active and social Signor Vittorio Manassei, who has named it Filipopoli, in honour of the present possessor of the estate. As the sun set we sate upon the treeless slope opposite the unpicturesque castle, which, indeed, has greatly disappointed us; yet, at this hour, there was the inevitable charm which eventide in Italy brings even to the least promising scenery; the deep purple Monte Voltore, its long lines blending with the plain, across which the last crimson lights were flickering; the dark copse-wood around; the smoke rising from the hamlet of Filipopoli; the goats and flocks wandering in the valley-common below,—

[1] Castel del Lago Pèsole is reputed to have been built by the Emperor Frederick II; but according to Antonini it is of much older date. Frederick probably rebuilt or enlarged it.

these, joined to somewhat of a wild-world solitude in the scene, threw a sentiment of beauty even over Castel del Lago Pèsole.

October 1.—We set out on our return to Naples. Signor Manassei and his son accompanied us in a carriage; and first we wound up by a good road to the top of the hill called Della Madonna del Carmine, whence we took leave of Monte Voltore, and the seaward plain of Basilicata. Beyond this, the mountains of Principato Ultra were very interesting; glimpses of blue worlds of light and shade, enchanting vales and hollows, which we longed to penetrate.

At Avigliano we left Signor Manassei, and drove on to Potenza, the present capital of the province, and as ugly a town for form, detail, and situation, as one might wish to avoid. Here we hired a caratella to take us to Eboli (for seven ducats), and merely resting to dine, drove on towards Vietri di Basilicata, where we arrived late and halted for the night.

October 2.—Vietri di Basilicata appears full of really fine scenery and material for good landscape, and left a strong impression of beauty on our minds, though every succeeding hour brought fresh charms to view. It is hardly possible to find a more beautiful day's drive in any part of the Regno di Napoli than this, the road passing through a constant succession of lovely scenes till it reaches Eboli. At sunset the blue gulf of Salerno was visible, and we soon reached the convent-inn of Eboli; which ten years ago I can recollect thinking a horrible place, though it seems to me now rather a comfortable inn.

October 4.—Yesterday we passed at Pæstum:—the morning drive by the beautiful Persano and its plain; the hours of lingering among the bright solitudes of ancient Posidonium; the return at evening when the western sun was golden, and the mountains fading red; the bustling and noisy Salerno by night.

To-day—by beautiful La Cava, and crowded Nocera, and ' railroad ' from Pompeii to Parthenope.

Our tour is done: it has wanted the romance of Calabria, and something has it been too hurried:—yet it has had its pleasures, and has added many agreeable memories to an already large store.

POSTSCRIPT

Four years after the above journals were written, namely, on the 14th August, 1851, a frightful earthquake visited the provinces of the Regno di Napoli, which are partly described in them, and the centre of this alarming convulsion appears to have been the unfortunate city of Melfi. I subjoin the following extract (No. 1), out of many which have appeared in the public papers, which will give some idea of the sad change which has passed over places so full of prosperity and enjoyment at the time of our visit in 1847. I am inclined to think that the account quoted below (No. 1) is in some respects exaggerated, but at all events the calamity has been most fearful. On reading this and other notices of the event in October last, I wrote to Signor Vittorio Manassei, who most obligingly forwarded me a letter from which I have extracted all which bears on the subject (No. 2). His occupation as agent for the estates of Prince Doria occasioning him to reside generally on the spot, his relation of the casualties may be fully depended on, both as to the number of lives lost at Melfi, and with regard to Barile, which I cannot help thinking he would have mentioned had it met with the fate stated in the notice extracted from the 'Athenæum Journal.'

No. 1.

From the Athenæum Journal, September 13, 1851.

NAPLES, *August 27, 1851.*

The details of the terrible earthquake which took place at Melfi on the fourteenth of this month reach Naples but slowly. Each post brings notice of an accumulated amount of suffering, an augmented list of deaths, and particulars of a devastation far surpassing anything that has occurred in the Italian peninsula for many years. I have seen several persons from Melfi, and from their narratives will endeavour to give you some idea of this awful visitation.

The morning of the 14th of August was very sultry, and a leaden atmosphere prevailed. It was remarked that an unusual silence appeared to extend over the animal world. The hum of insects ceased, the feathered tribes were mute, not a breath of wind moved the arid vegetation. About half-past two o'clock the town of Melfi rocked for about six seconds, and nearly every building fell in. The number of edifices actually levelled with the earth is 163, of those partially destroyed 98, and slightly damaged 180. Five monastic establishments were destroyed, and seven churches, including the cathedral. The awful event occurred at a time when most of the inhabitants of a better condition were at dinner; and the result is, that out of the whole population only a few peasants labouring in the fields escaped. More than 700 dead bodies have already been dug out of the ruins, and it is supposed that not less than 800 are yet entombed. A college accommodating 65 boys and their teachers is no longer traceable. But the melancholy event does not end here. The adjoining village of Ascoli has also suffered, 32 houses having fallen in, and the church being levelled with the ground. More than 200 persons perished there. Another small town, Barile, has actually disappeared; and a lake has arisen from the bowels of the earth, the waters being warm and brackish.

I proceed to give a few anecdotes as narrated by persons who have arrived in Naples from the scene of horror.—'I was travelling,' says one, 'within a mile of Melfi, when I observed three cars drawn by oxen. In a moment the two most distant fell into the earth: from the third I observed a man and a boy descend and run into a vineyard which skirted the road. Shortly after, I think about three seconds, the third car was swallowed up. We stopped our carriage, and proceeded to the spot where the man and boy stood. The former I found stupefied—he was both deaf and dumb; the boy appeared to be out of his mind, and spoke wildly, but eventually recovered. The poor man still remains speechless.' Another informant says:—'Melfi, and all around, present a singular and melancholy appearance; houses levelled or partially fallen in, here and there the ground broken up,

large gaps displaying volcanic action, people wandering about stupefied, men searching in the ruins, women weeping, children here and
there crying for their parents, and some wretched examples of
humanity carrying off articles of furniture. The authorities are
nowhere to be found.' A third person states—'I am from Melfi, and
was near a monastery when the earthquake occurred. A peasant
told me that the water in a neighbouring well was quite hot; a few
moments after I saw the monastery fall. I fell on the ground and
saw nothing more. I thought I had had a fit.'

No. 2.

From a letter written by Signor Vittorio Manassei, March 27, 1852.

'That although the Castle of Melfi has been ruined by the earthquake of August the 14th, 1851, at least one-fifth part of it having been
thrown down, namely, the towers of the outer side, with much of the
modern palace, the great gallery, the rooms occupied by Il Signor Lear,
the other gallery, and all that side of the building occupied by the family:
yet, notwithstanding, no person who was in the castle at the time
of the earthquake perished, every individual having been enabled to
escape into the vine-garden after the first shock, and before the second
commenced, by which all the walls already shaken by the first undulating movement were at once overthrown.

'That the campanile of the cathedral fell down to one-third of
its height: that the octagonal church, and the great Casa Manna, (both
of which are particularly marked in one of the views taken by Signor
Lear on the spot) exists no longer. Such is the case also with the
Town Hall, (Palazzo Pubblico) the Palazzi Aquilecchia-Aranea,
Severini, and many others. Thus it is too, almost without exception,
with all the smaller houses of Melfi, which are all of them destroyed;
and when Signor L. was at Melfi, they were building (he may perhaps
recollect) a great Taverna; this, but lately completed, was greatly
frequented by passengers—and at the first shock of the earthquake
there perished in it 62 individuals, and 25 horses; this building is
now literally a shapeless heap of stones. Not more than 840 persons
were killed in Melfi.

'At Venosa, though the earthquake was very sensibly felt, no loss of life
occurred, and the family of Signor Rapolla were not sufferers in any way.

'At Rio Nero, the palazzo of the Signor Catena (where Signor Lear was staying) fell down, except the lower floor, but no one of that family was killed. In the town, between 90 and 100 lost their lives.

'In Atella, comparatively little damage was done. San Michele, that is the church, of Monte Voltore fell down, but the monastery itself was hardly injured.

'At the Castle of Lago Pèsole (where Signor Vittorio Manassei happened to be at the time of the earthquake) the shocks were much felt; but although the older part of the building was greatly shaken, the inhabited side was hardly affected.

'At Monteverde, and at Lacedogna, but little injury resulted from the shocks; and although all the towns from Atella in a line to the Adriatic were more or less visited, yet but few were damaged beyond Melfi. Minervino, and all the surrounding places known to Signor L., escaped injury.

'NAPLES, *March* 27, 1852.'

Index

211

Index